Modern Russian 1

Clayton L. Dawson
Charles E. Bidwell
Assya Humesky

Georgetown University Press, Washington, D.C. 20057

Library of Congress Cataloging in Publication Data

Dawson, Clayton L.
  Modern Russian.

  Includes indexes.
  1. Russian language—Grammar—1950-
2. Russian language—Spoken Russian. I. Bidwell,
Charles Everett, 1923-   joint author. II. Humesky,
Assya, joint author. III. Title.
PG2112.D36 1977   491.7'83'421   77-5837
ISBN 0-87840-169-5 (v. 1)

ABOUT *Modern Russian*

In February 1960 the University of Michigan sponsored a conference of scholars to "develop criteria for a two-year college sequence of specialized materials for learning the Russian language." In its proposal to the U.S. Office of Education for funds to support the conference, the University of Michigan stated its view that "The urgency of our national need to improve and increase the study of the Russian language in our schools and colleges and the comparative dearth and inadequacy of existing materials for this purpose dictate the collaboration of the U.S. Office of Education with the Russian language specialists . . . in the production of a complete two-year college level course in Russian." The proposal advised that "pertinent decisions regarding personnel, institutional sponsorship, and methodology for the production of such a course should be made only on a broadly established basis of consensus among a widely representative group of scholars and specialists in this field." The twenty-seven scholars and specialists listed on the page opposite collaborated at the conference to achieve that consensus, and designated nine persons, similarly listed, as an Advisory Committee to the project.

Recommendations arising from the February 1960 conference and from the Advisory Committee resulted in the naming and empowering of the Working Committee: Dr. Clayton L. Dawson, Professor and Chairman of the Slavic Department at Syracuse University (project coordinator); Dr. Charles E. Bidwell, Associate Professor and Chairman of the Department of Slavic Languages and Literatures, University of Pittsburgh; and Dr. Assya Humesky, Associate Professor of Russian Language and Literature, University of Michigan. Syracuse University undertook to house and administer the entire project, and assumed responsibility for the preparation of the new materials. Both the University of Michigan conference and the University of Syracuse project to produce the two-year course were supported by the U.S. Office of Education, under authority of Title VI of the National Defense Education Act.

The University of Michigan, the University of Pittsburgh, and Syracuse University cooperated by granting leaves of absence to Drs. Humesky, Bidwell, and Dawson respectively. Along with these universities, The American University, the Foreign Service Institute, Georgetown University, Indiana University, St. John's University, the State University College at New Paltz, New York, and the University of Washington participated in the field testing of materials prior to publication, providing helpful suggestions and encouragement. Generous help was provided in typing, advising, and recording by a large group of native Russians teaching in the Slavic Department of Syracuse University. Professors Robert L. Baker of Indiana University and Tatiana Cizevska of the University of Illinois contributed timely information on culture and current usage out of their recent experience in the Soviet Union. Finally, special critical evaluations and recommendations were provided by Professors Baker, Richard Burgi of Princeton University, Kurt Klein of the University of Illinois, and Laurence Thompson of the University of Washington.

Modern Russian, together with the recordings and the teacher's manual prepared to accompany it, unique in both content and techniques in the Russian field, is the fruition of this cooperative group effort.

Introduction: Using *Modern Russian*

The materials of *Modern Russian*, like those of its prototype, the Modern Language Association's *Modern Spanish*, provide a new kind of language course based on audio-lingual principles and aimed at speaking proficiency within the framework of the traditional language program. *Modern Russian* consists of two volumes of eighteen lessons each, designed for a two-year course meeting from three to five hours a week.

Stressing the fundamental structural features of the contemporary spoken language, the thirty-six lessons present a total vocabulary of some 2700 items. Magnetic tape recordings, available to accompany the written materials, are an integral part of the two-year program. In addition, long-playing disk recordings of basic portions of the lessons are obtainable for home study.

Audio-lingual principles assume that fluency in a foreign language is acquired less by intellectual analysis than by intensive practice. Awareness of structure is acquired not by memorizing rules and paradigms but by imitation and repetition of basic language patterns and by performance of drills carefully constructed to capitalize on the learner's natural inclination to analogize from material already learned. Language learning thus properly begins with listening and repeating and only later proceeds to reading and writing. These first two stages are of primary importance if the student is to gain even a minimum control of spoken Russian; for this reason we recommend strongly that most material be presented and practiced with books closed, both in class and in the laboratory.

A lesson consists of the following parts designed to be used as suggested:

Preparation for Conversation. Anticipating the Conversation to follow, this part presents the basic elements of the Conversation in the order of their appearance, together with parallel English equivalents and, where needed, with phonetic transcription. This material provides a basis for understanding and assimilating the Conversation. Supplementary related words and phrases are also given here.

Conversations. Simulating situations of contemporary Soviet life, these introduce the basic lexical and structural items of the lesson in dialogue form and in colloquial Russian. The first four lessons contain a single Conversation each; the remaining lessons each contain a pair of Conversations. **Notes** explain points of cultural difference and of usage and style. For the first five lessons a parallel English equivalent of each Conversation is provided. A phonetic transcription of the Russian is also given as an aid to proper pronunciation in learning the materials; this is presented consistently in the first ten lessons, but only to clarify special problems thereafter. The Conversations, basic to each lesson, are best assimilated to the point of complete memorization. These are recorded on the tapes—and on the records as well—for individual repeated listening and imitation. They are presented in four stages: (1) the entire dialogue at natural speed without pauses; (2) the individual sentences, broken down from the end, with pauses for student repetition; (3) complete utterances, again with pauses for student repetition; and (4) the entire dialogue once again at natural speed without pauses.

Basic Sentence Patterns. These are sets of patterned sentences, deriving from the Conversations and illustrating the major structural points of the lesson with the use of new and review vocabulary. They are to be mastered through repeated practice. The Basic Sentence Patterns are paralleled by English equivalents.

Pronunciation Practice. To instill habits of correct pronunciation, every lesson provides pronunciation drills, frequently contrastive ones. Additional pronunciation drills, not appearing in the text, are given in the *Teacher's Manual* and on the tapes. Lessons 6 through 11 each present an **Intonation Practice** treating the fundamental patterns of simple sentences.

Structure and Drills. These form the grammatical heart of the course, generally treating four or five major structural points per lesson. Each structural point is developed in five to twelve different drills, with an average of ten responses. The student imitates the models given (generally there are two, the first with an English equivalent), by responding orally to sentences, questions, and/or cues in Russian provided by the teacher. The drills are widely varied: repetition, substitution, question-answer, subject reversal, transformation, structure replacement, integration, expansion, and progressive substitution. All drills are fully recorded on the tapes with appropriate pauses for student responses, followed by the confirming responses. To make the procedure clear, the desired responses for the first two lessons are printed in full. A discussion of a structural point generally follows the drills in which it has been developed.

Reading and Writing. Essentially a recapitulation of the lexical and structural items in the lesson and a review of past items, this part is a reworking of the Conversation materials and provides practice in reading. The portions presented in handwritten form invite practice in dictation or copying (easily self-corrected), as well as in reading a cursive script. Translation of the readings is *not* recommended; comprehension can best be checked by questions in Russian as provided in the *Teacher's Manual.*

Experience suggests that presentation of dialogues is most effective when delivered at a normal conversational speed in natural word groupings (not as words in isolation), with a natural intonation. Class choral repetition is helpful in presenting new Conversations in order to bring the class into active participation, and choral recitation of the parts of the dialogue by designated groups of the class provides a useful check on memorizing the Conversations. Memorizing the Conversations, though not indispensable, does result in higher achievement in the structural drills. Intensive drill on the Preparation for Conversation and class practice on the Conversation, followed by the use of the tape in the language laboratory and/or the records at home, can make memorizing the Conversation a relatively simple task.

Practice in writing—whether mere copying or writing out drill responses specifically assigned for that purpose—should not be neglected, despite the strong oral emphasis of *Modern Russian*. The writing of selected drills tends to reinforce mastery of the structure and to check on progress being made.

Normally a lesson will take five meetings to cover, though clearly the longer the time spent on a lesson, the more complete the mastery of it is likely to be. The first four lessons are shorter and may therefore be covered in four sessions each. Where classes meet only three hours a week, drills which cannot be covered in class may be assigned for performance in a language laboratory. A course of three class hours a week has been successfully given by Syracuse University with these materials on just such a basis.

Contents

Recordings for *Modern Russian*

Modern Russian 1

Cassette	Side A: Lesson	Page	Minutes	Side B: Lesson	Page	Minutes
1	1	3	45	2	19	31
2	3	35	46	4	49	31
3	5	61	30	5	74	25
4	6	83	43	6	99	39
5	7	109	28	7	122	29
6	7	127	25	7	131	27
7	8	139	54	8	156	55
8	9	167	29	9	180	27
9	9	185	26	9	189	24
10	10	195	26	10	209	25
11	10	213	26	10	216	26
12	11	225	23	11	237	24
13	11	240	30	11	245	30
14	12	253	40	12	268	36
15	13	279	30	13	293	30
16	13	299	24	13	303	23
17	14	309	25	14	320	24
18	14	323	29	14	327	28
19	15	335	49	15	351	51
20	16	361	47	16	376	46
21	17	389	26	17	401	24
22	17	403	27	17	409	27
23	18	419	24	18	424	23
24	18	436	31	18	441	31

Modern Russian 2

Cassette	Side A: Lesson	Page	Minutes	Side B: Lesson	Page	Minutes
25	19	483	41	19	498	37
26	20	507	45	20	523	43
27	21	533	46	21	546	47
28	22	553	23	22	563	22
29	22	566	29	22	570	25
30	23	577	47	23	591	47
31	24	599	44	24	612	43
32	25	619	36	25	631	35
33	25	635	24	25	638	19
34	26	643	50	26	657	46

Modern Russian 2 (continued)

Cassette	Side A: Lesson	Page	Minutes	Side B: Lesson	Page	Minutes
35	27	667	44	27	679	44
36	28	687	46	28	701	47
37	29	709	31	29	720	30
38	29	725	24	29	728	24
39	30	735	30	30	746	30
40	30	750	26	30	754	25
41	31	761	46	31	776	44
42	32	787	46	32	801	44
43	33	811	45	33	825	43
44	34	833	27	34	845	27
45	34	849	24	34	852	23
46	35	859	41	35	873	40
47	36	883	22	36	886	21
48	36	896	30	36	902	28

Modern Russian 1

NOTES

The Russian sound system

Russian sounds may be divided into two basic groups: vowels and consonants.

A. The vowels

Russian has five basic vowel sounds, all of them shorter than the very approximate English vowels given here for the sake of a rough comparison.[1]

[a]	star	[tám, vás]
[o]	port	[ón, nós]
[e]	met	[étu, jél]
[i]	machine	[i, iván]
[u]	lunar, soon	[nú, kúm]

As aids to pronunciation, we also give two additional symbols to represent positional variants of [a] and [i].

[ə]	sofa, about	[pápə, ókələ]
[ɨ]	ship, weary	[bɨk, sɨn]

> Sound Drill 1: Practice the Russian examples illustrating the vowel sounds, imitating your instructor (or the tape) as accurately as you can.[2]

B. The consonants

Russian consonants fall into two main groups, which we call "hard" and "soft." Hard consonants are pronounced with the main body of the tongue flattened, creating a hollow, open, mouth cavity. Soft consonants, conversely, are pronounced with the tongue raised in an arc, creating a narrowed mouth cavity and a restricted passage of air.

The consonants may be divided into four subgroups: those which occur in both soft and hard varieties regardless of what sound follows, those whose hardness or softness depends on the sound that follows, those which are only hard, and those which are only soft.

---

[1] In illustrating the sounds we use a transcription based on Latin characters, some slightly modified in form.
[2] Sound Drills 1–5 are recorded on tape and printed in the Teacher's Manual.

1. Consonants which occur in both hard and soft varieties regardless of the sound that follows.[1]

[m]	moose	[móst, tám]
[m̦]	amuse	[m̦ésta, m̦áta]
[b]	boots	[bába, búdu]
[b̦]	beauty	[b̦ít, ab̦éda]
[p]	poor	[pápka, sláp]
[p̦]	pure	[sp̦í, p̦ós]
[v]	voice	[vám, slóva]
[ɣ]	view	[ɣíza, ɣétka]
[f]	food	[fú, slóf]
[f̦]	feud	[f̦ín, astáf̦]
[n]	now	[nós, vón]
[n̦]	menu	[n̦ós, n̦ét]
[d]	do	[dá, díma]
[d̦]	adieu, should you	[d̦ád̦a, d̦íma]
[t]	stool	[tót, tút]
[ț]	costume, what youth	[țók, máț]
[z]	zoom	[zóna, váza]
[ʒ̦]	presume (British), he's young	[ʒ̦imá, vaʒ̦mú]
[s]	swim	[sók, vús]
[ș]	assume, this youth	[șádu, p̦ișmó]
[r]	trilled r (as in Spanish or Italian)	[ruká, urók]
[r̦]	soft trilled r (no equivalent)	[r̦iká, gavar̦ú]
[l]	belt	[lámpa, stól]
[l̦]	million	[l̦águ, stál̦]

> Sound Drill 2: Practice the Russian examples illustrating these hard and soft consonant pairs, imitating your instructor (or the tape) as accurately as you can. Note that Russian consonants do not have the slight puff of breath characteristic of such English consonants as p, t, and k in certain positions.

2. Consonants whose hardness or softness ordinarily depends on the sound that follows.

The consonants [k], [g], and [x] are ordinarily pronounced hard, but are replaced by their soft alternates [k̦], [g̦], and [x̦] respectively when followed by the vowels [e] and [i]:

[k]	skill, scat	[kák, drúk]
[k̦]	acute, cure	[k̦inó, k̦ém]
[g]	go	[gúm, gólas]
[g̦]	argue	[nógi, nag̦é]
[x]	(no English equivalent; something like the Scotch or German **ch** in lo**ch** or a**ch**)	[xudój, áx]
[x̦]	(soft variety; no equivalent)	[x̦ím̦ik, branx̦ít]

> Sound Drill 3: Practice the Russian examples illustrating these sounds, imitating your instructor (or the tape) as accurately as you can.

---

[1] In the transcription, a small hook under the letter marks the soft consonant. Notice that the soft consonant has somewhat the effect of a "y-like" glide following the consonant.

3. Consonants which occur only in a hard variety regardless of the sound that follows:

[c]	its, waltz	[caɾícə, aʈéc]
[š]	shrimp	[škáf, šútkə]
[ž]	azure, leisure	[žúk, užé]

Sound Drill 4: Practice the Russian examples illustrating these sounds, imitating your instructor (or the tape) as accurately as you can. Note that the Russian [c] is a single sound unit, and that both [š] and [ž] are articulated farther back in the throat than the comparable English sounds.

4. Consonants which occur only in a soft variety, regardless of the sound that follows:

[č]	cheap	[čás, dóč]
[šč]	fresh cheese or wash sheets (pronounced as a single sound unit)	[ščí, jiščó]
[j]	yes, boy	[já, mój]

Sound Drill 5: Practice the Russian examples illustrating these sounds, imitating your instructor (or the tape) as accurately as you can.

The Russian (Cyrillic) alphabet and the writing system

Russian does not use the Latin alphabet employed by English and such Western European languages as French, German, Spanish, and Italian. Rather, Russian uses another alphabet, called the Cyrillic. It is basically modeled after the Greek alphabet, but is supplemented by additional symbols for certain sounds occurring in the Slavic languages but not in Greek. Other Slavic peoples using the Cyrillic alphabet include the Ukrainians, Byelorussians, Bulgarians, Macedonians, and Serbs; while the Czechs, Poles, Slovaks, Slovenes, and Croats use the Latin alphabet.

The Russian (Cyrillic) alphabet is given below in its conventional order, together with typical pronunciations of the letters and illustrative examples. Note that most letters are pronounced in more than one way, depending upon where they occur or the place of stress in the word.[1]

THE ALPHABET	TYPICAL PRONUNCIATION	EXAMPLES
А а	[a]	а, тáм
	[ə]	мáма
Б б	[b]	бáк, бáба
	[ḅ]	óбе, тебé
	[p]	бóб, бáбка
В в	[v]	вáм, вóт
	[ɣ]	вéк
	[f]	в тóм
Г г	[g]	готóва, тóга
	[g̓]	бéре, тóге
	[k]	бéг, мóг
	[v]	тогó, какóго

[1] Stress is marked with an acute (′) accent over the vowel.

Д д	[d]	да́, до́м
	[ḍ]	гдé, водé, одéт
	[t]	обéд, гóд, вóдка
Е е	[e]	обéд, вéтка, тé
	[je]	éм, éдет
	[i]	дóме, бедá
	[ji]	едá, егó
Ё ё	[o]	мёд, тёте
	[jo]	её, моё
Ж ж	[ž]	да́же, жа́ба
	[š]	ёж, одёжка
З з	[z]	завóд, ба́за
	[ẓ]	зевóк, везёт
	[s]	вóз, га́з
И и	[i]	и́, зима́, ги́д
	[ji]	мои́, твои́
	[ɨ]	живёт
Й й	[j]	мóй, такóй, ма́йка, йóд
К к	[k]	ка́к, вóдка
	[ḳ]	кéм, Кита́й
Л л	[l]	лóжка, ви́лка, ви́дел
	[ḷ]	лёд, лéто, болéли
М м	[m]	мóй, та́м
	[ṃ]	мéл, тéми
Н н	[n]	но, она́
	[ṇ]	нéт, они́
О о	[o]	дóм, завóд, вóдка
	[a]	окнó, слова́
	[ə]	ма́ло, молокó
П п	[p]	пойдём
	[p̣]	пи́л, пéние
Р р	[r]	рука́, ми́р
	[ṛ]	рекá, мóре
С с	[s]	скажи́, ва́с, доска́
	[ṣ]	сéл, Семён, неси́
Т т	[t]	та́м, привéт
	[ṭ]	тéм, тёк
У у	[u]	у́тро, куда́, иду́
Ф ф	[f]	фóрма, фа́кт
	[f̣]	Фёкла, Фили́пп
Х х	[x]	а́х, хóлодно, хлéб
	[x̣]	хи́мик, Хитрóв

Ц ц	[c]	отец, царица
Ч ч	[č]	чай, почта, врач
Ш ш	[š]	шар, шум, хорошо
Щ щ	[šč]	щи, борщ, еще
Ъ ъ	(hard sign)[1]	
Ы ы	[i]	ты, вы, было, рады
Ь ь	(soft sign)[1]	
Э э	[e]	это, этот, эти, поэт
Ю ю	[u]	Ваню, всю, бюро
	[ju]	юбка, свою, мою
Я я	[a]	пять, опять, говорят
	[i]	пяти, тяжело
	[ja]	я, твоя, стоял
	[ji]	язык
	[jə]	пения, до свидания

Remarks on stress

A. Stress in the word

A stressed vowel is one pronounced with greater intensity or loudness than an unstressed vowel. Words of more than one syllable can have only one syllable which is stressed in Russian. This contrasts sharply with English, where many words have more than one stress, for example:

ENGLISH pròpagánda

RUSSIAN пропаганда [prəpagándə]

When words are combined in a sentence in Russian, certain short words may receive no stress. For example, prepositions such as **у** and **на**, and the negative particle **не** are normally pronounced as though they were part of the following word:

у неё   [uṇijó]

на почту   [napóčtu]

не видел   [ṇiγíḍil]

B. The major segment

A Russian sentence may consist of a single word or of one or more groups of words. Each group contains one word which has an even stronger stress than any of the other stressed words in the group. We call the groups *major segments* and the strongest stress in each group the *major stress*. We call the remaining word stresses in the major segment *secondary stresses*. The boundary between major segments represents a point where a short slowing up or pause may be made in speaking. In our transcription, the major sentence stress will be indicated by a double accent mark ("), and the secondary or word stress will have a single acute accent mark ('). On the material printed in Cyrillic, only the single accent mark will be used for both major sentence stress and word stress.

---

[1] The hard sign **твёрдый знак** and soft sign **мягкий знак** have no sound value. For a description of their function, see page 9.

Division of a sentence into major segments will often depend on the individual speaking style and tempo. A given sentence in rapid speech will be spoken with fewer major segments than the same utterance in slow deliberate speech. But the segmentation is not arbitrary—there are some places where a major segment boundary may be made and others where it will be rare or nonexistent. For example, a major segment boundary does not occur between a preposition and the following word, and it rarely occurs between an adjective and the noun it qualifies.

In neutral, unemphatic style, the major stress usually falls on the last word of each major segment. In statements, a shift of the major stress to another word in the segment shifts the emphasis to that word:

NEUTRAL	Я иду́ домо́й.	[já idú damój]	I'm going *home*.
SPECIAL	Я иду́ домо́й.	[já idũ damój]	I *am* going home.
or	Я иду́ домо́й.	[jã idú damój]	*I*'m going home.

To sum up, we indicate the degrees of stress (loudness) as follows:

1. Major stress (one per major segment)—double accent mark on transcription, single accent mark on Cyrillic.
2. Secondary or word stress (no more than one per word)—single acute accent mark.
3. No stress—no accent mark.

EXAMPLE Я иду́ на по́чту.   [já idú napõčtu]

Above all, the student should bear in mind that the best guide to accurate pronunciation is the way a native speaker actually pronounces the words, not the written representation of stress.

Discrepancies between the sound system and the writing system

A. Use of the same consonant letter to write both hard and soft consonant varieties

As we know, most Russian consonant sounds come in hard and soft varieties. It is a peculiarity of the writing system and the alphabet, however, that the same letter often represents both a hard and soft consonant in writing. For example, both hard [n] and soft [ņ] are written н in Cyrillic; only the following letter can tell us whether it is hard or soft. Compare нóс [nós] with нёс [ņós].

B. Double set of vowel letters in the writing system

To preserve the distinction between hard and soft consonants in the writing system, the Russian alphabet employs a double set of vowel letters which may be termed "hard-" and "soft-series" vowel letters. In themselves the vowels are neither hard nor soft; rather, they indicate the hardness or softness of the preceding consonant. Thus "hard-series" vowel letter а typically follows a hard consonant, and "soft-series" vowel letter я typically follows a soft consonant.

HARD SERIES	SOFT SERIES
а	я
э	е
ы	и
о	ё
у	ю

	HARD CONSONANT PLUS VOWEL					SOFT CONSONANT PLUS VOWEL				
WRITTEN	ба	бо	бу	бэ	бы	бя	бё	бю	бе	би
PRONOUNCED	[ba	bo	bu	be	bɨ]	[b̡a	b̡o	b̡u	b̡e	b̡i]
WRITTEN	да	до	ду	дэ	ды	дя	дё	дю	де	ди
PRONOUNCED	[da	do	du	de	dɨ]	[d̡a	d̡o	d̡u	d̡e	d̡i]
WRITTEN	ма	мо	му	мэ	мы	мя	мё	мю	ме	ми
PRONOUNCED	[ma	mo	mu	me	mɨ]	[m̡a	m̡o	m̡u	m̡e	m̡i]
WRITTEN	та	то	ту	тэ	ты	тя	тё	тю	те	ти
PRONOUNCED	[ta	to	tu	te	tɨ]	[t̡a	t̡o	t̡u	t̡e	t̡i]

The special symbol ь indicates the softness of a preceding consonant when no vowel letter follows.[1] Remember that this sign is not a vowel, i.e., it has no independent sound value. It is merely an alphabetic device to show that the preceding consonant is soft. It is written principally at the end of a word or between consonants.

	HARD CONSONANT NOT FOLLOWED BY VOWEL		SOFT CONSONANT NOT FOLLOWED BY VOWEL	
WRITTEN	стóл	table	стóль	so much
PRONOUNCED	[stól]		[stól̡]	
WRITTEN	брáт	brother	брать	to take
PRONOUNCED	[brát]		[brát̡]	
WRITTEN	ýгол	corner	ýголь	coal
PRONOUNCED	[úgəl]		[úgəl̡]	
WRITTEN	пóлка	shelf	пóлька	polka
PRONOUNCED	[pólkə]		[pól̡kə]	

C. Soft-series vowel letters at the beginning of a word or following another vowel letter

The soft-series vowel letters я, ё, е, and ю, also serve another function. At the beginning of a word following another vowel letter, they are written to represent the consonant sound [j] (written elsewhere й) plus a vowel. Thus я in these positions is equivalent to й plus a; ё is equivalent to й plus о; е is equivalent to й plus э, and ю is equivalent to й plus у.

WRITTEN	я́ма	моя́	ёж	моё	éсть	моéй	юг	мою́
PRONOUNCED	[jámə	majá	jóš	majó	jés̡t̡	majéj	júk	majú]

The soft-series vowel letter и differs from the others in that there is usually no preceding [j] sound in initial position, and there is a rather weak [j] between vowels:

и́мя	мой
[ím̡ə]	[mají] *or* [maí]

D. The hard sign ъ and soft sign ь

There are two letters in the Russian alphabet with no independent sound value. They are called **твёрдый знак** *hard sign* ъ and **мягкий знак** *soft sign* ь.

---

[1] See item D below, for fuller treatment of this symbol.

1. THE SOFT SIGN

Of the two symbols, the soft sign ь is much more frequently encountered and serves two major purposes:

a. To indicate consonant softness at the end of a word or before another consonant: пять [p̣áṭ] *five*, то́лько [tólkə] *only*, чита́ть [čitáṭ] *to read*.

b. To indicate that a preceding consonant is soft *and* that the next vowel is preceded by the sound [j]: семья́ [s̢imjá] *family*, пьёт [p̣jót] *he drinks*.

Note: Although the soft sign is sometimes written after the consonants ж and ш for historic reasons, these consonants are nevertheless pronounced hard: мужья́ [mužjá] *husbands*, идёшь [iḍóš] *you're going*.

2. THE HARD SIGN

The hard sign ъ in modern Russian is only used after prefixes ending in a consonant followed by a soft-series vowel. It indicates that a [j] sound precedes this vowel: съе́л [sjél] *he ate up*, отъе́зд [atjést] *departure*.

PREPARATION FOR CONVERSATION   Студе́нт и студе́нтка

Except in certain fixed expressions, nouns are first given in their nominative case form. The nominative case is primarily used to indicate the subject of a sentence or clause. Russian nouns are of three genders: masculine, feminine, and neuter. Masculine nouns usually terminate in a consonant letter, feminine ones in –а or –я, and neuters in –о or –е. The gender of nouns will be indicated in the Preparation for Conversation only where it is not obvious from the nominative form, as for example: дверь (f) *door*, де́нь (m) *day*. For the time being verbs and adjectives will be given only in the form in which they occur in the conversation.

студе́нт [studént]	student
и [i]	and
студе́нтка [studéntkə]	girl student, coed
Евге́ний [jivgéṇij]	Evgeny
Ни́на [ṇínə]	Nina
приве́т [pṛiγét]	greetings! regards! hi!
Приве́т, Ни́на![1]	Hi, Nina!
вы́ идёте [ví iḍoṭi]	you're going, you're on your way
куда́ [kudá]	where, where to, to what place
Куда́ вы́ идёте?	Where are you going?
уро́к [urók]	lesson, a lesson, the lesson[2]
на уро́к [nəurók]	to the lesson, to class
пе́ние [p̣éṇijə]	singing
уро́к пе́ния [urók p̣éṇijə]	singing class, a singing lesson
На уро́к пе́ния.	To a singing lesson.
я иду́ [já idú]	I'm going, I'm on my way
Я иду́ на уро́к пе́ния.	I'm going to a singing lesson.
а [a]	and, but, by the way, how about
домо́й [damój]	home, homeward
А вы́ домо́й?	And are you on your way home?

---

[1] Boldface sentences in the Preparation for Conversation are those that appear in the Conversation itself.
[2] Notice that Russian does not have definite or indefinite articles corresponding to English *the, a, an*.

нéт [ņét]	no
пóчта [póčtə]	post office
на пóчту [napóčtu]	to the post office
Нéт, я́ идý на пóчту.	No, I'm on my way to the post office.
письмó [p̧işmó]	a letter
послáть письмó [pasláţ p̧işmó]	to send a letter
Я́ идý на пóчту послáть письмó.	I'm going to the post office to send a letter.
собрáние [sabráņjə]	meeting, a meeting, the meeting
бы́ло [bílə]	was, there was
вчерá [fčirá]	yesterday
Вчерá бы́ло собрáние?	Was there a meeting yesterday?
скажи́те [skažíţi]	say! tell [me]!
Скажи́те, вчерá бы́ло собрáние?	Say, was there a meeting yesterday?
бы́ло [bílə]	there was
нé было [ņébilə]	there wasn't
Нéт, нé было.	No, there wasn't.
клýб [klúp]	club
в клýбе [fklúb̧i]	in the club, at the club
В клýбе? Нéт, нé было.	At the club? No, there wasn't.
завóд [zavót]	plant, factory
на завóде [nəzavóḑi]	at the plant, at the factory
А на завóде?	How about at the plant?
тáм [tám]	there
я́ нé был [já ņébil]	I wasn't
Я́ тáм нé был.	I wasn't there.
но [no]	but
Бы́ло, но я́ тáм нé был.	There was [a meeting], but I wasn't there.
нý [nú]	well
извини́те [izɣiņíţi]	excuse [me]
Нý, извини́те.	Well, excuse [me].
автóбус [aftóbus]	bus
мóй автóбус [mój aftóbus]	my bus
вóт идёт [vót iḑót]	here comes, there goes
Вóт идёт мóй автóбус.	Here comes my bus.
до свидáния [dəsɣidáņjə]	good-bye, I'll be seeing you
До свидáния.	Good-bye.

SUPPLEMENT

я́ идý [já idú]	I'm going
ты́ идёшь [tí iḑóš]	you're going[1]
óн идёт [ón iḑót]	he's going
онá идёт [aná iḑót]	she's going
мы́ идём [mí iḑóm]	we're going
вы́ идётè [ví iḑóţi]	you're going[1]
они́ идýт [aņí idút]	they're going

---

[1] **Ты́** *you* is used in addressing a close friend or a member of one's family. **Вы́** *you* is used in addressing a person where a more formal relationship exists, and it is also used whenever more than one person is addressed.

The following are some of the classroom words and expressions your instructor will be using. Be sure you are able to recognize them when you hear them.

ещё ра́з	[jiščó rás]	once again, once more
повтори́те	[pəftaŗíţi]	repeat!
пожа́луйста	[pažáləstə]	please
говори́те	[gəvaŗíţi]	speak! talk!
гро́мче	[grómči]	louder
всё вме́сте	[fşé vm̧ésţi]	all together
чита́йте	[čitájţi]	read!
хорошо́	[xərašó]	good, fine, all right
пло́хо	[plóxə]	bad, poor, not good
лу́чше	[lúčši]	better

Студе́нт и студе́нтка*,¹

Boy student and girl student

The following symbols are used in the transcription of the conversations to give the student some notion of the inflection of the voice at the end of a phrase or sentence:

↓ indicates a dropping off of the voice
↑ indicates a rise of the voice
| indicates voice level sustained

E. — Евге́ний (студе́нт)   Evgeny (a student)
H. — Ни́на (студе́нтка)   Nina (a girl student)

E.	1 Приве́т, Ни́на! Куда́ вы́ идёте?	p̧ŗiɣét ņínə ↓ kudá ví iḍóţi ↓	Hi, Nina! Where are you going?
H.	2 На уро́к пе́ния. А вы́ домо́й?	nəurók p̧éņijə ↓ a ví damój ↑	To a singing lesson. And you're on your way home?²
E.	3 Не́т, я́ иду́ на по́чту посла́ть письмо́.	ņét ↓ já idú napóčtu | paslát ṗişmó ↓	No, I'm on my way to the post office to send a letter.
H.	4 Скажи́те, вчера́ бы́ло собра́ние?	skažíţi ↓ fčirá bílə sabráņjə ↓	Say, was there a meeting yesterday?
E.	5 В клу́бе? Не́т, не́ было.	fklúṗi ↑ ņét ↓ ņébilə ↓	At the club?³ No, there wasn't.
H.	6 А на заво́де?	a nəzavóḍi ↑	How about at the plant? ⁴,⁵
E.	7 Бы́ло, но́ я́ та́м не́ был.	bílə | nó já tám ņébil ↓	There was, but I wasn't there.

---

* Superscript numerals in the Conversation refer to the Notes immediately following.

H.	8	Ну, извини́те.	nǔ | izyiņíți ↓	Well, excuse me. Here comes my
		Во́т идёт	vót iḍót	bus.
		мо́й авто́бус.	mój aftŏbus ↓	
E.	9	До свида́ния.	dəsyidáņjə ↓	I'll be seeing you.
H.	10	До свида́ния.	dəsyidáņjə ↓	Good-bye.

NOTES

[1] The terms **студе́нт** and **студе́нтка** refer only to university students, as compared with **учени́к** and **учени́ца** which designate pupils or students below university level. Russians make a much sharper distinction than we in the terms used for university level as opposed to pre-university level, for example:

UNIVERSITY LEVEL		PRE-UNIVERSITY LEVEL	
профе́ссор	*professor*	учи́тель (m) учи́тельница (f)	*teacher*
университе́т	*university*	шко́ла	*school*
ле́кция	*lecture*	уро́к	*lesson, class*

[2] Russian has two words **и** and **а** both meaning *and*. **И** is used as a simple connector:

студе́нт **и** студе́нтка   boy *and* girl student

whereas **а** is used to point up a contrast or to introduce a new topic:

Я иду́ на уро́к. **А** вы́ домо́й?   I'm going to a lesson. *And* you, are you going home?

[3] **Клу́б** means *club* in the sense of a group of working associates who meet for recreational or informal educational purposes. Clubs in the Soviet Union play a political-educational role in encouraging useful hobbies such as radio, photography, or airplane modeling; or in the study of technical subjects, mathematics, botany, zoology, and so forth. Recreational activities include amateur performances, dances, and games such as chess.

[4] It is not uncommon in the Soviet Union for university students to work in a factory during the day and attend classes in the evening. Unless they are excellent students, secondary school graduates generally must work for two years before entering the university.

[5] Notice that *at* in Russian is **на** in **на заво́де** *at the plant*, but **в** in **в клу́бе** *at the club*. Certain nouns require the preposition **на** in this meaning, while other nouns require **в**. In the same way, when these prepositions are used in the meaning *to*, **на** must be used with **заво́д** (**на заво́д** *to the plant*) and **в** must be used with **клу́б** (**в клу́б** *to the club*).

Basic sentence patterns

The material in this section gives some of the possible variants of utterances found in the conversation. It is designed to provide the student with certain basic patterns before an analysis of the structure is given and before he is asked to manipulate the specific grammatical items. In this way it is hoped that he will not only be able to observe the over-all structural patterns of Russian, but also have some ready-made utterances for active use when he begins to converse. The material should be thoroughly drilled as repetition practice with books closed as the first step. After this, it may be used for reading practice.

1. Куда́ вы́ идёте?	Where are you going?
— На уро́к пе́ния.	To a singing lesson.
— Я́ иду́ на уро́к пе́ния.	I'm going to a singing lesson.
— На по́чту.	To the post office.
— Я́ иду́ на по́чту.	I'm going to the post office.
— На собра́ние.	To a meeting.
— Я́ иду́ на собра́ние.	I'm going to a meeting.
— На заво́д.	To the plant.
— Я́ иду́ на заво́д.	I'm going to the plant.
2. Куда́ ты́ идёшь?	Where are you going?
— На по́чту посла́ть письмо́.	To the post office to send a letter.
— Я́ иду́ на по́чту посла́ть письмо́.	I'm going to the post office to send a letter.
— Домо́й.	Home.
— Я́ иду́ домо́й.	I'm going home.
— В клу́б.	To the club.
— Я́ иду́ в клу́б.	I'm going to the club.
3. Во́т идёт мо́й авто́бус.	Here comes my bus.
_____ Евге́ний.	_____ Evgeny.
_____ Ни́на.	_____ Nina.
_____ студе́нт.	_____ a student.
_____ студе́нтка.	_____ a girl student.
Во́т иду́т Евге́ний и Ни́на.	Here come Evgeny and Nina.
_____ студе́нт и студе́нтка.	_____ a boy and a girl student.

STRUCTURE AND DRILLS

The present tense of the first conjugation verb идти́

я́ иду́	I'm going, I'm on my way, I'm coming
ты́ идёшь	you're going, you're on your way, you're coming
о́н идёт	he's going
она́ идёт	she's going
мы́ идём	we're going
вы́ идёте	you're going
они́ иду́т	they're going

■ REPETITION DRILL

Listen to your instructor (or the tape) and repeat the above pronoun-verb model until you can say it perfectly.

■ REPETITION-SUBSTITUTION DRILL

Repeat after your instructor (or the tape) as accurately as you can, imitating both the individual words and the sentence intonation. Then, on hearing only the subject pronoun, give the full sentence.[1]

---

[1] Complete student answers are given in the first two lessons only. Although instructions for the drills are addressed to the student, he is advised to perform them without looking at the printed page, preferably with his book closed. Boldface type always indicates the "model" sentence to be spoken by the student; the corresponding lightface sentence is the "model" to be spoken by the teacher. The English translation appears in italic type.

TEACHER	STUDENT
I'm going home	*I'm going home.*
Я иду́ домо́й.	**Я иду́ домо́й.**
Ты идёшь домо́й.	Ты идёшь домо́й.
Óн идёт домо́й.	Óн идёт домо́й.
Она́ идёт домо́й.	Она́ идёт домо́й.
Мы идём домо́й.	Мы идём домо́й.
Вы идёте домо́й.	Вы идёте домо́й.
Они́ иду́т домо́й.	Они́ иду́т домо́й.

■ QUESTION-ANSWER DRILL

Answer the question, using **на по́чту** with both short and full answers. (In class two students may participate.)

TEACHER	STUDENT
Where are you going?	*To the post office.*
Where are you going?	*I'm going to the post office.*
Куда́ вы идёте?	**На по́чту.**
Куда́ вы идёте?	**Я иду́ на по́чту.**
Куда́ ты идёшь?	На по́чту.
Куда́ ты идёшь?	Я иду́ на по́чту.
Куда́ óн идёт?	На по́чту.
Куда́ óн идёт?	Óн идёт на по́чту.
Куда́ мы идём?	На по́чту.
Куда́ мы идём?	Мы идём на по́чту.
Куда́ она́ идёт?	На по́чту.
Куда́ она́ идёт?	Она́ идёт на по́чту.
Куда́ вы идёте?	На по́чту.
Куда́ вы идёте?	Я иду́ на по́чту.
Куда́ они́ иду́т?	На по́чту.
Куда́ они́ иду́т?	Они́ иду́т на по́чту.

■ QUESTION-ANSWER DRILL

Answer the question, using **на собра́ние,** with both short and full answers.

TEACHER	STUDENT
Where are you going, home?	*No, to a meeting.*
Where are you going, home?	*No, I'm going to a meeting.*
Куда́ вы идёте, домо́й?	**Нéт, на собра́ние.**
Куда́ вы идёте, домо́й?	**Нéт, я иду́ на собра́ние.**
Куда́ óн идёт, домо́й?	Нéт, на собра́ние.
Куда́ óн идёт, домо́й?	Нéт, óн идёт на собра́ние.
Куда́ она́ идёт, домо́й?	Нéт, на собра́ние.
Куда́ она́ идёт, домо́й?	Нéт, она́ идёт на собра́ние.
Куда́ мы идём, домо́й?	Нéт, на собра́ние.
Куда́ мы идём, домо́й?	Нéт, мы идём на собра́ние.
Куда́ они́ иду́т, домо́й?	Нéт, на собра́ние.
Куда́ они́ иду́т, домо́й?	Нéт, они́ иду́т на собра́ние.
Куда́ ты идёшь, домо́й?	Нéт, на собра́ние.
Куда́ ты идёшь, домо́й?	Нéт, я иду́ на собра́ние.

Answer two ways, using **на уро́к пе́ния.**

TEACHER	STUDENT
Where's Nina going?	*To a singing lesson.*
Where's Nina going?	*Nina's going to a singing lesson.*
Куда́ идёт Ни́на?	**На уро́к пе́ния.**
Куда́ идёт Ни́на?	**Ни́на идёт на уро́к пе́ния.**
Куда́ идёт Евге́ний?	На уро́к пе́ния.
Куда́ идёт Евге́ний?	Евге́ний идёт на уро́к пе́ния.
Куда́ идёт студе́нт?	На уро́к пе́ния.
Куда́ идёт студе́нт?	Студе́нт идёт на уро́к пе́ния.
Куда́ идёт студе́нтка?	На уро́к пе́ния.
Куда́ идёт студе́нтка?	Студе́нтка идёт на уро́к пе́ния.

■ SUBSTITUTION DRILLS

Items to be cued by the teacher are indicated in parentheses.

1. *The student is going to a meeting.*

Студе́нт идёт на собра́ние.	**Студе́нт идёт на собра́ние.**
(Студе́нт и студе́нтка) ____.	Студе́нт и студе́нтка иду́т на собра́ние.
(О́н) _____.	О́н идёт на собра́ние.
(Она́) _____.	Она́ идёт на собра́ние.
(Они́) _____.	Они́ иду́т на собра́ние.
(Евге́ний) _____.	Евге́ний идёт на собра́ние.
(Ни́на) _____.	Ни́на идёт на собра́ние.
(Евге́ний и Ни́на) _____.	Евге́ний и Ни́на иду́т на собра́ние.

2. *Here comes my bus.*

Во́т идёт мо́й авто́бус.	**Во́т идёт мо́й авто́бус.**
Во́т идёт Ни́на.	**Во́т идёт Ни́на.**
_____ (Евге́ний).	Во́т идёт Евге́ний.
_____ (студе́нт).	Во́т идёт студе́нт.
_____ (студе́нтка).	Во́т идёт студе́нтка.
_____ (мо́й авто́бус).	Во́т идёт мо́й авто́бус.
_____ (Евге́ний и Ни́на).	Во́т иду́т Евге́ний и Ни́на.
_____ (студе́нт и студе́нтка).	Во́т иду́т студе́нт и студе́нтка.

■ QUESTION-ANSWER DRILL

Answer the following questions, using a pronoun and **в клу́б** in the answer.

TEACHER	STUDENT
Where's the student going?	*He's on his way to the club.*
Куда́ идёт студе́нт?	**О́н идёт в клу́б.**
Куда́ иду́т студе́нтка и студе́нт?	Они́ иду́т в клу́б.
Куда́ идёт Евге́ний?	О́н идёт в клу́б.
Куда́ иду́т Ни́на и Евге́ний?	Они́ иду́т в клу́б.
Куда́ идёт Ни́на?	Она́ идёт в клу́б.
Куда́ иду́т студе́нт и студе́нтка?	Они́ иду́т в клу́б.

As you have noticed, the endings of the verb **идти́** in the present tense change for each person in the singular and plural. Thus the first person singular is **я иду́**, second person singular **ты́ идёшь**, third person singular **о́н** (*or* **она́**) **идёт**, and so forth.

The present stem of the verb is **ид–**, and the stress is on the endings throughout the conjugation. Note that the stem consonant **д** is hard in the first person singular and third person plural, but is soft in all the other forms.

	SINGULAR		PLURAL	
1	ид–у́	[id–ú]	ид–ём	[iḓ–óm]
2	ид–ёшь[1]	[iḓ–óš]	ид–ёте	[iḓ–óṭi]
3	ид–ёт	[iḓ–ót]	ид–у́т	[id–út]

This pattern of endings is typical of first conjugation verbs with the stress on the endings. There are only two conjugations in Russian; the second will be discussed later.

It is important to note that **идти́** means both *to be going* and *to be coming*. It describes motion in process and is generally restricted to going on foot.

---

[1] It is a convention in Russian to spell the second person singular ending with a **ь**, even though the consonant **ш** cannot be pronounced soft. Notice also that since the letter **ё** *always* carries the stress, it is unnecessary to mark the stress further.

NOTES

PREPARATION FOR CONVERSATION   Давно́ ва́с не ви́дел

не ви́дел	[n̡iɣíd̡il]	haven't seen, didn't see
ва́с	[vás]	you (dir obj)
давно́	[davnó]	for a long time, a long time ago
Давно́ ва́с не ви́дел.		I haven't seen you for a long time.
всю́ зи́му	[fs̡ú z̡ímu]	all winter, all winter long
Всю́ зи́му ва́с не ви́дел.		I haven't seen you all winter.
ка́к дела́	[kág d̡ilá]	how is everything
а́ *long*	[á]	ah, oh
А́, Кири́лл Па́влович! Ка́к дела́?		Ah, Kirill Pavlovich! How is everything?
хорошо́	[xəraší]	well, fine, good
спаси́бо	[spaş̡íbə]	thanks, thank you
Хорошо́, спаси́бо.		Fine, thanks.
больны́	[baļn̡í]	sick, ill
вы́ бы́ли	[ví bíļi]	you were
Вы́ бы́ли больны́.		You were sick.
я́ слы́шал	[já slíšəl]	I heard
Я́ слы́шал, вы́ бы́ли больны́.		I heard you were sick.
здоро́в	[zdaróf]	healthy, well, recovered
тепе́рь	[t̡ip̡ér̡]	now
Тепе́рь я́ здоро́в.		I'm well now.
вполне́	[fpalņé]	completely, fully, quite
уже́	[užé]	already, by now
Тепе́рь я́ уже́ вполне́ здоро́в.		I'm completely well now. (*Lit.* Now I already completely well.)
но	[no]	but
да́	[dá]	yes
Да́, но тепе́рь я́ уже́ вполне́ здоро́в.		Yes, but now I'm completely well. (*Lit.* Yes, but now I already completely well.)
горсове́т	[gorsaɣét]	gorsovet (city council)
в горсове́те	[vgorsaɣét̡i]	at the gorsovet
вы́ рабо́таете	[ví rabótəjit̡i]	you work, you've been working

19

Вы́ рабо́таете в горсове́те?	Do you work at the gorsovet?
всё ещё [fşó jiščó]	still, yet
Вы́ всё ещё рабо́таете в горсове́те?	Do you still work at the gorsovet?
я рабо́таю [já rabótəju]	I work
Да́, я всё ещё рабо́таю в горсове́те.	Yes, I still work at the gorsovet.
то́же [tóži]	too, also
жена́ [žiná]	wife
Да́, и жена́ то́же.	Yes, and my wife [does] too.
она́ рабо́тает [aná rabótəjit]	she works
Да́, и жена́ то́же рабо́тает.	Yes, and my wife works too.
слы́шать [slíšət]	to hear
э́то [étə]	that, it, this
ра́д [rát]	glad
Ра́д э́то слы́шать.	Glad to hear it.
Давно́?	For a long time?
о́сень (f) [óşiņ]	fall, autumn
с о́сени [sóşiņi]	since autumn, since fall
Да́, с о́сени.	Yes, since fall.
я спешу́ [já spişú]	I'm hurrying, I'm in a hurry
на авто́бус [nəaftóbus]	for the bus, to catch a bus
Я́ спешу́ на авто́бус.	I'm in a hurry to catch a bus.
Извини́те, я́ спешу́ на авто́бус.	Excuse me, I'm in a hurry to catch a bus.
приве́т жене́ [priɣéd žiņé]	regards to your wife, say hello to your wife
До свида́ния. Приве́т жене́.	Good-bye. [Give my] regards to your wife.
всего́ хоро́шего [fşivó xaróšivə]	good-bye
спаси́бо [spaşíbə]	thanks, thank you
Спаси́бо. Всего́ хоро́шего.	Thank you. Good-bye.

SUPPLEMENT

му́ж [múš]	husband
му́ж и жена́ [múš i žiná]	husband and wife
ты́ рабо́таешь [tí rabótəjiš]	you work, you've been working, you're working, you do work
где́ [gḍé]	where, at what place[1]
Где́ ты́ рабо́таешь?	Where do you work?
— Я́ рабо́таю в клу́бе.	I work at the club.
они́ рабо́тают [aņí rabótəjut]	they work
Где́ они́ рабо́тают?	Where do they work?
— Они́ рабо́тают на заво́де.	They work at a plant.
мы́ рабо́таем [mí rabótəjim]	we work
Мы́ рабо́таем на по́чте.	We work at the post office.

---

[1] There are two words for *where* in Russian: где́ and куда́. Где́ means *where* in the sense *at what place* as opposed to куда́ *to what place*.

Compare	Где́ вы́ рабо́таете?	— На заво́де.	В клу́бе.	На по́чте.
with	Куда́ вы́ идёте?	— На заво́д.	В клу́б.	На по́чту.

Давно́ ва́с не ви́дел

I haven't seen you for a long time

К.П. — Кири́лл Па́влович Цара́пкин
С.Ф. — Семён Фили́ппович Хитро́в

К.П.	1	Семён Фили́ппович! Всю́ зи́му ва́с не ви́дел.	şimón fiļípič ↓ fşú zĭmu vás ņiɣíḑil ↓	Semyon Filipovich![1] I haven't seen you all winter.
С.Ф.	2	А, Кири́лл Па́влович! Ка́к дела́?	ã ↓ ķiŗíl pãlič ↓ kág ḑilã ↓	Ah, Kirill Pavlovich![1] How is everything?[2]
К.П.	3	Хорошо́, спаси́бо. Я слы́шал, вы́ бы́ли больны́.	xərašŏ | spaşĭbə ↓ já slĭšəl | ví bĭļi baļnĭ ↓	Fine, thanks. I heard you were sick.
С.Ф.	4	Да́. Но тепе́рь я уже́ вполне́ здоро́в.	dã ↓ no ţiṛḗṛ | já užé fpalņḗ zdarŏf ↓	Yes. But now I'm completely well.[2]
К.П.	5	Вы́ всё ещё рабо́таете в горсове́те?	ví fşó jiščŏ rabótəjiţi vgorsaɣĕţi ↓	Are you still working at the gorsovet?[3]
С.Ф.	6	Да́, и жена́ то́же.	dã ↓ i žiná tŏži ↓	Yes, and my wife is too.
К.П.	7	Да́? Ра́д э́то слы́шать. Давно́?	dã ↑ rát étə slĭšəţ ↓ davnŏ ↑	Is that so? Glad to hear it. For a long time?
С.Ф.	8	С о́сени. Извини́те, я спешу́ на авто́бус.	sŏşiņi ↓ izɣiņĭţi ↓ já sṛišú nəaftŏbus ↓	Since fall. Excuse me, I'm hurrying to catch a bus.
К.П.	9	До свида́ния. Приве́т жене́.	dəsɣidãņjə ↓ pṛiɣéd žiņḗ ↓	Good-bye. [Give my] regards to your wife.
С.Ф.	10	Спаси́бо. Всего́ хоро́шего.	spaşĭbə ↓ fşivó xarŏšivə ↓	Thank you. Good-bye.[4]

NOTES   [1] Adult Russians commonly address each other by the first name and a middle name derived from the father's first name. **Па́влович** and **Фили́ппович** are middle names, or patronymics, formed by adding the suffix **-ович** to the stem of first names **Па́вел** *Paul* and **Фили́пп** *Philip*. Daughters of **Па́вел** and **Фили́пп** have patronymics **Па́вловна** and **Фили́пповна** respectively, with the feminine suffix

-овна. If the father's first name ends in -й, the patronymic suffix is spelled -евич (for the son) and -евна (for the daughter).

FATHER'S FIRST NAME		SON'S PATRONYMIC	DAUGHTER'S PATRONYMIC
Никола́й	Nicholas	Никола́евич	Никола́евна
Евге́ний	Eugene	Евге́ниевич	Евге́ниевна
Ива́н	John	Ива́нович	Ива́новна
Кири́лл	Cyril	Кири́ллович	Кири́лловна
Семён	Simon	Семёнович	Семёновна

Patronymics are usually shortened in speech, for example: **Семён Фили́ппович** is usually pronounced [şimón fiḷípič]; **Кири́лл Па́влович** [ķiŗíl páḷič]; **Ни́на Семёновна** [ṇínə şimónnə].

[2] Observe that the present tense forms of the verb *to be* (corresponding to English *am*, *is*, *are*) are usually not expressed in Russian:

Ка́к дела́?	How is everything? (*Lit.* How things?)
Я́ вполне́ здоро́в.	I'm completely well. (*Lit.* I completely well.)

[3] **Горсове́т** (short for **городско́й сове́т**) means city council and includes all of the administrative offices necessary to run a city.

[4] **Всего́ хоро́шего** and **до свида́ния** are used more or less interchangeably in saying *good-bye*. Note that both **всего́** and **хоро́шего** spell their last consonant with a г but pronounce it [v]: [fşivó xaróšivə]. This pronunciation of г as [v] is regular for adjective and pronoun endings spelled -ого and -его.

Basic sentence patterns

1. Где́ ты́ рабо́таешь?
  — Я́ рабо́таю в горсове́те.
  ——————— в клу́бе.
  ——————— на заво́де.
  ——————— на по́чте.

    Where do you work?
    I work at the gorsovet.
    —— at the club.
    —— in a plant.
    —— at the post office.

2. Ты́ давно́ та́м рабо́таешь?
  — Да́, давно́.
  — Да́, уже́ давно́.
  — Да́, с о́сени.
  — Да́, и жена́ то́же.
  — Да́, и му́ж то́же.

    Have you been working there long?
    Yes, I have.
    Yes, for a long time now.
    Yes, since fall.
    Yes, and my wife too.
    Yes, and my husband too.

3. Я́ всю́ зи́му ва́с не ви́дел.[1]
  Я́ давно́ ва́с не ви́дел.
  Я́ вчера́ ва́с не ви́дел.
  — Я́ то́же ва́с не ви́дел.

    I haven't seen you all winter.
    I haven't seen you in a long time.
    I didn't see you yesterday.
    I didn't see you either.

[1] The past tense form **ви́дел** is used only when the subject is masculine. It is replaced by **ви́дела** when the subject is feminine: Я́ всю́ зи́му ва́с не ви́дела. Я́ давно́ ва́с не ви́дела. Я́ вчера́ ва́с не ви́дела. Я́ то́же ва́с не ви́дела.

4. Извини́те. Я спешу́.　　　　　　　Excuse me, I'm in a hurry.
　　Я спешу́ на авто́бус.　　　　　　I'm hurrying to the bus.
　　_____ на заво́д.　　　　　　_____ to the plant.
　　_____ на по́чту.　　　　　　_____ to the post office.
　　_____ в клу́б.　　　　　　　_____ to the club.
　　_____ в горсове́т.　　　　　_____ to the gorsovet.
　　_____ домо́й.　　　　　　　_____ home.

Correspondence between cyrillic vowel letters and the vowel sounds

The Russian vowel letters have already been discussed, particularly with reference to their functions as indicators of softness or hardness of the preceding consonant. We have also discussed the particular function of the soft-series vowel letters, **я, е, и, ё, ю,** as indicators of the presence of a preceding [j] sound under certain conditions.

In the following paragraphs the Cyrillic vowel letters will be presented, with examples of their occurrence in both stressed and unstressed syllables. Observe carefully the correspondence between the Cyrillic vowel *letters* and their *sound values*, noting particularly that the position of a vowel in relation to the stressed syllable often determines its sound value.

A. The Cyrillic letters **и** and **ы** have approximately the same vowel sound in unstressed syllables as in stressed syllables, [i] and [ɨ] respectively. Except for **ш, ж,** and **ц,** all consonants before **и** are pronounced soft; all consonants before **ы** are pronounced hard.

и́ли	[íḷi]	or	высо́кий	[visóķij]	high
име́ть	[iṃéț]	to possess	но́вый	[nóvij]	new
лю́ди	[ḷúḑi]	people	была́	[bilá]	was
мину́та	[ṃinútə]	minute			
ты́	[tí]	you			

B. The Cyrillic letters **ю** and **у** have the same vowel sound in unstressed syllables as in stressed syllables: [u].

At the beginning of a word and after **ъ, ь,** or a vowel, however, the letter **ю** is pronounced [ju]. Consonants preceding **ю** are always pronounced soft; except for **ч** and **щ,** all consonants before **у** are pronounced hard.

у́лица	[úḷicə]	street	говорю́	[gəvaṛú]	I speak
ми́нус	[ṃínus]	minus	зна́ю	[znáju]	I know
друго́й	[drugój]	other	пью́т	[ṗjút]	they drink
рубли́	[rubḷí]	rubles	ю́га	[júgə]	of the south
пи́шут	[ṗíšut]	they write			
зву́к	[zvúk]	sound			
у́ксус	[úksus]	vinegar			
ую́тно	[ujútnə]	cozy			
мо́рю	[móṛu]	to the sea			
люби́ть	[ḷuḅíț]	to love			

C. The Cyrillic letter ё occurs only in stressed syllables and is consistently pronounced with the vowel sound [o].

At the beginning of a word and after ь, ъ, or a vowel, the letter ё is pronounced [jo]. Except for ш and ж, consonants preceding ё are pronounced soft.

нёс	[ņós]	he was carrying		ёлка	[jólkə]	spruce
тёмный	[ţómnij]	dark		приём	[pŗijóm]	reception
идёт	[idót]	he's going		пьёт	[pjót]	he drinks

Note: In our text ё will be consistently written with two dots to keep it distinct from e. Except in textbooks and dictionaries, Russians do not normally make a distinction between e and ё in writing.

D. The Cyrillic letter o has the sound value [o] only in stressed syllables. In the syllable immediately before the stress and at the very beginning of a word it is pronounced [a]. In all other positions the Cyrillic letter o is pronounced [ə]. Except for ч and щ, consonants before o are always pronounced hard.

оборóт	[abarót]	turn		онó	[anó]	it
хорошó	[xərašó]	good		вопрóс	[vaprós]	· question
городóк	[gəradók]	small town				
óлово	[óləvə]	tin				
молокó	[məlakó]	milk				
тóлько	[tólkə]	only				

E. The Cyrillic letter e has the sound [e] only in stressed syllables. In other positions it is pronounced as [i], varying in value from the sound of the English e in *e*mit or r*e*act to a shorter, more obscure sound as in the first syllable of d*i*spatch.

In certain grammatical endings it is pronounced by some speakers as short [i] and by others as [ə], for example, **пóле** [póļi] or [póļə]. Remember that at the beginning of a word, or following ь, ъ, or a vowel, the letter e is pronounced with a preceding [j] sound. Except for ш, ж, and ц, consonants before e are pronounced soft.

человéк	[čilaɣék]	person		бóлее	[bóļiji]	more
моéй	[majéj]	my		съéли	[sjéļi]	they ate up
дéло	[ḓélə]	business		отъéзда	[atjézdə]	of the departure
тепéрь	[ţiṗéŗ]	now		чьéй	[čjéj]	whose
переведите	[ṗiŗiɣiḓíţi]	translate				
меня	[miņá]	me				
éсли	[jésļi]	if				
ещё	[jiščó]	yet, still				

F. The Cyrillic letter э occurs chiefly in words of non-Russian origin and almost always at the beginning of a word. When stressed it has the sound value [e]; when unstressed it is heard as [i].

э́то	[étə]	this		энéргия	[iņérgijə]	energy
э́ти	[éţi]	these		этажи	[itaží]	floors
э́хо	[éxə]	echo				
экзáмен	[igzámin]	examination				
элемéнт	[iļiṃént]	element				

Some Russian speakers, however, tend to pronounce э as [e] wherever it occurs, for example, этáж [etáš] or [itáš].

G. The Cyrillic letter я has the vowel sound [a] in stressed syllables and the vowel sound [i] in unstressed syllables except for certain endings, where it has the value [ə]. Consonants preceding я are always pronounced soft. At the beginning of a word and after ь, ъ, or a vowel, the letter я is pronounced with a preceding [j] sound.

пять	[р̧áţ]	five		ясно	[jásnə]	clearly
поля	[pa̧lá]	fields		Ялта	[jáltə]	Yalta
меня	[m̧iṇá]	me		язы́к	[jizík]	language
моря	[ma̧rá]	seas				
пяти́	[р̧iţí]	five				
гляде́ть	[ģliḑéţ]	to gaze				
я	[já]	I				

STRUCTURE AND DRILLS

The present tense of the first conjugation verb рабóтать

я рабóтаю	I work, I'm working, I've been working
ты́ рабóтаешь	you work, you're working, you've been working
óн рабóтает	he works
онá рабóтает	she works
мы́ рабóтаем	we work
вы́ рабóтаете	you work
они́ рабóтают	they work

■ REPETITION DRILL

Listen to your instructor (or the tape) and repeat the above pronoun-verb model until you can say it perfectly.

■ REPETITION-SUBSTITUTION DRILLS

Repeat after your instructor (or the tape) as accurately as you can, imitating both the individual words and the sentence intonation. Then, on hearing only the subject cue, give the full sentence.

TEACHER

1. *I'm working now.*
   Я тепéрь рабóтаю.
   Они́ тепéрь рабóтают.
   Ты́ тепéрь рабóтаешь.
   Вы́ тепéрь рабóтаете.
   Мы́ тепéрь рабóтаем.
   Óн тепéрь рабóтает.
   Онá тепéрь рабóтает.

STUDENT

I'm working now.
Я тепéрь рабóтаю.
Они́ тепéрь рабóтают.
Ты́ тепéрь рабóтаешь.
Вы́ тепéрь рабóтаете.
Мы́ тепéрь рабóтаем
Óн тепéрь рабóтает.
Онá тепéрь рабóтает.

2. *I work too.* | *I work too.*
Я́ тóже рабóтаю. | **Я́ тóже рабóтаю.**
Вы́ тóже рабóтаете. | **Вы́ тóже рабóтаете.**
Ты́ тóже рабóтаешь. | Ты́ тóже рабóтаешь.
Женá тóже рабóтает. | Женá тóже рабóтает.
Онá тóже рабóтает. | Онá тóже рабóтает.
Мýж тóже рабóтает. | Мýж тóже рабóтает.
Óн тóже рабóтает. | Óн тóже рабóтает.
Мы́ тóже рабóтаем. | Мы́ тóже рабóтаем.
Они́ тóже рабóтают. | Они́ тóже рабóтают.

■ QUESTION-ANSWER DRILLS

Answer the questions in the negative according to the models given.

TEACHER	STUDENT
Do you work?	*No, I don't.*
Ты́ рабóтаешь?	**Нéт, не рабóтаю.**
Вы́ рабóтаете?	**Нéт, не рабóтаю.**
Женá рабóтает?	Нéт, не рабóтает.
Мýж рабóтает?	Нéт, не рабóтает.
Они́ рабóтают?	Нéт, не рабóтают.
Онá рабóтает?	Нéт, не рабóтает.
Óн рабóтает?	Нéт, не рабóтает.

Using **на пóчте,** answer with both short and full answers according to the models given.

Where do you work?	*At the post office.*
Where do you work?	*We work at the post office.*
Гдé вы́ рабóтаете?	**На пóчте.**
Гдé вы́ рабóтаете?	**Мы́ рабóтаем на пóчте.**
Гдé онá рабóтает?	На пóчте.
Гдé онá рабóтает?	Онá рабóтает на пóчте.
Гдé ты́ рабóтаешь?	На пóчте.
Гдé ты́ рабóтаешь?	Я́ рабóтаю на пóчте.
Гдé они́ рабóтают?	На пóчте.
Гдé они́ рабóтают?	Они́ рабóтают на пóчте.
Гдé óн рабóтает?	На пóчте.
Гдé óн рабóтает?	Óн рабóтает на пóчте.

■ SUBSTITUTION DRILL

He's been working there for a long time.	*He's been working there for a long time.*
Óн давнó тáм рабóтает.	**Óн давнó тáм рабóтает.**
Женá давнó тáм рабóтает.	**Женá давнó тáм рабóтает.**
(Евгéний) ________.	Евгéний давнó тáм рабóтает.
(Ни́на) ________.	Ни́на давнó тáм рабóтает.
(Онá) ________.	Онá давнó тáм рабóтает.
(Семён) ________.	Семён давнó тáм рабóтает.
(Они́) ________.	Они́ давнó тáм рабóтают.
(Кири́лл и Семён) ________.	Кири́лл и Семён давнó тáм рабóтают.
(Мýж) ________.	Мýж давнó тáм рабóтает.

Following the models, give both short and full answers.

TEACHER	STUDENT
Have you been working at the club long?	*Yes, for a long time, since fall.*
Have you been working at the club long?	*Yes, I've been working there since fall.*
Вы́ давно́ рабо́таете в клу́бе?	Да́, давно́, с о́сени.
Вы́ давно́ рабо́таете в клу́бе?	Да́, я́ рабо́таю та́м с о́сени.
О́н давно́ рабо́тает в клу́бе?	Да́, давно́, с о́сени.
О́н давно́ рабо́тает в клу́бе?	Да́, о́н рабо́тает та́м с о́сени.
О́ни давно́ рабо́тают в клу́бе?	Да́, давно́, с о́сени.
О́ни давно́ рабо́тают в клу́бе?	Да́, они́ рабо́тают та́м с о́сени.
О́на давно́ рабо́тает в клу́бе?	Да́, давно́, с о́сени.
О́на давно́ рабо́тает в клу́бе?	Да́, она́ рабо́тает та́м с о́сени.
Кири́лл давно́ рабо́тает в клу́бе?	Да́, давно́, с о́сени.
Кири́лл давно́ рабо́тает в клу́бе?	Да́, о́н рабо́тает та́м с о́сени.
Ты́ давно́ рабо́таешь в клу́бе?	Да́, давно́, с о́сени.
Ты́ давно́ рабо́таешь в клу́бе?	Да́, я рабо́таю та́м с о́сени.

DISCUSSION

Like **идти́**, the verb **рабо́тать** belongs to the first conjugation. It differs from **идти́** in that its present stem appears to end in a vowel (**рабо́та–**), whereas that of **идти́** ends in a consonant (**ид–**). This is only a convention of the writing system, however, since the actual present stem of **рабо́тать** ends in the consonant *sound* [j]. As we know, when [j] occurs between vowels it is expressed through the "soft-series" vowel letters which follow. Thus we may contrast the written stem and endings in the chart below with those of the transcription, which show the real division of stem and ending.

		WRITTEN FORMS	TRANSCRIPTION
STEM		рабо́та–	rabótəj–
SINGULAR	1	рабо́та–ю	rabótəj–u
	2	–ешь	–iš
	3	–ет	–it
PLURAL	1	–ем	–im
	2	–ете	–iţi
	3	–ют	–ut

It is only in the imperative forms that the [j] of the stem is written with a separate letter **й**: **рабо́тай (рабо́тайте)**! *work*!

Рабо́тать is typical of the "j-stem" verbs in that it has a fixed stress which falls on the same syllable of the stem in all forms.

The Russian handwriting system

A. The alphabet

PRINTED	WRITTEN		PRINTED	WRITTEN		PRINTED	WRITTEN
А а	*А а*		К к	*К к*		Х х	*Х х*
Б б	*Б б*		Л л	*Л л*		Ц ц	*Ц ц*
В в	*В в*		М м	*М м*		Ч ч	*Ч ч*
Г г	*Г г*		Н н	*Н н*		Ш ш	*Ш ш*
Д д	*Д д д*		О о	*О о*		Щ щ	*Щ щ*
Е е	*Е е*		П п	*П п*		Ъ ъ	*ъ*
Ё ё	*Ё ё*		Р р	*Р р*		Ы ы	*ы*
Ж ж	*Ж ж*		С с	*С с*		Ь ь	*ь*
З з	*З з з*		Т т	*Т т*		Э э	*Э э*
И и	*И и*		У у	*У у*		Ю ю	*Ю ю*
Й й	*Й й*		Ф ф	*Ф ф*		Я я	*Я я*

B. Reading practice

Conversations from Lessons 1 and 2 are given below in handwritten form as an introduction to the handwriting system. Now that you are familiar with the conversations, you should have no real difficulty reading them. Refer to the printed versions if necessary.

Студент и студентка.

— Привет, Нина! Куда вы идёте? — На урок пения. А вы домой? — Нет, я иду на почту послать письмо. — Скажите, вчера было собрание? — В клубе?

Нет, не было. – А на заводе? – Было, но я там не был. – Ну, извините. Вот идёт мой автобус. – До свидания! – До свидания!

Давно вас не видел.

– Семён Филиппович! Всю зиму вас не видел. – А, Кирилл Павлович! Как дела? – Хорошо, спасибо. Вы, я слышал, были больны? – Да. Но теперь я вполне здоров. – Вы всё ещё работаете в горсовете? – Да, и жена тоже. – Да? Рад это слышать. Давно? – С осени. Извините, я спешу на автобус. – До свидания! Привет жене! – Спасибо. Всего хорошего!

C. How the letters are formed

1. SMALL LETTERS

о	а	д	б	ф

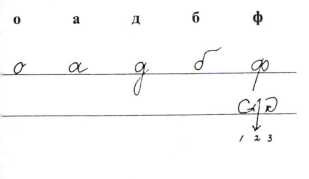

The first three letters are formed in practically the same way as in English. The letters **б** and **ф** begin the same way as **о**. In **б**, a vertical line then goes upward and curves at the top to the right. In **ф**, after the first circle, a straight vertical stroke goes downward and then back up along the same line, returning to the initial point and continuing up and clockwise to form another circle.

у	и	й

The letters **у** and **и** are formed like the English handwritten *y* and *u*; **й** is the same as **и**, but with the addition of a short half circle above. (Write it immediately lest you forget.)

ц	ш	щ

The letter **ц** is also written like **и**, except that it ends in a small loop below the line. Handwritten **ш** and **щ** consist of three vertical lines of equal height with a final drop to the line (unlike the English written *w*). The **щ** has a small tail loop like **ц**.

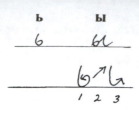

Make a small figure 6 to form the soft sign. The written ы starts with the same downstroke and loop as ь, swings up to a sharp peak, goes down again, and then curves to the right. Both letters are short compared with the handwritten в.

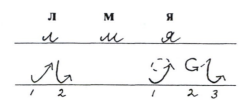

The first letter is written like one variant of the English handwritten *r*. The second is similar, but ends in a small circle, resembling a combination of ч and ь. (Some Russians replace ъ with an apostrophe.) The third differs from the first in that it does not have the short horizontal line at the top, but is rounded.

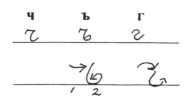

These three letters begin with a small hook slightly above the line (remember this when joining these letters to others). To form я, begin with the same upward stroke as in л and м. Then make a small counterclockwise circle at the top, returning to the same point and ending in a line down (я looks like л with a small loop to the left of its top). Do not make the Russian л as tall as an English *l*.

The first two letters, п and т, are formed much like the English handwritten *n* and *m*. The Russian к is written like the printed English *k*; it is never tall with a loop as in the English written *k*.

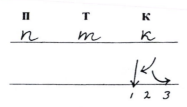

For н, start from the top down, then go back halfway up the same line, turning to the right and upward, then finally coming back down to the line. To form ю, follow the directions for н, but continue the last stroke back upward to form a circle.

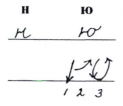

For handwritten э, begin at the top and make a half circle clockwise, then cut it in half by a small horizontal line. For ж, start at the top and make the same half circle, then slant back up to the right, then straight down and again up to the right; finish with another half circle (like the English written *c*) going in the opposite direction.

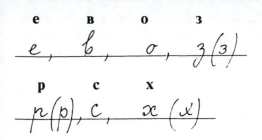

e	в	о	з
e,	*b*,	*o*,	*з* (з)

р	с	х
р (р),	*с*,	*x* (x)

These letters are all formed much the same way as in English. The letter **e** must be written *e* (never *ε*); the letter **в** must be written tall and kept distinct from **ь** (*b* versus *b*).

Note: Russians do not print words, even when they fill out official forms by hand.

■ HANDWRITING DRILL

Practice copying the small letters above until you can write them easily and accurately.

2. CAPITAL LETTERS[1]

А	В	Д	К
A	*B*	*D*	*K*

These are similar to the English letters with corresponding shapes.

Н	О	С	Х
H	*O*	*C*	*x*

Ж	И	Й	Л	М
Ж	*И*	*Й*	*Л*	*М*

These are the same as their corresponding small letters but taller and larger.

Ш	Щ	Ц	Э	Ю	Я
Ш	*Щ*	*Ц*	*Э*	*Ю*	*Я*

Г	П	Б	Ф
Г	*П*	*Б*	*Ф*

All four letters start with a basic line that curves downward, turning to the left. The fourth letter differs from the others only in that it starts with a small flourish at the top. The same stroke in the first, second, and third is the curved line from left to right that caps each letter. The second has another downward stroke, ending toward the right before the cap is added. The third letter has as its third stroke a large loop at the bottom (like a closed, looped figure 2). The fourth has two loops on either side of the down stroke which resemble a figure 8 on its side.

---

[1] Russian capital letters are used only at the beginning of the sentence, in proper names, and in the first word of a title. Russians do not capitalize the names of months, nationalities, centuries, professions, or ranks; nor do they capitalize the personal pronoun **я** within a sentence.

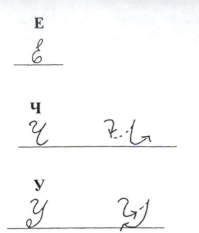

E

Ч

У

Certain varieties of the English written capital *E* are acceptable. Start outside and make the small top loop; the bottom half circle must be larger than the upper one.

For **Ч,** begin with an upward, clockwise curve, then make a downward, "u-shaped" curve, slanting back and down, finally curving to the right *on the line*.

Capital **У** is like the preceding letter, except that the curved downward stroke goes to the left. Unlike its small counterpart, capital **У** starts high above the base line and must not extend below the line.

■ HANDWRITING DRILL

Practice copying the capital letters until you can write them easily and accurately.

D. Summary remarks on the handwriting system

1. All Russian capital letters except **Щ** and **Ц** have their base on the line and extend above it; **Щ** and **Ц** each has a small loop which extends below the line.

2. Small handwritten letters are of two types: long and short.

a. *Long letters*
Three long letters have their base on the line and extend above it.

and

Five long letters have their base on the line and extend below it.

and

b. *Short letters*
All the remaining letters are of the same height and are written on the line except **щ** and **ц**, each of which has a short loop below the line.

3. Most letters are joined together in writing; however, and are usually not connected to the following letter.

4. The letters з, д, р, г, and х, may be handwritten in two ways.

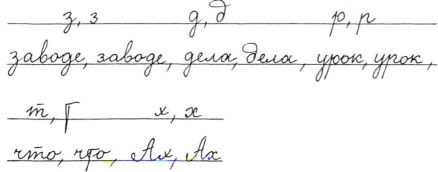

The first variant in each pair is the one used more frequently. Some Russians draw a horizontal line above *т̄* and below *ш̲* to make these letters stand out better. The student is advised to use the first variant of *т̄* because he cannot substitute the usual English written *t* for Russian *г̄*.

каши *хотите*

■ COPYING AND HANDWRITING PRACTICE

1. Copy the handwritten versions of the first two conversations, being careful to observe the connections of the letters. 2. Return to the first two conversations in printed form and copy each in handwriting.

Syllabification of words in Russian

Both in pronouncing words by syllable and in dividing them at the end of a written line, there are certain important principles that should be followed.

In pronunciation, the basic pattern is to end a syllable with a vowel wherever possible.

спа–си́–бо	[spa–şí–bə]	thanks
ра–бо́–та–е–те	[ra–bó–tə–ji–ţi]	[you] work
пи–сьмо́	[ṇi–şmó]	letter
ска–жи́–те	[ska–ží–ţi]	tell [me]! say!
по–вто–ри́–те	[pə–fta–ŗi–ţi]	repeat!

Consonant clusters beginning with р, л, н, and й are usually divided after these consonants. Final consonants are, of course, treated as part of the syllable which they end.

ка–ран–да́ш	[kə–ran–dáš]	pencil
чи–та́й–те	[či–táj–ţi]	read!
по́л–ка	[pól–kə]	shelf
у–ни–вер–си–те́т	[u–ṇi–yir–şi–ţét]	university

In dividing written words at the end of a line, these same general rules apply, but there is slightly more leeway in the division of clusters of consonants. For example, **сестра́** may be divided **се–стра́** (as in pronunciation), **сес–тра́**, or **сест–ра́**. Doubled letters are always divided when carried over to the next line, for example, **А́н–на** and **под–да́ть**. Single letters are never left at the end of one line or at the beginning of the next.

NOTES

PREPARATION FOR CONVERSATION	Лу́чше по́здно, чём никогда́

лу́чше [lúčši]	better
по́здно [póznə]	late
чём [čém]	than
никогда́ [ɲikagdá]	never
Лу́чше по́здно, чём никогда́.	Better late than never.
здра́вствуйте [zdrástujți] [1]	hello
Лёв, здра́вствуйте!	Hello, Lev!
вы́ спеши́те [ví spišíți]	you're hurrying
Куда́ вы́ спеши́те?	Where are you hurrying to?
университе́т [uɲiɣirşiţét]	university
в университе́т [vuɲiɣirşiţét]	to the university
Я́ спешу́ в университе́т.	I'm hurrying to the university.
концéрт [kancért]	concert
на концéрт [nəkancért]	to a concert
В университе́т, на концéрт.	To the university, to a concert.
Я́ спешу́ в университе́т, на концéрт.	I'm hurrying to the university, to a concert.
интерéсно [inţiŗésnə]	that's interesting
беспла́тно [ƀisplátnə]	free
Интерéсно. Это беспла́тно?	That's interesting. Is it free?
пойти́ [pajţí]	to go
[вы] хоти́те [ví xaţíţi]	you want
Хоти́те пойти́?	Do you want to go?
удово́льствие [udavóḷstɣijə]	pleasure
С удово́льствием! [sudavóḷstɣijəm]	With pleasure! or I'd love to!

---

[1] **Здра́вствуйте** is simplified in pronunciation to something that ranges from [zdrástujți] to [zdrásçți], depending on the tempo of speech and the informality of the speaker. Note also that **по́здно** is pronounced without д : [póznə]. Clusters of three or more consonants are usually simplified, and д and т are usually omitted between consonants except at the beginning of a word: **пра́здник** [prázɲik] *holiday.*

вы́ де́лаете [ví ḍéləɉiţi]	you're doing
что́ [štó]	what
Что́ вы́ де́лаете?	What are you doing?
кста́ти [kstáţi]	by the way, incidentally
Кста́ти, что́ вы́ тепе́рь де́лаете?	By the way, what are you doing now?
лаборато́рия [ləbəratóɾijə]	laboratory
в лаборато́рии [vləbəratóɾiji]	in a laboratory
Я рабо́таю в лаборато́рии.	I work in a laboratory.
та́к ску́чно [ták skúšnə] [1]	[it's] so dull, [it's] so boring
Там та́к ску́чно.	It's so boring there.
поступа́йте в университе́т [pəstupáɉţi vuṇiɣirṣiţét]	enroll at the university! enter the university!
так [tək]	in that case, then
Так поступа́йте в университе́т.	Then enroll at the university.
Что́ вы́!	You can't mean it! *or* You're not serious!
уже́ по́здно [užé póznə]	it's already late, it's too late
мне́ [mṇé]	for me, to me
Мне́ уже́ по́здно.	It's too late for me.
Мне́ тепе́рь уже́ по́здно.	It's too late for me now.
говоря́т [gəvaɾát]	they say, people say
[вы] зна́ете [ví znáɉiţi]	you know
зна́ете, говоря́т... [znáɉiţi gəvaɾát]	you know [what] they say . . .
Зна́ете, говоря́т: "Лу́чше по́здно, чéм никогда́".	You know [what] they say: "Better late than never."

SUPPLEMENT

ра́но	early
Ещё ра́но.	It's early yet *or* It's too early.
за́нят (m)	he's busy, occupied, tied up
занята́ (f)	she's busy, occupied, tied up
за́няты (pl)	we're busy, occupied, tied up
Вы́ за́няты?	Are you busy?
— Да́, я́ за́нят (*or* занята́).	Yes, I am.
ча́сто	often
Я́ ча́сто рабо́таю в лаборато́рии.	I often work in the laboratory.
ре́дко	rarely, seldom
Я́ ре́дко рабо́таю в лаборато́рии.	I rarely work in the laboratory.
иногда́	sometimes
Я́ иногда́ рабо́таю в лаборато́рии.	I sometimes work in the laboratory.
никогда́ не	never
Я́ никогда́ не рабо́таю в лаборато́рии.	I never work in the laboratory.

ADDITIONAL CLASSROOM EXPRESSIONS

отвеча́йте [atɣičáɉţi] *or* отве́тьте [atɣéţţi]	answer!
Откро́йте кни́ги. [atkróɉţi kṇígi]	Open your books.

---

[1] **Ску́чно** is pronounced [skúšnə] by some speakers, [skúčnə] by others.

Закро́йте кни́ги. [zakrójţi kņígi]	Close your books.
пра́вильно [práɣiļnə]	right, that's right
непра́вильно [ņipráɣiļnə]	wrong, that's wrong
господи́н [gəspaḑín]	Mr.
госпожа́ [gəspažá]	Miss, Mrs.
господа́ [gəspadá]	ladies and gentlemen, everybody, everyone
Закро́йте кни́ги, господа́.	Close your books, everyone.
Вы́ понима́ете? [ví pəņimájiţi]	Do you understand?
— Я́ понима́ю. [já pəņimáju]	I understand.

Лу́чше по́здно, чéм никогда́

Better late than never

М. — Ми́ла   Л. — Лёв

М.	1	Лёв, здра́вствуйте! Куда́ вы́ спеши́те?	ļ̌ĕf ↓ zdrắstujţi ↓ kudá ví sҏišĩţi ↓	Hello Lev. Where are you hurrying to?
Л.	2	В университе́т, на конце́рт.	vuņiɣirşiţĕt ↓ nəkancĕrt ↓	To the university, to a concert.
М.	3	Интере́сно. Э́то беспла́тно?	inţiҏĕsnə ↑ étə ḅisplắtnə ↑	That's interesting. Is it free?
Л.	4	Да́. Хоти́те пойти́?	dắ ↓ xaţíţi pajţí ↑	Yes. Do you want to go?[1]
М.	5	С удово́льствием!	sudavõ̧lstɣijəm ↓	I'd love to!
Л.	6	Кста́ти, что́ вы́ тепе́рь де́лаете?	kstắţi ↓ štó ví ţiҏĕҏ ḑĕ́ləjiţi ↓	By the way, what are you doing now?[2]
М.	7	Рабо́таю в лаборато́рии. Та́м та́к ску́чно!	rabótəju vləbəratõҏiji ↓ tám tắk skúšnə ↓	I work in a laboratory. It's so dull there!
Л.	8	Так поступа́йте в университе́т.	tək pəstupájţi vuņiɣirşiţĕt ↓	Enroll at the university then.[3]
М.	9	Что́ вы́! Мне́ тепе́рь уже́ по́здно.	štõ ví ↓ mņĕ ţiҏĕҏ užé põznə ↓	You're not serious! It's too late for me now.
Л.	10	Зна́ете, говоря́т: «Лу́чше по́здно, чéм никогда́».	znắjiţi ↓ gəvaҏắt	lúčši põznə ↑ čĕm ņikagdắ ↓	You know what they say: "Better late than never."

[1] Verbs in Russian almost always come in pairs called "imperfective" and "perfective." **Пойти** is the perfective member of the imperfective-perfective pair of verbs **идти** and **пойти**. The imperfective member of the verbal pair usually describes an action viewed as a process (**идти** *to be going*); the perfective usually describes an action in terms of its accomplishment or result (**пойти** *to go*). Verbal pairs usually have the same root, but differ in their prefix or in their stem. The system of paired verbs is called "aspect," and the choice of which verb to use—imperfective or perfective—depends on how the Russian speaker views the action.

In these early lessons, the student will encounter verbs of both aspects and will practice them as he meets them, without being expected to know both members of a particular pair or how one is formed in relation to the other.

[2] Russian adverbs, unlike those in English, are usually placed before the verb:

Что́ вы **тепе́рь** де́лаете?	What are you doing *now*?
Вчера́ бы́ло собра́ние?	Was there a meeting *yesterday*?
Я **та́м** не́ был.	I wasn't *there*.

It is also normal to place direct object pronouns before the verb.

Я всю зи́му **ва́с** не ви́дел.	I haven't seen *you* all winter.
Я давно́ **ва́с** не ви́дел.	I haven't seen *you* in a long time.
Ра́д **э́то** слы́шать.	Glad to hear *it*.

[3] The stressed word **та́к** in **та́к ску́чно** means *so* and differs from the unstressed так [tǝk] in **Так поступа́йте в университе́т**, which means *then, in that case*.

Basic sentence patterns

1. Куда́ ты́ спеши́шь? — Where are you hurrying to?
   - — В университе́т. — To the university.
   - — В клу́б. — To the club.
   - — На собра́ние. — To a meeting.
   - — На по́чту. — To the post office.
   - — На конце́рт. — To a concert.
   - — На уро́к. — To class.
   - — На уро́к пе́ния. — To a singing class.
   - — На авто́бус. — To the bus.
   - — На заво́д. — To the plant.
   - — Домо́й. — Home.

2. Куда́ вы́ спеши́те? — Where are you hurrying to?
   - — Я спешу́ в клу́б. — I'm hurrying to the club.
   - _____ в университе́т. — _____ to the university.
   - _____ на собра́ние. — _____ to the meeting.
   - _____ на по́чту. — _____ to the post office.
   - _____ на уро́к. — _____ to class.
   - _____ на уро́к пе́ния. — _____ to a singing class.
   - _____ на авто́бус. — _____ to the bus.
   - _____ на заво́д. — _____ to the plant.
   - _____ домо́й. — _____ home.

3. Хоти́те пойти́ на конце́рт?

     _____ на собра́ние?

     _____ на по́чту?

     _____ в клу́б?

     _____ в университе́т?

     _____ в университе́т, на конце́рт?

Want to go to the concert?

_____ to the meeting?

_____ to the post office?

_____ to the club?

_____ to the university?

_____ to the university, to a concert?

4. Хоти́те пойти́ в клу́б?

— С удово́льствием.

— Да́. Я́ давно́ та́м не́ был.

— Да́. Я́ давно́ та́м не была́.[1]

— Не́т, я за́нят.

— Не́т, я занята́.[1]

— Не́т, я уже́ та́м бы́л.

— Не́т, я уже́ та́м была́.[1]

— Не́т, та́м та́к ску́чно.

— Не́т, уже́ по́здно.

— Не́т, ещё ра́но.

Want to go to the club?

I'd love to.

Yes, I haven't been there for a long time.

Yes, _____.

No, I'm busy.

No, _____.

No, I was already there.

No, _____.

No, it's so boring there.

No, it's [too] late.

No, it's still early.

5. Что́ вы́ тепе́рь де́лаете?

— Рабо́таю в лаборато́рии.

     _____ на заво́де.

     _____ в клу́бе.

     _____ в горсове́те.

     _____ в университе́те.

     _____ на по́чте.

What do you do now?

I work in a laboratory.

_____ at the plant.

_____ at the club.

_____ at the gorsovet.

_____ at the university.

_____ at the post office.

6. Куда́ спеши́т Ле́в, на заво́д?

— Не́т, на собра́ние.

— Не́т, на уро́к пе́ния.

Куда́ спеша́т Ни́на и Кири́лл?

— Они́ спеша́т в клу́б.

— Они́ спеша́т в лаборато́рию.

Куда́ вы́ спеши́те, Евге́ний?

— Я́ спешу́ в университе́т.

— Я́ спешу́ на конце́рт.

Where's Lev hurrying to, the plant?

No, to a meeting.

No, to a singing lesson.

Where are Nina and Kirill hurrying to?

They're hurrying to the club.

They're hurrying to the laboratory.

Where are you hurrying to, Evgeny?

I'm hurrying to the university.

I'm hurrying to a concert.

The alternation of voiced and voiceless consonants

Besides the important feature of hardness and softness, the Russian consonant system is dominated by another significant element: the presence or absence of what is called "voice."

A *voiced* consonant is one pronounced with an accompanying vibration of the vocal cords. For example, the Russian [b, ḅ; v, ɣ; d, ḍ; z, ẓ] are all considered *voiced* consonants. So, too, are the English *b* in *boys*, *v* in *view*, *d* in *dog*, and *z* in *zip*.

In contrast, a *voiceless* (or *unvoiced*) consonant is one pronounced without this accompanying vibration of the vocal cords. For example, the Russian [p, ṗ; f, f̦; t, ṭ; s, ṣ] are all considered *voiceless* consonants in the system. Similarly, the English *p* in *poise*, *f* in *few*, *t* in *togs*, and *s* in *sip* are voiceless consonants.

The main difference between the Russian and English treatment of the voiced and voiceless consonants is that in Russian there is a systematic replacement of one by the other under prescribed circumstances while in English there is not. We can pronounce the English *gooseberry* with either

---

[1] Feminine speaker.

an [s] or a [z] sound, and both are acceptable. Russian, however, requires that the written д of **во́дка** be pronounced [t] because it occurs before [k], an unvoiced consonant: [vótkə].

Although all Russian consonant sounds may be characterized as voiced or voiceless, not all occur in opposed pairs. The following chart shows the regularly opposed pairs.

SOUNDS	*Voiced*	b	ḅ	v	ɣ	d	ḍ	z	ẓ	ž	g
	Voiceless	p	ṗ	f	ꜰ	t	ṭ	s	ş	š	k

The consonants [x, x̣, c, č, šč] are all voiceless, but do not have voiced counterparts that operate independently in the system. They can, however, affect the pronunciation of a preceding consonant. The consonants [r, ṛ, l, ḷ, m, ṃ, n, ṇ, j] possess voice, but have no corresponding voiceless counterparts. They are considered "neutral" because they do not determine the pronunciation of other consonants occurring in combination with them.

In terms of the Russian writing system, the paired voiced and voiceless consonants may be indicated as follows:

Voiced	б	бь	в	вь	д	дь	з	зь	ж	г
Voiceless	п	пь	ф	фь	т	ть	с	сь	ш	к

Since the writing system does not accurately reflect the spoken language, it is essential for the student to know which consonants are voiced, which are voiceless, and, especially, which are paired in terms of voice or absence of voice. This is important because, in certain positions, only consonant sounds of one or the other series are spoken, regardless of the spelling. The automatic alternation of voiced and voiceless consonant sounds operates, under the following conditions, within a word or combination of words spoken together as a unit.[1]

A. At the end of a word, consonants ordinarily voiced are replaced automatically by their unvoiced counterparts.

FINAL POSITION				NON-FINAL POSITION		
гото́в	[gatóf]	ready		гото́ва	[gatóvə]	ready
заво́д	[zavót]	plant		заво́ды	[zavódi]	plants
гри́б	[gṛíp]	mushroom		грибы́	[gṛibí]	mushrooms
о́чередь	[óčiṛiṭ]	line		о́череди	[óčiṛidi]	lines

B. Consonants in clusters, either within one word or in adjacent words pronounced without a break, are assimilated to the extent that the entire cluster is pronounced either voiceless or voiced.

Note, in the following examples, that it is the *second or last* voiced or voiceless consonant in the series that determines how the preceding consonant(s) will be pronounced.

1. VOICELESS CLUSTERS

	SPELLED			PRONOUNCED		
вч	in	вчера́	yesterday	[fč]	in	[fčirá]
зд		по́езд	train	[st]		[pójist]
бк		коро́бка	box	[pk]		[karópkə]
вст		в столе́	in the desk	[fst]		[fstaḷé]
дк		во́дка	vodka	[tk]		[vótkə]
вк		в клу́бе	at the club	[fk]		[fklúḅi]

---

[1] Since the neutral consonants р, л, н, м, and й do not play a part in the alternation of voiced and voiceless consonants, they will be excluded from this discussion.

40   LESSON 3

2. VOICED CLUSTERS

кд	in	ка́к дела́	how are things	[gd̦]	in	[ká gd̦ilá]
сьб		про́сьба	request	[z̦b]		[pró z̦bə]
кж		та́кже	likewise, too	[gž]		[tá gži]

The consonant в (вь) must be considered a special case. Although it undergoes unvoicing (i.e., it is pronounced as [f] or [f̦] either in final position or when followed by an unvoiced consonant), it does not cause a normally voiceless consonant preceding it to become voiced. Thus, both зва́ли (with cluster [zv]) and свали́ (with cluster [sv]) exist in Russian.

To summarize, we may say that the assimilation of consonants is a regressive process in Russian: the last element affects that which precedes it. Thus, in the following series, Position 2 determines the quality of Position 1 in terms of voice or its lack.

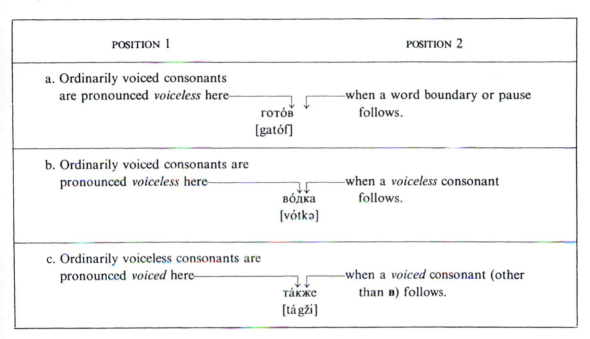

POSITION 1	POSITION 2
a. Ordinarily voiced consonants are pronounced *voiceless* here— гото́в [gatóf]	—when a word boundary or pause follows.
b. Ordinarily voiced consonants are pronounced *voiceless* here— во́дка [vótkə]	—when a *voiceless* consonant follows.
c. Ordinarily voiceless consonants are pronounced *voiced* here— та́кже [tá gži]	—when a *voiced* consonant (other than в) follows.

■ VOICING AND UNVOICING DRILLS

Read the following Cyrillic words, noting the automatic changes in pronunciation that take place in certain positions.

1. UNVOICING AT END OF WORDS

б pronounced [p]

ра́б	[ráp]
сла́б	[sláp]
гри́б	[gr̦íp]
сто́лб	[stólp]
ло́б	[lóp]
зу́б	[zúp]
ду́б	[dúp]
ря́б	[r̦áp]

бь pronounced [p̦]

скорбь	[skórp̦]
зя́бь	[z̦áp̦]
дро́бь	[dróp̦]
го́лубь	[gólup̦]
зы́бь	[zíp̦]
ря́бь	[r̦áp̦]
гра́бь	[gráp̦]
О́бь	[óp̦]

в pronounced [f]

Хрущёв	[xruščóf]
Лёв	[l̦éf]
Турге́нев	[turgé ṇif]
жи́в	[žíf]
но́в	[nóf]
сло́в	[slóf]
о́стров	[óstrəf]
не́рв	[ṇérf]
рёв	[ɹ̦óf]
обры́в	[abríf]
сня́в	[sṇáf]

вь pronounced [f̦]		г pronounced [k]		д pronounced [t]	
прибáвь	[pr̦ibáf̦]	шáг	[šák]	рáд	[rát]
застáвь	[zastáf̦]	снéг	[sn̦ék]	сáд	[sát]
бурáвь	[buráf̦]	бéрег	[b̦ér̦ik]	обéд	[ab̦ét]
любóвь	[ļubóf̦]	лёг	[ļók]	лёд	[ļót]
морквь	[markóf̦]	кнг	[kn̦ík]	вд	[v̦ít]
брóвь	[bróf̦]	пирóг	[p̦irók]	гóд	[gót]
крóвь	[króf̦]	дрýг	[drúk]	гóрод	[górət]
нóвь	[nóf̦]	крýг	[krúk]	рд	[r̦át]
чéрвь	[čérf̦]	юг	[júk]	стд	[stít]
óбувь	[óbuf̦]				

дь pronounced [ț]		ж pronunced [š]		з pronounced [s]	
клáдь	[kláț]	гарáж	[garáš]	рáз	[rás]
глáдь	[gláț]	этáж	[itáš]	глáз	[glás]
тетрáдь	[țitráț]	нарéжь	[nar̦éš]	гáз	[gás]
лóшадь	[lóšiț]	ёж	[jóš]	расскáз	[raskás]
плóщадь	[plóščiț]	стрж	[str̦íš]	внз	[vn̦ís]
мéдь	[m̦éț]	нóж	[nóš]	колхóз	[kalxós]
óчередь	[óčir̦iț]	ýж	[úš]	морóз	[marós]
бýдь	[búț]	мýж	[múš]	сою́з	[sajús]
		зáмуж	[zámuš]		

зь pronounced [ș]			
мáзь	[máș]	сýзь	[súș]
лáзь	[láș]	грзь	[gr̦áș]
слéзь	[sļéș]	свзь	[sv̦áș]
рéзь	[r̦éș]	кнзь	[kn̦áș]
слзь	[sļíș]	бзь	[b̦áș]
врóзь	[vróș]		

2. UNVOICING BEFORE AN UNVOICED CONSONANT

в pronounced [f]		б pronounced [p]		г pronounced [k]	
всю́	[fșú]	óбщий	[ópščij]	бéгство	[b̦ékstvə]
вчерá	[fčirá]	рбка	[rípkə]	кóгтя	[kókțə]
вхóд	[fxót]	рбчик	[r̦ápčik]	нóгтя	[nókțə]
автóбус	[aftóbus]	удóбство	[udópstvə]	жёгший	[žókšij]
овцá	[afcá]	хлéбца	[xļépcə]	ЗАГС	[záks]
продавщца	[prədafščícə]	корóбка	[karópkə]	дёгтя	[d̦ókțə]
в чáс	[fčás]	вообщé	[vəapščé]	лгте	[ļákți]
в корóбке	[fkarópk̦i]			пострги	[pastr̦íkši]
вполнé	[fpalņé]				

д pronounced [t]		ж pronounced [š]		з pronounced [s]	
лóдка	[lótkə]	книжка	[kṇíškə]	блйзко	[bḷískə]
похóдка	[paxótkə]	неужто	[ṇiúštə]	скáзка	[skáskə]
блюдце	[bḷútcə]	лóжка	[lóškə]	пóезд	[pójist]
молодцы́	[məlatcí]	надéжд	[naḍéšt]	визг	[ɣísk]
вóдка	[vótkə]	нужд	[núšt]	мóзг	[mósk]
загáдка	[zagátkə]	немнóжко	[ṇimnóškə]	дрóзд	[dróst]
нáдпись	[nátṛiş]			из тáнка	[istánkə]
под снéгом	[patsṇégəm]			слёзка	[sḷóskə]
над собóй	[nətsabój]				

3. VOICING BEFORE A VOICED CONSONANT

к pronounced [g]		с pronounced [z]		т pronounced [d]	
тáкже	[tágži]	сгорáть	[zgaráṭ]	от гóрода	[adgórədə]
как делá	[kagḍilá]	сбить	[zḅíṭ]	от брáта	[adbrátə]
вокзáл	[vagzál]	сгóвор	[zgóvər]	отбóй	[adbój]
экзáмен	[igzámin]	сбóр	[zbór]	отжáть	[adžáṭ]
анекдóт	[aṇigdót]	сбóрник	[zbórṇik]	óтзыв	[ódzif]
к женé	[gžiṇé]	сдáча	[zdáčə]	от зáвисти	[adzáɣişṭi]
к зимé	[gziṃé]	с горы́	[zgarí]	óтжил	[ódžil]
к бáбе	[gbáḅi]			отбрóсы	[adbrósi]
к дóму	[gdómu]			от жены́	[adžiní]
кáк бы	[kágbi]			отгадáть	[adgadáṭ]

сь pronounced [ẕ]		ть pronounced [ḍ]	
прóсьба	[próẕbə]	селитьба	[şiḷíḍbə]
косьбá	[kaẕbá]	женитьба	[žiṇíḍbə]
		молотьбá	[məlaḍbá]

STRUCTURE AND DRILLS

The present tense of the second conjugation verb спешить

я спешу́	I'm hurrying, I'm in a hurry
ты́ спеши́шь	you're hurrying, you're in a hurry
óн спеши́т	he's hurrying
онá спеши́т	she's hurrying
мы́ спеши́м	we're hurrying
вы́ спеши́те	you're hurrying
они́ спешáт	they're hurrying

1. Listen to your instructor (or the tape) and repeat the preceding pronoun-verb model until you can say it perfectly.

2. *I'm hurrying to a lesson.*
   т: Я спешу́ на уро́к.
   s: **Я спешу́ на уро́к.**
   Они́ спеша́т на уро́к.
   Вы́ спеши́те на уро́к.
   Она́ спеши́т на уро́к.
   Мы́ спеши́м на уро́к.
   О́н спеши́т на уро́к.
   Ты́ спеши́шь на уро́к.

■ QUESTION-ANSWER DRILLS

1. *Where are you hurrying to?*
   We're hurrying to a concert.
   т: Куда́ вы́ спеши́те?
   s: **Мы́ спеши́м на конце́рт.**
   т: Куда́ о́н спеши́т?
   s: **О́н спеши́т на конце́рт.**
   Куда́ они́ спеша́т?
   Куда́ ты́ спеши́шь?
   Куда́ она́ спеши́т?
   Куда́ мы́ спеши́м?

2. *Where are you hurrying, home?*
   No, I'm hurrying to the post office.
   т: Куда́ вы́ спеши́те, домо́й?
   s: **Не́т, я́ спешу́ на по́чту.**
   т: Куда́ она́ спеши́т, домо́й?
   s: **Не́т, она́ спеши́т на по́чту.**
   Куда́ они́ спеша́т, домо́й?
   Куда́ о́н спеши́т, домо́й?
   Куда́ ты́ спеши́шь, домо́й?

Using **в университе́т**, Student 1 first replies with a short answer, then Student 2 replies with a full answer.

Using **на авто́бус,** answer the question with both short and full answers.

3. *Where are you hurrying to?*
   To the university.
   I'm hurrying to the university.
   т: Куда́ вы́ спеши́те?
   s₁: **В университе́т.**
   s₂: **Я́ спешу́ в университе́т.**
   Ни́на, Кири́лл, куда́ вы́ спеши́те?
   Куда́ ты́ спеши́шь?
   Куда́ о́н спеши́т?
   Куда́ она́ спеши́т?
   Куда́ они́ спеша́т?

4. *Where are you going in such a hurry?*
   To catch a bus.
   I'm hurrying to catch a bus.
   т: Куда́ вы́ та́к спеши́те?
   s₁: **На авто́бус.**
   s₂: **Я́ спешу́ на авто́бус.**
   Куда́ о́н та́к спеши́т?
   Куда́ они́ та́к спеша́т?
   Куда́ мы́ та́к спеши́м?
   Куда́ ты́ та́к спеши́шь?
   Куда́ она́ та́к спеши́т?

5. *Where are you hurrying to, the laboratory?*
   No, I'm hurrying to the club.
   т: Куда́ вы́ спеши́те, в лаборато́рию?
   s: **Не́т, я́ спешу́ в клу́б.**
   т: Куда́ ты́ спеши́шь, в лаборато́рию?
   s: **Не́т, я́ спешу́ в клу́б.**

   Куда́ о́н спеши́т, в лаборато́рию?
   Куда́ они́ спеша́т, в лаборато́рию?
   Куда́ ты́ спеши́шь, в лаборато́рию?
   Куда́ она́ спеши́т, в лаборато́рию?
   Куда́ вы́ спеши́те, в лаборато́рию?

---

[1] Beginning with this lesson, both the teacher and student sentences are included in the same column.

Спешить is a second conjugation verb with the stress on the endings.

	SINGULAR	PLURAL
1	спеш–у́	спеш–и́м
2	–и́шь	–и́те
3	–и́т	–а́т

Second conjugation verbs have linking vowel и, (спеши́шь, спеши́т, спеши́м, спеши́те) where first conjugation verbs have e or ё (рабо́таешь, идёшь). Where first conjugation verbs have the third person plural ending in –ут or –ют (иду́т, рабо́тают), second conjugation verbs have –ат or –ят (спеша́т, говоря́т). It is only in the first person singular that first and second conjugation verbs share the common ending –y or –ю.

Examples of other second conjugation verbs so far encountered:[1]

> слы́шать   *to hear*
> слы́ш–у, слы́ш–ишь, слы́ш–ит, слы́ш–им, слы́ш–ите, слы́ш–ат
> говори́ть   *to speak, say*
> говор–ю́, говор–и́шь, говор–и́т, говор–и́м, говор–и́те, говор–я́т
> стоя́ть   *to stand*
> сто–ю́, сто–и́шь, сто–и́т, сто–и́м, сто–и́те, сто–я́т

Masculine, feminine, and plural endings of short-form adjectives

MASCULINE SUBJECT	Я (ты́, о́н) за́нят.	I'm (you're, he's) busy.
	_____ ра́д.	_____ glad.
	_____ здоро́в.	_____ well.
	_____ бо́лен.	_____ sick.
FEMININE SUBJECT	Я (ты́, она́) занята́.	I'm (you're, she's) busy.
	_____ ра́да.	_____ glad.
	_____ здоро́ва.	_____ well.
	_____ больна́.	_____ sick.
PLURAL SUBJECT	Мы́ (вы́, они́) за́няты.	We're (you're, they're) busy.
	_____ ра́ды.	_____ glad.
	_____ здоро́вы.	_____ well.
	_____ больны́.	_____ sick.

■ REPETITION DRILL

Listen to your instructor (or the tape) and repeat the above models until you can say them perfectly.

---

[1] These verbs are given here primarily to show ending and stress patterns. They will be drilled later.

Repeat after your instructor (or the tape) as accurately as you can, imitating both the individual words and the sentence intonation. Then, on hearing only the subject cue, supply the full utterance according to the given model.

1. *I'm busy now.*
   т: Я тепе́рь за́нят.
   s: **Я тепе́рь за́нят.**
   т: Она́ тепе́рь занята́.
   s: **Она́ тепе́рь занята́.**
   (они́, вы, Ни́на, жена́, му́ж, мы, Ми́ла)

2. *Are you glad to hear it?*
   т: Ты ра́д э́то слы́шать?
   s: **Ты ра́д э́то слы́шать?**
   т: Она́ ра́да э́то слы́шать?
   s: **Она́ ра́да э́то слы́шать?**
   (Семён, они́, Цара́пкин, вы, Ми́ла)

3. *I'm completely well.*
   т: Я вполне́ здоро́в.
   s: **Я вполне́ здоро́в.**
   т: Они́ вполне́ здоро́вы.
   s: **Они́ вполне́ здоро́вы.**
   (вы, жена́, она́, Евге́ний)

4. *I'm sick.*
   т: Я бо́лен.
   s: **Я бо́лен.**
   т: Она́ больна́.
   s: **Она́ больна́.**
   (Ми́ла и Семён, вы, Евге́ний, мы, Ни́на)

1. *Lev, are you busy?*
   No, I'm not busy.
   т: Ле́в, ты за́нят?
   s: **Не́т, я не за́нят.**
   т: Ни́на, ты занята́?
   s: **Не́т, я не занята́.**
   (Ми́ла, Хитро́в, Кири́лл Па́влович, Ни́на Семёновна, Семён)

2. *Nina, are you still sick?*
   No, I'm completely well now.
   т: Ни́на, вы всё ещё больны́?
   s: **Не́т, я тепе́рь вполне́ здоро́ва.**
   т: Кири́лл, ты всё ещё бо́лен?
   s: **Не́т, я тепе́рь вполне́ здоро́в.**
   Семён Фили́ппович, вы всё ещё больны́?
   Ми́ла, ты всё ещё больна́?
   Евге́ний, ты всё ещё бо́лен?
   Кири́лл Па́влович, вы всё ещё больны́?

I'm glad to hear that.
т: Я ра́д э́то слы́шать.
s: **Я ра́д э́то слы́шать.**
т: (Мы) _____.
s: **Мы ра́ды э́то слы́шать.**
   (они́, Кири́лл, жена́, Семён Фили́ппович, она́, Ни́на и Ми́ла, о́н)

MASCULINE	FEMININE	PLURAL
–	–a	–ы

The short-form adjectives agree with their subject in gender or number. Note that those used with masculine subjects have no ending, those used with feminine subjects end in –a, and those used with plural subjects end in –ы.[1]

Note that the stress may shift to the ending, particularly in the feminine form: **Она́ занята́.** (Compare it with **Он за́нят.**)

If the stem ends in more than one consonant, the masculine form may contain a vowel that does not appear in the other forms. This vowel appears between the last two consonants of the stem. Compare **он бо́лен** with **она́ больна́, вы больны́.** The soft sign is written in the feminine and plural forms to indicate that the **л** is soft.

ЧТЕ́НИЕ И ПИСЬМО́   READING AND WRITING

The conversation for Lesson 3 is presented here in handwritten form for reading and copying practice.

Лучше поздно, чем никогда

—Лев! Здравствуйте! Куда вы спешите?
—В университет, на концерт. —Интересно. Это бесплатно? —Да. Хотите пойти? —С удовольствием. —Кстати, что вы теперь делаете? —Работаю в лаборатории. Там так скучно. —Так поступайте в университет. —Что вы! Мне теперь уже поздно! —Знаете, говорят: „Лучше поздно, чем никогда."

---

[1] The neuter short adjective ending o is excluded from this discussion for practical reasons since the subjects used with these adjectives are mostly masculine, feminine, or plural.

NOTES

PREPARATION FOR CONVERSATION | Разгово́р в общежи́тии

общежи́тие [apščiží̧ijǝ] — dormitory
в общежи́тии [vǝpščiží̧iji] — in the dormitory
разгово́р [rǝzgavór] — conversation
Разгово́р в общежи́тии. — Conversation in the dormitory.
войти́ (pfv)[1] [vaj̧í] — to enter, come in, go in
мо́жно [móžnǝ] — it's possible, one may
Мо́жно войти́? — May I come in?

коне́чно [ka̧éšnǝ] [2] — of course, certainly
заходи́ть [zǝxa̧í̧] — to drop in, stop by, call [on someone]
заходи́ [zǝxa̧í] — come in!
заперта́ [zǝ̧irtá] [3] — locked
две́рь (f) [d̠ǿ̧] — door
Две́рь не заперта́. — The door isn't locked.
Заходи́! Две́рь не заперта́. — Come in! The door isn't locked.

бы́ть [bí̧] — to be
я была́ [já bilá] — I (f) was, I've been
зна́ть [znát̠] — to know
ты зна́ешь [tí znájiš] — you know
Зна́ешь, где́ я была́? — Know where I've been?
всё у́тро [fşó útrǝ] — all morning
Зна́ешь, где́ я была́ всё у́тро? — Know where I've been all morning?

го́род [górǝt] — city, town
в го́роде [vgórǝ̧i] — in the city, in town, downtown
Я была́ в го́роде. — I've been downtown.

пода́рок [padárǝk] — gift, present
я покупа́ла [já pǝkupálǝ] — I (f) was buying
покупа́ть [pǝkupá̧] — to buy, to be buying

---

[1] The abbreviation *pfv* will be used for the perfective aspect and *ipfv* for the imperfective.
[2] **Коне́чно** is pronounced [ka̧éšnǝ] by many speakers.
[3] Two pronunciations are possible: [zǝ̧irtá] and [zá̧irtǝ].

Я покупа́ла пода́рок.   I was buying a present.

    Ни́не [ɲíɲi]   [for] Nina

Я покупа́ла пода́рок Ни́не.   I was buying Nina a present.

    áx [áx]   oh!

Áx, да́!   Oh, yes!

    де́нь (m) [ḍéṇ]   day

    де́нь рожде́ния [ḍéṇ raždéṇijə]   birthday (*lit.* day of birth)

    у неё [uṇijó]   she has (*lit.* by her)

У неё де́нь рожде́ния.   She has a birthday *or* It's her birthday.

    за́втра [záftrə]   tomorrow

У неё за́втра де́нь рожде́ния.   She has a birthday tomorrow.

    купи́ть (pfv) [kuṗíṭ]   to buy

    ты́ купи́ла [tí kuṗílə]   you (f) bought

Что́ ты́ купи́ла?   What did you buy?

    посмотре́ть (pfv) [pəsmatṛéṭ]   to take a look

    [ты́] хо́чешь [tí xóčiš]   you want

Хо́чешь посмотре́ть?   Want to take a look?

    коро́бка [karópkə]   box (cardboard)

    в коро́бке [fkarópḳi]   in the box

    ту́т [tút]   here

Во́т ту́т, в коро́бке.   It's here in the box.

    портфе́ль (m) [partṡél]   briefcase

    доста́ть (pfv) [dastáṭ]   to get

    ты́ доста́ла [tí dastálə]   you (f) got

Где́ ты́ доста́ла?   Where'd you get [it]?

Портфе́ль! Где́ ты́ доста́ла?   A briefcase! Where'd you get it?

    ГУ́М [gúm]   GUM (State Department Store)

    в ГУ́Ме [vgúṃi]   at GUM

    краси́вый [kraṡívij]   handsome, pretty, lovely

    пра́вда [právdə]   isn't it (*lit.* truth)

Пра́вда, краси́вый?   Handsome, isn't it?

В ГУ́Ме. Пра́вда, краси́вый?   At GUM. Handsome, isn't it?

    о́чень [óčiṇ]   very

О́чень краси́вый.   Very handsome.

    до́лго [dólgə]   long, a long time

    стоя́ть [stajáṭ]   to stand, to be standing

    ты́ стоя́ла [tí stajálə]   you (f) stood

Ты́ до́лго стоя́ла?   Did you stand for a long time?

    о́чередь (f) [óčiṛiṭ]   line, turn

    в о́череди [vóčiṛiḍi]   in line

Ты́ до́лго стоя́ла в о́череди?   Did you stand in line a long time?

Не́т, не о́чень.   No, not very [long].

де́лать [ḍélət]	to do, to be doing
Что́ вы́ де́лали?	What did you do? *or* What were you doing?
— Ничего́. ṇičivó]	Nothing.
Где́ вы́ бы́ли?	Where were you?
слу́жба [slúžbə]	job, work, service
— На слу́жбе.	At work.
Что́ вы́ купи́ли?	What did you buy?
материа́л [məṭirjál]	material
пла́тье [pláṭjə]	dress
— Материа́л на пла́тье.	Material for a dress *or* Dress material.
костю́м [kasṭúm]	suit
— Материа́л на костю́м.	Material for a suit *or* Suit material.

ADDITIONAL CLASSROOM EXPRESSIONS

да́льше [dáļši]	continue! go on! (*lit.* further)
Чита́йте да́льше!	Go on reading!
пиши́те [ṗišíṭi] *or* напиши́те [neṗišíṭi]	write!
на доске́ [nədaşḱé]	on the board
Напиши́те на доске́!	Write on the board!
иди́те [iḍíṭi]	go!
к доске́ [gdaşḱé]	to the board
Иди́те к доске́!	Go to the board!
измени́те [izṃiṇíṭi]	change! make a change!
замени́те [zəṃiṇíṭi]	substitute! make a substitution!

Разгово́р в общежи́тии

Conversation in the dormitory

C. — Са́ша (студе́нт)
О. — О́ля (студе́нтка)

C.	1 Кто́ та́м?	któ tắm ↓	Who's there?
О.	2 Э́то я, О́ля. Мо́жно войти́?	étə jắ ↓ őļə ↓ móžnə vajṭí ↓	It's me, Olya. May I come in?
C.	3 Коне́чно. Заходи́. Две́рь не заперта́.	kaṇéšnə ↓ zəxaḍí ↓ dγéṛ ṇizəṗirtắ ↓	Of course. Come in. The door isn't locked.
О.	4 Зна́ешь, где́ я была́ всё у́тро? В го́роде. Покупа́ла пода́рок Ни́не.	znájiš gḍé já bilắ ↓ fşó űtrə ↓ vgőrəḍi ↓ pəkupálə padắrək ṇíṇi ↓	Know where I've been all morning? Downtown. I was buying a present for Nina.

C.	5	Áx, дá! У неё зáвтра дéнь рождéния. А чтó ты́ купи́ла?	áx dã́ ↓ uɲijó záftrə ḍéɲ raẑḍéɲijə ↓ a štó tí kupílə ↓	Oh, yes! It's her birthday tomorrow. And what did you buy?
O.	6	Хóчешь посмотрéть? Вóт тýт, в корóбке.	xóčiš pəsmatṛéṭ ↑ vót tṹt ↓ fkarópḳi ↓	Want to take a look? It's here in the box.
C.	7	Портфéль! Гдé ты́ достáла?	partḟéḷ ↓ gḍé tí dastálə ↓	A briefcase! Where did you get it?
O.	8	В ГУ́Ме. Прáвда, краси́вый?	vgṹṃi ↓ právdə kraʂívij ↑	In GUM.[2] Handsome, isn't it?
C.	9	Óчень. Ты́ дóлго стоя́ла в óчереди?	óčiɲ ↓ tí dólgə stajálə vóčiṛiḍi ↓	Very. Did you stand in line a long time?
O.	10	Нéт, не óчень.	ɲét ↑ ɲióčiɲ ↓	No, not very.

NOTES

[1] Informally Russians address each other using nicknames based on the first name, for example: **Сáша** for **Алексáндр, Óля** for **Óльга**. Such names are comparable to our Bob for Robert, Gene for Eugene, Betty for Elizabeth, and so forth. Others are:

Жéня	*for*	Евгéний	Eugene	Ми́ла	*for*	Людми́ла	Ludmilla
Вáня		Ивáн	John	Гáля		Гал
и́на	Galina
Лёва		Лéв	Leo	Тáня		Татья́на	Tatiana
Кóля		Николáй	Nicholas	Кáтя		Екатери́на	Katherine
Пéтя		Пётр	Peter	Зи́на		Зинаи́да	Zinaida
Алёша		Алексéй	Alexis	Лю́ба		Любóвь	Amy
Сéня		Семён	Simon	Мáша		Мари́я	Mary
Бóря		Бори́с	Boris	Лéна		Елéна	Helen
Волóдя		Влади́мир	Vladimir	Ли́за		Елизавéта	Elizabeth

[2] **ГУМ (Госудáрственный универсáльный магази́н)** is the State Department Store, which is located in Red Square opposite the Moscow Kremlin. Note that, although GUM itself is written with capital letters, its declensional endings are written with small letters: **в ГУ́Ме** *in GUM*.

Basic sentence patterns

1. Ктó тáм?
   — Э́то я́, Óля.
   _____ Евгéний.
   _____ Ни́на.
   _____ Кири́лл Пáвлович.
   _____ Семён Фили́ппович.

Who's there?
It's me, Olya.
_____ Evgeny.
_____ Nina.
_____ Kirill Pavlovich.
_____ Semyon Filippovich.

_____ Царáпкин.	_____ Tsarapkin.
_____ Хитрóв.	_____ Khitrov.
_____ Мúла.	_____ Mila.
_____ Лéв.	_____ Lev.

2. Сáша, гдé ты был всё ýтро?
   — Я был на собрáнии.
   _____ на урóке пéния.
   _____ на завóде.
   _____ на пóчте.
   _____ на концéрте.

Where were you all morning, Sasha?
I've been at a meeting.
_____ at a singing lesson.
_____ at the plant.
_____ at the post office.
_____ at a concert.

3. Óля, гдé ты былá всё ýтро?
   — Я былá в гóроде.
   _____ в ГУ́Ме.
   _____ в общежúтии.
   _____ в университéте.
   _____ в горсовéте.
   _____ в клýбе.
   _____ в лаборатóрии.

Where were you all morning, Olya?
I was in town.
_____ at GUM.
_____ in the dormitory.
_____ at the university.
_____ at the gorsovet.
_____ at the club.
_____ at the laboratory.

4. Чтó ты дéлал в гóроде, Сáша?
   — Я покупáл подáрок.
   — Я покупáл подáрок Нúне.
   — Я стоя́л в óчереди.
   — Я покупáл портфéль.
   — Я покупáл материáл на костю́м.

What were you doing in town, Sasha?
I was buying a present.
I was buying Nina a present.
I was standing in line.
I was buying a briefcase.
I was buying suit material.

5. А чтó ты дéлала, Óля?
   — Я тóже былá в гóроде.
   — Я тóже покупáла подáрок.
   — Я тóже стоя́ла в óчереди.
   — Я покупáла плáтье.
   — Я покупáла материáл на плáтье.
   — Я покупáла материáл на костю́м.

And what were you doing, Olya?
I was in town, too.
I was buying a present, too.
I was standing in line, too.
I was buying a dress.
I was buying dress material.
I was buying suit material.

6. Гдé вы э́то достáли?
   — В гóроде.
   — В ГУ́Ме.
   — В университéте.
   — В общежúтии.
   — В клýбе.
   — В лаборатóрии.

Where did you get that?
In town.
At GUM.
At the university.
At the dormitory.
At the club.
At the laboratory.

Introductory remarks on the Russian case system

By now you have noted that Russian nouns may vary their endings in accordance with the way they function in a sentence. Thus, in the following examples, the Russian word for _laboratory_ changes its ending according to whether it indicates location or destination.

LOCATION	Онá рабóтает в лаборатóрии.	She works in a laboratory.
DESTINATION	Онá идёт в лаборатóрию.	She's on her way to the laboratory.

Compare the examples with English, where the word *laboratory* does not change but a different preposition is used: *in* for location and *to* for destination.

In Russian the same preposition (**в**) is used but a different "case" form of the noun is required: prepositional case for location and accusative case for destination.

There are six cases in Russian, used in both the singular and the plural. They are given below together with a brief comment on their primary function.

CASE NAME	ABBREVIATION	PRIMARY FUNCTION TO INDICATE
NOMINATIVE	NOM or N	grammatical subject of sentence
ACCUSATIVE	ACC or A	direct object, complete goal of action
GENITIVE	GEN or G	possession, absence, limitation
PREPOSITIONAL[1]	PREP or P	location or focus of activity
DATIVE	DAT or D	indirect object, person affected (in impersonal constructions)
INSTRUMENTAL	INSTR or I	instrument or means of accomplishment of activity

The nominative form is customarily used in citing nouns, pronouns, and adjectives in dictionaries or otherwise out of context.

Remarks on stems and endings: the concept of "zero" ending

Since Russian, like Latin and German, relies heavily on changes in the forms of its nouns, adjectives, and verbs for grammatical purposes, the student must be able to identify and manipulate both stems and grammatical endings.

Briefly stated, the stem is the part of a word that remains relatively constant; the ending is the part that varies to show grammatical changes. Compare the following sets, observing that both existent endings and the absence of endings provide important grammatical information.

Москва́	Moscow	в Москву́	to Moscow
окно́	window	на окне́	on the window
одно́ сло́во	one word	мно́го сло́в	many words
сто́л	table	на столе́	on the table
о́н здоро́в	he's well	она́ здоро́ва	she's well
о́н бы́л	he was	она́ была́	she was

The concept of the nonexistent or "zero" ending is a very important one for Russian. Nouns, verbs, adjectives, and numerals all have forms where a "zero" ending contrasts with explicit endings.

---

[1] The prepositional case is also frequently called the *locative* case. It is the one case in Russian that is *never* used *without* a preposition.

For example, most masculine nouns have a "zero" ending in their nominative singular case form. A "zero" ending also occurs after the suffix л in the masculine past tense form, contrasting with the feminine ending –a, the neuter ending –o, and the plural ending –и. Furthermore, most feminine and neuter nouns have a "zero" ending in the genitive plural, in contrast with all of their case forms that occur with an ending. Compare сло́во *word*, слова́ *words* with слов *of the words*; and кни́га *book*, кни́ги *books* with книг *of the books*.

STRUCTURE AND DRILLS

Past tense of the verb бы́ть *to be*

MASCULINE SUBJECT	Я́ бы́л та́м.	I was there.
	Ты́ бы́л та́м.	You were there.
	О́н бы́л та́м.	He was there.
	Портфе́ль бы́л та́м.	The briefcase was there.
FEMININE SUBJECT	Я́ была́ та́м.	I was there.
	Ты́ была́ та́м.	You were there.
	Она́ была́ та́м.	She was there.
	Коро́бка была́ та́м.	The box was there.
NEUTER SUBJECT	Собра́ние бы́ло та́м.	The meeting was there.
PLURAL SUBJECT	Мы́ бы́ли та́м.	We were there.
	Вы́ бы́ли та́м.	You were there.[1]
	Они́ бы́ли та́м.	They were there.
	Ле́в и Ни́на бы́ли та́м.	Lev and Nina were there.

■ REPETITION DRILL

Listen to your instructor (or the tape) and repeat the above models until you can reproduce them accurately.

■ REPETITION-SUBSTITUTION DRILL

I was at the plant.
т: Я́ бы́л на заво́де.
s: **Я́ бы́л на заво́де.**
  (о́н, они́, Са́ша, Ни́на, О́ля и Ле́в, вы́,
  она́, мы́)

---

[1] Note that вы́, the plural-polite pronoun *you*, is treated grammatically as a plural even when it refers to a single person. Thus, Где́ вы́ доста́ли? can be addressed to one person who is not an intimate friend, or to more than one person. Ты́, on the other hand, can only be addressed to one person.

1. *Were they in the dormitory too?*
   Yes, they were.
   т: Они тоже были в общежитии?
   s: Да, были.
   т: Он тоже был в общежитии?
   s: Да, был.
   (Лев и Кирилл, она, Саша, Оля)

2. *Have you already been to the club, Nina?*
   Yes, I have.
   т: Вы уже были в клубе, Нина?
   s: Да, была.
   т: Вы уже были в клубе, Лев?
   s: Да, был.
   Ты уже была в клубе, Мила?
   Ты уже был в клубе, Саша?
   Вы уже были в клубе, Оля?

3. *Where were you, Sasha?*
   I was in the laboratory.
   т: Где ты был, Саша?
   s: **Я был в лаборатории.**
   т: Где ты была, Нина?
   s: **Я была в лаборатории.**
   Где вы были, Кирилл?
   Где вы были, Мила?
   Где он был?
   Где она была?
   Где мы были?
   Где они были?

4. *Nina, where have you been all morning?*
   I've been in town.
   т: Нина, где вы были всё утро?
   s: **Я была в городе.**
   т: Саша, где ты был всё утро?
   s: **Я был в городе.**
   Оля, где ты была всё утро?
   Кирилл, где ты был всё утро?
   Лев, где вы были всё утро?
   Оля и Нина, где вы были всё утро?
   Лев и Кирилл, где вы были всё утро?

5. *Was she at work?*
   Yes, she was.
   т: Она была на службе?
   s: **Да, была.**
   т: Они были на службе?
   s: **Да, были.**
   Муж был на службе?
   Они были на службе?
   Кирилл был на службе?
   Жена была на службе?
   Кирилл и Лев были на службе?

DISCUSSION

The past tense differs from the present and future in Russian in that it is not based on personal endings but on gender-number endings. The past tense of the verb **быть** *to be* illustrates this principle.

SINGULAR			PLURAL
Masculine	*Feminine*	*Neuter*	
был	был-а	был-о	был-и

Я та́м не́ **был**.	I (*m*) wasn't there.
Вы́ **бы́ли** больны́.	You were sick.
Она́ **была́** в го́роде.	She was in town.
Вчера́ **бы́ло** собра́ние.	There was a meeting yesterday.

In the last example, **бы́ло** agrees with the neuter noun **собра́ние**.

The accusative form of inanimate masculine and neuter nouns

MODELS

Я спешу́ на уро́к.	I'm hurrying to a lesson.
_____ на уро́к пе́ния.	_____ to a singing lesson.
_____ на конце́рт.	_____ to a concert.
_____ на авто́бус.	_____ to the bus.
_____ на заво́д.	_____ to the plant.
_____ на собра́ние.	_____ to a meeting.

Я иду́ в университе́т.	I'm on my way to the university.
_____ в клу́б.	_____ to the club.
_____ в горсове́т.	_____ to the gorsovet.
_____ в го́род.	_____ to town.
_____ в ГУ́М.	_____ to GUM.
_____ в общежи́тие.	_____ to the dormitory.

Ты́ уже́ ви́дел го́род?	Have you already seen the city?
_____ пода́рок?	_____ the present?
_____ портфе́ль?	_____ the briefcase?
_____ клу́б?	_____ the club?
_____ ГУ́М?	_____ GUM?
_____ университе́т?	_____ the university?
_____ письмо́?	_____ the letter?
_____ общежи́тие?	_____ the dormitory?

Где́ вы́ доста́ли пода́рок?	Where did you get the present?
_____ портфе́ль?	_____ the briefcase?
_____ письмо́?	_____ the letter?

■ REPETITION DRILLS

Repeat the models after your instructor (or the tape), noting that the accusative form is like the nominative for these masculine and neuter nouns referring to inanimate things. Note also that certain nouns require the preposition **в** and others require **на.**

1. *She's going to class.*
   т: Она́ идёт на уро́к.
   s: **Она́ идёт на уро́к.**
   т: _____ (на по́чту).
   s: **Она́ идёт на по́чту.**
   (на конце́рт, на заво́д,
   на собра́ние, на уро́к пе́ния)

2. *She's going to the club.*
   т: Она́ идёт в клуб.
   s: **Она́ идёт в клуб.**
   т: _____ (в горсове́т).
   s: **Она́ идёт в горсове́т.**
   (в ГУ́М, в го́род, в общежи́тие,
   в университе́т, в клуб)

3. *We're hurrying to the bus.*
   т: Мы спеши́м на авто́бус.
   s: **Мы спеши́м на авто́бус.**
   т: _____ (в ГУ́М).
   s: **Мы спеши́м в ГУ́М.**
   (на уро́к, в общежи́тие,
   на конце́рт, в университе́т,
   на заво́д, в го́род, на собра́ние,
   в клуб)

4. *I've already seen the present.*
   т: Я уже́ ви́дел пода́рок.
   s: **Я уже́ ви́дел пода́рок.**
   т: _____ (общежи́тие).
   s: **Я уже́ ви́дел общежи́тие.**
   (го́род, ГУ́М, письмо́, клуб,
   университе́т, портфе́ль)

DISCUSSION

Masculine and neuter nouns such as **уро́к, портфе́ль, собра́ние,** and **письмо́,** which refer to other than living beings, have the same form in the accusative case as in the nominative. The accusative case is used in Russian for the direct object of a verb, or for the object of certain prepositions such as **в** or **на,** used in conjunction with verbs of motion. It is important to remember that in the meaning *to,* certain nouns require the preposition **в** while others require the preposition **на.**

в го́род	to town	на конце́рт	to the concert
в ГУ́М	to GUM	на авто́бус	to the bus
в общежи́тие	to the dormitory	на уро́к	to class
в клуб	to the club	на по́чту	to the post office
в университе́т	to the university	на собра́ние	to the meeting

Разговор в общежитии

— Кто там? — Это я, Оля. Можно войти?
— Конечно. Заходи. Дверь не заперта. — Знаешь,
где я была всё утро? В городе, покупала
подарок Нине. — Ах да! У неё завтра день
рождения. А что ты купила? — Хочешь посмотреть? Вот тут в коробке. — Портфель?
Где ты достала? — В ГУМе. Правда красивый? — Очень. Ты долго стояла в очереди?
— Нет, не очень.

NOTES

PREPARATION FOR CONVERSATION   **Что́ на обе́д?**

обе́д [aḅét]   dinner
на обе́д [nəaḅét]   for dinner
Что́ на обе́д?   What's for dinner?
ка́к насчёт [kák naščót]   how about
Ка́к насчёт обе́да?   How about dinner?
Ка́к насчёт обе́да, Оле́г?   How about dinner, Oleg?

откры́та [atkrítə]   open
столо́вая [stalóvəjə]   dining hall, cafe, restaurant, dining room
Столо́вая откры́та.   The dining hall's open.
Столо́вая давно́ откры́та.   The dining hall's been open for a long time.

обе́дать [aḅédət]   to dine, eat dinner
идём [iḍóm]   let's go!
Идём обе́дать!   Let's go eat dinner!
Хорошо́. Идём обе́дать.   Fine. Let's go eat dinner!

го́лоден [gólədin]   hungry
Я уже́ го́лоден.   I'm already hungry.

сего́дня [şivódṇə]¹   today
Что́ сего́дня на обе́д?   What's for dinner today?
интере́сно [inţiŗésnə]   I wonder (*lit.* [it is] interesting [to me])
Интере́сно, что сего́дня на обе́д?   I wonder what's for dinner today.

смотре́ть [smatŗéţ]   to look
Ты́ смотре́л?   Did you look?

всегда́ [fşigdá]   always
Как всегда́.   [Same] as always.

пи́ща [píščə]   fare, food, diet
на́ша [nášə]   our

¹ Note that г is pronounced [v] in **сего́дня** [şivódṇə] *today*.

61

щи́ (pl) [ščí]	schi (sauerkraut soup, cabbage soup)
да [də]¹	and
ка́ша [kášə]	kasha (cooked cereal, porridge)

«Щи́ да ка́ша — пи́ща на́ша».   "Schi and kasha is our diet."

бо́льше [bólˌši]	more, bigger
бо́льше не́т [bólˌši n̯ét]	there isn't any more, it's all gone
ры́ба [ríbə]	fish

Была́ ры́ба, но бо́льше не́т.   There was fish, but it's all gone.

| доса́да [dasádə] | annoyance, aggravation, disappointment, vexation |

Во́т доса́да!   How annoying! *or* What a nuisance!

| не хо́чется [n̯ixóčitcə] | [one] doesn't feel like |
| туда́ [tudá] | there, to that place |

Не хо́чется идти́ туда́.   I don't feel like going there.

| да́же [dáži] | even |

Да́же идти́ туда́ не хо́чется.   I don't even feel like going there.

SUPPLEMENT

| голодна́ (f) [gəladná] | hungry |

Ни́на, ты голодна́?   Nina, are you hungry?

| го́лодны (pl) [gólədn̯i] | hungry |

Вы́ го́лодны?   Are you hungry?

| бо́рщ [bóršč] | borsch (beet soup) |

Что́ на обе́д, бо́рщ?   What's for dinner, borsch?

| ко́фе (m) [kóf̯i]² | coffee |

Хо́чешь ко́фе?   Want some coffee?

| пи́ть [p̯íṭ] | to drink |

Я́ пи́л ко́фе.   I was drinking (*or* drank) coffee.

| ча́й (m) [čáj] | tea |

Я́ пи́л ча́й.   I was drinking (*or* drank) tea.

| неда́вно [n̯idávnə] | awhile ago, recently, not long ago |

Я́ неда́вно пи́л ча́й.   I drank tea awhile ago.

| молоко́ [məlakó] | milk |

Я́ неда́вно пи́л молоко́.   Awhile ago I drank some milk.

---

¹ Do not confuse unstressed да [də] *and* with stressed да́ [dá] *yes.*

² Ко́фе is considered a masculine noun by some speakers; others treat it as a neuter. It is one of a small number of indeclinable nouns, i.e., nouns that use the same form in all cases.

Что́ на обе́д?

What's for dinner?

О. — Оле́г

Л. — Лёв

Л. 1 Ка́к насчёт обе́да, Оле́г? Столо́вая давно́ откры́та.	kák naščót aḅẽ́də aḷék ↓ stalóvəjə davnó atkr̆ítə ↓	How about dinner, Oleg? The dining hall's been open for a long time.[1]
О. 2 Хорошо́. Идём обе́дать. Я́ уже́ го́лоден.	xərašő ↓ iḍőm aḅédəţ ↓ já užé gől̆ədin ↓	Fine. Let's go eat dinner. I'm already hungry.
Л. 3 Интере́сно, что́ сего́дня на обе́д. Ты́ смотре́л?	inţir̆ésnə ↓ štó şivódņə nəaḅét ↓ tí smatr̆ẽl ↑	I wonder what's for dinner today. Did you look?
О. 4 Да́. Ка́к всегда́, «Щи́ да ка́ша — пи́ща на́ша». Была́ ры́ба, но бо́льше не́т.	dã́ ↓ kák fşigdã́ ↓ ščí də kắšə | ṛíščə nắšə ↓ biĺá r̆íbə ↓ no bóḷşi ņḗt ↓	Yes. Same as always, "Schi and kasha is our diet."[2] There was fish, but it's all gone.
Л. 5 Во́т доса́да! Да́же идти́ туда́ не хо́чется.	vót dasắdə ↓ dắži iţţí tudá | ņixő̆čitcə ↓	How annoying! I don't even feel like going there.

NOTES

[1] **Столо́вая** is a feminine adjective which functions as a noun. It is derived from **столо́вая ко́мната** *table room*. **Столо́вая** is used here as *dining hall*, but it also means [*second class*] *restaurant* as well as dining room.

[2] «**Щи́ да ка́ша — пи́ща на́ша**» is a colloquial expression illustrating the humble food that comprises the Russian rural diet. **Щи́** is a soup made of sauerkraut or cabbage. **Ка́ша** is cooked cereal, which may be served at any meal and eaten with butter, salt, or gravy; or with milk and sugar. **Бо́рщ** is a vegetable soup, primarily made of beets.

пообе́дать   [pəabédət]
Вы́ уже́ пообе́дали?
  ребя́та   [ribatə]
Приве́т, ребя́та!
Приве́т, ребя́та! Вы́ уже́ пообе́дали?

  ещё   [jiščó]
Не́т ещё.

  опя́ть   [apáṭ]
  в столо́вой   [fstalóvəj]
В столо́вой опя́ть щи́ и ка́ша.

  селёдка   [şilótkə]
А я́ купи́л селёдку.
  как ра́з   [kakrás]
А я́ как ра́з купи́л селёдку.
А я́ как ра́з купи́л селёдку. Хоти́те?

  друго́е де́ло   [drugójə ḍélə]
Э́то друго́е де́ло!
Селёдка — э́то друго́е де́ло!

  у на́с е́сть   [unás jéşṭ]
  хле́б   [xḷép]
Хле́б у на́с е́сть.
  огурцы́   [agurcí]
Огурцы́ то́же.
Хле́б у на́с е́сть. Огурцы́ то́же.

  же   [ži]
Где́ же они́?
  шка́ф   [škáf]
  в шкафу́   [fškafú]
Где́ же они́? В шкафу́?

  окно́   [aknó]
  на окне́   [nəakņé]
Не́т, на окне́.

  наре́жь!   [naṛéš]
Наре́жь огурцы́!
Оле́г, наре́жь огурцы́!

  я́щик   [jáščik]
  в я́щике   [vjáščiķi]
Но́ж в я́щике.
  сто́л   [stól]
  в столе́   [fstaḷé]
Но́ж в столе́, в я́щике.

to eat dinner, have dinner
Have you had dinner already?
    children, kids, fellows, guys
Hi, fellows!
Hi, fellows! Have you had dinner already?

    yet, still; else, some more, another
Not yet.

    again
    at (or in) the dining hall
At the dining hall it's schi and kasha again.

    herring
But I bought herring.
    just, it just happens
Well, it just happens I bought herring.
Well, it just happens I bought herring. Want
    some?

    another matter, a different thing
That's different!
Herring! That's different!

    we have (lit. by us there is)
    bread
We have bread.
    cucumbers
Cucumbers too.
We have bread. Cucumbers too.

    (unstressed emphatic particle)
Where are they?
    cupboard, wardrobe, dresser
    in the cupboard
Where are they, in the cupboard?

    window
    on the window [ledge]
No, on the window [ledge].

    slice!
Slice the cucumbers!
Oleg, slice the cucumbers!

    drawer, box [wooden]
    in the drawer
The knife's in the drawer.
    desk, table
    in the desk, in the table
The knife's in the desk drawer.

вúжу [ɣížu]	I see
не вúжу [n̩iɣížu]	I don't see
Не вúжу.	I don't see [it].
вúлка [ɣílkə]	fork
вúлки [ɣílk̩i]	forks
Тýт тóлько вúлки.	There are just forks here.
лóжка [lóškə]	spoon
лóжки [lóšk̩i]	spoons
тóлько [tól̩kə]	only, just
Тýт тóлько вúлки и лóжки.	There are just forks and spoons here.
на столé [nəstal̩é]	on the table, on the desk.
Вóт он, на столé.	Here it is, on the desk.

SUPPLEMENT

смотрéть в окнó	to look out the window, look in the window
Óн смотрéл в окнó.	He was looking out (or in) the window.

Вы́ ужé пообéдали?

Have you had dinner already?

К. — Кирúлл   О. — Олéг   Л. — Лéв

К.	1	Привéт, ребя́та! Вы́ ужé пообéдали?	pr̩iɣét ↑ r̩ib̩átə ↓ vi užé pəab̩édal̩i ↓	Hi, fellows! Have you had dinner already?
О.	2	Нéт ещё. В столóвой опя́ть щи и кáша.	n̩ét jiščó ↓ fstalóvəj ap̩át̩ ščí i kašə ↓	Not yet. At the dining hall it's schi and kasha again.
К.	3	А я́ как рáз купúл селёдку. Хотúте?	a já kakrás ǀ kup̩íl s̩il̩ótku ↓ xat̩ít̩i ↑	Well it just so happens I bought herring. Want some?
Л.	4	Селёдка — э́то другóе дéло.	s̩il̩ótkə ↓ étə drugójə d̩élə ↓	Herring![1] That's different!
О.	5	Хлéб у нáс éсть. Огурцы́ тóже.	xl̩ép unás jés̩t̩ ↓ agurcí tóži ↓	We have bread. Cucumbers too.
К.	6	Гдé же онú? В шкафý?	gd̩éži an̩í ↓ fškafű ↑	Where are they, in the cupboard?[2]
О.	7	Нéт, на окнé.	n̩ét ↓ nəakn̩é ↓	No, on the window [ledge].

Л.	8	Олéг, нарéжь огурцы́. Нóж в столé, в я́щике.	aļék ↓ naŗéš agurcĭ ↓ nóš fstaļé | vjắščiķi ↓	Oleg, slice the cucumbers. The knife is in the desk drawer.[3]
О.	9	Не ви́жу. Ту́т тóлько ви́лки и лóжки.	ņiɣĭžu ↑ tút tóļkə ɣĭlķi | i lóšķi ↓	I don't see it. There are just forks and spoons here.
К.	10	Вóт óн, на столé.	vót ón ↓ nəstaļé ↓	Here it is, on the desk.

NOTES

[1] Herring is a very common food in the Russian diet; it is served not only as an appetizer, but as a main course as well.

[2] Each room in a university dormitory has its **шкáф,** which may serve both as a cupboard and as a wardrobe. (Built-in closets are not to be found in the Soviet Union, nor are they generally found elsewhere in Europe.) Each floor in the dormitory has a kitchen where students can prepare tea, snacks, or light meals.

[3] **Я́щик** is used here as *drawer*, but it also means *box*. It differs from **корóбка,** which designates a small box or one made of cardboard, in that it is usually larger and made of wood. Note also that **стóл** means both *table* and *desk;* the latter comes from **пи́сьменный стóл** *writing table.*

Basic sentence patterns

1. Интерéсно, чтó сегóдня на обéд? Wonder what's for dinner today?
   — Щи́ и кáша. Schi and kasha.
   — Бóрщ и кáша. Borsch and kasha.
   — Селёдка. Herring.
   — Ры́ба. Fish.
   — Бóрщ и ры́ба. Borsch and fish.

2. Óн недáвно пи́л чáй. He drank tea awhile ago.
   Онá _____ пилá ____. She drank _____.
   Они́ _____ пи́ли ____. They drank _____.
   Óн недáвно пи́л кóфе. He drank coffee awhile ago.
   Онá _____ пилá ____. She drank _____.
   Они́ _____ пи́ли ____. They drank _____.
   Óн недáвно пи́л молокó. He drank milk awhile ago.
   Онá _____ пилá ____. She drank _____.
   Они́ _____ пи́ли ____. They drank _____.

3. Столóвая откры́та? Is the dining hall open?
   Лаборатóрия откры́та? _____ laboratory open?
   Пóчта откры́та? _____ post office open?
   Корóбка откры́та? _____ box open?

Дверь откры́та?	Is the door open?
Заво́д откры́т?	_____ plant open?
Клуб откры́т?	_____ club open?
Я́щик откры́т?	_____ drawer open?
Горсове́т откры́т?	_____ gorsovet open?
Портфе́ль откры́т?	_____ briefcase open?
Собра́ние откры́то?	_____ meeting open?
Окно́ откры́то?	_____ window open?
Общежи́тие откры́то?	_____ dormitory open?

4. Вы́ уже́ го́лодны?

— Да́, я́ уже́ го́лоден.

— Да́, я́ уже́ голодна́.

— Да́, мы́ уже́ го́лодны.

— Не́т, я́ ещё не го́лоден.

— Не́т, я́ ещё не голодна́.

— Не́т, мы́ ещё не го́лодны.

Are you already hungry?

Yes, I'm already hungry.

Yes, _____.

Yes, we're already hungry.

No, I'm not hungry yet.

No, _____.

No, we're not hungry yet.

5. Вы́ уже́ пообе́дали?

— Да́, я́ уже́ пообе́дал.

— Да́, я́ уже́ пообе́дала.

— Да́, мы́ уже́ пообе́дали.

— Ещё не́т.

Вы́ уже́ обе́дали?

— Не́т, я́ ещё не обе́дал.

— Не́т, я́ ещё не обе́дала.

— Не́т, мы́ ещё не обе́дали.[1]

Have you already had dinner?

Yes, I've already had dinner.

Yes, _____.

Yes, we've already had dinner.

Not yet.

Have you already had dinner?

No, I haven't had dinner yet.

No, _____.

No, we _____.

6. У на́с е́сть хле́б.

_____ бо́рщ.

_____ ры́ба.

_____ ка́ша.

_____ щи́.

_____ огурцы́.

_____ ча́й.

_____ ко́фе.

_____ молоко́.

We have bread.

_____ borsch.

_____ fish.

_____ kasha.

_____ schi.

_____ cucumbers.

_____ tea.

_____ coffee.

_____ milk.

7. Где́ же но́ж?

— На столе́.

— В я́щике.

— На окне́.

— В столе́, в я́щике.

— В портфе́ле.

— В коро́бке.

— В шкафу́.

Where's the knife?

On the table.

In the drawer.

On the window sill.

In the desk (_or_ table) drawer.

In the briefcase.

In the cardboard box.

In the cupboard.

---

[1] In both the question and answer, either the imperfective **обе́дал** or the perfective **пообе́дал** may be used. The difference in meaning is slight, with **пообе́дал** focusing on the completion of the activity: _Have you already finished eating dinner?_ Note, however, that in the negative answers, only **обе́дал** is used.

Pronunciation practice: hard versus soft consonants

A.   [t] vs. [ţ]   Usual Cyrillic spelling т; also ть, д, or дь.

Note the pronunciation of hard [t] in the following:

[napóčtu]	на по́чту	to the post office
[stuḑént]	студе́нт	student

and compare it with soft [ţ]:

[sp̦iș̌iţi]	спеши́те	you're hurrying
[paslá̦t]	посла́ть	to send, mail

The formation of Russian hard [t] differs from that of English *t* in that the tip of the tongue closes off the air stream by making contact against the back surface of the upper teeth, whereas English *t* is formed by stopping the air stream farther back, on the ridge of the gums behind the teeth. Soft Russian [ţ], on the other hand, is formed by a closure of the front part of the blade of the tongue (not the tip) against the ridge of the gums and has the effect on the ear of being followed by a y-like glide. In addition, neither Russian hard [t] nor soft [ţ] (nor any other Russian consonant, for that matter) ever has the puff of breath that usually accompanies English *t*.

> Sound Drill: Practice the Russian paired examples illustrating hard [t] and soft [ţ], imitating your instructor (or the tape) as accurately as you can. Be sure to avoid the puff of breath that often accompanies the English *t*.

B.   [d] vs. [ḑ]   Usual Cyrillic spelling д; sometimes дь, т, or ть.

Note the pronunciation of hard [d] in the following:

[davnó]	давно́	for a long time
[zdaróvi]	здоро́вы	healthy
[kudá]	куда́	where to
[idú]	иду́	I'm going

and compare it with soft [ḑ]:

[ɣíḑil]	ви́дел	saw
[ḑilá]	дела́	affairs
[nɔzavóḑi]	на заво́де	at the plant
[iḑót]	идёт	is going

Russian hard [d] is made with the tongue in the same position as Russian hard [t] and [n], that is, well forward of the position for making the corresponding English sounds and with the tongue touching the teeth. Russian soft [ḍ] is made with the tongue in the same position as for Russian [ṭ] and [ṇ].

> Sound Drill: Practice the Russian paired examples illustrating hard [d] and soft [ḍ], imitating your instructor (or the tape) as accurately as you can.

C.   [n] vs. [ṇ]   Usual Cyrillic spelling **н**; sometimes **нь**.

Note the pronunciation of hard [n] in the following:

[nəurók]	на уро́к	to the lesson
[napóčtu]	на по́чту	to the post office
[nú]	ну́	well

and compare it with soft [ṇ]:

[ṇínə]	Ни́на	Nina
[dəsyidáṇjə]	до свида́ния	good-bye
[fpalṇé]	вполне́	fully, completely
[ḍéṇ]	де́нь	day

Russian hard [n] is formed, like Russian hard [t], by closing off the air stream with the tip of the tongue which strikes the back surface of the upper teeth. (Be careful not to make an English *n*, where the air stream is closed farther back on the gums above the upper teeth!)

Russian soft [ṇ] is formed like Russian soft [ṭ], that is, with the front part of the upper surface of the tongue against the ridge of the gums above the upper teeth and with the tip of the tongue touching the teeth. It has the effect of being followed by a y-like glide and sounds something like English *ny* in such words as ca*ny*on and o*ni*on; however, the y-like glide in Russian must *never* be separated and made a separate consonant sound as it is in English.

> Sound Drill: Practice the Russian examples illustrating hard [n] and soft [ṇ], imitating your instructor (or the tape) as accurately as you can. Notice particularly that before [k] and [g], Russian [n] does not take on the *ng* sound that occurs in such English words as *bank* and *finger*.

Grammatical gender of nouns

All Russian nouns belong to one of three genders: masculine, feminine, or neuter. Besides distinctions based on natural gender, such as we find in English, Russian assigns *all* nouns to one of the three categories.

MASCULINE		FEMININE		NEUTER	
студе́нт	student	студе́нтка	student	письмо́	letter
клу́б	club	жена́	wife	окно́	window
уро́к	lesson	по́чта	post office	пла́тье	dress
ча́й	tea	ры́ба	fish	собра́ние	meeting
го́род	city	пра́вда	truth	общежи́тие	dormitory
учи́тель	teacher	лаборато́рия	laboratory		

It is essential for the student of Russian to know the gender of each noun he encounters. This is important because such words as adjectives and past tense verbs vary their form in agreement with the gender of the noun they accompany.

EXAMPLE

MASCULINE SUBJECT   Мо́й портфе́ль бы́л та́м.   My briefcase was there.
FEMININE SUBJECT   Моя́ жена́ была́ та́м.   My wife was there.
NEUTER SUBJECT   Моё письмо́ бы́ло та́м.   My letter was there.

The gender of most nouns can be predicted from the written nominative singular form. Nouns whose final letter in the nominative singular is a hard consonant, **ч**, **щ**, or **й** (i.e., with a zero ending), are masculine. Similarly, most nouns ending in **–а** or **–я** are feminine, and nouns ending in **–о**, **–ё**, or **–е** are neuter.

MASCULINE		FEMININE		NEUTER	
му́ж	husband	сестра́	sister	у́тро	morning
обе́д	dinner	зима́	winter	перо́	pen
сто́л	table	коро́бка	box (cardboard)	де́ло	business
но́ж	knife	шко́ла	school	мо́ре	sea
Ива́н	Ivan	Ири́на	Irina	по́ле	field
клю́ч	key	Росси́я	Russia	житьё	existence
бо́рщ	borsch	Га́ля	Galya	бельё	linen
ча́й	tea	семья́	family		

Nouns ending in **–а** or **–я** are masculine, however, if they refer to a male person: **дя́дя** *uncle*, **де́душка** *grandfather*, **Ва́ня** *Vanya* (*Johnny*), **Ми́ша** *Misha* (*Mike*), **Стёпа** *Styopa* (*Steve*), **Гри́ша** *Grisha* (*Greg*), **Ва́ся** *Vasya*. Most of these are nicknames.

Nouns whose gender can*not* be ascertained from the written form alone are those whose nominative singular ends in the soft sign **–ь**. Most of these nouns are feminine, but many are masculine. They will be identified as m (masculine) or f (feminine) in the glossaries, for example, **о́сень** (f) *fall*, **о́чередь** (f) *line*, **две́рь** (f) *door*, **портфе́ль** (m) *briefcase*, **де́нь** (m) *day*; otherwise the gender of nouns will not ordinarily be indicated.

Verbal aspects

Compared with the highly complex system of tenses in English, the Russian verb is structurally very simple. English makes considerable use of such auxiliary verbs as *do*, *have*, *be*, and *will* in forming its many compound tenses. Russian uses only a single compound tense used to form one kind of future; otherwise, past, present, and future in Russian verbs are expressed by simple, one-word verb forms.

To illustrate the economy of forms in the Russian system, compare the following:

RUSSIAN	ENGLISH
рабо́тал	worked, was working, did work, used to work, have worked, had worked, had been working

Similarly, all of the following English verbal concepts *can* be expressed in Russian by the simple present verb **рабо́таю**: [I] work, [I] am working, [I] do work, [I] have been working, [I] have worked.

Despite its structural simplicity, however, the Russian verb possesses an added dimension called "aspect," which enables it to make refinements comparable to the English. The system of "aspects" involves two contrasting categories: *imperfective aspect* versus *perfective aspect*. The aspect a Russian speaker uses depends on the way he views the action.

Broadly speaking, the *imperfective aspect* focuses on the activity as a process, without regard to its terminating point in time. The *perfective aspect*, on the other hand, focuses on the activity as a completed (or to be completed) action marked off in time, often emphasizing the result rather than the process. Compare the use of the two aspects in the past tense of the verbs **покупа́ть** and **купи́ть**:

IMPERFECTIVE	Я покупа́ла пода́рок.	I was buying a present.
PERFECTIVE	Что́ же вы́ купи́ли?	And what did you buy?

Note also the differences between the following:

IMPERFECTIVE	Мы́ неда́вно пи́ли ча́й.	We *drank* (or *were drinking*) tea not long ago.
PERFECTIVE	Мы́ уже́ вы́пили ча́й.	We already *drank* (or *finished drinking*) the tea.
IMPERFECTIVE	Она́ смотре́ла в окно́.	She *was looking* out the window.
PERFECTIVE	Она́ посмотре́ла в окно́.	She *took a look* out the window.
IMPERFECTIVE	Что́ вы́ де́лали?	What *did* you *do*? *Or* What *were* you *doing*?
PERFECTIVE	Что́ вы́ сде́лали?	What *did* you *do*? *Or* What *did* you get *done*? *Or* What *have* you *done*?

Imperfective and perfective verbs often differ structurally only in that one is prefixed and the other not. Both imperfective and perfective verbs may be used in the past and future. In the present, only imperfective verbs are used.

	PAST	PRESENT	FUTURE
IMPERFECTIVE	я смотре́л *I was looking* *I looked*	я смотрю́ *I'm looking* *I look*	я бу́ду смотре́ть *I'll be looking* *I'll look*
PERFECTIVE	я посмотре́л *I took a look*		я посмотрю́ *I'll take a look*

Note that it is almost always the perfective verb that is prefixed:

IMPERFECTIVE	PERFECTIVE	IMPERFECTIVE	PERFECTIVE
пи́ть	вы́пить	смотре́ть	посмотре́ть
де́лать	сде́лать	идти́	пойти́

STRUCTURE AND DRILLS

Replacement of nouns by third person pronouns: о́н, она́, оно́, and они́

MODELS

Где́ Кири́лл? — Во́т о́н.	Where's Kirill? Here he is.
Где́ портфе́ль? — Во́т о́н.	Where's the briefcase? Here it is.
Где́ Ири́на? — Во́т она́.	Where's Irina? Here she is.
Где́ коро́бка? — Во́т она́.	Where's the box? Here it is.
Где́ общежи́тие? — Во́т оно́.	Where's the dormitory? Here it is.
Где́ письмо́? — Во́т оно́.	Where's the letter? Here it is.
Где́ Кири́лл и Ири́на? — Во́т они́.	Where are Kirill and Irina? Here they are.
Где́ огурцы́? — Во́т они́.	Where are the cucumbers? Here they are.

■ REPETITION DRILL

Repeat the above models after your instructor (or the tape) until you can answer the questions automatically according to the pattern.

■ QUESTION-ANSWER DRILLS

1. *Where's the student?*
   He's here.
   т: Где́ студе́нт?
   s: **О́н ту́т.**
   т: Где́ студе́нтка?
   s: **Она́ ту́т.**
   (Ни́на, Цара́пкин, Евге́ний, Ми́ла, жена́, му́ж, Оле́г, О́ля, Ле́в)

2. *Where's the briefcase?*
   It's there.
   т: Где́ портфе́ль?
   s: **О́н та́м.**
   т: Где́ по́чта?
   s: **Она́ та́м.**
   (письмо́, собра́ние, клу́б, лаборато́рия, общежи́тие, селёдка, две́рь, коро́бка, о́чередь, ча́й, окно́, ло́жка, ви́лка, я́щик, пода́рок)

3. *Where's the knife, on the table?*
   Yes, it's on the table.
   т: Где́ но́ж, на столе́?
   s: **Да́, о́н на столе́.**
   т: Где́ ча́й, на столе́?
   s: **Да́, о́н на столе́.**
   (бо́рщ, портфе́ль, коро́бка, селёдка, ло́жки, ви́лки, огурцы́, письмо́, ча́й, материа́л, молоко́, обе́д, хле́б, ры́ба)

4. *Is the knife there?*
   Yes, it's there.
   т: Но́ж та́м?
   s: **Да́, о́н та́м.**
   т: Ры́ба та́м?
   s: **Да́, она́ та́м.**
   (письмо́, огурцы́, ча́й, собра́ние, сто́л, авто́бус, конце́рт, пода́рок, портфе́ль, ры́ба, пла́тье, шка́ф)

DISCUSSION

The masculine pronoun о́н substitutes for masculine nouns such as сто́л *table*, Ва́ня *Vanya*, уро́к *lesson*, and де́нь *day*.

The feminine pronoun она́ substitutes for feminine nouns such as жена́ *wife*, селёдка *herring*, лаборато́рия *laboratory*, and о́чередь *line* or *turn*.

The neuter pronoun **онó** substitutes for neuter nouns such as **письмó** *letter*, **окнó** *window*, **у́тро** *morning*, and **пла́тье** *dress*.

Óн and **она́** mean *he* and *she* respectively when referring to person and *it* when referring to things. **Онó** means only *it*, since one does not use **онó** in referring to persons.[1]

Interrogatives кто́ and что́

MODELS

Кто́ та́м бы́л?	Who was there?
— Та́м была́ Ни́на.	Nina was there.
— Та́м бы́л Ива́н.	Ivan was there.
— Та́м бы́ли Ни́на и Ива́н.	Nina and Ivan were there.
Что́ бы́ло на столе́?	What was on the table?
— На столе́ бы́л пода́рок.	There was a present on the table.
— На столе́ была́ ры́ба.	There was a fish on the table.
— На столе́ бы́ло письмо́.	There was a letter on the table.
— На столе́ бы́ли огурцы́.	There were cucumbers on the table.

■ REPETITION DRILL

Repeat the above models after your instructor (or the tape) until the verb agreement becomes automatic. (Note that in the question **бы́л** is used with **кто́** and **бы́ло** with **что́**.)

■ CUED QUESTION-ANSWER DRILLS

The following drills should be performed as simple repetition drills until the student(s) can answer automatically. (During the repetition stage the teacher may ask for both group and individual responses.)

1. (*Mila*) *Who was there?*
   Mila was there.
   т: (Ми́ла) Кто́ та́м бы́л?
   s: **Та́м была́ Ми́ла.**
   т: (Хитро́в) Кто́ та́м бы́л?
   s: **Та́м бы́л Хитро́в.**
   (му́ж, жена́, Ни́на, Ле́в, Евге́ний, Семён, Оле́г и О́ля, Ни́на и Ива́н. студе́нт и студе́нтка)

2. (*a table*) *What was there?*
   There was a table there.
   т: (сто́л) Что́ та́м бы́ло?
   s: **Та́м бы́л сто́л.**
   т: (ры́ба) Что́ та́м бы́ло?
   s: **Та́м была́ ры́ба.**
   (письмо́, уро́к, собра́ние, конце́рт, пода́рок, бо́рщ, пла́тье, коро́бка, огурцы́, ча́й, хле́б, ви́лки и ло́жки)

---

[1] The Russian pronouns **óн, она́,** and **онó** are used only in reference to a specific masculine, feminine, or neuter noun. They are never used to translate the empty English introductory *it* in such sentences as: *It's late.* The *it* of such sentences is simply omitted in Russian.

EXAMPLES	Уже́ по́здно.	It's already late.
	Та́м бы́ло интере́сно?	Was it interesting there?
	Ещё ра́но.	It's still early.

3. (Nina) *Who was standing there?*
   Nina was standing there.

   т: (Ни́на) Кто́ та́м стоя́л?
   s: **Та́м стоя́ла Ни́на.**
   т: (Лёв и Ми́ла) Кто́ та́м стоя́л?
   s: **Та́м стоя́ли Лёв и Ми́ла.**
   (студе́нт, студе́нтка, Оле́г, О́ля, Царапкин, Хитро́в, студе́нт и студе́нтка)

DISCUSSION

In terms of grammatical agreement, **кто́** *who* is treated as masculine singular even though the person asking the question may know that the referent will be a female person or more than one person. Similarly, **что́** is treated as neuter singular. Note that **что́** *what* is pronounced [štó].

Introductory э́то

MODELS

Что́ э́то?	What's that?
— Э́то письмо́.	It's a letter.
А э́то что́?	And what's this?
— Э́то пода́рок О́ле.	It's a present for Olya.
Э́то ты́, Кири́лл?	Is that you, Kirill?
— Не́т, э́то я́, Лёв.	No, it's me, Lev.
Э́то друго́е де́ло.	That's different.
Что́ э́то, огурцы́?	What are those, cucumbers?

■ CUED QUESTION-ANSWER DRILLS

The item to be substituted is to be given first, followed by the question and then the student answer.

1. (*a letter*) *What's that?*
   It's a letter.
   т: (письмо́) Что́ э́то?
   s: **Э́то письмо́.**
   т: (я́щик) Что́ э́то?
   s: **Э́то я́щик.**
   (сто́л, ры́ба, ка́ша, селёдка, две́рь, окно́, портфе́ль, ча́й, ко́фе, авто́бус, но́ж)

2. (*Evgeny*) *Who's there?*
   It's me, Evgeny.
   т: (Евге́ний) Кто́ та́м?
   s: **Э́то я́, Евге́ний.**
   т: (Ни́на) Кто́ та́м?
   s: **Э́то я́, Ни́на.**
   (Кири́лл, Лёв, Семён, Царапкин, Ми́ла, Хитро́в, Кири́лл, О́льга, Оле́г, Семён Фили́ппович)

DISCUSSION

The introductory word **э́то** usually indicates something not previously described or specified, but about which some statement is to be made. It can be translated as *this, that, these, those,* and sometimes (particularly in a rejoinder) *it.*

The irregular present tense of хотéть

Я хочý пойти на концéрт.　　　　　I want to go to the concert.

Ты хóчешь _____.　　　　You want _____.

Óн хóчет _____.　　　　He wants _____.

Мы хотим _____.　　　　We want _____.

Вы хотите _____.　　　　You want _____.

Они хотя́т _____.　　　　They want _____.

■ REPETITION DRILL

Repeat the model after your instructor (or the tape) until you can reproduce all forms accurately.

■ REPETITION-SUBSTITUTION DRILL

She wants to go to the concert.

т: Онá хóчет пойти на концéрт.

s: **Онá хóчет пойти на концéрт.**

(Кирилл, ты, я, Нина, мы, они, вы, Олéг
и Сáша)

■ QUESTION-ANSWER DRILL

Don't you want to go there?
No, I don't.

т: Вы не хотите идти тудá?

s: **Нéт, не хочý.**

т: Óн не хóчет идти тудá?

s: **Нéт, не хóчет.**

(ты, Сáша, Евгéний, они, Мила, вы, Нина
и Олéг)

DISCUSSION

The verb **хотéть** has an irregular present tense. It follows a first conjugation pattern in the singular and a second conjugation pattern in the plural. Note that the final stem consonant is **ч** in the singular and **т** in the plural, and that the stress is on the endings except for the second and third persons singular.

SINGULAR	PLURAL
хочý	хотим
хóчешь	хотите
хóчет	хотя́т

The past tense

MASCULINE SUBJECT	Óн бы́л в го́роде.	He was in town.
	Я́ давно́ ва́с не ви́дел.	I haven't seen you in a long time.
	Ты́ купи́л селёдку?	Did you buy herring?
	Сего́дня му́ж не́ был на слу́жбе.	My husband wasn't at work today.
FEMININE SUBJECT	Она́ давно́ ва́с не ви́дела.	She hasn't seen you in a long time.
	Ни́на, ты́ была́ в го́роде?	Nina, were you in town?
	Да́, я́ покупа́ла пла́тье.	Yes, I was buying a dress.
	Я́ до́лго стоя́ла в о́череди.	I stood in line for a long time.
NEUTER SUBJECT	Вчера́ бы́ло собра́ние.	There was a meeting yesterday.
	Письмо́ бы́ло на столе́.	The letter was on the table.
	Молоко́ стоя́ло на окне́.	The milk was standing on the window sill.
PLURAL SUBJECT	А где́ вы́ бы́ли?	And where have you been?
	Они́ стоя́ли в о́череди.	They were standing in line.
	Что́ вы́ де́лали?	What have you been doing?
	Мы́ неда́вно пи́ли ча́й.	We drank tea awhile ago.
	Ло́жки бы́ли на столе́.	The spoons were on the table.

■ REPETITION DRILL

Repeat the above models, observing the basic pattern. The past tense is regularly signaled by the suffix –л, usually added to a vowel-ending stem. The endings that follow are gender-number endings, with zero for masculine, –a for feminine, –o for neuter, and –и for plural. Note that the past tense forms always have a hard л in the singular, but a soft л in the plural: пи́л [p̣íl] versus пи́ли [p̣íḷi], стоя́л [stajál] versus стоя́ли [stajáḷi].

■ REPETITION-SUBSTITUTION DRILLS

1. *We drank tea not long ago.*
   т: Мы́ неда́вно пи́ли ча́й.
   s: **Мы́ неда́вно пи́ли ча́й.**
   (му́ж, они́, Евге́ний, Ни́на, О́ля, вы́, студе́нт и студе́нтка, жена́)

2. *Ivan was hurrying to the meeting.*
   т: Ива́н спеши́л на собра́ние.
   s: **Ива́н спеши́л на собра́ние.**
   (ты́, Ни́на, му́ж, вы́, жена́, она́, я́, мы́, му́ж и жена́, они́, о́н, она́)

3. *He hasn't seen you in a long time.*
   т: Óн давно́ ва́с не ви́дел.
   s: **Óн давно́ ва́с не ви́дел.**
   (мы́, му́ж, жена́, О́ля, Га́ля, мы́, они́, Цара́пкин)

■ TRANSFORMATION DRILLS

1. *The borsch is on the table.*
   The borsch was on the table.
   т: Бо́рщ на столе́.
   s: **Бо́рщ бы́л на столе́.**

   т: Пла́тье на столе́.
   s: **Пла́тье бы́ло на столе́.**
   (но́ж, коро́бка, письмо́, пода́рок, ло́жка, ло́жки, ка́ша, ча́й, обе́д, щи́, хле́б)

2. *The herring is in the cupboard.*
   The herring was in the cupboard.
   т: Селёдка в шкафу́.
   s: **Селёдка была́ в шкафу́.**

т: Материа́л в шкафу́.
s: **Материа́л бы́л в шкафу́.**
(огурцы́, ры́ба, ка́ша, ча́й, ви́лки,
ло́жки, хле́б, портфе́ль, письмо́,
коро́бка)

■ QUESTION-ANSWER DRILLS

1. *Where was Evgeny?*
   He was at the meeting.
   т: Где́ бы́л Евге́ний?
   s: **Он бы́л на собра́нии.**
   т: Где́ была́ Ни́на?
   s: **Она́ была́ на собра́нии.**
   (О́ля, Кири́лл, студе́нтка, жена́, Ле́в и
   Оле́г, студе́нт и студе́нтка)

2. *What was she doing?*
   She was standing in line.
   т: Что́ она́ де́лала?
   s: **Она́ стоя́ла в о́череди.**
   т: Что́ он де́лал?
   s: **Он стоя́л в о́череди.**
   Что́ они́ де́лали?
   Что́ вы́ де́лали, Семён?
   Что́ вы́ де́лали, Ми́ла?
   Что́ ты́ де́лал, Са́ша?
   Что́ ты́ де́лала, Ни́на?

3. *Where's Olya, downtown?*
   No, but she was downtown.
   т: Где́ О́ля, в го́роде?
   s: **Не́т, но она́ была́ в го́роде.**
   т: Где́ Евге́ний, в го́роде?
   s: **Не́т, но о́н бы́л в го́роде.**
   (Цара́пкин, Кири́лл Па́влович, о́н,
   они́, она́)

■ TRANSFORMATION DRILL

Where was Olya standing?
Where was she standing?
т: Где́ стоя́ла О́ля?
s: **Где́ она́ стоя́ла?**[1]
т: Где́ стоя́л Евге́ний?
s: **Где́ о́н стоя́л?**
Где́ стоя́ли Кири́лл и Семён?
(Ни́на, Ле́в, Ми́ла, му́ж и жена́)

■ QUESTION-ANSWER DRILLS

1. *What did you buy, Oleg?*
   I bought bread and herring.
   т: Что́ вы́ купи́ли, Оле́г?
   s: **Я купи́л хле́б и селёдку.**
   т: Что́ вы́ купи́ли, О́ля?
   s: **Я купи́ла хле́б и селёдку.**
   Что́ вы́ купи́ли, ребя́та?
   Что́ купи́л Ле́в?
   Что́ купи́ла О́ля?
   Что́ купи́ла жена́?
   Что́ купи́л му́ж?

2. *What were you doing, Olya?*
   I was buying a briefcase.
   т: Что́ вы́ де́лали, О́ля?
   s: **Я покупа́ла портфе́ль.**
   т: Что́ вы́ де́лали, Ле́в?
   s: **Я покупа́л портфе́ль.**
   (Ми́ла, Кири́лл, Ни́на, Семён, Са́ша)

---

[1] In где́ questions of this type the pronoun must *precede* the verb: **Где́ она́ стоя́ла?** A noun, however, may appear either before or after the verb: **Где́ О́льга стоя́ла?** (*Or* **Где́ стоя́ла О́льга?**)

The past tense of Russian verbs is expressed by the past tense suffix –л plus the appropriate gender or number ending to agree with the subject.

With most verbs the past tense suffix is added to a form of the stem ending in a vowel: бы́–л, ду́ма–л, покупа́–л, ви́де–л, стоя́–л, говори́–л, and so forth.

Stress. The stress is usually the same in all four forms of past tense, but may shift to the ending in the feminine form, particularly with the shorter verbs. Compare был, бы́ло, бы́ли with была́ (f); also пил, пи́ло, пи́ли with пила́ (f). In the combinations не́ был, не́ было, and не́ были, the stress shifts from the verb to the negative particle не. Note, however, that it remains on the verb in the feminine form не была́.

REFERENCE LIST OF PAST TENSE FORMS				
Infinitive	*Masculine*	*Feminine*	*Neuter*	*Plural*
бы́ть be	бы́л	был–а́	бы́л–о	бы́л–и
пи́ть drink	пи́л	пил–а́	пи́л–о	пи́л–и
зна́ть know	зна́л	зна́л–а	зна́л–о	зна́л–и
посла́ть send	посла́л	посла́л–а	посла́л–о	посла́л–и
де́лать do	де́лал	де́лал–а	де́лал–о	де́лал–и
доста́ть get	доста́л	доста́л–а	доста́л–о	доста́л–и
слы́шать hear	слы́шал	слы́шал–а	слы́шал–о	слы́шал–и
рабо́тать work	рабо́тал	рабо́тал–а	рабо́тал–о	рабо́тал–и
обе́дать dine	обе́дал	обе́дал–а	обе́дал–о	обе́дал–и
пообе́дать dine	пообе́дал	пообе́дал–а	пообе́дал–о	пообе́дал–и
покупа́ть buy	покупа́л	покупа́л–а	покупа́л–о	покупа́л–и
купи́ть buy	купи́л	купи́л–а	купи́л–о	купи́л–и
спеши́ть hurry	спеши́л	спеши́л–а	спеши́л–о	спеши́л–и
ви́деть see	ви́дел	ви́дел–а	ви́дел–о	ви́дел–и
смотре́ть look	смотре́л	смотре́л–а	смотре́л–о	смотре́л–и
посмотре́ть look	посмотре́л	посмотре́л–а	посмотре́л–о	посмотре́л–и
хоте́ть want	хоте́л	хоте́л–а	хоте́л–о	хоте́л–и

ЧТЕ́НИЕ И ПИСЬМО́ READING AND WRITING

А, а А вы куда? Как дела на заводе?

Б, б Было собрание. Рыбы больше нет. Вы были больны.

В, в Давно вас не видел. Вы здоровы?

Г, г Говорят, обед готов. Где огурцы?

Д, д, д   Да. До свидания. Где вы достали?
Hа заводе.

Е, е   Привет жене! Очень интересно.
Есть хочется.

Ё, ё   Вот идёт Семён. Всё утро там
был.

Ж, ж   Жена на службе. Можно войти?
Пожалуйста. Скажите, где нож?

З, з, з   Здравствуйте! Вы здоровы?
Пожалуйста, заходите.

И, и   Извините, Иван Иванович!
Спасибо, Ирина.

Й, й   Это мой чай. Красивый материал.
Читайте! Нью Йорк.

К, к   Коля, кто там? Как дела?
Куда идёт Кирилл?

Л, л   Лев и Кирилл были на службе.
Люба купила платье.

М, м   Мы там были. Там мой материал.
Семён в ГУМе.

Н, н   Нет. Ну, ничего, Нина. Где Ирина
Ивановна?

О, о   Он идёт домой. Вот мой автобус.
Вполне здоров. Обед готов.

П, п   Пожалуйста! Это платье. Куда
вы спешите?

Р, р, р   Красивый материал. Говорят,
Ирина в городе.

С, с   Семён всю зиму не был на службе.
Где стол? Можно посмотреть?
До свидания.

Т, т   Ты тут? Вот идёт автобус.
Что ты!

У, у   У нас есть огурцы. Я спешу.
Я иду на почту.

Ф, ф   Семён Филиппович на службе. Где
Африка? Софья Филипповна там.
Портфель тут.

Х, х   Хорошо. Заходите. Хотите
посмотреть?

Ц, ц   Огурцы на столе. Где концерт?
Царапкин там.

Ч, ч   Что вы! Чай на столе. Очень
красивый. Как насчёт обеда? Иван
Иванович стоял в очереди.

Ш, ш   Куда ты спешишь? Хорошо. Каша
хорошая. Шура спешит на концерт.

Щ, щ   Борщ ещё не готов. Нож в ящике.
Где Хрущёв? Щи на столе.

ъ   Кто это съел? Ты съел огурцы?

ы   Где вы были?

ь   Вот очередь. Нарежь огурцы Где портфель? Ты теперь работаешь?

Э, э   Это ты, Коля? Нет, это я, Нина. Это ужасно!

Ю, ю   Юрий всю зиму был болен. Я работаю на почте.

Я, я   Я иду домой. До свидания. Говорят, Коля опять болен. Он стоял в очереди. Где Ялта?

NOTES

PREPARATION FOR CONVERSATION | Пе́рвый де́нь в университе́те

пе́рвый де́нь
Пе́рвый де́нь в университе́те.
де́вять
почти́
Уже́ почти́ де́вять.

the first day
The first day at the university.
nine
almost
It's almost nine already.

пора́
Пора́ идти́.

time, it's time
It's time to be going.

гото́в (m), гото́ва (f)
Но я́ ещё не гото́ва.

ready
But I'm not ready yet.

ру́чка
моя́ ру́чка
[я] зна́ю
Не зна́ю, где́ моя́ ру́чка.

pen, penholder
my pen
I know
I don't know where my pen is.

по́лка
на по́лке
во́н та́м
А во́н та́м, на по́лке, не она́?

shelf, bookcase
on the shelf, on the bookcase
over there, over yonder
But over there on the shelf, isn't [that] it?

тетра́дь (f)
э́ти тетра́ди
всё э́ти тетра́ди
тебе́
заче́м
заче́м тебе́
И заче́м тебе́ всё э́ти тетра́ди?

notebook
these notebooks, those notebooks
all those notebooks
for you, to you
why, what for, for what purpose
why do you need
And why do you need all those notebooks?

пра́вда
Да́, пра́вда.

truth; it's the truth, that's right
Yes, you're right.

кни́га
кни́ги
взя́ть (pfv)

book
books
to take

[я] возьму́	I'll take
Я возьму́ то́лько кни́ги.	I'll take just the books.
одну́ тетра́дь	one notebook
Возьму́ то́лько кни́ги и одну́ тетра́дь.	I'll take just the books and one notebook.
возьми́	take!
каранда́ш	pencil
И каранда́ш возьми́.	And take a pencil.
И ещё каранда́ш возьми́.	And take a pencil too.
пошли́	let's go! we're off!
Ну́, пошли́!	Well, let's go!
всё	all, everything (*here* all set)
Ну́ всё, пошли́!	Well, all set, let's go!
Во́т и университе́т!	Here's the university!
ре́ктор	the chancellor, the president (of the university)
óн бу́дет говори́ть	he'll speak
Где́ бу́дет говори́ть ре́ктор?	Where will the chancellor speak?
зда́ние [zdáɲjə]	building
большо́е зда́ние	the large building
ты́ ви́дишь	you see
Ты́ ви́дишь большо́е зда́ние?	Do you see the large building?
Во́н та́м. Ви́дишь большо́е зда́ние?	Over there. Do you see the large building?
библиоте́ка	library
про́тив библиоте́ки	opposite the library
Во́н та́м. Ви́дишь большо́е зда́ние про́тив библиоте́ки?	Over there. Do you see the large building opposite the library?
Да́, ви́жу.	Yes, I see.
тогда́	then, in that case
пока́	so long
Ну́, тогда́ пока́.	Well, so long then.

SUPPLEMENT

перо́	pen point, pen
Где́ перо́?	Where's a pen? *or* Where's a pen point?
чей (m)	whose
Чей э́то каранда́ш?	Whose pencil is this?
— Мо́й.	Mine.
чья (f)	whose
Чья́ э́то кни́га?	Whose book is this?
— Моя́.	Mine.
чьё (n)	whose
Чьё э́то письмо́?	Whose letter is this?
— Моё.	Mine.
за́л	hall (room within a building)
Во́т за́л, где́ бу́дет говори́ть ре́ктор.	Here's the hall where the chancellor will speak.

Пе́рвый де́нь в университе́те

Н. — Никола́й (Ко́ля), бра́т
Г. — Гали́на (Га́ля), сестра́

Н.	1	Га́ля,	gắļə ↓
		уже́ почти́ де́вять.	užé pačţí ḍếɣiţ ↓
		Пора́ идти́.	pará iţţí ↓
Г.	2	Но я́ ещё не гото́ва.	no já jiščó ņigatốvə ↓
		Не зна́ю,	ņiznắju |
		где́ моя́ ру́чка.¹	gḍé majá rűčkə ↓
Н.	3	А во́н та́м,	a vón tắm |
		на по́лке,	napốlķi ↓
		не она́?	ņianắ ↑
		И заче́м тебе́	i začém ţiḅé |
		всё э́ти тетра́ди?	fşé éţi ţitrắḍi ↓
Г.	4	Да́, пра́вда.	dắ ↓ prắvdə ↓
		Возьму́ то́лько кни́ги	vaẓmú tốļkə kņ́igi |
		и одну́ тетра́дь.	i adnú ţitrắţ ↓
Н.	5	И ещё каранда́ш возьми́.	i jiščó kərandắš vaẓmí ↓
Г.	6	Ну́ всё.	nú fşố ↓
		Пошли́!²	pašļí ↓

* * *

Н.	7	Во́т и университе́т!	vót i uņiɣirşiţẽt ↓
Г.	8	Где́ бу́дет говори́ть ре́ктор?³	gḍé búḍit gəvaŗíţ ŗёktər ↓
Н.	9	Во́н та́м.	vón tắm ↓
		Ви́дишь большо́е зда́ние	ɣíḍiš baļšójə zdáņjə |
		про́тив библиоте́ки?	próţif ḅibļiaţếķi ↓
Г.	10	Да́, ви́жу.	dắ ↓ ɣížu ↓
Н.	11	Ну́, тогда́ пока́.	nú tagdá pakắ ↓

NOTES

¹ Of the two words for *pen*, **ру́чка** is more commonly used in the Soviet Union now than **перо́**. More specifically, **ру́чка** means *penholder* and **перо́** *pen point*. Notice that these terms all refer to the old-fashioned type of pen used with an inkwell. *Fountain pen* is **авторучка**.

² **Пошли́** *let's go* is actually the plural past tense form of **пойти́** *to go, to set off* used as a special imperative in highly colloquial style. Compare it with the English expression *we're off*.

³ **Ре́ктор** is comparable to our *university* or *college president* or *chancellor*. At the beginning of each academic year freshmen assemble in a large hall to hear an address given by him.

америка́нский	American (adj only)
америка́нский студе́нт	an American student
Óн америка́нский студе́нт.	He's an American student.
тво́й пе́рвый де́нь	your first day
пройти́ (pfv I)	to pass, go by
прошёл	passed, went [by]
Ка́к прошёл тво́й пе́рвый де́нь?	How did your first day go?
ничего́	all right (*lit.* nothing)
Ничего́.	All right.
оди́н (m)	one, a
америка́нец	American
оди́н америка́нец	an American
Та́м бы́л оди́н америка́нец.	There was an American there.
ле́кция	lecture, class (at university level)
на ле́кции	at the lecture, in class
у на́с на ле́кции	at our lecture, in our class
У на́с на ле́кции бы́л оди́н	There was an American at our lecture.
америка́нец.	
ты́ зна́ешь	you know
Зна́ешь, у на́с на ле́кции	You know, there was an American at our
бы́л оди́н америка́нец.	lecture.
о́н стои́т	he's standing, he stands
Óн та́м стои́т.	He's standing over there.
то́т, та́, то́; те́	that (over there, yon); that person, that one
во́н то́т	that person over there, the one over there
Во́н то́т, что та́м стои́т?	That fellow standing over there?
мо́жет бы́ть [móž(id)bíţ]	maybe, perhaps
Мо́жет бы́ть, во́н то́т, что	That fellow standing over there perhaps?
та́м стои́т?	
Та́к э́то Фили́пп Гра́нт.	Why that's Philip Grant.
его́	him; his
Ты́ его́ зна́ешь?	Do you know him?
познако́миться [pəznakómitcə]	to become acquainted, meet, be introduced
Интере́сно познако́миться.	[It'd be] interesting to meet [him].
Ты́ его́ зна́ешь? Интере́сно	Do you know him? [It'd be] interesting
познако́миться.	to meet [him].
Э́то моя́ сестра́.	This is my sister.
Приве́т, Фили́пп. Э́то моя́ сестра́	Hi Philip. This is my sister Galya.
Га́ля.	
бра́т	brother
Э́то мо́й бра́т Ко́ля.	This is my brother, Kolya.
сейча́с[1]	now, just now, right away
Я́ ва́с сейча́с ви́дел.	I saw you just now.

---

[1] This word may be pronounced either [şijčás] or [şičás].

ка́жется	it seems
Я ва́с, ка́жется, сейча́с ви́дел.	It seems I saw you just now.
аудито́рия	auditorium, lecture room, classroom
в аудито́рии	in the auditorium
в то́й аудито́рии	in that auditorium, in the auditorium there
Я ва́с, ка́жется, сейча́с ви́дел в то́й аудито́рии.	It seems I saw you just now in the auditorium there.
Да́, я та́м была́.	Yes, I was there.
по-ру́сски	Russian
вы́ говори́те	you speak
Вы́ говори́те по-ру́сски.	You speak Russian.
А вы́ хорошо́ говори́те по-ру́сски.	You speak Russian well, by the way.
вы́ ду́маете	you think
мне́ ка́жется	it seems to me
Вы́ ду́маете? А мне́ ка́жется — не о́чень.	You think so? It seems to me I don't [speak it] very [well].
что́ вы́ (что́ вы́ говори́те)!	you're not serious! what do you mean (*lit.* what are you saying)!
Ну́ что́ вы́! Вполне́ хорошо́.	Why what do you mean! [You speak] quite well.
вы́ учи́ли	you studied
ру́сский язы́к	Russian, language Russian
Где́ вы́ учи́ли ру́сский язы́к?	Where did you study Russian?
шко́ла	school (below university level)
в шко́ле	in school
Где́ вы́ учи́ли ру́сский язы́к, в шко́ле?	Where did you study Russian, in school?
Не́т, в университе́те.	No, at the university.

SUPPLEMENT

Аме́рика	America
О́н учи́л ру́сский язы́к в Аме́рике.	He studied Russian in America.
америка́нка	[an] American (f)
Кто́ она́, америка́нка?	What is she, an American?
я говорю́	I speak
Я говорю́ по-ру́сски.	I speak Russian.
Я говорю́ по-англи́йски.	I speak English.
Я не говорю́ по-англи́йски.	I don't speak English.
непло́хо	not badly, not too badly
Вы́ непло́хо говори́те по-ру́сски.	You don't speak Russian too badly.

Американский студент

Н. — Николай (Коля)
Г. — Галина (Галя)
Ф. Г. — Филипп Грант (американец)

Н.	1	Ка́к прошёл тво́й пе́рвый де́нь, Га́ля?	kák prašól ↓ tvój p̦érvij d̦é n̦ ↓ gã ̣l ̦ə ↓
Г.	2	Ничего́. Зна́ешь, у на́с на ле́кции бы́л оди́н америка́нец.[1]	n̦ičivó ↓ znãjiš ↓ unás nal̦ékciji | bíl ad̦ín am̦ir̦ikã ̣n̦ic ↓
Н.	3	Мо́жет бы́ть, во́н то́т, что та́м стои́т? Так э́то Фили́пп Гра́нт.	móž(id)bíț vón tót ↓ štə tám stajít ↑ tək étə f̦il̦íp gr̃ant ↓
Г.	4	Ты́ его́ зна́ешь? Интере́сно познако́миться.	tí jivó znãjiš ↑ in̦țir̦ésnə pəznakó m̦itcə ↓
Н.	5	Приве́т, Фили́пп! Э́то моя́ сестра́ Га́ля.	pr̦iγét f̦il̦íp ↓ étə majá șistrá gã ̣l ̦ə ↓
Ф. Г.	6	Здра́вствуйте![2] Я́ ва́с, ка́жется, сейча́с ви́дел в то́й аудито́рии.	zdrã stujți ↓ já vás kã žitcə șičás γíd̦il | ftój aud̦itó r̦iji ↓
Г.	7	Да́, я́ та́м была́. А вы́ хорошо́ говори́те по-ру́сски.	dã ↓ já tám bilã ↓ a ví xərašó gəvar̦íți parũsk̦i ↓
Ф. Г.	8	Вы́ ду́маете? А мне́ ка́жется — не о́чень.	ví dũməjiți ↓ a mn̦é kã žitcə n̦ó čin̦ ↓
Н.	9	Ну́, что́ вы́! Вполне́ хорошо́.	nú štó ví ↓ fpaln̦é xərašó ↓
Г.	10	Где́ вы́ учи́ли ру́сский язы́к, в шко́ле?[3]	gd̦é vi uč́íl̦i rúsk̦ij jizík ↓ fškó l̦i ↑
Ф. Г.	11	Не́т, в университе́те.	n̦ét ↓ vun̦iγir̦șițéți ↓

NOTES   [1] The nouns **америка́нец** and **америка́нка** refer to an American male and female respectively. The adjective **америка́нский** can never be used alone to refer to the person. Thus **америка́нский студе́нт** or **америка́нская студе́нтка** is used for *an American student*, but only **америка́нец** or **америка́нка** for *an American*. Notice that none of these words is capitalized in Russian.

[2] When introduced, Russians usually say simply **здрáвствуйте** *hello*. With older people or distinguished individuals, however, one should use the more polite forms corresponding to our *Very pleased to meet you:* **Óчень прия́тно** (*or* **Óчень прия́тно познакóмиться** [**с вáми**]).

[3] **Рýсский язы́к** is used for *Russian* here, but the adverbial form **по-рýсски** is used with such verbs as **говори́ть** *to speak*, **читáть** *to read*, and **писáть** *to write*.

Compare	Вы́ знáете **рýсский язы́к?**	Do you know Russian?
	Гдé вы́ учи́ли **рýсский язы́к?**	Where did you study Russian?
with	Вы́ говори́те **по-рýсски?**	Do you speak Russian?
	Вы́ читáете **по-рýсски?**	Do you read Russian?

Basic sentence patterns

1. Э́то мóй пéрвый дéнь в университéте.	It's my first day at the university.
____________ в шкóле.	____________ in school.
____________ в лаборатóрии.	____________ in the laboratory.
____________ в общежи́тии.	____________ in the dormitory.
____________ на завóде.	____________ at the plant.
____________ на слýжбе.	____________ on the job.
2. Порá идти́, Кóля. Ты́ ужé готóв?	Time to be going, Kolya. Are you ready yet?
— Дá, готóв.	Yes, I am.
— Нéт ещё.	Not yet.
— Дá, я́ ужé готóв.	Yes, I'm ready.
— Нéт, я́ ещё не готóв.	No, I'm not ready yet.
3. Порá идти́, Гáля. Ты́ ужé готóва?	Time to be going, Galya. Are you ready yet?
— Дá, готóва.	Yes, I am.
— Нéт ещё.	Not yet.
— Дá, я́ ужé готóва.	Yes, I'm ready.
— Нéт, я́ ещё не готóва.	No, I'm not ready yet.
4. Порá идти́, ребя́та. Вы́ ужé готóвы?	Time to be going, fellows. Are you ready yet?
— Дá, мы́ готóвы.	Yes, we are.
— Нéт ещё.	Not yet.
— Дá, мы́ ужé готóвы.	Yes, we're ready.
— Нéт, мы́ ещё не готóвы.	No, we're not ready yet.
5. Ужé порá идти́ на лéкцию?	Is it already time to go to the lecture?
— Дá, ужé порá.	Yes, it's already time.
— Дá, давнó порá.	Yes, it's long since time.
— Дá, ужé дéвять.	Yes, it's already nine.
— Дá, почти́ дéвять.	Yes, it's almost nine.
— Дá, пошли́.	Yes, let's go.
— Нéт, ещё рáно.	No, it's early still.
6. Идём в университéт.	Let's go to the university.
_____ в библиотéку.	_____ to the library.
_____ в аудитóрию.	_____ to the auditorium.

Идём в клу́б.	Let's go to the club.
——— в общежи́тие.	——— to the dormitory.
——— в лаборато́рию.	——— to the laboratory.
——— в го́род.	——— to town.

7. Я спешу́ на рабо́ту. — I'm hurrying to work.
——— на по́чту. — ——— to the post office.
——— на конце́рт. — ——— to the concert.
——— на ле́кцию. — ——— to the lecture.
——— на собра́ние. — ——— to the meeting.

8. Это моя́ сестра́ Га́ля. — This is my sister Galya.
——— мо́й бра́т Ко́ля. — ——— my brother Kolya.
——— моя́ жена́. — ——— my wife.
——— мо́й му́ж. — ——— my husband.

9. Я ва́с ви́дел на ле́кции. — I saw you at the lecture.
——— на собра́нии. — ——— at the meeting.
——— на конце́рте. — ——— at the concert.
——— на заво́де. — ——— at the plant.
——— в го́роде. — ——— downtown.
——— в ГУ́Ме. — ——— in GUM.

10. О́н тепе́рь в университе́те. — He's at the university now.
——— в клу́бе. — ——— at the club ———.
——— в общежи́тии. — ——— in the dormitory ———.
——— в аудито́рии. — ——— in the auditorium ———.
——— в библиоте́ке. — ——— at the library ———.

11. Вы́ не говори́те по-ру́сски? — You don't speak Russian, do you?
Вы́ непло́хо говори́те по-ру́сски. — You don't speak Russian [too] badly.
——— хорошо́ ———. — You speak Russian well.
——— всегда́ ———. — You always speak Russian.
——— то́же ———. — You also speak Russian.
——— опя́ть ———. — You're speaking Russian again.
——— о́чень хорошо́ ———. — You speak Russian very well.
——— вполне́ хорошо́ ———. — You speak Russian quite well.

12. Вы́ говори́те по-англи́йски? — Do you speak English?
— Да́, говорю́. — Yes, I do.
— Да́, я́ говорю́ по-англи́йски. — Yes, I speak English.
— Да́, но не о́чень хорошо́. — Yes, but not very well.
— Не́т, не говорю́. — No, I don't.
— Не́т, я́ не говорю́ по-англи́йски. — No, I don't speak English.

13. Вы́ понима́ете по-англи́йски? — Do you understand English?
— Да́, понима́ю. — Yes, I do.
— Да́, я́ понима́ю по-англи́йски. — Yes, I understand English.
— Не́т, не понима́ю. — No, I don't.
— Не́т, я́ не понима́ю по-англи́йски. — No, I don't understand English.

14. Вы́ купи́ли селёдку? — Did you buy herring?
——— ры́бу? — ——— fish?
——— кни́гу? — ——— a book?
——— тетра́дь? — ——— a notebook?

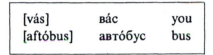

_____ хлéб?	_____ bread?
_____ чáй?	_____ tea?
_____ кóфе?	_____ coffee?
_____ молокó?	_____ milk?
_____ огурцы́?	_____ cucumbers?
_____ тетрáди?	_____ notebooks?

Pronunciation practice: hard versus soft consonants

A.   [s] vs. [ş]   Usual Cyrillic spelling **с**; sometimes **сь, з**, or **зь**.

Note the pronunciation of hard [s] in the following:

[vás]	вáс	you
[aftóbus]	автóбус	bus

and compare it with soft [ş]:

[şiṃón]	Семён	Simon
[fşú]	всю́	all
[ṛişmó]	письмó	letter

Russian hard [s] is fairly similar to English *s*. Soft [ş] is made by bringing the front part of the blade of the tongue toward the upper gum ridge. It has the effect of being followed by a y-like glide.

> Sound Drill: Practice the Russian paired examples illustrating hard [s] and soft [ş], imitating your instructor (or the tape) as accurately as you can.

B.   [z] vs. [ẓ]   Usual Cyrillic spelling **з**; sometimes **зь, с**, or **сь**.

Note the pronunciation of hard [z] in the following:

[zdrástujṭi]	здрáвствуйте	hello
[zdaróvi]	здорóвы	healthy
[nəzavóḍi]	на завóде	at the plant

and compare it with soft [ẓ]:

[ẓímu]	зи́му	winter
[ẓínə]	Зи́на	Zina

Russian [z] and [ẓ] are made with the vocal organs in the same position as for Russian [s] and [ş], but, in addition, they are voiced.

> Sound Drill: Practice the Russian paired examples illustrating hard [z] and soft [ẓ], imitating your instructor (or the tape) as accurately as you can.

C.   [r] vs. [ŗ]   Usual Cyrillic spelling **р**; sometimes **рь**.

Note the pronunciation of hard [r] in the following:

[zdrástujʈi]	здрáвствуйте	hello
[nəurók]	на урóк	to the lesson
[zdaróvi̯]	здорóвы	healthy
[xərašó]	хорошó	good, well

and compare it with soft [ŗ]:

[ḳiŗíl]	Кирúлл	Kirill
[gəvaŗát]	говоря́т	they say
[ʈiṇéŗ]	тепéрь	now

Russian hard [r] is unlike any variety of American English *r*. It is something like the "rolled" Scottish *r* and practically identical with the *r* of Spanish, Italian, modern Greek, Serbo-Croatian, or Polish. In pronouncing Russian [r], the tongue is trilled or vibrated, making one or more taps against the ridge of the gums behind the upper teeth. (American children sometimes make such a trill in imitating the sound of a machine gun or an airplane engine.) Soft [ŗ] is formed similarly, but the middle surface of the tongue is arched higher giving the effect of a y-like glide.[1]

> Sound Drill: Practice the Russian paired examples illustrating hard [r] and soft [ŗ], imitating your instructor (or the tape) as accurately as you can.

Intonation practice

Introductory remarks

Within any major segment of speech some syllables are spoken at a higher relative pitch level than others. We designate these as 1 low, 2 middle, 3 high, and 4 extra-high, with the extra-high level occurring much less frequently than the other three.

These levels are indicated graphically by a line which we call the *intonation contour*, drawn above the major segment through the primary and secondary stress points and ending in an arrow. An upward stroke indicates a slight rise in the voice (typical of certain kinds of questions), and a downward stroke indicates a falling of the voice. The primary stress point is indicated by a small circle and the secondary stress points by small black dots on the intonation contour directly above the stressed syllables.

EXAMPLE

4
3
2
1

Нúна былá в ГУ́Ме.

---

[1] One hears something like the Russian [r] in certain imitations of upper-class British speech, for example, in the pronunciation of *terribly* when the *r* sounds almost like a *d*.

Intonation drills

A. *Statements with falling contours.* In contours of this type the high peak occurs in the first part of the segment, dropping gradually thereafter and making the sharpest drop on or immediately before the syllable with primary stress. The basic range is from 2 or 3 down to 1, although the starting point may be an upward rise from level 2 to level 3. These countours are typical of neutral statements, exclamations, and commands.

Imitate the teacher or tape as accurately as you can.

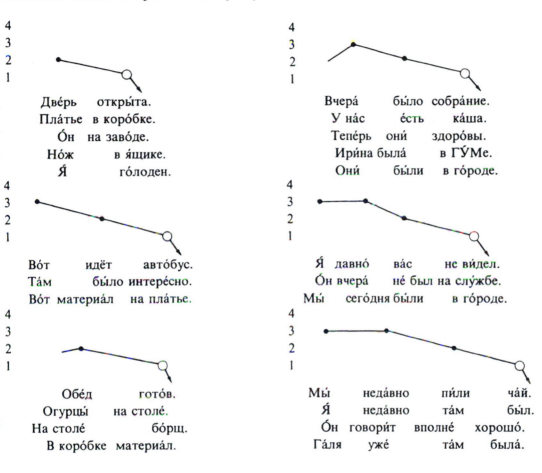

Дверь	открыта.
Платье	в коробке.
Он	на заводе.
Нож	в ящике.
Я	голоден.

Вчера	было собрание.
У нас	есть	каша.
Теперь	они	здоровы.
Ирина была	в ГУМе.
Они	были	в городе.

Вот	идёт	автобус.
Там	было интересно.
Вот материал	на платье.

Я давно	вас	не видел.
Он вчера	не был на службе.
Мы	сегодня были	в городе.

Обед	готов.
Огурцы	на столе.
На столе	борщ.
В коробке	материал.

Мы	недавно	пили	чай.
Я	недавно	там	был.
Он	говорит	вполне	хорошо.
Галя	уже	там	была.

B. *Questions with falling contours.* The contour is similar to that of statements, but the range is wider, starting with level 4 and dropping gradually thereafter to level 2. The primary stress may be either on the question word itself or on the last stressed syllable. This contour is typical of questions beginning with a question word. Note that the voice does not *rise* at the end as it often does in English.

Imitate your teacher or the tape as accurately as you can.

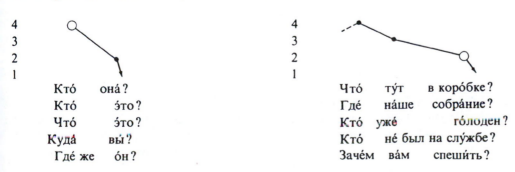

Кто	она?
Кто	это?
Что	это?
Куда	вы?
Где же	он?

Что	тут	в коробке?
Где	наше	собрание?
Кто	уже	голоден?
Кто	не был на службе?
Зачем	вам	спешить?

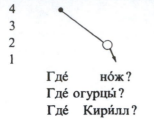

```
4  ●━━━
3      ╲
2       ╲
1        ○→
```
Где́   но́ж?
Где́ огурцы́?
Где́   Кири́лл?

```
4      ●╲╲
3         ╲  ●
2             ╲
1              ○→
```
Куда́   вы́   идёте?
Где́   вы́   бы́ли?
Кто́   ва́с   ви́дел?
Что́   вы́   де́лали?
Где́   они́   стоя́ли?
Что́   вы́   ви́дели?
Что́   бы́ло в коро́бке?

The four noun declensions in Russian:
стол–, окно́–, жена́–, and две́рь-class nouns

According to the patterning of their case endings, Russian nouns may be divided into four basic types. We shall use a model noun to represent each basic type.

1. сто́л–class	2. окно́–class	3. жена́–class	4. две́рь–class

1. **Сто́л**-class nouns are masculine. Their nominative singular ends in a consonant letter (including **–й**) or **–ь**.

> EXAMPLES
> авто́бус, приве́т, уро́к, Кири́лл, Семён, му́ж, клу́б, университе́т, бо́рщ, ча́й, де́нь, портфе́ль.

2. **Окно́**-class nouns are neuter. Their nominative singular ends in the letter **–о, –е,** or **–ё.**

> EXAMPLES
> письмо́, у́тро, де́ло, пла́тье, собра́ние, пе́ние *singing*, общежи́тие, бельё *linen*.

3. **Жена́**-class nouns are chiefly feminine; a few that refer to males are masculine. Their nominative singular ends in the letter **–а** or **–я.**

> EXAMPLES
> слу́жба, ры́ба, селёдка, лаборато́рия, коро́бка, пра́вда, Ни́на, Ми́ла, Га́ля, Ко́ля *Kolya*, Ми́ша *Misha*, дя́дя *uncle*.

4. **Две́рь**-class nouns are feminine. Their nominative singular always ends in the letter **–ь.**

> EXAMPLES
> две́рь, о́сень, о́чередь, тетра́дь.

■ EXERCISE

Arrange four columns with the following heads:

1. сто́л   2. окно́   3. жена́   4. две́рь

Put each of these nouns in its proper column:
телефо́н, убо́рщица, де́ло, о́чередь, пла́тье, шко́ла, ле́кция, собра́ние, ча́й, окно́, язы́к, клю́ч, исто́рия, каранда́ш, ка́рта, о́сень, фи́льм, геро́й, неде́ля, перо́, свида́ние, учи́тельница, пе́ние, у́гол, мо́ре, тетра́дь, молоко́, результа́т, слу́жба, Лёв, ка́ша, огуре́ц, де́нь, портфе́ль, Ко́ля.

The accusative singular of nouns ending in –а and –я

MODELS

Я купи́л селёдку.	I bought herring.
_____ ры́бу.	_____ fish.
_____ ру́чку.	_____ a pen.
_____ ви́лку.	_____ a fork.
_____ ло́жку.	_____ a spoon.
_____ по́лку.	_____ a bookcase.
_____ кни́гу.	_____ a book.

Я ви́жу Ни́ну.	I see Nina.
_____ Ми́лу.	_____ Mila.
_____ студе́нтку.	_____ the coed.
_____ сестру́.	_____ my sister.
_____ жену́.	_____ my wife.
_____ О́лю.	_____ Olya.
_____ Ко́лю.	_____ Kolya.
_____ Са́шу.	_____ Sasha.

Я иду́ в лаборато́рию.	I'm going to the laboratory.
_____ в аудито́рию.	_____ to the lecture hall.
_____ в библиоте́ку.	_____ to the library.
_____ в шко́лу.	_____ to school.
_____ на по́чту.	_____ to the post office.
_____ на слу́жбу.	_____ to work.
_____ на ле́кцию.	_____ to the lecture.

■ **REPETITION DRILLS**

Repeat the above models, noting that when nouns ending in –а or –я in the nominative singular serve as the direct object or the object of a preposition after a motion verb, the endings –а and –я are replaced by –у and –ю respectively.

■ **RESPONSE DRILLS**

1. *Where's the vodka?*
   Did you buy vodka?
   т: Где́ во́дка?
   s: **Вы́ купи́ли во́дку?**
   т: Где́ ры́ба?
   s: **Вы́ купи́ли ры́бу?**
   (кни́га, ви́лка, ло́жка, по́лка, селёдка, ру́чка)

2. *There's the post office.*
   Yes, I see the post office.
   т: Та́м по́чта.
   s: **Да́, я́ ви́жу по́чту.**
   т: Та́м лаборато́рия.
   s: **Да́, я́ ви́жу лаборато́рию.**
   (коро́бка, ры́ба, ка́ша, аудито́рия, ло́жка, ви́лка, Ни́на, О́ля)

3. *The school's open.*
   I'm going to school.
   т: Шко́ла откры́та.
   s: **Я́ иду́ в шко́лу.**

   т: Аудито́рия откры́та.
   s: **Я́ иду́ в аудито́рию.**
   (лаборато́рия, библиоте́ка, шко́ла, аудито́рия)

4. *Nina was at the lecture.*
   Did you see Nina?
   т: Ни́на была́ на ле́кции.
   s: **Вы́ ви́дели Ни́ну?**

т: Ко́ля бы́л на ле́кции.
s: **Вы́ ви́дели Ко́лю?**
   (сестра́, Ми́ла, О́ля, Га́ля, Са́ша,
   студе́нтка Ни́на)

■ CUED QUESTION-ANSWER DRILL

   (*a lecture*)   *Where are you going?*
                     To a lecture.
т: (ле́кция)   Куда́ вы́ идёте?
s: **На ле́кцию.**
т: (библиоте́ка)   Куда́ вы́ идёте?
s: **В библиоте́ку.**
   (слу́жба, по́чта, шко́ла, аудито́рия,
   лаборато́рия, ле́кция)

DISCUSSION

NOMINATIVE SINGULAR	ACCUSATIVE SINGULAR
–a and –я	–y and –ю
жена́ ры́ба селёдка Га́ля О́ля Ко́ля	жену́ ры́бу селёдку Га́лю О́лю Ко́лю

The direct object of a verb or the object of a preposition accompanying a motion verb is in the accusative case. **Жена́**-class nouns replace **–a** and **–я** of the nominative singular with **–y** and **–ю** respectively in the accusative singular. Note that while most of these nouns are feminine, some are masculine: **Та́м бы́л Ко́ля** *Kolya was there*; **Я́ ви́дел Ко́лю** *I saw Kolya*.

Inanimate **сто́л**- and **окно́**-class nouns have accusatives which are like their nominatives both in the singular and the plural:

Я́ ви́жу сто́л.   I see the table.
_____ столы́.   ____ the tables.
_____ окно́.   ____ the window.
_____ о́кна.   ____ the windows.
_____ огуре́ц.   ____ the cucumber.
_____ огурцы́.   ____ the cucumbers.

All **две́рь**-class nouns (animate and inanimate) have singular accusatives like their nominative singular. (In the plural, the accusative is like the nominative only if the noun is inanimate.)

Я́ ви́жу две́рь.   I see the door.
_____ две́ри.   ____ the doors.
_____ Любо́вь Петро́вну.   ____ Lyubov Petrovna.

The second conjugation verb говори́ть

PAST	говори́л, говори́ла, говори́ло, говори́ли
PRESENT	говорю́, говори́шь, говори́т, говори́м, говори́те, говоря́т

■ SUBSTITUTION DRILLS

1. *You talked for a long time.*
   т: Вы́ до́лго говори́ли.
   s: **Вы́ до́лго говори́ли.**
   (о́н, она́, они́, ты́, мы́, вы́, я́)

2. *He speaks Russian.*
   т: О́н говори́т по-ру́сски.
   s: **О́н говори́т по-ру́сски.**
   (они́, вы́, я́, мы́, ты́, она́, мы́, о́н)

■ QUESTION-ANSWER DRILLS

1. *Do you speak Russian?*
   Yes, I do.
   т: Вы́ говори́те по-ру́сски?
   s: **Да́, говорю́.**
   т: Она́ говори́т по-ру́сски?
   s: **Да́, говори́т.**
   (ты́, они́, Фили́пп, вы́, америка́нец, Гра́нт)

2. *How do I speak Russian?*
   You don't speak Russian [too] badly.
   т: Ка́к я́ говорю́ по-ру́сски?
   s: **Вы́ непло́хо говори́те по-ру́сски.**
   т: Ка́к они́ говоря́т по-ру́сски?
   s: **Они́ непло́хо говоря́т по-ру́сски.**
   (о́н, мы́, ты́, она́, вы́, я́, Фили́пп, америка́нец Гра́нт)

3. *Does she speak English?*
   No, she doesn't.
   т: Она́ говори́т по-англи́йски?
   s: **Не́т, не говори́т.**
   т: Ты́ говори́шь по-англи́йски?
   s: **Не́т, не говорю́.**
   (Ко́ля, вы́, бра́т, они́, сестра́, ты́)

■ CUED QUESTION-ANSWER DRILLS

1. (*Tsarapkin*) *Who's speaking?*
   It's Tsarapkin speaking.
   т: (Цара́пкин) Кто́ говори́т?
   s: **Говори́т Цара́пкин.**
   т: (Ни́на) Кто́ говори́т?
   s: **Говори́т Ни́на.**
   (Кири́лл Па́влович, ре́ктор, Ни́на, Евге́ний, Ле́в)

2. (*the chancellor*) *Who spoke?*
   The chancellor spoke.
   т: (ре́ктор) Кто́ говори́л?
   s: **Говори́л ре́ктор.**
   т: (его́ жена́) Кто́ говори́л?
   s: **Говори́ла его́ жена́.**
   (америка́нец Гра́нт, Хитро́в, Никола́й, Ми́ла, Евге́ний, Ни́на, Га́ля)

DISCUSSION

The second conjugation verb говори́ть, unlike спеши́ть, has its stem ending in a soft consonant. The spelling ending of the first person singular of говори́ть is –ю, and that of the third person plural is –ят: говорю́, говоря́т. Since спеши́ть has its stem ending in a hard consonant, the first person singular has the ending –у and the third person plural has the ending –ат: спешу́, спеша́т. The stress pattern is the same in both verbs. The endings for the other persons are written the same for both verbs: –ишь, –ит, –им, –ите. Note from the transcription following that р is soft throughout in говори́ть, and that ш is hard throughout in спеши́ть. (It is only a convention of the spelling system that и and not ы is written after hard consonant ш.)

говор–ю́	[gəvaɹ–ú	спеш–у́	[spiš–ú
–и́шь	–íš	–и́шь	–íš
–и́т	–ít	–и́т	–ít
–и́м	–ím	–и́м	–ím
–и́те	–íʈi	–и́те	–íʈi
–я́т	–át]	–а́т	–át]

Possessive modifiers

MODELS

NONCHANGING FORMS

Э́то **его́** сто́л.	This is his table.
Э́то **её** сто́л.	This is her table.
Э́то **и́х** сто́л.	This is their table.
Э́то **его́** по́лка.	This is his bookshelf.
Э́то **её** по́лка.	This is her bookshelf.
Э́то **и́х** по́лка.	This is their bookshelf.
Э́то **его́** письмо́.	This is his letter.
Э́то **её** письмо́.	This is her letter.
Э́то **и́х** письмо́.	This is their letter.

CHANGING FORMS

Че́й э́то портфе́ль?	Whose briefcase is this?
— Э́то **мо́й** портфе́ль.	It's my briefcase.
— Э́то **тво́й** портфе́ль.	It's your briefcase.
Чья́ э́то кни́га?	Whose book is this?
— Э́то **моя́** кни́га.	It's my book.
— Э́то **твоя́** кни́га.	It's your book.
Чьё э́то письмо́?	Whose letter is this?
— Э́то **моё** письмо́.	It's my letter.
— Э́то **твоё** письмо́.	It's your letter.
Че́й э́то сто́л?	Whose table is this?
— Э́то **на́ш** сто́л.	It's our table.
— Э́то **ва́ш** сто́л.	It's your table.
Чья́ э́то по́лка?	Whose shelf is this?
— Э́то **на́ша** по́лка.	It's our shelf.
— Э́то **ва́ша** по́лка.	It's your shelf.
Чьё э́то общежи́тие?	Whose dormitory is this?
— Э́то **на́ше** общежи́тие.	It's our dormitory.
— Э́то **ва́ше** общежи́тие.	It's your dormitory.

Repeat the above models observing the pattern. Note that there are two types of modifiers:

    1. Those that do not change their form to agree with the word they modify: **его́, её, их.**

    2. Those that change their form according to the word they modify: **чей, чья, мой, моя́, наш, ваш, твой.**

    Observe also that **твой, твоя́,** and **твоё** relate to **ты,** while **ваш, ва́ша,** and **ва́ше** relate to **вы.**

■ QUESTION-ANSWER DRILLS

1. *Where's my briefcase?*
   Your briefcase is on the table.
   т: Где́ мо́й портфе́ль?
   s: **Ва́ш портфе́ль на столе́.**
   т: Где́ мо́й материа́л?
   s: **Ва́ш материа́л на столе́.**
   (я́щик, бо́рщ, каранда́ш, ча́й, но́ж)

2. *Where's our dinner?*
   Your dinner is there.
   т: Где́ на́ш обе́д?
   s: **Ва́ш обе́д та́м.**
   т: Где́ на́ш бо́рщ?
   s: **Ва́ш бо́рщ та́м.**
   (ча́й, заво́д, шка́ф, сто́л, хле́б)

3. *Where's my sister?*
   Your sister's here.
   т: Где́ моя́ сестра́?
   s: **Ва́ша сестра́ ту́т.**
   т: Где́ моя́ кни́га?
   s: **Ва́ша кни́га ту́т.**
   (две́рь, жена́, ру́чка, шко́ла, тетра́дь, коро́бка, аудито́рия)

4. *Where's our school?*
   Our school is there.
   т: Где́ на́ша шко́ла?
   s: **На́ша шко́ла та́м.**
   т: Где́ на́ша кни́га?
   s: **На́ша кни́га та́м.**
   (по́лка, две́рь, столо́вая)

5. *Where's my husband?*
   Your husband is there.
   т: Где́ мо́й му́ж?
   s: **Тво́й му́ж та́м.**
   т: Где́ мо́й сто́л?
   s: **Тво́й сто́л та́м.**
   (пода́рок, я́щик, бра́т, портфе́ль, шка́ф)

6. *Where's your material?*
   My material is there.
   т: Где́ тво́й материа́л?
   s: **Мо́й материа́л та́м.**
   т: Где́ тво́й сто́л?
   s: **Мо́й сто́л та́м.**
   (каранда́ш, бо́рщ, му́ж, обе́д)

■ SUBSTITUTION DRILL

    Whose pencil is that?
    т: Че́й э́то каранда́ш?
    s: **Че́й э́то каранда́ш?**
    т: _____(перо́)?
    s: **Чьё э́то перо́?**

(материа́л, пла́тье, ры́ба, я́щик, бо́рщ, две́рь, окно́, письмо́, но́ж, коро́бка, портфе́ль, сто́л, по́лка)

■ QUESTION-ANSWER DRILLS

1. *Whose letter is that?*
   That's my letter.
   т: Чьё э́то письмо́?
   s: **Э́то моё письмо́.**
   т: Чья́ э́то кни́га?
   s: **Э́то моя́ кни́га.**
   (портфе́ль, две́рь, окно́, но́ж, я́щик, коро́бка, сто́л, пла́тье)

2. *Whose pen is that, yours?*
   Yes, that's my pen.
   т: Чьё э́то перо́, ва́ше?
   s: **Да́, э́то моё перо́.**
   т: Че́й э́то портфе́ль, ва́ш?
   s: **Да́, э́то мо́й портфе́ль.**
   (кни́га, две́рь, я́щик, тетра́дь, окно́, каранда́ш, по́лка)

3. *Whose dress is that, yours?*
   Yes, it's my dress.
   т: Чьё э́то пла́тье, твоё?
   s: **Да́, э́то моё пла́тье.**
   т: Чья́ э́то ка́ша, твоя́?
   s: **Да́, э́то моя́ ка́ша.**
   (нож, стол, обе́д, ры́ба, костю́м, ча́й,
   коро́бка)

4. *Is that your pencil?*
   No, it's his pencil.
   т: Э́то ва́ш каранда́ш?
   s: **Не́т, э́то его́ каранда́ш.**
   т: Э́то ва́ше перо́?
   s: **Не́т, э́то его́ перо́.**
   (портфе́ль, стол, две́рь, ча́й, кни́га,
   письмо́, жена́, нож, сестра́, окно́,
   материа́л)

5. *Is that your dress?*
   No, that's her dress.
   т: Э́то твоё пла́тье?
   s: **Не́т, э́то её пла́тье.**
   т: Э́то тво́й му́ж?
   s: **Не́т, э́то её му́ж.**
   (твоя́ тетра́дь, перо́, ча́й, письмо́,
   сестра́, окно́, материа́л)

6. *Is this our bread?*
   No, that's their bread.
   т: Э́то на́ш хле́б?
   s: **Не́т, э́то и́х хле́б.**
   т: Э́то на́ша селёдка?
   s: **Не́т э́то и́х селёдка.**
   (стол, ча́й, кни́га, окно́, материа́л, но́ж,
   коро́бка, обе́д, по́лка, пи́ща)

■ PROGRESSIVE SUBSTITUTION DRILLS

TEACHER

STUDENT

1. *This is my briefcase.*
   Э́то мо́й портфе́ль.
   _____ (кни́га).
   _____ (письмо́).
   __ (твоё) _____.
   _____ (тетра́дь).
   _____ (каранда́ш).
   __ (ва́ш) _____.
   _____ (по́чта).
   _____ (общежи́тие).

This is my briefcase.
Э́то мо́й портфе́ль.
Э́то моя́ кни́га.
Э́то моё письмо́.
Э́то твоё письмо́.
Э́то твоя́ тетра́дь.
Э́то тво́й каранда́ш.
Э́то ва́ш каранда́ш.
Э́то ва́ша по́чта.
Э́то ва́ше общежи́тие.

2. *This is our dormitory.*
   Э́то на́ше общежи́тие.
   _____ (по́лка).
   _____ (пода́рок).
   __ (мо́й) _____.
   _____ (сестра́).
   _____ (окно́).
   __ (твоё) _____.
   _____ (коро́бка).
   _____ (материа́л).
   __ (ва́ш) _____.
   _____ (шко́ла).
   _____ (общежи́тие).
   __ (на́ше) _____.
   _____ (пи́ща).
   _____ (сто́л).

This is our dormitory.
Э́то на́ше общежи́тие.
Э́то на́ша по́лка.
Э́то на́ш пода́рок.
Э́то мо́й пода́рок.
Э́то моя́ сестра́.
Э́то моё окно́.
Э́то твоё окно́.
Э́то твоя́ коро́бка.
Э́то тво́й материа́л.
Э́то ва́ш материа́л.
Э́то ва́ша шко́ла.
Э́то ва́ше общежи́тие.
Э́то на́ше общежи́тие.
Э́то на́ша пи́ща.
Э́то на́ш сто́л.

3. *Here's our chancellor.*

т: Вóт нáш рéктор.

s: **Вóт нáш рéктор.**

т: _____ (общежѝтие).

s: **Вóт нáше общежѝтие.**

___ (вáше) _____.

Вóт вáше общежѝтие.

_____ (автóбус).

_____ (урóк).

_____ (лéкция).

Вóт нáше письмó.

___ (моё) _____.

_____ (перó).

_____ (портфéль).

___ (твóй) _____.

_____ (письмó).

_____ (кнѝга).

_____ (карандáш).

_____ (плáтье).

DISCUSSION

There are two types of *possessive modifiers* in Russian:

1. Those that do *not* change their form to agree with the word they accompany.

егó	his, its
её	her, hers, its
и́х	their, theirs

Note that **егó** is pronounced [jivó].

EXAMPLES

егó портфéль	егó сестрá	егó письмó	егó тетрáди
её портфéль	её сестрá	её письмó	её тетрáди
и́х портфéль	и́х сестрá	и́х письмó	и́х тетрáди

2. Those with grammatical endings which change to agree in gender, number, and case with the word they accompany:

MASCULINE	FEMININE	NEUTER	
чéй	чья́	чьё	whose
мóй	моя́	моё	my, mine
твóй	твоя́	твоё	your, yours
нáш	нáша	нáше	our, ours
вáш	вáша	вáше	your, yours

Note that **твóй, твоя́,** and **твоё** refer to **ты́,** while **вáш, вáша,** and **вáше** refer to **вы́.**

EXAMPLES

чéй карандáш	чья́ сестрá	чьё письмó
whose pencil	*whose sister*	*whose letter*
мóй карандáш	моя́ сестрá	моё письмó
my pencil	*my sister*	*my letter*
вáш карандáш	вáша сестрá	вáше письмó
your pencil	*your sister*	*your letter*

The perfective future of the first conjugation verbs пойти and взять

Я пойду́ на конце́рт.	I'll go to a concert.
Ты́ пойдёшь _____.	You'll go _____.
О́н пойдёт _____.	He'll go _____.
Мы́ пойдём_____.	We'll go _____.
Вы́ пойдёте _____.	You'll go _____.
Они́ пойду́т _____.	They'll go _____.

■ REPETITION DRILL

Repeat the model after your instructor (or the tape) until you can reproduce all the forms accurately. Note that the endings are exactly like the present tense endings of the imperfective verb идти́, but that the meaning is future.

■ SUBSTITUTION DRILLS

1. *I'm going to go to a dinner.*
   т: Я́ пойду́ на обе́д.
   s: **Я́ пойду́ на обе́д.**
   т: (Они́) _____.
   s: **Они́ пойду́т на обе́д.**
      (она́, ты́, вы́, мы́, Са́ша,
      Ко́ля и Га́ля, я́)

2. *I'll go to the library tomorrow.*
   т: Я́ пойду́ в библиоте́ку за́втра.
   s: **Я́ пойду́ в библиоте́ку за́втра.**
   т: (О́н)_____.
   s: **О́н пойдёт в библиоте́ку за́втра.**
      (мы́, бра́т, сестра́, ты́, вы́, они́,
      бра́т и сестра́, я́)

■ TRANSFORMATION DRILL

I'm going to the dormitory.
I'll go to the dormitory.
т: Я́ иду́ в общежи́тие.
s: **Я́ пойду́ в общежи́тие.**

т: Ты́ идёшь в общежи́тие.
s: **Ты́ пойдёшь в общежи́тие.**
   (мы́, Никола́й, Га́ля, они́, вы́, о́н)

■ QUESTION-ANSWER DRILL

Are you going to the club today?
No, I'll go there tomorrow.
т: Вы́ идёте в клу́б сего́дня?
s: **Не́т, я́ пойду́ туда́ за́втра.**

т: Они́ иду́т в клу́б сего́дня?
s: **Не́т, они́ пойду́т туда́ за́втра.**
   (Евге́ний, ты́, мы́, она́, сестра́, Ни́на,
   Цара́пкин)

Я́ возьму́ то́лько кни́ги.	I'll just take books.
Ты́ возьмёшь _____.	You'll ____ take ____.
О́н возьмёт _____.	He'll ____ take ____.
Мы́ возьмём _____.	We'll ____ take ____.
Вы́ возьмёте _____.	You'll ____ take ____.
Они́ возьму́т _____.	They'll ____ take ____.

Repeat the model after your instructor (or the tape) until you can reproduce all the forms accurately. The pattern of endings is the same as for the present tense of **идти** and the perfective future of **пойти**. Note that since **взять** is a perfective verb, the meaning of the forms is future.

■ SUBSTITUTION DRILLS

1. *They'll take these notebooks.*
   т: Они возьму́т э́ти тетра́ди.
   s: **Они возьму́т э́ти тетра́ди.**
   т: (Я)_____.
   s: **Я возьму́ э́ти тетра́ди.**
   (Га́ля, ты́, вы́, мы́, сестра́, Оле́г и Кири́лл, ты́, я́)

2. *I'll take these books.*
   т: Я возьму́ э́ти кни́ги.
   s: **Я возьму́ э́ти кни́ги.**
   т: (Она́)_____.
   s: **Она́ возьмёт э́ти кни́ги.**
   (Кири́лл, ты́, мы́, они́, бра́т, О́ля, Са́ша и Ко́ля, я́, вы́)

■ CUED QUESTION-ANSWER DRILL

(*I*) *Who'll take these notebooks?*
     I will.
т: (я) Кто́ возьмёт э́ти тетра́ди?
s: **Я возьму́.**
т: (о́н) Кто́ возьмёт э́ти тетра́ди?
s: **О́н возьмёт.**
  (они́, мы́, вы́, ты́, Са́ша, Ни́на, бра́т)

DISCUSSION

The perfective verb **пойти** is the aspect pair of the imperfective verb **идти**. Both **пойти** and **взять** *to take* are first conjugation perfective verbs which take the same set of endings in their perfective future as **идти** does in the present.

SINGULAR	пойд—у́	I'll go	возьм—у́	I'll take
	—ёшь	you'll go	—ёшь	you'll take
	—ёт	he (she)'ll go	—ёт	he (she)'ll take
PLURAL	—ём	we'll go	—ём	we'll take
	—ёте	you'll go	—ёте	you'll take
	—у́т	they'll go	—у́т	they'll take

For convenience, we may call such endings as these "present-future" endings. Although they are the same for both imperfective and perfective verbs, they have different meanings, depending on the aspect of the verb. When the verb is imperfective, the endings signalize the present tense; when the verb is perfective, the endings signalize the future. It is important to note that the perfective future has in it the particular limitations inherent in the perfective aspect. It describes a future action in terms of its realization, completion, or result; thus it contrasts with the imperfective, which focuses on either the process itself or its repetition.

The second conjugation verb видеть

MODELS

Ни́на ви́дела О́лю в ГУ́Ме.　　　Nina saw Olya in GUM.
Ле́в ви́дел＿＿＿＿＿＿.　　　　Lev saw ＿＿＿＿＿＿.
Мы́ ви́дели ＿＿＿＿＿＿.　　　　We saw ＿＿＿＿＿＿.

Иногда́ я́ ви́жу Ко́лю в клу́бе.　　Sometimes I see Kolya at the club.
＿＿＿＿ ты́ ви́дишь ＿＿＿＿.　　＿＿＿＿＿ you see ＿＿＿＿＿.
＿＿＿＿ о́н ви́дит ＿＿＿＿.　　　＿＿＿＿＿ he sees ＿＿＿＿＿.
＿＿＿＿ мы́ ви́дим ＿＿＿＿.　　＿＿＿＿＿ we see ＿＿＿＿＿.
＿＿＿＿ вы́ ви́дите ＿＿＿＿.　　＿＿＿＿＿ you see ＿＿＿＿＿.
＿＿＿＿ они́ ви́дят ＿＿＿＿.　　＿＿＿＿＿ they see ＿＿＿＿＿.

■ REPETITION DRILL

Repeat the given models, noting that in the first person singular, present tense, **ж** replaces the final stem consonant **д**, which occurs in all other forms.

■ SUBSTITUTION DRILLS

1. *I often see Nina in town.*
   т: Я́ ча́сто ви́жу Ни́ну в го́роде.
   s: **Я́ ча́сто ви́жу Ни́ну в го́роде.**
   т: (Мы́)＿＿＿＿＿＿＿＿＿＿＿.
   s: **Мы́ ча́сто ви́дим Ни́ну в го́роде.**
   (Никола́й, ты́, я́, вы́, моя́ сестра́, они́, мо́й бра́т)

2. *He often used to see Nina in town.*
   т: О́н ча́сто ви́дел Ни́ну в го́роде.
   s: **О́н ча́сто ви́дел Ни́ну в го́роде.**
   т: (Вы́)＿＿＿＿＿＿＿＿＿＿＿.
   s: **Вы́ ча́сто ви́дели Ни́ну в го́роде.**
   (моя́ сестра́, Га́ля, мо́й бра́т, мы́, они́, на́ша учи́тельница)

■ TRANSFORMATION DRILLS

1. *I rarely saw Galya there.*
   I rarely see Galya there.
   т: Я́ ре́дко та́м ви́дел Га́лю.
   s: **Я́ ре́дко та́м ви́жу Га́лю.**
   т: Они́ ре́дко та́м ви́дели Га́лю.
   s: **Они́ ре́дко та́м ви́дят Га́лю.**
   (о́н, мы́, вы́, я́, сестра́, ты́, они́, мы́, я́)

2. *We sometimes see Nina there.*
   We sometimes saw Nina there.
   т: Мы́ иногда́ та́м ви́дим Ни́ну.
   s: **Мы́ иногда́ та́м ви́дели Ни́ну.**
   т: Никола́й иногда́ та́м ви́дит Ни́ну.
   s: **Никола́й иногда́ та́м ви́дел Ни́ну.**
   (я́, ты́, вы́, они́, сестра́, бра́т, мы́)

■ QUESTION-ANSWER DRILL

Do you see the knife?
No, I don't.
т: Ты́ ви́дишь но́ж?
s: **Не́т, не ви́жу.**
т: Вы́ ви́дите но́ж?
s: **Не́т, не ви́жу.**
   (они́, о́н, она́, ты́, вы́)

DISCUSSION

　　The verb **ви́деть** differs from the other second conjugation verbs already discussed (**спеши́ть** and **говори́ть**) in that there is an alternation of stem consonants in the first person singular of the present tense. In **ви́деть,** the **д** is automatically replaced by **ж** in the first person singular and the ending is **–у.** Compare the three patterns of second conjugation verbs:

	спеши́ть *to hurry*	говори́ть *to speak*	ви́деть *to see*
PRESENT STEM	спеш–	говор–	ви́д–
	спеш–у́ –и́шь –и́т –и́м –и́те –а́т	говор–ю́ –и́шь –и́т –и́м –и́те –я́т	ви́ж–у ви́д–ишь –ит –им –ите –ят
PAST STEM	спеши́–	говори́–	ви́де–
	спеши́–л –ла –ло –ли	говори́–л –ла –ло –ли	ви́де–л –ла –ло –ли

Second person imperatives: familiar versus plural-polite forms

MODELS

Скажи́, где́ ты́ вчера́ бы́л?
Скажи́те, где́ вы́ вчера́ бы́ли?

Say, where were you yesterday?
Say, _____?

Извини́, я́ спешу́ на авто́бус.
Извини́те, я́ спешу́ на авто́бус.

Excuse me, I'm hurrying to catch a bus.
Excuse me, _____.

Заходи́. Давно́ тебя́ не ви́дел.
Заходи́те. Давно́ вас не ви́дел.

Come in, I haven't seen you in a long time.
Come in, _____.

Наре́жь, пожа́луйста, огурцы́.
Наре́жьте, пожа́луйста, огурцы́.

Please slice the cucumbers.
_____ slice _____.

Возьми́ э́ти кни́ги.
Возьми́те э́ти кни́ги.

Take these books.
Take _____.

Здра́вствуй, Оле́г!
Здра́вствуйте, ребя́та!

Hello, Oleg!
Hello, fellows!

■ REPETITION DRILL

Repeat the given models, noting that the plural-polite imperative is exactly like the familiar imperative except for the addition of the unstressed suffix **–те.**[1]

---

[1] At this stage the student is not expected to form the imperative; rather, he should recognize those which he encounters and either add or delete the formal-plural suffix **–те.** Thus, given the familiar imperative **чита́й!** *read!* he will be expected to know that the formal-plural is **чита́йте!**

1. *Slice the bread!*
  т: Наре́жь хлеб!
  s: Наре́жьте хлеб!
  т: Заходи́, пожа́луйста!
  s: Заходи́те, пожа́луйста!
  Скажи́, вчера́ бы́ло собра́ние?
  Возьми́ то́лько одну́ тетра́дь!
  Здра́вствуй, Лёв!
  Извини́, во́т мо́й авто́бус!
  Не говори́!
  Посмотри́!
  Поступа́й в университе́т!
  Чита́й!
  Повтори́!
  Не спеши́!

2. *Look, here comes Nina.*
  т: Смотри́те, во́т идёт Ни́на.
  s: Смотри́, во́т идёт Ни́на.
  т: Возьми́те э́ти кни́ги.
  s: Возьми́ э́ти кни́ги.
  Заходи́те, две́рь не заперта́.
  Наре́жьте хлеб и огурцы́.
  Извини́те, я́ спешу́ на уро́к.
  Не говори́те!
  Посмотри́те!
  Поступа́йте в университе́т!
  Чита́йте по-ру́сски!

DISCUSSION

Imperatives call primarily for action rather than a verbal response. The most common type is the second person imperative.

EXAMPLES

Пожа́луйста, заходи́те!	Come in, please!
Извини́те. Во́т идёт мо́й авто́бус.	Excuse me. Here comes my bus.
Смотри́, во́т идёт Смирно́в.	Look, there goes Smirnov.
Наре́жь огурцы́.	Cut the cucumbers.
Скажи́те, вчера́ бы́ло собра́ние?	Tell me, was there a meeting yesterday?

The familiar imperative (used in addressing **ты**) differs structurally from the formal-plural imperative (used in addressing **вы**) only in that the unstressed suffix –**те** is added in the latter form.

FAMILIAR	FORMAL-PLURAL	
наре́жь	наре́жьте	cut!
смотри́	смотри́те	look!
спроси́	спроси́те	ask!
отве́ть	отве́тьте	answer!
повтори́	повтори́те	repeat!
измени́	измени́те	change!
замени́	замени́те	substitute!
здра́вствуй	здра́вствуйте	hello (*lit*. be healthy)!

— Здравствуйте, Олег Филиппович! Здравствуйте, Лев Павлович! — Куда вы так спешите? На лекцию? — Нет, на почту. А вы куда? — Я иду домой. — Скажите, вчера было собрание? — Да. И было очень интересно. — Извините. Вот идёт мой автобус. Всего хорошего! — До свидания! Привет жене!

— Здравствуйте, Кирилл Павлович! — А, Семён Филиппович! Давно вас не видел. Говорят, вы были больны? — Да. Всю зиму не был на службе. — А теперь вы здоровы? — Вполне. — А как жена, здорова? — Спасибо, здорова.

— Нина! Обед готов? Что ты! Мы недавно пили чай. — Да, но я уже голоден. У нас есть рыба? — Нет. Рыбы больше нет. — А борщ у нас есть? — Да. И каша тоже. Нарежь огурцы. Они на столе. — Хорошо. А где нож? — Он в столе, в ящике.

NOTES

PREPARATION FOR CONVERSATION   **Я забы́л свой портфе́ль**

свой портфе́ль	my briefcase
забы́ть (pfv I)	to forget, leave (inadvertently)
Я забы́л свой портфе́ль.	I forgot my briefcase.
телефо́н (телефо́ны)	telephone (telephones)
звони́ть (II)[1]	to ring, to phone
звони́т телефо́н	the phone is ringing.
Ма́ша (variant of Мари́я)	Masha
Ма́ша, звони́т телефо́н.	Masha, the phone is ringing.
к телефо́ну	to (*or* toward) the telephone
подойти́ (pfv I)	to approach, go up to
Подойди́ к телефо́ну!	Go to the phone!
Подойди́, пожа́луйста, к телефо́ну!	Go answer the phone, please!
алло́ [aļó]	hello
слу́шать (I)	to listen
Алло́! Я слу́шаю.	Hello! (*Lit.* Hello! I'm listening.)
попроси́ть (pfv II)	to ask, request
Попроси́те Ива́на Никола́евича к телефо́ну!	Ask Ivan Nikolaevich [to come] to the phone!
Попроси́те, пожа́луйста, Ива́на Никола́евича к телефо́ну!	Please ask Ivan Nikolaevich to come to the phone!
Кто говори́т?	Who's speaking? *or* Who's calling?
Сейча́с. А кто говори́т?	Right away. And who's calling?
Ку́рочкин.	Kurochkin.
у телефо́на	on the phone, on the line (*lit.* at the phone)
Я у телефо́на, Бори́с Миха́йлович.	Hello (*lit.* I'm on the line), Boris Mikhailovich.
де́ло (дела́)	thing(s), matter(s)
в чём	in what
В чём де́ло?	What's the matter?

---

[1] The symbols (I) and (II) stand for the first and second conjugations. Henceforth verb aspect will be indicated only for perfective verbs. Thus, (I) means that the verb is imperfective and first conjugation; (pfv I) means that the verb is perfective and first conjugation.

у вáс
ли
не забы́л ли я́
Не забы́л ли я́ у вáс свóй портфéль?
узнáть (pfv II)
Я́ хотéл узнáть, не забы́л ли я́ у вáс свóй
портфéль.

at your place; you have
whether, if (question particle)
didn't I forget, whether or not I forgot
Didn't I leave my briefcase at your place?
to find out, learn, recognize
I wanted to find out whether or not I left my
briefcase at your place.

минýтку
нигдé
Минýтку. Нéт, нигдé не ви́жу.

just a minute
nowhere, not . . . anywhere
Just a minute. No, I don't see it anywhere.

остáвить (pfv II)
Мóжет бы́ть вы́ в университéте остáвили?

to leave
Maybe you left it at the university?

подýмать (pfv I)
о, об, обо (*plus* prepositional case)
об э́том
Кáк я́ об э́том не подýмал!

to think, think a bit
about, of, on (concerning)
about that, of that
How is it I didn't think of that!

тудá
войти́ тудá
смóчь (pfv I)
я́ смогý
Но я́ не смогý тудá войти́.

there, to that place
to get in (*lit.* to enter there)
to be able, can
I'll be able
But I won't be able to get in.

двéри (pl of двéрь)
Двéри ужé зáперты.

doors, door, doorway
The doors are already locked.

убóрщица (убóрщицы)
А убóрщица?
откры́ть (pfv I)
мóчь (I)
онá мóжет
А убóрщица? Онá мóжет откры́ть.

cleaning woman (cleaning women)
How about the cleaning woman?
to open
to be able, can
she can
How about the cleaning woman? She can
open [the doors].

клю́ч (ключи́)
у неё éсть   [uɲijó jéṣt]
У неё éсть ключи́.

key(s)
she has
She has the keys.

о нéй
Конéчно. Я́ о нéй забы́л.
совсéм
Конéчно. Я́ о нéй совсéм забы́л.

about her
Of course. I forgot about her.
completely, altogether
Of course. I forgot all about her.

SUPPLEMENT

вахтёр (вахтёры)
Гдé вахтёр? Óн мóжет откры́ть двéри.

custodian(s) (compare Fr. *concierge*)
Where's the custodian? He can open the
door[s].

звонóк (звонки́)
Чтó э́то, звонóк?
позвони́ть (pfv II)
Онá позвони́ла домóй.

bell(s), doorbell(s)
What's that, the bell?
to phone, call on the phone
She telephoned home.

Я забы́л свой портфе́ль

И.Н. — Ива́н Никола́евич (профе́ссор Орло́в)
М.И. — Мари́я Ива́новна Орло́ва (Ма́ша, его́ жена́)
Б.М. — Бори́с Миха́йлович (профе́ссор Ку́рочкин)

И. Н.	1	Ма́ша, звони́т телефо́н! Подойди́, пожа́луйста.	mắšə ↓ zvaṇít ţiḷifṍn ↓ pədajḍǐ pažáləstə ↓
М. И.	2	Алло́! Я слу́шаю!¹	aḷő ↑ já slűšəju ↓
Б. М.	3	Попроси́те, пожа́луйста, Ива́на Никола́евича к телефо́ну.	pəpraṣǐţi pažáləstə | ivánə ṇikalắjičə kţiḷifónu ↓
М. И.	4	Сейча́с. А кто́ говори́т?	ṣičắs ↓ a któ gəvaŗít ↓
Б. М.	5	Ку́рочкин.	kűrəčķin ↓
И. Н.	6	Я у телефо́на, Бори́с Миха́йлович. В чём де́ло?	já uţiḷifṍnə | baŗís ṃixálič ↓ fčóm ḍélə ↓
Б. М.	7	Я хоте́л узна́ть, не забы́л ли я́ у ва́с свой портфе́ль.²	já xaţél uznắţ | ṇizabǐl ḷi já uvás | svój partfḗḷ ↓
И. Н.	8	Мину́тку. Не́т, нигде́ не ви́жу.³ Мо́жет быть, вы́ в университе́те оста́вили.	ṃinűtku ↓ ṇḗt ↓ ṇigḍé ṇiɣǐžu ↓ móž(id)bíţ | ví vuṇiɣirṣiţḗţi astáɣiḷi ↓
Б. М.	9	Ка́к я об э́том не поду́мал! Но я не смогу́ туда́ войти́. Две́ри уже́ за́перты.⁴	kắk já abétəm ṇipadúməl ↓ no já ṇismagú tudá vajţí ↑ dɣéŗi užé zắṗirti ↓
И. Н.	10	А убо́рщица? Она́ мо́жет откры́ть, у неё́ есть ключи́.	a ubőrščicə ↓ anắ móžit atkríţ ↓ uṇijó jéşţ kḷučǐ ↓ ·
Б. М.	11	Коне́чно! Я о ней совсе́м забы́л.	kaṇḗšnə ↓ já aṇéj safşém zabǐl ↓

NOTES

¹ Russians answer the telephone in various ways, corresponding to our *hello:*

Я у телефо́на.

Алло́! *or* Алло́, я слу́шаю.

Да́? *or* Да́, я слу́шаю.

[Я] слу́шаю.

Despite its spelling, **алло́** is pronounced with a single л, usually soft: [aḷó].

[2] The possessive modifier **свóй** is equivalent to **мóй** in this sentence. **Свóй** means *one's own* and can refer to any person. It is not used to modify the subject of a sentence, but refers *back to the subject for its meaning:*

Я́ забы́л **свóй** портфéль.	I forgot *my* briefcase.
Ты́ забы́л **свóй** портфéль.	You forgot *your* briefcase.
Онá забы́ла **свóй** портфéль.	She forgot *her* briefcase.

[3] Note that **нигдé** *nowhere* is used in a double negative construction in Russian. This is true of all such negative constructions: **никогдá**, **ничегó**, **никудá**, and so forth.

Я́ егó **нигдé не** ви́жу.	I don't see it (*or* him) anywhere.
Вы́ **никогдá не** говори́те по-рýсски.	You never speak Russian.
Я́ **ничегó** об э́том **не** знáю.	I don't know anything about it.
Я́ **никудá не** идý.	I'm not going anywhere.

[4] Russians often use the plural form **двéри** to mean a *single door* as well as more than one door. In the meaning *doorway*, the plural is used:

Óн стоя́л в **дверя́х**. He stood in the *doorway*.

PREPARATION FOR CONVERSATION — Студéнты писáли о нарóдах СССР

нарóды СССР	the peoples of the U.S.S.R.
о нарóдах СССР	about the peoples of the U.S.S.R.
писáть (I)	to write
Студéнты писáли о нарóдах СССР.	The students wrote about the peoples of the U.S.S.R.
результáт (результáты)	result(s)
неплохóй	not half bad, pretty good
неплохи́е результáты	pretty good results
по-мóему	in my opinion, I think
По-мóему, результáты неплохи́е.	In my opinion the results are pretty good.
Вы́ о чём э́то? (*full form* Вы́ о чём э́то говори́те?)	What's that you're talking about?
экзáмен (экзáмены)	examination(s)
Вы́ о чём э́то? Об экзáменах?	What are you talking about? The examinations?
рабóта (рабóты)	work(s), paper(s) (written)
о рабóтах студéнтов	about the students' papers
Нéт, о рабóтах студéнтов.	No, about the students' papers.
Они́ писáли о нарóдах СССР.	They wrote about the peoples of the U.S.S.R.
вóт кáк!	really! you don't say! is that so!
Гдé и́х рабóты?	Where are their papers?
Вóт кáк! Гдé и́х рабóты?	Is that so! Where are their papers?

стул (сту́лья)
здесь
Во́т зде́сь, на сту́ле.

chair(s)
here
Right here on the chair.

ага́ [ahá]
Ага́, ви́жу!

aha! ahhh!
Aha, I see!

яку́т (яку́ты)
э́тот (m), э́та (f), э́то (n)
Э́та рабо́та о яку́тах.
украи́нец (украи́нцы)
э́ти рабо́ты
Э́ти рабо́ты об украи́нцах.
Э́та рабо́та о яку́тах, э́ти об украи́нцах.

Yakut(s)
this, that
This paper is on the Yakuts.
Ukrainian(s)
these papers
These papers are on the Ukrainians.
This paper is on the Yakuts, and these are on the Ukrainians.

написа́ть (pfv I)
А о чём написа́л Козло́в?

to write
And what did Kozlov write about?

грузи́н (грузи́ны)
Козло́в написа́л о грузи́нах.
отли́чно
О грузи́нах. И отли́чно написа́л.

Georgian(s)
Kozlov wrote about the Georgians.
excellently
About the Georgians. And he wrote excellently.

молоде́ц (молодцы́)
Он молоде́ц!

one who does an outstanding job
He's terrific!

Ра́д э́то слы́шать!

Glad to hear it.

дово́лен, дово́льна, –о, –ы
профе́ссор (профессора́)
Все́ профессора́ дово́льны.
им
Все́ профессора́ им дово́льны.
Все́ на́ши профессора́ им дово́льны.

pleased, satisfied
professor(s)
All the professors are pleased.
by him, with him
All the professors are pleased with him.
All our professors are pleased with him.

ру́сские
о ру́сских
А во́т рабо́та о ру́сских.

the Russians
on the Russians, about the Russians
And here's a paper on the Russians.

Петро́ва
Э́то Петро́ва написа́ла.

Miss Petrov
Miss Petrov wrote that.

мно́го
о не́й
Да́? Я о не́й уже́ мно́го слы́шал.

much, a lot, a good deal
about her
Yes? I've already heard a good deal about her.

лу́чшие студе́нты
Она́ и Козло́в — лу́чшие студе́нты.
факульте́т (факульте́ты)
на факульте́те
на э́том факульте́те
Она́ и Козло́в — лу́чшие студе́нты на э́том факульте́те.

the best students
She and Kozlov are the best students.
department(s)
in the department
in this department
She and Kozlov are the best students in this department.

сочинéние

composition

Мы́ писáли сочинéние.

We were writing a composition.

учи́тель (учителя́)

teacher(s) (below university level)

Óн вáш учи́тель?

Is he your teacher?

учи́тельница (учи́тельницы)

female teacher(s) (below university level)

Онá вáша учи́тельница?

Is she your teacher?

грýппа (грýппы)

group(s), section(s)

в грýппе

in the group, in the section

Они́ лýчшие студéнты в э́той грýппе.

They're the best students in this group.

Студéнты писáли о нарóдах СССР

И. Н. — Ивáн Николáевич

Б. М. — Бори́с Михáйлович

Б. М.	1	По-мóему,	pamõjimu |
		результáты неплохи́е.	ŗizuļtáti ŋiplaχíji↓
И. Н.	2	Вы́ о чём э́то?	ví ačõm étə ↓
		Об экзáменах?	abɨgzáɱinəx ↓
Б. М.	3	Нéт,	ŋḗt ↓
		о рабóтах студéнтов.	arabótəx stuḑéntəf ↓
		Они́ писáли	aŋí ŗisáḷi
		о нарóдах СССР.[1]	anaródəx éséséŗ ↓
И. Н.	4	Вóт кáк!	võt kák ↓
		Гдé и́х рабóты?	gḑé íx rabõti ↓
Б. М.	5	Вóт здéсь,	vód zḑéş ↓
		на стýле.	nastũḷi˙↓
И. Н.	6	Агá,	ahã̌ ↓
		ви́жу.	γĭžu ↓
		Э́та рабóта о яку́тах,	étə rabótə ajikũtəx |
		э́ти об украи́нцах.	éţi abukraíncəx ↓
		А о чём написáл Козлóв?	a ačóm nəŗisál kazlõf ↑
Б. М.	7	О грузи́нах.	agruẓínəx ↓
		И отли́чно написáл!	i atļĭčnə nəŗisál ↓
		Óн молодéц![2]	ón məlaḑéc ↓
И. Н.	8	Рáд э́то слы́шать.	rắt étə slĭšəţ ↓
		Кáжется,	kắžitcə |
		всé нáши профессорá	fşé náši prəʃisarắ
		и́м довóльны.[3]	im davóļni ↓

Б. М.	9	А вóт рабóта о рýсских.	a vót rabótə arúsķix ↓
		Э́то Петрóва написáла.⁴	étə ρitrŏvə nəρisálə ↓

И. Н.	10	Дá?	dắ ↑
		Я о нéй ужé мнóго слы́шал.	já aņéj užé mnŏgə slíšəl ↓
		Онá и Козлóв —	aná i kazlŏf ↑
		лýчшие студéнты	lúcšiji stuďĕnti ‖
		на э́том факультéте.⁵	naétəm fəkuļţĕţi ↓

NOTES

[1] In the abbreviation **CCCP** *U.S.S.R.*, the letters stand for Союз Совéтских Социалистѝческих Респýблик *Union of Soviet Socialist Republics.* Unlike **ГУМ**, **CCCP** is not declined:

Compare **в ГУМе** *in GUM* with **в CCCP** *in the U.S.S.R.*

[2] The noun **молодéц** is a term of praise that can be applied to anyone who does a good job or comes through successfully. It is often used when we would say: *nice going! fine! good boy! good girl!* i.e., as an exclamation of approval.

[3] **Профéссор** is grammatically masculine, but may refer to a woman as well as a man:

Онá нáш профéссор. She's our professor.

Compare it with the masculine noun **учѝтель**, which has a corresponding feminine equivalent **учѝтельница**. Note, however, that the masculine plural **учителя́** can refer to a mixed group of teachers, but that the feminine plural **учѝтельницы** refers only to women teachers.

[4] **Петрóва** is the feminine form of **Петрóв** and may mean Miss or Mrs. Petrov, depending upon the context. It is not considered impolite to refer to a man or woman simply by using the last name; for example, **Вóт идёт Царáпкина** means *Here comes Miss* (or *Mrs.*) *Tsarapkin.* In addressing the person, however, either the first name and patronymic or the nickname is usual. **Господѝн** and **госпожá** are used by Russians only when referring to foreigners or by emigré Russians.

[5] **Факультéт** does *not* mean *faculty* in the American sense, but corresponds to the branches of the university we call *schools, divisions,* or *departments.* For example, **филологѝческий факультéт** (филфáк for short) means *department of languages and literatures,* and **медицѝнский факультéт** *school of medicine.*

Basic sentence patterns

1. Где огурцы́?
   ___ и́х рабо́ты?
   ___ ключи́?
   ___ ви́лки?
   ___ ло́жки?
   ___ кни́ги?
   ___ тетра́ди?

   Where are the cucumbers?
   _____ their papers?
   _____ the keys?
   _____ the forks?
   _____ the spoons?
   _____ the books?
   _____ the notebooks?

2. Где студе́нты?
   ___ учи́тельницы?
   ___ учителя́?
   ___ профессора́?

   Where are the students?
   _____ the women teachers?
   _____ the teachers?
   _____ the professors?

3. Во́т ключи́.
   ___ тетра́ди.
   ___ кни́ги.
   ___ ви́лки.
   ___ ло́жки.
   ___ огурцы́.
   ___ и́х рабо́ты.

   Here are the keys.
   _____ the notebooks.
   _____ the books.
   _____ the forks.
   _____ the spoons.
   _____ the cucumbers.
   _____ their papers.

4. Где пи́сьма?
   — Во́т здесь, на сту́ле.
   _____ на окне́.
   _____ на столе́.
   _____ на по́лке.

   Where are the letters?
   Here on the chair.
   ___ on the window sill.
   ___ on the desk (or table).
   ___ on the shelf.

5. Где пи́сьма?
   — Во́т здесь, в я́щике.
   _____ в портфе́ле.
   _____ в кни́ге.
   _____ в тетра́ди.
   _____ в коро́бке.

   Where are the letters?
   Here in the drawer.
   ___ in the briefcase.
   ___ in the book.
   ___ in the notebook.
   ___ in the box.

6. Я́ о не́й мно́го слы́шал.
   ___ нём _____.
   ___ ни́х _____.
   ___ ва́с _____.

   I've heard a lot about her.
   _____ him.
   _____ them.
   _____ you.

7. О ко́м ты́ говори́шь?
   — О вахтёре.
   — О Кири́лле.
   — О Цара́пкине.
   — О Ни́не.
   — О Ко́ле.
   — О Га́ле.
   — О Са́ше.

   Whom are you talking about?
   About the custodian.
   About Kirill.
   About Tsarapkin.
   About Nina.
   About Kolya.
   About Galya.
   About Sasha.

8. О ко́м они́ говоря́т?   Whom are they talking about?
   — О профе́ссоре.   About the professor.
   — Об Ива́не.   About Ivan.
   — Об убо́рщице.   About the cleaning lady.
   — Об учи́теле.   About the teacher.
   — Об О́ле.   About Olya.
   — Об америка́нке.   About the American [woman].
   — Об америка́нце.   About the American [man].

9. О́н говори́л о Евге́нии.   He was talking about Evgeny.
   _____ о Мари́и.   _____ about Maria.
   _____ о тетра́ди.   _____ about the notebook.
   _____ о лаборато́рии.   _____ about the laboratory.
   _____ о собра́нии.   _____ about the meeting.
   _____ о сочине́нии.   _____ about the composition.
   _____ о две́ри.   _____ about the door.
   _____ о ле́кции.   _____ about the lecture.
   _____ об общежи́тии.   _____ about the dormitory.
   _____ об о́сени.   _____ about autumn.
   _____ об о́череди.   _____ about the line.

10. О чём вы́ говори́те?   What are you talking about?
    — О клу́бе.   About the club.
    — О заво́де.   About the plant.
    — О борще́.   About the borsch.
    — О конце́рте.   About the concert.
    — О портфе́ле.   About the briefcase.
    — О шка́фе.   About the cupboard.
    — О ча́е.   About tea.
    — О селёдке.   About herring.

11. О чём ты́ говори́шь?   What are you talking about?
    — О шко́ле.   About school.
    — О письме́.   About a letter.
    — О молоке́.   About the milk.
    — Об университе́те.   About the university.
    — Об экза́мене.   About the exam.
    — Об авто́бусе.   About the bus.
    — Об обе́де.   About dinner.
    — Об окне́.   About the window.

12. О чём писа́ли студе́нты?   What did the students write about?
    — Они́ писа́ли о наро́дах СССР.   They wrote about the peoples of the U.S.S.R.
    _____ о яку́тах.   _____ about the Yakuts.
    _____ о грузи́нах.   _____ about the Georgians.
    _____ об украи́нцах.   _____ about the Ukrainians.
    _____ об америка́нцах.   _____ about the Americans.
    _____ об америка́нках.   _____ about American women.

Pronunciation practice: hard versus soft consonants

A.   [p] vs. [p̦]   Usual Cyrillic spelling п; also пь, б, or бь.

Note the pronunciation of hard [p] in the following:

[napóčtu]	на по́чту	to the post office
[pažáləstə]	пожа́луйста	please

and compare it with soft [p̦]:

[sp̦iši̧ti]	спеши́те	you're hurrying
[p̦érvij]	пе́рвый	first

These are labial consonants, formed (like the English *p*) by completely closing the lips. Soft [p̦] has the effect of a *y*-like glide following it.

> Sound Drill: Practice the Russian paired examples illustrating hard [p] and soft [p̦], imitating your instructor (or the tape) as accurately as you can. Be sure to avoid the puff of breath that often accompanies the English *p*. Note that before [i], a *w*-like off-glide is often heard after hard [p].

B.   [b] vs. [b̦]   Usual Cyrillic spelling б; also бь, п, or пь.

Note the pronunciation of hard [b] in the following:

[bróṣit]	бро́сить	to drop
[aftóbus]	авто́бус	bus
[spaṣíbə]	спаси́бо	thank you

and compare it with soft [b̦]:

[nəab̦ét]	на обе́д	for dinner
[fklúb̦i]	в клу́бе	at the club
[naslúžb̦i]	на слу́жбе	at work

Russian [b], like the corresponding English sound, is made by completely closing the lips. The soft [b̦] will usually have the effect of a *y*-like glide following it.

> Sound Drill: Practice the Russian paired examples illustrating hard [b] and soft [b̦], imitating your instructor (or the tape) as accurately as you can. Note that before [i], a *w*-like off-glide is often heard after hard [b].

C.   [m] vs. [m̡]   Usual Cyrillic spelling м; sometimes мь.

Note the pronunciation of hard [m] in the following:

[z̡ímu]	зи́му	winter
[mój]	мой	my
[p̡iʂmó]	письмо́	letter

and compare it with soft [m̡]:

[s̡im̡ón]	Семён	Semyon
[m̡ílə]	Ми́ла	Mila

Russian [m], like Russian [b] and [p] and the corresponding sounds in English, is made with a complete closure of the lips. The soft [m̡] usually has the effect of a y-like glide following it.

> Sound Drill: Practice the Russian paired examples illustrating hard [m] and soft [m̡], imitating your instructor (or the tape) as accurately as you can. Note that before [ɨ], a w-like off-glide is often heard after hard [m].

Intonation practice: part I—questions without question words

Questions with a rising contour. This contour is characteristic of questions without question words; these sentences usually present an alternative which can be answered "yes" or "no." In such questions the final word carries the major stress. The pitch begins at about level 2 and rises to a peak on the major stress. It is either sustained or, in unstressed final syllables, it may drop.

Practice the following drills, imitating the tape or the instructor.

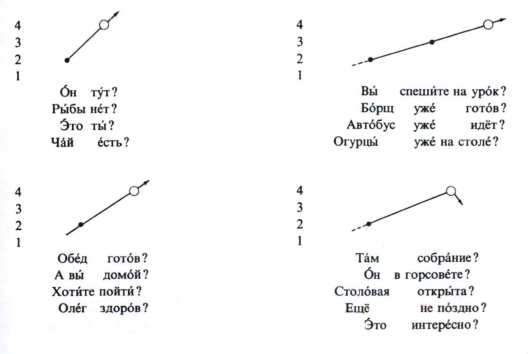

4
3
2
1

Óн   ту́т?
Ры́бы не́т?
Э́то ты́?
Ча́й   е́сть?

4
3
2
1

Вы́   спеши́те на уро́к?
Бо́рщ   уже́   гото́в?
Авто́бус   уже́   идёт?
Огурцы́   уже́ на столе́?

4
3
2
1

Обе́д   гото́в?
А вы́   домо́й?
Хоти́те пойти́?
Оле́г   здоро́в?

4
3
2
1

Та́м   собра́ние?
Óн   в горсове́те?
Столо́вая   откры́та?
Ещё   не по́здно?
Э́то   интере́сно?

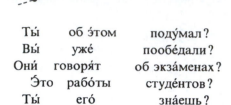

Вы́	уже́	идёте?
Она́	рабо́тает в шко́ле?	
Две́ри	ещё	не за́перты?
Э́то	ту́т	в коро́бке?
Вы́	идёте	на по́чту?

Ты́	об э́том	поду́мал?
Вы́	уже́	пообе́дали?
Они́	говоря́т	об экза́менах?
Э́то	рабо́ты	студе́нтов?
Ты́	его́	зна́ешь?

■ TRANSFORMATION DRILL

Pronounce the following questions as statements.

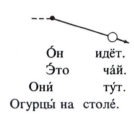

О́н	идёт?
Э́то	ча́й?
Они́	ту́т?
Огурцы́	на столе́?

О́н	идёт.
Э́то	ча́й.
Они́	ту́т.
Огурцы́	на столе́.

■ TRANSFORMATION DRILL

Pronounce the following statements as questions.

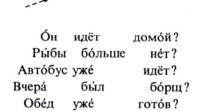

О́н	идёт	домо́й.
Ры́бы	бо́льше	не́т.
Авто́бус	уже́	идёт.
Вчера́	бы́л	бо́рщ.
Обе́д	уже́	гото́в.

О́н	идёт	домо́й?
Ры́бы	бо́льше	не́т?
Авто́бус	уже́	идёт?
Вчера́	бы́л	бо́рщ?
Обе́д	уже́	гото́в?

STRUCTURE AND DRILLS

The nominative plural of nouns

MODELS

Ка́к дела́?	How are *things*?
У на́с е́сть **огурцы́**.	We have *cucumbers*.
Ту́т то́лько **ви́лки** и **ло́жки**.	Here are only *forks* and *spoons*.
Где́ её **тетра́ди** и **кни́ги**?	Where are her *notebooks* and *books*?

Двéри ужé зáперты.	The *doors* are already locked.
У негó éсть ключи́.	He has *keys*.
Результáты неплохи́е.	The *results* aren't bad.
Гдé и́х рабóты?	Where are their *papers*?
О чём писáли студéнты?	What did the *students* write about?
Гдé учителя́?	Where are the *teachers*?
Всё профессорá и́м довóльны.	All the *professors* are pleased with him.
Всё здáния бы́ли зáперты.	All the *buildings* were locked.

NOMINATIVE PLURAL: TABLE OF BASIC NOUN ENDINGS

	жена́-class nouns and most стол-class nouns	окно́-class nouns and some стол-class nouns	двéрь-class nouns
HARD STEMS	–ы	–a	
SOFT STEMS	–и	–я	–и

Notes

1. The ending –и occurs instead of –ы in the hard stem стол- and жена́-class nouns whose final consonant is ж, ш, к, г, or х: ножи́, карандаши́, америка́нки, кни́ги, ло́жки.

2. Some стол-class nouns take the nominative plural ending –a or –я, which is practically always stressed: профессорá, учителя́, городá.

3. Many nouns have a different place of stress in the plural than they have in the singular. Compare женá with жёны, окнó with óкна, письмó with пи́сьма, гóрод with городá, and сестрá with сёстры.

4. Some стол-class nouns have an inserted vowel in the nominative singular which does not appear elsewhere in the declension. Compare the singular дéнь with the plural дни́, звонóк with звонки́, and подáрок with подáрки. Most nouns ending in –ец in the nominative singular have this feature. Compare америка́нец with америка́нцы, украи́нец with украи́нцы, and огурéц with огурцы́.

5. A few стол- and окно́-class nouns have their stems softened and expanded in the plural by the addition of [j]. The nominative plural of such nouns is written with –ь *plus* я (–ья). Compare перó with пéрья, брáт with брáтья, and сту́л with сту́лья. In the plural of му́ж, the soft sign is written but the ж is not pronounced soft: мужья́ [mužjá].

■ STRUCTURE REPLACEMENT DRILLS

Nominative singular to nominative plural.

1. *Where was the bus?*
   Where were the buses?
   т: Гдé бы́л автóбус?
   s: Гдé бы́ли автóбусы?
   т: Гдé былá шкóла?
   s: Гдé бы́ли шкóлы?
   (завод, стол, материал, телефон, университет, концерт, экзамен, работа, группа)

2. *There was a book on the shelf.*
   There were books on the shelf.
   т: На пóлке былá кни́га.
   s: На пóлке бы́ли кни́ги.
   т: На пóлке бы́л я́щик.
   s: На пóлке бы́ли я́щики.
   (коробка, тетрадь, вилка, портфель, ключ)

3. *Where's the key?*
   Where are the keys?
   т: Где́ клю́ч?
   s: **Где́ ключи́?**
   т: Где́ ключи́?
   s: **Где́ ло́жки?**
   (дверь, полка, ручка, портфель,
   очередь)

4. *Orlov was here.*
   The Orlovs were here.
   т: Орло́в бы́л зде́сь.
   s: **Орло́вы бы́ли зде́сь.**
   т: Ку́рочкин бы́л зде́сь.
   s: **Ку́рочкины бы́ли зде́сь.**
   (Царапкин, американка, Хитро́в,
   уборщица, студент, студентка,
   учительница)

■ MIXED STRUCTURE REPLACEMENT DRILLS

Nominative plural to nominative singular and vice versa.

1. *The windows are there.*
   The window is there.
   т: О́кна та́м.
   s: **Окно́ та́м.**
   т: Окно́ та́м.
   s: **О́кна та́м.**
   (города́, го́род, профе́ссор,
   профессора́)

2. *The knives were in the drawer.*
   The knife was in the drawer.
   т: Ножи́ бы́ли в я́щике.
   s: **Но́ж бы́л в я́щике.**
   т: Каранда́ш бы́л в я́щике.
   s: **Карандаши́ бы́ли в я́щике.**
   (нож, карандаши, ножи, карандаш)

■ MIXED STRUCTURE REPLACEMENT DRILL

Nominative singular to nominative plural and vice versa.

Where was the bell?
Where were the bells?
т: Где́ бы́л звоно́к?
s: **Где́ бы́ли звонки́?**
т: Где́ бы́ли украи́нцы?
s: **Где́ бы́л украи́нец?**
(огурец, звонки, американец, украинец,
огурцы, подарок)

■ MIXED STRUCTURE REPLACEMENT DRILLS

Nominative plural to nominative singular and vice versa.

1. *The chairs are here.*
   The chair is here.
   т: Сту́лья зде́сь.
   s: **Сту́л зде́сь.**
   т: Бра́т зде́сь.
   s: **Бра́тья зде́сь.**
   (пе́рья, мужья́, бра́тья, му́ж, перо́, сту́л)

2. *Where's the chair?*
   Where are the chairs?
   т: Где́ сту́л?
   s: **Где́ сту́лья?**
   т: Где́ бра́тья?
   s: **Где́ бра́т?**
   (муж, перья, стулья, брат, мужья)

■ STRUCTURE REPLACEMENT DRILLS

1. *The students have already found out about it.*
   The student has already found out about it.

   т: Студе́нты уже́ узна́ли об э́том.
   s: **Студе́нт уже́ узна́л об э́том.**
   т: Убо́рщицы уже́ узна́ли об э́том.
   s: **Убо́рщица уже́ узна́ла об э́том.**

   (учи́тельницы, жёны, мужья́, бра́тья,
   сёстры, учителя́, профессора́, амери-
   ка́нки, америка́нцы)

2. *The student already found out about it.*
   The students already found out about it.

   т: Студе́нт уже́ узна́л об э́том.
   s: **Студе́нты уже́ узна́ли об э́том.**
   т: Жена́ уже́ узна́ла об э́том.
   s: **Жёны уже́ узна́ли об э́том.**

   (муж, брат, сестра́, учи́тель, убо́рщица,
   профе́ссор, украи́нец, америка́нка)

3. *You don't know where the knife is, do you?*
   You don't know where the knives are, do you?

   т: Ты не зна́ешь, где нож?
   s: **Ты не зна́ешь, где ножи́?**
   т: Ты не зна́ешь, где каранда́ш?
   s: **Ты не зна́ешь, где карандаши́?**

   (портфель, книга, ключ, тетрадь, вилка,
   платье, сочинение, подарок, стул)

■ QUESTION-ANSWER DRILLS

1. *Was Professor Orlov there?*
   All the professors were there.

   т: Профе́ссор Орло́в был там?
   s: **Все профессора́ бы́ли там.**
   т: Студе́нт Козло́в был там?
   s: **Все студе́нты бы́ли там.**
   Студе́нтка Петро́ва была́ там?
   На́ш грузи́н был там?
   На́ш украи́нец был там?
   На́ш яку́т был там?
   На́ша гру́ппа была́ там?
   Ва́ш учи́тель был там?

2. *He's a student, but who are they?*
   They're students too.

   т: О́н студе́нт, а кто́ они́?
   s: **Они́ то́же студе́нты.**
   т: Она́ учи́тельница, а кто́ они́?
   s: **Они́ то́же учи́тельницы.**
   О́н профе́ссор, а кто́ они́?
   Она́ убо́рщица, а кто они́?
   О́н учи́тель, а кто́ они́?
   О́н украи́нец, а кто́ они́?
   О́н грузи́н, а кто́ они́?
   О́н яку́т, а кто́ они́?
   Она́ америка́нка, а кто́ они́?
   О́н америка́нец, а кто́ они́?

■ MIXED STRUCTURE REPLACEMENT DRILLS

Nominative plural to nominative singular and vice versa.

1. *You don't know where the pens are, do you?*
   You don't know where the pen is, do you?

   т: Ты не зна́ешь, где ру́чки?
   s: **Ты не зна́ешь, где ру́чка?**
   т: Ты не зна́ешь, где пла́тья?
   s: **Ты не зна́ешь, где пла́тье?**

   (сочинения, собрания, стулья, учителя,
   шкафы, перья, тетради)

2. *Is there a chair there?*
   Are there any chairs there?

   т: Та́м есть сту́л?
   s: **Та́м есть сту́лья?**
   т: Та́м есть перо́?
   s: **Та́м есть пе́рья?**

   (коро́бка, шка́ф, окно́, огуре́ц, ло́жка,
   я́щик)

NOUNS: TABLE OF NOMINATIVE PLURAL ENDINGS			
стóл-class	окнó-class	женá-class	двéрь-class
–ы or –и (in most instances)	–a or –я	–ы or –и	only –и
–á or –я́ (in some instances)			

1. All **двéрь**-class nouns spell their nominative plural ending with –и (usually unstressed), which replaces –ь of the nominative singular: **двéрь, двéри; óчередь, óчереди; тетрáдь, тетрáди.**

2. Most **окнó**-class nouns spell their nominative plural ending with –a (replacing nominative singular –o) or –я (replacing nominative singular –e or –ё): **окнó, óкна; дéло, делá; собрáние, собрáния; плáтье, плáтья.**

3. Some **стóл**-class nouns spell their nominative plural ending with –a or –я, which is almost always stressed: **профéссор, профессорá; гóрод, городá; учи́тель, учителя́; крáй, края́** *regions*. Note that the plural ending –я replaces –ь and –й of the nominative singular in the spelling of these forms.

4. All **женá**-class nouns and most **стóл**-class nouns spell their nominative plural ending with –ы or –и: **женá, жёны; стóл, столы́; автóбус, автóбусы; сестрá, сёстры; клю́ч, ключи́.** Note that nouns ending in –я, –й, or –ь in the nominative singular replace these letters with –и in the nominative plural: **истóрия, истóрии** *history*; **чáй, чаи́; портфéль, портфéли.**

Hard stem **женá**- and **стóл**-class nouns take the ending –и instead of –ы if their stem ends in к, г, х, ш, or ж: **урóк, урóки; кни́га, кни́ги; нóж, ножи́; карандáш, карандаши́; корóбка, корóбки.** Note that к, г, and х are then pronounced soft before –и.

Inserted vowels and alternation of stems

As compared with endings, which regularly change, stems are relatively stable. However, some stems show a regular pattern of alternation, with a vowel occurring in certain forms and not in others. In the examples below, note that the nominative singular contains the inserted vowel o or e as its next to last letter, while the nominative plural occurs without the inserted vowel.

NOMINATIVE SINGULAR	NOMINATIVE PLURAL	BASIC STEM
америкáнец	америкáнцы	**америкáнц–**
молодéц	молодцы́	**молодц–**
украи́нец	украи́нцы	**украи́нц–**
звонóк	звонки́	**звонк–**
огурéц	огурцы́	**огурц–**

The vowel is inserted between the last two stem consonants and serves not only to break the cluster, but also, frequently, to carry the stress. Such inserted "cluster-breaking" vowels typically occur in case forms with a zero ending, i.e., in the nominative singular of **стол**-class nouns and in the genitive plural of **жена**- and **окно**-class nouns.

Expanded stems in the plural

Although singular and plural stems are usually the same, some nouns have a plural stem that differs in certain respects. For example, some **окно**- and **стол**-class nouns with a singular stem ending in a hard consonant, soften this consonant (if it can be softened) and add a [j] for the plural stem. Note that in the Cyrillic writing system, the [j] is expressed by means of ь followed by the soft-series vowel letter я for the nominative plural.

NOMINATIVE SINGULAR		NOMINATIVE PLURAL	
брат	[brát]	братья	[brátjə]
перо	[p̡iró]	перья	[p̡ét̡jə]
муж	[múš]	мужья	[mužjá]
стул	[stúl]	стулья	[stúl̡jə]

The nominative plural of possessive modifiers

MODELS

Чьи это ключи?
Мои ключи в портфеле.
Это **твои** тетради.
Всё **наши** профессора им довольны.
Где **ваши** книги?
Где **их** работы?

Whose keys are these?
My keys are in the briefcase.
Those are *your* notebooks.
All *our* professors are pleased with him.
Where are *your* books?
Where are *their* papers (*lit.* works)?

■ STRUCTURE REPLACEMENT DRILLS

1. *Is that your key?*
Are those your keys?
т: Это ваш ключ?
s: **Это ваши ключи?**
т: Это ваше сочинение?
s: **Это ваши сочинения?**
(платье, окно, портфель, коробка, дверь, карандаш, нож, тетрадь, стол)

2. *Whose book is that?*
Whose books are those?
т: Чья это книга?
s: **Чьи это книги?**
т: Чьё это перо?
s: **Чьи это перья?**
(стол, работа, сочинение, огурец, материал, нож, карандаш, полка, портфель, ключ)

Whose pens are these?
These are our pens.
т: Чьи э́то пе́рья?
s: **Э́то на́ши пе́рья.**

т: Чьи́ э́то карандаши́?
s: **Э́то на́ши карандаши́.**
(кни́ги, тетра́ди, сочине́ния, рабо́ты, материа́лы, коро́бки, я́щики, ножи́)

■ MIXED STRUCTURE REPLACEMENT DRILL

Singular to plural and vice versa.

Where is your brother?
Where are your brothers?
т: Где́ твой бра́т?
s: **Где́ твои́ бра́тья?**

т: Где́ твои́ сёстры?
s: **Где́ твоя́ сестра́?**
(ру́чка, портфе́ли, по́лка, экза́мены, сто́л, учителя́, две́рь, ключи́, ножи́, каранда́ш, тетра́дь)

■ QUESTION-ANSWER DRILLS

1. *Are those his keys?*
   No, those are my keys.
   т: Э́то его́ ключи́?
   s: **Не́т, э́то мои́ ключи́.**
   т: Э́то его́ огурцы́?
   s: **Не́т, э́то мои́ огурцы́.**
   (портфе́ль, портфе́ли, коро́бка, кни́ги, рабо́та, пе́рья, но́ж, студе́нты, перо́)

2. *Whose notebooks are these?*
   Yours.
   т: Чьи́ э́то тетра́ди?
   s: **Твои́.**
   т: Чья́ э́то кни́га?
   s: **Твоя́.**
   (сто́л, сочине́ние, шкафы́, коро́бки, рабо́та, перо́, пе́рья, но́ж, карандаши́)

■ RESPONSE DRILLS

1. *Here's my sister.*
   These are her books.
   т: Во́т моя́ сестра́.
   s: **Э́то её кни́ги.**
   т: Во́т мо́й бра́т.
   s: **Э́то его́ кни́ги.**
   (мои́ студе́нты, мои́ сёстры, моя́ учи́тельница, мо́й му́ж, мои́ бра́тья, мо́й профе́ссор, мои́ профессора́)

2. *This is my pencil.*
   And whose is this?
   т: Э́то мо́й каранда́ш.
   s: **А э́то че́й?**
   т: Э́то мои́ тетра́ди.
   s: **А э́то чьи́?**
   (окно́, ножи́, ключи́, сочине́ние, ча́й, по́лка, кни́ги, портфе́ль, хле́б, ру́чка)

■ PROGRESSIVE SUBSTITUTION DRILL

1. *Where is your brother?*
   т: Где́ ва́ш бра́т?
   s: **Где́ ва́ш бра́т?**
   т: _____ (бра́тья)?
   s: **Где́ ва́ши бра́тья?**
   т: _____ (сёстры)?
   s: **Где́ ва́ши сёстры?**
   __ (твоя́) ____?
   _____ (му́ж)?
   _____ (учи́тельница)?

   Где́ твоя́ учи́тельница?
   _____ (о́кна)?
   __ (на́ше) __?
   _____ (авто́бус)?
   _____ (ключи́)?

2. *This is my briefcase.*

т: Это мо́й портфе́ль.

s: Это мо́й портфе́ль.

т: ____ (его́) _____.

s: Это его́ портфе́ль.

т: _____ (каранда́ш).

s: Это его́ каранда́ш.

_____ (перо́).

____ (мой) ____.

Это мой пе́рья.

_____ (коро́бка).

____ (его́) _____.

_____ (коро́бки).

_____ (учи́тель).

____ (йх) _____.

_____ (учителя́).

____ (её) _____.

DISCUSSION

All possessive modifiers of the changing type have nominative plurals that end in –и.

whose чьй	*my, mine* мой	*your, yours* твой	*our, ours* на́ши	*your, yours* ва́ши

The third person possessives, **его́**, **её**, and **йх**, never change their form and thus have no special forms for the plural.

Где́ её рабо́ты?	Where are her papers?
Где́ его́ рабо́ты?	Where are his papers?
Где́ йх рабо́ты?	Where are their papers?

The prepositional case:
singular and plural endings of nouns

MODELS

Где́ вы́ учи́ли ру́сский язы́к, в шко́ле?	Where did you study Russian, *in school?*
— Не́т, в университе́те.	No, *at the university.*
Я ва́с ви́дел на ле́кции.	I saw you *at the lecture.*
Я ва́с ви́дел в аудито́рии.	I saw you *in the auditorium.*
Во́т но́ж, на столе́.	Here's the knife *on the table.*
Она́ была́ в го́роде.	She was *in town.*
Это твой кни́ги на по́лке?	Are these your books *on the shelf?*
О́н и Петро́ва — лу́чшие студе́нты в э́той гру́ппе.	He and Miss Petrov are the best students *in this group.*
Во́т йх рабо́ты, здесь на сту́ле.	Here are their papers *on the chair.*
Вы́ до́лго стоя́ли в о́череди?	Did you stand *in line* long?
О ко́м вы́ ду́маете?	*Whom* are you thinking *about?*
— О Мари́и.	*About Maria.*
— Об Ива́не.	*About Ivan.*
— О Льве́.	*About Lev.*
Студе́нты писа́ли о наро́дах СССР.	The students wrote *about the peoples of the* U.S.S.R.
Козло́в писа́л о грузи́нах.	Kozlov wrote *about the Georgians.*

	most **стол-**, **окно-**, and **жена́**-class nouns –е	**две́рь**-class nouns and all nouns ending in –ий, –ия, and –ие in the nominative singular –и
SINGULAR	на столе́ в шко́ле об окне́ об учи́теле о пла́тье	в о́череди о Евге́нии на ле́кции об общежи́тии в зда́нии
PLURAL	HARD STEMS –ах SOFT STEMS –ях	–ях
	на стола́х в шко́лах об о́кнах об учителя́х	в очередя́х в дверя́х на ле́кциях об общежи́тиях в зда́ниях

Note: The prepositional case is always used with a preposition, usually one of the following:

в (*or* **во**)	in, at
на	on, at
о (*or* **об**, *or* **обо**)	about, concerning, on, of

The alternate form of **в** is **во**, used before certain consonant clusters: **во всём** *in everything*, **во Фра́нции** *in France*.

Alternate forms of **о** are **об** and **обо**. **Об** is used before words beginning with **а**, **о**, **у**, **э**, and **и**: **об э́том**, **об украи́нцах**. **Обо** occurs only in a few fixed phrases, such as **обо мне́** *about me* and **обо всём** *about everything*.

■ REPETITION DRILL

Repeat the models given above until you are familiar with the endings of the prepositional case.

■ CUED SUBSTITUTION DRILLS

1. (*Lev*) *She was talking about Lev.*
    т: (Лёв) Она́ говори́ла о Льве́.
    s: **Она́ говори́ла о Льве́.**
    т: (бра́т) (Она́) _____.
    s: **Она́ говори́ла о бра́те.**
    (сестра, муж, профессор, Галя, город, книга, карандаш, нож, дело, полка, чай)

2. (*Ivan*) *We were thinking about Ivan.*
    т: (Ива́н) Мы́ ду́мали об Ива́не.
    s: **Мы́ ду́мали об Ива́не.**
    т: (обе́д) (Мы́) _____.
    s: **Мы́ ду́мали об обе́де.**
    (урок, учитель, университет, Орлов, экзамен, учительница, общежитие, осень)

Cue should be given before the question is asked.

1. (*Kirill*) *Who are you thinking about?*
    About Kirill.
    т: (Кири́лл) О ко́м вы́ ду́маете?
    s: **О Кири́лле.**
    т: (Ко́ля)   О ко́м вы́ ду́маете?
    s: **О Ко́ле.**
    (Га́ля, Козло́в, Семён, Мария, Маша,
    Нина, Евгений, Царапкин, Борис, Ку-
    рочкин, Николай)

2. (*Ivan*) *Whom are you talking about?*
    About Ivan.
    т: (Ива́н) О ко́м ты́ говори́шь?
    s: **Об Ива́не.**
    (Оля, учитель, учительница, Орлов,
    американка, уборщица)

3. (*Professor Orlov*) *Whom is he asking about?*
    About Professor Orlov.
    т: (профéссор Орло́в) О ко́м о́н спра́шивает?
    s: **О профéссоре Орло́ве.**
    (Иван, Нина, Коля, американка, Мария, учитель, учительница, Олег, Николай)

■ QUESTION-ANSWER DRILLS

1. *Have you forgotten about Lev?*
    No, I haven't forgotten about Lev.
    т: Ты́ забы́л о Льве́?
    s: **Не́т, я́ не забы́л о Льве́.**
    т: Ты́ забы́л о звонке́?
    s: **Не́т, я́ не забы́л о звонке́.**
    (об америка́нце, об украи́нце, о Льве́,
    о звонке́, о пода́рке, об америка́нце)

2. *Were you thinking about Lev?*
    Yes, I was thinking about Lev.
    т: Ты́ ду́мал о Льве́?
    s: **Да́, я́ ду́мал о Льве́.**
    т: Ты́ ду́мал об учи́теле?
    s: **Да́, я́ ду́мал об учи́теле.**
    (о профессоре Орлове, о сестре, о
    Гале, о брате, о Коле, об Иване
    Петровиче, об Ирине Петровне)

■ STRUCTURE REPLACEMENT DRILLS

1. *She forgot about the students.*
    She forgot about the student.
    т: Она́ забы́ла о студе́нтах.
    s: **Она́ забы́ла о студе́нте.**
    т: Она́ забы́ла о профессора́х.
    s: **Она́ забы́ла о профéссоре.**
    (о братьях, о сёстрах, о книгах, о
    школах, о лекциях, о перьях, о платьях,
    о работах)

2. *Ivan didn't write about the schools.*
    Ivan didn't write about the school.
    т: Ива́н не писа́л о шко́лах.
    s: **Ива́н не писа́л о шко́ле.**
    т: Ива́н не писа́л о профессора́х.
    s: **Ива́н не писа́л о профéссоре.**
    (об учителях, о братьях, о книгах, об
    уроках, об университетах, о городах,
    об очередях, о грузинах)

3. *Do you want to find out about the exam?*
    Do you want to find out about the exams?
    т: Вы́ хоти́те узна́ть об экза́мене?
    s: **Вы́ хоти́те узна́ть об экза́менах?**
    т: Вы́ хоти́те узна́ть об уро́ке?
    s: **Вы́ хоти́те узна́ть об уро́ках?**
    (об автобусе, об обеде, об учителе, о
    лекции, о собрании)

4. *What have you heard about her brother?*
    What have you heard about her brothers?
    т: Что́ вы́ слы́шали о её бра́те?
    s: **Что́ вы́ слы́шали о её бра́тьях?**
    т: Что́ вы́ слы́шали о её сестре́?
    s: **Что́ вы́ слы́шали о её сёстрах?**
    (о его профессоре, о его учителе, о сё
    учительнице, о его сочинении, о её
    работе)

The sisters forgot about the brothers.
The brothers forgot about the sisters.

т: Сёстры забыли о братьях.
s: **Братья забыли о сёстрах.**
т: Профессора забыли о студентах.
s: **Студенты забыли о профессорах.**
Мужья забыли о жёнах.
Студенты забыли об учителях.
Уборщицы забыли о профессорах.
Грузины забыли о якутах.
Украинцы забыли о грузинах.
Учителя забыли об учительницах.

The book is in the drawer.
The books are in the drawers.

т: Книга в ящике.
s: **Книги в ящиках.**
т: Ручка на столе.
s: **Ручки на столах.**
Ключ в портфеле.
Подарок в коробке.
Студент на лекции.
Сестра на экзамене.
Студенты в аудитории.
Учитель в библиотеке.

(*The meetings*)   *What did they write about?*
                   About the meetings.

т: (собрания)   **О чём они писали?**
s: **О собраниях.**
т: (народы СССР) **О чём они писали?**
s: **О народах СССР.**
(книги, его работы, языки, лекции,
экзамены, американцы, учителя,
города СССР)

DISTRIBUTION OF ENDINGS IN THE PREPOSITIONAL CASE

1. *Singular:* –е and –и

   a. Most **стол-**, **окно-**, and **жена-**class nouns take –е as their ending in the prepositional singular: **на столе, об окне, о жене, о рыбе, в городе, о платье, о Гале, об Иване, о Льве.**[1]

   Hard consonants are regularly replaced by their soft counterparts before –е in the prepositional singular. Compare **стол** [stól] with **на столе** [nəstaļé] and **окно** [aknó] with **в окне** [vakņé]. **Ж, ш,** and **ц** remain hard in this position since they have no soft counterparts: **уборщица** [ubórščicə], **об уборщице** [abubórščici].

   b. All **дверь-**class nouns and those nouns with a nominative singular ending in –ий, –ия, or –ие spell their prepositional singular ending with –и: **о двери, в очереди, об осени, о собрании, о пении, об Евгении, о здании.**

2. *Plural:* –ах and –ях

   a. Nouns whose stems end in a hard consonant or **ч** or **щ** spell their prepositional plural ending –ах: **о ключах, о щах, о столах, о жёнах, о книгах, о полках, о профессорах, об украинцах, о письмах.**

   b. All others take the ending –ях in the prepositional plural: **о дверях, о портфелях, об учителях, о платьях, о братьях, о перьях, о собраниях, о сочинениях.**

   Note that –ь is written in the prepositional plural only if it is also written in the nominative plural: Compare **о мужьях** (nom pl **мужья**) with **об очередях** (nom pl **очереди**).

---

[1] Note that the name **Лёв** *Lev* has the inserted vowel е in the nominative singular only. In the other forms, ь must be inserted to preserve the softness of the л: о Льве.

Prepositions в and на with the prepositional case

Где ваш брат?	Where's your brother?
— На работе.	At work.
— На обеде.	At a dinner.
— На концерте.	At a concert.
— На почте.	At the post office.
— На экзамене.	At an exam.
— На уроке.	At a lesson.
— На собрании.	At a meeting.
— На лекции.	At a lecture.
— На заводе.	At the plant.
— На службе.	At work.
Где ваша сестра?	Where's your sister?
— В университете.	At the university.
— В школе.	At school.
— В лаборатории.	At the laboratory.
— В библиотеке.	At the library.
— В ГУМе.	At GUM.
— В городе.	Downtown or In town.
— В аудитории.	In the auditorium.
— В клубе.	At the club.
— В общежитии.	In the dormitory.
— В горсовете.	At the gorsovet.

■ REPETITION DRILL

Repeat the models given, noting that with certain nouns only **на** can be used, with others only **в**.

■ STRUCTURE REPLACEMENT DRILL

They're now at the exams.
They're now at the exam.
т: Они теперь на экзаменах.
s: **Они теперь на экзамене.**

т: Они теперь на лекциях.
s: **Они теперь на лекции.**
(на собраниях, на заводах, на уроках, в библиотеках, в аудиториях, в общежитиях, в лабораториях, в школах, в клубах)

■ CUED QUESTION-ANSWER DRILLS

1. (*singing lesson*) *Where were you?*
   At a singing lesson.
   т: (урок пения) Где вы были?
   s: **На уроке пения.**
   т: (работа) Где вы были?
   s: **На работе.**
   (обед, завод, почта, экзамен, концерт, собрание, служба, лекция)

2. (*laboratory*) *Just where is she?*
   At the laboratory.
   т: (лаборатория) Где же она?
   s: **В лаборатории.**
   т: (город) Где же она?
   s: **В городе.**
   (ГУМ, школа, клуб, аудитория, библиотека, университет, общежитие)

3.   (work)   *Where is he now?*
                    At work.
    т: (рабо́та) Где́ о́н тепе́рь?
    s: **На рабо́те.**
    т: (шко́ла) Где́ о́н тепе́рь?
    s: **В шко́ле.**
    (университет, почта, экзамен, лаборато́рия, собрание, завод, концерт, город, урок, обед, лекция)

4.   (meetings)   *Where did they hear about it?*
                    At the meetings.
    т: (собра́ния) Где́ они́ об э́том слы́шали?
    s: **На собра́ниях.**
    т: (экза́мены) Где́ они́ об э́том слы́шали?
    s: **На экза́менах.**
    (заводы, города, уроки, школы, библиотеки, университеты, лаборатории)

■ RESPONSE DRILL

There's the school.
Kolya's in school.
т: Во́т шко́ла.
s: **Ко́ля в шко́ле.**
т: Во́т заво́д.
s: **Ко́ля на заво́де.**
   (почта, клуб, аудитория, университет, ГУМ, лаборатория, библиотека, школа, общежитие)

■ CUED QUESTION-ANSWER DRILL

   (plant)   *Where's Ivan?*
               At the plant.
т: (завод)   Где́ Ива́н?
s: **На заво́де.**
т: (школа)   Где́ Ни́на?
s: **В шко́ле.**
  (университет) Где́ ре́ктор?
  (работа)   Где́ Са́ша?

  (лекция)   Где́ студе́нты?
  (город)   Где́ Ле́в?
  (аудитория)   Где́ Кири́лл?
  (экзамен)   Где́ профе́ссор Орло́в?
  (лабора́тория) Где́ Ми́ла?
  (концерт)   Где́ тво́й бра́т?
  (обед)   Где́ твоя́ сестра́?
  (общежитие)   Где́ студе́нтки?

■ PROGRESSIVE SUBSTITUTION DRILLS

1. *Irina Ivanovna was in town.*
   т: Ири́на Ива́новна была́ в го́роде.
   s: **Ири́на Ива́новна была́ в го́роде.**
   т: (Ва́ша сестра́)_____.
   s: **Ва́ша сестра́ была́ в го́роде.**
                   _____ (по́чте).
     ____ (бра́т) _____.
                   _____ (собра́нии).
     (Его́) _____.
     ____ (учителя́) _____.
                  _____ (экза́менах).
     ____ (студе́нты) _____.
     (На́ши) _____.
                   _____ (экза́мене).
     ____ (профессора́) _____.
                   _____ (университе́те).

2. *My brother is downtown.*
   т: Мо́й бра́т в го́роде.
   s: **Мо́й бра́т в го́роде.**
   т: ____ (сестра́) _____.
   s: **Моя́ сестра́ в го́роде.**
                 _____ (шко́ле).
     ____ (бра́тья) _____.
                 _____ (заво́де).
     (Её) _____.
                 _____ (ле́кциях).
                 _____ (ГУ́Ме).
     ____ (му́ж) _____.
     (Тво́й) _____.
                 _____ (общежи́тии).

English *in* (i.e., *in the interior*) is usually rendered by Russian в and English *on* (*on the surface*) by Russian на.

в столе́	in the desk (*or* table)
на столе́	on the desk (*or* table)
в кни́ге	in the book
на кни́ге	on the book

However, the English concept *at* may be rendered by either на or в, especially if the place described is viewed in terms of its function or the activity carried on there. In such instances, the choice between на or в is not dictated by the idea of position "inside" or "outside," but is fixed for a particular noun and must be memorized by the student as a set phrase. As a general rule, в is more commonly used if the place is a building or enclosure, and на is used if the place is described in terms of the activity carried on there.

1. **на**

на собра́нии, на собра́ниях	at a meeting, at meetings
на экза́мене, на экза́менах	at the exam, at exams
на заво́де, на заво́дах	at the plant, at plants
на уро́ке, на уро́ках	at the lesson, at lessons
на ле́кции, на ле́кциях	at the lecture, at lectures
на по́чте	at the post office
на слу́жбе	at work, on the job
на рабо́те	at work
на обе́де	at a dinner

2. **в**

в клу́бе, в клу́бах	at the club, at (*or* in) clubs
в библиоте́ке, в библиоте́ках	at (*or* in) the library, at (*or* in) libraries
в шко́ле, в шко́лах	at (*or* in) school, in schools
в университе́те, в университе́тах	at the university, at universities
в ГУ́Ме	at (*or* in) GUM

The personal pronouns and interrogatives кто́, что́ in the prepositional case

MODELS

О чём они́ писа́ли?	*What* did they write about?
О ко́м вы́ говори́те?	*Whom* are you talking about?
Она́ говори́ла обо мне́.	She was talking about *me*.
_____ о тебе́.	_____ about *you*.
_____ о ва́с.	_____ about *you*.
_____ о на́с.	_____ about *us*.
Я́ о нём мно́го слы́шал.	I've heard a lot about *him*.
_ о не́й _____.	_____ about *her*.
_ о ни́х _____.	_____ about *them*.

■ REPETITION DRILL

Practice the models until you are familiar with all the forms.

1. *Were you thinking about Nina?*
   Yes, I was thinking about her.
   т: Вы́ ду́мали о Ни́не?
   s: **Да́, я́ ду́мал о не́й.**
   т: Вы́ ду́мали о Ко́ле?
   s: **Да́, я́ ду́мал о нём.**
      (об учи́тельнице, о Га́ле,
      об Ива́не, о его́ сестре́,
      о её бра́те)

2. *Who was he writing about, me?*
   Yes, about you.
   т: О ко́м о́н писа́л, обо мне́?
   s: **Да́, о тебе́.**
   т: О ко́м о́н писа́л, о тебе́?
   s: **Да́, обо мне́.**
      (о ва́с, о ни́х, о нём, о не́й,
      о на́с, о тебе́)

■ RESPONSE DRILLS

1. *She was thinking about me.*
   About whom?
   т: Она́ ду́мала обо мне́.
   s: **О ко́м?**
   т: Она́ ду́мала об уро́ке.
   s: **О чём?**
      (о шко́ле, о Га́ле, о тебе́,
      о на́с, об экза́менах, об учи́теле,
      о собра́нии, о сестре́)

2. *Oh, you're here!*
   We were just talking about you.
   т: А́, вы́ здесь!
   s: **Мы́ как ра́з говори́ли о ва́с.**
   т: А́, ты́ здесь!
   s: **Мы́ как ра́з говори́ли о тебе́.**
      (он, они́, она́, Ко́ля, Ни́на,
      Га́ля)

■ CUED QUESTION-ANSWER DRILL

(*You*) *Whom was he asking about?*
    About you.
т: (вы́) О ко́м о́н спра́шивал?
s: **О ва́с.**
т: (ты́) О ко́м о́н спра́шивал?
s: **О тебе́.**
  (я, она́, мы, вы, он, они́)

■ QUESTION-ANSWER DRILL

Who is he?
I haven't heard of him.
т: Кто́ о́н?
s: **Я́ о нём не слы́шал.**

т: Кто́ вы́?
s: **Я́ о ва́с не слы́шал.**
  (они́, ты, она́, он,
  вы, она́)

■ RESPONSE DRILLS

1. *I've heard a lot about American women.*
   What have you heard about them?
   т: Я́ мно́го слы́шал об америка́нках.
   s: **Что́ вы́ о ни́х слы́шали?**
   т: Я́ мно́го слы́шал о ва́с.
   s: **Что́ вы́ обо мне́ слы́шали?**
      (о его́ сестре́, о его́ учителя́х, о её
      бра́те, об украи́нцах, о его́ учи́теле, об
      америка́нцах, о её профе́ссоре, о её
      му́же, о его́ жене́)

2. *She's terrific.*
   The professors speak highly of her.
   т: Она́ молоде́ц.
   s: **Профессора́ о не́й хорошо́ говоря́т.**
   т: Вы́ молоде́ц.
   s: **Профессора́ о ва́с хорошо́ говоря́т.**
      (он, мы, вы все, они́, ты, я)

I didn't think about that.

т: Я об э́том не поду́мал.

s: **Я об э́том не поду́мал.**

(Óн) _____.

_____ (о не́й) _____.

(Вы́) _____.

_____ (обо мне́) _____.

_____ (не слы́шали).

_____ (о на́с) _____.

(Они́) _____.

Они́ о на́с не слы́шали.

_____ (о тебе́) _____.

_____ (не писа́ли).

(Она́) _____.

_____ (о ва́с) _____.

_____ (не забы́ла).

(Мы́) _____.

_____ (о ни́х) _____.

(Óн) _____.

_____ (об э́том) _____.

_____ (не поду́мал).

Remarks on stress shift in nouns

A change in the position of the stress occurs frequently in the Russian declension of nouns, but it follows fairly regular patterns. The most typical of these patterns are given below.

1. Stress shift from stem in the singular to endings in the plural.

NOM SG	PREP SG	NOM PL	PREP PL
го́род	в го́роде	города́	в города́х
де́ло	о де́ле	дела́	о дела́х
му́ж	о му́же	мужья́	о мужья́х
учи́тель	об учи́теле	учителя́	об учителя́х
профе́ссор	о профе́ссоре	профессора́	о профессора́х
шка́ф	о шка́фе	шкафы́	о шкафа́х

2. Stress shift from endings in the singular to stem in the plural:

NOM SG	PREP SG	NOM PL	PREP PL
жена́	о жене́	жёны	о жёнах
сестра́	о сестре́	сёстры	о сёстрах
зима́	о зиме́	зи́мы	о зи́мах
окно́	на окне́	о́кна	на о́кнах
перо́	о пере́	пе́рья	о пе́рьях
письмо́	о письме́	пи́сьма	о пи́сьмах

3. Stress shift from stem in the nominative singular to endings in all the singular and plural forms where a vowel ending exists.

NOM SG	PREP SG	NOM PL	PREP PL
сто́л	на столе́	столы́	на стола́х
звоно́к	о звонке́	звонки́	о звонка́х
каранда́ш	о карандаше́	карандаши́	о карандаша́х
клю́ч	о ключе́	ключи́	о ключа́х
но́ж	о ноже́	ножи́	о ножа́х
огуре́ц	об огурце́	огурцы́	об огурца́х
язы́к	о языке́	языки́	о языка́х

The third group of nouns actually have their stress consistently on the endings, where there actually are endings. Where the ending is zero (as in the nominative singular) the stress is of necessity on the stem, usually on the last syllable.

— Мы неда́вно пи́ли чай, но я опя́ть го́лоден. — Уже́ мо́жно обе́дать, обе́д на столе́. У нас сего́дня борщ, ка́ша, ры́ба и огурцы́.

Ива́н Никола́евич всю зи́му не́ был на слу́жбе. Он был бо́лен. Его́ жена́, Мари́я Ива́новна, то́же была́ больна́. Тепе́рь Ива́н Никола́евич и Мари́я Ива́новна здоро́вы.

Ни́на Ива́новна вчера́ была́ в го́роде. Она́ покупа́ла материа́л на костю́м. Она́ до́лго стоя́ла в о́череди и купи́ла о́чень краси́вый материа́л.

— Кто там? — Это я. — Мари́я Ива́новна? — Да. — Здра́вствуйте, заходи́те пожа́луйста! Ра́да вас ви́деть. — Зна́ете, я была́ в го́роде. Покупа́ла материа́л на костю́м. Хоти́те посмотре́ть? — Коне́чно. — Пра́вда краси́вый? — О́чень. Где вы купи́ли? — В ГУМе.

— Как идёт рабо́та на заво́де? — Хорошо́. А как ва́ши дела́? — То́же хорошо́, спаси́бо. — Ну, до свида́ния! — Всего́ хоро́шего!

— Семён, нарежь, пожалуйста, огурцы!
— Хорошо. А где они? — Там, на окне.
— А где нож, в шкафу? — Нет в столе,
в ящике.

— Олег, ты слы́шал? Говоря́т, Ни́на больна́.
— Не́т, она́ здоро́ва. Смотри́, во́т она́ идёт.
— Ни́на, куда́ вы́ идёте?
— А́, здра́вствуйте. Я иду́ в э́то зда́ние. Та́м сейча́с бу́дет говори́ть ре́ктор.
— Пошли́ и мы́, Оле́г. Э́то интере́сно.

Сего́дня у на́с на ле́кции бы́л оди́н америка́нец. Он учи́л ру́сский язы́к в университе́те в Аме́рике и вполне́ хорошо́ говори́т по-ру́сски. Интере́сно с ни́м познако́миться. Но ка́к? Мо́жет быть за́втра о́н бу́дет в столо́вой.

— Хоти́те пойти́ на конце́рт, Ми́ла?
— С удово́льствием. Кста́ти, э́то беспла́тно?
— Да́. Ну, пока́. Я́ сейча́с спешу́ на собра́ние в клу́б.
— До свида́ния.

NOTES

PREPARATION FOR CONVERSATION | Где мой слова́рь?

слова́рь (словари́) (m)	dictionary (dictionaries)
Где мой слова́рь?	Where's my dictionary?
у тебя́	you have; at your place.
У тебя́ мой слова́рь?	Do you have my dictionary?
Влади́мир, у тебя́ мой слова́рь?	Vladimir, do you have my dictionary?
у меня́	I have; at my place
Нет, не у меня́.	No, I don't.
он у Семёнова	Semyonov has it
ра́зве	really; are you sure!
Ра́зве он не у Семёнова?	Are you sure Semyonov doesn't have it?
у него́ [uɲivó]	he has; at his place
у него́ нет	he doesn't have it
Нет, у него́ нет.	No, he doesn't have it.
спра́шивать (I)	to ask, inquire
(pfv спроси́ть)	
то́лько что [tóɫkəštə]	just, just now
Я то́лько что спра́шивал.	I just asked.
Нет, у него́ нет. Я то́лько что́ спра́шивал.	No, he doesn't have it. I just asked.
он у Козло́ва	Kozlov has it
Тогда́, мо́жет бы́ть, он у Козло́ва?	Then maybe Kozlov has it?
заня́тия (pl)	studies, classes
на заня́тиях	at classes
Козло́ва не́ было.	Kozlov was absent (or missing).
Козло́ва сего́дня не́ было на заня́тиях.	Kozlov didn't attend his classes today.
Мо́жет бы́ть, ты оста́вил свой слова́рь в библиоте́ке?	Maybe you left your dictionary at the library?
Я та́м не́ был.	I haven't been there.

пошёл, пошла́, пошло́, пошли́ (irreg past of пойти́)	went
Я пошёл домо́й.	I went home.
по́сле заня́тий	after classes
По́сле заня́тий я пошёл домо́й.	After classes I went home.
сра́зу	immediately, right away, at once
Сра́зу по́сле заня́тий я пошёл домо́й.	Right after classes I went home.
како́й-то слова́рь	a dictionary, some sort of dictionary
В столо́вой я ви́дел како́й-то слова́рь.	I saw a dictionary in the dining hall.
у нас в столо́вой	in our dining hall
У нас в столо́вой я ви́дел како́й-то слова́рь.	I saw a dictionary in our dining hall.
подожда́ть (pfv I)	to wait (a limited amount of time)
Подожди́, у нас в столо́вой я ви́дел како́й-то слова́рь.	Wait a second, I saw a dictionary in our dining hall.
наве́рно	probably, likely
Это, наве́рно, мой слова́рь.	It's probably my dictionary.
посмотрю́	I'll take a look
Это, наве́рно, мой. Пойду́ посмотрю́.	It's probably mine. I'll go take a look.
магази́н	store
до́лжен, должна́, должно́, должны́	must, have to, got to (*lit.* obliged, obligated)
Я до́лжен пойти́ в магази́н.	I've got to go to the store.
ко́е-что́ [kójə štó]	a thing or two, a couple of things
А я до́лжен пойти́ в магази́н ко́е-что́ купи́ть.	And I've got to go to the store to buy a couple of things.

SUPPLEMENT

исто́рия	history
У меня́ тепе́рь исто́рия.	I have history now.
литерату́ра	literature
У меня́ тепе́рь литерату́ра.	I have literature now.
геогра́фия	geography
У меня́ тепе́рь геогра́фия.	I have geography now.
матема́тика	mathematics
У меня́ тепе́рь матема́тика.	I have mathematics now.
фи́зика	physics
У меня́ тепе́рь фи́зика.	I have physics now.
хи́мия	chemistry
У меня́ тепе́рь хи́мия.	I have chemistry now.

Где мо́й слова́рь?

Н. — Никола́й   В. — Влади́мир

Н.	1	Влади́мир, у тебя́ мо́й слова́рь?	vlaḑîmir ↓ uţiḅấ mój slaváṛ ↓
В.	2	Нет, не у меня́. А ра́зве о́н не у Семёнова?[1]	ṇḗt ↓ ṇiuṃiṇấ ↓ a rázɣi ón ṇiuşiṃőnəvə ↓
Н.	3	Нет, у него́ нет. Я то́лько что спра́шивал.	ṇḗt ↓ uṇivó ṇḗt ↓ já tóḷkəštə spráširəl ↓
В.	4	Тогда́, мо́жет бы́ть, о́н у Козло́ва?	tagdá móžidbíṭ ón ukazlővə ↓
Н.	5	Козло́ва сего́дня не́ было на заня́тиях.[2]	kazlóvə şivódṇə ṇébilə nəzaṇấṭijəx ↓
В.	6	Мо́жет бы́ть, ты́ оста́вил сво́й слова́рь в библиоте́ке?	móžidbíṭ ti astáɣil svój slaváṛ vḅibḷiaṭḗ̆ḳi ↓
Н.	7	Я та́м не́ был.[3] Сра́зу по́сле заня́тий пошёл домо́й.	já tám ṇḗbil ↓ srázu pósḷi zaṇấṭij pašól damőj ↓
В.	8	Подожди́, у на́с в столо́вой я ви́дел како́й-то слова́рь.	pədažḑĭ ↓ unás fstalővəj | já ɣíḑil kakójtə slaváṛ ↓
Н.	9	Э́то, наве́рно, мо́й. Пойду́ посмотрю́.	étə naɣérnə mőj ↓ pajdú pəsmatṛű ↓
В.	10	А я́ до́лжен пойти́ в магази́н ко́е-что́ купи́ть.[4]	a já dólžin pajṭí vməgaȝín ↑ kójə štó kuṛíṭ ↓

NOTES

[1] **Ра́зве** is a word used to express surprise or incredulity, such as: *you don't mean to say! it isn't possible! really!* and so forth.

[2] Note the use of the plural **заня́тия** to mean *class*. This is the usual word for classes or studies at the university. **Ле́кция** may also be used to refer to university classes, but it is more often used in its literal sense (*lecture*) to describe an event outside class, such as a talk by a visiting lecturer. Compare also **уро́к** (literally *lesson*), used both to mean any kind of *private lesson* and *class* at the pre-university level.

Студе́нты тепе́рь на заня́тиях.	The students are in classes now.
Я иду́ на ле́кцию.	I'm going to a lecture.
Ученики́ на уро́ках.	The pupils are in class (*lit.* at their lessons).

Contrast **Я та́м не́ был** *I haven't been there* with **Козло́ва сего́дня не́ было на заня́тиях** *Kozlov wasn't at his classes today.* In the second example, a neuter verb and a genitive case subject are used to emphasize Kozlov's absence, i.e., to point out that he was missing.

⁴ **До́лжен** is a short-form adjective used together with the infinitive to mean *must, has* (or *have*) *to.* Its literal meaning is *obliged* or *obligated.*

PREPARATION FOR CONVERSATION   **В магази́не**

ка́рта	map
Евро́па	Europe
ка́рты Евро́пы	maps of Europe
у ва́с е́сть	you have
У ва́с е́сть ка́рты Евро́пы?	Do you have maps of Europe?
продавщи́ца	saleslady
ожида́ть (I)	to expect
Не́т, но мы́ ожида́ем за́втра.	No, but we're expecting them tomorrow.
неде́ля (неде́ли)	week(s)
на сле́дующей неде́ле	next week
Не́т, но мы́ ожида́ем на сле́дующей неде́ле.	No, but we're expecting them next week.
на э́той неде́ле	this week
Не́т, но мы́ ожида́ем на э́той неде́ле.	No, but we're expecting them this week.
Кита́й	China
ка́рта Кита́я	a map of China
У ва́с е́сть ка́рта Кита́я?	Do you have a map of China?
У ва́с не́т ка́рты Кита́я?	Don't you have a map of China?
А ка́рты Кита́я у ва́с не́т?	And you don't have a map of China?
то́же	too, also; either
А ка́рты Кита́я у ва́с то́же не́т?	And you don't have a map of China either?
е́сть	there is, there are
У на́с е́сть ка́рта Кита́я.	We do have a map of China.
пожа́луйста	please, you're welcome
во́т пожа́луйста	here you are
Во́т, пожа́луйста.	Here you are.
и	also, too
мне́ нужна́ ка́рта	I need a map
Но мне́ нужна́ и ка́рта Евро́пы.	But I need a map of Europe, too.
всё-таки	nevertheless, still, just the same
Но мне́ всё-таки нужна́ и ка́рта Евро́пы.	But just the same I need a map of Europe, too.
кио́ск	stand, newsstand
спроси́ть (pfv II) (ipfv спра́шивать)	to ask, inquire
А вы́ спроси́те в кио́ске.	Ask at the newsstand.
у́гол (gen sg угла́)	corner

на углу́	on the corner
А вы́ спроси́те в кио́ске на углу́.	Ask at the newsstand on the corner.
та́м то́же не́т	[it's] not there either
Я́ уже́ та́м бы́л. Та́м то́же не́т.	I've already been there. They don't have it there either.
а́тлас	atlas
Ка́к насчёт а́тласа?	How about an atlas?
Ка́к тогда́ насчёт а́тласа?	How about an atlas then?
дорого́й	expensive, dear
А́тлас, наве́рно, о́чень дорого́й?	An atlas is probably very expensive, isn't it?
Не́т, не о́чень.	No, not very.
принести́ (pfv I)	to bring
я́ принесу́	I'll bring
Не́т, не о́чень. Сейча́с принесу́.	No, not very. I'll bring one right away.

SUPPLEMENT

у неё е́сть	she has
У неё е́сть а́тлас?	Does she have an atlas?
у ни́х е́сть	they have
У ни́х е́сть а́тлас?	Do they have an atlas?
кусо́к (gen sg куска́)	piece
Хоти́те ещё кусо́к хле́ба?	Want another piece of bread?
стака́н	glass
Хоти́те ещё стака́н молока́?	Want another glass of milk?
ча́шка	cup
Хоти́те ещё ча́шку ко́фе?	Want another cup of coffee?

В магази́не

В. — Влади́мир
П. — Продавщи́ца

В.	1	У ва́с е́сть ка́рты Евро́пы?	uvás jéʂţ ká̱rt̻i jivrő̱p̻i ↓
П.	2	Не́т, но мы́ ожида́ем на сле́дующей неде́ле.	ņḗt ↓ no mí aži̱dájim | nas̻lédujuščij ņi̱d̻ḗ̱l̻i ↓
В.	3	А ка́рты Кита́я у ва́с то́же не́т?[1]	aká̱rt̻i ķitá̱jə ↓ uvás tő̱ži ņét ↓
П.	4	Не́т, е́сть.[2] Во́т, пожа́луйста.[3]	ņḗt↓ jéʂţ↓ vő̱t↓ pažá̱ləstə↓

В.	5 Хорошо́.	xərašő ↓
	Но мне́ всё-таки нужна́	no mŋé fʂőtəķi nužná |
	и ка́рта Евро́пы.	i kártə jivrőpi ↓
П.	6 А вы́ спроси́те	a ví spraʂíţi
	в кио́ске на углу́.⁴	fķiósķi nəuglű ↓
В.	7 Я́ уже́ та́м бы́л.	já užé tám bĭl ↓
	Та́м то́же не́т.	tám tőži ŋét ↓
П.	8 Ка́к тогда́ насчёт а́тласа?	kák taɡdá naščót átləsə ↓
В.	9 А́тлас, наве́рно,	átlas naɣérnə
	о́чень дорого́й?	óčiŋ dəraɡőj ↓
П.	10 Не́т, не о́чень.	ŋét ↓ ŋiőčiŋ ↓
	Сейча́с принесу́.	ʂičás prɨŋisű ↓

NOTES

¹ Note that **то́же** means *too* or *also* in affirmative sentences, but *neither* or *not . . . either* in negative ones:

Compare	Жена́ то́же рабо́тает в горсове́те.	My wife works at the gorsovet, too.
with	Ка́рты Кита́я у ва́с то́же не́т?	You don't have a map of China either?
	Я́ то́же его́ не зна́ю.	Neither do I know him *or* I don't know him either.

² In answering negative questions, Russians *usually* begin their answer with **не́т** regardless of whether the answer is affirmative or negative:

А ка́рты Кита́я у ва́с то́же не́т?	And you don't have a map of China either?
— Не́т, е́сть.	Yes, we do.
Ты́ та́м не́ был?	Weren't you there?
— Не́т, бы́л.	Yes, I was.
— Не́т, не́ был.	No, I wasn't.

³ **Пожа́луйста** is a polite word used in various situations:

Пожа́луйста, заходи́те.	Come in, please.
Во́т, пожа́луйста.	Here you are.
Пожа́луйста.	You first (at a door or entrance).
Спаси́бо. — Пожа́луйста.	Thank you. You're welcome.

⁴ A few **сто́л**-nouns like **шка́ф** and **у́гол** have a second prepositional case ending in stressed **–у́**, which occurs only when they are used with prepositions **на** and **в**.

Compare	Кио́ск на углу́.	The newsstand is *on the corner.*
with	Я́ говорю́ об угле́.	I'm talking *about the corner.*
Compare	Огурцы́ в шкафу́.	The cucumbers are *in the cupboard.*
with	Я́ говорю́ о шка́фе.	I'm talking *about the cupboard.*

Basic sentence patterns

1. У вáс éсть словáрь?　　　　　　　　　Do you have a dictionary?
— Дá, éсть.　　　　　　　　　　　　　Yes, I do.
— Дá, у меня́ éсть словáрь.　　　　　　　Yes, I have a dictionary.
У тебя́ éсть словáрь?　　　　　　　　　Do you have a dictionary?
— Дá, éсть.　　　　　　　　　　　　　Yes, I do.
— Дá, у меня́ éсть словáрь.　　　　　　　Yes, I have a dictionary.
У негó éсть словáрь?　　　　　　　　　Does he have a dictionary?
— Дá, éсть.　　　　　　　　　　　　　Yes, he does.
— Дá, у негó éсть словáрь.　　　　　　　Yes, he has a dictionary.
У неё éсть словáрь?　　　　　　　　　Does she have a dictionary?
— Дá, éсть.　　　　　　　　　　　　　Yes, she does.
— Дá, у неё éсть словáрь.　　　　　　　Yes, she has a dictionary.
У нáс éсть словáрь?　　　　　　　　　Do we have a dictionary?
— Дá, éсть.　　　　　　　　　　　　　Yes, we do.
— Дá, у нáс éсть словáрь.　　　　　　　Yes, we have a dictionary.
У нúх éсть словáрь?　　　　　　　　　Do they have a dictionary?
— Дá, éсть.　　　　　　　　　　　　　Yes, they do.
— Дá, у нúх éсть словáрь.　　　　　　　Yes, they have a dictionary.

2. У вáс éсть словáрь?　　　　　　　　　Do you have a dictionary?
— Нéт, у меня́ нéт словаря́.　　　　　　　No, I don't have a dictionary.
У тебя́ éсть словáрь?　　　　　　　　　Do you have a dictionary?
— Нéт, у меня́ нéт словаря́.　　　　　　　No, I don't have a dictionary.
У негó éсть словáрь?　　　　　　　　　Does he have a dictionary?
— Нéт, у негó нéт словаря́.　　　　　　　No, he doesn't have a dictionary.
У неё éсть словáрь?　　　　　　　　　Does she have a dictionary?
— Нéт, у неё нéт словаря́.　　　　　　　No, she doesn't have a dictionary.
У нáс éсть словáрь?　　　　　　　　　Do we have a dictionary?
— Нéт, у нáс нéт словаря́.　　　　　　　No, we don't have a dictionary.
У нúх éсть словáрь?　　　　　　　　　Do they have a dictionary?
— Нéт, у нúх нéт словаря́.　　　　　　　No, they don't have a dictionary.

3. У вáс éсть портфéль?　　　　　　　　Do you have a briefcase?
— Дá, у меня́ éсть портфéль.　　　　　　Yes, I have a briefcase.
— Нéт, у меня́ нéт портфéля.　　　　　　No, I don't have a briefcase.

4. У вáс éсть рýчка?　　　　　　　　　Do you have a pen?
— Дá, у меня́ éсть рýчка.　　　　　　　Yes, I have a pen.
— Нéт, у меня́ нéт рýчки.　　　　　　　No, I don't have a pen.

5. У вáс éсть молокó?　　　　　　　　　Do you have milk?
— Дá, у нáс éсть молокó.　　　　　　　Yes, we have milk.
— Нéт, у нáс нéт молокá.　　　　　　　No, we don't have any milk.

6. Чтó у вáс тепéрь?　　　　　　　　　What do you have now?
— У меня́ тепéрь литератýра.　　　　　　I have literature now.
＿＿＿＿＿＿＿＿ рýсский язы́к.　　　　＿＿＿ Russian ＿＿＿.
＿＿＿＿＿＿＿＿ геогрáфия.　　　　　＿＿＿ geography ＿＿.
＿＿＿＿＿＿＿＿ истóрия.　　　　　＿＿＿ history ＿＿＿.
＿＿＿＿＿＿＿＿ математика.　　　　＿＿＿ mathematics ＿＿＿.
＿＿＿＿＿＿＿＿ физика.　　　　　＿＿＿ physics ＿＿＿.
＿＿＿＿＿＿＿＿ хúмия.　　　　　＿＿＿ chemistry ＿＿.

7. Козло́ва сего́дня не́т.

 Влади́мира _____.

 Евге́ния _____.

 Кири́лла _____.

 Семёна _____.

 Льва́ _____.

 Оле́га _____.

 Никола́я _____.

Kozlov is absent today.

Vladimir _____.

Evgeny _____.

Kirill _____.

Semyon _____.

Lev _____.

Oleg _____.

Nikolay _____.

8. Ко́ли вчера́ не́ было на заня́тиях.

 Га́ли _____.

 Ни́ны _____.

 Ми́лы _____.

 Мари́и _____.

 Ма́ши _____.

 О́ли _____.

Kolya was absent from classes yesterday.

Galya _____.

Nina _____.

Mila _____.

Maria _____.

Masha _____.

Olya _____.

9. Его́ там не́ было?

 — Не́т, не́ было.

 — Не́т, о́н та́м бы́л.

 Её та́м не́ было?

 — Не́т, не́ было.

 — Не́т, она́ та́м была́.

 И́х та́м не́ было?

 — Не́т, не́ было.

 — Не́т, они́ та́м бы́ли.

Wasn't he there?

No, he wasn't.

Yes, he was there.

Wasn't she there?

No, she wasn't.

Yes, she was there.

Weren't they there?

No, they weren't.

Yes, they were there.

10. Че́й э́то портфе́ль?

 — Влади́мира.

 — Семёнова.

 — Оле́га.

 — Семёна.

 — Профе́ссора Орло́ва.

 — Бра́та.

 — Хитро́ва.

 — Цара́пкина.

 — Учи́теля.

 — Никола́я.

 — Евге́ния.

Whose briefcase is that?

Vladimir's.

Semyonov's.

Oleg's.

Semyon's.

Professor Orlov's.

My brother's.

Khitrov's.

Tsarapkin's.

The teacher's.

Nikolay's.

Evgeny's.

11. Чьи́ э́то ключи́?

 — Убо́рщицы.

 — Продавщи́цы.

 — Сестры́.

 — Жены́.

 — Мари́и.

 — Учи́тельницы.

 — Ни́ны Петро́вны.

Whose keys are these?

The cleaning lady's.

The saleslady's.

My sister's.

My wife's.

Maria's.

The teacher's (f).

Nina Petrovna's.

12. Это дело Ни́ны.   That's Nina's business.
    _____ О́ли.   _____ Olya's _____.
    _____ Га́ли.   _____ Galya's _____.
    _____ Ко́ли.   _____ Kolya's _____.
    _____ Са́ши.   _____ Sasha's _____.
    _____ продавщи́цы.   _____ the saleslady's _____.
    _____ убо́рщицы.   _____ the cleaning lady's _____.
    _____ вахтёра.   _____ the custodian's _____.
    _____ Козло́ва.   _____ Kozlov's _____.
    _____ ре́ктора.   _____ the chancellor's _____.
    _____ Льва́.   _____ Lev's _____.

Pronunciation practice:
hard versus soft consonants

A.   [v] vs. [ɣ]   Usual Cyrillic spelling в; sometimes г or вь.

Note the pronunciation of hard [v] in the following:

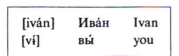

| [iván] | Ива́н | Ivan |
| [ví] | вы́ | you |

and compare it with soft [ɣ]:

| [dəsɣidánjə] | до свида́ния | good-bye |
| [ɣíḍil] | ви́дел | saw |

Russian [v], like the corresponding English sound, is made by bringing the upper teeth close to the lower lip. Before [o] (and especially [ɨ]) there is often the auditory effect of a w-like off-glide. Soft [ɣ], on the other hand, has the auditory effect of being followed by a y-like off-glide.

Sound Drill: Practice the Russian paired examples illustrating hard [v] and soft [ɣ], imitating your instructor (or the tape) as accurately as you can.

B.   [f] vs. [f̡]   Usual Cyrillic spelling ф; also в; sometimes вь or фь.

Note the pronunciation of hard [f] in the following:

[t̡il̡ifón]	телефóн	telephone
[áfrikə]	Áфрика	Africa
[fpaln̡é]	вполнé	completely

and compare it with soft [f̡]:

[f̡il̡íp]	Филúпп	Philip
[praf̡ésər]	профéссор	professor
[partf̡él̡]	портфéль	briefcase

Russian [f], like the corresponding English sound, is made by bringing the upper teeth close to the lower lip. Soft [f̡] has the effect of a y-like glide following it.

> Sound Drill: Practice the Russian paired examples illustrating hard [f] and soft [f̡], imitating your instructor (or the tape) as accurately as you can. Note that before [o] (and especially [i]), a w-like off-glide is often heard after hard [f].

C.   [l] vs. [l̡]   Usual Cyrillic spelling л; sometimes ль.

Note the pronunciation of hard [l] in the following:

[γíd̡il]	вúдел	saw
[n̡ébil]	нé был	wasn't
[d̡ilá]	делá	affairs
[fpaln̡é]	вполнé	completely

and compare it with soft [l̡]:

[l̡éf]	Лéв	Lev
[baln̡í]	больнú	sick
[partf̡él̡]	портфéль	briefcase
[uč̡ít̡il̡]	учúтель	teacher

Russian hard [l] is made with the tip of the tongue against the back of the upper teeth and with the middle of the tongue lowered or hollowed out. English has a somewhat similar *l* in words like ba*ll*, bu*ll*, and who*l*e. In Russian the tongue muscles are tenser and the tongue hollower.

Russian soft [l̡] is formed with the front part of the blade of the tongue (not the tip) in contact with the ridge of the gums behind the upper teeth. Soft [l̡] has somewhat the effect of being followed by a y-like glide as in English mi*lli*on.

> Sound Drill: Practice the Russian paired examples illustrating hard [l] and soft [l̡], imitating your instructor (or the tape) as accurately as you can.

Intonation practice: part II—questions without question words

Questions with a rising-falling contour. This contour is typical of questions where the major stress is not on the last word. The pitch rises to a high peak at level 4 on the major stress and then drops to a point somewhere between levels 1 and 2.

Practice the following drills, imitating the tape or the instructor.

Вы́ говори́те по-ру́сски?
Э́то ты́, О́ля?
Вчера́ бы́ло собра́ние?
О́н давно́ бо́лен?

Вы́ слы́шали об э́том?
Она́ мо́жет пойти́?
Вы́ до́лго рабо́тали?
Вы́ хоти́те ко́фе?

■ TRANSFORMATION DRILL

Pronounce the following statements as questions.

О́н не́ был на экза́мене.
Она́ доста́ла огурцы́.
У на́с е́сть ко́фе.
Э́то ва́ша кни́га.

О́н не́ был на экза́мене?
Она́ доста́ла огурцы́?
У на́с е́сть ко́фе?
Э́то ва́ша кни́га?

■ TRANSFORMATION DRILL

Pronounce the following questions as statements.

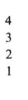

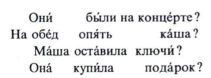

Они́ бы́ли на конце́рте?
На обе́д опя́ть ка́ша?
Ма́ша оста́вила ключи́?
Она́ купи́ла пода́рок?

Они́ бы́ли на конце́рте.
На обе́д опя́ть ка́ша.
Ма́ша оста́вила ключи́.
Она́ купи́ла пода́рок.

To have in Russian: affirmative y constructions in the present tense

MODELS

У вác éсть карандáш?	Do you have a pencil?
— Дá, éсть.	Yes, I do.
— Дá, у меня́ éсть карандáш.	Yes, I have a pencil.
У вác éсть кни́га?	Do you have a book?
— Дá, éсть.	Yes, I do.
— Дá, у меня́ éсть кни́га.	Yes, I have a book.
У вác éсть перó?	Do you have a pen [point]?
— Дá, éсть.	Yes, I do.
— Дá, у меня́ éсть перó.	Yes, I have a pen [point].
У вác éсть тетрáди?	Do you have notebooks?
— Дá, éсть.	Yes, I do.
— Дá, у меня́ éсть тетрáди.	Yes, I have notebooks.
У тебя́ мóй карандáш?	Do you have my pencil?
— Дá, у меня́.	Yes, I do.
— Дá, óн у меня́.	Yes, I have it.
У тебя́ моя́ кни́га?	Do you have my book?
— Дá, у меня́.	Yes, I do.
— Дá, онá у меня́.	Yes, I have it.
У тебя́ моё перó?	Do you have my pen [point]?
— Дá, у меня́.	Yes, I do.
— Дá, онó у меня́.	Yes, I have it.
У тебя́ мои́ тетрáди?	Do you have my notebooks?
— Дá, у меня́.	Yes, I do.
— Дá, они́ у меня́.	Yes, I have them.
У вác сегóдня экзáмен?	Do you have an exam today?
— Дá, у нác сегóдня экзáмен.	Yes, we have an exam today.
У вác сегóдня лéкция?	Do you have a lecture today?
— Дá, у нác сегóдня лéкция.	Yes, we have a lecture today.
У вác сегóдня собрáние?	Do you have a meeting today?
— Дá, у нác сегóдня собрáние.	Yes, we have a meeting today.
У вác сегóдня экзáмены?	Do you have examinations today?
— Дá, у нác сегóдня экзáмены.	Yes, we have examinations today.

■ REPETITION DRILL

Repeat the models after your instructor or the tape until you are familiar with the patterns.

■ REPETITION-SUBSTITUTION DRILL

We do have cucumbers.
т: У нác éсть огурцы́.
s: **У нác éсть огурцы́.**
    (борщ, кáша, чáй, кóфе, селёдка, мо-
локó, ры́ба, телефóн, ключи́, словáрь)

1. *Do you have a pencil?*
   Yes, I do.
   т: У тебя́ есть каранда́ш?
   s: Да́, есть.
   т: У тебя́ есть кни́га?
   s: Да́, есть.
   (ру́чка, нож, тетра́дь, а́тлас, портфе́ль, молоко́, борщ, селёдка)

2. *Do you have fish?*
   Yes, we have fish.
   т: У ва́с есть ры́ба?
   s: Да́, у на́с есть ры́ба.
   т: У ва́с есть огурцы́?
   s: Да́, у на́с есть огурцы́.
   (столы́, а́тлас, ка́рта Евро́пы, карандаши́, кни́ги, тетра́ди, материа́л на пла́тье)

3. *Do you have a pencil?*
   Yes, I have a pencil.
   т: У тебя́ есть каранда́ш?
   s: Да́, у меня́ есть каранда́ш.
   т: У тебя́ есть ру́чка?
   s: Да́, у меня́ есть ру́чка.
   (кни́га, тетра́дь, по́лка, портфе́ль, коро́бка, тетра́ди, нож)

4. *Do we have fish?*
   Yes, we do.
   т: У на́с есть ры́ба?
   s: Да́, есть.
   т: У на́с есть ключи́?
   s: Да́, есть.
   (ка́рта Евро́пы, ви́лки, ло́жки, ка́рта Кита́я, кни́ги, карандаши́, пе́рья)

■ QUESTION-ANSWER DRILLS

1. *Do you have my keys?*
   Yes, I do.
   т: Мои́ ключи́ у тебя́?
   s: Да́, у меня́.
   т: Мои́ ключи́ у Козло́ва?
   s: Да́, у него́.
   (у неё, у них, у вас, у него́, у тебя́, у Влади́мира, у Ни́ны)

2. *Do you have my notebook?*
   Yes, I have it.
   т: У тебя́ моя́ тетра́дь?
   s: Да́, она́ у меня́.
   т: У тебя́ мой а́тлас?
   s: Да́, он у меня́.
   (моя́ ру́чка, моя́ ка́рта Кита́я, мой нож, мои́ пи́сьма, моё письмо́, моя́ ло́жка, моё сочине́ние, мой каранда́ш)

3. *What do you have now, history?*
   Yes, I have history now.
   т: Что́ у тебя́ тепе́рь, исто́рия?
   s: Да́, у меня́ тепе́рь исто́рия.

   т: Что́ у тебя́ тепе́рь, хи́мия?
   s: Да́, у меня́ тепе́рь хи́мия.
   (экза́мен, собра́ние, уро́к пе́ния, исто́рия, матема́тика, литерату́ра, фи́зика, геогра́фия)

DISCUSSION

The concept *to have* is most commonly expressed in Russian by means of the preposition y plus the genitive case form of the noun or pronoun to indicate the possessor. The thing had or possessed is in the nominative case and is the grammatical subject of the Russian sentence.

У ва́с есть кни́га?	Do you have a book? (*Lit.* By you is a book?)
— У меня́ есть кни́га.	I have a book.
У на́с есть ры́ба.	We have fish *or* We do have fish.
У ва́с есть огурцы́?	Do you have cucumbers?
— Да́, есть.	Yes, we do.
У Влади́мира есть портфе́ль.	Vladimir has a briefcase.

Есть is required in those constructions where the speaker wishes to establish or affirm the presence or existence of the subject under discussion. If it is used in the question it must be repeated in the answer. It is omitted when some other part of the sentence is focused on.

Чтó у тебя́ тепéрь, рýсский язы́к?	*What* do you have now, *Russian?*
— Нéт, у меня́ тепéрь **истóрия**.	No, I have *history* now.
У вáс мóй словáрь?	Do *you* have my dictionary?
У вáс **мóй** словáрь?	Do you have *my* dictionary?
У вáс **словáрь**?	Is it a *dictionary* you have?

To have had in Russian: affirmative y constructions in the past tense

MODELS

У вáс бы́л экзáмен?	Did you have an exam?
——————— урóк?	——————— a lesson?
——————— урóк пéния?	——————— a singing lesson?
——————— англи́йский язы́к?	——————— English?
——————— рýсский язы́к?	——————— Russian?
У вáс былá лéкция?	Did you have a lecture?
——————— истóрия?	——————— history?
——————— матемáтика?	——————— mathematics?
——————— геогрáфия?	——————— geography?
——————— литератýра?	——————— literature?
У вáс бы́ло собрáние?	Did you have a meeting?
——————— сочинéние?	——————— a composition?
——————— пéние?	——————— singing?
У вáс бы́ли экзáмены?	Did you have exams?
——————— урóки?	——————— lessons?
——————— собрáния?	——————— meetings?
——————— лéкции?	——————— lectures?
——————— заня́тия?	——————— classes?

■ REPETITION DRILL

Repeat the above models, noting that for the past tense the appropriate form of **бы́л, былá, бы́ло,** or **бы́ли** must be used to agree with the noun denoting the thing had or possessed.

■ QUESTION-ANSWER DRILLS

1. *Did you already have an exam?*
   Yes, we did.
   т: У вáс ужé бы́л экзáмен?
   s: **Дá, бы́л.**
   т: У вáс ужé бы́ло собрáние?
   s: **Дá, бы́ло.**
   (лекция, урок пения, география, экзамены, физика, математика, химия)

2. *Did you have exams yesterday?*
   Yes, we did have exams yesterday.
   т: У вáс вчерá бы́ли экзáмены?
   s: **Дá, у нáс вчерá бы́ли экзáмены.**
   т: У вáс вчерá бы́л урóк?
   s: **Дá, у нáс вчерá бы́л урóк.**
   (собрание, уроки, лекция, история, литература, экзамен, русский язык, занятия)

■ STRUCTURE REPLACEMENT DRILLS

1. *I have a box.*
   I had a box.
   т: У меня́ éсть коро́бка.
   s: **У меня́ была́ коро́бка.**
   т: У меня́ éсть портфéль.
   s: **У меня́ был портфéль.**
   (каранда́ш, по́лка, перо́, ру́чка, тетра́ди,
   нож, ножи́, ключ, ключи́)

2. *We're having a meeting today.*
   We had a meeting today.
   т: У на́с сего́дня собра́ние.
   s: **У на́с сего́дня бы́ло собра́ние.**
   т: У на́с сего́дня пéние.
   s: **У на́с сего́дня бы́ло пéние.**
   (ру́сский язы́к, экза́мен, экза́мены,
   сочинéние, уро́к, ры́ба, бо́рщ, ка́ша)

■ QUESTION-ANSWER DRILLS

1. *We had an exam, did you?*
   So did we.
   т: У на́с был экза́мен, а у ва́с?
   s: **У на́с то́же был.**
   т: У на́с была́ лéкция, а у ва́с?
   s: **У на́с то́же была́.**
   (экза́мены, сочинéние, ру́сский язы́к,
   пéние, исто́рия, геогра́фия, собра́ние,
   заня́тия)

2. *Did you already have singing?*
   Yes, I did.
   т: У тебя́ ужé бы́ло пéние?
   s: **Да́, бы́ло.**
   т: У тебя́ ужé была́ матема́тика?
   s: **Да́, была́.**
   (пéние, уро́ки, исто́рия, фи́зика, хи́мия,
   сочинéние)

■ CUED QUESTION-ANSWER DRILL

(*a meeting*) *What did you have yesterday?*
   We had a meeting.
т: (собра́ние) Что́ у ва́с вчера́ бы́ло?
s: **У на́с бы́ло собра́ние.**
т: (экза́мены) Что́ у ва́с вчера́ бы́ло?
s: **У на́с бы́ли экза́мены.**
(ру́сский язы́к, заня́тия в лаборато́рии,
сочинéние, пéние, лéкция. рабо́та в
лаборато́рии)

DISCUSSION

To express the concept *to have* in the past tense in an affirmative sentence, Russian uses the appropriate form af **был, была́, бы́ло,** or **бы́ли** to agree with the grammatical subject, i.e., the thing *had.*

У на́с был бо́рщ.	*We had borsch.*
_____ была́ ры́ба.	_____ *fish.*
_____ бы́ло собра́ние.	_____ *a meeting.*
_____ бы́ли экза́мены.	_____ *exams.*

The most typical affirmative response to questions using this construction is a short answer containing the confirming **да́** plus the appropriate verb form.

У тебя́ был экза́мен?	*Did you have an exam?*
—Да́, был.	*Yes, I did.*

The genitive singular of nouns

Это ключи профессора.   These are the professor's keys.
_____ вахтёра.   _____ the custodian's ____.
_____ ректора.   _____ the chancellor's ____.
_____ брата.   _____ Brother's ____.
_____ Владимира.   _____ Vladimir's ____.
_____ Николая.   _____ Nikolay's ____.
_____ учителя.   _____ the teacher's ____.

Где ключи сестры?   Where are Sister's keys?
_____ учительницы?   _____ the teacher's ____?
_____ продавщицы?   _____ the saleslady's ____?
_____ уборщицы?   _____ the cleaning lady's ____?
_____ американки?   _____ the American woman's ____?
_____ Марии?   _____ Maria's ____?

Спроси насчёт письма.   Ask about the letter.
_____ окна.   _____ the window.
_____ молока.   _____ the milk.
_____ пения.   _____ the singing.
_____ сочинения.   _____ the composition.
_____ общежития.   _____ the dormitory.
_____ собрания.   _____ the meeting.

TABLE OF GENITIVE SINGULAR ENDINGS				
стол- and окно-class nouns		жена-class nouns		дверь-class nouns
–а or –я		–ы or –и		–и
стола	Николая	жены	Гали	двери
телефона	чая	карты	Коли	очереди
звонка	учителя	сестры	Марии	осени
студента	платья	Европы	истории	тетради
дела	собрания	Нины	каши	
окна	сочинения		книги	
пера			коробки	
письма			студентки	

Notes

1. **Стол**–class nouns ending in –ь and –й and **окно**–class nouns ending in –e or –ё in the nominative singular take –я in the genitive singular. All other **стол**– and **окно**–class nouns take –а in the genitive singular. **Окно**–class nouns have the same ending as in the nominative plural, but the stress may differ. Compare **письма** (nominative plural) with **письма** (genitive singular) and **дела** (nominative plural) with **дела** (genitive singular).

2. **Жена́**– and **дверь**-class nouns have the same ending in the genitive singular as in the nominative plural. But note that with **жена́**-class nouns, the stress may differ. Compare **жёны** (nominative plural) with **жены́** (genitive singular) and **сёстры** (nominative plural) with **сестры́** (genitive singular).

■ REPETITION DRILL

Repeat the above models after your instructor or the tape until you are familiar with the pattern of genitive singular endings.

■ CUED QUESTION-ANSWER DRILL

   (*Kurochkin*)   *Whose briefcase is that?*
                 Kurochkin's.
т: (Ку́рочкин) Чей э́то портфе́ль?
s: **Ку́рочкина.**
т: (Влади́мир) Чей э́то портфе́ль?
s: **Влади́мира.**
   (Ни́на, Козло́в, Никола́й, учи́тель, америка́нец, Орло́в, америка́нка, Ива́н, Мари́я)

■ INTEGRATION DRILLS

1. *This is a book. This is a student.*
   This is a student's book.
   т: Э́то кни́га. Э́то студе́нт.
   s: **Э́то кни́га студе́нта.**
   т: Э́то каранда́ш. Э́то Орло́в.
   s: **Э́то каранда́ш Орло́ва.**
   Э́то тетра́дь. Э́то Влади́мир.
   Э́то портфе́ль. Э́то профе́ссор.
   Э́то рабо́та. Э́то грузи́н.
   Э́то студе́нты. Э́то профе́ссор Орло́в.
   Э́то сочине́ние. Э́то Козло́в.

2. *This is a dictionary. This is the teacher.*
   This is the teacher's dictionary.
   т: Э́то слова́рь. Э́то учи́тель.
   s: **Э́то слова́рь учи́теля.**
   т: Э́то ка́рта. Э́то Кита́й.
   s: **Э́то ка́рта Кита́я.**
   Э́то ключи́. Э́то Никола́й.
   Э́то результа́ты. Э́то собра́ние.
   Э́то ка́рта. Э́то Евро́па.
   Э́то а́тлас. Э́то Евге́ний.
   Э́то учи́тель. Э́то шко́ла.
   Э́то ру́чка. Э́то америка́нец.
   Э́то кни́га. Э́то продавщи́ца.
   Э́то стака́н. Э́то молоко́.

3. *Here's a briefcase. Here's a teacher.*
   Here's a teacher's briefcase.
   т: Во́т портфе́ль. Во́т учи́тельница.
   s: **Во́т портфе́ль учи́тельницы.**
   т: Во́т убо́рщица. Во́т шко́ла.
   s: **Во́т убо́рщица шко́лы.**
   Во́т ка́рта. Во́т Евро́па.
   Во́т дверь. Во́т аудито́рия.
   Во́т учи́тель. Во́т гру́ппа.
   Во́т окно́. Во́т америка́нка.
   Во́т кни́га. Во́т продавщи́ца.
   Во́т пла́тье. Во́т Ни́на.
   Во́т ви́лка. Во́т Ми́ла.
   Во́т ча́шка. Во́т ча́й.

4. *This is a dictionary. This is a professor.*
   This is the professor's dictionary.
   т: Э́то слова́рь. Э́то профе́ссор.
   s: **Э́то слова́рь профе́ссора.**
   т: Э́то портфе́ль. Э́то Ко́ля.
   s: **Э́то портфе́ль Ко́ли.**
   Э́то сто́л. Э́то Мари́я.
   Э́то рабо́та. Э́то Га́ля.
   Э́то обе́д. Э́то Ко́ля.
   Э́то о́кна. Э́то библиоте́ка.
   Э́то пла́тье. Э́то продавщи́ца.
   Э́то слова́рь. Э́то Га́ля.
   Э́то две́ри. Э́то ГУ́М.

5. *Here's the library. Here's the university.*
   Here's the university library.
   т: Вот библиотéка. Вот университéт.
   s: **Вот библиотéка университéта.**
   т: Вот кни́га. Вот учи́тель.
   s: **Вот кни́га учи́теля.**
   Вот портфéль. Вот профéссор Ку́рочкин.
   Вот кáрта. Вот здáние.
   Вот кни́ги. Вот Николáй.
   Вот сочинéние. Вот Евгéний.
   Вот студéнты. Вот профéссор Орлóв.
   Вот материáлы. Вот собрáние.
   Вот чáшка. Вот кóфе.

6. *The teacher is here. But where is her husband?*
   Where's the teacher's husband?
   т: Учи́тельница ту́т. А гдé её му́ж?
   s: **Гдé му́ж учи́тельницы?**
   т: Профéссор Орлóв ту́т. А гдé егó
      студéнты?
   s: **Гдé студéнты профéссора Орлóва?**
   Владúмир ту́т. А гдé егó сестрá?
   Козлóв ту́т. А гдé егó брáт?
   Учи́тель Хитрóв ту́т. А гдé егó женá?
   Николáй ту́т. А гдé егó брáт?
   Ни́на ту́т. А гдé её му́ж?
   Марúя ту́т. А гдé её учи́тель?

DISCUSSION

Unlike the prepositional case, the genitive is used both with and without a preposition. Used without a preposition, it indicates a relationship of possession or descriptive limitation.

му́ж сестры́	sister's husband
кни́га Ивáна	Ivan's book, a book of Ivan's
ру́чка Марúи	Maria's pen, a pen of Maria's
кáрта Еврóпы	a map of Europe
нарóд Китáя	the people of China
учи́тель пéния	a singing teacher, a teacher of singing
урóк геогрáфии	a geography lesson
стакáн молокá	a glass of milk

Note that, unlike the English possessive, the Russian genitive normally *follows* the noun indicating what is possessed or described.

The genitive of кто́, что́, and the personal pronouns

MODELS

У **вáс** éсть словáрь?	Do *you* have a dictionary?
У **тебя́** éсть словáрь?	Do *you* have a dictionary?
У **когó** мóй áтлас?	*Who* has my atlas?
— У **меня́**.	*I* do.
— У **негó**.	*He* does.
— У **неё**.	*She* does.
— У **нáс**.	*We* do.
— У **ни́х**.	*They* do.
Насчёт **чегó** онú спрáшивали?	*What* was it they were asking about?

NOM	я	ты́	óн оно́	онá	мы́	вы́	онú	кто́	что́
GEN	меня́	тебя́	егó (негó)	её (неё)	нáс	вáс	úх (нúх)	когó	чегó

The alternate third person pronouns, **него́**, **неё**, and **ни́х**, are used only when the personal pronouns are preceded by a preposition: **у него́**, **у неё**, and **у ни́х**. Note that г in **его́**, **него́**, **кого́**, and **чего́** is pronounced [v]: [jivó], [ņivó], [kavó], and [čivó].

■ REPETITION DRILL

Repeat the above models after your instructor or the tape.

■ QUESTION-ANSWER DRILLS

1. *Where is he, at the university?*
   Yes, he has exams today.
   т: Где́ о́н, в университе́те?
   s: **Да́, у него́ сего́дня экза́мены.**
   т: Где́ она́, в университе́те?
   s: **Да́, у неё сего́дня экза́мены.**
   (они, Кирилл, Галя, студенты)

2. *And where are you going, to a lecture?*
   Yes, I have history now.
   т: А вы́ куда́, на ле́кцию?
   s: **Да́, у меня́ сейча́с исто́рия.**
   т: А они́ куда́, на ле́кцию?
   s: **Да́, у ни́х сейча́с исто́рия.**
   (Ирина, ты, ваш студент, твоя сестра, Коля, твои братья, Ирина и Галя)

3. *What does Galya have now?*
   She has history now.
   т: Что́ у Га́ли тепе́рь?
   s: **У неё тепе́рь исто́рия.**
   т: Что́ у тебя́ тепе́рь?
   s: **У меня́ тепе́рь исто́рия.**
   (у них, у Коли, у нас, у Козлова, у вас)

■ CUED QUESTION-ANSWER DRILLS

1. (*We*) *Who has Russian now?*
   We do.
   т: (мы́) У кого́ тепе́рь ру́сский язы́к?
   s: **У на́с.**
   т: (они́) У кого́ тепе́рь ру́сский язы́к?
   s: **У ни́х.**
   (вы, она, я, он, они, ты, мы, они, он)

2. (*They*) *Who has my dictionary?*
   They have your dictionary.
   т: (они́) У кого́ мо́й слова́рь?
   s: **У ни́х.**
   т: (о́н) У кого́ мо́й слова́рь?
   s: **У него́.**
   (она, вы, он, я, мы, они)

■ STRUCTURE REPLACEMENT DRILLS

1. *Vladimir has the key.*
   He has the key.
   т: Клю́ч у Влади́мира.
   s: **Клю́ч у него́.**
   т: Клю́ч у сестры́.
   s: **Клю́ч у неё.**
   (у студента, у жены, у Коли и Гали, у брата, у Козлова и Семёнова, у Николая, у Марии)

2. *My sister has an atlas.*
   She has an atlas.
   т: У сестры́ е́сть а́тлас.
   s: **У неё е́сть а́тлас.**
   т: У Никола́я е́сть а́тлас.
   s: **У него́ е́сть а́тлас.**
   (у Коли и Гали, у Любови, у студента, у Семёна, у Семёнова, у Козлова и Семёнова, у Владимира)

1. *Is Galya at classes?*
   No, she has a meeting now.
   т: Га́ля на заня́тиях?
   s: **Нет, у неё сейча́с собра́ние.**
   т: Ива́н на заня́тиях?
   s: **Нет, у него́ сейча́с собра́ние.**
   (Ни́на, её сестра́, Никола́й, они́, Ири́на, Лев, Семёнов, студе́нт, Любо́вь, Ко́ля, Бори́с, Мари́я)

2. *Do you have Russian now?*
   No, I have singing.
   т: У вас тепе́рь ру́сский язы́к?
   s: **Нет, у меня́ тепе́рь пе́ние.**
   т: У Ири́ны тепе́рь ру́сский язы́к?
   s: **Нет, у неё тепе́рь пе́ние.**
   (у меня́, у нас, у Влади́мира, у них)

The genitive case in нет constructions

MODELS

Кого́ здесь нет?	Who isn't here? *or* Who's missing?
— Здесь нет Козло́ва.	Kozlov isn't here.
_____ Никола́я.	Nikolay _____.
_____ Ко́ли.	Kolya _____.
_____ Ни́ны.	Nina _____.
_____ Мари́и.	Maria _____.

Он здесь?	Is he here?
— Нет, его́ нет.	No, he isn't.
Она́ здесь?	Is she here?
— Нет, её нет.	No, she isn't.

Борща́ бо́льше нет.	There's no more borsch.
Хле́ба _____.	_____ bread.
Ча́я _____.	_____ tea.
Молока́ _____.	_____ milk.
Ры́бы _____.	_____ fish.
Ка́ши _____.	_____ kasha.
Селёдки _____.	_____ herring.

У вас нет карандаша́?	You don't have a pencil, do you?
_____ а́тласа?	_____ an atlas _____?
_____ словаря́?	_____ a dictionary ___?
_____ пера́?	_____ a pen _____?
_____ молока́?	_____ milk _____?
_____ ка́рты Евро́пы?	_____ a map of Europe ____?
_____ тетра́ди?	_____ a notebook _____?
_____ кни́ги?	_____ a book _____?

■ REPETITION DRILL

Repeat the above models after your instructor (or the tape), noting that the subject of sentences using **нет** is always in the genitive case in Russian.

These drills should first be performed as simple repetition drills, then repeated as structure replacement drills.

1. *The map is on the table.*
   There isn't any map on the table!
   т: Ка́рта на столе́.
   s: **Ка́рты нет на столе́!**
   т: Ры́ба на столе́.
   s: **Ры́бы нет на столе́!**
   (нож, каша, письмо, коробка, чай, перо, портфель, сочинение, вилка, словарь)

2. *Professor Orlov is here.*
   Professor Orlov isn't here.
   т: Профе́ссор Орло́в здесь.
   s: **Профе́ссора Орло́ва здесь нет.**
   т: Он здесь.
   s: **Его́ здесь нет.**
   (уборщица, она, брат, Мария, он, Маша, она, украинец, он, Коля, он, Николай)

3. *Do you have a map of China?*
   You don't have a map of China, do you?
   т: У ва́с е́сть ка́рта Кита́я?
   s: **У ва́с нет ка́рты Кита́я?**
   т: У ва́с е́сть нож?
   s: **У ва́с нет ножа́?**
   (ключ, атлас, ручка, тетрадь, карта Америки, шкаф, коробка, перо, словарь)

1. (*Kozlov*) *Who's not here yet?*
   Kozlov.
   т: (Козло́в) Кого́ ещё нет?
   s: **Нет Козло́ва.**
   т: (Ни́на) Кого́ ещё нет?
   s: **Нет Ни́ны.**
   (Влади́мир, учи́тельница, Никола́й, профе́ссор Орло́в, Ива́н, му́ж Мари́и, учи́тель, убо́рщица, бра́т Ни́ны)

2. (*phone*) *What's missing here?*
   There's no phone here.
   т: (телефо́н) Чего́ здесь нет?
   s: **Здесь нет телефо́на.**
   т: (молоко́) Чего́ здесь нет?
   s: **Здесь нет молока́.**
   (полка, стул, атлас, словарь, звонок, ключ, нож, хлеб, стол)

1. *Where's the fish?*
   There isn't any fish left.
   т: Где́ ры́ба?
   s: **Ры́бы бо́льше нет.**
   т: Где́ ча́й?
   s: **Ча́я бо́льше нет.**
   (каша, борщ, селёдка, молоко, хлеб)

2. *Is Kozlov here?*
   No, Kozlov isn't here.
   т: Козло́в здесь?
   s: **Нет, Козло́ва здесь нет.**
   т: Ку́рочкин здесь?
   s: **Нет, Ку́рочкина здесь нет.**
   (Нина, Коля, ректор, вахтёр, профессор Орлов, Олег, Мария, Николай, Кирилл)

3. *Do you have a map of Europe?*
   No, I don't have a map of Europe.
   т: У вáс éсть кáрта Еврóпы?
   s: **Нéт, у меня́ нéт кáрты Еврóпы.**
   т: У вáс éсть áтлас?
   s: **Нéт, у меня́ нéт áтласа.**
   (словарь, ключ, перо, портфель, телефон, тетрадь, сестра, брат)

4. *Is Kozlov here?*
   Kozlov is absent (or *missing*) *today.*
   т: Козлóв здéсь?
   s: **Козлóва сегóдня нéт.**
   т: Николáй здéсь?
   s: **Николáя сегóдня нéт.**
   (Коля, Владимир, Иван, Оля, Хитров,
   Мария, Борис, Нина, Курочкин)

5. *Is there a library there?*
   No, there's no library there.
   т: Тáм éсть библиотéка?
   s: **Нéт, тáм нéт библиотéки.**
   т: Тáм éсть пóчта?
   s: **Нéт, тáм нéт пóчты.**
   (завод, университет, общежитие, зал,
   школа, телефон, магазин, аудитория,
   клуб, киоск, лаборатория)

DISCUSSION

Нéт means both *no* (as the opposite of **дá**) and *there is* (or *are*) *no* or *there isn't* (or *aren't*) *any.* Historically it comes from a combination of **не** plus **éсть.**

When **нéт** is used in constructions with the genitive it focuses on the lack or absence of the subject. It differs from constructions using the nominative plus **не,** where the focus is not on the absence but on some other element of the sentence.

Compare   **Егó** здéсь **нéт.**   He's not here (i.e., he's missing *or* absent).
with   **Óн не** здéсь, а в гóроде.   He's not here; he's in town.

The genitive case in past tense нé было constructions

MODELS

Когó тáм **нé было?**	*Who wasn't* there (i.e., who was missing)?
— Тáм нé было Козлóва.	Kozlov wasn't there.
_____ Николáя.	Nikolay _____.
_____ Кóли.	Kolya _____.
_____ Мар#и.	Maria _____.
_____ Ни́ны.	Nina _____.
_____ Óли.	Olya _____.
Егó тáм нé было?	Wasn't he there?
— Нéт, нé было.	No, he wasn't.
Её тáм нé было?	Wasn't she there?
— Нéт, нé было.	No, she wasn't.
Чегó тáм нé было?	What was missing? *or* What wasn't there?
— Тáм нé было борщá.	There wasn't any borsch.
_____ чáя.	_____ tea.
_____ хлéба.	_____ bread.
_____ молокá.	_____ milk.

— Там не́ было ры́бы.	There wasn't any fish.
_____ ка́ши.	_____ kasha.
_____ селёдки.	_____ herring.
У меня́ не́ было карандаша́.	I didn't have a pencil.
_____ а́тласа.	_____ an atlas.
_____ словаря́.	_____ a dictionary.
_____ портфе́ля.	_____ a briefcase.
_____ пера́.	_____ a pen.
_____ сочине́ния.	_____ a composition.
_____ ка́рты Евро́пы.	_____ a map of Europe.
_____ тетра́ди.	_____ a notebook.
_____ кни́ги.	_____ a book.

REPETITION DRILL

Repeat the above models after your instructor (or the tape), noting that for the past tense **не́ было** corresponds to **не́т** of the present and that here too the subject is in the genitive case. **Не́ было** is pronounced with a single stress which falls on **не́**: [n̡ébilə].

■ REPETITION-STRUCTURE REPLACEMENT DRILLS

1. *There's no fish.*
   There was no fish.
   т: Ры́бы не́т.
   s: **Ры́бы не́ было.**
   т: Авто́буса не́т.
   s: **Авто́буса не́ было.**
   (материала, очереди, портфеля, словаря, карты Китая, коробки, работы, борща, собрания)

2. *We don't have [any] work.*
   We didn't have [any] work.
   т: У на́с не́т рабо́ты.
   s: **У на́с не́ было рабо́ты.**
   т: У на́с не́т клу́ба.
   s: **У на́с не́ было клу́ба.**
   (собрания, учителя, карты СССР, телефона, библиотеки, аудитории, экзамена, урока, лекции)

■ QUESTION-ANSWER DRILLS

1. *Was the custodian there?*
   No, he wasn't.
   т: Вахтёр та́м бы́л?
   s: **Не́т, его́ не́ было.**
   т: Его́ жена́ та́м была́?
   s: **Не́т, её не́ было.**
   (Коля и Галя, ваш муж, её брат, она, он, они, продавщица, наш студент)

2. *Did you have a meeting?*
   No, we didn't have a meeting.
   т: У ва́с бы́ло собра́ние?
   s: **Не́т, у на́с не́ было собра́ния.**
   т: У ва́с бы́л уро́к пе́ния?
   s: **Не́т, у на́с не́ было уро́ка пе́ния.**
   (работа, лекция, история, экзамен, ключ, атлас, сочинение)

3. *Was there borsch?*
   No, there wasn't.
   т: Бо́рщ бы́л?
   s: **Не́т, не́ было.**
   т: Ры́ба была́?
   s: **Не́т, не́ было.**
   (экзамен, каша, борщ, селёдка, кофе, обед, урок пения, хлеб, очередь, звонок, собрание)

■ RESPONSE DRILL

Kozlov wasn't there.
Who wasn't there?

т: Козло́ва та́м не́ было.

s: **Кого́ та́м не́ было?**

т: А́тласа та́м не́ было.

s: **Чего́ та́м не́ было?**

(очереди, Коли, портфеля, Николая, киоска, Владимира, карты Китая, Ни́ны)

■ STRUCTURE REPLACEMENT DRILLS

1. *There was fish on the table.*
   There wasn't any fish on the table.

   т: На столе́ была́ ры́ба.

   s: **На столе́ не́ было ры́бы.**

   т: На столе́ бы́л обе́д.

   s: **На столе́ не́ было обе́да.**

   (чай, каша, молоко, подарок, сочинение, селёдка, хлеб, словарь, ручка,
   атлас, платье)

2. *We had a meeting yesterday.*
   We didn't have a meeting yesterday.

   т: У на́с вчера́ бы́ло собра́ние.

   s: **У на́с вчера́ не́ было собра́ния.**

   т: У на́с вчера́ бы́л экза́мен.

   s: **У на́с вчера́ не́ было экза́мена.**

   (химия, математика, концерт, физика,
   урок пения, лекция, история)

3. *I had a dictionary.*
   I didn't have a dictionary.

   т: У меня́ бы́л слова́рь.

   s: **У меня́ не́ было словаря́.**

   т: У меня́ была́ кни́га.

   s: **У меня́ не́ было кни́ги.**

   (урок, пение, география, лекция, экзамен, история, урок физики, литература)

■ PROGRESSIVE SUBSTITUTION DRILLS

1. *I have a pencil.*

   т: У меня́ е́сть каранда́ш.

   s: **У меня́ е́сть каранда́ш.**

   т: _____ (не́т) _____.

   s: **У меня́ не́т карандаша́.**

   _____ (е́сть) _____.

   _____ (не́ было) _____.

   _____ (е́сть) _____.

   (У тебя́) _____.

   _____ (тетрадь).

   _____ (не́т) _____.

   _____ (е́сть) _____.

   _____ (не́ было) _____.

   _____ (е́сть) _____.

2. *He has a briefcase.*

т: У него́ есть портфе́ль.

s: У него́ есть портфе́ль.

т: _____ (нет) _____.

s: У него́ нет портфе́ля.

_____ (не́ было) ____.

_____ (нет) _____.

_____ (есть) _____.

_____ (не́ было) ____.

_____ (есть) _____.

(У неё) _____.

_____ (ка́рта).

У неё есть ка́рта.

_____ (нет) _____.

_____ (есть) _____.

_____ (не́ было) ____.

_____ (есть) _____.

(Та́м) _____.

_____ (дверь).

_____ (нет) _____.

_____ (есть) _____.

_____ (не́ было) ____.

_____ (есть) _____.

DISCUSSION

Нет of the present tense is replaced in the past tense by **не́ было** in constructions focusing on the absence of a thing or person. The noun or pronoun indicating the missing thing or person is in the genitive case.

However, the nominative may be used for the subject (together with **не** plus **был, была́, бы́ло,** or **бы́ли**) if the focus is not on the absence itself, but on some other element of the sentence.

Compare Ни́на давно́ не была́ в клу́бе. Nina hasn't been at the club in a long time.

with Ни́ны не́ было в клу́бе. Nina wasn't at the club.

Compare Ива́н был не на ле́кциях, а на собра́нии. Ivan wasn't at lectures; he was at the meeting.

with Ива́на не́ было на собра́нии. Ivan wasn't at the meeting.

ЧТЕ́НИЕ И ПИСЬМО́

Вчера я забыл в университете свой портфель. А в портфеле были ключи. Я думал, что наша уборщица может открыть двери, но она тоже забыла ключи. Я - профессор, но уборщица! Как она забыла?!

- Кто там? Мария Петровна? - Нет, это Нина Ивановна. - Я, давно вас не видела. Заходите, пожалуйста! - Спасибо. А где ваша сестра? На службе? - Нет, она в городе.

— Ты куда? — В общежитие, а ты? Я тоже. Ты не знаешь, вчера было собрание? — Да, было, но я там не был. — А где ты был? — На концерте.

— Ася, ты готова? — Нет ещё. Где моя ручка? — Вот она. Смотри, уже почти девять! Пора идти! — Ну, хорошо, хорошо, я уже готова. До свидания, мама!

— Здравствуйте, Иван Иванович! — А, Мария Петровна! Здравствуйте! — Как ваша жена? Всё ещё больна? — Нет, уже здорова. Вчера была на службе. — Рада это слышать. Ну, пока! Я спешу на автобус.

— Нина, о чём вы думаете? — Об экзамене. — Зачем о нём думать? Он уже прошёл. — Да, но я, кажется, не очень хорошо написала. — Нет, я слышал, что вы отлично написали. — Вот как! Я очень рада.

— Алло! Коля? Нет, это Лев. — Здравствуйте, Лев! Ну, как Коля? Здоров? — Да, он уже вполне здоров. — Я очень рад это слышать. Он где теперь? — Кажется, в библиотеке. — Кстати, у вас вчера был экзамен? — Да. Мы писали о народах СССР. — Это интересно. Вы уже знаете результаты? — Нет ещё.

— Кто у телефона? — Иван Иванович Орлов. — А, здравствуйте, Иван Иванович. Как прошёл экзамен? — Очень хорошо. Студенты отлично написали. — Рад это слышать. Я вижу, что наши студенты молодцы.

— О ком вы говорите, о Гранте? — Нет, о Козлове. Он опять отлично написал. — Я слышал, что он молодец. — Да. Знаете о чём он написал? — Нет, не знаю. О чём? — О грузинах и их истории. — Вот как! Это интересно. Могу ли я посмотреть? — Конечно. Вот его работа.

— Дверь открыта? — Нет. — А где твой ключ? — В портфеле. — А портфель где? — В университете. — Ну хорошо, тогда возьми мой ключ. — Спасибо.

— У меня завтра экзамен. Где мой словарь? — На столе. — Его тут нет. — Тогда, может быть, он на полке. — Не вижу. А, вот он, на стуле.

NOTES

PREPARATION FOR CONVERSATION   Замо́лвите за меня́ слове́чко!

за меня́	for me, in my behalf
слове́чко (var of сло́во)	word
замо́лвить слове́чко	to put in a good word
Замо́лвите за меня́ слове́чко!	Put in a good word for me!
с *or* со (*plus* gen)	from, off, since
с рабо́ты	from work
Вы́ с рабо́ты идёте?	Are you coming from work?
Здра́вствуйте, Ни́на! С рабо́ты идёте?	Hello, Nina! Are you coming from work?
Не́т, я́ в горсове́те была́.	No, I've been to the gorsovet.
ко́мната	room
Не́т, я́ в горсове́те была́, насчёт ко́мнаты.	No, I've been to the gorsovet about a room.
како́й	what, which
Како́й ко́мнаты?	What room?
В чём де́ло?	What's the matter?
заявле́ние	application
заявле́ние на ко́мнату	application for a room
пода́ть (pfv irreg)	to give, serve, submit
пода́ть заявле́ние	to submit an application
Я́ подала́ заявле́ние на ко́мнату.	I submitted an application for a room.
жда́ть (ipfv I)	to wait
на́до	it's necessary, one has to
На́до та́к до́лго жда́ть.	You have to wait so long.
Я́ подала́ заявле́ние на ко́мнату, но на́до та́к до́лго жда́ть.	I submitted an application for a room, but you have to wait so long.
во́т что́!	so that's it!
А́х, во́т что́!	Oh, so that's it!
дру́г (nom pl друзья́)	friend
хоро́ший дру́г	good friend

167

Та́м рабо́тает мо́й хоро́ший дру́г
Алексе́ев.
   ведь [γiṭ] (unstressed)
Зна́ете, ведь та́м рабо́тает мо́й хоро́ший
дру́г Алексе́ев.

Чт́о вы́ говори́те!

Ива́н Ива́нович, замо́лвите за меня́
слове́чко!
   ми́лый
Ива́н Ива́нович, ми́лый, замо́лвите за меня́
слове́чко!

   предложи́ть (pfv II)
   ва́м
Я́ хоте́л ва́м э́то предложи́ть.
   как ра́з
Я́ как ра́з хоте́л ва́м э́то предложи́ть.

   большо́е спаси́бо
Большо́е ва́м спаси́бо!

   что та́м!
Ну́ что та́м!

   ста́рый
   ста́рые друзья́
Мы́ ведь ста́рые друзья́.

My good friend Alexeev works there.
   after all, the thing is, as a matter of fact,
You know, as a matter of fact, my good
friend Alexeev works there.

You don't say!

Ivan Ivanovich, put in a good word for me!
   kind, dear, nice
My dear Ivan Ivanovich, put in a good word
for me!

   to suggest, propose
   to you, for you
I wanted to suggest that to you.
   just, the very thing
That's the very thing I wanted to suggest to
you.

   thanks very much, thanks a lot
Thank you very much!

   what for!
Whatever for!

   old
   old friends
We're old friends after all.

SUPPLEMENT

   сло́во (pl слова́)
Э́то ру́сское сло́во?
   рестора́н
Вы́ идёте в рестора́н?
   теа́тр
   Большо́й теа́тр
Вы́ идёте в Большо́й теа́тр?
   кварти́ра
У ва́с е́сть кварти́ра?
   до́м
Э́то ва́ш до́м?

   па́рк
Куда́ вы́ идёте? — В па́рк.

   word
Is that a Russian word?
   restaurant
Are you going to a restaurant?
   theater
   the Bolshoi Theater
Are you going to the Bolshoi Theater?
   apartment
Do you have an apartment?
   house, building
Is that your house? *or* Is that the building
where you live?
   park
Where are you going? To the park.

Замóлвите за меня́ словéчко!

И.И. — Ивáн Ивáнович
Н. — Ни́на

И. И.	1	Здрáвствуйте, Ни́на!	zdrắstujţi ņínə ↓
		С рабóты идёте?	srabŏti iḍóţi ↓
Н.	2	Нéт,	ņḗt ↓
		я́ в горсовéте былá,	já vgorsaɣḗţi bilá↓
		насчёт кóмнаты.	naščót kŏmnəţi ↓
И. И.	3	Какóй кóмнаты?	kakŏj kómnəţi ↓
		В чём дéло?	fčóm ḍélə ↓
Н.	4	Я́ подалá заявлéние	já pədalá zəjivļéņjə
		на кóмнату,	nakŏmnətu ↓
		нó нáдо тáк дóлго	nó nádə tắg dólgə
		ждáть!¹	ždáţ ↓
И. И.	5	Áх, вóт чтó!	áx vŏt štó ↓
		Знáете,	znắjiţi ↓
		ведь тáм рабóтает	ɣiţ tám rabótəjit
		мóй хорóший дрýг Алексéев.	mój xaróšij drúk aḷikşḗjif ↓
Н.	6	Чтó вы́ говори́те!	štó ví gəvaŗíţi ↓
		Ивáн Ивáнович,	iván ivắnich ↓
		ми́лый,	ṃílij ↓
		замóлвите за меня́ словéчко!	zamŏlɣiţi zəṃiņá slaɣéčkə ↓
И. И.	7	Я́ как рáз хотéл	já kak rás xaţél
		вáм э́то предложи́ть.	vám étə pŗidlaží̧ţ ↓
Н.	8	Большóе вáм спаси́бо!	baḷšŏjə vám spaşíbə ↓
И. И.	9	Нý чтó тáм!	nú štŏ tám ↓
		Мы́ ведь стáрые друзья́!	mí ɣiţ stáriji druẓjá ↓

NOTES ¹ In order to obtain a room in a government-owned house, it is necessary to apply to the regional soviet or, in this instance, to the *city council* горсовéт. Waiting lists are very long since housing is one of the major problems in the large cities of the U.S.S.R.

PREPARATION FOR CONVERSATION   **В горсовéте**

секретáрь (m)	secretary
Óн нáш секретáрь.	He's our secretary.
Онá нáш секретáрь.	She's our secretary.
у себя́	in one's room, in one's office

товáрищ	comrade, friend, colleague
Товáрищ Алексéев у себя́?	Is comrade Alexeev in?
Скажи́те, товáрищ Алексéев у себя́?	Tell [me], is comrade Alexeev in?
Москвá	Moscow
Нéт, óн сейчáс в Москвé.	No, he's in Moscow at the moment.
А Вóлков здéсь?	Well, is Volkov here?
проходи́ть (II) (pfv пройти́)	to pass, go by
Дá, проходи́те пожáлуйста!	Yes, go on in, please!
Á, привéт! Давнó тебя́ не ви́дел!	Hi! I haven't seen you in a long time!
кáк живёшь [kág žiγóš]	how are you? how's it going?
Здрáвствуй, кáк живёшь?	Hello, how are you?
Ничегó.	All right.
прóсьба [prózbə]	request, favor
мáленькая	small, little
У меня́ мáленькая прóсьба.	I have a small favor [to ask].
получи́ть (pfv II)	to obtain, receive, get
дéвушка	young lady, girl (in late teens)
однá дéвушка	a certain young lady
Тýт однá дéвушка кóмнаты получи́ть не мóжет.	There's a certain young lady who can't get a room.
никáк	in no way, by no means, not in any way
Тýт однá дéвушка никáк кóмнаты получи́ть не мóжет.	There's a certain young lady who simply can't get a room.
Дá? Ктó онá? Гдé рабóтает?	Is that so? Who is she? Where does she work?
студéнтка–заóчница	correspondence-school student
фáбрика	factory
Онá студéнтка-заóчница, рабóтает на фáбрике.	She's a correspondence-school student and works at a factory.
Агá, на фáбрике. Э́то хорошó.	Ahhh, at a factory. That's good.
сдéлать (pfv I)	to do, get done
чтó-нибудь	something, anything
Мы́ чтó-нибудь сдéлаем.	We'll do something [about it].
Вóт спаси́бо!	Well, thanks.

SUPPLEMENT

жи́ть (ipfv I)	to live
Гдé вы́ живёте?	Where do you live?
— Я́ живу́ прóтив пáрка.	I live across from the park.
откýда	from where
Откýда вы́ идёте? — С рабóты.	Where are you coming from? From work.
из or изо (plus gen)	from, out of
Откýда вы́ идёте? — Из гóрода.	Where are you coming from? From town.
от or ото (plus gen)	from

Я получи́л письмо́ от бра́та.	I received a letter from my brother.
до (*plus* gen)	up to, until, before
Óн звони́л до рабо́ты.	He called (*or* telephoned) before work.
о́коло (*plus* gen)	near, by, about
Я живу́ о́коло па́рка.	I live near the park.
без *or* безо (*plus* gen)	without
Я без бра́та не пойду́.	I won't go without my brother.
для (*plus* gen)	for
Вы́ э́то сде́лаете для меня́?	Will you do that for me?

В горсове́те

И.И. — Ива́н Ива́нович
С. — Секрета́рь (Ири́на Петро́вна)
В. — Во́лков (Пётр Ники́тич)

И.И.	1	Здра́вствуйте,	zdrǎstujṭi |
		Ири́на Петро́вна!	iṛínə ṗitrǒvnə ↓
		Скажи́те,	skažíṭi ↓
		това́рищ Алексе́ев у себя́?¹	taváṛišč aḷikṣéjif uṣiḅǎ ↑
С.	2	Не́т,	ņḗt ↓
		о́н сейча́с в Москве́.	ón ṣičás vmaskṿḗ ↓
И.И.	3	А Во́лков зде́сь?	a vólkəv zḏéṣ ↑
С.	4	Да́,	dǎ ↓
		проходи́те, пожа́луйста!	prəxaḏíṭi pažáləstə ↓
И.И.	5	А́,	ǎ ↓
		приве́т, Во́лков!	pṛiɣét vólkəf ↓
		Давно́ тебя́ не ви́дел.	davnǒ ṭiḅá ņiɣíḏil ↓
В.	6	Здра́вствуй,	zdrǎstuj ↓
		ка́к живёшь?	kág žiɣǒš ↓
И.И.	7	Ничего́.	ņičivǒ ↓
		У меня́ ма́ленькая про́сьба.	uṃiṇá máḷiṇkəjə prǒẓbə ↓
		Ту́т одна́ де́вушка	tút adná ḏévuškə |
		ко́мнаты получи́ть не мо́жет.	kǒmnəti pəlučíṭ ņimóžit ↓
В.	8	Да́?	dǎ ↑
		Кто́ она́?	ktǒ aná ↓
		Где́ рабо́тает?	gḏé rabǒtəjit ↓

И.И.	9 Она́ студе́нтка-зао́чница, рабо́тает на фа́брике.	aná studéntkə zaŏčŗicə ↓ rabótəjit nafãbŗiķi ↓
В.	10 Ага́, на фа́брике. Э́то хорошо́. Мы́ что́-нибудь сде́лаем.²	ahã ↓ nafãbŗiķi ↓ étə xərašŏ ↓ mí štóŗibuḍ zḍélǝjim ↓
И.И.	11 Во́т спаси́бо.	võt spaşíbə ↓

NOTES

¹ Here **това́рищ** means *comrade* in the political sense, i.e., a party member. It is very common in official situations, however, for Soviet citizens to use the word (especially in the plural) without any necessary implication that persons so addressed are party members. A foreigner should never use **това́рищ** in addressing a Soviet citizen.

Това́рищ is also used in the nonpolitical sense, meaning *comrade* or *friend*, but it implies a more casual relationship than **дру́г** *friend*. One may have many **това́рищи,** but few **друзья́.**

Both **дру́г** and **това́рищ,** like **профе́ссор** and **секрета́рь,** are grammatically masculine, but may refer to both men and women:

О́н мо́й хоро́ший дру́г.	He's my good friend.
Она́ мо́й хоро́ший дру́г.	She's my good friend.
Това́рищ Петро́в бы́л зде́сь.	Comrade Petrov was here.
Това́рищ Петро́ва была́ зде́сь.	Comrade Petrov (f) was here.

² Students who work at factories and take correspondence courses have a priority in obtaining lodgings. The Soviet **студе́нт-зао́чник** or **студе́нтка-зао́чница** differs somewhat from the American correspondence-school student in that the latter does his entire work through correspondence. The Soviet correspondence-school student must meet at least once or twice a year for laboratory sessions, summary lectures, consultations on future work, and examinations.

Basic sentence patterns

1. Вы́ идёте с рабо́ты?	Are you coming from work?
— Не́т, с конце́рта.	No, from a concert.
— Не́т, с обе́да.	No, from a dinner.
— Не́т, с экза́мена.	No, from an exam.
— Не́т, с уро́ка пе́ния.	No, from a singing lesson.
— Не́т, с собра́ния.	No, from a meeting.
— Не́т, с по́чты.	No, from the post office.
— Не́т, с ле́кции.	No, from a lecture.
2. Вы́ идёте из клу́ба?	Are you coming from the club?
— Не́т, из рестора́на.	No, from the restaurant.
— Не́т, из теа́тра.	No, from the theater.
— Не́т, из па́рка.	No, from the park.
— Не́т, из университе́та.	No, from the university.

— Нет, из ГУМа.   No, from GUM.
— Нет, из горсовета.   No, from the gorsovet.
— Нет, из общежития.   No, from the dormitory.
— Нет, из библиотеки.   No, from the library.
— Нет, из лаборатории.   No, from the laboratory.

3. Я его видел до урока.   I saw him before the lesson.
_____ концерта.   _____ the concert.
_____ обеда.   _____ dinner (or noon).[1]
_____ чая.   _____ tea.[2]
_____ экзамена.   _____ the exam.
_____ собрания.   _____ the meeting.
_____ лекции.   _____ the lecture.
_____ работы.   _____ work.
_____ службы.   _____ work.

4. После урока он пошёл домой.   After the lesson he went home.
_____ концерта _____.   _____ the concert _____.
_____ собрания _____.   _____ the meeting _____.
_____ чая _____.   _____ the tea _____.
_____ экзамена _____.   _____ the exam _____.

5. Сразу после обеда мы пошли домой.   Right after the dinner we went home.
_____ собрания _____.   _____ the meeting _____.
_____ лекции _____.   _____ the lecture _____.
_____ работы _____.   _____ work _____.
_____ школы _____.   _____ school _____.

6. Это для вас.   This is for you.
_____ тебя.   _____ you.
_____ нас.   _____ us.
_____ него.   _____ him.
_____ неё.   _____ her.
_____ них.   _____ them.

7. Мы это сделаем для Ивана.   We'll do it for Ivan.
_____ Нины.   _____ Nina.
_____ профессора Орлова.   _____ Professor Orlov.
_____ учителя.   _____ the teacher.
_____ учительницы.   _____ the teacher.

8. Они без вас не пойдут.   They won't go without you.
_____ нас _____.   _____ us.
_____ тебя _____.   _____ you.
_____ меня _____.   _____ me.
_____ него _____.   _____ him.

9. Мы без неё не пойдём.   We won't go without her.
_____ Ивана _____.   _____ Ivan.
_____ Ирины _____.   _____ Irina.
_____ Коли _____.   _____ Kolya.

---

[1] Обед is frequently used in the sense *noon*. Thus до обеда may mean both *before dinner* and *before noon*. Similarly, после обеда means both *after dinner* and *afternoon*, as well as *in the afternoon*.
[2] Чай is often used to refer to breakfast or morning tea.

10. Где вы́ бы́ли?
  — У профе́ссора Орло́ва.
  — У дру́га.
  — У Ива́на.
  — У Петра́.

Where have you been?
To see Professor Orlov.
To see a friend.
To see Ivan.
To see Pyotr.

11. Где вы́ обе́дали?
  — У Никола́я.
  — У бра́та.
  — У сестры́.
  — У Ни́ны.
  — У Га́ли.
  — У Мари́и Ива́новны.

Where did you eat dinner?
At Nikolay's.
At my brother's.
At my sister's.
At Nina's.
At Galya's.
At Maria Ivanovna's.

12. Отку́да вы́?
  — Из Ленингра́да.
  — Из Кита́я.
  — Из Москвы́.
  — Из Евро́пы.
  — Из Аме́рики.
  — Из СССР.

Where are you from?
From Leningrad.
From China.
From Moscow.
From Europe.
From America.
From the U.S.S.R.

13. Отку́да вы́ идёте?
  — Из ГУ́Ма.
  — Из го́рода.
  — Из магази́на на углу́.
  — Из библиоте́ки.
  — С рабо́ты.
  — С по́чты.
  — С фа́брики.
  — С заво́да.

Where are you coming from?
From GUM.
From town.
From the store on the corner.
From the library.
From work.
From the post office.
From the factory.
From the plant.

14. Отку́да вы́ э́то получи́ли?
  — Из клу́ба.
  — Из библиоте́ки.
  — Из лаборато́рии.
  — С фа́брики.
  — С заво́да.

Where did you get that?
From the club.
From the library.
From the laboratory.
From the factory.
From the plant.

15. От кого́ вы́ э́то получи́ли?
  — От профе́ссора Орло́ва.
  — От америка́нца.
  — От Влади́мира.
  — От Петра́.
  — От Евге́ния.

From whom did you get that?
From Professor Orlov.
From an American.
From Vladimir.
From Pyotr.
From Evgeny.

16. От кого́ вы́ э́то слы́шали?
  — От секретаря́.
  — От учи́теля.
  — От сестры́.
  — От Ири́ны.
  — От Мари́и Ива́новны.

From whom did you hear that?
From the secretary.
From the teacher.
From my sister.
From Irina.
From Maria Ivanovna.

17. Где ваш дом?

   — Около парка.

   — Около университета.

   — Около театра.

   — Около ресторана.

   — Около общежития.

   — Около почты.

   — Около фабрики.

   — Около школы.

   — Около библиотеки.

Where's your house?

Near the park.

Near the university.

Near the theater.

Near the restaurant.

Near the dormitory.

Near the post office.

Near the factory.

Near the school.

Near the library.

18. Где библиотека? — Против театра.

Где общежитие? — Против парка.

Где киоск? — Против ресторана.

Где театр? — Против университета.

Где ресторан? — Против ГУМа.

Где клуб? — Против библиотеки.

Где ваш дом? — Против школы.

Где магазин? — Против почты.

Где большой зал? — Против лаборатории.

Где школа? — Против фабрики.

Где лаборатория? — Против аудитории.

Where's the library? Across from the theater.

Where's the dorm? Across from the park.

Where's the newsstand? Across from the restaurant.

Where's the theater? Across from the university.

Where's the restaurant? Across from GUM.

Where's the club? Across from the library.

Where's your house? Across from the school.

Where's the store? Across from the post office.

Where's the large hall? Across from the laboratory.

Where's the school? Across from the factory.

Where's the laboratory? Across from the auditorium.

19. Вы спрашивали насчёт обеда?

   _____ борща?

   _____ чая?

   _____ молока?

   _____ рыбы?

   _____ каши?

   _____ селёдки?

   _____ водки?

Did you ask about dinner?

_____ borsch?

_____ tea?

_____ milk?

_____ fish?

_____ kasha?

_____ herring?

_____ vodka?

20. А как насчёт собрания?

   _____ сочинения?

   _____ карты?

   _____ литературы?

   _____ географии?

   _____ атласа?

   _____ портфеля?

And how about the meeting?

_____ the composition?

_____ a map?

_____ literature?

_____ geography?

_____ an atlas?

_____ a briefcase?

21. Вы насчёт урока?

   _____ экзамена?

   _____ собрания?

   _____ комнаты?

   _____ квартиры?

   _____ работы?

Are you here about the lesson?

_____ the exam?

_____ the meeting?

_____ the room?

_____ the apartment?

_____ the work?

Pronunciation practice: hard consonants [k], [g], and [x] and their soft counterparts [ķ], [g̑], and [x̧].

Hard consonants [k], [g], and [x] are regularly replaced by their soft counterparts [ķ], [g̑], and [x̧] before vowels [e] and [i].

A. Hard [k] and soft counterpart [ķ]
    Usual Cyrillic spelling к; sometimes г.

Note the pronunciation of hard [k] in the following:

[maskvá]	Москва́	Moscow
[kudá]	куда́	where (to)
[urók]	уро́к	lesson
[skaží]	скажи́	tell me

and compare it with soft [ķ]:

[γílķi]	ви́лки	forks
[fkarópķi]	в коро́бке	in the box
[uróķi]	уро́ки	lessons
[ņiķítə]	Ники́та	Nikita
[carápķin]	Цара́пкин	Tsarapkin

Russian hard [k] is made in much the same way as English *k* except that there is not the slight h-like puff of breath typical of the English *k*.

> Sound Drill: Practice the Russian examples illustrating hard [k] and soft [ķ], imitating your instructor (or the tape) as accurately as you can. Notice that hard [k] occurs before [o], [a], [u], and [ə], whereas soft [k] occurs before [e] and [i]. At the end of a word, only hard [k] occurs—never soft [ķ].

B. Hard [g] and soft counterpart [g̑]
    Usual Cyrillic spelling г; sometimes к.

Note the pronunciation of hard [g] in the following:

| [gəvaŗát] | говоря́т | they say |
| [vgúɱi] | в ГУ́Ме | at GUM |

and compare it with soft [g̑]:

| [jivg̑éņij] | Евге́ний | Evgeny |
| [g̑ít] | гид | guide |

Russian hard [g] and soft [g̑] are made with the vocal organs in the same position as for hard [k] and soft [ķ], but they are voiced.

C. Hard [x] and soft counterpart [x̢]
Usual Cyrillic spelling **x**; rarely **г**.

Note the pronunciation of hard [x] in the following:

[xərašó]	хорошó	good
[zəxaḍíṭi]	заходи́те	come in

and compare it with soft [x̢]:

[x̢itróf]	Хитрóв	Khitrov
[sx̢émə]	схéма	scheme

The sound [x] does not occur in English (though it does appear in German a*ch*, Ba*ch*, and
Bu*ch*, or in Spanish mu*j*er and hi*j*o). It is formed in the same part of the mouth as [k] and [g]; but,
instead of completely closing off the air stream, the back of the tongue merely approaches the back
part of the roof of the mouth so that the air stream vibrates in the constricted passage thus produced.
The soft counterpart [x̢] is produced slightly further forward in the mouth.

Intonation practice: emphatic statements with rising-falling intonation curve

Emphatic statements with rising-falling contours are those in which the major stress is not in the
final position, but is shifted forward to a medial position in the sentences. The intonation contour
is similar to that of questions without question words which have their major stress in the medial
position, except that the entire contour is on a lower level and the drop after the major stress is
sharper.

EMPHATIC INTONATION   QUESTION INTONATION

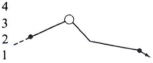   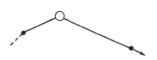

Óн **нé был** на слýжбе!	Óн **нé был** на слýжбе?
Они́ **бы́ли** на завóде.	Они́ **бы́ли** на завóде?
Она́ **доста́ла** материа́л.	Она́ **доста́ла** материа́л?
У на́с **éсть** ча́й.	У на́с **éсть** ча́й?

A. Listen to the tape and practice the intonation in the following emphatic statements.

B. Now practice these same sentences as questions. Remember that the rising-falling contour is neutral for questions and does not imply any special emphasis.

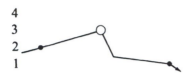

Она́ **купи́ла** материа́л!
Ива́н **опя́ть** ту́т!
Вчера́ **бы́ло** собра́ние!
Мари́я **не была́** в ГУ́Ме!
Оле́г **давно́** бо́лен!

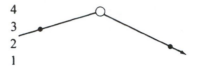

Она́ купи́ла материа́л?
Ива́н опя́ть ту́т?
Вчера́ бы́ло собра́ние?
Мари́я не была́ в ГУ́Ме?
Оле́г давно́ бо́лен?

C. Using the same basic sentences, practice them as neutral statements now. Note that here the intonation curve has a falling contour and that the primary stress is on the last stressed syllable.

D. Practice the following set of longer statements with neutral intonation. Again the contour is falling and the primary stress is on the last stressed syllable of the utterance.

Она́ купи́ла материа́л.
Ива́н опя́ть ту́т.
Вчера́ бы́ло собра́ние.
Мари́я не была́ в ГУ́Ме.
Оле́г давно́ бо́лен.

Бори́с мо́жет э́то принести́.
Никола́й был вчера́ в библиоте́ке.
Она́ смо́жет откры́ть две́ри.
Оле́г хоте́л принести́ слова́рь.
Козло́в был вчера́ на заня́тиях.
Она́ пойдёт за́втра в клу́б.

E. Practice the same sentences, changing them to emphatic statements with a rising-falling contour and with the primary stress shifted to the second element.

F. Now practice the same sentences, changing them to *questions*. Again the contour is rising-falling and the primary stress is on the second element. Note the sharper peak and drop that is typical of the question, as contrasted with the emphatic statements.

Бори́с **мо́жет** э́то принести́!
Никола́й **был** вчера́ в библиоте́ке!
Она́ **смо́жет** откры́ть две́ри!
Оле́г хоте́л принести́ слова́рь!
Козло́в **был** вчера́ на заня́тиях!
Она́ **пойдёт** за́втра в клу́б!

Бори́с мо́жет э́то принести́?
Никола́й был вчера́ в библиоте́ке?
Она́ смо́жет откры́ть две́ри?
Оле́г хоте́л принести́ слова́рь?
Козло́в был вчера́ на заня́тиях?
Она́ пойдёт за́втра в клу́б?

The preposition y: further uses with the genitive case

MODELS

Она́ стоя́ла у две́ри.	She was standing at (or by) the door.
_____ у окна́.	_____ at (or by) the window.
_____ у стола́.	_____ at (or by) the table.
_____ у шка́фа.	_____ at (or by) the cupboard.
_____ у телефо́на.	_____ at (or by) the phone.

Я был у бра́та.	I was at my brother's place.
___ у Оле́га.	___ at Oleg's place.
___ у Петра́.	___ at Pyotr's ___.
___ у профе́ссора Орло́ва.	___ at Professor Orlov's ___.
___ у дру́га.	___ at a friend's ___.
___ у Льва́.	___ at Lev's ___.
___ у Никола́я.	___ at Nikolay's ___.
___ у сестры́.	___ at my sister's ___.
___ у Мари́и Ива́новны.	___ at Maria Ivanovna's ___.
___ у Га́ли.	___ at Galya's ___.
___ у Ко́ли.	___ at Kolya's ___.

Он э́то доста́л у Козло́ва.	He got it from Kozlov.
_____ у учи́теля.	_____ from the teacher.
_____ у секретаря́.	_____ from the secretary.
_____ у Ири́ны.	_____ from Irina.
_____ у Мари́и.	_____ from Maria.
_____ у Га́ли.	_____ from Galya.
_____ у Коли.	_____ from Kolya.

У кого́ вы э́то узна́ли?	From whom did you find that out?
— У профе́ссора Орло́ва.	From Professor Orlov.
— У бра́та.	From my brother.
— У му́жа.	From my husband.
— У Петра́.	From Pyotr.
— У Евге́ния.	From Evgeny.
— У секретаря́.	From the secretary.
— У това́рища Алексе́ева.	From comrade Alexeev.
— У сестры́.	From my sister.
— У О́ли.	From Olya.
— У убо́рщицы.	From the cleaning woman.
— У жены́.	From my wife.

У кого́ вы спра́шивали?	Whom did you ask? Or Of whom did you inquire?
— У Кири́лла.	Kirill.
— У Влади́мира.	Vladimir.
— У Цара́пкина.	Tsarapkin.
— У Во́лкова.	Volkov.
— У Семёна Фили́пповича.	Semyon Filippovich.

— У учи́теля.	The teacher.
— У Никола́я.	Nikolay.
— У Ми́лы.	Mila.
— У Ма́ши.	Masha.
— У Мари́и Петро́вны.	Maria Petrovna.
— У продавщи́цы.	The saleslady.

Ка́к у ва́с прошёл экза́мен?	How did your exam go?
____ у Оле́га _____?	_____ Oleg's _____?
____ у него́ _____?	_____ his _____?
____ у Ни́ны _____?	_____ Nina's _____?
____ у неё _____?	_____ her _____?
____ у ни́х _____?	_____ their _____?
____ у Никола́я _____?	_____ Nikolay's __?

■ REPETITION-DRILL

Repeat the above models after your instructor or the tape until you are familiar with the various y constructions illustrated.

■ CUED SUBSTITUTION DRILLS

1. (window) *There was a girl standing at the window.*
   т: (окно́) У окна́ стоя́ла де́вушка.
   s: **У окна́ стоя́ла де́вушка.**
   т: (две́рь) (У) _____.
   s: **У две́ри стоя́ла де́вушка.**
   (полка, стол, шкаф, карта, телефон, окно, дверь)

2. (brother) *Yesterday he visited his brother.*
   т: (бра́т) Вчера́ о́н бы́л у бра́та.
   s: **Вчера́ о́н бы́л у бра́та.**
   т: (сестра́) (Вчера́) _____.
   s: **Вчера́ о́н бы́л у сестры́.**
   (друг, Николай, Коля, Ирина, Мила, Мария Ивановна, учитель, товарищ Волков)

3. (Pyotr) *Have you already asked* (or *inquired of*) *Pyotr?*
   т: (Пётр) Вы́ уже́ спра́шивали у Петра́?
   s: **Вы́ уже́ спра́шивали у Петра́?**
   т: (О́льга) (Вы́) _____?
   s: **Вы́ уже́ спра́шивали у О́льги?**
   (она, Владимир, они, Нина, Коля, он, Курочкин, Иван Иванович)

4. (you) *He left the briefcase at your place.*
   т: (вы́) О́н забы́л у ва́с портфе́ль.
   s: **О́н забы́л у ва́с портфе́ль.**
   т: (они́) (О́н) _____.
   s: **О́н забы́л у ни́х портфе́ль.**
   (она, я, ты, Иван, Нина, её муж, Борис, Ирина)

■ SUBJECT REVERSAL DRILLS

1. *They're at Professor Orlov's.*
   Professor Orlov is at their place.
   т: Они́ у профе́ссора Орло́ва.
   s: **Профе́ссор Орло́в у ни́х.**
   т: Я́ у бра́та.
   s: **Бра́т у меня́.**
   Мы́ у Льва́ Ники́тича.
   О́н у Га́ли.
   Они́ у сестры́.
   Она́ у учи́теля.
   Я́ у сестры́.

2. *Kozlov was visiting Pyotr.*
   Pyotr was visiting Kozlov.
   т: Козло́в бы́л у Петра́.
   s: **Пётр бы́л у Козло́ва.**
   т: Козло́в бы́л у Льва́ Ники́тича.
   s: **Ле́в Ники́тич бы́л у Козло́ва.**
   Ко́ля бы́л у Га́ли.
   Бра́т бы́л у сестры́.
   Учи́тель бы́л у учи́тельницы.
   Мари́я была́ у профе́ссора.

1. *Did Irina get that?*
   Yes, and I [got it] from Irina.

T: Это Ири́на доста́ла?

S: **Да́, а я́ у Ири́ны.**

T: Это учи́тель доста́л?

S: **Да́, а я́ у учи́теля.**

    (брат, Козлов, учительница, ректор, Иван, её муж, продавщица, секретарь, Лев Никитич)

2. *Did Pyotr find that out?*
   Yes, and I [found out] from Pyotr.

T: Это Пётр узна́л?

S: **Да́, а я́ у Петра́.**

T: Это Никола́й узна́л?

S: **Да́, а я́ у Никола́я.**

    (Мария, Владимир, её сестра, Семёнов, его жена, Коля, профессор Петров, Лев Никитич)

■ CUED QUESTION-ANSWER DRILL

  (*teacher*)   *Whom did you ask?*
                The teacher.

T: (учи́тель)   У кого́ вы́ спра́шивали?

S: **У учи́теля.**

T: (учи́тельница) У кого́ вы́ спра́шивали?

S: **У учи́тельницы.**

  (американец, её муж, уборщица, Коля, профессор Петров, Ирина, Галя, Лев Никитич)

■ RESPONSE DRILL

Kolya's coming.
Wonder how his exam went.

T: Ко́ля идёт.

S: **Интере́сно, ка́к у него́ прошёл экза́мен?**

T: Мари́я идёт.

S: **Интере́сно, ка́к у неё прошёл экза́мен?**

  (Николай, Ирина и Оля, Галя, Иван Иванович, Маша)

■ CUED QUESTION-ANSWER DRILLS

1.   (*Kolya*) *Where's the briefcase?*
             On Kolya's desk.

T: (Ко́ля) Где́ портфе́ль?

S: **У Ко́ли на столе́.**

T: (они́) Где́ портфе́ль?

S: **У ни́х на столе́.**

  (я, ты, она, мы, вы, он, Галя, Николай, учительница, учитель)

2.   (*window*) *Where was Nina standing?*
             At the window.

T: (окно́) Где́ стоя́ла Ни́на?

S: **У окна́.**

T: (телефо́н) Где́ стоя́ла Ни́на?

S: **У телефо́на.**

  (дверь, шкаф, карта, полка, стол, окно)

DISCUSSION

The preposition **y** is always followed by the genitive case. Besides its use in *to have* constructions (e.g., **у меня́ е́сть**), it has several other functions.

1. In a purely spatial sense with inanimate nouns, it indicates close proximity.

    О́н стоя́л **у окна́.**   He was standing at (*or* by) the window.

    Подожди́ **у две́ри.**   Wait at (*or* by) the door.

2. With nouns and pronouns referring to people, it designates a place in terms of the person located there. Thus it functions like the French *chez* and may be translated *at the house* (or *office* or *place*) *of*. Forms of the verb **бы́ть** plus **y** often correspond to the English concept *to visit*.

    Я́ оста́вил **у ва́с** портфе́ль.   I left the briefcase at your place.

    Она́ была́ **у бра́та.**   She was at her brother's *or* She was visiting her brother.

3. Used with nouns and pronouns referring to people, and in conjunction with such verbs as **узнáть, спрáшивать,** and **достáть, у** indicates the source of a thing.

У когó вы́ э́то достáли?	*From whom* did you get that?
— У Ири́ны.	*From Irina.*
У когó ты́ э́то узнáл?	*From whom* did you find that out?
— У Кóли.	*From Kolya.*
У когó вы́ спрáшивали?	*Whom* did you ask? or *Of whom* did you inquire?
— У секретаря́.	*The secretary.*

4. The use of **у** plus the genitive form of a noun or pronoun sometimes substitutes for a possessive modifier, especially if there is no real possession involved.

Кáк прошёл **у тебя́** урóк?	How did *your* lesson go?
Ктó **у вáс** учи́тель?	Who's *your* teacher?

Prepositions meaning *from:* из, с, and от

Óн идёт из пáрка.	He's coming from the park.
_____ из теáтра.	_____ from the theater.
_____ из ресторáна.	_____ from the restaurant.
_____ из университéта.	_____ from the university.
_____ из общежи́тия.	_____ from the dormitory.
_____ из библиотéки.	_____ from the library.
_____ из лаборатóрии.	_____ from the laboratory.
_____ из шкóлы.	_____ from the school.

Онá идёт с концéрта.	She's coming from the concert.
_____ с урóка.	_____ from a lesson.
_____ с завóда.	_____ from the plant.
_____ с обéда.	_____ from dinner.
_____ с собрáния.	_____ from the meeting.
_____ с фáбрики.	_____ from the factory.
_____ с рабóты.	_____ from work.
_____ со слýжбы.	_____ from work.
_____ с лéкции.	_____ from the lecture.
_____ с пóчты.	_____ from the post office.

Óн получи́л письмó от брáта.	He received a letter from his brother.
_____ от дрýга.	_____ from a friend.
_____ от Николáя.	_____ from Nikolay.
_____ от сестры́.	_____ from his sister.
_____ от жены́.	_____ from his wife.
_____ от Óли.	_____ from Olya.
_____ от Мари́и.	_____ from Maria.

Óн получи́л от неё письмо́ из Москвы́.	He got a letter from her from Moscow.
——————— от него́ ———————.	——————— from him ———————.
——————— от ни́х ———————.	——————— from them ———————.
.——————— от меня́ ———————.	——————— from me ———————.
——————— от на́с ———————.	——————— from us ———————.
——————— от ва́с ———————.	——————— from you ———————.
——————— от тебя́ ———————.	——————— from you ———————.

■ REPETITION DRILL

Repeat the above models, noting that the preposition **из** *from* is the directional opposite of the preposition **в** *to,* and that the preposition **с** *from* is the directional opposite of the preposition **на** *to.*

■ STRUCTURE REPLACEMENT DRILLS

1. *He's going to the park.*
   He's coming from the park.
   т: О́н идёт в па́рк.
   s: **О́н идёт из па́рка.**
   т: О́н идёт в рестора́н.
   s: **О́н идёт из рестора́на.**
   (в библиоте́ку, в общежи́тие, в теа́тр, в горсове́т, в клу́б, в шко́лу, в университе́т, в аудито́рию, в магази́н)

2. *They're going to the concert.*
   They're coming from the concert.
   т: Они́ иду́т на конце́рт.
   s: **Они́ иду́т с конце́рта.**
   т: Они́ иду́т на слу́жбу.
   s: **Они́ иду́т со слу́жбы.**
   (на уро́к, на по́чту, на собра́ние, на обе́д, на фа́брику, на экза́мен, на рабо́ту, на ле́кцию)

■ RESPONSE DRILL

Vladimir was in Moscow recently.
Did you get a letter from Vladimir?
т: Влади́мир неда́вно бы́л в Москве́.
s: **Вы́ получи́ли от Влади́мира письмо́?**
т: Ири́на неда́вно была́ в Москве́.
s: **Вы́ получи́ли от Ири́ны письмо́?**
(Кири́лл, он, она́, они́, я, мы, Са́ша, Ни́на, она́)

■ STRUCTURE REPLACEMENT DRILLS

1. *She sent a letter to Moscow.*
   She received a letter from Moscow.
   т: Она́ посла́ла письмо́ в Москву́.
   s: **Она́ получи́ла письмо́ из Москвы́.**
   т: Она́ посла́ла письмо́ в Ленингра́д.
   s: **Она́ получи́ла письмо́ из Ленингра́да.**
   Она́ посла́ла письмо́ в Аме́рику.
   Она́ посла́ла письмо́ в Кита́й.
   Она́ посла́ла письмо́ в Евро́пу.
   Она́ посла́ла письмо́ в СССР.

2. *They were at the concert.*
   They're coming from the concert.
   т: Они́ бы́ли на конце́рте.
   s: **Они́ иду́т с конце́рта.**
   т: Они́ бы́ли в па́рке.
   s: **Они́ иду́т из па́рка.**
   (в библиоте́ке, на фа́брике, на по́чте, в магази́не, на ле́кции, на экза́мене, в рестора́не, в теа́тре, на собра́нии, в общежи́тии)

1. *I was at my brother's place.*
I heard it from my brother.

т: Я был у бра́та.

s: **Я э́то слы́шал от бра́та.**

т: Я был у сестры́.

s: **Я э́то слы́шал от сестры́.**

(у дру́га, у Ни́ны, у профе́ссора Орло́ва, у Са́ши, у ре́ктора, у него́, у неё, у них)

2. *The spoons are in the drawer.*
Take the spoons from the drawer.

т: Ло́жки в я́щике.

s: **Возьми́ ло́жки из я́щика.**

т: Ло́жки на столе́.

s: **Возьми́ ло́жки со стола́.**

(в шкафу́, на шкафу́, в коро́бке, на сту́ле, на по́лке, в портфе́ле, в я́щике)

■ CUED QUESTION-ANSWER DRILL

(*Moscow*) *Where did he phone from?*
From Moscow.

т: (Москва́) Отку́да о́н звони́л?

s: **Из Москвы́.**

т: (Ленингра́д) Отку́да о́н звони́л?

s: **Из Ленингра́да.**

(магази́н на углу́, ГУМ, горсове́т, университе́т, общежи́тие, го́род, шко́ла, библиоте́ка)

■ STRUCTURE REPLACEMENT DRILL

He was at the plant.
He phoned from the plant.

т: О́н бы́л на заво́де.

s: **О́н звони́л с заво́да.**

т: О́н бы́л на слу́жбе.

s: **О́н звони́л со слу́жбы.**

(на по́чте, на рабо́те, на фа́брике, на слу́жбе)

■ RESPONSE DRILL

My friend is in Moscow.
I received a letter from Moscow.

т: Мо́й дру́г в Москве́.

s: **Я получи́л письмо́ из Москвы́.**

т: Мо́й дру́г в Ленингра́де.

s: **Я получи́л письмо́ из Ленингра́да.**

(в Кита́е, в Москве́, в Евро́пе, в Аме́рике, в СССР)

DISCUSSION

All three prepositions, **из**, **с**, and **от**, mean *from*, but each is limited in its sphere of usage: nouns or pronouns referring to people require **от**, but for places and things **из** and **с** are generally used. **Из** is used with inanimate nouns which take the preposition **в**, whereas **с** is used with nouns which take **на**.

Она́ идёт **в го́род.**	She's going *to town.*
Она́ идёт **из го́рода.**	She's coming *from town.*
Она́ идёт **на ле́кцию.**	She's going *to the lecture.*
Она́ идёт **с ле́кции.**	She's coming *from the lecture.*

Notes

1. The preposition **с** has a variant form **со**, used before certain consonant clusters:

Она́ идёт **со слу́жбы.**	She's coming *from* work.
Возьми́ каранда́ш **со стола́**!	Take the pencil *from* the table!

2. The prepositions **из** and **от** also have variants **изо** and **ото,** but these occur far less frequently, for example:

изо дня́ в де́нь	day in, day out
де́нь **ото** дня́	from day to day

3. All prepositions are pronounced as a unit with the word that follows. Prepositions **от** and **из,** like most short prepositions, are normally pronounced without a stress: **от него́** [atɲivó], **из го́рода** [izgórədə]. When preposition **с** precedes a word beginning with another **с,** it is pronounced without a break as a long [s]: **с собра́ния** [ssabráɲjə].

Other prepositions requiring the genitive case

MODELS

Я его́ ви́дел по́сле уро́ка.	I saw him after the lesson.
_____ конце́рта.	_____ the concert.
_____ экза́мена.	_____ the exam.
_____ обе́да.	_____ dinner.
_____ собра́ния.	_____ the meeting.
_____ ле́кции.	_____ the lecture.
_____ рабо́ты.	_____ work.
_____ шко́лы.	_____ school.

Я хочу́ э́то сде́лать до уро́ка.	I want to get it done before the lesson.
_____ до конце́рта.	_____ before the concert.
_____ до экза́мена.	_____ before the exam.
_____ до собра́ния.	_____ before the meeting.
_____ до ле́кции.	_____ before the lecture.

Для кого́ э́то?	Who is this for?
— Для меня́.	For me.
— Для тебя́.	For you.
— Для него́.	For him.
— Для неё.	For her.
— Для ни́х.	For them.
— Для ва́с.	For you.
— Для на́с.	For us.
— Для профе́ссора.	For the professor.
— Для учи́тельницы.	For the teacher.

Где́ о́н живёт?	Where does he live?
— О́н живёт про́тив па́рка.	He lives opposite the park.
_____ теа́тра.	_____ the theater.
_____ рестора́на.	_____ the restaurant.
_____ общежи́тия.	_____ the dormitory.
_____ по́чты.	_____ the post office.
_____ шко́лы.	_____ the school.
_____ фа́брики	_____ the factory.
_____ библиоте́ки.	_____ the library.

Где они живут?		Where do they live?
— Они живут около парка.		They live near the park.
_____ театра.		_____ the theater.
_____ ресторана.		_____ the restaurant.
_____ завода.		_____ the plant.
_____ общежития.		_____ the dormitory.
_____ почты.		_____ the post office.
_____ школы.		_____ the school.
_____ фабрики.		_____ the factory.
_____ библиотеки.		_____ the library.

Как насчёт хлеба?		How about bread?
_____ борща?		_____ borsch?
_____ чая?		_____ tea?
_____ молока?		_____ milk?
_____ рыбы?		_____ fish?
_____ каши?		_____ kasha?
_____ селёдки?		_____ herring?

■ REPETITION DRILL

Repeat the given models, noting that all six prepositions (после, до, для, против, около, and насчёт) require the genitive form of the noun or pronoun following.

■ QUESTION-ANSWER DRILLS

1. *When did you see her, after the concert?*
   No, before the concert.
   т: Когда вы её видели, после концерта?
   s: Нет, до концерта.
   т: Когда вы её видели, после лекции?
   s: Нет, до лекции.
   (после работы, после собрания, после школы, после урока, после обеда, после службы)

2. *Where did she wait for him, at the club?*
   No, opposite the club.
   т: Где она его ждала, в клубе?
   s: Нет, против клуба.
   т: Где она его ждала, в библиотеке?
   s: Нет, против библиотеки.
   (на фабрике, в общежитии, на заводе, на почте, в ресторане, в аудитории, в лаборатории, в клубе)

3. *Where did you wait, in the restaurant?*
   No, on the corner near the restaurant.
   т: Где вы ждали, в ресторане?
   s: Нет, на углу около ресторана.
   т: Где вы ждали, в библиотеке?
   s: Нет, на углу около библиотеки.
   (на почте, в парке, на фабрике, в горсовете, на заводе, в школе)

4. *Do you live near the park?*
   Just opposite the park.
   т: Вы живёте около парка?
   s: Как раз против парка.
   т: Вы живёте около школы?
   s: Как раз против школы.
   (около завода, около клуба, около горсовета, около библиотеки, около ресторана, около общежития, около театра)

5. *When did he call, before the meeting?*
   No, after the meeting.
   т: Когда он звонил, до собрания?
   s: Нет, после собрания.

   т: Когда он звонил, до обеда?
   s: Нет, после обеда.
   (до лекции, до работы, до концерта, до урока, до клуба, до службы, до школы)

1. *Where is he?*
   We won't go without him.
   т: Где́ же о́н?
   s: **Мы́ без него́ не пойдём.**
   т: Где́ же Ири́на?
   s: **Мы́ без Ири́ны не пойдём.**
     (они, Кирилл, она, Саша, Олег)

2. *He isn't here yet.*
   I won't go without him.
   т: Его́ ещё не́т.
   s: **Я́ без него́ не пойду́.**
   т: Га́ли ещё не́т.
   s: **Я́ без Га́ли не пойду́.**
     (Бориса, Нины, её, их, секретаря, его)

3. *Where is he?*
   We bought this for him.
   т: Где́ о́н?
   s: **Мы́ э́то купи́ли для него́.**
   т: Где́ Ни́на?
   s: **Мы́ э́то купи́ли для Ни́ны.**
     (она, Кирилл, Евгений, Алексеев, они,
     Мария Ивановна)

4. *You can buy fish here.*
   How about fish?
   т: Здесь мо́жно купи́ть ры́бу.
   s: **Ка́к насчёт ры́бы?**
   т: Здесь мо́жно купи́ть хле́б.
   s: **Ка́к насчёт хле́ба?**
     (селёдку, молоко, чай, словарь, атлас,
     карту, ручку, стол)

1. *The theater's over there, opposite the post office.*
   The post office is over there, opposite the theater.
   т: Теа́тр вон та́м, про́тив по́чты.
   s: **По́чта вон та́м, про́тив теа́тра.**
   т: Лаборато́рия вон та́м, проти́в аудито́рии.
   s: **Аудито́рия вон та́м, про́тив лаборато́рии.**
     Библиоте́ка вон та́м, против рестора́на.
     Общежи́тие вон та́м, против шко́лы.
     Шко́ла вон та́м, против заво́да.
     Па́рк вон та́м, против фа́брики.
     Магази́н вон та́м, против теа́тра.

2. *He did it for us.*
   We did it for him.
   т: О́н э́то сде́лал для на́с.
   s: **Мы́ э́то сде́лали для него́.**
   т: Она́ э́то сде́лала для ва́с.
   s: **Вы́ э́то сде́лали для неё.**
     Я́ э́то сде́лал для тебя́.
     Они́ э́то сде́лали для него́.
     Мы́ э́то сде́лали для неё.
     Ко́ля э́то сде́лал для Га́ли.
     Сестра́ э́то сде́лала для бра́та.
     Бори́с э́то сде́лал для Ива́на.

3. *He won't go without me.*
   I won't go without him.
   т: О́н без меня́ не пойдёт.
   s: **Я́ без него́ не пойду́.**
   т: Они́ без неё не пойду́т.
   s: **Она́ без ни́х не пойдёт.**
     Мы́ без тебя́ не пойдём.
     Она́ без ни́х не пойдёт.
     Вы́ без на́с не пойдёте.
     Я́ без него́ не пойду́.

DISCUSSION

Unlike most of the shorter prepositions, which are ordinarily pronounced with no stress, the prepositions о́коло, про́тив, по́сле, and насчёт are pronounced with stress. Although weaker than the stress of the word following, they serve to maintain the [o] vowel quality, which in the unstressed prepositions до and от is reduced to [a] or [ə].

Note, however, that if the speaker wishes to point up a contrast, even the shorter prepositions may be pronounced with a stress:

Вы́ та́м бы́ли по́сле конце́рта?
— Не́т, до́ конце́рта.

Were you there *after* the concert?
No, *before* the concert.

Verbs with infinitives ending in –чь: мочь and смочь

IMPERFECTIVE PRESENT

Я могу́ откры́ть окно́.	I can open the window.
Ты мо́жешь _____.	You can _____.
Он мо́жет _____.	He can _____.
Мы мо́жем _____.	We can _____.
Вы мо́жете _____.	You can _____.
Они́ мо́гут _____.	They can _____.

IMPERFECTIVE PAST

Он не мо́г откры́ть две́ри.	He couldn't open the door.
Она́ не могла́ _____.	She couldn't _____.
Они́ не могли́ _____.	They couldn't _____.

PERFECTIVE FUTURE

Я не смогу́ пойти́ на собра́ние.	I won't be able to go to the meeting.
Ты не смо́жешь _____.	You won't be able _____.
Он не смо́жет _____.	He won't be able _____.
Мы не смо́жем _____.	We won't be able _____.
Вы не смо́жете _____.	You won't be able _____.
Они́ не смо́гут _____.	They won't be able _____.

PERFECTIVE PAST

Он не смо́г пойти́ в клу́б.	He was unable to go to the club.
Она́ не смогла́ _____.	She was unable _____.
Они́ не смогли́ _____.	They were unable _____.

■ REPETITION DRILL

Repeat the above models, observing particularly the replacement of the stem consonant г by ж in the second and third persons singular and in the first and second persons plural. Note also the pattern of stress shift in both past and non-past forms.

■ SUBSTITUTION DRILLS

1. *I can't write without a pencil.*
   т: Я не могу́ писа́ть без карандаша́.
   s: **Я не могу́ писа́ть без карандаша́.**
   (она, мы, вы, ты, они, он)

2. *I won't be able to get into the building without a key.*
   т: Без ключа́ я не смогу́ войти́ в зда́ние.
   s: **Без ключа́ я не смогу́ войти́ в зда́ние.**
   (ты, мы, вы, он, я, она, они)

3. *My husband couldn't get any coffee.*
   т: Му́ж не смог доста́ть ко́фе.
   s: **Му́ж не смог доста́ть ко́фе.**
   (девушки, он, Саша, она, жена, Пётр Иванович, студентки, вы)

4. *She couldn't attend classes.*
   т: Она́ не могла́ бы́ть на заня́тиях.
   s: **Она́ не могла́ бы́ть на заня́тиях.**
   (они, мы, вы, Нина, Ирина, Козлов, Коля, Владимир, студенты)

Were you at the concert, Nina?
No, I couldn't go.

т: Ни́на, вы́ бы́ли на конце́рте?
s: **Нéт, я́ не смогла́ пойти́.**

т: Cа́ша, ты́ бы́л на конце́рте?
s: **Нéт, я́ не смо́г пойти́.**

Óля, ты́ была́ на конце́рте?
Пётр Ива́нович бы́л на конце́рте?
Ири́на Петро́вна была́ на конце́рте?
Они́ бы́ли на конце́рте?

■ RESPONSE DRILLS

1. *I'm not busy now.*
   I'll be able to go to the club.

   т: Я́ тепéрь не за́нят.
   s: **Я́ смогу́ пойти́ в клу́б.**
   т: Ты́ тепéрь не за́нят.
   s: **Ты́ смо́жешь пойти́ в клу́б.**
       (они, вы, Оля, мы, Саша, девушки)

2. *I'm busy now.*
   I can't go to the club.

   т: Я́ тепéрь за́нят.
   s: **Я́ не могу́ пойти́ в клу́б.**
   т: Ты́ тепéрь за́нят.
   s: **Ты́ не мо́жешь пойти́ в клу́б.**
       (они, вы, Оля, мы, Саша, девушки)

3. *I don't have a pencil.*
   I can't write.

   т: У меня́ нéт карандаша́.
   s: **Я́ не могу́ писа́ть.**
   т: У ва́с нéт карандаша́.
   s: **Вы́ не мо́жете писа́ть.**
       (у неё, у них, у тебя, у него, у меня,
       у них)

4. *My sister was sick.*
   She couldn't work.

   т: Моя́ сестра́ была́ больна́.
   s: **Она́ не могла́ рабо́тать.**
   т: Мо́й му́ж бы́л бо́лен.
   s: **Óн не мо́г рабо́тать.**
       (жена и сестра, мой брат, мои сёстры,
       вахтёр, уборщица)

5. *She doesn't have a room.*
   She simply can't get a room.

   т: У неё нéт ко́мнаты.
   s: **Она́ ника́к не мо́жет получи́ть ко́мнату.**
   т: У меня́ нéт ко́мнаты.
   s: **Я́ ника́к не могу́ получи́ть ко́мнату.**
       (у нас, у них, у тебя, у вас, у Нины,
       у меня)

DISCUSSION

Only a small number of Russian verbs have infinitives ending in –чь. All belong to the first conjugation, and all have basic stems ending in г or к. So far we have encountered only мо́чь (imperfective) and смо́чь (perfective) *can, to be able.*

In the present-future of мо́чь and смо́чь, the basic г of the stem is replaced by ж in the second and third persons singular and in the first and second persons plural.

Compare	я́ могу́	я́ смогу́
	они́ мо́гут	они́ смо́гут
with	ты́ мо́жешь	ты́ смо́жешь
	óн мо́жет	óн смо́жет
	мы́ мо́жем	мы́ смо́жем
	вы́ мо́жете	вы́ смо́жете.

Note that the stress is on the ending only in the first person singular: могу́, смогу́; otherwise it falls on the o of the stem: e.g., мо́жешь, смо́жешь, and so forth.

In the past tense, the suffix л does not appear in the masculine form, but does appear elsewhere.

я (ты, óн) мóг	я (ты, óн) смóг
я (ты, онá) моглá	я (ты, онá) смоглá
онó моглó	онó смоглó
мы (вы, они́) моглú	мы (вы, они́) смоглú

Note that in the past tense the stress is on the ending, where there is an ending vowel.

Further past tense drills

MODELS

Вы уже знáли об этом?	Did you already know about it?
— Нет, не знáл.	No, I didn't know.
— Нет, не знáла.	No, _____.
Вы уже послáли письмó?	Have you already sent the letter?
— Да, уже послáл.	Yes, I already sent it.
— Да, уже послáла.	Yes, _____.
Где вы рабóтали?	Where did you work?
— Я рабóтал на фáбрике.	I worked in a factory.
— Я рабóтала на фáбрике.	I _____.
Вы уже пообéдали?	Have you already had dinner?
— Нет, я ещё не обéдал.	No, I haven't yet.
— Нет, я ещё не обéдала.	No, _____.
Вы уже посмотрéли её кóмнату?	Have you already looked at her room?
— Нет, я ещё не смотрéл.	No, I haven't yet.
— Нет, я ещё не смотрéла.	No, _____.
Вы слýшали лéкции в университéте?	Did you attend lectures at the university?
— Да, слýшал.	Yes, I did.
— Да, слýшала.	Yes, ____.
Вы уже спроси́ли егó?	Have you already asked him?
— Нет, я ещё не спрáшивал.	No, I haven't yet.
— Нет, я ещё не спрáшивала.	No, _____.
Вы уже написáли письмó?	Have you already written the letter?
— Нет, я ещё не написáл.	No, I haven't yet written it.
— Нет, я ещё не написáла.	No, _____.

■ REPETITION DRILL

Repeat the above models, noting that often (but not always) a past imperfective verb is used in a negative answer to a question using a perfective verb.

■ SUBSTITUTION DRILLS

1. *Grant studied Russian at the university.*
   т: Грáнт учи́л рýсский язы́к в университéте.
   s: **Грáнт учи́л рýсский язы́к в университéте.**
   (вы, мы, Сáша, онá, студéнтки, студéнты, Кири́лл, дéвушки, Ни́на)

2. *He was asking where this building was.*
   т: Óн спрáшивал, где э́то здáние.
   s: **Óн спрáшивал, где э́то здáние.**
   (онá, мы, Влади́мир, Орлóв, Мáша, они́)

3. *Orlov left your dictionary at my place.*

   т: Орло́в оста́вил ва́ш слова́рь у меня́.

   s: **Орло́в оста́вил ва́ш слова́рь у меня́.**

   (они, учитель, девушки, Оля, Саша)

5. *I waited for you for a long time.*

   т: Я́ до́лго ва́с жда́л.

   s: **Я́ до́лго ва́с жда́л.**

   (мы, он, она, они, Саша, Владимир, девушки)

7. *She took the atlas from the library.*

   т: Она́ взяла́ а́тлас из библиоте́ки.

   s: **Она́ взяла́ а́тлас из библиоте́ки.**

   (мы, он, Нина, Кирилл, они)

4. *I wrote a letter home yesterday.*

   т: Я́ вчера́ написа́л письмо́ домо́й.

   s: **Я́ вчера́ написа́л письмо́ домо́й.**

   (мы, Евгений, Маша, девушки, Лев, Борис, они)

6. *I already submitted an application for a room.*

   т: Я́ уже́ по́дал заявле́ние на ко́мнату.[1]

   s: **Я́ уже́ по́дал заявле́ние на ко́мнату.**

   (Борис, Нина, они, он, вы, мой друг, мы)

8. *I wanted to suggest that to you.*

   т: Я́ хоте́л ва́м э́то предложи́ть.

   s: **Я́ хоте́л ва́м э́то предложи́ть.**

   (Орлов, учительница, профессора, мы, Иван Иванович, мой друг, мои друзья)

■ STRUCTURE REPLACEMENT DRILLS

1. *She wanted to write a composition.*
   She wrote a composition.

   т: Она́ хоте́ла написа́ть сочине́ние.

   s: **Она́ написа́ла сочине́ние.**

   т: Она́ хоте́ла купи́ть пла́тье.

   s: **Она́ купи́ла пла́тье.**

   (узнать результаты, открыть окно, достать материал, посмотреть его работу, пить чай)

3. *They can buy the present.*
   They bought the present.

   т: Они́ мо́гут купи́ть пода́рок.

   s: **Они́ купи́ли пода́рок.**

   т: Они́ мо́гут спроси́ть у Влади́мира.

   s: **Они́ спроси́ли у Влади́мира.**

   (замолвить словечко, получить книги из Москвы, это сделать, послать письмо)

2. *He forgot to open the window.*
   He opened the window.

   т: О́н забы́л откры́ть окно́.

   s: **О́н откры́л окно́.**

   т: О́н забы́л написа́ть сочине́ние.

   s: **О́н написа́л сочине́ние.**

   (спросить у Олега, оставить у неё подарок, послать письмо, взять словарь, купить хлеб, достать материал)

■ QUESTION-ANSWER DRILLS

1. *Don't you want to see the room, Nina?*
   I already did.

   т: Ни́на, ты́ не хо́чешь посмотре́ть ко́мнату?

   s: **Я́ уже́ посмотре́ла.**

   т: Ко́ля, ты́ не хо́чешь посмотре́ть ко́мнату?

   s: **Я́ уже́ посмотре́л.**

   Са́ша, ты́ не хо́чешь пообе́дать в столо́вой?

   О́льга, ты́ не хо́чешь пообе́дать в столо́вой?

   Семён, ты́ не хо́чешь купи́ть ка́рту Кита́я?

   О́ля, ты́ не хо́чешь купи́ть ка́рту Кита́я?

---

[1] The masculine and plural forms have two possible stresses: по́дал (*or* пода́л) and по́дали (*or* пода́ли). The feminine has stress on the last syllable only: подала́.

2. *Nina, have you already had dinner?*
   No, I haven't yet had dinner.
   т: Ни́на, ты́ уже́ пообе́дала?
   s: **Нет, ещё не обе́дала.**
   т: Ко́ля, ты́ уже́ пообе́дал?
   s: **Нет, ещё не обе́дал.**

Ири́на, ты́ уже́ спроси́ла об э́том?
Семён, ты́ уже́ спроси́л об э́том?
О́ля, ты́ уже́ посмотре́ла его́ рабо́ту?
Бори́с, ты́ уже́ посмотре́л его́ рабо́ту?
Ми́ла, ты́ уже́ поду́мала об э́том?
Влади́мир, ты́ уже́ поду́мал об э́том?

ЧТЕ́НИЕ И ПИСЬМО́

Вчера́ мы обе́дали в рестора́не о́коло па́рка. Бы́ли мои́ друзья́, Бори́с и его́ жена́ Ми́ла. По́сле обе́да мы пи́ли ча́й. Они́ спра́шивали меня́ о заня́тиях в университе́те. Я спра́шивал Ми́лу о рабо́те в лаборато́рии. По́сле ча́я мы пошли́ домо́й.

Все́ студе́нты говоря́т об экза́менах. Они́ писа́ли о наро́дах СССР. Результа́ты, ка́жется, неплохи́е. Но все́, коне́чно, хотя́т зна́ть, кто написа́л лу́чше. „Об э́том ра́но спра́шивать," – говоря́т профессора́ Орло́в и Куро́чкин.

В магази́не на углу́ нет ка́рт Евро́пы. Их ожида́ют на сле́дующей неде́ле. Но есть ка́рты СССР и Кита́я. На по́лке я ви́жу большо́й а́тлас. Мо́жет быть, он не о́чень дорого́й, но я не хочу́ его́ покупа́ть сейча́с.

– Вот на сту́ле како́й-то а́тлас. Ты не зна́ешь, чей он? – Мо́жет бы́ть Козло́ва? – У него́ нет а́тласа. – Тогда́, наве́рно, э́то Семёнова. – Да, мо́жет бы́ть.

— Привет, Саша! Где ты достал тетради? — В магазине на углу. — Вот как! А я вчера там был и не видел. — Но сегодня уже есть. — А карты? — Кажется, тоже есть.

— Владимир, ты куда? — В город. — Ты думаешь, магазины уже открыты? — Конечно. Сейчас уже девять часов. — Ну, тогда я тоже пойду. Ведь сегодня день рождения Ирины. — Я не забыл. Я хочу для неё кое-что купить.

— Мне нужна "История СССР." У вас есть? — Нет, ожидаем на следующей неделе. — А как насчёт "Истории Китая"? "История Китая" у нас есть. Вот она. — А скажите, карта Европы у вас тоже есть? — Да, сейчас принесу.

— Где Пётр Иванович? Ты не знаешь? — Кажется, сразу после обеда он пошёл домой. — Разве он забыл, что у нас сейчас экзамен? — Наверно забыл.

— Маша, обед готов? — Ещё нет. — А я уже голоден. — Подожди, пожалуйста, минутку. Каша ещё не готова. — А что ещё на обед? — Борщ и рыба.

— Оля, я вижу, ты была в ГУМе? — Да, только что была. — Ты не забыла купить ручку? — Вот, досада! Забыла. — А что это в коробке? — Подарок для тебя. Видишь, об этом я не забыла.

— Вот селёдка. И хлеб есть, и огурцы. — Но где у тебя ножи и вилки? — Кажется, в ящике. — В ящике нет. В шкафу тоже не вижу. — Тогда посмотри на полке. — Да, вот они. И хлеб тоже здесь.

NOTES

PREPARATION FOR CONVERSATION

В суббо́ту бу́дут та́нцы

суббо́та [subótə]	Saturday
в суббо́ту [fsubótu]	on Saturday
бу́дут (fut of бы́ть)	will be
та́нцы (sg та́нец)	dance, dancing, dances
В суббо́ту бу́дут та́нцы.	There'll be a dance on Saturday.
до́ма	at home
сиде́ть (II)	to be sitting, to sit
я сижу́, они́ сидя́т	I sit, they sit
вре́мя (n)	time
ве́сь (m), вся́ (f), всё (n)	all
Ты́ всё вре́мя сиди́шь до́ма.	You sit at home all the time.
Зи́на, ты́ всё вре́мя сиди́шь до́ма.	Zina, you sit at home all the time.
пойдём (imperative)	let's go!
Пойдём в клу́б!	Let's go to the club!
Пойдём в суббо́ту в клу́б!	Let's go to the club on Saturday!
Та́м всегда́ та́к ску́чно!	It's always so boring there!
Не́т, спаси́бо. Та́м всегда́ та́к ску́чно!	No, thanks. It's always so boring there!
ра́з	occasion, time
на э́тот ра́з	this time, on this occasion
Да́, но́ на э́тот ра́з бу́дут та́нцы.	Yes, but this time there'll be dancing.
Та́нцы? Э́то друго́е де́ло!	Dancing? That's a different story!
танцева́ть (I)	to dance
я танцу́ю, они́ танцу́ют	I dance, they dance
люби́ть (II)	to love, like
я люблю́, они́ лю́бят	I love, I like; they love, they like
Я люблю́ танцева́ть.	I love to dance.
Та́нцы? Э́то друго́е де́ло! Танцева́ть я люблю́.	Dancing? That's different! I love to dance.

вме́сте	together
всё вме́сте	all together
Пойдём всё вме́сте!	Let's all go together!
Пойдём всё вме́сте: я, ты, Влади́мир и Оле́г.	Let's all go together: you and I, Vladimir and Oleg!
Ты Оле́га зна́ешь?	Do you know Oleg?
Немно́го.	Slightly (*lit.* a little).
Я его́ немно́го зна́ю.	I know him slightly.
ку́рс	class (year), course
на одно́м ку́рсе	in the same class
Мы на одно́м ку́рсе.	We're in the same class.
знако́м	acquainted, familiar
ма́ло	little, too little, very little, few
Мы ма́ло знако́мы.	We're barely acquainted.
Мы на одно́м ку́рсе, но ма́ло знако́мы.	We're in the same class, but we're barely acquainted.
па́рень (m) (pl па́рни)	lad, boy, fellow
Воло́дя говори́т, что он хоро́ший па́рень.	Volodya says he's a nice boy.
това́рищ по ко́мнате	roommate
Они́ това́рищи по ко́мнате.	They're roommates.
уви́деть (pfv II)	to see, catch sight of
я уви́жу, они́ уви́дят	I'll see, they'll see
Уви́дим.	We'll see.
зна́чит	it means; so, then
так зна́чит	so then, well then
Так зна́чит, в суббо́ту?	So, on Saturday, then?
Уви́дим. Так зна́чит, в суббо́ту?	We'll see. So, on Saturday, then?
ско́лько (*plus* gen)	how much, how many
во ско́лько	at what time
Во ско́лько?	At what time?
В де́вять.	At nine.
ве́чер (pl вечера́)	evening(s)
ве́чером	in the evening
сего́дня ве́чером	this evening
Что ты де́лаешь сего́дня ве́чером?	What are you doing this evening?
фи́льм	film, picture, movie
война́	war
ми́р	peace; world
Я иду́ на фильм «Война́ и ми́р».	I'm going to the movie *War and Peace*.
Говоря́т, хоро́ший.	They say it's good.

с ни́м	with him
Вы́ с ни́м знако́мы?	Are you acquainted with him?
с не́й	with her
Вы́ с не́й знако́мы?	Are you acquainted with her?
с ни́ми	with them
Вы́ с ни́ми знако́мы?	Are you acquainted with them?
познако́мить (pfv II)	to introduce, acquaint
я познако́млю, они́ познако́мят	I'll introduce, they'll introduce
Я́ ва́с познако́млю с не́й.	I'll introduce you to her.
сюда́	here, over [here], this way, in this direction
О́н идёт сюда́.	He's coming over [here].
назва́ть (pfv I)	to name
назову́, назову́т	I'll name, they'll name
Назови́те дни́ неде́ли!	Name the days of the week!
понеде́льник*	Monday
вто́рник	Tuesday
среда́	Wednesday
четве́рг	Thursday
пя́тница	Friday
суббо́та [subótə]	Saturday
воскресе́нье	Sunday

В суббо́ту бу́дут та́нцы

Ка́тя	1	Зи́на,	ẓínə ↓
		ты́ всё вре́мя сиди́шь до́ма.	tí fşó vŗéṃə şiḍíš dŏ́mə ↓
		Пойдём в суббо́ту в клу́б.	pajḍóm fsubótu fklú̆p ↓
Зи́на	2	Не́т, спаси́бо.	ņĕ́t ↓ spaşíbə ↓
		Та́м всегда́ та́к ску́чно!	tám fşigdá ták skú̆šnə ↓
Ка́тя	3	Да́,	dã́ ↓
		но́ на э́тот ра́з	nó naĕ́tət rás |
		бу́дут та́нцы.[1]	búdut tã́nci ↓
Зи́на	4	Та́нцы?	tã́nci ↑
		Э́то друго́е де́ло!	étə drugŏ́jə ḍélə ↓
		Танцева́ть я́ люблю́.	tənciváṭ já ḷubḷú̆ ↓
Ка́тя	5	Пойдём всё вме́сте:	pajḍóm fşé vṃĕ́şṭi ↓
		я́,	jã́ |
		ты́,	tí |
		Влади́мир	vlaḍíṃir |
		и Оле́г.[2]	i aḷĕ́k ↓
		Ты́ Оле́га зна́ешь?	tí aḷégə znã́jiš ↑

---

* Note that Russians consider Monday the first day of the week and Sunday the last. This is reflected in the names: **вто́рник** (from **второ́й** *second*), **четве́рг** (from **четвёртый** *fourth*), and **пя́тница** (from **пя́тый** *fifth*).

Зи́на	6	Немно́го.	n̦imnốgə ↓
		Мы́ на одно́м ку́рсе,	mí nəadnóm kűrşi ↓
		но ма́ло знако́мы.[3]	no málə znakỗmi ↓
Ка́тя	7	Воло́дя говори́т,	valódə gəva̧rít |
		что о́н хоро́ший па́рень.[4, 5]	štə ón xarốšij pǎ̧r̦in̦ ↓
		Они́ това́рищи по ко́мнате.	an̦í tava̧rišči pakỗmnə̧ti ↓
Зи́на	8	Уви́дим.	uɣíḑim ↓
		Так зна́чит, в суббо́ту?	tagznáčit fsubốtu ↓
		Во ско́лько?	vaskốl̦kə ↓
Ка́тя	9	В де́вять.	vd̦éɣi̧ț ↓
		А что́ ты́ де́лаешь	a štó tí ḑéləjiš |
		сего́дня ве́чером?	şivódn̦ə ɣéčirəm ↓
Зи́на	10	Я иду́ на фи́льм «Война́ и ми́р».	já idú naf̦íl̦m vajná i m̦ir ↓
		Говоря́т, хоро́ший.	gəva̧r̦át xarốšij ↓

NOTES

[1] **Та́нцы** is ordinarily used in the plural unless a specific type of dance is referred to:

| *Compare* | Пойдём на та́нцы. | Let's go to the dance. |
| *with* | Не́т, э́то не ру́сский та́нец. | No, that's not a Russian dance. |

[2] In Russian it is correct and not at all impolite to start with oneself in referring to a group:

Пойдём всё вме́сте: я, ты́, Влади́мир и Оле́г.

Russians do not put a comma after the next to the last item in a series if the conjunction **и** precedes the last item. If the **и** is omitted, then the comma must be used: **я, ты́, Влади́мир, Оле́г.**

[3] In the expression **на одно́м ку́рсе**, the noun **ку́рс** is used to mean *class year* (comparable to such terms as *freshman* or *sophomore*). **Ку́рс** can also mean *course*, as in **ку́рс исто́рии** *history course*.

[4] **Воло́дя** is a nickname for **Влади́мир**. Similarly, **Ка́тя** is short for **Екатери́на**, and **Зи́на** for **Зинаи́да**.

[5] The word **па́рень** *boy*, *lad*, or *fellow* was formerly restricted to a country or working-class boy. Since World War II its usage has been extended to refer to any young man.

PREPARATION FOR CONVERSATION   **Оле́г ду́мает пойти́ в кино́**

кино́ (n indeclinable) [k̦inó]	movies, cinema
в кино́ [fk̦inó]	to the movies, at the movies
Оле́г ду́мает пойти́ в кино́.	Oleg is thinking of going to the movies.

чита́ть (I)	to read
я чита́ю, они́ чита́ют	I read, they read
Что́ ты чита́ешь?	What are you reading?
Что́ ты чита́ешь, исто́рию?	What are you reading, history?
«Евге́ний Оне́гин»	*Eugene Onegin*
Я чита́ю «Евге́ния Оне́гина».	I'm reading *Eugene Onegin*.
стихи́	verses, poetry
Во́т ка́к, стихи́!	You don't say! Poetry!
Я чита́ю «Войну́ и ми́р».	I'm reading *War and Peace*.
А я сейча́с чита́ю «Войну́ и ми́р».	Well, I'm reading *War and Peace* now.
рома́н	novel
э́тот рома́н	that novel, this novel
Я люблю́ э́тот рома́н.	I love that novel.
его́ (acc of о́н, оно́)	it, him
мно́го ра́з	many times
Я мно́го ра́з чита́л его́.	I've read it many times.
идёт фи́льм	a film is playing (*or* showing)
В кино́ идёт америка́нский фи́льм.	There's an American film showing at the movies.
Кста́ти, в кино́ идёт америка́нский фи́льм.	Incidentally, there's an American film showing at the movies.
Кста́ти, зна́ешь, в кино́ идёт америка́нский фи́льм.	Incidentally, you know, there's an American film showing at the movies.
Кста́ти, зна́ешь, в кино́ идёт америка́нский фи́льм «Война́ и ми́р».	Incidentally, you know the American film *War and Peace* is showing at the movies.
Я о́чень хочу́ его́ посмотре́ть.	I want very much to see it.
Да́, зна́ю. Я о́чень хочу́ его́ посмотре́ть.	Yes, I know. I want very much to see it.
когда́	when
Ты́ когда́ ду́маешь пойти́?	When is it you're thinking of going?
послеза́втра [posⁱizáftrə]	the day after tomorrow
и́ли	or
За́втра и́ли послеза́втра.	Tomorrow or the day after.
почему́	why
А почему́ ты́ спра́шиваешь?	Why do you ask?
за́втра ве́чером	tomorrow evening, tomorrow night
Зи́на идёт за́втра ве́чером.	Zina's going tomorrow evening.
Я слы́шал, что́ Зи́на идёт за́втра ве́чером.	I heard Zina was going tomorrow evening.
Я то́же пойду́ за́втра.	I'll go tomorrow, too.
Да́? Тогда́ я то́же пойду́ за́втра.	Really? Then I'll go tomorrow, too.

счита́ть (I) [ščitáṭ]	to count, consider
счита́ю, счита́ют [ščitáju, ščitájut]	I count, they count
от одного́ до десяти́	from one to ten
Счита́йте от одного́ до десяти́!	Count from one to ten!
оди́н	one
два́	two
три́	three
четы́ре	four
пя́ть	five
ше́сть	six
се́мь	seven
во́семь	eight
де́вять	nine
де́сять	ten
час	hour, o'clock, one o'clock
Во ско́лько вы́ пое́дете?	At what time will you go?
— В ча́с.	At one [o'clock].
— В два́.	At two.
— В три́.	At three.
— В четы́ре.	At four.
— В пя́ть.	At five.
— В ше́сть.	At six.
— В се́мь.	At seven.
— В во́семь.	At eight.
— В де́вять.	At nine.
— В де́сять.	At ten.

Оле́г ду́мает пойти́ в кино́

В. — Влади́мир   О. — Оле́г

В.	1	Здра́вствуй, Оле́г!	zdrắstuj aļék ↓
		Что́ ты́ чита́ешь?	štó tí čitájiš ↓
		Исто́рию?	istőṛiju ↑
O.	2	Не́т,	ņḗt ↓
		«Евге́ния Оне́гина».[1]	jivgéņijə aņḗginə ↓
В.	3	Во́т ка́к,	vőt kák ↑
		стихи́!	sṭiх̧ĩ ↓
		А я́ сейча́с чита́ю	a jắ şičás čitáju ǀ
		«Войну́ и ми́р».	vajnú i ṃĩr ↓
O.	4	Я́ люблю́ э́тот рома́н.	já ļubļű étət ramán ↓
		Мно́го ра́з чита́л его́.	mnógə rắs čitál jivó ↓

B.	5	Кстáти, знáешь,	kstáʈi znǎjiš ↓
		в кинó идёт	fķinó iḏőt │
		америкáнский фильм	aṃiŗikánsķij fǐḷm
		«Войнá и мир».	vajná i ṃǐr
O.	6	Дá,	dǎ ↓
		знáю.	znǎju ↓
		Я óчень хочý егó посмотрéть.	já óčiṇ xačú jivó pəsmatŗéʈ ↓
B.	7	Ты когдá дýмаешь пойти?	tí kagdǎ dúmajiš pajʈí ↓
O.	8	Зáвтра	zǎftrə ↓
		или послезáвтра.	íḷi posḷizǎftrə ↓
		А почемý ты спрáшиваешь?	a pəčimú tí sprǎšivəjiš ↓
B.	9	Я слышал,	já slǐšəl │
		что Зина идёт	štə ẓínə iḏót │
		зáвтра вéчером.	zǎftrə γéčirəm ↓
O.	10	Дá?	dǎ ↑
		Тогдá я тóже пойдý зáвтра.	tagdá já tőži pajdú zǎftrə ↓

NOTES

¹ «Евгéний Онéгин» is Alexander Pushkin's (1799-1837) famous novel in verse, written during the 1820's. Note that titles of books, movies, plays, and so forth are declined in Russian unless preceded by the nouns *book*, *movie*, *play*, and so forth.

Compare	Я читáю «Войнý и мир».	I'm reading *War and Peace*.
with	Я читáю ромáн «Войнá и мир».	I'm reading the novel *War and Peace*.

Basic sentence patterns

1. Ты знáешь Олéга?	Do you know Oleg?
_____ Евгéния?	_____ Evgeny?
_____ Кирилла?	_____ Kirill?
_____ Царáпкина?	_____ Tsarapkin?
_____ Алексéева?	_____ Alexeev?
_____ Львá?	_____ Lev?
_____ секретаря?	_____ the secretary?
_____ Сáшу?	_____ Sasha?
_____ Кóлю?	_____ Kolya?
_____ Волóдю?	_____ Volodya?
_____ Гáлю?	_____ Galya?
_____ Нину?	_____ Nina?
_____ Марию?	_____ Maria?
_____ Ирину Петрóвну?	_____ Irina Petrovna?

2. Вы егó знáете?	Do you know him?
__ её _____?	_____ her?
__ их _____?	_____ them?
__ меня _____?	_____ me?
__ нáс _____?	_____ us?

3. Попроси́те Ива́на Николáевича к телефóну.

Ask Ivan Nikolaevich to come to the phone.

_____ Бори́са Михáйловича _____.	____ Boris Mikhailovich _____.
_____ Влади́мира _____.	____ Vladimir _____.
_____ профéссора Орлóва _____.	____ Professor Orlov _____.
_____ Евгéния _____.	____ Evgeny _____.
_____ секретаря́ _____.	____ the secretary _____.
_____ учи́теля Смирнóва _____.	____ Teacher Smirnov _____.
_____ Кóлю _____.	____ Kolya _____.
_____ Волóдю _____.	____ Volodya _____.
_____ Сáшу _____.	____ Sasha _____.
_____ Мари́ю _____.	____ Maria _____.
_____ Ни́ну _____.	____ Nina _____.
_____ Гáлю _____.	____ Galya _____.
_____ Ири́ну Петрóвну _____.	____ Irina Petrovna _____.

4. Чтó вы́ читáете?

What are you reading?

— Ромáн.	A novel.
— Стихи́.	Poetry.
— «Евгéния Онéгина».	*Eugene Onegin.*
— «Бори́са Годунóва».	*Boris Godunov.*
— «Дóктора Живáго».	*Doctor Zhivago.*
— «Войнý и ми́р».	*War and Peace.*
— «Áнну Карéнину».	*Anna Karenina.*
— Истóрию.	History.
— Геогрáфию.	Geography.

5. Я́ люблю́ чáй.

I'm very fond of tea.

_____ бóрщ.	_____ borsch.
_____ хлéб.	_____ bread.
_____ молокó.	_____ milk.
_____ огурцы́.	_____ cucumbers.
_____ щи́.	_____ schi.
_____ кáшу.	_____ kasha.
_____ ры́бу.	_____ fish.
_____ селёдку.	_____ herring.

6. На слéдующей недéле я́ бýду в Москвé.

Next week I'll be in Moscow.

_____ ты́ бýдешь ____.	_____ you'll be _____.
_____ óн бýдет ____.	_____ he'll be _____.
_____ мы́ бýдем ____.	_____ we'll be _____.
_____ вы́ бýдете ____.	_____ you'll be _____.
_____ они́ бýдут ____.	_____ they'll be _____.

7. Я́ бýду читáть «Евгéния Онéгина».

I'll be reading *Eugene Onegin.*

Ты́ бýдешь _____.	You'll be _____.
Óн бýдет _____.	He'll be _____.
Мы́ бýдем _____.	We'll be _____.
Вы́ бýдете _____.	You'll be _____.
Они́ бýдут _____.	They'll be _____.

8. Я люблю́ танцева́ть.
   Ты лю́бишь _____.
   Она́ лю́бит _____.
   Мы́ лю́бим _____.
   Вы́ лю́бите _____.
   Они́ лю́бят _____.

I love to dance.
You love ____.
She loves ____.
We love ____.
You love ____.
They love ____.

9. Я́ всё вре́мя сижу́ до́ма.
   Ты́ _____ сиди́шь __.
   О́н _____ сиди́т ____.
   Мы́ _____ сиди́м ____.
   Вы́ _____ сиди́те ___.
   Они́ _____ сидя́т ____.

I sit (or stay) home all the time.
You sit (or stay) _____.
He sits (or stays) _____.
We sit (or stay) _____.
You sit (or stay) _____.
They sit (or stay) _____.

10. Я́ его́ уви́жу сего́дня ве́чером.
    Ты́ __ уви́дишь _____.
    Она́ _ уви́дит _____.
    Мы́ _ уви́дим _____.
    Вы́ __ уви́дите _____.
    Они́ _ уви́дят _____.

I'll see him this evening.
You'll see _____.
She'll see _____.
We'll see _____.
You'll see _____.
They'll see _____.

11. Я́ всегда́ её ви́жу в теа́тре.
    Ты́ _____ ви́дишь _____.
    О́н _____ ви́дит _____.
    Мы́ _____ ви́дим _____.
    Вы́ _____ ви́дите _____.
    Они́ _____ ви́дят _____.

I always see her at the theater.
You __ see _____.
He ___ sees _____.
We ___ see _____.
You ___ see _____.
They __ see _____.

12. Я́ за́втра куплю́ молоко́.
    Ты́ _____ ку́пишь _____.
    Она́ ___ ку́пит _____.
    Мы́ ____ ку́пим _____.
    Вы́ _____ ку́пите _____.
    Они́ ____ ку́пят _____.

I'll buy milk tomorrow.
You'll buy _____.
She'll buy _____.
We'll buy _____.
You'll buy _____.
They'll buy _____.

13. Я́ оста́влю портфе́ль в клу́бе.
    Ты́ оста́вишь _____.
    О́н оста́вит _____.
    Мы́ оста́вим _____.
    Вы́ оста́вите _____.
    Они́ оста́вят _____.

I'll leave the briefcase at the club.
You'll leave _____.
He'll leave _____.
We'll leave _____.
You'll leave _____.
They'll leave _____.

14. Я́ спрошу́ об э́том у Льва́.
    Ты́ спро́сишь _____.
    О́н спро́сит _____.
    Мы́ спро́сим _____.
    Вы́ спро́сите _____.
    Они́ спро́сят _____.

I'll ask Lev about it.
You'll ask _____.
He'll ask _____.
We'll ask _____.
You'll ask_____.
They'll ask _____.

15. Како́й сего́дня де́нь?
    — Сего́дня воскресе́нье.
    _____ понеде́льник.
    _____ вто́рник.
    _____ среда́.

What day is today?
Today is Sunday.
_____ Monday.
____ Tuesday.
_____ Wednesday.

— Сегодня четверг.		Today is Thursday.
_____ пятница.		_____ Friday.
_____ суббота.		_____ Saturday.

16. Пойдём в воскресенье в клуб.

    _____ в понедельник _____.

    _____ во вторник _____.

    _____ в среду _____.

    _____ в четверг _____.

    _____ в пятницу _____.

    _____ в субботу _____.

Let's go to the club on Sunday.

    _____ on Monday.

    _____ on Tuesday.

    _____ on Wednesday.

    _____ on Thursday.

    _____ on Friday.

    _____ on Saturday.

17. Она весь день сидела дома.

    ____ весь вечер _____.

    ____ всё утро _____.

    ____ всё лето _____.

    ____ всю зиму _____.

    ____ всю неделю _____.

    ____ всё время _____.

She stayed home all day.

    _____ all evening.

    _____ all morning.

    _____ all summer.

    _____ all winter.

    _____ all week.

    _____ all the time.

Pronunciation practice: unpaired consonants [š], [ž], [c], [č], [šč], and [j]

Some consonants occur without soft or hard counterparts. Three consonants are always pronounced hard: [š], [ž], and [c]. Three are always pronounced soft: [č], [šč], and [j].

A.   Hard consonant [š]

   Usual Cyrillic spelling ш; also ж, шь, or жь.

Note the pronunciation of hard [š] in the following:

[ví spišíţi]	вы спешите	you're hurrying
[já slíšəl]	я слышал	I heard
[xərašó]	хорошо	good

The Russian consonant [š] is always hard. It differs from the corresponding English sound (usually spelled *sh* in words like *sh*op, cru*sh*, and bu*sh*) in that the tip of the tongue is curled slightly up and back, and the sound is made farther back in the mouth.

> Sound Drill: Practice the Russian examples illustrating [š], imitating your instructor (or the tape) as accurately as you can. Remember that even when Cyrillic е, и, and ь are written after ш, they are still pronounced hard.

B.   Hard consonant [ž]
      Usual Cyrillic spelling ж; sometimes жь.

Note the pronunciation of hard [ž] in the following:

[žiná]	жена́	wife
[naslúžɓi]	на слу́жбе	at work

Russian [ž] is a hard consonant formed with the tongue in the same position as for [š], but it is pronounced voiced. It is similar to the English *s* in *leisure* and *pleasure*, except that the Russian sound is made with the tip of the tongue curled up and back and is produced farther back in the mouth. (Russian [ž] is articulated in approximately the same position in the mouth as American English *r*.)

> Sound Drill: Practice the Russian examples illustrating [ž], imitating your instructor (or the tape) as accurately as you can. Remember that even when Cyrillic e, ё, and и are written after ж, they are still pronounced hard.

C.   Hard consonant [c]
      Usual Cyrillic spelling ц.

Note the pronunciation of hard [c] in the following:

[kancért]	конце́рт	concert
[agurcí]	огурцы́	cucumbers
[aṭéc]	оте́ц	father

The Russian sound [c] is like the *ts* in English ca*ts*, and in the foreign-derived words *ts*et*se* and *ts*ar. The tip of the tongue touches the gum ridge behind the upper teeth. It is always pronounced hard.

> Sound Drill: Practice the Russian examples illustrating [c], imitating your instructor (or the tape) as accurately as you can. Remember that even when Cyrillic e and и are written after ц, they are still pronounced hard.

D.   Soft consonant [č]
      Usual Cyrillic spelling ч; sometimes чь.

Note the pronunciation of soft [č] in the following:

[čáj]	чай	tea
[napóčtu]	на по́чту	to the post office
[fčirá]	вчера́	yesterday
[óčiṇ]	о́чень	very

Russian [č] is formed much like English *ch* in *ch*eap or *ch*in, but without the puff of breath which occurs with English *ch* in the above words.

> Sound Drill: Practice the Russian examples illustrating [č], as well as the paired sets contrasting [č] and soft [ṭ], imitating your instructor (or the tape) as accurately as you can. Remember that even when Cyrillic a, o, and y are written after ч, they are still pronounced soft.

E.   Soft consonant [šč]

Usual Cyrillic spelling щ; sometimes щь or сч (rarely ждь).

Note the pronunciation of soft [šč] in the following:

[ščí]	щи́	schi
[bóršč]	бо́рщ	borsch
[naščót]	насчёт	with regard to
[jáščik]	я́щик	drawer, box
[ṛíščə]	пи́ща	food, fare

The Russian sound represented by [šč] is pronounced either as a long soft [š] or as a soft [š] followed by a [č], also soft. It sounds something like the *sch* in English mi*sch*ief, pronounced rapidly with *sh* instead of *s*. The sound [šč] is considered soft in the Russian sound system and has no hard counterpart.

> Sound Drill: Practice the Russian examples illustrating long soft [šč], imitating your instructor (or the tape) as accurately as you can. Remember that even when Cyrillic **a** and **y** are written after **щ**, they are still pronounced soft.

F.   Soft consonant [j][1]

Note the pronunciation of soft [j] in the following:

[já]	я́	I
[mój]	мо́й	my
[dəsγidáṇjə]	до свида́ния	good-bye
[angínəj]	анги́ной	with a sore throat

Russian [j] is pronounced much like the English *y* in *y*ou and bo*y*, except that the Russian sound is made with the tongue much tenser and more elevated, particularly after a vowel. Russian [j] is considered a soft consonant and has no hard counterpart.

> Sound Drill: Practice the Russian examples illustrating [j], imitating your instructor (or the tape) as accurately as you can.

Intonation practice: review of falling intonation contours

Reread the discussion on intonation contours in Lesson 6.

A. Review of statements with falling contours.

О́н здесь.	He's here.
Алексе́ев у себя́.	Alexeev's in.
Она́ на собра́нии.	She's at a meeting.
Влади́мир у телефо́на.	Vladimir's on the phone.

---

[1] In the Cyrillic writing system, the consonant sound [j] is ordinarily expressed by the separate letter **й** after a vowel only when there is no vowel immediately following, i.e., at the end of a word or just before another consonant: мо́й [mój], тро́йка [trójkə]. It is most often expressed through use of the soft-series vowel letters, particularly at the beginning of a word or between vowels: я́ [já], мою́ [majú].

Вилки в шкафу́.	The forks are in the cupboard.
Она́ в магази́не.	She's at the store.
А́тлас дорого́й.	The atlas is expensive.
О́н в Москве́.	He's in Moscow.
Пойду́ посмотрю́.	I'll go take a look.
Во́т рестора́н.	Here's the restaurant.
Вчера́ бы́л конце́рт.	Yesterday there was a concert.
У на́с е́сть бо́рщ.	We have borsch.
Тепе́рь она́ больна́.	She's sick now.
Вахтёр стоя́л у две́ри.	The custodian stood at the door.
Мы́ уже́ обе́дали.	We've already had dinner.
О́н сейча́с в Москве́.	He's in Moscow now.
У меня́ ма́ленькая про́сьба.	I have a small favor to ask.
Она́ рабо́тает на фа́брике.	She works at a factory.
Я иду́ с рабо́ты.	I'm coming from work.
Замо́лвите за меня́ слове́чко.	Put in a good word for me.
Большо́е ва́м спаси́бо.	Thanks very much.
Мы́ ведь ста́рые друзья́.	We're old friends, after all.
Я давно́ ва́с не ви́дел.	I haven't seen you in a long time.
Она́ опя́ть купи́ла пла́тье.	She has bought a dress again.
О́н вполне́ тепе́рь здоро́в.	He's completely well now.
Мы́ неда́вно пи́ли ча́й.	We drank tea awhile ago.
Ни́на до́лго стоя́ла в о́череди.	Nina stood in line a long time.
На́до та́к до́лго жда́ть.	One has to wait so long.
Ведь та́м рабо́тает Алексе́ев.	Alexeev works there, after all.

B. Review of questions with falling contours (question-word questions).

Кто́ та́м?	Who's there?
Кто́ спра́шивает?	Who's calling?
Где́ вахтёр?	Where's the custodian?
Где́ кио́ск?	Where's a newsstand?
Что́ э́то?	What's that?
Куда́ идёшь?	Where are you going?
Заче́м спеши́ть?	What's the hurry?
Ка́к Ни́на?	How's Nina?
Где́ она́ была́?	Where was she?
Кто́ та́м стоя́л?	Who was standing there?
Что́ э́то в шкафу́?	What's that in the cupboard?
У кого́ вы́ бы́ли?	Whom did you go to see?
Что́ вы́ де́лали?	What were you doing?
Кто́ э́то говори́т?	Who's that talking?
Куда́ они́ спеша́т?	Where are they hurrying to?
Отку́да вы́ идёте?	Where are you coming from?
Заче́м тебе́ спеши́ть?	What's your hurry?
О ко́м о́н спра́шивал?	Who was he asking about?
Что́ сего́дня на обе́д?	What's for dinner today?
О чём написа́л Козло́в?	What did Kozlov write about?
Куда́ вы́ та́к спеши́те?	Where are you going in such a hurry?
Что́ вы́ тепе́рь де́лаете?	What are you doing now?

Что́ э́то та́м в углу́?	What's that in the corner there?
Где́ ты́ э́то доста́ла?	Where did you get that?
Ка́к тепе́рь насчёт обе́да?	How about dinner now?
Отку́да вы́ э́то получи́ли?	Where did you get that?
У кого́ вы́ э́то узна́ли?	From whom did you learn that?
Заче́м тебе́ э́ти тетра́ди?	What do you need these notebooks for?
Где́ стои́т на́ш ре́ктор?	Where's our chancellor standing?
Ка́к прошёл тво́й уро́к?	How did your lesson go?
Ка́к тогда́ насчёт а́тласа?	How about an atlas then?

STRUCTURE AND DRILLS

The accusative of кто́, что́, and the personal pronouns

MODELS

Что́ вы́ та́м ви́дели?	What did you see there?
Кого́ вы́ та́м ви́дели?	Whom did you see there?
Все́ профессора́ меня́ зна́ют.	All the professors know me.
_____ тебя́ _____.	_____ you.
_____ его́ _____.	_____ him.
_____ её _____.	_____ her.
_____ на́с _____.	_____ us.
_____ ва́с _____.	_____ you.
_____ и́х _____.	_____ them.
Спроси́те его́, ка́к пройти́ в ГУ́М.	Ask him how to get to GUM.
_____ её _____.	___ her _____.
_____ и́х _____.	___ them _____.
Не смотри́ на него́!	Don't look at him (or it)!
_____ на неё!	_____ her (or it)!
_____ на ни́х!	_____ them!
Замо́лвите за меня́ слове́чко!	Put in a good word for me!
_____ за него́ _____!	_____ for him!
_____ за неё _____!	_____ for her!
_____ за на́с _____!	_____ for us!
_____ за ни́х _____!	_____ for them!

■ REPETITION DRILL

Repeat the above models, noting that the accusative is like the genitive for all personal pronouns and кто́, but that что́ has an accusative like the nominative. Note also that after prepositions the third person pronouns are него́, неё, and ни́х; otherwise they are его́, её, and и́х.

■ STRUCTURE REPLACEMENT DRILL

Ask Ivan Nikolaevich [to come] to the phone.
Ask him [to come] to the phone.
т: Попроси́те Ива́на Никола́евича к
  телефо́ну.
s: **Попроси́те его́ к телефо́ну.**

т: Попроси́те Га́лю к телефо́ну.
s: **Попроси́те её к телефо́ну.**
(вахтёра, Воло́дю, Ни́ну, Мари́ю Пет-
ро́вну, Евге́ния, Ка́тю, Зи́ну, Петра́,
Никола́я)

Where's your dictionary?
I left it at home.

т: Где́ ва́ш слова́рь?
s: **Я его́ забы́л до́ма.**
т: Где́ ва́ша ка́рта?
s: **Я её забы́л до́ма.**

(ва́ше перо́, ваш нож, ва́ша кни́га, ва́ши тетра́дки, ва́ши словари́, ва́ша рабо́та, ваш а́тлас, ваш портфе́ль, ва́ше сочине́ние, ва́ши ключи́)

■ RESPONSE DRILLS

1. *Ah, there you are!*
   We've been expecting you for a long time.
   т: А́, во́т вы́!
   s: **Мы́ ва́с давно́ ожида́ем.**
   т: А́, во́т ты́!
   s: **Мы́ тебя́ давно́ ожида́ем.**
   (она́, они́, Ко́ля, убо́рщица, учи́тель Семёнов, Ни́на, О́льга Петро́вна, Ле́в Ники́тич)

2. *Here's the dress material.*
   Where did you get it?
   т: Во́т материа́л на пла́тье.
   s: **Где́ вы́ его́ доста́ли?**
   т: Во́т ка́рта Кита́я.
   s: **Где́ вы́ её доста́ли?**
   (а́тлас Аме́рики, ка́рты Евро́пы, каранда́ш, огурцы́, ры́ба, кни́ги, портфе́ль, тетра́ди, слова́рь)

3. *Kozlov was there.*
   I saw him.
   т: Козло́в та́м бы́л.
   s: **Я его́ ви́дел.**
   т: Она́ та́м была́.
   s: **Я её ви́дел.**
   (ты, он, вы, они, Никола́й, твои́ сёстры, Ка́тя, профе́ссор Орло́в, твои́ бра́тья)

4. *Zina isn't ready yet.*
   Wait for her.
   т: Зи́на ещё не гото́ва.
   s: **Подожди́ её.**
   т: Я ещё не гото́в.
   s: **Подожди́ меня́.**
   (мы, Оле́г и Зи́на, бра́т, она́, сестра́, они́, твоя́ жена́, он, тво́й муж)

5. *He's here.*
   Do you know him?
   т: О́н ту́т.
   s: **Ты́ его́ зна́ешь?**
   т: Она́ ту́т.
   s: **Ты́ её зна́ешь?**
   (Ири́на, Ко́ля, Козло́в, мо́й бра́т, моя́ сестра́, мои́ бра́тья, мои́ сёстры)

6. *He's not here yet.*
   We're expecting him.
   т: Его́ ещё не́т.
   s: **Мы́ его́ ожида́ем.**
   т: Учи́тельницы ещё не́т.
   s: **Мы́ её ожида́ем.**
   (их, Ко́ли, Никола́я, продавщи́цы, его́, профе́ссора, Семёнова и его́ жены́)

7. *There's Zina over there.*
   Ask her.
   т: Во́н та́м Зи́на.
   s: **Спроси́те её.**
   т: Во́н та́м Воло́дя.
   s: **Спроси́те его́.**
   (Ири́на Петро́вна, убо́рщицы, мо́й бра́т, моя́ сестра́, учителя́, учи́тельница, Оле́г, студе́нты)

8. *We saw the factory.*
   What did you see?
   т: Мы́ ви́дели заво́д.
   s: **Что́ вы́ ви́дели?**
   т: Мы́ ви́дели Зи́ну.
   s: **Кого́ вы́ ви́дели?**
   (а́тлас, ка́рты, Воло́дю, фи́льм, ва́шу сестру́, её бра́та, библиоте́ку, учителя́, результа́ты экза́мена, Мари́ю, ко́мнату)

DISCUSSION

The accusative of personal pronouns and кто́ has the same form as the genitive. The accusative of что́, however, is like the nominative.

NOM	я	ты	он, оно	она	мы	вы	они	кто	что
ACC	меня́	тебя́	его́ (него́)	её (неё)	нас	вас	их (них)	кого́	что́

The alternate forms, **него́**, **неё**, and **них**, are used only with prepositions: **Посмотри́ на него́!** *Look at him!* **Замо́лвите за неё слове́чко!** *Put in a good word for her!*

The accusative singular of nouns

MODELS

Кого́ вы́ та́м ви́дели?	Whom did you see there?
— Бори́са.	Boris.
— Влади́мира.	Vladimir.
— Профе́ссора Орло́ва.	Professor Orlov.
— Евге́ния.	Evgeny.
— Никола́я.	Nikolay.
— Ко́лю.	Kolya.
— Воло́дю.	Volodya.
— Са́шу.	Sasha.
— Ири́ну.	Irina.
— Мари́ю.	Maria.
— Любо́вь.	Lyubov.
Что́ вы́ купи́ли?	What did you buy?
— Хле́б.	Bread.
— Ча́й.	Tea.
— Молоко́.	Milk.
— Ка́рту Кита́я.	A map of China.
— Ры́бу.	Fish.
— Селёдку.	Herring.
— Тетра́дь.	A notebook.
Куда́ о́н пошёл?	Where did he go?
— На уро́к.	To class.
— На конце́рт.	To a concert.
— В клу́б.	To the club.
— В па́рк.	To the park.
— На собра́ние.	To a meeting.
— В общежи́тие.	To the dormitory.
— На фа́брику.	To the factory.
— В шко́лу.	To school.
— В библиоте́ку.	To the library.
— В лаборато́рию.	To the laboratory.
— На ле́кцию.	To the lecture (*or* class).
Когда́ вы́ бу́дете до́ма.	When will you be home?
— В воскресе́нье.	On Sunday.
— В понеде́льник.	On Monday.

— Во вто́рник.	On Tuesday.
— В сре́ду.	On Wednesday.
— В четве́рг.	On Thursday.
— В пя́тницу.	On Friday.
— В суббо́ту.	On Saturday.

Я бу́ду у ни́х ве́сь де́нь.	I'll be at their place all day.
_____ ве́сь ве́чер.	_____ all evening.
_____ всё у́тро.	_____ all morning.
_____ всё ле́то.	_____ all summer.
_____ всю зи́му.	_____ all winter.
_____ всю весну́.	_____ all spring.
_____ всю о́сень.	_____ all autumn.
_____ всю неде́лю.	_____ all week.

■ **REPETITION DRILL**

Repeat the given models, noting that the accusative singular is like the nominative singular except for:

1. Animate **сто́л**-nouns, which use the genitive singular endings.
2. **Жена́**-nouns, which have the endings –y and –ю in the accusative singular.

■ **CUED SUBSTITUTION DRILL**

(Oleg)	*Do you know Oleg?*
т: (Оле́г)	Вы́ зна́ете Оле́га?
s:	**Вы́ зна́ете Оле́га?**
т: (профе́ссор Орло́в) (Вы́) _____?	
s:	**Вы́ зна́ете профе́с-сора Орло́ва?**

(Никола́й, учи́тель, Семе́нов, его́ сестра́, америка́нец Гра́нт, Са́ша, студе́нт Козло́в, Евге́ний, его́ това́рищ, секрета́рь)

■ **RESPONSE DRILLS**

1. *We have no bread.*
   I bought bread today.
   т: У на́с не́т хле́ба.
   s: **Я сего́дня купи́л хле́б.**
   т: У на́с не́т ча́я.
   s: **Я сего́дня купи́л ча́й.**
   (нет рыбы, нет молока, нет кофе, нет селёдки, нет атласа, нет словаря, нет карты Европы)

2. *There's Professor Orlov over there.*
   I know Professor Orlov.
   т: Во́н та́м профе́ссор Орло́в.
   s: **Я зна́ю профе́ссора Орло́ва.**
   т: Во́н та́м Любо́вь Петро́вна.
   s: **Я зна́ю Любо́вь Петро́вну.**
   (Володя, Курочкин, Борис Михайлович, Ирина Ивановна, Коля, его секретарь)

■ **QUESTION-ANSWER DRILLS**

1. *Where's the key?*
   I left the key on the table.
   т: Где́ клю́ч?
   s: **Клю́ч я оста́вил на столе́.**
   т: Где́ кни́га?
   s: **Кни́гу я оста́вил на столе́.**
   (молоко, тетрадь, ручка, словарь, письмо, коробка, материал)

2. *Was the exam on Monday?*
   No, on Tuesday.
   т: Экза́мен бы́л в понеде́льник?
   s: **Не́т, во вто́рник.**
   т: Экза́мен бы́л во вто́рник?
   s: **Не́т, в сре́ду.**
   (в среду, в четверг, в пятницу)

1. *Where's the park?*
   I want to go to the park.
   т: Где парк?
   s: **Я хочу пойти в парк.**
   т: Где общежитие?
   s: **Я хочу пойти в общежитие.**
   (ГУМ, школа, фабрика, клуб, большой зал, библиотека)

2. *Maybe Katya heard about that.*
   Ask Katya.
   т: Может быть Катя слышала об этом.
   s: **Спросите Катю.**
   т: Может быть Лев слышал об этом.
   s: **Спросите Льва.**
   (Любовь Петровна, Евгений, профессор Курочкин, Пётр Иванович, его товарищ по комнате, Оля, учитель Семёнов)

3. *Nina and Katya were there.*
   I saw only Katya.
   т: Там были Нина и Катя.
   s: **Я видел только Катю.**
   т: Там были Орлов и Курочкин.
   s: **Я видел только Курочкина.**
   (Володя и Олег, брат и сестра, Оля и Николай, студент и студентка, уборщица и вахтёр, муж и жена)

4. *Over there is the university.*
   I've already seen the university.
   т: Вон там университет.
   s: **Я уже видел университет.**
   т: Вон там общежитие.
   s: **Я уже видел общежитие.**
   (почта, лаборатория, дверь, здание библиотеки, её комната, их аудитория, магазин)

DISCUSSION

Only **жена**-nouns and animate **стол**-nouns have accusatives which differ from the nominative. Animate **стол**-nouns have accusatives exactly like their genitives. **Жена**-nouns have accusatives ending in –y (for nominatives ending in –a) and –ю (for nominatives ending in –я).

NOUN ENDINGS IN THE ACCUSATIVE SINGULAR				
стол-nouns		**окно**-nouns	**жена**-nouns	**дверь**-nouns
Inanimate (same as nominative)	Animate (same as genitive)	(same as nominative)	–y and –ю	(same as nominative)
стол	Козлова	окно	жену	дверь
портфель	мужа	дело	сестру	очередь
карандаш	украинца	утро	Зину	Любовь
ГУМ	якута	перо	уборщицу	осень
танец	профессора	собрание	Колю	тетрадь
фильм	студента	сочинение	Галю	
Китай	брата	платье	неделю	
угол	Льва	пение	Катю	
атлас	Кирилла		Володю	
	Евгения		историю	
	парня			

A few **жена**-nouns with the stress on the ending in the nominative singular shift the stress back to the stem in the accusative singular. Compare **зима** with **зиму** *winter*, **среда** with **среду** *Wednesday*, and **доска** with **доску** *board*.

Summary remarks. The accusative functions primarily to indicate the goal of a verbal action, i.e., the direct object of a transitive verb. Used in conjunction with such prepositions as **в** and **на**, it indicates the goal to which the action is directed.

The accusative is also frequently used in expressions of time, where it may occur either with or without a preposition, for example, **в суббо́ту, на э́тот раз, всю зи́му.** When used without a preposition, it indicates the complete span of time encompassed by the activity.

Second conjugation verbs with a stem consonant change in the first person singular present-future

Вы́ давно́ здесь сиди́те?	Have you been sitting here long?
— Да́, всё у́тро сижу́ здесь.	Yes, I've been sitting here all morning.
Вы́ за́втра уви́дите Ни́ну?	Will you see Nina tomorrow?
— Да́, уви́жу.	Yes, I will.
Попроси́те его́ к телефо́ну.	Ask him to the phone.
— Хорошо́, сейча́с попрошу́.	O.K., I'll do it right away.
Спроси́те Ку́рочкина об э́том.	Ask Kurochkin about that.
— Я́ за́втра его́ спрошу́.	I'll ask him tomorrow.
Что́ вы́ ку́пите в ГУ́Ме?	What are you going to buy at GUM?
— Я́ куплю́ пода́рок Ни́не.	I'll buy a present for Nina.
Вы́ лю́бите ча́й?	Do you like tea?
— Да́, о́чень люблю́.	Yes, I'm very fond of it.
Где́ вы́ оста́вите клю́ч?	Where will you leave the key?
— Я́ оста́влю его́ в я́щике.	I'll leave it in the drawer.
Вы́ меня́ познако́мите?	Will you introduce me?
— Да́, познако́млю.	Yes, I will.

■ REPETITION DRILL

Repeat the above models, noting that there are two types of change which may take place in the first person singular of second conjugation verbs:

1. Replacement of the final stem consonant by an automatic alternate (compare **ты́ ви́дишь, о́н ви́дит** with **я́ ви́жу**).

2. The addition of a soft л (compare **ты́ лю́бишь, о́н лю́бит** with **я́ люблю́**).

■ SUBSTITUTION DRILLS

1. *You sit home all the time.*
   т: Ты́ всё вре́мя сиди́шь до́ма.
   s: **Ты́ всё вре́мя сиди́шь до́ма.**
   (она, мы, вы, они, Катя, я, моя жена, ваши братья)

2. *Zina loves to dance.*
   т: Зи́на лю́бит танцева́ть.
   s: **Зи́на лю́бит танцева́ть.**
   (мы все, наши студентки, я, вы, ты, эта девушка, Петр и Мила, я)

3. *I'll leave the key with Pyotr.*
   т: Я́ оста́влю клю́ч у Петра́.
   s: **Я́ оста́влю клю́ч у Петра́.**
   (она, ты, мы, вы, я, они)

4. *I sometimes see Zina at the movies.*
   т: Я́ иногда́ ви́жу Зи́ну в кино́.
   s: **Я́ иногда́ ви́жу Зи́ну в кино́.**
   (Олег, ты, они, вы, я, мои друзья, мы, мой товарищ по комнате)

5. *When shall I see you again?*

т: Когда́ я опя́ть ва́с уви́жу?

s: Когда́ я́ опя́ть ва́с уви́жу?

(он, мы, Воло́дя, я, эти америка́нцы, они́)

6. *I'll ask him for the key.*

т: Я попрошу́ у него́ клю́ч.

s: Я́ попрошу́ у него́ клю́ч.

(ты, они́, мы, вы, я, Ива́н, она́, наши студе́нты)

7. *I'll ask them about that.*

т: Я спрошу́ и́х об э́том.

s: Я́ спрошу́ и́х об э́том.

(мы, вы, Катя, де́вушки, ты, он, я, студе́нтки)

8. *We'll buy bread tomorrow.*

т: Мы́ за́втра ку́пим хле́б.

s: Мы́ за́втра ку́пим хле́б.

(я, ты, вы, она́, я, они́, он, я, мы, вы, ты, я)

9. *I'll introduce him to her.*

т: Я его́ познако́млю с не́й.

s: Я́ его́ познако́млю с не́й.

(они́, мы, Катя, я, ты, вы, Оле́г, де́вушки, Воло́дя)

■ STRUCTURE REPLACEMENT DRILLS

1. *Whom did you ask about this?*
   Whom will you ask about this?

т: Кого́ ты́ спроси́л об э́том?

s: Кого́ ты́ спро́сишь об э́том?

т: Кого́ вы́ спроси́ли об э́том?

s: Кого́ вы́ спро́сите об э́том?

(мы, они́, я, она́, он)

2. *I left the dictionary on his desk.*
   I'll leave the dictionary on his desk.

т: Я оста́вил слова́рь у него́ на столе́.

s: Я́ оста́влю слова́рь у него́ на столе́.

т: Она́ оста́вила слова́рь у него́ на столе́.

s: Она́ оста́вит слова́рь у него́ на столе́.

(мы, они́, Катя, вы, Евге́ний, ты, я, студе́нт, америка́нец)

3. *She bought suit material.*
   She'll buy suit material.

т: Она́ купи́ла материа́л на костю́м.

s: Она́ ку́пит материа́л на костю́м.

т: Я купи́л материа́л на костю́м.

s: Я́ куплю́ материа́л на костю́м.

(Воло́дя, они́, вы, сестра́, я, Козло́в)

4. *Zina used to sit home all the time.*
   Zina sits at home all the time.

т: Зи́на всё вре́мя сиде́ла до́ма.

s: Зи́на всё вре́мя сиди́т до́ма.

т: Вы́ всё вре́мя сиде́ли до́ма.

s: Вы́ всё вре́мя сиди́те до́ма.

(я, она́, эти студе́нты, ты, они́, мы, он)

5. *She loved you.*
   She loves you.

т: Она́ ва́с люби́ла.

s: Она́ ва́с лю́бит.

т: О́н ва́с люби́л.

s: О́н ва́с лю́бит.

(мой бра́т, я, они́, мы, этот америка́нец)

6. *They often used to see Oleg.*
   They often see Oleg.

т: Они́ ча́сто ви́дели Оле́га.

s: Они́ ча́сто ви́дят Оле́га.

т: Я ча́сто ви́дел Оле́га.

s: Я́ ча́сто ви́жу Оле́га.

(он, студе́нтка, Зи́на, мы, наши де́вушки, вы, ты, я)

DISCUSSION

Second conjugation verbs undergo a stem change in the first person singular present-future if their stem ends in д, т, с, з, б, п, в, ф, or м.

1. Dentals д, т, с, and з are automatically replaced by their palatal alternates ж, ч, ш, and ж respectively, and the first person singular ending is spelled –у.
2. Labials б, п, в, ф, and м add a soft л before the first person singular ending –ю.

	GROUP 1		GROUP 2			
INFINITIVE	ви́деть to see (ipfv)	спроси́ть to ask (pfv)	люби́ть to love (ipfv)	купи́ть to buy (pfv)	оста́вить to leave (pfv)	познако́мить to introduce (pfv)
SG 1	ви́жу	спрошу́	люблю́	куплю́	оста́влю	познако́млю
2	ви́дишь	спро́сишь	лю́бишь	ку́пишь	оста́вишь	познако́мишь
3	ви́дит	спро́сит	лю́бит	ку́пит	оста́вит	познако́мит
PL 1	ви́дим	спро́сим	лю́бим	ку́пим	оста́вим	познако́мим
2	ви́дите	спро́сите	лю́бите	ку́пите	оста́вите	познако́мите
3	ви́дят	спро́сят	лю́бят	ку́пят	оста́вят	познако́мят

Note that the change in stem occurs only in the first person singular.

If the stress is on the last syllable of the infinitive, it will fall on the ending of the first person singular, but will often shift back one syllable in all other forms of the present-future. Compare **спроси́ть, спрошу́** with **спро́сишь, спро́сит, спро́сим, спро́сите, спро́сят**. If the stress of the infinitive falls on a syllable other than the last, it will remain on that same syllable in all forms, for example, **оста́вить, оста́влю, оста́вишь, оста́вит, оста́вим, оста́вите, оста́вят**.

In the past tense, the stress is consistently on the same syllable as in the infinitive, for example, **ви́деть, ви́дел, ви́дела, ви́дело, ви́дели; люби́ть, люби́л, люби́ла, люби́ло, люби́ли**.

The future of бы́ть
and the formation of the imperfective future

MODELS

Я бу́ду та́м в суббо́ту.	I'll be there on Saturday.
Ты́ бу́дешь _____.	You'll be _____.
О́н бу́дет _____.	He'll be _____.
Мы́ бу́дем _____.	We'll be _____.
Вы́ бу́дете _____.	You'll be _____.
Они́ бу́дут _____.	They'll be _____.

Что́ вы́ бу́дете де́лать?
— Мы́ бу́дем рабо́тать.

What will you be doing?
We'll be working.

Что́ ты́ бу́дешь де́лать?
— Я́ бу́ду чита́ть.

What will you be doing?
I'll be reading *or* I'll read.

Что́ Оле́г бу́дет де́лать?
— О́н бу́дет писа́ть пи́сьма.

What will Oleg be doing?
He'll be writing letters.

Что́ они́ бу́дут де́лать?
— Они́ бу́дут танцева́ть.

What will they be doing?
They'll be dancing.

Что́ мы́ бу́дем де́лать?
— Мы́ бу́дем пи́ть ча́й.

What shall we do?
We'll drink tea.

Repeat the given models, noting that the future of **быть** may be used alone (in the sense of *will* or *shall be*) or in combination with imperfective infinitives to form the imperfective future. Remember that the future forms of **быть** can never be combined with perfective infinitives.

■ QUESTION-ANSWER DRILLS

1. *Will you be home this evening?*
   No, I won't.
   т: Вы́ бу́дете до́ма сего́дня ве́чером?
   s: **Не́т, не бу́ду.**
   т: Оле́г бу́дет до́ма сего́дня ве́чером?
   s: **Не́т, не бу́дет.**
   (они, ты, твой брат, ваша сестра)

2. *Will you be working tomorrow?*
   Yes, I will.
   т: Ты́ бу́дешь рабо́тать за́втра?
   s: **Да́, бу́ду.**
   т: Секрета́рь бу́дет рабо́тать за́втра?
   s: **Да́, бу́дет.**
   (эта студентка, вы, мы, ваши товарищи, вахтёр)

3. *What are you going to do, drink tea?*
   Yes, we're going to drink tea.
   т: Что́ Вы́ бу́дете де́лать, пи́ть ча́й?
   s: **Да́, мы́ бу́дем пи́ть ча́й.**
   т: Что́ вы́ бу́дете де́лать, танцева́ть?
   s: **Да́, мы́ бу́дем танцева́ть.**
   (писать сочинение, читать стихи, говорить с ними, ждать секретаря, слушать лекции, обедать в ресторане)

■ STRUCTURE REPLACEMENT DRILLS

1. *I didn't ask about that.*
   I won't ask about that.
   т: Я́ об э́том не спра́шивал.
   s: **Я́ об э́том не бу́ду спра́шивать.**
   т: Она́ об э́том не спра́шивала.
   s: **Она́ об э́том не бу́дет спра́шивать.**
   (ты, мы, он, вы, они, учительница, профессора, украинец, студенты)

2. *I didn't think about that.*
   I won't think about that.
   т: Я́ об э́том не ду́мал.
   s: **Я́ об э́том не бу́ду ду́мать.**
   т: Вы́ об э́том не ду́мали.
   s: **Вы́ об э́том не бу́дете ду́мать.**
   (они, мы, ты, я, жена, мои товарищи)

3. *We drank tea.*
   We'll drink tea.
   т: Мы́ пи́ли ча́й.
   s: **Мы́ бу́дем пи́ть ча́й.**
   т: Ты́ пи́л ча́й.
   s: **Ты́ бу́дешь пи́ть ча́й.**
   (они, вы, она, он, я, муж и жена, моя сестра, мой товарищ, студенты, этот парень)

1. *Who'll be there? Volodya?*
   Yes, Volodya will be there.
   т: Кто́ та́м бу́дет? Воло́дя?
   s: **Да́, та́м бу́дет Воло́дя.**
   т: Кто́ та́м бу́дет? Студе́нты?
   s: **Да́, та́м бу́дут студе́нты.**
   (Мария, ваш брат, учителя, твои
   товарищи, продавщицы, Зина)

2. *What will you be doing?*
   I'll be reading.
   т: Что́ вы́ бу́дете де́лать?
   s: **Я́ бу́ду чита́ть.**
   т: Что́ о́н бу́дет де́лать?
   s: **О́н бу́дет чита́ть.**
   (они, мы, ты, она, твой товарищ,
   студенты, твоя сестра)

3. *Will you drink tea?*
   No, I won't.
   т: Ты́ бу́дешь пи́ть ча́й?
   s: **Не́т, не бу́ду.**
   т: Она́ бу́дет пи́ть ча́й?
   s: **Не́т, не бу́дет.**
   (мы, они, он, вы, твой товарищ, эти
   парни, учительницы)

4. *Will you be dancing?*
   Yes, I will.
   т: Вы́ бу́дете танцева́ть?
   s: **Да́, бу́ду.**
   т: Она́ бу́дет танцева́ть?
   s: **Да́, бу́дет.**
   (ты, мы, студенты, твой товарищ,
   украинцы, твоя сестра, грузины, этот
   парень)

■ STRUCTURE REPLACEMENT DRILLS

1. *I'm reading War and Peace.*
   I'll be reading War and Peace.
   т: Я́ чита́ю «Войну́ и ми́р».
   s: **Я́ бу́ду чита́ть «Войну́ и ми́р».**
   т: О́н чита́ет «Войну́ и ми́р».
   s: **О́н бу́дет чита́ть «Войну́ и ми́р».**
   (они, мы, ты, она, студенты, вы, мой
   товарищ)

2. *What were you doing?*
   What will you be doing?
   т: Что́ вы́ де́лали?
   s: **Что́ вы́ бу́дете де́лать?**
   т: Что́ вы́ писа́ли?
   s: **Что́ вы́ бу́дете писа́ть.**
   (читали, покупали, пили, спрашивали)

3. *We're sitting by the window.*
   We'll be sitting by the window.
   т: Мы́ сиди́м у окна́.
   s: **Мы́ бу́дем сиде́ть у окна́.**
   т: Я́ сижу́ у окна́.
   s: **Я́ бу́ду сиде́ть у окна́.**
   (они, Козлов, Катя, ты, вы, студентки, он)

4. *Zina's at the dance.*
   Zina will be at the dance.
   т: Зи́на на та́нцах.
   s: **Зи́на бу́дет на та́нцах.**
   т: Они́ на та́нцах.
   s: **Они́ бу́дут на та́нцах.**
   (наши парни, я, мы, Володя и его
   товарищ)

5. *He was at the library.*
   He'll be at the library.
   т: О́н бы́л в библиоте́ке.
   s: **О́н бу́дет в библиоте́ке.**
   т: Вы́ бы́ли в библиоте́ке.
   s: **Вы́ бу́дете в библиоте́ке.**
   (все профессора, эта студентка, я, этот
   студент, мы, они)

As in the past tense, the imperfective and perfective aspects are sharply contrasted in the future. The imperfective future is used to describe future activity not specifically marked off in time, or activity expected to occur more than once in the future. Thus the focus is on the activity as a process or recurring phenomenon. This type of future is formed by means of the future of **быть** plus the imperfective infinitive.

The perfective future, on the other hand, describes future activity of a more concrete, realizable nature. It focuses on the completion or accomplishment of the activity, and it concerns itself more with the result than the process. It is a simple form, structurally like the present tense and employing the same personal endings as the present tense.

EXAMPLES

IPFV FUT	Я бу́ду ду́мать об э́том.	I'll be thinking about it.
PFV FUT	Я поду́маю об э́том.	I'll think about it *or* I'll think it over.
IPFV FUT	Мы́ что́-нибудь бу́дем де́лать.	We'll [be] do[ing] something.
PFV FUT	Мы́ что́-нибудь сде́лаем.	We'll do something *or* We'll get something done.
IPFV FUT	Они́ бу́дут мно́го спра́шивать.	They'll ask a lot of questions.
PFV FUT	Они́ спро́сят об э́том.	They'll ask about that.

In short, the imperfective aspect emphasizes the "doing," whereas the perfective emphasizes "getting the thing done."

Куда́ and где: directional versus locational concepts

Куда́ вы́ спеши́те?	Where are you hurrying to?
— Домо́й.	Home.
Где́ вы́ бы́ли ве́сь де́нь?	Where have you been all day?
— До́ма.	At home.
Куда́ она́ идёт?	Where's she going?
— Она́ идёт **на по́чту**.	She's on her way to the post office.
Где́ она́?	Where is she?
— Она́ **на по́чте**.	She's at the post office now.
Пойдём **в клу́б**.	Let's go to the club.
В клу́бе бу́дут та́нцы.	There'll be dancing at the club.
Я́ не хочу́ идти́ **туда́**.	I don't want to go there.
Кто́ **та́м** бу́дет?	Who'll be there?
Иди́ **сюда́**.	Come here.
О́н **здесь**.	He's here.

■ REPETITION DRILL

Repeat the given models, noting that the distinction between "directional" and "locational" concepts in Russian is observed both in the adverbs and in the case system.

■ CUED QUESTION-ANSWER DRILL

	(park)	*Where's she going?*
		To the park.
т:	(па́рк)	Куда́ она́ идёт?
s:		**В па́рк.**
т:	(па́рк)	Где́ она́ была́?
s:		**В парке.**
	(магази́н)	Куда́ вы́ идёте?
	(магази́н)	Где́ вы́ доста́ли костю́м?
	(лаборато́рия)	Куда́ вы́ спеши́те?
	(лаборато́рия)	Где́ она́ рабо́тает?
	(заво́д)	Куда́ о́н пошёл?
	(заво́д)	Где́ ва́ш му́ж?
	(по́чта)	Куда́ пошёл Ива́н?
	(по́чта)	Где́ о́н тепе́рь?
	(библиоте́ка)	Куда́ она́ спеши́ла?
	(библиоте́ка)	Где́ она́ тепе́рь?

■ RESPONSE DRILL

He was at the club.
Where?

т: Óн бы́л в клу́бе.
s: **Где́?**
т: Óн спеши́л на обе́д.
s: **Куда́?**

Я́ ду́маю пойти́ в кино́.
Они́ бу́дут танцева́ть в клу́бе.
Я́ забы́л слова́рь в столо́вой.
Они́ иду́т домо́й.

Я́ пойду́ в магази́н.
Мы́ спеши́ли на рабо́ту.
Я́ оста́вил сво́й портфе́ль до́ма.
Пойдём в библиоте́ку.
Вы́ спроси́те в магази́не на углу́.
Óн забы́л ключи́ на заво́де.
Я́ спеши́л на по́чту.
Мы́ идём на та́нцы.
Студе́нты сейча́с на экза́менах.

■ STRUCTURE REPLACEMENT DRILLS

1. *He's here.*
   He's coming this way (or *here*).
   т: Óн зде́сь.
   s: **Óн идёт сюда́.**
   т: Óн на рабо́те.
   s: **Óн идёт на рабо́ту.**
   (он в библиотеке, на концерте, здесь, там, дома)

2. *I'm at work.*
   I'm on my way to work.
   т: Я́ на рабо́те.
   s: **Я́ иду́ на рабо́ту.**
   т: Я́ на уро́ке.
   s: **Я́ иду́ на уро́к.**
   (на заводе, на почте, на лекции, на собрании, на службе, на экзамене, на обеде)

3. *He's going to town.*
   He's been in town.
   т: Óн идёт в го́род.
   s: **Óн бы́л в го́роде.**
   т: Óн идёт в магази́н.
   s: **Óн бы́л в магази́не.**
   (в ГУМ, в школу, в библиотеку, в университет, в кино, в клуб, в общежитие)

1. *He's already been downtown.*
   I'm going downtown now.
   т: Óн ужé бы́л в гóроде.
   s: **Тепéрь я́ иду́ в гóрод.**
   т: Óн ужé бы́л на рабóте.
   s: **Тепéрь я́ иду́ на рабóту.**
      (в библиотеке, на заводе, на уроке, в школе, на экзамене, в общежитии, в ГУМе, на собрании)

2. *I forgot my briefcase at the library.*
   I'm going to the library.
   т: Я́ забы́л портфéль в библиотéке.
   s: **Я́ иду́ в библиотéку.**
   т: Я́ забы́л портфéль в университéте.
   s: **Я́ иду́ в университéт.**
      (в школе, в ГУМе, в магазине, в общежитии, дома, в горсовете)

3. *It's time to go to school.*
   Well, here we are at school already.
   т: Порá идти́ в шкóлу.
   s: **Ну́ вóт, мы́ ужé в шкóле.**

   т: Порá идти́ на рабóту.
   s: **Ну́ вóт, мы́ ужé на рабóте.**
      (в библиотеку, в университет, в магазин, на службу, на почту)

■ QUESTION-ANSWER DRILL

Was he at home?
Yes, but where were you?
т: Óн бы́л дóма?
s: **Дá, а гдé вы́ бы́ли?**
т: Óн спеши́л на обéд?
s: **Дá, а куда́ вы́ спеши́ли?**
   Óн бы́л в кинó?

Óн спеши́л в кинó?
Óн э́то слы́шал в шкóле?
Óн пошёл в шкóлу?
Óн э́то читáл в библиотéке?
Óн спеши́л в библиотéку?
Óн бы́л в пáрке?
Óн пошёл в пáрк?

DISCUSSION

The distinction between *where to* and *where at* is observed both in the adverbs (куда́ versus гдé; домóй versus дóма) and in the case system. For example, prepositions в and на must be followed by the accusative if destination is involved and by the prepositional if only location is involved.

1. **Куда́** question with destinational (*where to*) adverb or *accusative case* in the answer:

Куда́ вы́ идёте?	Where are you going [to]?
— Домóй.	Home[ward].
— В клýб.	To the club.
— На пóчту.	To the post office.
— В шкóлу.	To school.
— На слýжбу.	To work.

2. **Гдé** question with locational (*where at*) adverb or *prepositional case* in the answer:

Гдé вы́ бы́ли?	Where were you?
— Дóма.	At home.
— В клýбе.	At the club.
— На пóчте.	At the post office.
— В шкóле.	At school.
— На слýжбе.	At work.

KEY QUESTION WORD	TYPE OF VERB	TYPE OF ADVERB	CASE REQUIRED AFTER в AND на
куда́	*destinational* e.g. идти́, пойти́, спеши́ть	*destinational* домо́й, туда́, сюда́	*accusative* на по́чту, в шко́лу
где́	*locational* e.g. бы́ть, жи́ть, сиде́ть, рабо́тать	*locational* до́ма, та́м, здесь	*prepositional* на по́чте, в шко́ле

ЧТЕ́НИЕ И ПИСЬМО́

– Вы не зна́ете, фильм „Война́ и мир" уже́ идёт? – Да. Я его́ ви́дел. – А где он идёт? В го́роде? – Нет, здесь, в кино́ на углу́. – Ах, здесь! Тогда́ я пойду́ сего́дня ве́чером.

– Почему́ ты не́ был на ле́кции? – Я был бо́лен. А о чём говори́л профе́ссор? – О рома́не „Война́ и мир". Ты чита́л э́тот рома́н? – Коне́чно, чита́л. А когда́ у нас бу́дет экза́мен? – На сле́дующей неде́ле.

– Ка́тя, хоти́те за́втра ве́чером пойти́ в клуб? – Нет, не хо́чется. В клу́бе о́чень ску́чно. – Что вы! Там бу́дут та́нцы. – Я не люблю́ танцева́ть. – Как тогда́ насчёт кино́? Сего́дня идёт фильм „Бори́с Годуно́в". – А, это интере́сно. – Так пойдём? – Хорошо́.

– За́втра мы идём на „Евге́ния Оне́гина". – Это америка́нский фильм? – Нет, ру́сский. Говоря́т, хоро́ший. – А вы не знаете, этот фильм будет долго идти? — Кажется, всю неделю. — Тогда я пойду в субботу.

— Галя, ты всё время сидишь дома. Пойдём завтра в театр. — Не могу. Я и Володя идём завтра вечером на танцы. — Ты и Володя? А я и не знала, что вы знакомы. — Мы уже давно знакомы.

— Ты был сегодня в общежитии? — Нет ещё. Сразу после занятий пошёл в кино. — Да? А что там идёт? — Американский фильм „Война и мир". — Вот как! Хороший? — Да. У нас такие фильмы редко видишь.

— Зина, вы знакомы? Это мой товарищ Олег. — Конечно, знакомы. Мы на одном курсе. — Вот как? Я не знала. — Да, знакомы и вечером идём вместе в кино.

— Вы не знаете, столовая уже открыта? — Да, и я уже пообедал. — А что было сегодня на обед? Наверно, как всегда, щи? — Да, щи и, конечно, каша. Была рыба, но больше нет. — Вот досада! Даже идти не хочется.

— Зина, почему ты всё время сидишь дома? — А куда здесь можно пойти? — В клуб, в кино. — В клубе скучно. — Нет, не всегда, в пятницу будут танцы. — А это другóе дéло. Танцевать я люблю.

— Кирилл, кто это? — Это Филипп, студент из Америки. — Ты знаком с ним? — Да, мы часто обедаем вместе в столовой. — Он хороший парень? — Да, очень. Хочешь, я тебя познакомлю с ним? — Конечно. Буду очень рад.

— Назовите дни недели. — Дни недели: понедельник, вторник, среда, четверг, пятница, суббота, воскресенье. — Какой сегодня день? — Сегодня среда. — Какой день был вчера? — Вчера был вторник. — А какой день будет завтра? — Завтра будет четверг. — А послезавтра? — Послезавтра будет пятница.

Я хочу пойти в кино. Я спросила, что идёт в кино и узнала, что идёт «Война и мир». Я уже видела этот фильм. Может быть пойти в клуб? Там, наверно, будут танцы.

Вчера на лекции профессор Орлов очень интересно говорил о народах СССР: о якутах и грузинах. На следующей неделе он будет говорить об украинцах. Олег уже слышал его много раз, а я только один раз.

У Козлова и его товарища в четверг экзамены. Они всё утро сидели в библиотеке. Сейчас они идут в ресторан. После обеда они опять пойдут в библиотеку.

Я спросил товарища, где можно достать американский словарь Вебстера. Он не знал. Мы спросили в библиотеке, но там такого словаря не было. Тогда мы спросили в магазине на углу, но там тоже не было, и продавщица не знала, где его можно купить.

Николай и Галя весь день сидели в библиотеке. Они были очень голодны. Они хотели пообедать в столовой, но там были только борщ и каша. Тогда Николай и Галя пошли в ресторан.

NOTES

PREPARATION FOR CONVERSATION   **В кино́**

до́брый	kind, good
До́брый ве́чер.	Good evening.
До́брый ве́чер, Зи́на.	Good evening, Zina.
Вы́ что́ ту́т де́лаете?	What are you doing here?
Оле́г! Вы́ что́ ту́т де́лаете?	Oleg! What are you doing here?
карти́на (gen pl карти́н)	picture
э́та карти́на	this (*or* that *or* the) picture
Я́ хочу́ посмотре́ть э́ту карти́ну.	I want to see this picture.
Я́ то́же хочу́ посмотре́ть э́ту карти́ну.	I, too, want to see the picture.
да во́т [dəvót]	well, why
Да во́т то́же хочу́ посмотре́ть э́ту карти́ну.	Why, I want to see the picture, too.
Во́т ка́к!	Is that so!
ходи́ть (II)	to go, attend
хожу́, хо́дят	I go, they go
Вы́ никогда́ не хо́дите в кино́.	You never go to the movies.
А я́ ду́мала, что вы́ никогда́ не хо́дите в кино́.	But I thought you never went to the movies.
Ка́к ви́дите, хожу́.	As you see, I do.
встре́тить (pfv II)	to meet, encounter
встре́чу, встре́тят	I'll meet, they'll meet
Я́ ва́с встре́тил.	I met you.
уда́ча	luck, good luck
во́т уда́ча	what luck, what a lucky break
И во́т уда́ча — ва́с встре́тил.	And what a lucky break—I've met you.
ка́ждый	each, every
Вы́ меня́ ви́дите ка́ждый де́нь.	You see me every day.
Почему́ уда́ча? Вы́ меня́ ви́дите ка́ждый де́нь.	Why is it a lucky break? You see me every day.
Да́, но на заня́тиях.	Yes, but in class.

поговори́ть (pfv II)	to talk (a bit), have a talk
поговорю́, поговоря́т	I'll have a talk, they'll have a talk
не поговори́шь	one can't talk, you can't talk (*lit.* you won't talk)
Та́м не поговори́шь.	You can't talk there.
Да́, но на заня́тиях. Та́м не поговори́шь.	Yes, but [only] in class. You can't [really] talk there.
А о чём же вы́ хоти́те поговори́ть?	And what is it you want to talk about?
мно́гое	many things, lots of things
О мно́гом.	About a lot of things.
себя́	oneself (refl pron)
о себе́	about oneself
о ва́с, о себе́	about you, about myself
наприме́р	for example
Наприме́р о ва́с, о себе́.	For example, about you, about myself.
успе́ть (pfv I)	to succeed, manage, make it
успе́ю, успе́ют	I'll manage, they'll manage
Не успе́ем.	We won't succeed *or* We won't be able to.
вре́мени не́т	there's no time
Не успе́ем, вре́мени не́т.	We won't be able to [because] there isn't time.
открыва́ть (I)	to open
открыва́ю, открыва́ют	I'm opening, they're opening
Уже́ две́ри открыва́ют.	They're opening the doors already.
Не успе́ем, вре́мени не́т. Уже́ две́ри открыва́ют.	We won't be able to [because] there isn't time. They're opening the doors already.

SUPPLEMENT

опа́здывать (I)	to come late, to be late
опа́здываю, опа́здывают	I come late, they come late
Вы́ всегда́ опа́здываете.	You always come late.
опозда́ть (pfv I)	to be late
опозда́ю, опозда́ют	I'll be late, they'll be late
я́ опозда́л(а)	I'm late, I was late
Извини́те, что я опозда́л(а).	Excuse me for being late.
но́чь (f)	night
но́чью	at night
споко́йный	quiet, calm, serene
Споко́йной но́чи![1]	Good night!
игра́ть в (*plus* acc)	to play (a game)
Вы́ игра́ете в ка́рты?	Do you play cards?
Вы́ игра́ете в те́ннис? [ftéɲis]	Do you play tennis?
Вы́ игра́ете в футбо́л? [ffudból]	Do you play soccer?
Вы́ игра́ете в бейсбо́л? [vbejzból]	Do you play baseball?
Вы́ игра́ете в хокке́й? [fxaķéj]	Do you play hockey?
весна́	spring
Вы́ бу́дете та́м всю́ весну́?	Will you be there all spring?
весно́й	in spring

---

[1] **Споко́йной но́чи**, like **всего́ хоро́шего**, is in the genitive case. This is usual with farewells and wishes for happiness.

Весно́й мы́ ча́сто игра́ем в те́ннис.	In spring we often play tennis.
ле́то	summer
Вы́ бу́дете та́м всё ле́то?	Will you be there all summer?
ле́том	in summer
Ле́том мы ча́сто игра́ем в бейсбо́л.	In summer we often play baseball.
зимо́й	in winter
Зимо́й мы́ ча́сто игра́ем в хокке́й.	In winter we often play hockey.
о́сенью	in autumn
О́сенью мы́ ча́сто игра́ем в футоол.	In autumn we often play soccer.
ско́ро	soon
В магази́не ско́ро бу́дут ка́рты.	They'll soon have maps in the store.

В кино́

Оле́г   1 До́брый ве́чер, Зи́на!

Зи́на   2 Оле́г! Вы́ что́ ту́т де́лаете?

Оле́г   3 Да во́т то́же хочу́ посмотре́ть э́ту карти́ну.

Зи́на   4 Во́т ка́к! А я ду́мала, что вы́ никогда́ не хо́дите в кино́.[1, 2]

Оле́г   5 Ка́к ви́дите, хожу́. И во́т уда́ча — ва́с встре́тил.

Зи́на   6 Почему́ уда́ча? Вы́ меня́ ви́дите ка́ждый де́нь.

Оле́г   7 Да́, но на заня́тиях. Та́м не поговори́шь.

Зи́на   8 А о чём же вы́ хоти́те поговори́ть?

Оле́г   9 О мно́гом. Наприме́р о ва́с, о себе́.[3]

Зи́на 10 Не успе́ем, вре́мени не́т. Уже́ две́ри открыва́ют.[4]

NOTES

[1] Note that in a subordinate clause, Russians use the present tense if the present tense is really meant. Compare the English, *I thought you never went to the movies*, where a past tense verb *went* is required because it is preceded by a past tense verb *thought* in the main clause. The Russian past tense is only used to describe events in the past that no longer occur in the present. **Я ду́мала, что вы́ никогда́ не ходи́ли в кино́** would mean *I thought you never used to go* (or *had gone*) *to the movies.*

Activities begun in the past and continuing in the present require the present tense in Russian. For example:

Вы́ давно́ здесь живёте?	Have you been living here long?
Я здесь рабо́таю с о́сени.	I've been working here since fall.

[2] **Ходи́ть** differs from **идти́** in that it describes the activity of going in general terms, *to go* or *to attend*, whereas **идти́** is more specific and means *to be going* or *to be on one's way*

Compare	Я хожу́ на собра́ния.	I go to the meetings (I attend meetings).
with	Я иду́ на собра́ние.	I'm going to a meeting (I'm on my way to a meeting).

With such adverbs as **ча́сто**, **ре́дко**, **никогда́**, and **иногда́**, the verb **ходи́ть** is normally used: **Вы́ ча́сто хо́дите в па́рк?** *Do you often go to the park?*

[3] Note that the reflexive personal pronoun **себе́** (rather than **мне́**) must be used here since the subject of the sentence and the object of the preposition **о** are the same:

Я́ не хочу́ говори́ть о **себе́**.	I don't want to talk about *myself*.

The single form **себе́** can refer to any of the personal pronouns:

Она́ ду́мает то́лько о **себе́**.	She thinks only of *herself*.
Они́ ду́мают то́лько о **себе́**.	They think only of *themselves*.
Вы́ ду́маете то́лько о **себе́**.	You think only of *yourself* (or *yourselves*).

Себе́ has no nominative form. It is usually cited in the accusative-genitive form **себя́**.

[4] If one is late to a motion-picture performance, he will not be allowed to enter while the picture is being shown; nor is it customary to leave before the picture is over. If this were done at a play, it would be considered *uncultured* **некульту́рно**.

PREPARATION FOR CONVERSATION   **По́сле кино́**

ну́ ка́к?	well, how about it?
понра́виться (pfv II)[1]	to like (*lit.* to appeal to)
Ну́ ка́к? Понра́вилось?	Well, how about it? Did you like it?
тако́й	such, so, like that
Я́ таки́х карти́н ещё не ви́дела.	I haven't seen any pictures like that before.
О́чень. Я́ таки́х карти́н ещё не ви́дела.	Very much. I haven't seen any pictures like that before.
Я́ то́же.	Neither have I *or* Same here.
Толсто́й (gen sg Толсто́го)	Tolstoy
понима́ние	understanding
Я́ не ожида́л тако́го понима́ния Толсто́го.	I didn't expect such understanding of Tolstoy.
Я́ не ожида́л от америка́нцев тако́го понима́ния Толсто́го.	I didn't expect such understanding of Tolstoy from the Americans.
игра́ть (I)	to play
Кто́ игра́л Ната́шу?	Who played Natasha?
и́мя (gen *and* prep sg и́мени, nom *and* acc pl имена́, gen pl имён)	name, first name
Я́ забы́ла и́мя.	I forgot the name *or* I've forgotten the name.
А кто́ игра́л Ната́шу? Я́ забы́ла и́мя.	But who played Natasha? I forgot the name.

---

[1] The verb **понра́виться** is a reflexive verb which is typically used in constructions requiring the dative case. The form **понра́вилось** is neuter past tense, and it may be literally translated as *it appealed* or *it made a favorable impression*.

помнить (II)
помню, помнят
Я тоже имени не помню.

to remember
I remember, they remember
I don't remember her name either.

выговорить (pfv II)
выговорю, выговорят
не выговоришь

to pronounce, say
I'll pronounce, they'll pronounce
one can't pronounce, you can't pronounce
(*lit.* you won't pronounce)

У них имена — не выговоришь.

They have names you can't pronounce.

Американцы не могут выговорить русских имён.

Americans can't pronounce Russian names.

А американцы, наверно, русских имён не могут выговорить.

Americans probably can't pronounce Russian names either.

Наверно.

Probably.

Вы часто ходите в кино или в клуб?
Скажите, вы часто ходите в кино или в клуб?

Do you often go to the movies or to the club?
Tell me, do you often go to the movies or to the club?

В кино — часто, а в клуб — нет.

To the movies, often; but to the club, no.

на танцы
разве что   [rázɣištə]
Разве что на танцы.

to dances, to a dance
unless maybe
Unless maybe to a dance.

Так вы любите танцевать?

Then you like to dance?

Хотите пойти в субботу?

Do you want to go Saturday?

С удовольствием.

I'd be glad to *or* I'd love to.

договориться (pfv II)
договорились
Значит, договорились.

to agree, come to an understanding
we've agreed, it's agreed, it's a date
Then it's a date.

SUPPLEMENT

фамилия
Как ваша фамилия?
— Моя фамилия Петров.
Как ваше имя?
— Моё имя Пётр.
имя и отчество
Как ваше имя и отчество?[1]
—Моё имя и отчество Пётр Иванович.

last name, family name
What's your last name?
My last name is Petrov.
What's your first name?
My first name is Pyotr.
first name and patronymic
What are your first name and patronymic?
My first name and patronymic are Pyotr Ivanovich.

звать (I)
зову, зовут
Как вас зовут?

to call
I call, they call
What's your name? (*Lit.* What do they call you?)

— Меня зовут Борис Петрович Орлов.

My name is Boris Petrovich Orlov.

---

[1] Russians usually omit the conjunction и in speech.

После кино́

Оле́г 1 Ну́ ка́к? Понра́вилось?[1]

Зи́на 2 О́чень. Я таки́х карти́н ещё не ви́дела.

Оле́г 3 Я то́же. Не ожида́л от америка́нцев тако́го понима́ния Толсто́го.[2]

Зи́на 4 Да́. А кто́ игра́л Ната́шу? Я забы́ла и́мя.[3],[4]

Оле́г 5 Я то́же и́мени не по́мню. У ни́х имена́ — не вы́говоришь.[5]

Зи́на 6 А америка́нцы, наве́рно, ру́сских имён не мо́гут вы́говорить.[6]

Оле́г 7 Наве́рно. Скажи́те, вы́ ча́сто хо́дите в кино́ и́ли в клу́б?

Зи́на 8 В кино́ — ча́сто, а в клу́б — не́т. Ра́зве что на та́нцы.

Оле́г 9 Так вы́ лю́бите танцева́ть? Хоти́те пойти́ в суббо́ту?

Зи́на 10 С удово́льствием.

Оле́г 11 Зна́чит, договори́лись.

NOTES

[1] The verb нра́виться (perfective понра́виться) is the usual word for *to like* and expresses a milder appreciation than люби́ть, which means both *to like* and *to love*. In connection with something experienced for the first time, нра́виться, понра́виться must be used: Ну́, понра́вилось? *Well, did you like it?* Люби́ть describes a stronger, more deep-seated emotion or attitude: Я люблю́ танцева́ть *I'm very fond of dancing*. In the sense of *to love*, only люби́ть can be used.

[2] Ле́в Толсто́й (1828-1910) is one of the major figures in Russian literature. His long novel «Война́ и ми́р» *War and Peace* was written in the early 1860's. Notice that Толсто́й is adjectival in its declension, e.g., Толсто́го (gen sg).

[3] The noun и́мя, like вре́мя and a handful of other Russian nouns with the nominative ending in –мя, is neuter. И́мя usually applies to the first name, but is sometimes used in reference to both first and last names, especially when speaking of prominent personalities. In asking a person's name, the adverb ка́к is used:

Ка́к ва́ше и́мя?	What's your first name?
Ка́к ва́ше и́мя и о́тчество?	What are your first name and patronymic?
Ка́к ва́ша фами́лия?	What's your last name?
Ка́к его́ зову́т?	What's his name?

[4] Note that Russians use the perfective past of certain verbs when, in corresponding situations, the present tense is more common in English:

Я забы́л её и́мя.	I forget her name *or* I've forgotten. ...
Я опозда́л. Извини́те.	I'm late (*lit.* I came late). Excuse me.
Я уста́л.	I'm tired *or* I've become tired.

[5] The second person singular perfective future without the pronoun ты́ is often used in negative constructions in Russian to make a general or impersonal statement. In English this is normally expressed by *you can't* or *one can't*:

На лекциях не поговоришь.   You can't talk at lectures.
У них имена — не выговоришь. They have names you can't pronounce.

⁶ **Русский** is the only name for a nationality that can serve as both adjective and noun in Russian:

Он русский, а не американец.   He's a Russian, not an American.
Он хорошо знает русский язык.   He knows the Russian language well.

Compare **американец** *an American* with **американский** *American* in the following sentences:

Он американец.   He's an American.
Он американский студент.   He's an American student.

Remember that none of the words referring to nationalities is capitalized in Russian: **русский, американский, американец, английский.** Only the names of countries are capitalized: **Советский Союз** *Soviet Union*, **Америка, Англия, Россия.**

Basic sentence patterns

1. Там много профессоров.   There are a lot of professors there.
   _____ столов.   _____ tables _____.
   _____ автобусов.   _____ buses _____.
   _____ киосков.   _____ newsstands ____.
   _____ магазинов.   _____ stores _____.
   _____ клубов.   _____ clubs _____.
   _____ заводов.   _____ plants _____.
   _____ атласов.   _____ atlases _____.

2. У нас нет карандашей.   We don't have any pencils.
   _____ ножей.   _____ knives.
   _____ ключей.   _____ keys.
   _____ щей.   _____ schi.
   _____ словарей.   _____ dictionaries.
   _____ тетрадей.   _____ notebooks.

3. Здесь нет картин.   There are no pictures here.
   _____ книг.   _____ books _____.
   _____ карт.   _____ maps _____.
   _____ школ.   _____ schools _____.
   _____ библиотек.   _____ libraries _____.
   _____ учительниц.   _____ teachers _____.
   _____ фабрик.   _____ factories _____.

4. Там не было коробок.   There weren't any boxes there.
   _____ полок.   _____ shelves _____.
   _____ досок.   _____ blackboards _____.
   _____ вилок.   _____ forks _____.
   _____ ложек.   _____ spoons _____.
   _____ чашек.   _____ cups _____.

Та́м не́ было ру́чек. | There weren't any pens there.
_____ о́кон. | _____ windows _____.
_____ пи́сем. | _____ letters _____.

5. У ни́х не́ было ле́кций. | They didn't have any lectures.
_____ аудито́рий. | _____ auditoriums.
_____ лаборато́рий. | _____ laboratories.
_____ заня́тий. | _____ classes.
_____ собра́ний. | _____ meetings.
_____ общежи́тий. | _____ dormitories.
_____ сочине́ний. | _____ compositions.
_____ заявле́ний. | _____ applications.

6. Вы́ купи́ли костю́м? | Did you buy a suit?
— Не́т, я не купи́л костю́ма. | No, I didn't buy a suit.
Вы́ купи́ли пода́рок? | Did you buy a present?
— Не́т, я не купи́л пода́рка. | No, I didn't buy a present.
Вы́ купи́ли ча́й? | Did you buy tea?
— Не́т, я не купи́л ча́я. | No, I didn't buy tea.
Вы́ купи́ли селёдку? | Did you buy herring?
— Не́т, я не купи́л селёдки. | No, I didn't buy herring.
Вы́ купи́ли ка́рту? | Did you buy a map?
— Не́т, я не купи́л ка́рты. | No, I didn't buy a map.
Вы́ купи́ли тетра́дь? | Did you buy a notebook?
— Не́т, я не купи́л тетра́ди. | No, I didn't buy a notebook.
Вы́ купи́ли молоко́? | Did you buy milk?
— Не́т, я не купи́л молока́. | No, I didn't buy milk.

7. Вы́ доста́ли шкафы́? | Did you get the cupboards?
— Не́т, я не доста́л шкафо́в. | No, I didn't get the cupboards.
Вы́ доста́ли а́тласы? | Did you get the atlases?
— Не́т, я не доста́л а́тласов. | No, I didn't get the atlases.
Вы́ доста́ли кни́ги? | Did you get the books?
— Не́т, я не доста́л кни́г. | No, I didn't get the books.
Вы́ доста́ли карти́ны? | Did you get the pictures?
— Не́т, я не доста́л карти́н. | No, I didn't get the pictures.
Вы́ доста́ли коро́бки? | Did you get the boxes?
— Не́т, я не доста́л коро́бок. | No, I didn't get the boxes.
Вы́ доста́ли портфе́ли? | Did you get the briefcases?
— Не́т, я не доста́л портфе́лей. | No, I didn't get the briefcases.
Вы́ доста́ли словари́? | Did you get the dictionaries?
— Не́т, я не доста́л словаре́й. | No, I didn't get the dictionaries.
Вы́ доста́ли тетра́ди? | Did you get the notebooks?
— Не́т, я не доста́л тетра́дей. | No, I didn't get the notebooks.

8. Я́ не ви́жу ножа́. | I don't see any knife.
_____ портфе́ля. | _____ briefcase.
_____ словаря́. | _____ dictionary.
_____ а́тласа. | _____ atlas.
_____ письма́. | _____ letter.

9. Я не покупа́л хле́ба.   I didn't buy any bread.

_____ молока́.   _____ milk.

_____ ры́бы.   _____ fish.

_____ бума́ги.   _____ paper.

_____ материа́ла.   _____ material.

_____ ча́я.   _____ tea.

10. Я жду́ профе́ссора Орло́ва.   I'm waiting for Professor Orlov.

Ты́ ждёшь _____.   You're waiting for_____.

О́н ждёт _____.   He's waiting for _____.

Мы́ ждём _____.   We're waiting for _____.

Вы́ ждёте _____.   You're waiting for _____.

Они́ ждут _____.   They're waiting for _____.

11. Я его́ подожду́.   I'll wait for him.

Ты́ ____ подождёшь.   You'll wait ____.

Она́ ____ подождёт.   She'll wait ____.

Мы́ ____ подождём.   We'll wait ____.

Вы́ ____ подождёте.   You'll wait ____.

Они́ ____ подожду́т.   They'll wait____.

12. Я принесу́ по́чту.   I'll bring [in] the mail.[1]

Ты́ принесёшь _____.   You'll bring [in] ____.

О́н принесёт _____.   He'll bring [in] _____.

Мы́ принесём _____.   We'll bring [in] ____.

Вы́ принесёте _____.   You'll bring [in] ____.

Они́ принесу́т _____.   They'll bring [in] ____.

13. Я не успе́ю написа́ть пи́сьма.   I won't have time to write letters.

Ты́ не успе́ешь _____.   You won't have time _____.

О́н не успе́ет _____.   He won't have time _____.

Мы́ не успе́ем _____.   We won't have time _____.

Вы́ не успе́ете _____.   You won't have time _____.

Они́ не успе́ют _____.   They won't have time _____.

14. Я открыва́ю о́кна ка́ждый де́нь.   I open the windows every day.

Ты́ открыва́ешь _____.   You open _____.

Она́ открыва́ет _____.   She opens _____.

Мы́ открыва́ем _____.   We open _____.

Вы́ открыва́ете _____.   You open _____.

Они́ открыва́ют _____.   They open _____.

15. Ка́к ва́ше и́мя?   What's your first name?

— Моё и́мя Никола́й.   My first name is Nikolay.

_____ Гали́на.   _____ Galina.

_____ Мари́я.   _____ Maria.

16. Ка́к ва́ша фами́лия?   What's your last name?

— Моя́ фами́лия Петро́в.   My last name is Petrov.

_____ Петро́ва.   _____ Petrova.

_____ Орло́в.   _____ Orlov.

---

[1] Notice that по́чта means *mail* as well as *post office*.

— Моя́ фами́лия Орло́ва.   My last name is Orlova.
_____ Ку́рочкин.   _____ Kurochkin.
_____ Ку́рочкина.   _____ Kurochkina.

17. Ка́к ва́ше и́мя и о́тчество?   What are your first name and patronymic?
— Моё и́мя и о́тчество Пётр Ники́тич.   My first name and patronymic are Pyotr
                                                                                      Nikitich.

_____ Влади́мир Ива́нович.   _____ Vladimir Ivanovich.
_____ Зинаи́да Петро́вна.   _____ Zinaida Petrovna.
_____ Ири́на Миха́йловна.   _____ Irina Mikhailovna.

18. До́брое у́тро, Зи́на!   Good morning, Zina!
До́брый де́нь, Зи́на!   Good afternoon, Zina!
До́брый ве́чер, Зи́на!   Good evening, Zina!
Споко́йной но́чи, Зи́на!   Good night, Zina!

19. Зимо́й мы́ ча́сто игра́ем в ка́рты.   In winter we often play cards.
Весно́й _____ .   In spring _____ .
О́сенью мы́ ре́дко игра́ем в ка́рты.   In autumn we rarely play cards.
Ле́том _____ .   In summer _____ .

Pronunciation practice: double consonants

In English double consonants are heard only at a boundary between two words. Written double consonant *letters* within the word (as in *Bill*, *hammer*) are pronounced as single consonants.

Compare   **Will Lee** go?   *with*   **Will 'e** go?
                 Ann names.   **Ann A**mes.
                 Kiss Sal.   **Kiss A**l.

In Russian, however, double consonants are heard not only across word boundaries, but also within words.

Compare   [attáṇi] от Та́ни   *with*   [atáṇi] от А́ни
              from Tanya   from Anya

              [ánnə] А́нна   [ivánə] Ива́на
              Anna   of Ivan

Double consonants occur in Russian mainly at the point where a prefix or preposition joins the rest of the word, but they may also occur at other places within a word (e.g., [ánnə]).

Note, however, that not every *written* sequence of two identical letters necessarily indicates a double consonant in pronunciation. Russians tend to pronounce many double letter sequences with a single consonant, especially in foreign-derived words. Thus, **профе́ссор** and **суббо́та** contain only single consonants in pronunciation. Usage varies in this respect. Many Russians pronounce **гру́ппа** with a single [p], though orthographic handbooks prescribe [pp]. In rapid speech double consonants often tend to be replaced by single consonants.

> Sound Drill: Practice the Russian examples illustrating the contrast between double and single consonants, imitating your instructor (or the tape) as accurately as you can. Be sure to pronounce the double consonants as *long* consonants, without a break in the middle.

Intonation practice:
review of rising and rising-falling contours

Reread the discussion on rising and rising-falling intonation contours in Lessons 7, 8, and 9.

A. Review of questions with rising contours (questions without a question word).

Óн здéсь?	Is he here?
Вóлков у себя́?	Is Volkov in?
Она́ в гóроде?	Is she in town?
Влади́мир на рабóте?	Is Vladimir at work?
Лóжки в я́щике?	Are the spoons in the drawer?
А́тлас дорогóй?	Is the atlas expensive?
Они́ на собра́нии?	Are they at a meeting?
Она́ студéнтка?	Is she a student?
Вы́ друзья́?	Are you friends?

Автóбус ужé идёт?	Is the bus coming already?
Та́м бы́ло интерéсно?	Was it interesting there?
Ты́ идёшь домóй?	Are you going home?
Óн пошёл в магази́н?	Did he go to the store?
Вы́ бы́ли больны́?	Were you sick?
Вы́ рабóтаете в горсовéте?	Do you work at the gorsovet?
У тебя́ тепéрь истóрия?	Do you have history now?
Бóрщ ужé готóв?	Is the borsch ready yet?
Лóжки ужé на столé?	Are the spoons already on the table?
Вы́ ужé пообéдали?	Have you already eaten dinner?
Ты́ егó зна́ешь?	Do you know him?
Вы́ спеши́те на автóбус?	Are you hurrying to the bus?
Това́рищ Алексéев у себя́?	Is comrade Alexeev in?
Óн сейча́с в Москвé?	Is he in Moscow now?
Они́ егó зна́ют?	Do they know him?
Вы́ о нéй слы́шали?	Have you heard about her?
Она́ сейча́с рабóтает?	Is she working now?

B. Review of questions with rising-falling contours (questions without question words).

Она́ купи́ла материа́л?	Did she buy the material?
Ири́на опя́ть больна́?	Is Irina sick again?
У ни́х éсть кóмната?	Do they have a room?
Они́ бы́ли на заня́тиях?	Did they attend classes?
Она́ доста́ла слова́рь?	Did she get hold of the dictionary?
Студéнты узна́ли об э́том?	Did the students find out about it?
Олéг давнó бóлен?	Has Oleg been ill long?
У ва́с сегóдня экза́мены?	Are your exams today?
Са́ша бы́л в шкóле?	Was Sasha in school?

Онá ужé купи́ла словáрь?	Has she already bought the dictionary?
Óльга Петрóвна опя́ть больнá?	Is Olga Petrovna sick again?
Мари́я Ивáновна былá в ГУ́Ме?	Was Maria Ivanovna at GUM?
У Ивáна Ивáновича éсть кóмната?	Does Ivan Ivanovich have a room?
Вы́ вчерá слу́шали концéрт?	Did you listen to the concert yesterday?
Лéв ужé получи́л письмó?	Has Lev already received the letter?
Олéг ужé давнó бóлен?	Has Oleg been ill a long time now?
Студéнты ужé узнáли об э́том?	Did the students already find out about it?
Онá ужé подалá заявлéние?	Has she already submitted an application?

C. Review of emphatic statements with rising-falling contours.

Олéг **давнó** здорóв!	Oleg has *long* since recovered!
Ми́ла **опя́ть** здéсь!	Mila is here *again*!
У неё **éсть** кóмната!	She *does* have a room!
Женá **всегдá** дóма!	My wife's *always* home!
Они́ **не хотя́т** обéдать!	They *don't want* to eat dinner!

Онá ужé **достáла** материáл!	She already *got* the material!
Ни́на ужé **подалá** заявлéние!	Nina already *has* submitted her application!
Олéг ужé **получи́л** письмó!	Oleg's already *received* the letter!
Вы́ о нéй **опя́ть** забы́ли!	You forgot about her *again*!
У ни́х ужé **éсть** кóмната!	They already *have* a room.
Товáрищ Алексéев **опя́ть** не обéдал!	Comrade Alexeev didn't have his dinner *again*
Библиотéка **давнó** запертá!	The library has *long* since been closed!
Мы́ ужé **спрáшивали** у негó!	We already *asked* him!
Я́ ужé **написáл** письмó!	I already *wrote* the letter!

■ TRANSFORMATION DRILLS

Change the following emphatic statements (with rising-falling contours) to questions (with rising-falling contours on a higher pitch level).

Ми́ла опя́ть здéсь!	Ми́ла опя́ть здéсь?
Они́ бы́ли в Москвé!	Они́ бы́ли в Москвé?
У неё éсть кóмната!	У неё éсть кóмната?
Кáтя купи́ла материáл!	Кáтя купи́ла материáл?
Зи́на всегдá дóма!	Зи́на всегдá дóма?

Ни́на ужé подалá заявлéние!	Ни́на ужé подалá заявлéние?
Брáт ужé послáл письмó!	Брáт ужé послáл письмó?
Товáрищ Вóлков опя́ть бóлен!	Товáрищ Вóлков опя́ть бóлен?
Óкна у ни́х всегдá зáперты!	Óкна у ни́х всегдá зáперты?
Сестрá ужé получи́ла письмó!	Сестрá ужé получи́ла письмó?
Ты́ возьмёшь э́ти кни́ги!	Ты́ возьмёшь э́ти кни́ги?

The present-future of first conjugation verbs patterned like рабо́тать and идти́

FIRST CONJUGATION PRESENT-FUTURE ENDINGS		EXAMPLES	
		идти́ (ipfv) *to be going*	рабо́тать (ipfv) *to work*
SINGULAR 1	–у or –ю	иду́	рабо́таю
2	–ешь (–ёшь)	идёшь	рабо́таешь
3	–ет (–ёт)	идёт	рабо́тает
PLURAL 1	–ем (–ём)	идём	рабо́таем
2	–ете (–ёте)	идёте	рабо́таете
3	–ут or –ют	иду́т	рабо́тают

Note that the second person singular ending is conventionally spelled with a final –ь even though ш is always pronounced hard.

MODELS

1. *First conjugation verbs which pattern like* рабо́тать *in the present-future:*

Что́ вы́ де́лаете?	What are you doing?
— Я ничего́ не де́лаю.	I'm not doing anything.
Вы́ его́ зна́ете?	Do you know him?
— Да́, зна́ю.	Yes, I do.
О чём вы́ ду́маете?	What are you thinking about?
— Я ду́маю об экза́менах.	I'm thinking about the exams.
Вы́ понима́ете, о чём о́н говори́т?	Do you understand what he's talking about?
— Не́т, не понима́ю.	No, I don't.
Когда́ вы́ э́то сде́лаете?	When will you do this?
— Я э́то сде́лаю за́втра.	I'll get it done tomorrow.
Что́ вы́ покупа́ете?	What are you buying?
— Я покупа́ю материа́л на костю́м.	I'm buying material for a suit.
Когда́ вы́ узна́ете об э́том?	When will you find out about it?
— Я узна́ю послеза́втра.	I'll find out the day after tomorrow.
Что́ вы́ чита́ете?	What are you reading?
— Я чита́ю стихи́.	I'm reading poetry.
Где́ вы́ сего́дня обе́даете?	Where are you eating dinner today?
— Я обе́даю в столо́вой.	I'm eating dinner in the dining hall.
Вы́ не успе́ете на авто́бус.	You won't make the bus on time.
— Не́т, успе́ю.	Yes, I will.
Кого́ вы́ ожида́ете?	Whom are you expecting?
— Я ожида́ю дру́га из Москвы́.	I'm expecting a friend from Moscow.

Вы́ игра́ете в те́ннис?	Do you play tennis?
— Да́, игра́ю.	Yes, I do.
Вы́ не опозда́ете на конце́рт?	Won't you be late for the concert?
— Не́т, не опозда́ю.	No, I won't be late.
Вы́ ча́сто опа́здываете на рабо́ту?	Are you often late to work?
— Не́т, я́ никогда́ не опа́здываю.	No, I'm never late.

2. *First conjugation verbs which pattern like* **идти́** *in the present-future:*

Вы́ пойдёте за́втра в теа́тр?	Will you be going to the theater tomorrow?
— Не́т, я́ пойду́ послезá́втра.	No, I'll go the day after.
Вы́ зайдёте в библиоте́ку?	Will you drop in at the library?
— Да́, я́ зайду́ туда́ по́сле заня́тий.	Yes, I'll drop by there after classes.
Кого́ вы́ ждёте?	Whom are you waiting for?
— Я́ жду́ Оле́га.	I'm waiting for Oleg.
Вы́ войдёте в до́м?	Are you going to go into the house?
— Не́т, не войду́.	No, I'm not.
Вы́ меня́ здéсь подождёте?	Will you wait for me here?
— Да́, подожду́.	Yes, I will.
Вы́ принесёте свóй словáрь?	Will you bring your dictionary?
— Да́, принесу́.	Yes, I will.
Вы́ возьмёте э́ти кни́ги?	Will you take these books?
— Да́, возьму́.	Yes, I will.
Где́ вы́ живёте?	Where do you live?
— Я́ живу́ про́тив па́рка.	I live across from the park.

■ REPETITION DRILL

Repeat the given models, noting the two types of verb patterns.

■ SUBSTITUTION DRILLS [1]

1. *I don't know.*
   Я́ не зна́ю.
   Вы́ не зна́ете.
   (мы, ты, Мила, студенты, вы, я, вахтёр)

2. *She's rarely late to work.*
   Она́ ре́дко опа́здывает на рабо́ту.
   Вы́ ре́дко опа́здываете на рабо́ту.
   (ты, мы, они, я, Мила, вы, ты)

3. *Won't you be late to the concert?*
   Ты́ не опозда́ешь на конце́рт?
   Вы́ не опозда́ете на конце́рт?
   (мы, она, они, ты, я, ваш брат, ваши
   друзья)

4. *You won't make it to the bus on time.*
   Вы́ не успе́ете на авто́бус.
   О́н не успе́ет на авто́бус.
   (я, они, ты, она, мы, Галя, вы, Пётр)

5. *In the afternoon we play cards.*
   По́сле обе́да мы́ игра́ем в ка́рты.
   По́сле обе́да они́ игра́ют в ка́рты.
   (я, вы, её друзья, ты, студенты, моя
   сестра, мы)

---

[1] Henceforth the drills will appear without the labels *T* (for teacher) and *S* (for student). In Substitution Drills, the word to be replaced will be indicated by boldface type in the models; in all other drills, the student's response appears in boldface.

1. *What's Oleg doing?*
   He's reading a letter.
   Что Олег делает?
   Он читает письмо.
   Что ты делаешь?
   Я читаю письмо.
   (студенты, учительница, учителя, продавщица, ты, они, вы, секретарь, студентки)

2. *When will you go home?*
   I'm already on my way.
   Когда ты пойдёшь домой?
   Я уже иду.
   Когда он пойдёт домой?
   Он уже идёт.
   (они, вы, она, студенты, продавщица, эти девушки, уборщица)

3. *Where is your application?*
   I'll bring it right away.
   Где твоё заявление?
   Я сейчас принесу.
   Где её заявление?
   Она сейчас принесёт.
   (ваше, их, его, её, их, твоё)

■ STRUCTURE REPLACEMENT DRILLS

1. *I waited a little.*
   I'll wait a little.
   Я немного подождал.
   Я немного подожду.
   Она немного подождала.
   Она немного подождёт.
   (мы, он, ты, они, вы, профессор, студенты, сестра, учителя)

2. *What were you buying?*
   What are you buying?
   Что ты покупал?
   Что ты покупаешь?
   Что она покупала?
   Что она покупает?
   (вы, он, они, мы, учитель, профессора, учительница)

3. *I'm on my way to a lecture.*
   I'll go to a lecture.
   Я иду на лекцию.
   Я пойду на лекцию.
   Он идёт на лекцию.
   Он пойдёт на лекцию.
   (мы, она, ты, они, вы, я и мой товарищ, учитель)

■ SUBSTITUTION DRILLS

1. *I'll bring coffee right away.*
   Я сейчас принесу кофе.
   Жена сейчас принесёт кофе.
   (брат, они, мы, Нина и Катя)

2. *I'll wait for him on the corner.*
   Я подожду его на углу.
   Мы подождём его на углу.
   (мой брат, ребята, ты, я, она, Владимир, вы, мы)

■ RESPONSE DRILLS

1. *I have to buy a couple of things.*
   I'll drop in this store.
   Я должен кое-что купить.
   Я зайду в этот магазин.

   Она должна кое-что купить.
   Она зайдёт в этот магазин.
   (мы должны, они должны, он должен, я должна)

2. *I live near the park.*
   Do you live near the park too?
   Я живу́ о́коло па́рка.
   Ты́ то́же живёшь о́коло па́рка?
   Я покупа́ю материа́л.
   Ты́ то́же покупа́ешь материа́л?
   Я де́лаю уро́ки.
   Я ду́маю о заня́тиях.
   Я жду́ дру́га.
   Я чита́ю «Войну́ и ми́р».
   Я игра́ю в те́ннис.
   Я рабо́таю на фа́брике.

3. *We'll think about it.*
   Will you think about it too?
   Мы́ поду́маем об э́том.
   Вы́ то́же поду́маете об э́том?
   Мы́ подождём на углу́.
   Вы́ то́же подождёте на углу́?
   Мы́ принесём пода́рки.
   Мы́ пойдём в кино́.
   Мы́ возьмём тетра́ди.
   Мы́ войдём в ко́мнату.
   Мы́ зайдём в библиоте́ку.

DISCUSSION

According to the pattern of their present-future endings, most first conjugation verbs drilled and discussed so far fall into two groups:

1. Those like **идти́**, with the written present-future stem ending in a consonant, to which the stressed endings –у́, –ёшь, –ёт, –ём, –ёте, –у́т are added: жд-у́, жд-ёшь, жд-ёт, жд-ём, жд-ёте, жд-у́т. The stem consonant is hard before the endings of the first person singular and the third person plural, but is soft before the other endings. Compare [ždú], [ždút] with [žḍóš], [žḍót], [žḍóm], [žḍóți]. Other verbs which pattern similarly are пойти́, войти́, подойти́, подожда́ть, принести́, взя́ть, жи́ть.

Note that in contrast with the present-future, the infinitive-past tense stem of the verbs in this group may be considerably different. Compare жи́ть, жи́л with живу́, живёшь; and взя́ть, взя́л with возьму́, возьмёшь.

2. Those like **рабо́тать**, with the written present-future stem ending in a vowel, to which the unstressed endings –ю, –ешь, –ет, –ем, –ете, –ют are added: чита́-ю, чита́-ешь, чита́-ет, чита́-ем, чита́-ете, чита́-ют.[1] Other verbs which pattern similarly are ду́мать, поду́мать, зна́ть, узна́ть, де́лать, сде́лать, покупа́ть, обе́дать, пообе́дать, понима́ть, слу́шать, спра́шивать, ожида́ть.

The genitive plural of nouns

The endings of the genitive plural present more complications than those of any other case. For this reason only the most basic ones will be treated in this lesson.

MODELS

Та́м бы́ло мно́го студе́нтов.	There were lots of students there.
_____ профессоро́в.	_____ professors ___.
_____ столо́в.	_____ tables _____.
_____ кио́сков.	_____ newsstands __.
_____ а́тласов.	_____ atlases _____.
_____ пода́рков.	_____ presents _____.

[1] In structural terms, the present-future stem of such verbs actually ends in the consonant *sound* [j], which, as we know, is not written with an independent symbol when it occurs between vowels. The soft-series vowel letters of the endings thus contain not only the ending, but also the final consonant of the present-future stem, e.g., [čitáj-, čitáj-u, čitáj-ut]. The imperative of verbs of this type is the one form in which the [j] of the stem is represented by a separate letter in Cyrillic (–й), e.g., чита́й! чита́йте! спра́шивай! спра́шивайте!

У нас нет ножей.	We don't have any knives.
_____ карандашей.	_____ pencils.
_____ ключей.	_____ keys.
_____ товарищей.	_____ friends.
_____ портфелей.	_____ briefcases.
_____ словарей.	_____ dictionaries.

Там мало дверей.	There are few doors there.
_____ очередей.	_____ lines _____.
_____ тетрадей.	_____ notebooks ____.

Так много дел!	So many things to do!
_____ слов!	_____ words!
_____ книг!	_____ books!
_____ картин!	_____ pictures!
_____ комнат!	_____ rooms!

Там много окон.	There are lots of windows there.
_____ писем.	_____ letters _____ .

У меня нет вилок.	I don't have any forks.
_____ полок.	_____ shelves.
_____ ложек.	_____ spoons.
_____ ручек.	_____ pens.
_____ сестёр.	_____ sisters.

У нас не было лекций.	We didn't have any lectures.
_____ лабораторий.	_____ laboratories.
_____ аудиторий.	_____ auditoriums.
_____ собраний.	_____ meetings.
_____ общежитий.	_____ dormitories.
_____ занятий.	_____ classes.

TYPICAL ENDINGS FOR NOUNS IN THE GENITIVE PLURAL (Endings are based on the plural stem)			
стол-nouns	**окно**-nouns	**жена**-nouns	**дверь**-nouns
HARD STEMS –ов SOFT STEMS –ей	(zero) –й	(zero) –й or –ь	–ей
столов студентов атласов уроков профессоров	дел слов окон писем	жён книг девушек сестёр коробок	
ключей товарищей ножей карандашей портфелей словарей	собраний сочинений общежитий заявлений занятий зданий	лекций историй лабораторий аудиторий недель	тетрадей очередей дверей ночей

1. Most **стол**-nouns ending in a hard consonant take the ending –**ов** in the genitive plural. Those ending in **ж, ш**, or a soft consonant other than **й**, take the ending –**ей**.

2. All **дверь**-nouns take the ending –**ей** in the genitive plural.

3. Most **окно́**- and **жена́**-nouns have a zero ending in the genitive plural. In structural terms this usually makes their genitive plural form identical with their plural stem: **жён, кни́г, карти́н, де́л, имён**. The stem may be slightly modified, however, in two ways:

    a. A vowel may be inserted between the last two consonants of the stem as in **о́кон** (stem **окн–**), **студе́нток** (stem **студе́нтк–**), **де́вушек** (stem **де́вушк–**), and **сестёр** (stem **сестр–**).

    b. If the stem ends in the sound [j], orthographic conventions require that it be written **й**: **собра́ний** (stem [sabránij–]), **ле́кций** (stem [ĺékcij–]). If the stem ends in a soft consonant other than [j], **ч**, or **щ**, the symbol **ь** must be written to indicate the basic softness of the stem final consonant: **неде́ль** (stem [ņiḑéĺ–]).

■ CUED SUBSTITUTION DRILLS

1. (*atlases*) *And how about the atlases?*
(а́тласы) **А ка́к насчёт а́тласов?**
(столы́) **А ка́к насчёт столо́в?**
(романы, экзамены, стихи, ящики, уроки, фильмы, шкафы, костюмы)

2. (*pencils*) *The students have no pencils.*
(карандаши́) У студе́нтов не́т карандаше́й.
(ножи́) **У студе́нтов не́т ноже́й.**
(ключи, словари, портфели, тетради, карандаши, ножи)

■ CUED QUESTION-ANSWER DRILL

(*teachers*) *From whom did she hear it?*
From the teachers.
(учителя́) От кого́ она́ э́то слы́шала?
От учителе́й.
(продавщи́цы) От кого́ она́ э́то слы́шала?
От продавщи́ц.

(их жёны, его сёстры, уборщицы, зао́чницы, профессора, студенты, учительницы, учителя, студентки, американки)

■ QUESTION-ANSWER DRILLS

1. *Where are the keys?*
There are no keys here.
Гдé ключи́?
Здéсь нéт ключе́й.
Гдé ножи́?
Здéсь нéт ноже́й.
(карандаши, сочинения, книги, словари, тетради, письма, вилки, ложки)

2. *Were there any maps there?*
No, there weren't any maps there.
Та́м бы́ли ка́рты?
Нéт, та́м ка́рт нé было.
Та́м бы́ли тетра́ди?
Нéт, та́м тетра́дей нé было.
(полки, коробки, девушки, книги, картины, вилки, ложки, окна, письма)

3. *Do you have any pencils?*
No, we don't have any pencils.
Карандаши́ у ва́с éсть?
Нéт, карандаше́й у на́с нéт.
А́тласы у ва́с éсть?
Нéт, а́тласов у на́с нéт.
(тетради, полки, романы, стихи, словари, портфели, шкафы, костюмы)

The teachers were at our house.
We were at the teachers'.
Учителя́ бы́ли у нас.
Мы́ бы́ли у учителе́й.
Студе́нты бы́ли у нас.
Мы́ бы́ли у студе́нтов.

(профессора́, его́ сёстры, убо́рщицы, их жёны, продавщи́цы, студе́нтки, учи́тель-ницы, америка́нки, секретари́)

■ INTEGRATION DRILL

These are dresses. These are sisters.
These are the sisters' dresses.
Это пла́тья.   Это сёстры.
Это пла́тья сестёр.
Это портфе́ли.   Это профессора́.
Это портфе́ли профессоро́в.
Это тетра́ди.   Это студе́нты.
Это кни́ги.   Это учителя́.
Это ко́мнаты.   Это продавщи́цы.
Это ключи́.   Это убо́рщицы.
Это карандаши́. Это учи́тельницы.

■ STRUCTURE REPLACEMENT DRILLS

We don't have a dormitory.
We don't have any dormitories.
У нас нет общежи́тия.
У нас нет общежи́тий.
У нас нет собра́ния.
У нас нет собра́ний.

(ле́кции, уро́ка, авто́буса, заня́тий, сто-ла́, учи́теля, ка́рты, сочине́ния, ко́мнаты, ключа́, шка́фа, ру́чки)

■ STRUCTURE REPLACEMENT DRILL

Here are the bookcases.
There are a lot of bookcases here.
Вот по́лки.
Здесь мно́го по́лок.
Вот магази́ны.
Здесь мно́го магази́нов.

(ножи́, заво́ды, карандаши́, зда́ния, о́кна, рестора́ны, телефо́ны, две́ри, общежи́тия, ко́мнаты)

The accusative plural of nouns

MODELS

Мы́ должны́ купи́ть а́тласы.	We have to buy atlases.
_____ портфе́ли.	_____ briefcases.
_____ тетра́ди.	_____ notebooks.
_____ карандаши́.	_____ pencils.
_____ ло́жки.	_____ spoons.
_____ ви́лки.	_____ forks.
_____ пе́рья.	_____ pen points.
_____ сту́лья.	_____ chairs.
_____ пла́тья.	_____ dresses.

Вы́ ви́дели их студе́нтов?	Did you see their students?
_____ профессоро́в?	_____ professors?
_____ това́рищей?	_____ friends?
_____ учителе́й?	_____ teachers?
_____ студе́нток?	_____ girl students?
_____ сестёр?	_____ sisters?

■ REPETITION DRILL

Repeat the given models, noting that where the direct object is inanimate, the accusative form is like the nominative, but where the direct object is animate, the accusative form is like the genitive.

■ QUESTION-ANSWER DRILLS

1. *Where are your keys?*
   We forgot the keys.
   Где ва́ши ключи́?
   Мы́ забы́ли ключи́.
   Где ва́ши кни́ги?
   Мы́ забы́ли кни́ги.

   (карандаши, тетради, словари, карты, атласы, портфели)

2. *Where are the students?*
   We saw the students at the club.
   Где студе́нты?
   Мы́ ви́дели студе́нтов в клу́бе.
   Где студе́нтки?
   Мы́ ви́дели студе́нток в клу́бе.

   (учителя́, профессора́, её сёстры, девушки, его товарищи, американки, секретари́, якуты)

■ RESPONSE DRILLS

1. *Here are cucumbers for you.*
   Where did you get such cucumbers?
   Во́т, пожа́луйста, огурцы́.
   Где́ вы́ доста́ли таки́е огурцы́?
   Во́т, пожа́луйста, пе́рья.
   Где́ вы́ доста́ли таки́е пе́рья?

   (ручки, карандаши, стулья, чашки, ложки, вилки, ножи)

2. *Look, there go the students!*
   I see students every day.
   Посмотри́, та́м иду́т студе́нты.
   Я́ ви́жу студе́нтов ка́ждый де́нь.
   Посмотри́, та́м иду́т продавщи́цы.
   Я́ ви́жу продавщи́ц ка́ждый де́нь.

   (учителя, её сёстры, их жёны, учительницы, девушки, секретари, студентки)

3. *Here are his compositions.*
   I've already read his compositions.
   Во́т его́ сочине́ния.
   Я́ уже́ чита́л его́ сочине́ния.
   Во́т его́ стихи́.
   Я́ уже́ чита́л его́ стихи́.

   (работы, книги, романы, заявления, письма)

4. *The shelves are ready.*
   Want to take a look at the shelves?
   По́лки гото́вы.
   Хоти́те посмотре́ть по́лки?
   О́кна гото́вы.
   Хоти́те посмотре́ть о́кна?

   (двери, столы, стулья, ящики, общежития, дома, комнаты, квартиры)

■ STRUCTURE REPLACEMENT DRILL

1. *Ask the teacher.*
   Ask the teachers.
   Спроси́те учи́теля.
   Спроси́те учителе́й.
   Спроси́те его́ сестру́.
   Спроси́те его́ сестёр.

   (продавщицу, профессора, студентку, учительницу, вахтёра, американку)

2. *Where did you see the factory?*
   Where did you see the factories?
   Где́ вы́ ви́дели фа́брику?
   Где́ вы́ ви́дели фа́брики?
   Где́ вы́ ви́дели студе́нта?
   Где́ вы́ ви́дели студе́нтов?

   (автобус, очередь, картину, студентку, девушку, профессора, его сестру, его товарища, лабораторию, ручку, вахтёра)

3. *I just met my sister.*
   I just met my sisters.
   Я́ то́лько что встре́тил сестру́.
   Я́ то́лько что встре́тил сестёр.
   Я́ то́лько что встре́тил това́рища.
   Я́ то́лько что встре́тил това́рищей.

   (учительницу, учителя, профессора, студентку, секретаря)

1. *Singular*
   a. Inanimate **стóл**-nouns and all **окнó**- and **двéрь**-nouns have accusative singular forms exactly like the nominative singular: стóл, чáй, окнó, плáтье, двéрь, Любóвь, мáть *mother*.
   b. Animate **стóл**-nouns borrow the genitive singular endings (–а, –я) for the accusative singular: товáрища, Владúмира, студéнта, Николáя, учúтеля, пáрня.
   c. Only **женá**-nouns have endings in the accusative singular distinct from those of the nominative or genitive singular (–у, –ю); these are used for *both* animate and inanimate nouns: женý, кнúгу, сестрý, Гáлю, истóрию, Кóлю, лéкцию.

2. *Plural*
   a. *All* inanimate nouns have accusative plural forms exactly like the nominative plural: столы́, словарú, кнúги, лéкции, óкна, сочинéния, двéри.
   b. *All* animate nouns have accusative plural forms exactly like the genitive plural: студéнтов, учителéй, жён, профессорóв, сестёр, товáрищей, матерéй *mothers*.

The genitive case with не бýдет constructions

MODELS

Зáвтра не бýдет урóка.	There won't be a lesson tomorrow.
_____ урóков.	_____ any lessons _____.
_____ лéкции.	_____ a lecture _____.
_____ лéкций.	_____ any lectures _____.
_____ собрáния.	_____ a meeting _____.
_____ собрáний.	_____ any meetings _____.

■ REPETITION DRILL

Repeat the given models, noting that the genitive is required in future **не бýдет** constructions.

■ STRUCTURE REPLACEMENT DRILLS

We had no classes yesterday.
We won't have any classes tomorrow.
Вчерá у нáс нé было урóков.
Зáвтра у нáс не бýдет урóков.

Вчерá у нáс нé было лéкции.
Зáвтра у нáс не бýдет лéкции.
   (собрания, занятий, урока, экзамена, экзаменов, собраний)

■ QUESTION-ANSWER DRILLS

1. *Will there be bread in the store?*
   No, there won't be any bread.
   В магазúне бýдет хлéб?
   Нéт, хлéба не бýдет.
   В магазúне бýдет молокó?
   Нéт, молокá не бýдет.
      (селёдка, чай, рыба, ножи, тетради)

2. *But will Zina be there?*
   No, Zina won't be there.
   А Зúна тáм бýдет?
   Нéт, Зúны тáм не бýдет.
   А Олéг тáм бýдет?
   Нéт, Олéга тáм не бýдет.
      (их жёны, её брат, профессора, Козлов, Алексеев, учителя, вахтёр, девушки, секретарь, его товарищи, студентки)

Just as **нét** and **нé было** are accompanied by the genitive in the present and past, so, too, **не бýдет** is accompanied by the genitive in the future to indicate a missing thing or person.

Compare the affirmative and negative sentences below, noting that the nominative subject in the affirmative examples is replaced by the genitive in the corresponding negative examples and that the negative **не бýдет** (like **нé было** of the past tense) is a fixed form.

AFFIRMATION	NEGATIVE
У нáс зáвтра бýдет лéкция.	У нáс зáвтра не бýдет лéкции.
We'll have a lecture tomorrow.	*We won't have a lecture tomorrow.*
У нúх зáвтра бýдут урóки.	У нúх зáвтра не бýдет урóков.
They'll have classes tomorrow.	*They won't have classes tomorrow.*

The genitive case for the direct object of negated verbs

MODELS

Я не хочý молокá. I don't want any milk.
_____ чáя. _____ tea.
_____ борщá. _____ borsch.
_____ рýбы. _____ fish.
_____ селёдки. _____ herring.

Мы́ такúх картúн ещё не вúдели. We haven't seen pictures like that before.
_____ фúльмов _____. _____ films _____.
_____ портфéлей _____. _____ briefcases _____.
_____ домóв _____. _____ houses _____.
_____ теáтров _____. _____ theaters _____.
_____ квартúр _____. _____ apartments _____.
_____ аудитóрий _____. _____ auditoriums _____.
_____ библиотéк _____. _____ libraries _____.
_____ общежúтий _____. _____ dormitories _____.
_____ здáний _____. _____ buildings _____.

Мы́ ещё не знáем всéх студéнтов. We don't know all the students yet.
_____ дéвушек. _____ girls _____.
_____ вахтёров. _____ custodians _____.
_____ учителéй. _____ teachers _____.
_____ студéнток. _____ coeds _____.
_____ секретарéй. _____ secretaries _____.
_____ слóв. _____ words _____.

■ REPETITION DRILL

Repeat the given models, noting that after negated verbs the direct object is in the genitive case.

1. *I like novels.*
   I don't like novels.
   Я люблю́ рома́ны.
   Я не люблю́ рома́нов.
   Я люблю́ хи́мию.
   Я не люблю́ хи́мии.
   (стихи, осень, весну, зиму, географию,
   физику, литературу)

2. *Why is she opening the door?*
   Why doesn't she open the door?
   Почему́ она́ открыва́ет две́рь?
   Почему́ она́ не открыва́ет две́ри?
   Почему́ она́ открыва́ет окно́?
   Почему́ она́ не открыва́ет окна́?
   (о́кна, ящик, коробки, книгу, атлас,
   двери, тетрадь, тетради)

■ QUESTION-ANSWER DRILLS

1. *Did he get the books?*
   No, he didn't get the books.
   Óн доста́л кни́ги?
   Не́т, о́н не доста́л кни́г.
   Óн доста́л ключи́?
   Не́т, о́н не доста́л ключе́й.
   (тетрадь, словари, костюм, тетради,
   вилки, ножи, ложки, коробки,
   карандаши)

2. *Did you buy the suit?*
   No, I didn't buy the suit.
   Ты́ купи́ла костю́м?
   Не́т, я́ не купи́ла костю́ма.
   Ты́ купи́ла материа́л?
   Не́т, я́ не купи́ла материа́ла.
   (атлас, портфель, платье, ручку, чай,
   карандаш, карту)

3. *Did you see his dictionary?*
   No, I didn't see his dictionary.
   Вы́ ви́дели его́ слова́рь?
   Не́т, я́ его́ словаря́ не ви́дел.

   Вы́ ви́дели его́ тетра́дь?
   Не́т, я́ его́ тетра́ди не ви́дел.
   (книги, комнату, роман, портфель,
   квартиру, картину, картины)

■ RESPONSE DRILL

She probably forgot his name.
No, she didn't forget his name.
Она́, наве́рно, забы́ла его́ и́мя.
Не́т, она́ не забы́ла его́ и́мени.
Она́, наве́рно, забы́ла ключи́.
Не́т, она́ не забы́ла ключе́й.
(перо, ручку, подарок, ключ, его день
рождения, его фамилию, его отчество)

DISCUSSION

Although, according to strict grammatical rules, the direct object of negated verbs should be in the genitive case, there are some exceptions. The most common of these are:

1. In informal spoken Russian the accusative singular of жена́-nouns is often used instead of the expected genitive:

   Я́ не чита́л э́ту кни́гу (*or* **Я́ не чита́л э́той кни́ги**)   *I haven't read this book.*

2. If the negated verb is followed by an infinitive, the accusative is often used instead of the expected genitive:

   Я́ не могу́ откры́ть окно́ (*or* **Я́ не могу́ откры́ть окна́**)   *I can't open the window.*

Demonstrative э́тот in the nominative, accusative, genitive, and prepositional cases

	SINGULAR			PLURAL
	Masculine	*Neuter*	*Feminine*	
NOM	э́тот	э́то	э́та	э́ти
ACC	*inanimate* э́тот *animate* э́того [étəvə]	э́то	э́ту	*inanimate* э́ти *animate* э́тих
GEN	э́того [étəvə]		э́той	э́тих
PREP	(об) э́том		э́той	э́тих

MODELS

Э́тот слова́рь не мо́й.　　　　　This dictionary isn't mine.
Э́то письмо́ не моё.　　　　　　This letter _____.
Э́та кни́га не моя́.　　　　　　This book _____.
Э́та тетра́дь не моя́.　　　　　This notebook _____.
Э́ти тетра́ди не мои́.　　　　　These notebooks aren't mine.

Вы́ ви́дите э́того студе́нта?　　Do you see that student?
_____ э́ту студе́нтку?　　　_____ that coed?
_____ э́тих студе́нтов?　　_____ those students?
_____ э́тих студе́нток?　　_____ those coeds?

Возьми́ э́тот рома́н!　　　　　Take this novel!
_____ э́ту кни́гу!　　　　　____ this book!
_____ э́то письмо́!　　　　　____ this letter!
_____ э́ту тетра́дь!　　　　　____ this notebook!
_____ э́ти стихи́!　　　　　____ these verses!

Я́ не ви́дел э́того рома́на.　　I haven't seen this novel.
_____ э́той кни́ги.　　　　_____ this book.
_____ э́того письма́.　　　_____ this letter.
_____ э́той тетра́ди.　　　_____ this notebook.
_____ э́тих стихо́в.　　　_____ these verses.

Я́ не слы́шал об э́том рома́не.　I haven't heard about this novel.
_____ э́той кни́ге.　　_____ this book.
_____ э́том де́ле.　　_____ this affair.
_____ э́той про́сьбе.　_____ this request.
_____ э́тих стиха́х.　_____ these verses.

■ REPETITION DRILL

Repeat the given models, noting particularly that genitive endings are used for the animate masculine accusative in the singular and for all animate accusatives in the plural.

1. *Whose key is this?*
This one here?
Чéй э́то клю́ч?
Во́т э́тот?
Чьи́ э́то стихи́?
Во́т э́ти?
(окно́, словáрь, двéрь, кни́ги, ко́мната, рабо́та, рома́н, портфéль, сочинéние, но́ж)

2. *Here's our room.*
No, this room isn't ours.
Во́т нáша ко́мната.
Нéт, э́та ко́мната не нáша.
Во́т нáша двéрь.
Нéт, э́та двéрь не нáша.
(клю́ч, окно́, автобус, карандаши́, ножи́, словáрь)

3. *I'll see you on Friday.*
This Friday?
Я́ вáс уви́жу в пя́тницу.
В э́ту пя́тницу?

Я́ вáс уви́жу в четвéрг.
В э́тот четвéрг?
(в суббо́ту, в понедéльник, в срéду, в воскресéнье, во вто́рник)

■ STRUCTURE REPLACEMENT DRILLS

1. *This is my table.*
This table is mine.
Э́то мо́й сто́л.
Э́тот сто́л мо́й.
Э́то моя́ ко́мната.
Э́та ко́мната моя́.
(мо́й портфéль, мои́ кни́ги, моя́ кáрта, моё перо́, мои́ клю́чи, моё сочинéние, моя́ двéрь)

2. *This is my table.*
My table is this one here.
Э́то мо́й сто́л.
Мо́й сто́л во́т э́тот.
Э́то моя́ ко́мната.
Моя́ ко́мната во́т э́та.
(мо́й портфéль, мои́ кни́ги, моя́ кáрта, мои́ клю́чи, моё окно́, моя́ двéрь)

■ TRANSFORMATION DRILLS

1. *These dictionaries are [available] in the library.*
This dictionary is [available] in the library.
Э́ти словари́ éсть в библиотéке.
Э́тот словáрь éсть в библиотéке.
Э́ти рома́ны éсть в библиотéке.
Э́тот рома́н éсть в библиотéке.
(кни́ги, кáрты, áтласы, пи́сьма, словари́, сочинéния, рома́ны)

2. *What did you find out from these students?*
What did you find out from this student?
Что́ ты́ узнáл от э́тих студéнтов?
Что́ ты́ узнáл от э́того студéнта?
Что́ ты́ узнáл от э́тих профéссоров?
Что́ ты́ узнáл от э́того профéссора?
(учителéй, убо́рщиц, парнéй, учи́тельниц, дéвушек, студéнток)

3. *Have you already seen these pictures?*
Have you already seen this picture?
Вы́ ужé ви́дели э́ти карти́ны?
Вы́ ужé ви́дели э́ту карти́ну?

Вы́ ужé ви́дели э́тих америкáнцев?
Вы́ ужé ви́дели э́того америкáнца?
(э́ти шкафы́, э́ти сочинéния, э́тих дéвушек, э́ти рабо́ты, э́тих студéнтов, э́тих студéнток)

■ EXPANSION DRILL

We were talking about the lecture.
We were talking about this (or that) lecture.
Мы́ говори́ли о лéкции.
Мы́ говори́ли об э́той лéкции.

Мы́ говори́ли об áтласе.
Мы́ говори́ли об э́том áтласе.
(об уро́ках, о кáрте, о клу́бе, о собрáнии, о концéрте, о ку́рсах, о фи́льмах, о карти́нах)

It is important to note the difference between the unchanging introductory э́то (see Lesson 5) and the declinable demonstrative э́тот, э́та, э́то, э́ти. Note the following, which are complete sentences; the voice drops at the end of each:

Э́то ко́мната.	This is a room.
Э́то перо́.	This is a pen.

Compare them with the following, which are not sentences; in speech the voice level is sustained:

э́та ко́мната	this room
э́то перо́	this pen

Whereas unchanging э́то is independent of the other elements in the sentence, the demonstrative э́тот must agree in number, gender, and case with its noun referent. Note the following:

Э́то бы́л не мо́й слова́рь.	It wasn't my dictionary.
Э́тот слова́рь бы́л не мо́й.	That dictionary wasn't mine.

In the first case э́то is independent; бы́л and мо́й are masculine to agree with слова́рь. In the second case э́тот, бы́л, and мо́й are all masculine to agree with слова́рь.

ЧТЕ́НИЕ И ПИСЬМО́

Ка́тя лю́бит танцева́ть. В суббо́ту она́ и Оле́г пойду́т вме́сте в клу́б, там бу́дут та́нцы. По́сле та́нцев они́ хотя́т посмотре́ть америка́нский фи́льм. Оле́г уже́ его́ ви́дел, а Ка́тя нет.

Зи́на была́ в магази́не. Там она́ встре́тила Ка́тю. Ка́тя купи́ла материа́л на костю́м. Материа́л был краси́вый, но дорого́й. За́втра де́вушки опя́ть пойду́т в магази́н, но уже́ вме́сте.

Влади́мир и Зи́на на одно́м ку́рсе. Они́ ча́сто по́сле ле́кций хо́дят вме́сте в рестора́н. Сего́дня по́сле обе́да они́ иду́т

в клуб. Там будут танцы народов
СССР.

— Можно войти? — Конечно, заходите!
Вы же знаете, наша дверь никогда не
заперта. — Я хотел спросить насчёт
концерта. Когда он будет? — В девять.
И, знаете, это бесплатно. — Вот хорошо!
Я не знал.

Га́ля всё вре́мя сиди́т до́ма. В клу́бе всегда́ то́лько та́нцы, а танцева́ть она́
не лю́бит. В кино́ она́ то́же не хо́дит. Она́ давно́ ви́дела все́ э́ти фи́льмы. Говоря́т,
что ско́ро бу́дет идти́ америка́нский фи́льм. Э́то друго́е де́ло. Тогда́ Га́ля не бу́дет
сиде́ть до́ма. Она́ пойдёт посмотре́ть э́тот фи́льм.

Оле́г чита́ет «Евге́ния Оне́гина», а Влади́мир «Войну́ и ми́р». Оле́г то́же чита́л
«Войну́ и ми́р», и да́же мно́го ра́з. Он говори́т, что о́чень лю́бит э́тот рома́н.

Воло́дя и Оле́г — това́рищи по ко́мнате. Ка́тя и Зи́на то́же живу́т вме́сте. Зи́на
и Оле́г на одно́м ку́рсе, но ма́ло знако́мы: то́лько «здра́вствуйте» и «до свида́ния».
Но в суббо́ту они́ ду́мают всё вме́сте пойти́ на та́нцы.

— Куда́ вы́ спеши́те, Га́ля?
— В библиоте́ку. Я́ всегда́ хожу́ туда́ по́сле ле́кций.
— Почему́ же я́ ва́с никогда́ та́м не ви́дел?
— Не зна́ю. Я́ чита́ю в э́той библиоте́ке ка́ждый де́нь.
— И я́ то́же. Где́ вы́ лю́бите сиде́ть?
— Я́ сижу́ всегда́ у окна́.
— Тепе́рь бу́ду зна́ть.

— Куда́ вы́ идёте та́к по́здно?
— Я́ спешу́ в общежи́тие. Та́м бу́дут все́ на́ши ребя́та.
— А что́ вы́ бу́дете та́м де́лать?
— Игра́ть в ка́рты.
— Но́чью?
— Да́, та́м мо́жно игра́ть то́лько но́чью.

NOTES

PREPARATION FOR CONVERSATION **Мы́ попу́тчики**

попу́тчик [papúččik]	traveling companion, fellow traveler
Мы́ попу́тчики.	We're traveling companions.
проводни́к, –а́; –и́, –о́в[1]	conductor, guide
биле́т	ticket
Ва́ш биле́т.	Your ticket.
граждани́н, –а; гра́ждане, гра́ждан[1]	citizen
Ва́ш биле́т, граждани́н.	Your ticket, sir.
ме́сто, –а; места́, ме́ст	place, seat, berth; position, job, space, room
Ме́сто во́семь здесь.	Berth eight is here.
ваго́н	railroad car
мя́гкий	soft
мя́гкий ваго́н	soft car, first-class car
Мя́гкий ваго́н, ме́сто во́семь здесь.	First-class car, berth eight is here.
Спаси́бо. О́, кого́ я ви́жу?!	Thank you. Oh, who's that I see?
е́хать (unidirectional ı), е́ду, е́дут	to be going (by vehicle)
И вы́ е́дете?	Are you going, too?
Га́ля! И вы́ е́дете?	Galya! Are you going, too?
Да́. Здра́вствуйте.	Yes. Hello.
иска́ть (ı), ищу́, и́щут	to look for, seek
Во́т ищу́ свое́ ме́сто. Проводни́к!	I'm just looking for my seat. Conductor!
ве́рхний, –яя, –ее	upper
Ва́ше ме́сто ве́рхнее.	Your berth is the upper.
ни́жний, –яя, –ее	lower
проси́ть (ıı), прошу́, про́сят	to request, ask for

---

[1] Nouns with shifting stress or other unpredictable features in the declension are given in four forms: nominative singular genitive singular, nominative plural, and genitive plural.

Я проси́ла ни́жнее.	I asked for a lower.
ка́сса	ticket window, box office, cash register
А я́ в ка́ссе проси́ла ни́жнее.	But I asked for a lower at the ticket window.
спа́ть (II), сплю́, спя́т	to sleep
неудо́бно	[it's] uncomfortable, [it's] inconvenient
наверху́	upstairs, on top, in the upper
Наверху́ спа́ть неудо́бно.	It's uncomfortable sleeping in an upper.
оши́бка	mistake, error
Э́то, наве́рно, оши́бка.	It's probably a mistake.
купе́ (indeclinable n) [kupé]	compartment, sleeping compartment
У меня́ то́же ме́сто в э́том купе́.	I also have a berth in this compartment.
Подожди́те! Э́то, наве́рно, оши́бка.	Wait a minute! It's probably a mistake.
У меня́ то́же ме́сто в э́том купе́.	I have a berth in this compartment, too.
удивля́ться (I)	to be surprised
Не удивля́йтесь!	Don't be surprised!
е́здить (multidirectional II), е́зжу, е́здят	to go (by vehicle), ride, travel
в одно́м купе́	in one compartment
Они́ е́здят в одно́м купе́.	They travel in the same compartment.
же́нщина	woman
мужчи́на [muščínə]	man
Же́нщины и мужчи́ны е́здят в одно́м купе́.	Women and men travel in the same sleeping compartment.
у на́с	in our country, in our society (lit. by us)
У на́с же́нщины и мужчи́ны е́здят в одно́м купе́.	In our country women and men travel in the same sleeping compartment.
Что́ вы́ говори́те!	You don't say!
пое́хать (pfv I), пое́ду, пое́дут	to go (by vehicle), ride, travel
Мы́ в одно́м купе́ пое́дем.	We'll travel in the same compartment.
с ва́ми	with you
мы́ с ва́ми	you and I
Мы́ с ва́ми в одно́м купе́ пое́дем?	Will you and I travel in the same compartment?
Так зна́чит, мы́ с ва́ми в одно́м купе́ пое́дем?	Then you mean you and I will travel in the same compartment?
Да́. А вы́ куда́ е́дете?	Yes. And where is it you're going?
В Москву́, а вы́?	To Moscow. And you?
Я́ то́же.	So am I.
Во́т мы́ и попу́тчики.	Well, so we're traveling companions.

SUPPLEMENT

сто́ить (II), сто́ит, сто́ят	to cost, be (in price)
Ско́лько сто́ит биле́т в Москву́?	How much is a ticket to Moscow?
жёсткий ваго́н	hard car, second-class car
в жёстком ваго́не	in (or on) the second-class car

У меня ме́сто в жёстком ваго́не.
   в мя́гком ваго́не
У меня́ ме́сто в мя́гком ваго́не.
   по́езд, –а ; поезда́, –о́в
   на по́езде
Вы́ е́дете на по́езде?
   внизу́
Где́ ва́ша ко́мната, наверху́ и́ли внизу́?
   плати́ть (II), плачу́, пла́тят
Плати́те в ка́ссе!
   заплати́ть (pfv II)
Вы́ уже́ заплати́ли?
   плати́ть (*or* заплати́ть) за (*plus* acc)
Ско́лько вы́ заплати́ли за биле́ты?
   ста́нция
   на ста́нции
   на ста́нцию
По́езд стои́т на ста́нции.

I have a seat in the second-class car.
   in (*or* on) the first-class car
I have a seat in the first-class car.
   train
   on the train, by train
Are you going on the train?
   downstairs, below
Where's your room, upstairs or downstairs?
   to pay
Pay at the ticket window!
   to pay
Did you already pay?
   to pay for
How much did you pay for the tickets?
   station
   at the station
   to the station
The train is in the station.

Мы́ попу́тчики

Гр. — Фили́пп Гра́нт, америка́нец
Г. — Га́ля
П. — Проводни́к [1]

П.   1 Ва́ш биле́т, граждани́н.[2] Мя́гкий ваго́н,[3] ме́сто во́семь зде́сь.

Гр.   2 Спаси́бо. О́, кого́ я́ ви́жу?! Га́ля! И вы́ е́дете?

Г.   3 Да́. Здра́вствуйте. Во́т ищу́ своё ме́сто. Проводни́к!

П.   4 Ва́ше ме́сто ве́рхнее.

Г.   5 А я́ в ка́ссе проси́ла ни́жнее. Наверху́ спа́ть неудо́бно.

Гр.   6 Подожди́те! Э́то, наве́рно, оши́бка! У меня́ то́же ме́сто в э́том купе́.

Г.   7 Не удивля́йтесь. У на́с же́нщины и мужчи́ны е́здят в одно́м купе́.[4]

Гр.   8 Что́ вы́ говори́те! Так зна́чит, мы́ с ва́ми в одно́м купе́ пое́дем?

Г.   9 Да́. А куда́ вы́ е́дете?

Гр. 10 В Москву́, а вы́?

Г. 11 Я́ то́же. Во́т мы́ и попу́тчики.

NOTES   [1] The **проводни́к** on Russian trains is the man in charge of an individual car. He differs from an American conductor in that the latter is responsible for several cars or the whole train. Thus job is something between that of a conductor and a porter. **Проводни́к** also means *gulde*.

Like all nouns ending in –анин, граждани́н loses –ин in the plural, and has the special nominative plural ending –e: гра́ждане. The stem thus ends in soft [ŋ] in the nominative plural, but in hard [n] elsewhere in the plural: мно́го гра́ждан, о гра́жданах.

Although the American student or tourist in the Soviet Union may hear the word граждани́н used by train and streetcar conductors, bus drivers, and policemen, he should not use it himself in addressing Soviet citizens. Under no circumstances should he use господи́н or госпожа́. The best way to get the attention of a stranger is by saying извини́те, прости́те, or скажи́те, пожа́луйста. Although the student probably will not use the terms himself, he may hear himself addressed as молодо́й челове́к or, in the case of a girl, де́вушка.

³ The so-called *soft car* мя́гкий ваго́н consists of first-class compartments with soft seats; each compartment accommodating four persons. Compartments in the *hard car* жёсткий ваго́н have hard seats; each compartment seats six persons and sleeps four. In selling tickets, no attempt is made to separate men from women in sleeping cars, and the American tourist may be surprised to find he is sharing a sleeping car on a Russian train with one or more persons of the opposite sex.

⁴ The verbs е́здить and е́хать describe going by vehicle or some means other than on foot. **Е́здить** is used for the general (multidirectional) activity and **е́хать** for the specific (unidirectional) activity. In this respect they parallel ходи́ть and идти́ exactly.

Compare	Мы́ ча́сто е́здим в Ки́ев.	We often go to Kiev.
	Мы́ ча́сто хо́дим в па́рк.	We often go to the park.
with	Мы́ е́дем в Ки́ев.	We're on our way to Kiev.
	Мы́ идём в па́рк.	We're on our way to the park.

PREPARATION FOR CONVERSATION   **В Москве́**

шофёр	driver (of car)
администра́тор	clerk, administrator
носи́льщик	porter
Носи́льщик!	Porter!
бага́ж	luggage, baggage
получи́ть (pfv II), получу́, полу́чат	to receive, get,
Получи́те мо́й бага́ж, пожа́луйста.	Get my luggage, please.
квита́нция	receipt, claim check
Во́т квита́нция.	Here's the claim check.
Носи́льщик! Получи́те мо́й бага́ж, пожа́луйста. Во́т квита́нция.	Porter! Get my luggage, please. Here's the claim check.
Сейча́с. А где́ вы́ бу́дете жда́ть?	Right away. Where will you wait?
ожида́ние	waiting, wait, expectation
за́л ожида́ния	waiting room
В за́ле ожида́ния.	In the waiting room.
ве́щь (f) (gen pl веще́й)	thing
Во́т ва́ши ве́щи.	Here are your things.
копе́йка (gen pl копе́ек)	kopeck
три́дцать [tr̝ítcət]	thirty
Три́дцать копе́ек, пожа́луйста.	Thirty kopecks, please.

256   LESSON 12

Вот ваши вещи. Тридцать копеек, пожалуйста.	Here are your things. Thirty kopecks, please.
такси (indecl n)	taxi
Такси!	Taxi!
багажник	baggage compartment, luggage carrier, trunk
положить (pfv II), положу, положат	to put
Я положу ваши вещи в багажник.	I'll put your things in the baggage compartment.
разрешить (pfv II), разрешу, разрешат	to permit, allow
Я положу ваши вещи в багажник, разрешите?	I'll put your things in the baggage compartment, O.K.?
вам куда?	where do you want to go?
Вам куда?	Where to?
гостиница	hotel
В гостиницу «Украина».	To the Hotel Ukraine.
приехать (pfv I), приеду, приедут	to arrive (by vehicle)
приехали	[we've] arrived, here we are
с вас	from you; you owe
рубль, рубля; –и, –ей (m)	ruble
Приехали. С вас рубль.	Here we are. That'll be one ruble.
Моя фамилия Грант.	My name is Grant.
номер, –а; номера, – ов	hotel room, number, issue
небольшой	small
заказать (pfv I), закажу, закажут	to order, make a reservation
Я заказал небольшой номер.	I ordered a small room.
люкс	deluxe class
Я заказал небольшой номер люкс.	I ordered a small room, deluxe class.
для одного	a single, for one
Я заказал небольшой номер люкс для одного.	I ordered a small single room, deluxe class.
этаж, –а; –и, –ей	story, floor
на пятом этаже	on the fifth floor
Ваш номер на пятом этаже.	Your room is on the fifth floor.
удобство	convenience, comfort
Все удобства.	[It has] all the conveniences.
ванная	bathroom
уборная	toilet, lavatory
вода	water
горячая вода	hot water
Все удобства: ванная, уборная, горячая вода.	All the conveniences: bath, lavatory, hot water.
направо	on the right, to the right
лифт	elevator
Лифт направо.	The elevator is to the right.
прекрасно	excellent, fine
Прекрасно.	Fine.

пешко́м	on foot
Я пойду́ пешко́м.	I'll go on foot.
нале́во	on the left, to the left
Где́ ли́фт?	Where's the elevator?
— Нале́во.	To the left.
пря́мо	straight, straight ahead, directly
Иди́те пря́мо.	Go straight ahead.
вокза́л [vagzál][1]	station, terminal
на вокза́л	to the station
на вокза́ле	in (or at) the station
Мы́ до́лго сиде́ли на вокза́ле.	We sat in the station a long time.
поезжа́й! поезжа́йте!	drive! go (by vehicle)!
Поезжа́йте в гости́ницу «Украи́на»!	Drive to the Hotel Ukraine!
Я́ е́ду в Ки́ев.	I'm going to Kiev.
Я́ е́ду в Ташке́нт.	I'm going to Tashkent.
Я́ е́ду в Ха́рьков.	I'm going to Kharkov.
Я́ е́ду во Владивосто́к.	I'm going to Vladivostok.
Я́ е́ду в Я́лту.	I'm going to Yalta.
Я́ е́ду в Оде́ссу.	I'm going to Odessa.
удо́бный (adv удо́бно)	convenient, comfortable
У ни́х удо́бная кварти́ра.	They have a comfortable apartment.

В Москве́

Гр. — Гра́нт
Нос. — Носи́льщик
Шоф. — Шофёр
Адм. — Администра́тор

Гр.   1 Носи́льщик! Получи́те мо́й бага́ж, пожа́луйста. Во́т квита́нция.

Нос.   2 Сейча́с. А где́ вы́ бу́дете жда́ть?

Гр.   3 В за́ле ожида́ния.

Нос.   4 Во́т ва́ши ве́щи. Три́дцать копе́ек, пожа́луйста. Такси́![1]

Шоф.   5 Я́ положу́ ва́ши ве́щи в бага́жник, разреши́те? Ва́м куда́?

Гр.   6 В гости́ницу «Украи́на».

Шоф.   7 Прие́хали. С ва́с ру́бль.

---

[1] Compare **вокза́л** with **ста́нция. Вокза́л** is a railway terminal or station building, whereas **ста́нция** can refer to any station. Notice that both require the preposition **на**:

| Он встретил жену́ на авто́бусной ста́нции. | He met his wife at the bus station. |
| Он встретил жену́ на вокза́ле. | He met his wife at the railway station. |

Гр. 8 Моя́ фами́лия Гра́нт. Я заказа́л небольшо́й но́мер люкс для одного́.[2]

Адм. 9 Да́, ваш но́мер на пя́том этаже́. Всё удо́бства: ва́нная, убо́рная, горя́чая вода́. Лифт напра́во.

Гр. 10 Прекра́сно.

NOTES

[1] Russians seldom check their luggage or use the help of porters. Tipping is officially forbidden in the Soviet Union, but most foreigners are expected to tip hotel servants, waiters, and check-room attendants.

[2] Only **люкс** guarantees hot water. At most hotels one gets only cold water, has no private bath, and has to share toilet facilities with other guests on the same floor. This is typical not only in the Soviet Union, but common in European countries as well.

Basic sentence patterns

1. Куда́ вы е́дете?
— В Москву́.
— Я е́ду в Москву́.
— В Ленингра́д.
— Мы е́дем в Ленингра́д.
— Зна́чит мы попу́тчики.
— Я то́же е́ду в Ленингра́д.
— Мы пое́дем в одно́м купе́.

Where are you going?
To Moscow.
I'm going to Moscow.
To Leningrad.
We're going to Leningrad.
Then we're traveling companions.
I'm on my way to Leningrad, too.
We'll ride in the same compartment.

2. Ва́ше ме́сто ве́рхнее и́ли ни́жнее?
— Ве́рхнее.
— Ни́жнее.
— Ни́жнее лу́чше, чем ве́рхнее.
— Неудо́бно спа́ть наверху́.
— Я в ка́ссе проси́л ни́жнее.

Do you have an upper or a lower?
An upper.
A lower.
The lower is better than the upper.
It's uncomfortable sleeping in an upper.
I asked for a lower at the ticket window.

3. Где́ вы бу́дете жда́ть?
— В за́ле ожида́ния.
— На углу́.
— О́коло кио́ска.
— В гости́нице.
— На ста́нции.
— На вокза́ле.

Where will you be waiting?
In the waiting room.
On the corner.
Near the newsstand.
At the hotel.
At the station.
At the station (*or* railway terminal).

4. Я положу́ ва́ши ве́щи на сто́л.
_____ на э́тот сту́л.
_____ на по́лку.
_____ в ко́мнату.

I'll put your things on the table.
_____ on this chair.
_____ on the bookcase.
_____ in the room.

Я положу́ ва́ши ве́щи в коро́бку.   I'll put your things in the box.
_____ в шкаф.   _____ in the dresser.
_____ в портфе́ль.   _____ in the briefcase.
_____ в я́щик.   _____ in the drawer.

5. Носи́льщик поло́жит ва́ши ве́щи в бага́жник.   The porter will put your things in the luggage
                                                                compartment.
_____ в такси́.   _____ in the taxi.
_____ в авто́бус.   _____ in the bus.
_____ в у́гол.   _____ in the corner.

6. Во́т ва́ша квита́нция.   Here's your receipt (or claim check).
____ ва́ш биле́т.   _____ your ticket.
____ ва́ша ва́нная.   _____ your bathroom.
____ ва́ш бага́ж.   _____ your luggage.
____ ва́ше ме́сто.   _____ your seat (or berth).
____ ва́ше купе́.   _____ your compartment.
____ ва́ши ве́щи.   Here are your things.

7. Э́то на́ш по́езд.   This is our train.
____ на́ша гости́ница.   _____ our hotel.
____ на́ша ста́нция.   _____ our station.
____ на́ш но́мер.   _____ our [hotel] room.
____ на́ша ко́мната.   _____ our room.

8. Я́ ищу́ своё ме́сто.   I'm looking for my seat (or berth).
_____ сво́й но́мер.   _____ my [hotel] room.
_____ своё купе́.   _____ my compartment.
_____ такси́.   _____ a taxi.

9. Мы́ и́щем кио́ск.   We're looking for a newsstand.
_____ проводника́.   _____ the conductor.
_____ шофёра.   _____ a taxi driver.
_____ администра́тора.   _____ the clerk in charge.
_____ носи́льщика.   _____ a porter.
_____ вахтёра.   _____ the custodian.

10. Где́ ли́фт?   Where's the elevator?
— Напра́во.   To the right.
— Иди́те напра́во.   Go to the right.
— Нале́во.   To the left.
— Иди́те нале́во.   Go to the left.
— Иди́те пря́мо.   Go straight ahead.

11. Куда́ вы́ е́дете?   Where are you going?
— В Ленингра́д.   To Leningrad.
— В Москву́.   To Moscow.
— В Ки́ев.   To Kiev.
— В Оде́ссу.   To Odessa.
— В Аме́рику.   To America.
— В СССР.   To the U.S.S.R.

12. Ва́м куда́?   Where to?
— В гости́ницу «Украи́на».   To the Hotel Ukraine.
— На ста́нцию.   To the station.

— На вокза́л.	To the railway terminal.
— В университе́т.	To the university.
— На по́чту.	To the post office.
— В Большо́й теа́тр.	To the Bolshoi Theater.
— В ГУ́М.	To GUM.

13. Ско́лько сто́ит биле́т в Москву́? How much is a ticket to Moscow?
_____ в Ленингра́д? _____ to Leningrad?
_____ в Ки́ев? _____ to Kiev?
_____ в Оде́ссу? _____ to Odessa?

14. Я́ е́ду то́лько до Москвы́. I'm only going as far as Moscow.
_____ до Ленингра́да. _____ as far as Leningrad.
_____ до Ки́ева. _____ as far as Kiev.
_____ до Ха́рькова. _____ as far as Kharkov.
_____ до Ташке́нта. _____ as far as Tashkent.
_____ до Владивосто́ка. _____ as far as Vladivostok.
_____ до Я́лты. _____ as far as Yalta.
_____ до Оде́ссы. _____ as far as Odessa.

15. Вы́ ча́сто е́здите в Москву́? Do you often go to Moscow?
_____ в Ленингра́д? _____ to Leningrad?
_____ в Ки́ев? _____ to Kiev?
_____ в Я́лту? _____ to Yalta?
_____ в Оде́ссу? _____ to Odessa?
_____ во Владивосто́к? _____ to Vladivostok?

16. Ско́лько э́то сто́ит? How much does this cost?
— Оди́н ру́бль. One ruble.
— Два́ рубля́. Two rubles.
— Три́ рубля́. Three rubles.
— Четы́ре рубля́. Four rubles.
— Пя́ть рубле́й. Five rubles.
— Ше́сть рубле́й. Six rubles.
— Се́мь рубле́й. Seven rubles.
— Во́семь рубле́й. Eight rubles.
— Де́вять рубле́й. Nine rubles.
— Де́сять рубле́й. Ten rubles.

17. Ско́лько с меня́? How much do I owe?
— Одна́ копе́йка. One kopeck.
— Две́ копе́йки. Two kopecks.
— Три́ копе́йки. Three kopecks.
— Четы́ре копе́йки. Four kopecks.
— Пя́ть копе́ек. Five kopecks.

18. С ва́с ше́сть копе́ек. You owe six kopecks.
_____ се́мь копе́ек. _____ seven kopecks.
_____ во́семь копе́ек. _____ eight kopecks.
_____ де́вять копе́ек. _____ nine kopecks.
_____ де́сять копе́ек. _____ ten kopecks.

Pronunciation practice: special consonant clusters

A. Hard [čš] (spelled чш, дш, or тш).

[lúčšij] лу́чший
better

[praséčšij] проше́дший
gone

[mláčšij] мла́дший
younger

[zablúčšij] заблу́дший
gone astray

[xúčšij] ху́дший
worse

[zaɣáčšij] завя́дший
wilted

[páčšij] па́дший
fallen

[cɣéčšij] цве́тший
bloomed

B. Long soft [čč] (spelled тч or дч).

[papúččik] попу́тчик
traveling companion

[gaʒéččik] газе́тчик
newsboy

[ščóččik] счётчик
meter

[raķéččik] раке́тчик
rocket technician

[zdáččik] сда́тчик
lessor

[baĺéččik] бале́тчик
ballet dancer

[şíččik] си́тчик
kind of cotton

[razɣéččik] разве́дчик
scout

[aččót] отчёт
account, report

[zavóččik] заво́дчик
factory owner

[óččij] о́тчий
father's

[kabáččik] каба́тчик
innkeeper

[buĺéččik] буфе́тчик
lunch counter attendant

[ɣiččiná] ветчина́
ham

C. Hard [dž]. This combination occurs when a prefix ending in д or т combines with a root which begins with the voiced consonant ж. It also occurs in foreign-derived words.

[ṇidžák] пиджа́к
jacket

[padžárij] поджа́рый
thin, haggard

[džás] джа́з
jazz

[adžiĺíšč] от жили́щ
from the dwellings

[džút] джу́т
jute

[ódžil] о́тжил
his time has passed

[džém] джем
jam

[adžéč] отже́чь
anneal; glass, metal

[padžéč] подже́чь
to set fire to

[ódžik] о́тжиг
annealing

[pədžigáţiĺ] поджига́тель
inciter

[aʒirbajdžán] Азербайджа́н
Azerbaidzhan (S.S.R.)

D. Hard [tc]. This combination occurs very frequently, especially in the infinitive and third person singular and plural of verbs with the reflexive particle –ся. It is spelled тс, тьс, дс, тц, or дц.

[dvátcət] два́дцать
twenty

[kanátci] кана́дцы
Canadians

[tŗítcət] три́дцать
thirty

[ţiþétci] тибе́тцы
Tibetans

[mítcə] мы́ться
to wash

[mójitcə] мо́ется
he washes

[mójutcə] мо́ются
they wash

[atcá] отца́
of father

[inarótci] иноро́дцы
foreigners

[l̦iṇingrátci] ленингра́дцы
people of Leningrad

[brátci] бра́тцы
brothers

STRUCTURE AND DRILLS

Two-stem first conjugation verbs

Many verbs of the first conjugation show a marked difference between the stem used to form the infinitive and past tense and that used to form the present-future. Verbs such as these we call "two-stem" verbs.

STEM взя–		STEM возьм–
INFINITIVE взя́ть	FUTURE возьму́, возьмёшь, возьмёт	
PAST взя́л, взяла́, взя́ли		

In order to manipulate the various forms of the Russian verb, it is essential to recognize certain broad rules of compatibility vis-à-vis stems and endings.

1. Infinitive and past tense endings begin with consonants (т and л) and, in almost all verbs, are added to a form of the stem ending in a vowel: жи́–ть, жи́–л.
2. Present-future endings begin with vowels and are added to a form of the stem ending in a consonant: жив–у́, жив–ёшь, жив–у́т.[1]

MODELS

Other two-stem verbs already encountered by the student in some of their forms.

посла́ть (pfv) *to send*
   Я уже́ посла́л письмо́.
   I already sent the letter.

пошлю́, пошлёшь, пошлю́т
   Я за́втра пошлю́ письмо́.
   I'll send the letter tomorrow.

сказа́ть (pfv) *to say, tell*
   Что вы сказа́ли?
   What did you say?

скажу́, ска́жешь, ска́жут
   Он ничего́ не ска́жет.
   He won't say anything.

заказа́ть (pfv) *to order*
   Она́ заказа́ла биле́ты.
   She ordered the tickets.

закажу́, зака́жешь, зака́жут
   Она́ зака́жет биле́ты.
   She'll order the tickets.

иска́ть (ipfv) *to look for*
   Вы меня́ иска́ли?
   Were you looking for me?

ищу́, и́щешь, и́щут
   Вы и́щете рабо́ту?
   Are you looking for work?

наре́зать (pfv) *to slice*
   Оле́г уже́ наре́зал хле́б.
   Oleg already sliced the bread.

наре́жу, наре́жешь, наре́жут
   Оле́г наре́жет хле́б.
   Oleg will slice the bread.

---

[1] In [j]–stem verbs, the present-future stem ends in the consonant *sound* [j].

писа́ть (ipfv) *to write*
    Мы́ писа́ли пи́сьма.
    We were writing letters.
написа́ть (pfv) *to write*
    Вы́ написа́ли домо́й?
    Have you written home?
жи́ть (ipfv) *to live*
    Вы́ до́лго та́м жи́ли?
    Did you live there long?
доста́ть (pfv) *to get*
    Вы́ доста́ли биле́ты?
    Did you get the tickets?
откры́ть (pfv) *to open*
    Вахтёр откры́л две́рь.
    The custodian opened the door.
закры́ть (pfv) *to close*
    Вы́ уже́ закры́ли о́кна?
    Did you already close the windows?
бы́ть *to be*
    Где́ вы́ бы́ли?
    Where were you?
забы́ть (pfv) *to forget*
    Она́ забы́ла о собра́нии.
    She forgot about the meeting.
пи́ть (ipfv) *to drink*
    Вы́ уже́ пи́ли ча́й?
    Have you had tea already?
танцева́ть (ipfv) *to dance*
    Вы́ мно́го танцева́ли?
    Did you dance much?
е́хать (ipfv) *to be going*
    Мы́ е́хали в Ташке́нт.
    We were on our way to Tashkent.
прие́хать (pfv) *to arrive*
    Они́ уже́ прие́хали.
    They've already arrived.

пишу́, пи́шешь, пи́шут
    Мы́ пи́шем пи́сьма.
    We're writing letters.
напишу́, напи́шешь, напи́шут
    Не́т, я́ за́втра напишу́.
    No, I'll write tomorrow.
живу́, живёшь, живу́т
    Вы́ давно́ здесь живёте?
    Have you lived here long?
доста́ну, доста́нешь, доста́нут
    О́н доста́нет биле́ты.
    He'll get the tickets.
откро́ю, откро́ешь, откро́ют
    Вахтёр откро́ет две́рь.
    The custodian will open the door.
закро́ю, закро́ешь, закро́ют
    Не́т, я́ сейча́с закро́ю.
    No, I'll do it now.
бу́ду, бу́дешь, бу́дут
    Где́ вы́ бу́дете после обе́да?
    Where will you be this afternoon?
забу́ду, забу́дешь, забу́дут
    Вы́ не забу́дете на́с?
    You won't forget us, will you?
пью́, пьёшь, пью́т
    Вы́ пьёте ко́фе?
    Do you drink coffee?
танцу́ю, танцу́ешь, танцу́ют
    Вы́ танцу́ете?
    Do you dance?
е́ду, е́дешь, е́дут
    Мы́ е́дем в Ташке́нт.
    We're on our way to Tashkent.
прие́ду, прие́дешь, прие́дут
    Они́ прие́дут в четве́рг.
    They'll arrive on Thursday.

■ SUBSTITUTION DRILLS

1. *I'm writing a letter*
    Я́ пишу́ письмо́.
    Они́ пи́шут письмо́.
    (мы, вы, ты, он, она, я, они)

2. *I'll write the letter.*
    Я́ напишу́ письмо́.
    Она́ напи́шет письмо́.
    (мы, они, ты, Евгений, я, вы, они)

3. *The custodian will open the doors.*
    Вахтёр откро́ет две́ри.
    Я́ откро́ю две́ри.
    (проводник, мы, они, ты, вы,
    носильщики, шофёр)

4. *I'm looking for a hotel.*
    Я́ ищу́ гости́ницу.
    Она́ и́щет гости́ницу.
    (мы, ты, Зина, они, вы, Филипп)

5. *I don't drink coffee.*

Я не пью кóфе.

Мы́ не пьём кóфе.

  (они, вы, Наташа, ты, муж, жена)

6. *They'll order the tickets.*

Они́ закáжут билéты.

Я́ закажу́ билéты.

  (Ирина, ты, вы, Козлов, они, я)

■ STRUCTURE REPLACEMENT DRILLS

1. *Do you dance much?*
   Did you dance much?

Вы́ мнóго танцу́ете?

Вы́ мнóго танцевáли?

Óн мнóго танцу́ет?

Óн мнóго танцевáл?

  (она, они, он, Галя)

2. *He forgot the keys.*
   He'll forget the keys.

Óн забы́л ключи́.

Óн забу́дет ключи́.

Ты́ забы́л ключи́.

Ты́ забу́дешь ключи́.

  (я, мы, вы, она)

3. *We lived in Kiev.*
   We live in Kiev.

Мы́ жи́ли в Ки́еве.

Мы́ живём в Ки́еве.

Я́ жи́л в Ки́еве.

Я́ живу́ в Ки́еве.

  (вы, они, Зина, я, мы)

4. *He was looking for you.*
   He's been looking for you.

Óн вáс искáл.

Óн вáс и́щет.

Я́ вáс искáл.

Я́ вáс ищу́.

  (они, мы, она, Алексеев, я)

5. *Oleg will get the tickets.*
   Oleg got the tickets.

Олéг достáнет билéты.

Олéг достáл билéты.

Я́ достáну билéты.

Я́ достáл билéты.

  (мы, они, вы, Наташа, ты, Волков)

■ QUESTION-ANSWER DRILLS

1. *Have you already sent the letter?*
   No, I'll send it tomorrow.

Вы́ ужé послáли письмó?

Нéт, я́ зáвтра пошлю́.

Онá ужé послáла письмó?

Нéт, онá зáвтра пошлёт.

  (Олег, ты, они, мы, Зина, вы)

2. *Have they already arrived?*
   No, they'll arrive today.

Они́ ужé приéхали?

Нéт, они́ приéдут сегóдня.

Вáш дру́г ужé приéхал?

Нéт, óн приéдет сегóдня.

  (ваши друзья, твоя сестра, украинцы)

■ MIXED STRUCTURE REPLACEMENT DRILL

Past tense to present-future and vice versa.

1. *He didn't say a thing.*
   He won't say a thing.

Óн ничегó не сказáл.

Óн ничегó не скáжет.

Вы́ ничегó не скáжете.

Вы́ ничегó не сказáли.

Онá ничегó не сказáла.

Мы́ ничегó не скáжем.

Они́ ничегó не сказáли.

Я́ ничегó не скажу́.

Ты́ ничегó не сказáл.

2. *I'll slice the bread.*
   I've sliced the bread.

Я́ нарéжу хлéб.

Я́ нарéзал хлéб.

Ты́ нарéзал хлéб.

Ты́ нарéжешь хлéб.

Мы́ нарéжем хлéб.

Олéг нарéзал хлéб.

Они́ нарéжут хлéб.

Вы́ нарéзали хлéб.

Óльга нарéжет хлéб.

Я́ нарéзал хлéб.

3. *They closed the windows.*
   They'll close the windows.
   Они́ закры́ли о́кна.
   Они́ закро́ют о́кна.
   Мы́ закро́ем о́кна.
   Мы́ закры́ли о́кна.

Я́ закры́л о́кна.
Ка́тя закры́ла о́кна.
Проводники́ закры́ли о́кна.
Вы́ закро́ете о́кна.

Genitive plural noun endings: special problems

1. Стóл-nouns with stems ending in the always-hard consonant ц take the ending –ов only if the stress falls on the ending: огурцо́в. If the stress falls on the stem, the ending is spelled –ев: америка́нцев, украи́нцев, та́нцев. Remember that this is merely a spelling convention and that ц is always *pronounced* hard: [aɱiɽiká̇ncif, ukrají̇ncif, agurcóf].

2. Particular problems arise in forming the genitive plural of certain стóл– and окнó-nouns with stems ending in the consonant sound [j].

   a. Стóл-nouns ending in й in the nominative singular take the genitive plural ending –ев (stressed: –ёв).

NOM SG		NOM PL	GEN PL
геро́й	hero	геро́и	геро́ев
ча́й	tea	чаи́	чаёв

   b. Most стóл- and окнó-nouns which terminate in *unstressed* –ья in the nominative plural take the ending –ев (retaining the preceding –ь). Most are nouns with only their plural stems ending in [j].

NOM PL		GEN PL
бра́тья	brothers	бра́тьев
сту́лья	chairs	сту́льев
пе́рья	pen points	пе́рьев
пла́тья	dresses	пла́тьев

   c. Those стóл-nouns whose nominative plural terminates in *stressed* –ья have a zero-ending genitive plural with e inserted before the final –й. Here –й is not an ending, strictly speaking, but the Cyrillic way of representing the stem consonant [j] after the inserted vowel.

NOM PL			GEN PL	
мужья́	[mužjá]	husbands	муже́й	[mužéj]
друзья́	[druẓjá]	friends	друзе́й	[druẓéj]
сыновья́	[sinaɣjá]	sons	сынове́й	[sinaɣéj]

3. A few стóл-nouns have zero-ending genitive plural forms which are identical with their nominative singular forms.

NOM SG		GEN PL	
оди́н ра́з	one time	мнóго ра́з	many times
оди́н солда́т	one soldier	мнóго солда́т	many soldiers
оди́н грузи́н	one Georgian	мнóго грузи́н	many Georgians

4. A few other nouns, such as **ребя́та** and **господа́** (plural of **господи́н**), have a zero ending in the genitive plural.

NOM PL		GEN PL
ребя́та	guys, fellows, kids	ребя́т
господа́	gentlemen, ladies and gentlemen	госпо́д

5. **Стол**-nouns ending in **–анин** or **–янин** in the nominative singular lose the suffix **–ин** in the plural and have a zero ending in the genitive plural.

NOM SG		NOM PL	GEN PL
граждани́н	citizen	гра́ждане	гра́ждан
англича́нин	Englishman	англича́не	англича́н
египтя́нин	Egyptian	египтя́не	египтя́н

■ RESPONSE DRILL

I don't see any chairs.
Where are the chairs?
Я не ви́жу сту́льев.
Где́ сту́лья?
Я не ви́жу америка́нцев.
Где́ америка́нцы?
(украинцев, грузин, ребят, платьев, перьев, её братьев, их мужей, его друзей, огурцов)

■ CUED QUESTION-ANSWER DRILL

(Georgians) Whom did you ask?
The Georgians.
(грузи́ны) У кого́ вы́ спра́шивали?
У грузи́н.
(мужья́) У кого́ вы́ спра́шивали?
У муже́й.
(друзья, братья, ребята, девушки, украинцы, американцы, парни, учителя́)

■ QUESTION-ANSWER DRILLS

1. *Don't you have any dresses?*
We do. The dresses are over there.
Не́т ли у ва́с пла́тьев?
Е́сть. Пла́тья во́н та́м.
Не́т ли у ва́с сту́льев?
Е́сть. Сту́лья во́н та́м.
(огурцов, перьев, ножей, словарей, карандашей, стульев, атласов, столов)

2. *Where are the dresses?*
I don't see any dresses.
Где́ пла́тья?
Я́ не ви́жу пла́тьев.
Где́ америка́нцы?
Я́ не ви́жу америка́нцев.
(стулья, перья, их мужья, его друзья, грузины, ребята, огурцы, её братья, украинцы)

3. *Can one get chairs there?*
No, there are no chairs there.
Та́м мо́жно доста́ть сту́лья?
Не́т, та́м не́т сту́льев.
Та́м мо́жно доста́ть пе́рья?
Не́т, у ни́х не́т пе́рьев.
(платья, огурцы, стулья, перья)

4. *Do they have dictionaries?*
No, they don't have any dictionaries.
У ни́х е́сть словари́?
Не́т, у ни́х не́т словаре́й.
У ни́х е́сть пе́рья?
Не́т, у ни́х не́т пе́рьев.
(стулья, платья, братья, портфели, ножи, карандаши, друзья, огурцы)

Their brothers were at our place.
We were at their brothers' place.
Йх бра́тья бы́ли у на́с.
Мы́ бы́ли у и́х бра́тьев.
Йх мужья́ бы́ли у на́с.
Мы́ бы́ли у и́х муже́й.

(их друзья́, грузи́ны, ребя́та, америка́нцы, украи́нцы, их жёны, их сёстры)

■ TRANSLATION DRILL

1. There are no pens here. 2. There are no chairs in the dormitory. 3. There are no Americans in the dormitory. 4. There are no Ukrainians in the dormitory. 5. There are no Georgians in the dormitory. 6. There are no dresses at GUM. 7. He has no brothers. 8. He has no friends. 9. The fellows have lots of time. 10. The husbands have no time. 11. I've read *War and Peace* many times. 12. We were at [our] friends'. 13. We were at our brothers' (places).

The use of the genitive after numbers

MODELS

С ва́с два́ рубля́.
_____ три́ _____.
_____ четы́ре__.

You owe two rubles.
_____ three ____.
_____ four ____.

Э́то сто́ит две́ копе́йки.
_____ три́ _____.
_____ четы́ре ____.

This costs two kopecks.
_____ three _____.
_____ four _____.

Биле́т сто́ит пя́ть рубле́й.
_____ ше́сть _____.
_____ се́мь _____.
_____ во́семь _____.
_____ де́вять _____.
_____ де́сять _____.

A ticket costs five rubles.
_____ six _____.
_____ seven ____.
_____ eight ____.
_____ nine _____.
_____ ten _____.

Я́ заплати́л пя́ть копе́ек.
_____ ше́сть _____.
_____ се́мь _____.
_____ во́семь ____.
_____ де́вять ____.
_____ де́сять ____.

I paid five kopecks.
_____ six _____.
_____ seven _____.
_____ eight _____.
_____ nine _____.
_____ ten _____.

■ REPETITION DRILL

Repeat the given models, noting that the genitive singular is required after **два́**, **две́**, **три́**, and **четы́ре**; and the genitive plural for **пя́ть** on up. Note also that **две́** replaces **два́** with all feminine nouns. Compare **две́ сестры́**, **две́ тетра́ди** with **два́ рубля́**, **два́ сло́ва**.

Response with consecutive numbers (one to ten).

1. *How much does this cost?*
   One ruble.
   Ско́лько э́то сто́ит?
   Оди́н ру́бль.
   Ско́лько э́то сто́ит?
   Два́ рубля́.

2. *How much do I owe?*
   One kopeck.
   Ско́лько с меня́?
   Одна́ копе́йка.
   Ско́лько с меня́?
   Две́ копе́йки.

3. *How many notebooks do you have?*
   I have one notebook.
   Ско́лько у вас тетра́дей?
   У меня́ одна́ тетра́дь.
   Ско́лько у вас кни́г?
   У меня́ две́ кни́ги.
   (бра́тьев, словаре́й, ру́чек, ко́мнат, ка-
   ранда́шей, пе́рьев, ви́лок, ло́жек)

4. *How much did you pay for it?*[1]
   One ruble, two kopecks.
   Ско́лько вы́ заплати́ли за э́то?
   Оди́н ру́бль две́ копе́йки.
   Ско́лько вы́ заплати́ли за э́то?
   Два́ рубля́ три́ копе́йки.

5. *How many days will you be in Moscow?*
   Only two days.
   Ско́лько дне́й вы́ бу́дете в Москве́?
   То́лько два́ дня́.
   Ско́лько дне́й вы́ бу́дете в Москве́?
   То́лько три́ дня́.

6. *How many weeks will you be in the U.S.S.R.?*
   Two weeks.
   Ско́лько неде́ль вы́ бу́дете в СССР?
   Две́ неде́ли.
   Ско́лько неде́ль вы́ бу́дете в СССР?
   Три́ неде́ли.

DISCUSSION

The number *one* differs from the other numbers in that it is treated as a modifier with separate forms for each gender: оди́н ру́бль, одна́ копе́йка, одно́ сло́во.

The other numbers when used in nominative and accusative constructions are accompanied by the genitive case: *genitive singular* for 2, 3, 4; and *genitive plural* for 5 and up. There is a special feminine form for two: две́; masculine and neuter nouns require два́. It is important to remember that compounds such as 21, 22, 31, 32, 101, and 102 require the noun form to agree with the last element of the compound only: три́дцать оди́н ру́бль *31 rubles*, три́дцать две́ копе́йки *32 kopecks*, три́дцать три́ студе́нта *33 students*.

Unidirectional versus multidirectional verbs of motion

MODELS

UNIDIRECTIONAL

Я́ иду́ в па́рк.	I'm going to the park.	(*on foot*)
Я́ е́ду в Москву́.	I'm going to Moscow.	(*by vehicle*)
Я́ шёл в па́рк.	I was on my way to the park.	(*on foot*)
Я́ е́хал в Москву́.	I was on my way to Moscow.	(*by vehicle*)

[1] Continue up to nine rubles, ten kopecks.

Я ча́сто хожу́ в па́рк.	I often go to the park.	(*on foot*)
Я ча́сто е́зжу в Москву́.	I often go to Moscow.	(*by vehicle*)
Я ча́сто ходи́л в па́рк.	I often went to the park.	(*on foot*)
Я ча́сто е́здил в Москву́.	I often went to Moscow.	(*by vehicle*)

UNIDIRECTIONAL		
INFINITIVE	**идти́** *to be going* (on foot)	**е́хать** *to be going* (by vehicle)
PRESENT	иду́, идёшь, идёт, идём, идёте, иду́т	е́ду, е́дешь, е́дет, е́дем, е́дете, е́дут
PAST	шёл, шла́, шло́, шли́	е́хал, –а, –о, –и

MULTIDIRECTIONAL		
INFINITIVE	**ходи́ть** *to go* (on foot)	**е́здить** *to go* (by vehicle)
PRESENT	хожу́, хо́дишь, хо́дит, хо́дим, хо́дите, хо́дят	е́зжу, е́здишь, е́здит, е́здим, е́здите, е́здят
PAST	ходи́л, –а, –о, –и	е́здил, –а, –о, –и

■ REPETITION DRILL

Repeat the given models, noting that **идти́** and **е́хать** describe motion in process or intended motion. Contrast them with **ходи́ть** and **е́здить**, which describe repeated motion, i.e., motion in more than one direction. In addition, remember that **идти́** and **ходи́ть** ordinarily indicate going on foot, while **е́хать** and **е́здить** indicate going by means of some vehicle.

■ SUBSTITUTION DRILLS

1. *She often goes to concerts.*
   Она́ ча́сто хо́дит на конце́рты.
   Студе́нты ча́сто **хо́дят** на конце́рты.
   (мы, я, ты, вы, они, Наташа, студентки)

2. *She's on her way to a concert.*
   Она́ идёт на конце́рт.
   Ты идёшь на конце́рт.
   (мы, я, они, Кирилл, вы)

3. *I often go to Kiev.*
   Я ча́сто е́зжу в Ки́ев.
   Они́ ча́сто **е́здят** в Ки́ев.
   (администратор, мы, ты, вы, эта женщина, я, они)

4. *Zina and Philip are on their way to Moscow.*
   Зи́на и Фили́пп е́дут в Москву́.
   Вы е́дете в Москву́.
   (я, мы, ты, она, наши студентки, Волков, вы, они)

■ STRUCTURE REPLACEMENT DRILLS

1. *I'm on my way to school.*
   I go to school.
   Я иду́ в шко́лу.
   Я хожу́ в шко́лу.
   Мы́ идём в шко́лу.
   Мы́ хо́дим в шко́лу.
   (Наташа, они, ты, я, вы, мой брат, мы все)

2. *I'm on my way to Leningrad.*
   I often go to Leningrad.
   Я е́ду в Ленингра́д.
   Я ча́сто е́зжу в Ленингра́д.
   Они́ е́дут в Ленингра́д.
   Они́ ча́сто е́здят в Ленингра́д.
   (мы, ты, товарищ Волков, проводник, вы, я, они)

3. *Were you on your way to the park?*
   Did you go to the park?
   Вы́ шли́ в па́рк?
   Вы́ ходи́ли в па́рк?
   Ты́ шёл в па́рк?
   Ты́ ходи́л в па́рк?
   (она шла, они шли, ты шла, Олег шёл)

4. *Were you on your way to Kiev?*
   Did you go to Kiev?
   Вы́ е́хали в Ки́ев?
   Вы́ е́здили в Ки́ев?
   Она́ е́хала в Ки́ев?
   Она́ е́здила в Ки́ев?
   (ты ехал, они ехали, Волков ехал,
   студентки ехали, ты ехала)

■ RESPONSE DRILLS

1. *We saw you on the bus.*
   Were you on your way downtown?
   Мы́ тебя́ ви́дели в авто́бусе.
   Ты́ е́хал в го́род?
   Мы́ ва́с ви́дели в авто́бусе.
   Вы́ е́хали в го́род?
   (её, его, тебя, вас, их)

2. *I saw you yesterday near the park.*
   Were you on your way to the park?
   Вчера́ я́ ва́с ви́дел о́коло па́рка.
   Вы́ шли́ в па́рк?
   Вчера́ я́ его́ ви́дел о́коло па́рка.
   О́н шёл в па́рк?
   (их, её, тебя, вас, его)

■ QUESTION-ANSWER DRILLS

1. *Where were you on Saturday morning?*
   I went to the library.
   Где́ ты́ бы́л в суббо́ту у́тром?
   Я́ ходи́л в библиоте́ку.
   Где́ она́ была́ в суббо́ту у́тром?
   Она́ ходи́ла в библиоте́ку.
   Где́ вы́, Ка́тя, бы́ли в суббо́ту у́тром?
   Где́ вы́, Оле́г, бы́ли в суббо́ту у́тром?
   Где́ ты́, Ири́на, была́ в суббо́ту у́тром?
   Где́ они́ бы́ли в суббо́ту у́тром?
   Где́ о́н бы́л в суббо́ту у́тром?
   Где́ вы́ бы́ли в суббо́ту у́тром?

2. *Where were you last week?*
   I went to Kharkov.
   Где́ ты́ бы́л на про́шлой неде́ле?
   Я́ е́здил в Ха́рьков.
   Где́ ты́ была́ на про́шлой неде́ле?
   Я́ е́здила в Ха́рьков.
   Где́ вы́, Оле́г, бы́ли на про́шлой неде́ле?
   Где́ вы́, Зи́на, бы́ли на про́шлой неде́ле?
   Где́ они́ бы́ли на про́шлой неде́ле?
   Где́ о́н бы́л на про́шлой неде́ле?
   Где́ она́ была́ на про́шлой неде́ле?

3. *Do you walk to work?*
   No, I go by bus.
   Вы́ хо́дите на́ работу пешко́м?
   Не́т, я́ е́зжу на авто́бусе.
   Они́ хо́дят на рабо́ту пешко́м?
   Не́т, они́ е́здят на авто́бусе.
   (она, ты, ваш брат, ваша сестра, они,
   вы)

4. *Are you going to the theater by cab?*
   No, we're going on foot.
   Вы́ е́дете в теа́тр на такси́?
   Не́т, мы́ идём пешко́м.
   Ты́ е́дешь в теа́тр на такси́?
   Не́т, я́ иду́ пешко́м.
   (она, они, Евгений, мы, ты, Катя)

DISCUSSION

Most non-prefixed, motion verbs have an added feature not found in other verbs: a double set of imperfectives used to distinguish between *unidirectional* motion and *multidirectional* motion.

The *unidirectional* imperfectives describe a single, one-way trip to a specific destination. It may refer to an action that is (or was) in process or to one intended in the near future.

Я́ сейча́с иду́ в па́рк.	I'm on my way to the park now.
За́втра я́ иду́ в кино́.	I'm going to the movies tomorrow.
Я́ е́ду в Москву́.	I'm on my way to Moscow.
За́втра я́ е́ду в Москву́.	I'm going to Moscow tomorrow.

The *multidirectional* imperfectives describe movement in more than one direction or unspecified as to destination. This may include one or more round trips, or movement in several directions.

Я не люблю ходи́ть.	I don't like to walk.
Я ходи́л в па́рк.	I went to the park (and returned).
Я е́здил в Ки́ев.	I went to Kiev (and returned).
Я ча́сто е́зжу в Ки́ев.	I often go to Kiev.

In addition to the distinction between *unidirectional* and *multidirectional* movement, Russian also distinguishes between movement under one's own power (**идти́, ходи́ть**) and movement by means of some conveyance (**е́хать, е́здить**).

While the verbs **е́хать** and **е́здить** are limited to the description of a person's travel by conveyance, the movement of the conveyance itself is usually described by means of **идти́** or **ходи́ть**.

Compare	Во́т идёт авто́бус.	Here comes the bus.
	Э́тот по́езд идёт в Ки́ев.	This train goes to Kiev.
	Поезда́ сего́дня не хо́дят.	Trains aren't running today.
with	Я е́ду в Ки́ев.	I'm going to Kiev.
	Мы́ е́здили на по́езде.	We went on the train.

The verb **идти́** is also used in many idioms.

В кино́ идёт хоро́ший фи́льм.	There's a good picture showing at the movies.
Идёт до́ждь. (Шёл до́ждь.)	It's raining. (It was raining.)
Идёт снег. (Шёл снег.)	It's snowing. (It was snowing.)
Э́тот костю́м ва́м идёт.	That suit becomes you.

The verbs **ходи́ть** and **е́здить** have perfectives which are very rarely used: **походи́ть** *to do a bit of walking* and **пое́здить** *to do a bit of riding*. The most frequently used perfectives are formed from **идти́** and **е́хать**: **пойти́** and **пое́хать**. These perfectives describe the accomplishment of setting out for one's destination with nothing said about the return.

Он пошёл в магази́н.	He went to the store *or* He set off for the store.
Он пое́хал в Москву́.	He went to Moscow *or* He set off for Moscow.

Now note the use of the imperfective past of **ходи́ть** and **е́здить**, which in similar situations, tell us that the person went and returned.

Он ходи́л в магази́н.	He went to the store (and is already back).
Он е́здил в Москву́.	He went to Moscow (and is already back).

Long-form adjectives: nominative singular and plural

MODELS

Э́то краси́вый костю́м.	That's a lovely suit.
_____ го́род.	_____ city.
Э́то краси́вое окно́.	That's a lovely window.
_____ общежи́тие.	_____ dormitory.
Э́то краси́вая карти́на.	That's a lovely picture.
_____ ко́мната.	_____ room.
Э́то краси́вые ве́щи.	Those are lovely things.
_____ дома́.	_____ houses.

Этот а́тлас ста́рый.	This atlas is old.
_____ дорого́й.	_____ expensive.
_____ хоро́ший.	_____ good.
Это пла́тье ста́рое.	This dress is old.
_____ дорого́е.	_____ expensive.
_____ хоро́шее.	_____ good.
Эта кни́га ста́рая.	This book is old.
_____ дорога́я.	_____ expensive.
_____ хоро́шая.	_____ good.
Эти кни́ги ста́рые.	These books are old.
_____ дороги́е.	_____ expensive.
_____ хоро́шие.	_____ good.
Како́й большо́й до́м!	What a large house!
_____ хоро́ший _____!	_____ nice _____!
Како́е большо́е зда́ние!	What a large building!
_____ хоро́шее _____!	_____ nice _____!
Кака́я больша́я кварти́ра!	What a large apartment!
_____ хоро́шая _____!	_____ nice _____!
Каки́е больши́е карти́ны!	What large pictures!
_____ хоро́шие _____!	_____ nice _____!
Где́ большо́й за́л?	Where's the large hall?
____ больша́я аудито́рия?	_____ the large auditorium?
____ большо́е общежи́тие?	_____ the large dormitory?
____ больши́е рестора́ны?	Where are the large restaurants?
Это второ́й уро́к.	This is the second lesson.
____ втора́я ле́кция.	_____ the second lecture.
____ второ́е собра́ние.	_____ the second meeting.
У меня́ ста́рый слова́рь.	I have an old dictionary.
_____ ста́рая тетра́дь.	_____ an old notebook.
_____ ста́рое пла́тье.	_____ an old dress.
Мы́ ста́рые друзья́.	We're old friends.
Бо́рщ горя́чий.	The borsch is hot.
_____ хоро́ший.	_____ good.
Вода́ горя́чая.	The water is hot.
_____ хоро́шая.	_____ good.
Молоко́ горя́чее.	The milk is hot.
_____ хоро́шее.	_____ good.
Щи́ горя́чие.	The schi is hot.
___ хоро́шие.	_____ good.
Ни́жний эта́ж за́нят.	The lower floor is occupied.
Ни́жняя кварти́ра занята́.	The lower apartment is occupied.
Ни́жнее ме́сто за́нято.	The lower berth is occupied.
Ни́жние этажи́ за́няты.	The lower floors are occupied.

Repeat the given models, noting the pattern of adjective endings. Observe that the stress may be consistently on the endings (as in **большо́й**, –о́е, –а́я, –и́е) or on the stem (as in **хоро́ший**, –ее, –ая, –ие), but that there is no shifting of stress within the various forms of a particular adjective. Soft-stem adjectives always have their stress on the stem.

■ EXPANSION DRILLS

1. *Where are the factories?*
   Where are the large factories?
   Где́ фа́брики?
   Где́ больши́е фа́брики?
   Где́ магази́н?
   Где́ большо́й магази́н?
   (теа́тр, слова́рь, лаборато́рия, общежи́тие, окно́, о́чередь, ста́нция, но́ж, шка́ф, кино́, па́рк, фа́брика, я́щик, рестора́н, библиоте́ка)

2. *Here are the boys.*
   Here are the Russian boys.
   Во́т па́рни.
   Во́т ру́сские па́рни.
   Во́т де́вушка.
   Во́т ру́сская де́вушка.
   (учителя́, слова́рь, ка́рта, фи́льм, рома́н, кни́ги, фа́брика)

■ QUESTION-ANSWER DRILL

Is the room large or small?
Small.
Ко́мната больша́я и́ли ма́ленькая?
Ма́ленькая.
Ва́ше ме́сто ве́рхнее и́ли ни́жнее?
Ни́жнее.
Огурцы́ хоро́шие и́ли плохи́е?

Ва́ш ваго́н жёсткий и́ли мя́гкий?
Кварти́ра ма́ленькая и́ли больша́я?
Фи́льм интере́сный и́ли ску́чный?
Ко́мнаты ма́ленькие и́ли больши́е?
Ста́нция больша́я и́ли ма́ленькая?

■ STRUCTURE REPLACEMENT DRILLS

1. *Here's the large auditorium.*
   Here's the small auditorium.
   Во́т больша́я аудито́рия.
   Во́т ма́ленькая аудито́рия.
   Во́т ску́чные кни́ги.
   Во́т интере́сные кни́ги.
   Во́т ве́рхнее ме́сто.
   Во́т плохи́е студе́нты.
   Во́т ма́ленькая ста́нция.
   Во́т хоро́ший студе́нт.
   Во́т мя́гкий ваго́н.
   Во́т ни́жнее ме́сто.
   Во́т жёсткий ваго́н.

2. *The atlases are expensive.*
   The atlas is expensive.
   А́тласы дороги́е.
   А́тлас дорого́й.
   Кни́ги интере́сные.
   Кни́га интере́сная.
   Портфе́ли хоро́шие.
   Общежи́тия больши́е.
   Пла́тья краси́вые.
   Словари́ дороги́е.
   Пе́рья плохи́е.
   Ко́мнаты ма́ленькие.
   Сту́лья удо́бные.

3. *You're a good friend.*
   You're good friends.
   Вы́ хоро́ший дру́г.
   Вы́ хоро́шие друзья́.
   Вы́ ста́рый дру́г.
   Вы́ ста́рые друзья́.
   Э́то ма́ленькая ко́мната.
   Э́то ма́ленькое окно́.

Во́т мя́гкий ваго́н.
Во́т жёсткий ваго́н.
У на́с больша́я аудито́рия.
У на́с хоро́шая аудито́рия.
Результа́т неплохо́й.
Ка́рта небольша́я.
До́м небольшо́й.

Russian adjectives follow a fairly simple pattern of endings in the spoken language. Because of the peculiarities of the spelling system, however, they appear complicated in writing. For convenience we group them according to their last stem consonant as hard stems, soft stems, and mixed stems.

1. *Hard stems* are those with stems ending in any *hard* consonant except ш, ж, к, г, or х: больно́й, краси́вый, ста́рый.
2. *Soft stems* are those with stems ending in soft н: ни́жний, ве́рхний.
3. *Mixed stems* are those with stems ending in к, г, х, ш, ж, ч, and щ: жёсткий, друго́й, большо́й, горя́чий.

ADJECTIVE ENDINGS IN THE NOMINATIVE SINGULAR AND PLURAL					
		SINGULAR			PLURAL
		Masculine	*Neuter*	*Feminine*	
HARD STEMS		–о́й (–ый) второ́й краси́вый	–ое второ́е краси́вое	–ая втора́я краси́вая	–ые вторы́е краси́вые
SOFT STEMS		–ий ни́жний	–ее ни́жнее	–яя ни́жняя	–ие ни́жние
MIXED STEMS	1. Stems ending in к, г, х	–о́й (–ий) друго́и ма́ленький	–ое друго́е ма́ленькое	–ая друга́я ма́ленькая	–ие други́е ма́ленькие
	2. Stems ending in ш, ж, ч, щ	–о́й (–ий) большо́й горя́чий	–о́е (–ее) большо́е горя́чее	–ая больша́я горя́чая	–ие больши́е горя́чие

Mixed stems ending in к, г, and х follow the same basic pattern of endings as hard stems, except that, instead of –ый (m) and –ые (pl), the endings are –ий and –ие respectively; the preceding к, г, or х is automatically softened. Compare краси́вый, краси́вые with ма́ленький, ма́ленькие.

Hard stems have the masculine ending –о́й if stressed, but –ый if unstressed. Compare второ́й, молодо́й with ста́рый, краси́вый.

Mixed stems ending in ш and ж have the masculine and neuter endings –о́й and –о́е if stressed, but –ий and –ее if unstressed. Compare большо́й, большо́е with хоро́ший, хоро́шее.

Note that some adjectives function as nouns and that some surnames are adjectival in form: столо́вая (for столо́вая ко́мната), ва́нная (for ва́нная ко́мната), Толсто́й, Достое́вский. The surname for Miss or Mrs. Tolstoy is Толста́я and for Miss or Mrs. Dostoevsky, Достое́вская. In the plural the Tolstoys are Толсты́е and the Dostoevskys Достое́вские.

— Доброе утро! — Здравствуйте! Куда вы едете? — В Москву. А вы куда? — Я тоже еду в Москву! — Вот, хорошо! Значит, мы попутчики.

— Здравствуй, Саша! Как живёшь? — Ничего, спасибо. — Это ваше общежитие? — Да. Моя комната на пятом этаже. — Ты живёшь один? — Нет, у меня есть два товарища по комнате: Володя Орлов и Олег Семёнов. Ты их знаешь? — Конечно, уже давно. Они очень хорошие ребята.

— Привет, Филипп! Что вы здесь делаете? — Жду Царапкина. — Это ваш товарищ по комнате? — Да, мы с осени живём вместе. — Я знаю Наташу Царапкину. Это его сестра? — Да. А вот и он идёт. Хотите познакомиться? — Да, конечно.

— Моя́ фами́лия Гра́нт. А ка́к ва́ша фами́лия?
— О́сипов. Я́ из Ленингра́да. А вы́ отку́да?
— Я́ из Аме́рики. То́лько прие́хал сего́дня.
— Во́т ка́к! О́чень ра́д с ва́ми познако́миться. Где́ ва́ша ко́мната?
— Во́т здесь, напра́во.
— Та́к мы́ това́рищи по ко́мнате! Во́т уда́ча: я́ как ра́з учу́ англи́йский язы́к.
— О, вы́ говори́те по-англи́йски?
— Немно́го.

— Скажи́те, вы́ пойдёте сего́дня в библиоте́ку?
— Да́, по́сле обе́да.

— Пожа́луйста, возьми́те для меня́ «Войну́ и ми́р».

— Хорошо́. Но вы́, ка́жется, неда́вно чита́ли э́тот рома́н?

— Да́, но таки́е ве́щи на́до чита́ть мно́го ра́з.

— Носи́льщик, возьми́те, пожа́луйста, мо́й бага́ж.

— Сейча́с. Вы́ хоти́те пое́хать на такси́?

— Да́, я о́чень спешу́.

— Во́н та́м такси́. Такси́! Положи́ть ве́щи в бага́жник?

— Да́, пожа́луйста. Во́т, возьми́те 10 копе́ек.

— Спаси́бо.

— Вы́ ча́сто хо́дите в кино́?

— Хожу́, но не ча́сто. Иногда́ в суббо́ту.

— Хоти́те пойти́ за́втра ве́чером?

— А что́ идёт?

— «Война́ и ми́р».

— Э́то, ка́жется, америка́нский фи́льм?

— Да́, и, говоря́т, хоро́ший.

— Пойдём. Интере́сно посмотре́ть.

— Я́ е́ду во Владивосто́к. Ка́жется, мы́ попу́тчики?

— Да́, но то́лько до Москвы́. Я́ е́ду в Москву́.

— Ско́лько вре́мени е́хать до Москвы́?

— Ше́сть часо́в. А ско́лько от Москвы́ до Владивосто́ка?

— Се́мь дней, ка́жется.

— Та́к до́лго? Когда́ же вы́ прие́дете?

— Сего́дня понеде́льник. Зна́чит я́ прие́ду во Владивосто́к на сле́дующей неде́ле, во вто́рник и́ли в сре́ду.

— Такси́!

— Ва́м куда́?

— В гости́ницу «Украи́на». То́лько я о́чень спешу́.

— Э́то пя́ть мину́т, не бо́льше.

— Ну во́т, мы́ уже́ е́дем пя́ть мину́т. Ещё далеко́?

— Не́т, сейча́с. Во́н, ви́дите, нале́во большо́й до́м? Э́то и е́сть гости́ница «Украи́на».

— Прекра́сно. Ско́лько с меня́?

— Два́дцать копе́ек.

— Пожа́луйста.

— Вы́ говори́те, что заказа́ли зде́сь но́мер?

— Да́, я заказа́л небольшо́й но́мер для одного́.

— Ка́к ва́ша фами́лия?

— Гра́нт. Фили́пп Гра́нт.

— Вы́ америка́нец?

— Да́. Я́ студе́нт Моско́вского университе́та.

— А, зна́чит вы́ не до́лго у на́с бу́дете.

— Не́т, то́лько два́ дня́.

NOTES

PREPARATION FOR CONVERSATION   **Читáйте «Вечéрнюю Москвý»**

вечéрний, –яя; –ее, –ие	evening
Читáйте «Вечéрнюю Москвý».	Read the *Evening Moscow*.
газéта	newspaper
посовéтовать (pfv I), посовéтую, –ешь, –ют	to advise
Какýю газéту вы́ мнé посовéтуете читáть?	What paper would you advise me to read?
извéстие	news, news report
«Извéстия» (pl)	*Izvestia* (name of newspaper)
«Прáвда»	*Pravda* (name of newspaper)
Ни́на, какýю газéту вы́ мнé посовéтуете читáть — «Прáвду», «Извéстия»?	Nina, which newspaper would you advise me to read, *Pravda* [or] *Izvestia*?
Нéт, читáйте «Вечéрнюю Москвý».	No, read the *Evening Moscow*.
объявлéние	notice, announcement, declaration
театрáльный	theater, theatrical
Тáм театрáльные объявлéния.	It has theater notices.
происшéствие	happening, occurrence, accident, event, incident
Тáм театрáльные объявлéния, происшéствия.	It has theater notices and [local] events.
тóт же, тá же, тó же, тé же	the same
вездé	everywhere
нóвость (f)	news, novelty
Нóвости вездé тé же.	The news is the same in all of them (*lit.* everywhere).
Тáм театрáльные объявлéния, происшéствия, а нóвости вездé тé же.	It has theater notices and local events, and the news is the same in all of them.
чáстный [čásnij]	private, personal
чáстные объявлéния	want ads, private ads
У вáс нéт чáстных объявлéний.	You don't have want ads.
продавáть (I), продаю́, –ёшь, –ю́т	to sell

лю́ди, люде́й	people
Ка́к же лю́ди продаю́т свои́ ве́щи?	Just how do people sell their things?
А скажи́те, во́т у ва́с не́т ча́стных объявле́ний, ка́к же лю́ди продаю́т свои́ ве́щи?	Tell me, since you don't have want ads, how do people sell their things?
подéржанный [paḍéržənij]	secondhand
Подéржанные ве́щи?	Secondhand things?
комиссио́нные магази́ны	commission stores (state-managed secondhand stores)
В комиссио́нных магази́нах.	In commission stores.
толку́чка	flea market, secondhand market
В комиссио́нных и́ли на толку́чках.	In commission stores or at the flea market.
знако́мые (acc, gen, *and* prep pl знако́мых)	acquaintances, friends
че́рез (*plus* acc)¹	through, across, by way of, in
Че́рез знако́мых.	Through friends.
просто́й (adv про́сто)	simple, simply
В комиссио́нных, на толку́чке, и́ли про́сто че́рез знако́мых.	In commission stores, at the flea market, or simply through friends.
А́х, во́т оно́ что́!	Oh, so that's it!
рекла́ма	advertisement, advertising
У ва́с ма́ло рекла́м.	You have so few advertisements.
заме́тить (pfv II), заме́чу, заме́тишь, –ят	to notice
Я заме́тил, что у ва́с ма́ло рекла́м.	I've noticed you have very few advertisements.
ме́жду про́чим	by the way, while we're on the subject
Ме́жду про́чим, я заме́тил, что у ва́с ма́ло рекла́м.	By the way, I've noticed you have very few ads.
журна́л	magazine, journal
У ва́с ма́ло рекла́м, да́же в журна́лах.	You have very few ads, even in magazines.
«Огонёк» (gen sg «Огонька́»)	*Ogonyok* (name of Soviet magazine—*lit.* small light)
У ва́с ма́ло рекла́м, да́же в журна́лах, наприме́р в «Огоньке́».	You have so few ads, even in magazines, for example, in *Ogonyok*.
о́черк	sketch, essay, feature story
США́ (*full form* Соединённые Шта́ты Аме́рики) [ešše á] or [ššá]	the U.S.A.
Вы́ чита́ли о́черк о США́?	Did you read the feature story on the U.S.A?
после́дний, –яя, –ее, –ие	last, latest
в после́днем но́мере	in the last issue
В после́днем но́мере бы́л о́черк о США́, вы́ чита́ли?	In the last issue there was a feature story on the U.S.A. Did you read it?

---

¹ The preposition **че́рез** is pronounced either with a weak stress on the first syllable or without stress altogether. It has the meaning *in* only in time expressions: **че́рез ча́с** *in an hour*.

Чита́л. А во́т вы́ наш журна́л «Аме́рика» зна́ете?	I did. But do you know our magazine *America*?
тру́дно (adj тру́дный)	hard, difficult
Да́, но его́ тру́дно доста́ть.	Yes, but it's hard to get hold of it.
ни	not (negative particle), no matter
в како́м кио́ске ни спро́сишь	no matter at which newsstand you ask
отве́т	answer
распро́дан, –а, –о, –ы	sold out
В како́м кио́ске ни спро́сишь, всегда́ оди́н отве́т: «Распро́даны».	No matter at what newsstand you ask, it's always the same answer: "They're sold out."
стра́нно (adj стра́нный)	strange
Стра́нно.	That's strange.
посо́льство	embassy
достава́ть (I), достаю́, –ёшь, –ю́т	to get, get hold of
Я могу́ достава́ть и́х в на́шем посо́льстве.	I can get them at our embassy.
Слу́шайте, я́ могу́ достава́ть и́х в на́шем посо́льстве.	Listen, I can get them at our embassy.
Во́т хорошо́!	Good!
бра́ть (I), беру́, –ёшь, –у́т (pfv взя́ть)	to take, get, borrow
Я́ тогда́ бу́ду бра́ть у ва́с.	Then I'll get them from you.

SUPPLEMENT

сове́товать (I), сове́тую, –ешь, –ют	to advise
Что́ вы́ мне́ сове́туете?	What would you advise me?
прочита́ть (pfv)	to read (through), to finish reading
Вы́ уже́ прочита́ли газе́ту?	Have you finished reading the newspaper?
лёгкий [ló̝xk̩ij]	easy, light
легко́ [l̩ixkó]	easy, easily
Не та́к легко́ доста́ть журна́л «Аме́рика».	It's not so easy to get hold of the magazine *America*.
челове́к (pl лю́ди)	person, human being, man
О́н хоро́ший челове́к.	He's a nice person.
Она́ хоро́ший челове́к.	She's a nice person.
ра́дио (indecl n)	radio
Послу́шаем ра́дио.	Let's listen to the radio.
но́вый	new
Что́ но́вого?	What's new?
молодо́й	young
Вы́ зна́ете э́того молодо́го челове́ка?	Do you know this young man?
у́лица	street
Во́т по́чта че́рез у́лицу.	There's the post office across the street.

Читайте «Вечёрнюю Москву́»

Ф. — Фили́пп   Н. — Ни́на

Ф. 1 Ни́на, каку́ю газе́ту вы́ мне́ посове́туете чита́ть — «Пра́вду», «Изве́стия»?[1]

Н. 2 Не́т, чита́йте «Вече́рнюю Москву́»: та́м театра́льные объявле́ния, происше́ствия, а но́вости везде́ те́ же.[2]

Ф. 3 Хорошо́. А скажи́те, во́т у ва́с не́т ча́стных объявле́ний, ка́к же лю́ди продаю́т свои́ ве́щи?

Н. 4 Поде́ржанные? В комиссио́нных, на толку́чке, и́ли про́сто че́рез знако́мых.[3]

Ф. 5 А́х, во́т оно́ что́! Ме́жду про́чим, я́ заме́тил, что у ва́с ма́ло рекла́м.[4] Да́же в журна́лах, наприме́р в «Огоньке́».[5]

Н. 6 Да́. Так вы́ уже́ знако́мы с «Огонько́м»? Кста́ти, в после́днем но́мере бы́л о́черк о США́, вы́ чита́ли?[6]

Ф. 7 Чита́л. А во́т вы́ на́ш журна́л «Аме́рика» зна́ете?[7]

Н. 8 Да́, но его́ тру́дно доста́ть. В како́м кио́ске ни спро́сишь, всегда́ оди́н отве́т: «Распро́даны».

Ф. 9 Стра́нно. Слу́шайте, я́ могу́ достава́ть и́х в на́шем посо́льстве.

Н. 10 Во́т хорошо́! Я́ тогда́ бу́ду бра́ть у ва́с.

NOTES

[1] «Пра́вда» Pravda (Truth) and «Изве́стия» Izvestia (News) are the two largest Soviet newspapers; the first is the official party newspaper and the second is the official government newspaper. Each issue is usually made up of four pages, limited to national and international items of political significance. Note that «Изве́стия» is plural: Я́ э́то чита́л в «Изве́стиях».

[2] «Вече́рняя Москва́» used to be the only paper in the Soviet Union that published local news items, including accidents. There is also a comparable newspaper in Leningrad called «Вече́рний Ленингра́д».

[3] Толку́чки are establishments where practically any secondhand item can be bought or sold. They are frowned on by the government and are frequently closed down or moved to the outskirts of town— to discourage people from patronizing them. Комиссио́нные магази́ны are government-supported secondhand stores where people may buy and sell used things. A seller must wait to receive his money until the item has actually been sold.

[4] The Soviet government is now doing a little more advertising of commodities than it did before World War II, using radio, posters, and occasionally even neon signs. Announcements on radio and television tell what goods have come into the state stores. In addition, bulletin boards have been installed in display windows; on these boards, individuals can post announcements of things for sale.

[5] «Огонёк» is a popular weekly illustrated magazine whose contents range from articles on national and international themes to fiction, verse, art reproductions, and crossword puzzles.

⁶ **США** (**Соединённые Штаты Америки**) is pronounced [ešše͡a] by some people and [šša] by others. Some speakers say **об США** [abešše͡a] and others **о США** [ašš͡a]. Like **СССР** this abbreviation is not declined: **в США, в СССР.** The basic rule for abbreviations is that they are not declined unless they contain a medial vowel: compare **об СССР** with **о ГУМе.**

⁷ **«Америка»** is an illustrated magazine with articles on life in the U.S.; it is printed in Russian and distributed in the Soviet Union by the U.S. Department of State. Soviet officials allow only a limited number to be sold, often returning large quantities to the American embassy, supposedly unsold. A very limited number of newsstands in the large cities are allowed to sell **«Америка»**, and, when the word gets around that a new issue has arrived, friends of the clerks who distribute and sell it usually buy up the few available copies. Secondhand copies sell readily in used-book stores.

PREPARATION FOR CONVERSATION   **Послушаем пластинки**

пластинка	phonograph record
послушать (pfv I) (*like* слушать)	to listen [to]
Послушаем пластинки.	Let's listen to records.
подруга	girl friend (of a girl)
Вы ещё не видели моих подруг.	You haven't seen my girl friends yet.
зайти (pfv I), зайду, –ёшь, –ут (past зашёл, зашла, –о, –и)	to drop in, stop by, call on
Зайдём в общежитие.	Let's drop in at the dormitory.
Хотите, зайдём в общежитие, познакомлю?	Want to drop in at the dormitory and I'll introduce you?
С большим удовольствием.	With great pleasure *or* I'd like to very much.
пропуск (pl –а, –ов)	pass, entry permit
дать (pfv irreg) (past дал, –а, –о, –и; fut дам, дашь, даст, дадим, дадите, дадут)	to give, let
А мне дадут пропуск?	But will they give me a pass?
Конечно.	Of course.
музыка	music
чаю (special gen)	[some] tea
выпить (pfv I), выпью, выпьешь, –ют	to drink, to finish drinking
Выпьем чаю, музыку послушаем.	We'll drink some tea and listen to music.
проигрыватель (m)	record player
У нас есть проигрыватель.	We have a record player.
уголок (var of угол)	corner
красный	red
красный уголок	recreation room

У на́с в кра́сном уголке́ е́сть про́игрыватель.	In our recreation room there's a record player.
Прекра́сно.	Fine.
пе́сня (gen pl пе́сен)	song
наро́дный	folk, popular
Та́м, наве́рно, е́сть ру́сские наро́дные пе́сни?	There probably are Russian folk songs there?
певе́ц (gen *and* acc sg певца́; nom pl певцы́, gen *and* acc pl певцо́в)	singer (m)
певи́ца	singer (f)
исполне́ние	performance
в исполне́нии	performed by
Да́, мно́го, и в исполне́нии лу́чших певцо́в и певи́ц.	Yes, lots, and performed by the best men and women singers.
Я люблю́ ва́ши наро́дные пе́сни.	I'm fond of your folk songs.
чёрный	black, dark
о́чи (*poetic for* глаза́)	eyes
Я та́к люблю́ ва́ши наро́дные пе́сни, наприме́р «О́чи чёрные».	I'm so fond of your folk songs, for example, "Dark Eyes."
рома́нс	love song (semi classical)
Да э́то ста́рый рома́нс.	Why, that's an old love song.
пе́ть (I), пою́, поёшь, пою́т	to sing
уже́ не	no longer
кото́рый	which, what, that
Да э́то ста́рый рома́нс, кото́рый уже́ не пою́т.	Why, that's an old love song that's no longer sung.
неуже́ли?	really? you don't say?
Неуже́ли?	Really?
услы́шать (pfv II) (*like* слы́шать)	to hear
мело́дия	melody, tune
У на́с в Аме́рике э́ту мело́дию ча́сто мо́жно услы́шать.	In America that tune may often be heard.
Да ну́?	No kidding?
джа́з	jazz, popular music
Мы́ лю́бим ва́ш джа́з.	We love your jazz.
А мы́ лю́бим ва́ш джа́з, то́лько пласти́нки тру́дно достава́ть.	By the way, we love your jazz, but it's hard to get records.
Я принесу́, у меня́ и́х мно́го.	I'll bring some; I have a lot of them.

SUPPLEMENT

приноси́ть (II), приношу́, прино́сишь, –ят	to bring
Óн ча́сто прино́сит пласти́нки.	He often brings records.
бе́лый	white
си́ний	dark blue

голубóй	light blue
зелёный	green
жёлтый	yellow
цвéт, –а (nom pl цветá)	color
какóго цвéта	what color, of what color

Какóго цвéта ваш костю́м? — What color is your suit?

— Си́него (*or* си́ний). — Dark blue.

вку́сный (adv вку́сно) — tasty, good (tasting), delicious

Хоти́те чáшку вку́сного кóфе? — Want a cup of good coffee?

глаз, –а; глазá, глаз — eye

У неё си́ние глазá. — She has dark blue eyes.

Послу́шаем пласти́нки

Н. — Ни́на   Ф. — Фили́пп

Н. 1 Фили́пп, вы́ ещё не ви́дели мои́х подру́г. Хоти́те, зайдём в общежи́тие, познакóмлю?

Ф. 2 С больши́м удовóльствием. А мнé даду́т прóпуск?[1]

Н. 3 Конéчно. Вы́пьем чáю, му́зыку послу́шаем. У нáс в крáсном уголкé éсть прои́грыватель.[2]

Ф. 4 Прекрáсно. Тáм, навéрно, éсть ру́сские нарóдные пéсни?

Н. 5 Дá, мнóго, и в исполнéнии лу́чших певцóв и певи́ц.

Ф. 6 Я тáк люблю́ вáши нарóдные пéсни, напримéр «Óчи чёрные».

Н. 7 «Óчи чёрные»? Да э́то стáрый ромáнс, котóрый ужé не поют.[3]

Ф. 8 Неужéли? А у нáс в Амéрике э́ту мелóдию чáсто мóжно услы́шать.

Н. 9 Да ну́? А мы́ лю́бим вáш джáз, тóлько пласти́нки тру́дно доставáть.[4]

Ф. 10 Я принесу́, у меня́ и́х мнóго.

NOTES

[1] One's *pass* or *entry permit* прóпуск must be shown to the custodian on entering or moving out of a dormitory. Another pass is needed to enter a university library. Also, foreign students must request a special permit for traveling outside the city; this permit must be shown when checking into a hotel.

[2] Крáсный уголóк *little red corner* refers to the recreation room in dormitories, factories, schools, universities, and clubs throughout the U.S.S.R. Each recreation room has a portrait of Lenin and sometimes one of Marx, Khrushchev, and others, and the rooms are frequently painted red. Крáсный originally meant *beautiful*, and in Orthodox tradition the крáсный у́гол was the right-hand corner of the room where icons or holy pictures were hung.

[3] The term **рома́нс** is derived from French; in Russian it describes a certain type of love lyric, set to music. Such well-known poets and composers as **Пу́шкин** and **Чайко́вский** have helped to create them. **Рома́нс** also refers to popular gypsy songs **цыга́нские рома́нсы**, but is not used in the English sense of *romance*. The word for *romance* is **рома́н** (which also means *novel* [book]).

[3] Russians are inclined to call any Western popular music **джа́з**. Foreign music has a special appeal to Russians, especially to those of the younger generation, and they are willing to pay high black market prices for foreign records.

Basic sentence patterns

1. Како́го цве́та ва́ше пла́тье?
   — Зелёного.
   — Жёлтого.
   — Бе́лого.
   — Чёрного.
   — Кра́сного.
   — Голубо́го.
   — Си́него.

   What color is your dress?
   Green.
   Yellow.
   White.
   Black.
   Red.
   Light blue.
   Dark blue.

2. Каку́ю газе́ту вы́ чита́ете?
   _____ кни́гу _____?
   Како́й журна́л _____?
   _____ рома́н _____?
   Како́е письмо́ _____?
   _____ объявле́ние _____?
   Каки́е стихи́ _____?
   _____ уро́ки _____?

   What newspaper are you reading?
   ____ book _____?
   What magazine _____?
   ____ novel _____?
   What letter _____?
   ____ notice _____?
   What verses _____?
   ____ lessons _____?

3. О чём вы́ говори́те?
   — О на́шем клу́бе.
   _____ факульте́те.
   _____ о́черке.
   _____ посо́льстве.

   What are you talking about?
   About our club.
   _____ department.
   _____ essay.
   _____ embassy.

4. О чём она́ узна́ла?
   — О твое́й ко́мнате.
   _____ кварти́ре.
   _____ уда́че.
   _____ оши́бке.
   _____ гру́ппе.

   What did she find out about?
   About your room.
   _____ apartment.
   _____ success (*or* good luck).
   _____ mistake.
   _____ group.

5. Не забу́дь о на́ших экза́менах.
   _____ ле́кциях.
   _____ пласти́нках.
   _____ про́игрывателях.
   _____ ра́дио.
   _____ пропуска́х.
   _____ веща́х.
   _____ квита́нциях.

   Don't forget about our exams.
   _____ lectures.
   _____ records.
   _____ record players.
   _____ radios.
   _____ passes.
   _____ things.
   _____ receipts.

6. В "Пра́вде" нет театра́льных объявле́ний.
_____ ча́стных _____.
В "Изве́стиях" нет интере́сных объявле́ний.
_____ таки́х _____.

There aren't any theater ads in *Pravda*.
_____ private _____.
There aren't any interesting ads in *Izvestia*.
_____ such _____.

7. Они́ прие́дут в сле́дующую пя́тницу.
_____ суббо́ту.
_____ сре́ду.
Я прие́ду в сле́дующий вто́рник.
_____ четве́рг.
_____ понеде́льник.
Мы прие́дем в сле́дующее воскресе́нье.

They'll arrive next Friday.
_____ Saturday.
_____ Wednesday.
I'll arrive next Tuesday.
_____ Thursday.
_____ Monday.
We'll arrive next Sunday.

8. Я таки́х карти́н ещё не ви́дел.
_____ люде́й _____.
_____ рекла́м _____.
_____ фа́брик _____.
_____ кио́сков _____.
_____ та́нцев _____.

I've never seen pictures like that before.
_____ people _____.
_____ advertisements _____.
_____ factories _____.
_____ newsstands _____.
_____ dances _____.

9. Я ищу́ небольшо́й я́щик.
_____ шкаф.
_____ стол.
_____ небольшу́ю по́лку.
_____ ко́мнату.
_____ гости́ницу.
_____ небольши́е коро́бки.
_____ стака́ны.
_____ ло́жки.

I'm looking for a small box.
_____ cupboard.
_____ table.
_____ a small shelf.
_____ room.
_____ hotel.
_____ some small boxes.
_____ glasses.
_____ spoons.

10. Мы бы́ли в большо́й аудито́рии.
_____ кварти́ре.
_____ ко́мнате.
_____ в большо́м го́роде.
_____ общежи́тии.
_____ за́ле.
_____ рестора́не.
_____ зда́нии.

We were in a large lecture hall.
_____ apartment.
_____ room.
_____ in a large town.
_____ dormitory.
_____ hall.
_____ restaurant.
_____ building.

11. Здесь нет друго́го проводника́?
_____ носи́льщика?
_____ друго́й продавщи́цы?
_____ учи́тельницы?

Isn't there another conductor here?
_____ porter _____?
_____ saleslady _____?
_____ teacher (f) _____?

12. Вы ско́ро встре́тите други́х профессоро́в.
_____ люде́й.
_____ секретаре́й.
_____ шофёров.
_____ америка́нцев.
_____ украи́нцев.
_____ ру́сских.

You'll soon meet other professors.
_____ people.
_____ secretaries.
_____ drivers.
_____ Americans.
_____ Ukrainians.
_____ Russians.

13. Мо́жно чита́ть? — Хорошо́, чита́йте!   Is it all right to read?   O.K. go ahead!

_____ писа́ть?	_____ пиши́те!	_____ write?	_____!
_____ говори́ть?	_____ говори́те!	_____ talk?	_____!
_____ спроси́ть?	_____ спроси́те!	_____ ask?	_____!
_____ игра́ть?	_____ игра́йте!	_____ play?	_____!
_____ рабо́тать?	_____ рабо́тайте!	_____ work?	_____!
_____ слу́шать?	_____ слу́шайте!	_____ listen?	_____!
_____ пи́ть?	_____ пе́йте!	_____ drink?	_____!
_____ пе́ть?	_____ по́йте!	_____ sing?	_____!
_____ откры́ть окно́?	_____ откро́йте!	_____ open the window? _____!	
_____ закры́ть две́рь?	_____ закро́йте!	_____ close the door? _____!	

14. Вы́ не ви́дели моего́ бра́та?   You didn't see my brother?

_____ дру́га?	_____ friend?
_____ на́шего шофёра?	_____ our driver?
_____ проводника́?	_____ guide (or conductor)?
_____ мои́х бра́тьев?	_____ my brothers?
_____ друзе́й?	_____ friends?
_____ на́ших профессоро́в?	_____ our professors?
_____ това́рищей?	_____ friends (or comrades)?

15. О́н бы́л у мое́й сестры́.   He was at my sister's place.

_____ подру́ги.	_____ girl friend's _____.
_____ на́шей учи́тельницы.	_____ our teacher's _____.
_____ америка́нки.	_____ American woman's _____.

16. Вы́ стоя́ли о́коло своего́ ваго́на.   You were standing near your coach.

_____ до́ма.	_____ house.
_____ багажа́.	_____ baggage.
_____ общежи́тия.	_____ dormitory.
_____ свое́й две́ри.	_____ your door.
_____ гости́ницы.	_____ hotel.
_____ лаборато́рии.	_____ laboratory.
_____ свои́х карти́н.	_____ your pictures.
_____ ка́рт.	_____ maps.

17. Я́ не сплю́.   I'm not asleep.
О́н не спи́т.   He's not asleep.
Мы́ не спи́м.   We're not asleep.
Они́ не спя́т.   They're not asleep.
Ты́ не спи́шь.   You're not asleep.
Вы́ не спи́те.   You're not asleep.

18. О́н ничего́ не заме́тит.   He won't notice a thing.
Она́ _____ не заме́тит.   She won't notice _____.
Вы́ _____ не заме́тите.   You won't notice _____.
Мы́ _____ не заме́тим.   We won't notice _____.
Я́ _____ не заме́чу.   I won't notice _____.
Ты́ _____ не заме́тишь.   You won't notice _____.

19. Я́ ва́с с не́й познако́млю.   I'll introduce you to her.
О́н _____ познако́мит.   He'll introduce _____.
Они́ _____ познако́мят.   They'll introduce _____.
Мы́ _____ познако́мим.   We'll introduce _____.

| Вы́ меня́ с не́й познако́мите? | Will you introduce me to her? |
| Ты́ _____ познако́мишь? | Will you introduce _____? |

20. Вы́ услы́шите одного́ из лу́чших певцо́в. You'll hear one of the best singers.

Ты́ услы́шишь _____.	You'll hear _____.
Óн услы́шит _____.	He'll hear _____.
Мы́ услы́шим _____.	We'll hear _____.
Я услы́шу _____.	I'll hear _____.
Они́ услы́шат _____.	They'll hear _____.

21. Я сейча́с получу́ ва́ши ве́щи. I'll get your things right away.

Óн _____ полу́чит _____.	He'll get _____.
Они́ _____ полу́чат _____.	They'll get _____.
Мы́ _____ полу́чим _____.	We'll get _____.
Вы́ _____ полу́чите _____.	You'll get _____.
Ты́ _____ полу́чишь_____.	You'll get _____.

22. Óн поло́жит ва́ш бага́ж в такси́. He'll put your baggage in the taxi.

Я положу́ _____.	I'll put _____.
Мы́ поло́жим _____.	We'll put _____.
Они́ поло́жат _____.	They'll put _____.
Шофёр поло́жит _____.	The driver will put _____.

23. Я за́втра посмотрю́ э́ту карти́ну. I'll see the picture tomorrow.

Мы́ _____ посмо́трим _____.	We'll see _____.
Зи́на _____ посмо́трит _____.	Zina will see _____.
Вы́ _____ посмо́трите _____.	You'll see _____.
Они́ _____ посмо́трят _____.	They'll see _____.
Ты́ _____ посмо́тришь _____.	You'll see _____.

24. Мы́ с не́й поговори́м об э́том. We'll have a talk with her about it.

Я _____ поговорю́ _____.	I'll have _____.
Вы́ _____ поговори́те _____.	You'll have _____.
Ты́ _____ поговори́шь _____.	You'll have _____.
Óн _____ поговори́т _____.	He'll have _____.
Они́ _____ поговоря́т _____.	They'll have _____.

Pronunciation practice: initial clusters with [r] or [r̥]

A. Clusters with [r] or [r̥] in second position in the cluster.

[brák] бра́к	[srók] сро́к	[tr̥í] три́
marriage	date, term	three
[brát] бра́т	[gráf] гра́ф	[tr̥étij] тре́тий
brother	count	third
[právdə] пра́вда	[grús] гру́з	[zr̥éɲijə] зре́ние
truth	load	sight
[prózbə] про́сьба	[kráj] кра́й	[sr̥idá] среда́
request	edge	Wednesday
[vrún] вру́н	[br̥ét] бре́д	[fsr̥édu] в сре́ду
liar	delirium	on Wednesday
[vráč] вра́ч	[br̥ivnó] бревно́	[gr̥éx] гре́х
physician	log	sin

[francús] француз Frenchman	[pṛiɣét] привéт greetings	[gṛáṣ] грязь dirt
[drúk] дрýг friend	[pṛámə] прямо straight	[kṛéslə] крéсло armchair
[drámə] дрáма drama	[vṛéṃə] врéмя time	[kriló] крылó wing
[trúdnə] трýдно difficult	[vṛát] в ряд into line	[xrám] хрáм temple
[trójkə] трóйка troika	[fṛigát] фрегáт frigate	[kṛík] крик shout
[zračók] зрачóк pupil of eye	[dṛévṇij] дрéвний ancient	[xṛén] хрéн horseradish
[srázu] срáзу immediately	[dṛimáṭ] дремáть to doze	

B. Clusters with [r] in first position in the cluster.

[rtúṭ] ртýть quicksilver	[rvánij] рвáный torn	[rváṭ] рвáть to tear	[rtá] ртá of a mouth

STRUCTURE AND DRILLS

The formation of the second person imperative

MODELS

Пожáлуйста, заходи.	Come in, please.
Пожáлуйста, заходите.	Come in, please.
Смотри, вóт идёт Нина.	Look, there goes (*or* here comes) Nina.
Смотрите, вóт идёт Нина.	Look, there goes (*or* here comes) Nina.
Подожди!	Wait a bit!
Подождите!	Wait a bit!
Пóй грóмче!	Sing louder!
Пóйте грóмче!	Sing louder!
Нарéжь огурцы!	Cut the cucumbers!
Нарéжьте огурцы!	Cut the cucumbers!
Напиши это!	Write it!
Напишите это!	Write it!
Не пиши!	Don't write!
Не пишите!	Don't write!
Открóй окнó!	Open the window!
Открóйте окнó!	Open the window!
Не открывáй окнá!	Don't open the window!
Не открывáйте окнá!	Don't open the window!
Танцýй!	Dance!
Танцýйте!	Dance!
Не пéй!	Don't drink!
Не пéйте!	Don't drink!
Иди домóй!	Go home!
Идите домóй!	Go home!

Second person imperatives are based on the present-future stem, which can best be found by dropping the endings –ут, –ют, –ат, and –ят from the third person plural.

The familiar-singular imperative ends in –и, –й, or –ь; the plural-polite imperative is formed by adding unstressed –те to the basic familiar-singular form. Of the three variants, only –и is a true ending; –й and –ь are properly part of the stem itself: –й is written to show that the stem ends in the consonant sound [j], and –ь is written to show that the final stem consonant is soft.

1. *Imperatives in* –й. Most verbs with an imperative in –й have a vowel preceding the written ending of the present-future. Their true stems, however, end in [j], spelled й in the imperative.

THIRD PERSON PLURAL		IMPERATIVE	
ду́ма-ют	[dúmaj-ut]	ду́май	ду́майте
чита́-ют	[čitáj-ut]	чита́й	чита́йте
танцу́-ют	[tancúj-ut]	танцу́й	танцу́йте
сто-я́т	[staj-át]	сто́й	сто́йте
по-ю́т	[paj-út]	по́й	по́йте
удивля́-ются	[u̯d̦ivl̦áj-utcə]	удивля́йся	удивля́йтесь

Imperatives based on the stem [p̦j–] *drink* have an inserted vowel: пе́й! вы́пей!

2. *Imperatives in* –ь *and* –и. The position of stress in the first person singular present-future plays a key role in determining whether the imperative wil be in –и or –ь.

a. If the first person singular ending is *stressed*, a stressed –и́ is added to the third plural stem.

THIRD PERSON PLURAL	FIRST PERSON SINGULAR	IMPERATIVE	
лю́б-ят	люблю́	люби́	люби́те
пойд-у́т	пойду́	пойди́	пойди́те
спро́с-ят	спрошу́	спроси́	спроси́те
пи́ш-ут	пишу́	пиши́	пиши́те

b. If the first person singular ending is *unstressed*, the imperative is spelled with –ь, which is a sign that the preceding consonant is pronounced soft (if possible).

THIRD PERSON PLURAL	FIRST PERSON SINGULAR	IMPERATIVE	
доста́н-ут	доста́ну	доста́нь	доста́ньте
забу́д-ут	забу́ду	забу́дь	забу́дьте
оста́в-ят	оста́влю	оста́вь	оста́вьте
встре́т-ят	встре́чу	встре́ть	встре́тьте
наре́ж-ут	наре́жу	наре́жь	наре́жьте

However, if the stem ends in a cluster of consonants, an unstressed –и is added: по́мн-ят, по́мню; the imperative is по́мни. An unstressed –и may also occur in imperatives from perfective verbs which have the stressed prefix вы́–: вы́говорят, вы́говорю; the imperative is вы́говори (like говори́ except for the stress).

Note on aspect: Although imperatives from both aspects may be used in affirmative commands, only imperfective imperatives are ordinarily used in negative commands.

Спроси́ его́!	Ask him!	Не спра́шивай его́!	Don't ask him!
Купи́ а́тлас!	Buy the atlas!	Не покупа́й а́тласа!	Don't buy an atlas!
Напиши́ мне́!	Write to me!	Не пиши́ мне́!	Don't write to me!
Откро́йте окно́!	Open the window!	Не открыва́йте окна́!	Don't open the window!

■ STRUCTURE REPLACEMENT DRILL

Read verses!
Чита́й стихи́!
Чита́йте стихи́!
По́й гро́мче!
По́йте гро́мче!
Купи́ а́тлас!
Бу́дь до́ма!

Спроси́ его́!
Оста́вь клю́ч!
Подожди́ меня́!
Доста́нь ка́рту!
Напиши́ письмо́!
Узна́й об э́том!

■ STRUCTURE REPLACEMENT DRILLS

1. *I'll do it.*
   Do it!
   Я́ сде́лаю э́то.
   Сде́лай э́то!
   Я́ стою́ на углу́.
   Сто́й на углу́!
   Я́ узна́ю об э́том.
   Я́ игра́ю в те́ннис.
   Я́ поду́маю об э́том.
   Я́ чита́ю стихи́.

2. *I'll open the door.*
   Open the door!
   Я́ откро́ю две́рь.
   Откро́й две́рь!
   Я́ пью́ ча́й.
   Пе́й ча́й!
   Я́ всегда́ покупа́ю в э́том магази́не.
   Я́ де́лаю уро́ки.
   Я́ танцу́ю.
   Я́ игра́ю в хокке́й.

3. *I'll bring the tea.*
   Bring the tea!
   Я́ принесу́ ча́й.
   Принеси́ ча́й!
   Я́ спрошу́ профе́ссора Орло́ва.
   Спроси́ профе́ссора Орло́ва!
   Я́ куплю́ а́тлас.
   Я́ посмотрю́ в окно́.
   Я́ подожду́ на углу́.
   Я́ напишу́ сочине́ние.
   Я́ возьму́ э́ту кни́гу.
   Я́ позвоню́ в клу́б.
   Я́ пойду́ на по́чту.

1. *I'm drinking tea.*
   You drink too!
   Я пью ча́й.
   И ты́ пе́й!
   Я откро́ю окно́.
   И ты́ откро́й!
   Я чита́ю стихи́.
   Я поду́маю об э́том.
   Я не ду́маю об экза́мене.
   Я не покупа́ю таки́х веще́й.
   Я стою́ в о́череди.
   Я спра́шиваю, когда́ не зна́ю.

2. *Why don't you listen?*
   Listen!
   Почему́ вы́ не слу́шаете?
   Слу́шайте!
   Почему́ ты́ не чита́ешь?
   Чита́й!
   Почему́ вы́ не захо́дите?
   Почему́ ты́ не пи́шешь?
   Почему́ вы́ не спра́шиваете?
   Почему́ ты́ не пьёшь?
   Почему́ вы́ не говори́те?
   Почему́ ты́ не идёшь?
   Почему́ вы́ не ду́маете?
   Почему́ ты́ не поёшь?
   Почему́ вы́ не поёте?

3. *You walk so much.*
   Don't walk so much!
   Ты́ та́к мно́го хо́дишь.
   Не ходи́ та́к мно́го!
   Вы́ та́к мно́го хо́дите.
   Не ходи́те та́к мно́го!
   Ты́ та́к мно́го пи́шешь.
   Вы́ та́к мно́го пи́шете.
   Ты́ та́к мно́го говори́шь.
   Вы́ та́к мно́го говори́те.

4. *Are you dancing again?*
   Don't do any more dancing!
   Ты́ опя́ть танцу́ешь?
   Не танцу́й бо́льше!
   Вы́ опя́ть танцу́ете?
   Не танцу́йте бо́льше!
   Ты́ опя́ть пьёшь?
   Вы́ опя́ть пьёте?
   Ты́ опя́ть спра́шиваешь?
   Вы́ опя́ть спра́шиваете?
   Ты́ опя́ть поёшь?
   Вы́ опя́ть поёте?

1. *Are you going to leave the dictionary at home?*
   Leave the dictionary at home!
   Ты́ оста́вишь слова́рь до́ма?
   Оста́вь слова́рь до́ма!
   Ты́ наре́жешь огурцы́?
   Наре́жь огурцы́!
   Ты́ доста́нешь а́тлас?
   Ты́ встре́тишь меня́ на углу́?
   Ты́ забу́дешь её?
   Ты́ бу́дешь гото́в?

2. *Are you going to open the window?*
   Open the window!
   Вы́ откро́ете окно́?
   Откро́йте окно́!
   Ты́ ку́пишь пла́тье?
   Купи́ пла́тье!
   Ты́ пойдёшь в магази́н?
   Вы́ напи́шите письмо́?
   Ты́ поду́маешь об э́том?
   Вы́ принесёте а́тлас?
   Ты́ подождёшь бра́та?
   Вы́ пойдёте на конце́рт?

3. *Are you going to meet us on the corner?*
   Meet us on the corner!
   Вы́ встре́тите на́с на углу́?
   Встре́тьте на́с на углу́!
   Ты́ ска́жешь твоё и́мя?

   Скажи́ твоё и́мя!
   Вы́ доста́нете ключи́?
   Ты́ посмо́тришь э́тот фи́льм?
   Вы́ ку́пите молоко́?
   Вы́ забу́дете об э́том?

May I bring the tea?
Fine, bring it!
Мо́жно принести́ ча́й?
Хорошо́, принеси́те!
Мо́жно написа́ть об э́том?
Хорошо́, напиши́те!

Мо́жно подожда́ть ва́с?
Мо́жно наре́зать огурцы́?
Мо́жно поду́мать немно́го?
Мо́жно посмотре́ть э́тот фи́льм?

■ STRUCTURE REPLACEMENT DRILLS

1. *Open the window!*
   Don't open the window!
   Откро́йте окно́!
   Не открыва́йте окна́!
   Купи́те ча́й!
   Не покупа́йте ча́я!
   Посмотри́те в окно́!
   Сде́лайте э́то!
   Спроси́те об э́том!
   Поду́майте об э́том!

2. *Buy a dictionary!*
   Don't buy a dictionary!
   Купи́ слова́рь!
   Не покупа́й словаря́!
   Посмотри́ в кни́гу!
   Не смотри́ в кни́гу!
   Напиши́ сочине́ние!
   Откро́й две́рь!
   Спроси́ его́!
   Поду́май о зиме́!

■ RESPONSE DRILLS

1. *We're playing cards.*
   You play, too!
   Мы́ игра́ем в ка́рты.
   И вы́ игра́йте!
   Мы́ не ду́маем об э́том.
   И вы́ не ду́майте!
   Мы́ чита́ем рома́ны.
   Мы́ бу́дем та́м.
   Мы́ танцу́ем ка́ждый ве́чер.
   Мы́ не пьём.
   Мы́ не поём.

2. *We're reading Tolstoy.*
   You read Tolstoy, too!
   Мы́ чита́ем Толсто́го.
   Вы́ то́же чита́йте Толсто́го!
   Мы́ покупа́ем в э́том магази́не.
   Вы́ то́же покупа́йте в э́том магази́не!
   Мы́ пи́шем сочине́ние.
   Мы́ поём.
   Мы́ ду́маем об э́том.
   Мы́ бу́дем та́м.
   Мы́ забу́дем об э́том.

SUMMARY OF RULES FOR FORMING THE BASIC **ты** IMPERATIVE

1. If the present-future stem ends in the sound [j], or (in spelling terms) if the endings of the present-future are immediately preceded by a vowel letter or ь, the imperative is spelled with **й**: **покупа́й!** (stem [pəkupáj–], first person singular **покупа́ю**). Note that the stress occasionally shifts back to the stem (compare **сто́й! сто́йте!** with **стою́**). Verbs like **пи́ть**, with ь directly before their present-future endings, have an inserted vowel in their stem: **пе́й, вы́пей** (stem [pj–], first person singular **пью́**).

2. If the present-future stem ends in any other consonant (but not a cluster), and if the stem is stressed in the first person singular, the imperative is spelled with –ь, as in **забу́дь!** (first person singular **забу́ду**). The –ь must be written, even though the consonant is one that cannot be soft, as in **наре́жь!**

3. If the present-future stem ends in a consonant cluster, even though the stress is on the stem in the first person singular present-future, the ending –и is added for the imperative, as in **по́мни!** (first person singular **по́мню**).

4. If the present-future stem ends in a consonant and the first person singular ending *is* stressed, the imperative ending is **–й**, as in **говори́!** (first person singular **говорю́**) and **иди́!** (first person singular **иду́**).

5. Perfective verbs with the stressed prefix **вы–** form their imperative in the same way as the imperative of the verb they derive from, for example, **вы́пей!** (compare **пей!**), **вы́говори!** (compare **говори́!**), **вы́режь!** (compare **режь!** *cut!* **наре́жь!** *slice!*).

The declension of adjectives: nominative, accusative, genitive, and prepositional cases

MODELS

Я́ купи́л но́вый костю́м.	I bought a new suit.
_____ но́вое ра́дио.	_____ a new radio.
_____ но́вую пласти́нку.	_____ a new record.
_____ но́вые пласти́нки.	_____ some new records.
Я́ ищу́ хоро́ший портфе́ль.	I'm looking for a good briefcase.
_____ хоро́шее ра́дио.	_____ a good radio.
_____ хоро́шую ко́мнату.	_____ a good room.
_____ хоро́шие пласти́нки.	_____ some good records.
Вы́ зна́ете э́того молодо́го челове́ка?	Do you know this young man?
_____ э́ту молоду́ю де́вушку?	_____ this young lady?
_____ э́тих молоды́х люде́й?	_____ these young people?
Вы́ лю́бите Достое́вского?	Are you fond of Dostoevsky?
_____ Толсто́го?	_____ Tolstoy?
_____ ру́сские рома́ны?	_____ Russian novels?
_____ таки́е стихи́?	_____ such verses?
_____ ста́рые рома́нсы?	_____ old love songs?
Я́ не люблю́ Достое́вского.	I don't like Dostoevsky.
_____ Толсто́го.	_____ Tolstoy.
_____ ру́сских рома́нов.	_____ Russian novels.
_____ таки́х стихо́в.	_____ such verses.
_____ ста́рых рома́нсов.	_____ old love songs.
Хоти́те ча́шку вку́сного ко́фе?	Want a cup of delicious coffee?
_____ хоро́шего ____?	_____ good _____?
_____ горя́чего ____?	_____ hot _____?
У ни́х не́т хоро́шего клу́ба.	They don't have a good club.
_____ общежи́тия.	_____ dormitory.
_____ хоро́шей библиоте́ки.	_____ a good library.
_____ лаборато́рии.	_____ laboratory.
_____ хоро́ших теа́тров.	_____ any good theaters.
_____ па́рков.	_____ parks.
_____ рестора́нов.	_____ restaurants.
Мы́ говори́ли об э́том но́вом зда́нии.	We were talking about that new building.
_____ большо́м ____.	_____ big _____.
_____ об э́том но́вом общежи́тии.	_____ about that new dormitory.
_____ большо́м _____.	_____ large _____.

Мы́ говори́ли об э́той но́вой гости́нице.	We were talking about that new hotel.
_____ большо́й _____.	_____ large _____.
_____ об э́тих но́вых магази́нах.	_____ about these new stores.
_____ больши́х_____.	_____ large _____.

Мы́ говори́м о после́днем но́мере «Пра́вды».
    _____ экза́мене.
    _____ собра́нии.
    _____ уро́ке.

We're speaking of the last issue of _Pravda_.
    _____ exam.
    _____ meeting.
    _____ lesson.

Мы́ говори́м о его́ после́дней кни́ге.
    _____ рабо́те.
    _____ о после́дних новостя́х.
    _____ изве́стиях.

We're talking about his latest book.
    _____ work.
    _____ about the latest news.
    _____ news reports.

		SINGULAR			PLURAL	
	Masculine		**Neuter**	**Feminine**		
ACC	_inanimate_ молодо́й ста́рый си́ний друго́й ру́сский большо́й хоро́ший	_animate_ молодо́го ста́рого си́него друго́го ру́сского большо́го хоро́шего	молодо́е ста́рое си́нее друго́е ру́сское большо́е хоро́шее	молоду́ю ста́рую си́нюю другу́ю ру́сскую большу́ю хоро́шую	_inanimate_ молоды́е ста́рые си́ние други́е ру́сские больши́е хоро́шие	_animate_ молоды́х ста́рых си́них други́х ру́сских больши́х хоро́ших
GEN	молодо́го ста́рого си́него друго́го ру́сского большо́го хоро́шего			молодо́й ста́рой си́ней друго́й	молоды́х ста́рых си́них други́х	
PREP	о молодо́м о ста́ром о си́нем о друго́м о ру́сском о большо́м о хоро́шем			ру́сской большо́й хоро́шей	ру́сских больши́х хоро́ших	

GENERAL OBSERVATIONS

    1. The endings of adjectives modifying masculine and neuter nouns are distinct from each other only in the nominative and accusative singular; in all the other cases, they share the same endings.

    2. Only adjectives modifying feminine nouns have endings in the accusative singular which are always distinct from those used in the nominative singular: –ую and –юю (но́вую, другу́ю, большу́ю. после́днюю, ве́рхнюю).

3. Adjectives modifying neuter and *inanimate* masculine nouns have the same endings in the accusative singular as in the nominative singular. Those adjectives modifying *animate* masculine nouns in the accusative singular have the same endings as in the genitive singular. Note that г in the endings –ого and –его is pronounced [v].

4. In the plural, adjectives modifying *inanimate* nouns use nominative plural endings; those modifying *animate* nouns use genitive plural endings.

■ RESPONSE DRILLS

1. *This room is a small one.*
   I asked for a large one.
   Э́тот но́мер ма́ленький.
   Я проси́л большо́й.
   Э́ти ножи́ ма́ленькие.
   Я проси́л больши́е.
   Э́та коро́бка ма́ленькая.
   Э́тот а́тлас ма́ленький.
   Э́та ло́жка ма́ленькая.
   Э́тот шка́ф ма́ленький.
   Э́та по́лка ма́ленькая.
   Э́та ка́рта ма́ленькая.

2. *You didn't happen to see the new record?*
   I'm looking for the new record.
   Вы́ не ви́дели но́вой пласти́нки?
   Я ищу́ но́вую пласти́нку.
   Вы́ не ви́дели голубо́го пла́тья?
   Я ищу́ голубо́е пла́тье.
   (си́него костю́ма, ру́сской газе́ты, аме-
   рика́нского журна́ла, жёлтой тетра́ди,
   ста́рого портфе́ля)

■ EXPANSION DRILL

Do you know that girl?
Do you know that lovely girl?
Вы́ зна́ете э́ту де́вушку?
Вы́ зна́ете э́ту краси́вую де́вушку?
Вы́ зна́ете э́того па́рня?
Вы́ зна́ете э́того краси́вого па́рня?
(э́ту пе́сню, э́ту же́нщину, э́того сту-
де́нта, это ме́сто, э́ту америка́нку, э́ту
мело́дию, э́тот го́род)

■ CUED QUESTION-ANSWER DRILL

(green)   *What color is this book?*
           Green.
(зелёный) Како́го цве́та э́та кни́га?
          Зелёного.
(бе́лый)   Како́го цве́та э́та кни́га?
          Бе́лого.
(кра́сный, жёлтый, си́ний, голубо́й,
чёрный)

■ QUESTION-ANSWER DRILLS

1. *Where's the American singer?*
   The American singer isn't here yet.
   Где́ америка́нский певе́ц?
   Америка́нского певца́ ещё не́т.
   Где́ америка́нская певи́ца?
   Америка́нской певи́цы ещё не́т.
   Где́ но́вый учи́тель?
   Где́ но́вая учи́тельница?
   Где́ ста́рый шофёр?
   Где́ вече́рняя газе́та?
   Где́ после́дний но́мер журна́ла?

2. *Are the new students here?*
   I don't see the new students.
   Но́вые студе́нты здесь?
   Я не ви́жу но́вых студе́нтов.
   Поде́ржанные ве́щи здесь?
   Я не ви́жу поде́ржанных веще́й.
   Вече́рние газе́ты здесь?
   Молоды́е лю́ди здесь?
   Жёлтые ча́шки здесь?
   Но́вые журна́лы здесь?
   Ста́рые пласти́нки здесь?
   Больши́е стака́ны здесь?

There was a lovely picture there.
There were many lovely pictures there.
Та́м была́ краси́вая карти́на.
Та́м бы́ло мно́го краси́вых карти́н.
Та́м бы́л но́вый до́м.
Та́м бы́ло мно́го но́вых домо́в.
Та́м бы́л небольшо́й шка́ф.

Та́м бы́ло просто́е пла́тье.
Та́м бы́л чёрный костю́м.
Та́м бы́ло но́вое общежи́тие.
Та́м бы́ло интере́сное объявле́ние.
Та́м была́ но́вая рекла́ма.

■ RESPONSE DRILLS

1. *You're a good student.*
   For a good student it isn't difficult.
   Вы́ хоро́ший студе́нт.
   Для́ хоро́шего студе́нта э́то не тру́дно.
   Вы́ хоро́шие студе́нты.
   Для́ хоро́ших студе́нтов э́то не тру́дно.
   Вы́ хоро́шая студе́нтка.
   Вы́ хоро́ший проводни́к.
   Вы́ хоро́ший администра́тор.
   Вы́ хоро́шая учи́тельница.
   Вы́ хоро́ший учи́тель.
   Вы́ хоро́шие учителя́.

2. *These things are expensive.*
   Don't buy expensive things.
   Э́ти ве́щи дороги́е.
   Не покупа́й дороги́х веще́й.
   Э́тот портфе́ль плохо́й.
   Не покупа́й плохо́го портфе́ля.
   Э́ти пласти́нки ста́рые.
   Э́то ра́дио дорого́е.
   Э́тот материа́л жёсткий.
   Э́тот рома́н ску́чный.

■ QUESTION-ANSWER DRILLS

1. *Did he ask about old magazines?*
   No, about new ones.
   О́н спра́шивал о ста́рых журна́лах?
   Не́т, о но́вых.
   О́н спра́шивал о ста́рой пласти́нке?
   Не́т, о но́вой.
   (о ста́ром рома́нсе, о ста́рых пе́снях,
   о ста́рой рабо́те, о ста́ром сочине́нии,
   о ста́ром заявле́нии, о ста́рых та́нцах)

2. *Are you talking about the small lecture hall?*
   No, about the large one.
   Вы́ говори́те о ма́ленькой аудито́рии?
   Не́т, о большо́й.
   Вы́ говори́те о ма́ленькой библиоте́ке?
   Не́т, о большо́й.
   (о ма́леньком шка́фе, о ма́леньком
   общежи́тии, о ма́ленькой лаборато́рии,
   о ма́леньком до́ме, о ма́ленькой
   оши́бке, о ма́леньком за́ле, о ма́лень-
   ком магази́не)

■ RESPONSE DRILLS

1. *Here's the recreation room.*
   They're waiting for us in the recreation room.
   Во́т кра́сный уголо́к.
   Они́ на́с жду́т в кра́сном уголке́.
   Во́т жёсткий ваго́н.
   Они́ на́с жду́т в жёстком ваго́не.
   (новое общежитие, старая аудитория,
   Большой театр, американское посоль-
   ство, новая квартира)

2. *Have you seen the new building?*
   *Everyone's been talking about the new
   building.*
   Вы́ ви́дели но́вое зда́ние?
   Всé говоря́т о но́вом зда́нии.
   Вы́ ви́дели америка́нских студе́нтов?
   Всé говоря́т об америка́нских студе́нтах.
   (новую гостиницу, вечернюю газету,
   последний номер «Известий», новое
   объявление, новое посольство, нового
   администратора, американский фильм)

	SINGULAR			PLURAL
	Masculine	*Neuter*	*Feminine*	
NOM	–о́й, –ый, –ий	–ое, –ее	–ая, –яя	–ые, –ие
ACC	(*inanimate* — nom) (*animate* — gen)		–ую, –юю	(*inanimate* — nom) (*animate* — gen)
GEN	–ого, –его		–ой, –ей	–ых, –их
PREP	–ом, –ем			

LONG-FORM ADJECTIVE ENDINGS IN NOMINATIVE, ACCUSATIVE, GENITIVE, AND PREPOSITIONAL CASES

Note: The letter г in the endings –ого and –его is pronounced [v].

REMARKS ON THE DISTRIBUTION OF ENDINGS IN THE GENITIVE AND PREPOSITIONAL CASES

1. *Masculine and neuter endings in the genitive and prepositional singular.*

a. Hard-stem adjectives and mixed stems ending in к, г, and х take –ого in the genitive and –ом in the prepositional: но́вого, но́вом; друго́го, друго́м.

b. Soft-stem adjectives take –его in the genitive and –ем in the prepositional: после́днего, после́днем.

c. Mixed stems ending in ш and ж take –о́го in the genitive and –о́м in the prepositional if the ending is stressed; if it is unstressed they take –его and –ем. Compare большо́го, большо́м with хоро́шего, хоро́шем.

2. *Feminine endings in the genitive-prepositional singular* (*genitive identical with prepositional*).

a. Hard stems and mixed stems ending in к, г, and х take –ой: но́вой, друго́й.

b. Soft stems take –ей: после́дней.

c. Mixed stems ending in ш and ж take –о́й if the ending is stressed; if it is unstressed they take –ей. Compare большо́й with хоро́шей.

3. *Plural endings in the genitive-prepositional* (*genitive identical with prepositional*).

a. Hard stems take the ending –ых in the genitive-prepositional: но́вых, молоды́х.

b. Soft stems and all mixed stems take the ending –их in the genitive-prepositional: после́дних, други́х, больши́х.

The declension of че́й and the possessive modifiers: nominative, accusative, genitive, and prepositional cases

MODELS

Че́й рома́н вы́ чита́ете?	Whose novel are you reading?
Чьё сочине́ние вы́ чита́ете?	Whose composition are you reading?
Чью́ кни́гу вы́ чита́ете?	Whose book are you reading?
Чьи́ стихи́ вы́ чита́ете?	Whose verses are you reading?

Вы́ зна́ете моего́ бра́та?	Do you know my brother?
_____ на́шего _____?	_____ our _____?
Вы́ зна́ете мою́ сестру́?	Do you know my sister?
_____ на́шу _____?	_____ our _____?
Вы́ зна́ете мои́х сестёр?	Do you know my sisters?
_____ на́ших _____?	_____ our _____?

Óн оста́вил сво́й слова́рь до́ма.	He left his dictionary home.
_____ свою́ кни́гу _____.	_____ his book _____.
_____ своё сочине́ние _____.	_____ his composition _____.
_____ сво́й пи́сьма _____.	_____ his letters _____.

Мы́ вчера́ бы́ли у твоего́ бра́та.	We were at your brother's place yesterday.
_____ у ва́шего _____.	_____ at your brother's place _____.
_____ у твое́й сестры́.	_____ at your sister's place _____.
_____ у ва́шей _____.	_____ at your sister's place _____.
_____ у твои́х друзе́й.	_____ at your friends' place _____.
_____ у ва́ших _____.	_____ at your friends' place _____.

Вы́ ещё не ви́дели на́шего го́рода.	You still haven't seen our city.
_____ на́шего общежи́тия.	_____ our dormitory.
_____ на́шей кварти́ры.	_____ our apartment.
_____ на́ших карти́н.	_____ our pictures.

Мы́ говори́ли о твоём до́ме.	We were talking about your house.
_____ ва́шем _____.	_____ your _____.
_____ твоём заявле́нии.	_____ your application.
_____ ва́шем _____.	_____ your _____.
_____ твое́й про́сьбе.	_____ your request.
_____ ва́шей _____.	_____ your _____.
_____ твои́х кни́гах.	_____ your books.
_____ ва́ших_____.	_____ your_____.

■ REPETITION DRILL

Repeat the above models, observing the pattern of endings.

■ RESPONSE DRILLS

1. *Here comes my brother.*
   Do you know my brother?
   Во́т идёт мо́й бра́т.
   Вы́ зна́ете моего́ бра́та?
   Во́т идёт моя́ сестра́.
   Вы́ зна́ете мою́ сестру́?
   (мои́ бра́тья, мои́ сёстры, мо́й дру́г, моя́ подру́га)

2. *Here's your briefcase.*
   You forgot your briefcase again.
   Во́т ва́ш портфе́ль.
   Вы́ опя́ть забы́ли сво́й портфе́ль.
   Во́т ва́ша кни́га.
   Вы́ опя́ть забы́ли свою́ кни́гу.
   (ва́ше заявле́ние, ва́ши ве́щи, ва́ша газе́та, ва́ш журна́л, ва́ши пласти́нки, ва́ша квита́нция, ва́ш биле́т)

3. *Take my notebook.*
   No, thanks, I'll take my own.
   Возьми́ мою́ тетра́дь.
   Не́т, спаси́бо. Я́ возьму́ свою́.
   Возьми́ моё ра́дио.
   Не́т, спаси́бо. Я́ возьму́ своё.
   (мо́й каранда́ш, мою́ ру́чку, мо́й слова́рь, моё перо́, мои́ тетра́ди, мою́ ка́рту, мои́ биле́ты)

1. *Whose mistake was she talking about?*
   About mine.
   О чьей ошибке она говорила?
   О моей.
   О чьём письме она говорила?
   О моём.
   (о чьих стихах, о чьём очерке, о чьей картине, о чьём сочинении, о чьих вещах, о чьих журналах, о чьём билете, о чьей просьбе)

2. *Are you reading your own application?*
   No, yours.
   Вы читаете своё заявление?
   Нет, ваше.
   Вы читаете своё сочинение?
   Нет, ваше.
   (своё письмо, свои стихи, свою работу, свой очерк, свою книгу)

■ EXPANSION DRILL

You haven't seen the city yet.
You haven't seen our city yet.
Вы ещё не видели города.
Вы ещё не видели нашего города.

Вы ещё не видели квартиры.
Вы ещё не видели нашей квартиры.
(дома, общежития, картин, комнаты, вокзала, университета, школы)

■ SUBJECT REVERSAL DRILL

Your brother was at my place yesterday.
I was at your brother's yesterday
Твой брат вчера был у меня.
Я вчера был у твоего брата.
Твои друзья вчера были у меня.
Я вчера был у твоих друзей.
(твои сёстры, твой друг, твоя подруга, твои братья)

■ STRUCTURE REPLACEMENT DRILL

I was reading your novel.
I was talking about your novel.
Я читал ваш роман.
Я говорил о вашем романе.
Я читал ваши стихи.
Я говорил о ваших стихах.
(вашу работу, ваше сочинение, ваш очерк, вашу книгу, ваше заявление, ваши работы)

	SINGULAR			PLURAL
	Masculine	*Neuter*	*Feminine*	
NOM	чей мой, твой, свой наш, ваш	чьё моё, твоё, своё наше, ваше	чья моя, твоя, своя наша, ваша	чьи мои, твои, свои наши, ваши
ACC	(*like* nom *or* gen)	(*like* nom)	чью мою, твою, свою нашу, вашу	(*like* nom *or* gen)
GEN	чьего моего, твоего, своего нашего, вашего		чьей моей, твоей, своей нашей, вашей	чьих моих, твоих, своих наших, ваших
PREP	(о) чьём (о) моём, твоём, своём (о) нашем, вашем			

Possessive adjectives all belong to the soft declension, with endings in the oblique cases (genitive, prepositional, dative, and instrumental) like those of the soft-stem adjectives. Note that, except for **наш** and **ваш**, which have their stress consistently on the stem, the possessive modifiers all have ending stress.

The reflexive possessive **свой, своё, своя, свои** *one's own* declines exactly like **мой** and **твой**. Rarely used in the nominative, it may substitute for **мой, твой, наш,** or **ваш** in those situations where subject and possessor are the same.

Я вам дал **мой (свой)** портфель.	I gave you *my* briefcase.
Мы говорим о **нашем (своём)** друге.	*We*'re talking about *our* friend.
Вы мне дали **вашу (свою)** книгу.	*You* gave me *your* book.
Вы мне дали **мою** книгу.	*You* gave me *my* book.

It is only when the subject is in the third person that **свой** plays a distinctive role. It differs in meaning from **его, её,** and **их**, the unchanging third person possessives.

Compare	Он забыл **свой** портфель.	He forgot his (own) briefcase.
with	Он забыл **его** портфель.	He forgot his (someone else's) briefcase.
Compare	Зина читала **свою** книгу.	Zina was reading her (own) book.
with	Зина читала **её** книгу.	Zina was reading her (someone else's) book.
Compare	Они говорили о **своих** друзьях.	They were talking about their (own) friends.
with	Они говорили об **их** друзьях.	They were talking about their (other's) friends.

Possessive modifiers are often omitted when it is clear from the context that the possessor and the subject are the same: **Я был у брата** (*or* **у моего брата**) *I was at my brother's place.*

Review of second conjugation verbs

PRESENT-FUTURE ENDINGS		позвонить (pfv) *to phone*	стоять (ipfv) *to stand*	слышать (ipfv) *to hear*	просить (ipfv) *to ask*	купить (pfv) *to buy*
SG	1	–ю or –у	позвоню	стою	слышу	прошу	куплю
	2	–ишь	позвонишь	стоишь	слышишь	просишь	купишь
	3	–ит	позвонит	стоит	слышит	просит	купит
PL	1	–им	позвоним	стоим	слышим	просим	купим
	2	–ите	позвоните	стоите	слышите	просите	купите
	3	–ят or –ат	позвонят	стоят	слышат	просят	купят

■ SUBSTITUTION DRILLS

1. *You never go to the movies.*
   Вы никогда не ходите в кино.
   Они никогда не ходят в кино.
   (мы, я, она, ты, его друзья, мой товарищ по комнате, вы)

2. *I hear the bell.*
   Я слышу звонок.
   Он слышит звонок.
   (мы, вы, ты, они, Наташа, студенты, мы все)

3. *She always asks that the windows be opened.*
Она́ всегда́ про́сит открыва́ть о́кна.
Они́ всегда́ про́сят открыва́ть о́кна.
   (я, вы, Зи́на, мы, ты, учи́тель,
   секрета́рь, учи́тельницы)

4. *I'll phone home tomorrow.*
За́втра **я́** позвоню́ домо́й.
За́втра **мы́** позвони́м домо́й.
   (она, вы, они, Олег, мы, я)

5. *Comrade Alexeev often goes to Kiev.*
Това́рищ Алексе́ев ча́сто е́здит в Ки́ев.
Э́ти проводники́ ча́сто е́здят в Ки́ев.
   (мы, они, я, вы, ты, эта женщина)

6. *I don't remember her name.*
Я́ не по́мню её и́мени.
Ты́ не по́мнишь её и́мени.
   (они, вы, студенты, мы, я)

7. *Volodya talks a lot at meetings.*
Воло́дя мно́го говори́т на собра́ниях.
Э́ти студе́нты мно́го говоря́т на
собра́ниях.
   (ты, вы, я, наш вахтёр, мы все)

■ STRUCTURE REPLACEMENT DRILLS

1. *Irina was looking out the window.*
Irina is looking out the window.
Ири́на смотре́ла в окно́.
Ири́на смо́трит в окно́.
Вы́ смотре́ли в окно́.
Вы́ смо́трите в окно́.
   (студенты, я, мы, ты, Коля)

2. *We often used to stand in line.*
We often stand in line.
Мы́ ча́сто стоя́ли в о́череди.
Мы́ ча́сто стои́м в о́череди.
Я́ ча́сто стоя́л в о́череди.
Я́ ча́сто стою́ в о́череди.
   (вы, люди, моя сестра, ты, мы, я)

■ QUESTION-ANSWER DRILLS

1. *I'm not asleep yet, how about you fellows?*
We're not asleep, either.
Я́ ещё не сплю́, а вы́, ребя́та?
Мы́ то́же не спи́м.
Я́ ещё не сплю́, а э́тот па́рень?
Он то́же не спи́т.
Я́ ещё не сплю́, а ты́, Ко́ля?
Я́ ещё не сплю́, а о́н?
Я́ ещё не сплю́, а ты́?
Я́ ещё не сплю́, а вы́, това́рищи?
Я́ ещё не сплю́, а э́ти лю́ди?
Я́ ещё не сплю́, а э́тот граждани́н?
Я́ ещё не сплю́, а на́ши попу́тчики?
Я́ ещё не сплю́, а вы́, де́вушки?

2. *She pays very little for her room, how about you?*
I also pay very little.
Она́ ма́ло пла́тит за ко́мнату, а вы́?
И я́ ма́ло плачу́.
Она́ ма́ло пла́тит за ко́мнату,
   а её сестра́?
И она́ ма́ло пла́тит.
   (а ты; а эта певица; а эти заочницы;
   а этот господин; а эта американка;
   а вы, ребята)

3. *When are you going to see that film?*
We'll see it tomorrow.
Когда́ вы́ посмо́трите э́тот фи́льм?
Мы́ посмо́трим его́ за́втра.
Когда́ певе́ц посмо́трит э́тот фи́льм?
Он посмо́трит его́ за́втра.
   (твои подруги, певица, ты, Володя и
   Пётр, твой товарищ по комнате, ты,
   секретарь, вы, эта девушка)

4. *Will you permit that?*
Of course we will.
Вы́ разреши́те э́то?
Коне́чно, мы́ разреши́м.
Ребя́та разреша́т э́то?
Коне́чно, они́ разреша́т.
   (секретарь, их братья, эта американка,
   Оля и Галя, ваша учительница, мой
   брат, его сестра, товарищ Царапкин)

She ought to receive a letter soon.
She'll receive a letter soon.
Она́ ско́ро должна́ получи́ть письмо́.
Она́ ско́ро полу́чит письмо́.
Вы́ ско́ро должны́ получи́ть письмо́.
Вы́ ско́ро полу́чите письмо́.

(братья, америка́нка, ты, учи́тельницы, я, граждани́н Семёнов, эти америка́нцы, мы, профессор)

■ STRUCTURE REPLACEMENT DRILL

1. *I met her at the station.*
   I'll meet her at the station.
   Я́ её встре́тил на вокза́ле.
   Я́ её встре́чу на вокза́ле.
   Проводни́к её встре́тил на вокза́ле.
   Проводни́к её встре́тит на вокза́ле.
   (шофёр, эта же́нщина, америка́нские певцы́, мы, друзья́, этот мужчи́на)

2. *Do you hear me?*
   Вы́ меня́ слы́шите?
   Ты́ меня́ слы́шишь?
   Вы́ меня́ встре́тите?
   Ты́ меня́ встре́тишь?
   Вы́ меня́ ви́дите?
   Вы́ меня́ извини́те?
   Вы́ меня́ услы́шите?
   Вы́ меня́ по́мните?
   Вы́ меня́ лю́бите?
   Вы́ меня́ познако́мите?

■ SUBJECT REVERSAL DRILLS

1. *I won't [be able to] hear the custodian.*
   The custodian won't [be able to] hear me.
   Я́ не услы́шу вахтёра.
   Вахтёр меня́ не услы́шит.
   Я́ не услы́шу сестёр.
   Сёстры меня́ не услы́шат.
   (секретаря́, тебя́, вас, ребя́т, певи́ц, певцо́в, студе́нток, Фили́ппа, де́вушек)

2. *He'll pay for them.*
   They'll pay for him.
   О́н запла́тит за ни́х.
   Они́ запла́тят за него́.
   О́н запла́тит за меня́.
   Я́ заплачу́ за него́.
   (тебя́, Зи́ну, ребя́т, неё, меня́, нас, вас, Козло́ва, них, попу́тчиков, этого челове́ка)

■ QUESTION-ANSWER DRILLS

1. *Will you study the Russian language?*
   I'm already studying Russian.
   Вы́ бу́дете учи́ть ру́сский язы́к?
   Я́ уже́ учу́ ру́сский язы́к.
   Э́тот студе́нт бу́дет учи́ть ру́сский язы́к?
   О́н уже́ у́чит ру́сский язы́к.
   (америка́нская певи́ца, ты, этот па́рень, твоя́ подру́га, америка́нский певе́ц, америка́нские певцы́, эта америка́нка, эти америка́нцы)

2. *Where will you put the records?*
   I'll put them on the table.
   Куда́ вы́ поло́жите пласти́нки?
   Я́ положу́ и́х на сто́л.
   Куда́ учи́тель поло́жит пласти́нки?
   О́н поло́жит и́х на сто́л.
   (она́, студе́нты, певе́ц, певи́ца, убо́рщицы, ты, мы, вы, де́вушки)

DISCUSSION

1. *Comparison between the present-future endings of first and second conjugation verbs.*

Verbs of the second conjugation have the vowels –и– and –я– (*or* –а–) in their present-future endings as compared with –е– (*or* –ё–) and –ю– (*or* –у–) for verbs of the first conjugation.

FIRST CONJUGATION						
зна́ю	зна́ешь	зна́ет	зна́ем	зна́ете	зна́ют	(e and ю)
иду́	идёшь	идёт	идём	идёте	иду́т	(ё and у)
SECOND CONJUGATION						
стою́	стои́шь	стои́т	стои́м	стои́те	стоя́т	(и and я)
слы́шу	слы́шишь	слы́шит	слы́шим	слы́шите	слы́шат	(и and а)

2. *Alternation of stems in the present-future of second conjugation verbs.*

Alternation of the final stem consonant occurs *only* in the first person singular. There are two types:

TYPE 1 (Stems ending in с, з, т, д, ст)	TYPE 2 (Stems ending in п, б, в, ф, м)
Compare спроси́ть, спро́сят *with* спрошу́ *Compare* ви́деть, ви́дят *with* ви́жу *Compare* встре́тить, встре́тят *with* встре́чу *Compare* заходи́ть, захо́дят *with* захожу́	*Compare* люби́ть, лю́бят *with* люблю́ *Compare* оста́вить, оста́вят *with* оста́влю *Compare* спа́ть, спя́т *with* сплю́ *Compare* познако́мить, познако́мят *with* познако́млю

3. *The present-future stem versus the infinitive-past stem.*

In second conjugation verbs the endings of the infinitive and past are consistently added to a form of the stem which ends in a vowel. This vowel is automatically dropped before the endings of the present-future.

INFINITIVE-PAST	PRESENT-FUTURE
смотре́-ть -л, -ла, -ли	**смотр**-ю́, -ишь, -ят
слы́ша-ть -л, -ла, -ли	**слы́ш**-у, -ишь, -ат
говори́-ть -л, -ла, ли	**говор**-ю́, -и́шь, -я́т

4. *Stress patterns in the present-future.*

The same three basic stress patterns that are found in first conjugation verbs are also found in second conjugation verbs:

a. Stress consistently falls on the ending: говорю́, говори́шь, говори́т, говори́м, говори́те, говоря́т.

b. Stress consistently falls on the stem: встре́чу, встре́тишь, встре́тит, встре́тим, встре́тите, встре́тят.

c. Stress falls on the ending in the first person singular, but shifts back to the stem in all other forms: прошу́, про́сишь, про́сит, про́сим, про́сите, про́сят.

Нина студентка-заочница; она работает на фабрике. Кирилл Павлович слышал, что Нина ищет комнату. Он был в горсовете у Алексеева и говорил о Нине. Алексеев сказал, что Нина не будет дома ждать.

Кирилл Павлович встретил Семёна Филипповича в магазине на углу. Семён Филиппович всю зиму был болен. Теперь он уже почти здоров, но всё ещё не работает. Его жена с осени работает в горсовете. Кирилл Павлович рад это слышать. Хорошо, что она работает.

Филипп Грант ехал в Москву. Он сидел в купе и читал „Вечернюю Москву". Галя тоже ехала в этом купе. Она читала журнал „Огонёк". Там был очерк о США. Галя мало знает об Америке. Она всегда с большим удовольствием читает журнал „Америка", но его трудно доставать: он всегда распродан.

Америка́нские пласти́нки о́чень тру́дно достава́ть. Га́ля купи́ла их на толку́чке. Сего́дня её подру́ги пойду́т в кра́сный уголо́к, где́ есть прои́грыватель. Они́ бу́дут та́м слу́шать му́зыку и танцева́ть. Га́ля принесёт свои́ но́вые пласти́нки.

— Зна́ешь, Оле́г, я встре́тил сего́дня Ка́тю.

— Где́? В библиоте́ке?

— Не́т, в кра́сном уголке́.

— Интере́сно, она́ ничего́ не спра́шивала обо мне́?

— Не́т, она́, как всегда́, говори́ла то́лько о себе́.

— Пра́вда, она́ ду́мает и говори́т всегда́ то́лько о себе́.

— Она́ и живёт то́лько для себя́.

— Ка́жется, ва́ши ребя́та лю́бят на́шу америка́нскую му́зыку?

— Да́, джа́з мы́ о́чень лю́бим. То́лько пласти́нки доста́ть тру́дно.

— А я́ о́чень люблю́ ва́ши наро́дные мело́дии и уже́ купи́л мно́го пласти́нок.

— Интере́сно, каки́е.

— Хоти́те послу́шать?

— Да́, коне́чно.

— Хорошо́, я принесу́ их сего́дня ве́чером. Е́сли хоти́те, я принесу́ и свои́ америка́нские.

— О, да́, пожа́луйста! Мы́ их с удово́льствием послу́шаем.

— Здесь идёт «Война́ и ми́р». Это америка́нский фи́льм.

— Зна́ю, но ты́ ви́дишь, Га́ля, кака́я о́чередь у ка́ссы? Мы́ мо́жем пойти́ на друго́й фи́льм.

— Не́т, я хочу́ то́лько на э́тот! Я́ так люблю́ э́тот рома́н!

— Ну, хорошо́, пойдём на э́тот.

— Во́т мо́й това́рищ по ко́мнате, Га́ля. Хо́чешь, я тебя́ познако́млю?

— Что́ ты́, Оле́г? Я́ ве́дь его́ хорошо́ зна́ю, э́то Никола́й Петро́в. Здра́вствуй, Ко́ля!

— А, Га́ля, приве́т! Что́ ты́ тут у на́с де́лаешь?

— Да во́т хочу́ посмотре́ть ва́ш кра́сный уголо́к. Оле́г говори́т, что́ у ва́с хоро́ший прои́грыватель и но́вые пласти́нки.

— Отли́чно. Сейча́с бу́дем слу́шать му́зыку и танцева́ть.

Ни́на хо́чет чита́ть журна́л «Аме́рика», но она́ не зна́ет, где его́ доста́ть. Когда́ она́ спра́шивает в кио́ске, ей всегда́ отвеча́ют, что о́н распро́дан. Я достаю́ э́тот журна́л у знако́мого америка́нца Гра́нта, но я́ не хочу́ ей говори́ть об э́том.

У Зи́ны е́сть хоро́ший прои́грыватель и мно́го пласти́нок. Она́ лю́бит наро́дные пе́сни и ста́рые рома́нсы. Сего́дня к ней зайдёт Фили́пп. О́н принесёт америка́нские пласти́нки, и они́ бу́дут слу́шать джа́з и танцева́ть.

Во́лков купи́л биле́ты в теа́тр, но Га́ля не мо́жет пойти́, она́ ве́чером рабо́тает. Во́лков говори́т, что тогда́ о́н то́же не пойдёт. О́н спра́шивает Га́лю, не зна́ет ли она́, кто́ хо́чет пойти́. Она́ отвеча́ет, что её подру́ги хоте́ли пойти́, но не доста́ли биле́тов. Она́ ду́мает, что они́ с удово́льствием ку́пят у Во́лкова э́ти биле́ты.

Пётр зашёл в клу́б послу́шать ле́кцию о ру́сских наро́дных пе́снях, но профе́ссор бы́л бо́лен и, ле́кции не́ было. Тогда́ о́н пошёл в ко́мнату, где стои́т прои́грыватель и мо́жно слу́шать пласти́нки. Там о́н встре́тил Зи́ну, и они́ до́лго вме́сте слу́шали ста́рые ру́сские рома́нсы в хоро́шем исполне́нии.

NOTES

PREPARATION FOR CONVERSATION   **На та́нцах**

уста́ть (pfv I), уста́ну, –ешь, –ут	to be tired (*or* exhausted), to get tired
Я уста́ла.	I'm tired *or* I'm exhausted.
уф!	ooh! ugh!
У́ф, уста́ла!	Ooh, I'm exhausted!
жа́рко (adj жа́ркий)	hot
Та́к жа́рко!	It's so hot!
У́ф, уста́ла! Та́к жа́рко!	Ooh, I'm exhausted! It's so hot!
отдохну́ть (pfv I), отдохну́, –ёшь, –у́т	to rest, have a rest
Отдохнём!	Let's rest! *or* We'll rest!
дава́ть (I), даю́, –ёшь, –ю́т	to give, let
дава́й! –те! (imper)	give! let's!
Дава́йте отдохнём!	Let's have a rest!
свобо́дный	free, unoccupied, vacant
Во́н та́м свобо́дные сту́лья.	Over there are some empty chairs.
впро́чем	then again, but then, however
А впро́чем, где́ Ка́тя и Воло́дя?	But then again, where are Katya and Volodya?
к (*or* ко) (*plus* dat)	toward, to
и́м (*or* ни́м) (dat of они́)	to them, for them
к ни́м	to them, to see them, to their place
Пойдём к ни́м!	Let's go see them! *or* Let's go join them!
мо́жет (*full form* мо́жет бы́ть)	maybe, perhaps
Мо́жет пойдём к ни́м?	Maybe we should join them?
предложи́ть (pfv II), предложу́, предло́жишь, –ат	to suggest, propose, offer
что́-то	something
Я хоте́л ва́м что́-то предложи́ть.	I wanted to suggest something to you.
Да́, я слу́шаю.	Yes, I'm listening.

перейти́ (pfv I), перейду́, –ёшь, –у́т	to go over, go across
перейти́ на «ты́»	to switch to "ты́," start using the familiar form of address

Дава́йте перейдём на «ты́». — Let's switch to "ты́."

Мы́ ведь уже́ хоро́шие друзья́. — We're already good friends after all.

согла́сен, согла́сна, –о, –ы	agreed, agreeable

Хорошо́, я́ согла́сна. — Fine, I'm willing.

Во́т и прекра́сно! — That's wonderful.

вы́пить (pfv I), вы́пью, вы́пьешь, вы́пьют	to drink, have a drink
на́до вы́пить	it's necessary to drink, we have to drink

За э́то на́до вы́пить! — We must drink to that!

хотя́	although
хотя́ бы	even if only, at least
лимона́д	lemonade

За э́то на́до вы́пить, хотя́ бы лимона́да. Хоти́те? — We must drink to that, even if only some lemonade. Want to?

Не «хоти́те», а «хо́чешь». — Not "вы́," "ты́." (*Lit.* Not "хоти́те," but "хо́чешь.")

забыва́ть (I), забыва́ю, –ешь, –ют	to forget

Не забыва́й, что мы́ на «ты́». — Don't forget we're using "ты́."

Не «хоти́те», а «хо́чешь». Не забыва́й, что мы́ на «ты́». — Not "вы́," "ты́." Don't forget we're using "ты́" now.

привы́кнуть (pfv I), привы́кну, –ешь, –ут (past привы́к, привы́кла, –о, –и)	to get used to, to be used to, to become accustomėd to

Я́ ещё не привы́к. — I'm not used to it yet.

Извини́, я́ ещё не привы́к. — Excuse me, I'm not used to it yet.

буфе́т	snack bar, sideboard

Пойдём в буфе́т. — Let's go to the snack bar.

SUPPLEMENT

дво́р	yard, backyard, courtyard
на дворе́	outside, outdoors, out; in the yard

Сего́дня на дворе́ о́чень жа́рко. — It's very hot out today.

свежо́	cool, chilly

На дворе́ свежо́. — It's cool outdoors *or* It's chilly out.

пого́да	weather

Кака́я сего́дня пого́да? — What's the weather today?

тепло́ (adj тёплый)	warm

Сего́дня тепло́. — It's warm today.

Сего́дня тёплая пого́да. — The weather is warm today.

хо́лодно (adj холо́дный)	cold

Сего́дня хо́лодно. — It's cold today.

Сего́дня холо́дная пого́да. — The weather is cold today.

отдыха́ть (I), отдыха́ю, –ешь, –ют	to rest, relax, vacation

Вы́ отдыха́ете? — Are you resting?

предлага́ть (I), предлага́ю, –ешь, –ют	to suggest, propose, offer
Что́ вы́ предлага́ете?	What are you suggesting?
переходи́ть (II) (*like* ходи́ть)	to go across, go over
Здесь мо́жно переходи́ть у́лицу?	Is it all right to cross the street here?
привы́чка	habit
Э́то стра́нная привы́чка.	That's a strange habit.
плохо́й	bad, poor
Э́то плоха́я привы́чка.	That's a bad habit.

На та́нцах

Зи́на 1 Уф, уста́ла! Та́к жа́рко![1]

Оле́г 2 Дава́йте отдохнём! Во́н та́м свобо́дные сту́лья.

Зи́на 3 Хорошо́! А впро́чем, где́ Ка́тя и Воло́дя? Мо́жет пойдём к ни́м?

Оле́г 4 Пойдём. Зна́ете, Зи́на, я́ хоте́л ва́м что́-то предложи́ть.

Зи́на 5 Да́, я́ слу́шаю.

Оле́г 6 Дава́йте перейдём на «ты́». Мы́ ведь уже́ хоро́шие друзья́.

Зи́на 7 Хорошо́, я́ согла́сна.

Оле́г 8 Во́т и прекра́сно! За э́то на́до вы́пить, хотя́ бы лимона́да.[2] Хоти́те?

Зи́на 9 Не «хоти́те», а «хо́чешь». Не забыва́й, что мы́ на «ты́».

Оле́г 10 Извини́, я́ ещё не привы́к.[3] Пойдём в буфе́т.[4]

NOTES

[1] Both **жа́ркий** and **горя́чий** mean *hot*, but ordinarily they are not interchangeable. In reference to weather, climate, and room temperature, only **жа́ркий** is used, for example, **Како́й жа́ркий де́нь!** *What a hot day!* **Горя́чий**, on the other hand, must be used in referring to objects or things that are hot, for example, **горя́чая вода́** *hot water*.

[2] Note that the genitive form **лимона́да** is used here. Nouns denoting divisible matter are used in the genitive case to indicate a portion of the whole amount, i.e., *some*. For example, compare **Я́ вы́пил молока́** *I drank some milk* with **Я́ вы́пил молоко́** *I drank up the milk*, i.e., all the milk. The word **лимона́д** is used by some Russians not only for *lemonade*, but for almost any soft drink.

[3] In this conversation we find two more examples of past tense verbs in Russian, both perfective, where present tense constructions are used in English:

Уф, уста́ла!	Ooh, I'm exhausted!
Я́ ещё не привы́к.	I'm not used to it yet.

[4] As used here, **буфе́т** is a snack bar or food counter with very limited fare, mostly cold. Although Khrushchev prohibited the sale of alcoholic beverages in snack bars, it is sometimes possible to obtain beer there. The word is also used to describe a cupboard or sideboard where dishes, utensils, table linens, snacks, and beverages are kept.

ша́хматы (pl only)
игра́
Игра́ в ша́хматы.
    за столо́м
Ка́жется, э́то Ка́тя и Воло́дя за столо́м.
Зи́на, смотри́: ка́жется, э́то Ка́тя и Воло́дя за столо́м.

    они́ игра́ют в ша́хматы
Да́, в ша́хматы игра́ют.

Пойдём к ни́м.

Я́ не зна́л, что ты́ игра́ешь.
Ка́тя, я́ и не зна́л, что ты́ игра́ешь.

    ещё ка́к (*or* ка́к ещё)!
И ещё ка́к!

    ма́т
    мне́ (dat of я́)
Она́ дала́ мне́ ма́т.
    два́ ра́за
Она́ два́ ра́за дала́ мне́ ма́т.

Да ну́! Э́то я́ до́лжен посмотре́ть.

    сади́ться (II), сажу́сь, сади́шься, –ятся
    вме́сто (*plus* gen)
Лу́чше ты́, Оле́г, сади́сь вме́сто меня́.

    с меня́ дово́льно
С меня́ уже́ дово́льно.

    сыгра́ть (pfv I), сыгра́ю, –ешь, –ют
    вдвоём
    почему́ бы не сыгра́ть
Почему́ бы ва́м вдвоём не сыгра́ть?
А почему́ бы ва́м, ребя́та, вдвоём не сыгра́ть?

    ва́м бу́дет ску́чно
    боя́ться (II) [bajátcə], бою́сь, бои́шься, –ятся
Бою́сь, что ва́м бу́дет ску́чно.
    пожа́луй
Пожа́луй. То́лько бою́сь, что ва́м бу́дет ску́чно.
Пожа́луй. То́лько бою́сь, что ва́м, де́вушки, бу́дет ску́чно.

chess, chessboard, chess set
game, play, playing
A game of chess.
    at the table
I guess that's Katya and Volodya at the table.
Look, Zina, I guess that's Katya and Volodya at the table.

    they're playing chess
Yes, they're playing chess.

Let's go join them!

I didn't know you play[ed].
Katya, I didn't even know you play[ed].

    and how!
And how!

    checkmate
    to me, for me
She beat me (*lit.* gave me checkmate).
    two times, twice
She beat me twice.

No kidding! That I've got to see!

    to sit down, take a seat
    instead of, in place of
You'd better sit down in my place, Oleg.

    I've had enough, I've had it
I've already had enough.

    to play, play a game
    two together
    why not play a game
Why don't you two play a game together?
Well, why don't you two boys play a game together?

    you'll be bored
    to be afraid

I'm afraid you'd be bored.
    that's an idea, I wouldn't mind, perhaps
That's an idea. But I'm afraid you'd be bored.

That's an idea. But I'm afraid you girls would be bored.

во́здух	air
све́жий	fresh, cool
на све́жий во́здух	out into fresh air
вы́йти (pfv I), вы́йду, вы́йдешь, –ут	to go out, get off (a vehicle), come out
(past вы́шел, вы́шла, –о, –и)	
Мы́ вы́йдем на све́жий во́здух.	We'll go out into the fresh air.
Мы́ вы́йдем немно́го на све́жий во́здух.	We'll go out for a bit of fresh air.
Хо́чешь, Зи́на?	Want to, Zina?
ла́дно	all right, O.K.
Ла́дно.	O.K.
приходи́ть (II) (*like* ходи́ть)	to come, arrive
на́м (dat pl of мы́)	to us, for us
Приходи́те к на́м.	Come see us *or* Come join us.
ко́нчить (pfv II), ко́нчу, –ишь, –ат	to finish
А вы́ приходи́те к на́м, когда́ ко́нчите.	And you come join us when you've finished.

SUPPLEMENT

конча́ть (I), конча́ю, –ешь, –ют	to finish
Когда́ вы́ конча́ете рабо́ту?	When do you finish working? *or* When are you through working?
и́з дому	from one's house, from home
Ва́м письмо́ и́з дому.	There's a letter for you from home.
выходи́ть (II) (*like* ходи́ть)	to go out, come out, get off (a vehicle)
О́н ре́дко выхо́дит и́з дому.	He rarely goes out of the house.
прийти́ (pfv I), приду́, –ёшь, –у́т	to come, arrive
(past пришёл, пришла́, –о́, –и́)	
Когда́ вы́ придёте к на́м?	When will you come to see us?
Ка́жется, ва́ш по́езд пришёл.	It seems your train has arrived.
гуля́ть (I), гуля́ю, –ешь, –ют	to walk (for pleasure), stroll
Вы́ ча́сто гуля́ете в па́рке?	Do you often stroll in the park?
погуля́ть (pfv I) (*like* гуля́ть)	to go for a stroll, go for a walk
Дава́йте погуля́ем.	Let's go for a walk (*or* stroll).

Игра́ в ша́хматы

З. — Зи́на	В. — Влади́мир
О. — Оле́г	К. — Ка́тя

О. 1 Зи́на, смотри́: ка́жется, э́то Ка́тя и Воло́дя за столо́м.

З. 2 Да́, в ша́хматы игра́ют.[1] Пойдём к ни́м.

О. 3 Ка́тя, я́ и не зна́л, что ты́ игра́ешь.

В. 4 И ещё ка́к! Уже́ два́ ра́за дала́ мне́ ма́т.

О. 5 Да ну! Это я должен посмотреть.

В. 6 Лучше ты, Олег, садись вместо меня. С меня уже довольно.

К. 7 А почему бы вам, ребята, вдвоём не сыграть?

О. 8 Пожалуй. Только боюсь, что вам, девушки, будет скучно.

К. 9 Нет, мы выйдем немного на свежий воздух. Хочешь, Зина?

З. 10 Ладно. А вы, ребята, приходите к нам, когда кончите.[2]

NOTES

[1] Chess has traditionally been a very popular game with Russians of all ages. The Soviet government prides itself on having the best chess players in the world. As a result of winning only second place at an international chess tournament, the government took measures to insure a crop of future champions by introducing a course in chess playing in Russian secondary schools.

[2] Notice that English often uses the present or even the past tense after *when*, whereas Russian more accurately uses the future:

Приходите к нам, **когда вы кончите.**	Come join us *when you finish* (or *when you've finished*—lit. *when you shall have finished*).

Basic sentence patterns

1. Давайте сыграем в карты.
   _____ в шахматы.
   _____ в футбол.
   _____ в теннис.
   _____ в бейсбол.
   _____ в хоккей.

Let's play a game of cards.
_____ of chess.
_____ of soccer.
_____ of tennis.
_____ of baseball.
_____ of hockey.

2. Давайте отдохнём.
   _____ перейдём на «ты».
   _____ пойдём в кино.
   _____ выпьем за это.
   _____ выйдем на свежий воздух.
   _____ сыграем в шахматы.
   _____ пойдём к ним.
   _____ пойдём в буфет.

Let's take a break *or* Let's rest a while.
____ switch to "ты."
____ go to the movies.
____ drink to that *or* Let's drink a toast to that.
____ go get some fresh air.
____ have a game of chess.
____ go join the others *or* Let's go see them.
____ go to the snack bar.

3. Я хотел вам что-то предложить.
   _____ ей _____.
   _____ им _____.
   _____ ему _____.
   Он хотел мне что-то предложить.
   _____ нам _____.

I had something I wanted to suggest to you.
_____ to her.
_____ to them.
_____ to him.
He had something he wanted to suggest to me.
_____ to us.

4. Мне́ нужна́ ка́рта Евро́пы.
    Ва́м _____.
    На́м _____.
    Тебе́ _____.
    И́м _____.
    Ему́ _____.
    Е́й _____.

I need a map of Europe.
You _____.
We _____.
You _____.
They _____.
He needs _____.
She _____.

5. Мне́ ну́жен но́вый а́тлас.
_____ слова́рь.
_____ секрета́рь.
Мне́ нужна́ но́вая продавщи́ца.
_____ ко́мната.
_____ ру́чка.
_____ тетра́дь.
Мне́ ну́жно но́вое ра́дио.
_____ перо́.
Мне́ нужны́ но́вые тетра́ди.
_____ по́лки.
_____ сту́лья.

I need a new atlas.
_____ dictionary.
_____ secretary.
I need a new saleslady.
_____ room.
_____ pen.
_____ notebook.
I need a new radio.
_____ pen [point].
I need new notebooks.
_____ shelves.
_____ chairs.

6. Мне́ хо́лодно.
____ жа́рко.
____ ску́чно.
Ва́м не хо́лодно?
_____ жа́рко?
_____ ску́чно?

I'm cold.
___ hot.
___ bored.
Aren't you cold?
_____ hot?
_____ bored?

7. Ка́к на дворе́?
— На дворе́ хорошо́.
_____ тепло́.
_____ хо́лодно.
_____ жа́рко.
_____ свежо́.

What's it like outdoors?
It's nice out.
___ warm__.
___ cold ___.
___ hot ___.
___ chilly__.

8. Ка́к сего́дня тепло́!
_____ хо́лодно!
_____ жа́рко!
_____ хорошо́!

How warm it is today!
____ cold _____!
____ hot _____!
____ nice _____!

9. Кака́я сего́дня пого́да?
— Пого́да сего́дня хоро́шая.
_____ плоха́я.
_____ тёплая.
_____ холо́дная.
_____ жа́ркая.

What's the weather like today?
The weather's nice today.
_____ bad ____.
_____ warm ___.
_____ cold ____.
_____ hot ____.

10. Ва́м письмо́ и́з дому.
_____ из Москвы́.
_____ из Ленингра́да.
_____ из Евро́пы.
_____ из Кита́я.
_____ из Аме́рики.
_____ из США.

There's a letter for you from home.
_____ from Moscow.
_____ from Leningrad.
_____ from Europe.
_____ from China.
_____ from America.
_____ from the U.S.A.

11. Я вам звони́л в час.
    _ ей _____.
    _ ему́ _____.
    Óн мне́ звони́л по́сле обе́да.
    — нам _____.
    — тебе́ _____.

    I called you at one.
    _____ her _____.
    _____ him _____.
    He called me after lunch (*or* in the afternoon).
    _____ us _____.
    _____ you _____.

12. Óн пришёл ко мне́.
    _____ к тебе́.
    _____ к нам.
    _____ к вам.
    _____ к ней.
    _____ к ним.
    Óн пришёл к себе́ домо́й.

    He came to see me.
    _____ you.
    _____ us.
    _____ you.
    _____ her.
    _____ them.
    He came back home *or* He's come home.

13. Когда́ вы ко́нчите рабо́тать?
    _____ он ко́нчит _____?
    _____ они́ ко́нчат _____?
    _____ мы ко́нчим _____?
    _____ ты ко́нчишь _____?
    _____ я ко́нчу _____?

    When will you be through working?
    ____ will he be _____?
    ____ will they be _____?
    ____ will we be _____?
    ____ will you be _____?
    ____ will I be _____?

14. Вы уже́ конча́ете обе́дать?
    Óн ___ конча́ет _____?
    Ты ___ конча́ешь _____?
    Они́ ___ конча́ют _____?
    Я уже́ конча́ю обе́дать.
    Мы ___ конча́ем _____.
    Она́ ___ конча́ет _____.

    Are you just about finished eating dinner?
    Is he _____ finished _____?
    Are you _____ finished _____?
    Are they _____ finished _____?
    I'm just about finished eating dinner.
    We're _____ finished _____.
    She's _____ finished _____.

15. Она́ даёт уро́ки англи́йского языка́.
    Они́ даю́т _____.
    Мы даём _____.
    Я даю́ _____.
    Вы даёте уро́ки ру́сского языка́?
    Óн даёт _____?
    Ты даёшь _____?

    She gives English lessons.
    They give _____.
    We give _____.
    I give _____.
    Do you give Russian lessons?
    Does he give _____?
    Do you give _____?

16. Они́ ему́ даду́т про́пуск.
    Вы _____ дади́те _____.
    Мы _____ дади́м _____.
    Ты _____ дашь _____.
    Она́ _____ даст _____.
    Я _____ дам _____.

    They'll give him a pass.
    You'll give _____.
    We'll give _____.
    You'll give _____.
    She'll give _____.
    I'll give _____.

17. Я вам дам знать.
    Óн ___ даст _____.
    Мы ___ дади́м ___.
    Они́ ___ даду́т ___.
    Вы мне́ дади́те знать?
    Ты ___ дашь _____?

    I'll let you know.
    He'll let _____.
    We'll let _____.
    They'll let _____.
    Will you let me know?
    Will you let _____?

18. Когда́ ко́нчишь, ты́ немно́го отдохнёшь?   When you finish, will you rest a bit?

_____ ко́нчите, вы́ _____ отдохнёте?   _____ you finish, will you rest ____?

Когда́ ко́нчу, я́ немно́го отдохну́.   When I finish, I'll rest a bit.

_____ ко́нчит, она́ _____ отдохнёт.   _____ she finishes, she'll rest _____.

_____ ко́нчим, мы́ _____ отдохнём.   _____ we finish, we'll rest _____.

_____ ко́нчат, они́ _____ отдохну́т.   _____ they finish, they'll rest _____.

19. Ле́том я́ отдыха́ю в Я́лте.   During the summer I vacation in Yalta.

_____ мы́ отдыха́ем ____.   _____ we vacation _____.

_____ ты́ отдыха́ешь ___.   _____ you vacation _____.

_____ они́ отдыха́ют ___.   _____ they vacation _____.

_____ вы́ отдыха́ете ____.   _____ you vacation _____.

_____ Хрущёв отдыха́ет _____.   _____ Khrushchev vacations ____.

20. Она́ к нему́ уже́ привы́кла.   She's already used to him.

____ к на́м _____.   _____ to us.

____ к ни́м _____.   _____ to them.

____ к ва́м _____.   _____ to you.

____ ко мне́ _____.   _____ to me.

____ к тебе́ _____.   _____ to you.

Pronunciation practice: final clusters with [r] or [ŗ]

A. Final clusters with [r] followed by a hard consonant.

[górp] го́рб hump	[čórt] чёрт devil	[fárs] фа́рс farce
[şérp] се́рб Serb	[óčirk] о́черк sketch, outline	[tórs] то́рс torso
[bórt] бо́рт shipboard	[párk] па́рк park	[kúrs] ку́рс course
[márt] ма́рт March	[γérx] ве́рх peak	[tórf] то́рф peat
[spírt] спи́рт alcohol, spirits	[syérx] све́рх above	[ņérf] не́рв nerve
[spórt] спо́рт sport	[mórš] мо́рж walrus	[nórm] но́рм of norms
[tórt] то́рт cake	[márš] ма́рш march	[ḍórn] дёрн turf

B. Final clusters with [ŗ] followed by a soft consonant.

Note: Although the writing system does not indicate it, the **p** preceding a soft consonant is pronounced soft.

[skóŗp] ско́рбь grief	[γéŗf] ве́рфь shipyard	[skátiŗt] ска́терть tablecloth
[ʃéŗş] фе́рзь queen (in chess)	[sṃéŗt] сме́рть death	[čétγiŗt] че́тверть quarter

C. Clusters with [r] in final position.

[ákr] áкр
acre

[žánr] жáнр
genre

[ţiátr] теáтр
theater

[métr] мéтр
meter

[aşótr] осётр
sturgeon

[litr] лúтр
liter

[smótr] смóтр
review

[céntr] цéнтр
center

[miņístr] минúстр
minister

[ţígr] тúгр
tiger

D. Clusters with [ṛ] in final position.

[şinţábṛ] сентя́брь
September

[akṭábṛ] октя́брь
October

[najábṛ] ноя́брь
November

[ḍikábṛ] декáбрь
December

[vnútṛ] внýтрь
inside

STRUCTURE AND DRILLS

The dative of ктó, чтó, the personal pronouns, and the reflexive personal pronoun себя́

NOM	КТÓ	ЧТÓ	Я	ТЫ	ÓН, ОНÓ	ОНÁ	МЫ	ВЫ	ОНÚ	(no nom)
DAT	КОМУ́	ЧЕМУ́	МНÉ	ТЕБÉ	ЕМУ́ (НЕМУ́)	ÉЙ (НÉЙ)	НÁМ	ВÁМ	ИМ (НИМ)	СЕБÉ

Notes

1. The alternate third person forms, **нему́**, **ней**, and **ним**, are used when a preposition precedes the pronoun: **к нему́**, **к ней**, and **к ни́м**.

2. The dative reflexive personal pronoun **себé** *to* (or *for*) *oneself* has no nominative. It is used when the subject and indirect object are the same: Я́ купи́л **себé** пласти́нку. (I bought a record *for myself*.)

MODELS

Я́ хотéл вáм чтó-то сказáть.
_____ ему́ _____.
_____ тебé _____.
_____ éй _____.
_____ и́м _____.

I wanted to tell you something.
_____ him _____.
_____ you _____.
_____ her _____.
_____ them _____.

Óн хотéл мнé чтó-то сказáть.
_____ нáм _____.

He wanted to tell me something.
_____ us _____.

Кому́ э́то письмо́? Мне́?
_____? Тебе́?
_____? На́м?
_____? Ва́м?
_____? Ему́?
_____? Е́й?
_____? И́м?

Who is that letter for? Me?
_____? You?
_____? Us?
_____? You?
_____? Him?
_____? Her?
_____? Them?

Я́ к ва́м приду́ в суббо́ту.
__ к нему́ _____.
__ к тебе́ _____.
__ к не́й _____.
__ к ни́м _____.

I'll come and see you on Saturday.
_____ him _____.
_____ you _____.
_____ her _____.
_____ them _____.

Приходи́те к на́м в суббо́ту.
_____ ко мне́ _____.

Come and see us on Saturday.
_____ me _____.

Я́ куплю́ ва́м э́ту пласти́нку.
_____ себе́ _____.
_____ тебе́ _____.
_____ ему́ _____.
_____ е́й _____.
_____ и́м _____.

I'll buy you this record.
_____ myself _____.
_____ you _____.
_____ him _____.
_____ her _____.
_____ them _____.

Она́ ку́пит себе́ но́вый портфе́ль.
_____ тебе́ _____.
_____ мне́ _____.
_____ на́м _____.

She'll buy herself a new briefcase.
_____ you _____.
_____ me _____.
_____ us _____.

■ CUED QUESTION-ANSWER DRILL

(you) To whom did the teacher say that?
    To you.
(вы́) Кому́ учи́тель э́то сказа́л?
    Ва́м.
(я) Кому́ учи́тель э́то сказа́л?
    Мне́.
(мы, ты, они, он, она)

■ RESPONSE DRILLS

1. *Oh, you're here already!*
   I'll bring you the paper.
   А́х, вы́ уже́ зде́сь!
   Я́ принесу́ ва́м газе́ту.
   А́х, она́ уже́ зде́сь!
   Я́ принесу́ е́й газе́ту.
      (ты, он, они, Галя, ректор)

2. *I don't know his house number.*
   He doesn't want to tell me.
   Я́ не зна́ю но́мера его́ до́ма.
   О́н мне́ не хо́чет говори́ть.
   Она́ не зна́ет но́мера его́ до́ма.
   О́н е́й не хо́чет говори́ть.
      (мы, профессор Алексеев, ты, вы,
      ректор, ребята)

3. *I wasn't home.*
   Who came to see me?
   Меня́ не́ было до́ма.
   Кто́ ко мне́ приходи́л?
   Бра́та не́ было до́ма.
   Кто́ к нему́ приходи́л?

   (нас, его, вас, девушек, тебя, певицы, их)

5. *He hasn't been to your place yet.*
   He'll come to see you.
   Он у ва́с ещё не́ был.
   Он придёт к ва́м.

4. *She's sick.*
   I'm on my way to see her.
   Она́ больна́.
   Я́ иду́ к ней.
   Мо́й това́рищ бо́лен.
   Я́ иду́ к нему́.

   (они, жена ректора, ты, секретарь, студенты, вы)

   Он у ни́х ещё не́ был.
   Он придёт к ни́м.

   (у нас, у неё, у них, у тебя, у меня, у него, у вас, у меня, у нас)

■ SUBJECT REVERSAL DRILL

1. *She bought him a present.*
   He bought her a present.
   Она́ купи́ла ему́ пода́рок.
   О́н купи́л е́й пода́рок.
   Мы́ купи́ли ему́ пода́рок.
   О́н купи́л на́м пода́рок.

   (я купи́л, ты купила, вы купили, они купили)

3. *I wrote him a letter.*
   He wrote me a letter.
   Я́ написа́л ему́ письмо́.
   О́н написа́л мне́ письмо́.
   Мы́ написа́ли ему́ письмо́.
   О́н написа́л на́м письмо́.

   (вы написали, ты написал, она написала, они написали, он написал, я написал)

2. *He'll bring her some lemonade.*
   She'll bring him some lemonade.
   О́н принесёт е́й лимона́да.
   Она́ принесёт ему́ лимона́да.
   Я́ принесу́ е́й лимона́да.
   Она́ принесёт мне́ лимона́да.

   (мы принесём, вы принесёте, они принесут, ты принесёшь, он принесёт)

The dative case in impersonal constructions

MODELS

Мне́ та́к жа́рко.	I'm so hot.
На́м _____.	We're____.
Ему́ _____.	He's ____.
Е́й _____.	She's ____.
И́м _____.	They're __.
Ва́м не жа́рко?	Aren't you hot?
Тебе́ _____?	_____ you __?
Ва́м не бу́дет ску́чно?	Won't you be bored?
Тебе́ _____?	_____ you _____?

Мне́ бу́дет ску́чно.	I'll be bored.
На́м _____.	We'll be ___.
Ему́ _____.	He'll be ___.
Е́й _____.	She'll be ___.
И́м _____.	They'll be ___.
Мне́ бы́ло хо́лодно.	I was cold.
На́м _____.	We were _____.
Ему́ _____.	He was _____.
Е́й _____.	She was _____.
И́м _____.	They were _____.
Тебе́ бы́ло хо́лодно?	Were you cold?
Ва́м _____?	_____ you ___?
Мне́ пора́ идти́.	It's time for me to be going.
На́м _____.	_____ us _____.
Заче́м ва́м спеши́ть?	What's your hurry? *or* Why should you hurry?
_____ тебе́ _____?	_____ your _____? *or* _____ you ___?
А мне́ мо́жно посмотре́ть?	May I look? *or* Is it O.K. for me to look?
___ на́м _____?	_____ we ___? *or* _____ us _____?
Мне́ та́м бы́ло хорошо́.	I was happy there *or* I felt good there.
Ему́ _____.	He _____ *or* He _____.
Мне́ хо́чется пи́ть.	I'm thirsty *or* I feel like having a drink.
На́м _____.	We're ___ *or* We _____.

■ REPETITION DRILL

Repeat the above models, noting that the person who is involved in each instance is expressed by the dative case in Russian.

■ CUED QUESTION-ANSWER DRILL

(*I*) *Who's thirsty?*
I am.
(я) Кому́ хо́чется пи́ть?
Мне́.
(она́) Кому́ хо́чется пи́ть?
Е́й.
(вы, ты, он, мы, они, я, она, вы, мы)

■ RESPONSE DRILLS

1. *We'll be dancing.*
We won't be bored.
Мы́ бу́дем танцева́ть.
На́м не бу́дет ску́чно.
Вы́ бу́дете танцева́ть.
Ва́м не бу́дет ску́чно.
(я, он, ты, она, они, он, вы, я)

2. *He went home.*
He was bored.
О́н пошёл домо́й.
Ему́ бы́ло ску́чно.
Она́ пошла́ домо́й.
Е́й бы́ло ску́чно.
(они, ты, вы, мы, я, он, ты, она)

1. *Where are you going?*
   Home. I'm bored here.
   Куда́ ты́ идёшь?
   Домо́й. Мне́ зде́сь ску́чно.
   Куда́ вы́ идёте?
   Домо́й. На́м зде́сь ску́чно.

   (он, они, мы, она, ты, вы, он)

2. *Why are you in such a hurry?*
   It's time for me to go home.
   Почему́ ты́ та́к спеши́шь?
   Мне́ пора́ домо́й.
   Почему́ о́н та́к спеши́т?
   Ему́ пора́ домо́й.

   (она, они, вы, ты, он, она, вы)

■ SUBSTITUTION DRILL

He knows that he'll be bored.
Он зна́ет, что́ ему́ бу́дет ску́чно.
Она́ зна́ет, что́ ей бу́дет ску́чно.

(мы, вы, я, они, Коля, ты, Галя, все)

■ STRUCTURE REPLACEMENT DRILLS

It's time for us to go.
It was time for us to go.
На́м пора́ идти́.
На́м пора́ бы́ло идти́.
Мне́ пора́ идти́.
Мне́ пора́ бы́ло идти́.

(ей, им, вам, нам, мне, тебе, ему, им, мне)

■ STRUCTURE REPLACEMENT DRILL

He wants to learn the results.
He's curious to know the results.
О́н хо́чет узна́ть результа́ты.
Ему́ интере́сно узна́ть результа́ты.
Мы́ хоти́м узна́ть результа́ты.
На́м интере́сно узна́ть результа́ты.

(они, ты, она, вы, я, мы, он, ты)

■ RESPONSE DRILLS

1. *I was at the flea market.*
   I found it interesting there.
   Я́ бы́л на толку́чке.
   Мне́ та́м бы́ло интере́сно.
   О́н бы́л на толку́чке.
   Ему́ та́м бы́ло интере́сно.

   (мы, она, вы, они, он, я)

2. *We danced for a long time.*
   We're hot.
   Мы́ до́лго танцева́ли.
   На́м жа́рко.
   О́н до́лго танцева́л.
   Ему́ жа́рко.

   (я, они, ты, она, вы, мы, я)

3. *You have time.*
   Why should you hurry?
   У ва́с е́сть вре́мя.
   Заче́м ва́м спеши́ть?
   У тебя́ е́сть вре́мя.
   Заче́м тебе́ спеши́ть?

   (у него, у нас, у них, у неё, у меня, у вас, у тебя, у них)

4. *We want to read.*
   May we read?
   Мы́ хоти́м чита́ть.
   На́м мо́жно чита́ть?
   О́н хо́чет чита́ть.
   Ему́ мо́жно чита́ть?

   (она, я, они, ты, вы, мы, он, я)

DISCUSSION

In impersonal constructions the dative case is used to identify the person affected or involved in the situation. Such dative constructions are especially common in conjunction with infinitives or short-form neuter adjectives ending in –o.

In the past and future, the neuter verb forms **бы́ло** and **бу́дет** are used. They usually precede the infinitive or short-form neuter adjective.

Тебе́ та́м не бу́дет интере́сно.	You won't find it interesting there.
Ему́ пора́ бы́ло идти́.	It was time for him to be going.
Мне́ бы́ло хо́лодно.	I was cold.
На́м бу́дет хо́лодно.	We'll be cold.

The dative personal referent may be omitted for a more general statement.

Жа́рко.	It's hot.
Пора́ идти́.	It's time to be going.
Мо́жно посмотре́ть?	Is it all right to look?
Ка́к интере́сно!	How interesting!

The dative case with ну́жен, нужна́, ну́жно, and нужны́

MODELS

Мне́ ну́жен а́тлас.	I need an atlas.
Мне́ ну́жен бы́л а́тлас.	I needed an atlas.
Мне́ ну́жен бу́дет а́тлас.	I'll need an atlas.
Мне́ нужна́ ка́рта Евро́пы.	I need a map of Europe.
Мне́ нужна́ была́ ка́рта Евро́пы.	I needed a map of Europe.
Мне́ нужна́ бу́дет ка́рта Евро́пы.	I'll need a map of Europe.
Мне́ ну́жно ра́дио.	I need a radio.
Мне́ ну́жно бы́ло ра́дио.	I needed a radio.
Мне́ ну́жно бу́дет ра́дио.	I'll need a radio.
Мне́ нужны́ ключи́.[1]	I need keys.
Мне́ нужны́ бы́ли ключи́.	I needed keys.
Мне́ нужны́ бу́дут ключи́.	I'll need keys.

■ REPETITION DRILL

Repeat the above models, noting the pattern in the present, past, and future.

■ CUED QUESTION-ANSWER DRILLS

1. (*I*) *Who needs an atlas?*
   I need an atlas.
   (я) Кому́ ну́жен а́тлас?
   Мне́ ну́жен а́тлас.
   (мы) Кому́ ну́жен а́тлас?
   На́м ну́жен а́тлас.
   (она́, он, мы, ты, они́, я, она́, ты)

2. (*chess set*) *What does he need?*
   He needs a chess set.
   (ша́хматы) Что́ ему́ ну́жно?
   Ему́ нужны́ ша́хматы.
   (но́ж) Что́ ему́ ну́жно?
   Ему́ ну́жен но́ж.
   (лимона́д, квита́нция, пласти́нки, бума́га, журна́л, молоко́, газе́та, каранда́ш, ру́чка)

3. (*cupboard*) *What will we need?*
   We'll need a cupboard.
   (шка́ф) Что́ на́м бу́дет ну́жно?
   На́м бу́дет ну́жен шка́ф.
   (по́лка) Что́ на́м бу́дет ну́жно?
   На́м бу́дет нужна́ по́лка.
   (ключи́, прои́грыватель, «Изве́стия», но́вое ме́сто, журна́л «Огонёк», «Вече́рняя Москва́», ша́хматы)

4. (*secretary*) *Whom did she need?*
   She needed the (or *a*) *secretary.*
   (секрета́рь) Кто́ ей бы́л ну́жен?
   Ей бы́л ну́жен секрета́рь.
   (убо́рщица) Кто́ ей бы́л ну́жен?
   Ей была́ нужна́ убо́рщица.
   (ре́ктор, продавщи́ца, това́рищ Волко́в, учи́тельница, вахтёр, Ната́ша и Зи́на, профе́ссор Орло́в)

---

[1] Some speakers stress the first syllable of the plural form: ну́жны.

1. *What dictionary does he need?*
   He needs this one.
   Какóй словáрь емý нýжен?
   Емý нýжен вóт э́тот.
   Какóй журнáл емý нýжен?
   Емý нýжен вóт э́тот.

   (пóлка, ромáн, перó, кни́га, сту́л,
   тетрáдь)

2. *Are there any cups here?*
   I need a cup.
   Тýт éсть чáшки?
   Мнé нужнá чáшка.
   Тýт éсть стакáны?
   Мнé нýжен стакáн.

   (лóжки, ножи́, ви́лки, карандаши́,
   пéрья, дóски, тетрáди)

■ RESPONSE DRILLS

1. *Here are some pencils.*
   We don't need pencils.
   Вóт карандаши́.
   Нáм карандаши́ не нужны́.
   Вóт пропускá.
   Нáм пропускá не нужны́.

   (словáрь, квитáнция, ключи́, ли́фт,
   такси́, телефóн, носи́льщики, кóфе)

2. *Oleg doesn't have an atlas.*
   Does he really need an atlas?
   У Олéга нéт áтласа.
   Рáзве емý нýжен áтлас?
   У Олéга нéт áтласов.
   Рáзве емý нужны́ áтласы?

   (нет тетрáдей, нет словарéй, нет пропускá, нет пера́, нет ключéй, нет столá,
   нет пóлки)

3. *Where can one get pencils?*
   She needs pencils.
   Гдé мóжно достáть карандаши́?
   Éй нужны́ карандаши́.
   Гдé мóжно достáть нóж?
   Éй нýжен нóж.

   (пéрья, материáл, корóбку, стóл,
   тетрáди, пóлку, словáрь, огурцы́)

4. *Where did you get paper?*
   I'll need paper.
   Гдé вы́ достáли бумáгу?
   Мнé нужнá бýдет бумáга.
   Гдé вы́ достáли кáрту Еврóпы?
   Мнé нужнá бýдет кáрта Еврóпы.

   (стол, карандаши́, пóлку, прóпуск,
   билéты, горя́чую вóду, молокó)

5. *The children got [hold of] some pencils.*
   They needed pencils.
   Ребя́та достáли карандаши́.
   И́м нужны́ бы́ли карандаши́.
   Ребя́та достáли сту́лья.
   И́м нужны́ бы́ли сту́лья.

   (стол, пóлку, кни́ги, словáрь, тетрáди,
   истóрию Китáя, кáрту Амéрики)

6. *He had no key.*
   He needed a key.
   У негó нé было ключá.
   Емý нýжен бы́л клю́ч.
   У негó нé было прóпуска.
   Емý нýжен бы́л прóпуск.

   (рубля́, копéйки, билéта, тетрáдей,
   рáдио, стакáна)

DISCUSSION

Ну́жен, нужна́, ну́жно, and нужны́ are the short forms of the long-form adjective ну́жный *necessary*. They are used in constructions where the dative indicates the person in need and the nominative indicates the thing needed: Мнé **нужна́** кáрта. (I need a map.—*Lit.* To me a map is necessary.)

In the past tense the appropriate form of бы́л, была́, бы́ло, or бы́ли is used in agreement with the short-form adjective and the noun indicating the thing needed.

Емý **нужна́** была́ кáрта.	He needed a map.
Емý **ну́жен** бы́л шофёр.	He needed a driver.
Емý **нужны́** бы́ли я́щики.	He needed some boxes.

In the future, the appropriate form of бу́дет (for singular) or бу́дут (for plural) is used with the short-form adjective.

Мне́ **нужна́ бу́дет** ка́рта.	I'll need a map.
Мне́ **нужны́ бу́дут** ка́рты.	I'll need maps.
Мне́ **ну́жно бу́дет** перо́.	I'll need a pen.

The neuter form **ну́жно** is also used in infinitive constructions.

Мне́ **ну́жно** спа́ть.	I need to sleep.
На́м **ну́жно бы́ло** спеши́ть.	We had to hurry.
Ему́ **ну́жно бу́дет** рабо́тать.	He'll need to work.

The imperfective verb дава́ть and its perfective да́ть

	дава́ть (imperfective)	да́ть (perfective)			
PAST	дава́л, дава́ла, дава́ло, дава́ли	да́л не́ дал [ɲédəl]	дала́ не дала́ [ɲidalá]	да́ло не́ дало [ɲédələ]	да́ли не́ дали [ɲédəli]
PRES	даю́, даёшь, даёт, даём, даёте, даю́т				
FUT	бу́ду дава́ть, бу́дешь дава́ть	да́м, да́шь, да́ст, дади́м, дади́те, даду́т			
IMPER	дава́й! дава́йте!	да́й! да́йте!			

MODELS

1. Imperfective verb дава́ть

О́н дава́л уро́ки ру́сского языка́.	He used to give Russian lessons.
Она́ дава́ла _____.	She used to give _____.
Мы́ дава́ли _____.	We used to give _____.
Я́ даю́ уро́ки англи́йского языка́.	I give English lessons.
Ты́ даёшь _____.	You give _____.
О́н даёт _____.	He gives _____.
Мы́ даём _____.	We give _____.
Вы́ даёте _____.	You give _____.
Они́ даю́т _____.	They give _____.
Я́ бу́ду дава́ть уро́ки ру́сского языка́.	I'll be giving Russian lessons.
Ты́ бу́дешь _____.	You'll be giving _____.
О́н бу́дет _____.	He'll be giving _____.
Мы́ бу́дем _____.	We'll be giving _____.
Вы́ бу́дете _____.	You'll be giving _____.
Они́ бу́дут _____.	They'll be giving _____.
Не дава́й и́м так мно́го воды́!	Don't give them so much water!
Не дава́йте _____!	Don't give _____!

2. Perfective verb да́ть

О́н мне́ да́л ключи́.	He gave me the keys.
О́н мне́ не́ дал ключе́й.	He didn't give me the keys.
Она́ мне́ дала́ ключи́.	She gave me the keys.
Она́ мне́ не дала́ ключе́й.	She didn't give me the keys.
Они́ мне́ да́ли ключи́.	They gave me the keys.
Они́ мне́ не́ дали ключе́й.	They didn't give me the keys.

Я́ ему́ да́м пя́ть рубле́й.	I'll give him five rubles.
Ты́ ____ да́шь _____.	You'll give _____.
Она́ ____ да́ст _____.	She'll give _____.
Мы́ ____ дади́м _____.	We'll give _____.
Вы́ ____ дади́те _____.	You'll give _____.
Они́ ____ даду́т _____.	They'll give _____.

Да́й мне́ э́ту кни́гу!	Give me that book!
Да́йте _____!	Give _____!

■ REPETITION DRILL

Repeat the above models, noting that the perfective verb да́ть has an irregular future. Note also that the imperfective verb дава́ть has a present tense based on an alternate form of the stem without –ва–.

■ STRUCTURE REPLACEMENT DRILLS

1. *I'll give [private] lessons.*
   I give [private] lessons.
   Я́ бу́ду дава́ть уро́ки.
   Я́ даю́ уро́ки.
   О́н бу́дет дава́ть уро́ки.
   О́н даёт уро́ки.
   (мои́ това́рищи, моя́ подру́га, мы, э́тот учи́тель, ты, я, э́ти де́вушки, вы, мой друг)

2. *Don't give him the key!*
   Give him the key!
   Не дава́й ему́ ключа́!
   Да́й ему́ клю́ч!
   Не дава́й е́й ры́бы!
   Да́й е́й ры́бу!
   Не дава́й и́м биле́тов!
   Не дава́й ему́ но́мера телефо́на!
   Не дава́й и́м словаря́!
   Не дава́й е́й пропуска́!
   Не дава́й ему́ а́тласа!

3. *I give singing lessons.*
   I used to give singing lessons.
   Я́ даю́ уро́ки пе́ния.
   Я́ дава́л уро́ки пе́ния.
   Мы́ даём уро́ки пе́ния.
   Мы́ дава́ли уро́ки пе́ния.
   (она́, они́, он, вы, мы)

4. *She gave him ten rubles.*
   She'll give him ten rubles.
   Она́ дала́ ему́ де́сять рубле́й.
   Она́ да́ст ему́ де́сять рубле́й.
   Я́ да́л ему́ де́сять рубле́й.
   Я́ да́м ему́ де́сять рубле́й.
   (я дала́, мы да́ли, они́ да́ли, вы да́ли, ты дала́, профессор Семёнов да́л, америка́нцы да́ли)

5. *She'll give him the tickets.*
   She gave him the tickets.
   Она́ да́ст ему́ биле́ты.
   Она́ дала́ ему́ биле́ты.
   Я́ да́м ему́ биле́ты.
   Я́ да́л ему́ биле́ты.
   (вахтёрша, мы, Ма́ша, певцы́, вы, она́, Алексе́ев)

6. *The teacher let him talk.*
   The teacher didn't let him talk.
   Учи́тель да́л ему́ говори́ть.
   Учи́тель не́ дал ему́ говори́ть.
   Она́ дала́ ему́ говори́ть.
   Она́ не дала́ ему́ говори́ть.

   (Орлов, мы, девушка, учителя, брат,
   сестра, Олег, жена)

7. *I placed an ad in the paper.*
   I'll place an ad in the paper.
   Я́ да́л объявле́ние в газе́ту.
   Я́ да́м объявле́ние в газе́ту.
   Мы́ да́ли объявле́ние в газе́ту.
   Мы́ дади́м объявле́ние в газе́ту.

   (вы, учитель, ты, этот человек, моя
   подруга, американцы, я, эта женщина,
   мы)

■ QUESTION-ANSWER DRILL

Does Kozlov have the atlas?
No, he gave it to me.
А́тлас у Козло́ва?
Не́т, о́н да́л его́ мне́.
А́тлас у ни́х?
Не́т, они́ да́ли его́ мне́.

   (у Коли, у неё, у Ирины, у него,
   у учительницы, у учителей, у Гали)

■ RESPONSE DRILL

He has a dictionary.
He'll give them the dictionary.
У него́ е́сть слова́рь.
О́н и́м да́ст слова́рь.
У меня́ е́сть слова́рь.
Я́ и́м да́м слова́рь.

   (у нас, у неё, у тебя, у меня, у вас, у них,
   у него, у нас)

DISCUSSION

The perfective verb **да́ть** has an irregular future which must be memorized: **да́м, да́шь, да́ст, дади́м, дади́те, даду́т.** Its imperative is **да́й! да́йте!** Its imperfective counterpart **дава́ть** has a present tense based on the stem [daj–]: **даю́, даёшь, даёт, даём, даёте, даю́т.**

The other forms of **дава́ть**, including the past tense, infinitive, and imperative are based on the longer stem [davá–]: **дава́л, дава́ть, дава́й.** All verbs with infinitives ending in –**ава́ть** follow this same pattern, for example, **продава́ть** *to sell*, **узнава́ть** *to recognize*, **сознава́ть** *to realize.*

Suggestions that include the speaker: part I—perfective verbs

MODELS

Пойдём в суббо́ту в клу́б!
Дава́й пойдём _____!
Дава́йте пойдём _____!

Вы́йдем немно́го на све́жий во́здух!
Дава́й вы́йдем _____!
Дава́йте вы́йдем _____!

Зайдём к ни́м!
Дава́й зайдём _____!
Дава́йте зайдём ____!

Отдохнём!
Дава́й отдохнём!
Дава́йте _____!

Let's go to the club on Saturday!
Let's go _____!
Let's go _____!

Let's go out and get a bit of fresh air!
Let's go out _____!
Let's go out _____!

Let's drop in on them!
Let's drop in _____!
Let's drop in _____!

Let's take a break! *or* Let's rest a bit!
Let's take _____! *or* Let's rest ____!
Let's take _____! *or* Let's rest ____!

Поговори́м об э́том де́ле!	Let's talk a bit about this matter!
Дава́й поговори́м _____!	Let's talk _____!
Дава́йте поговори́м ____!	Let's talk _____!
Сыгра́ем в ша́хматы!	Let's play a game of chess!
Дава́й сыгра́ем ____!	Let's play _____!
Дава́йте сыгра́ем __!	Let's play _____!

■ REPETITION DRILL

Repeat the above models, noting that either the first person plural perfective verb alone, or the verb combined with **дава́й** (familiar) or **дава́йте** (plural-polite) can be used. **Дава́й(те)** makes the suggestion more tentative and is somewhat comparable to English *How about it?* or *What do you say?*

■ STRUCTURE REPLACEMENT DRILLS

1. *We'll go to the park.*
   Let's go to the park!
   Мы́ пойдём в па́рк.
   Пойдём в па́рк!
   Мы́ подождём о́коло кио́ска.
   Подождём о́коло кио́ска!
   Мы́ забу́дем об этом.
   Мы́ зайдём в буфе́т.
   Мы́ посмо́трим в словаре́.
   Мы́ ку́пим этот материа́л.
   Мы́ оста́вим ему́ ключи́.
   Мы́ пойдём в кино́.

2. *We bought a dictionary.*
   Let's buy a dictionary!
   Мы́ купи́ли слова́рь.
   Ку́пим слова́рь!
   Мы́ поду́мали об этом.
   Поду́маем об э́том!
   Мы́ откры́ли окно́.
   Мы́ сыгра́ли в ша́хматы.
   Мы́ поговори́ли об э́том де́ле.
   Мы́ предложи́ли ему́ рабо́ту.
   Мы́ подожда́ли на углу́.
   Мы́ оста́вили ключи́ на столе́.
   Мы́ вы́пили лимона́да.

3. *Let's buy them a present!*
   Let's buy them a present, how about it?
   Ку́пим и́м пода́рок!
   Дава́й ку́пим и́м пода́рок.
   Поговори́м об э́том!
   Дава́й поговори́м об э́том.
   Пойдём отдохнём!
   Ко́нчим э́ту рабо́ту!
   Принесём сто́л!
   Прочита́ем объявле́ние!
   Зайдём в комиссио́нный магази́н!
   Оста́вим э́тот разгово́р!

4. *I want to go to the theater.*
   How about (us) going to the theater?
   Я́ хочу́ пойти́ в теа́тр.
   Дава́йте пойдём в теа́тр.
   Я́ хочу́ отдохну́ть.
   Дава́йте отдохнём.
   Я́ хочу́ вы́йти на све́жий во́здух.
   Я́ хочу́ спроси́ть об э́том.
   Я́ хочу́ подожда́ть.
   Я́ хочу́ поговори́ть.
   Я́ хочу́ пойти́ на та́нцы.
   Я́ хочу́ зайти́ в э́то зда́ние.

■ QUESTION-ANSWER DRILLS

1. *Well, how about the movies, shall we go?*
   O.K., let's go!
   Ну́, ка́к насчёт кино́, пойдём?
   Ла́дно, пойдём!
   Ну, ка́к насчёт кни́ги, ку́пим?
   Ла́дно, ку́пим!
   Ну, ка́к насчёт обе́да, пообе́даем?

   Ну, ка́к насчёт о́черка, напи́шем?
   Ну, ка́к насчёт ча́я, вы́пьем?
   Ну, ка́к насчёт рабо́ты, ко́нчим?
   Ну, ка́к насчёт пласти́нок, послу́шаем?
   Ну, ка́к насчёт биле́тов, возьмём?
   Ну, ка́к насчёт костю́мов, зака́жем?

2. *Want to go to the club Saturday?*
   O.K., let's go!
   Хоти́те пойти́ в суббо́ту в клуб?
   Хорошо́, дава́йте пойдём!
   Хоти́те немно́го отдохну́ть?
   Хорошо́, дава́йте отдохнём!

Хоти́те с не́й поговори́ть?
Хоти́те зайти́ к ни́м?
Хоти́те сыгра́ть в ша́хматы?
Хоти́те замо́лвить за ни́х слове́чко?
Хоти́те посмотре́ть э́тот фи́льм?
Хоти́те войти́ в за́л?

■ RESPONSE DRILLS

1. *Let's take a cab!*
   O.K., let's!
   Дава́йте возьмём такси́.
   Хорошо́, возьмём!
   Дава́йте перейдём на «ты».
   Хорошо́, перейдём!
   Дава́йте напи́шем ему́ письмо́.
   Дава́йте подождём авто́буса.
   Дава́йте отдохнём в па́рке.
   Дава́йте зака́жем биле́ты.
   Дава́йте послу́шаем ру́сские пе́сни.
   Дава́йте пойдём пообе́даем.
   Дава́йте вы́пьем лимона́да.

2. *I have to go to Kiev.*
   Me too. Let's go together!
   Я до́лжен пое́хать в Ки́ев.
   Я то́же. Дава́й пое́дем вме́сте!
   Я до́лжен написа́ть сочине́ние.
   Я то́же. Дава́й напи́шем вме́сте!
   Я до́лжен пойти́ в библиоте́ку.
   Я до́лжен спроси́ть об экза́менах.
   Я до́лжен зайти́ в магази́н.
   Я до́лжен вы́йти на све́жий во́здух.
   Я до́лжен попроси́ть его́ об э́том.
   Я до́лжен подожда́ть това́рища.
   Я до́лжен прочита́ть газе́ту.

3. *I'm going to go to the flea market.*
   Let's go together!
   Я пойду́ на толку́чку.
   Пойдём вме́сте!
   Я закажу́ биле́ты.
   Зака́жем вме́сте!

Я пообе́даю в столо́вой.
Я и́х подожду́.
Я послу́шаю пласти́нки.
Я посмотрю́ журна́л «Аме́рика».
Я погуля́ю в па́рке.
Я зайду́ на по́чту.

DISCUSSION

Most suggestions that include the speaker are expressed using the perfective form of the verb. The basic form is the subjectless first person plural verb.

In informal spoken Russian, however, дава́й or дава́йте often precedes the first person plural form: дава́й for addressing ты and дава́йте for addressing вы. Use of дава́й or дава́йте ▇▇ only adds an informal tone, but makes the suggestion more tentative and open to discussion. It is somewhat comparable to English suggestions prefaced by: *What [do you] say we . . . ? How about (us) . . . ? Why don't we . . . ?*

Compare	Послу́шаем пласти́нки.	Let's listen to records!
with	Дава́й послу́шаем пласти́нки.	What do you say we listen to records?

The unstressed suffix –те may also be added to the first person plural form of a few verbs, mostly verbs of motion. It makes the suggestion more formal and polite.

Пойдёмте в кино́.	Let's go to the movies! *or* Shall we go to the movies?
Вы́йдемте на све́жий во́здух.	Let's go out for some fresh air! *or* Shall we go out for some fresh air?

The subjectless first person plural of a very few imperfective verbs may also be used in making suggestions: идём, е́дем *let's be on our way! let's go!*

Adverbs and short-form neuter adjectives ending in -o

Óн споко́йный челове́к.	He's a quiet person.
Óн споко́йно рабо́тает.	He works quietly.
Э́то непра́вильный отве́т.	This is an incorrect answer.
Вы́ непра́вильно отве́тили.	You answered incorrectly.
Э́то неудо́бные сту́лья.	These are uncomfortable chairs.
На ни́х неудо́бно сиде́ть.	It's uncomfortable sitting on them.
Э́то просты́е слова́.	These are simple words.
И́х про́сто писа́ть.	They're simple to write.
Э́то тру́дная игра́.	This is a difficult game.
В неё тру́дно игра́ть.	It's difficult to play it.
Э́то ску́чный рома́н.	This is a boring novel.
Его́ ску́чно чита́ть.	It's boring reading it.
Э́то дорога́я ве́щь.	This is an expensive thing.
Она́ до́рого сто́ит.	It costs a lot (*lit.* dearly).
Э́то лёгкий язы́к.	This is an easy language.
Его́ легко́ учи́ть.	It's easy to learn.
Óн хоро́ший студе́нт.	He's a good student.
Óн хорошо́ рабо́тает.	He works well.

■ REPETITION DRILL

Repeat the given models, noting that short-form neuter adjectives and adverbs may be formed by dropping the long-form adjective endings and adding –o. Observe that sometimes the stress may differ. Compare **хоро́ший** with **хорошо́**, and **плохо́й** with **пло́хо**.

■ STRUCTURE REPLACEMENT DRILLS

1. *He lives quietly.*
   He's a quiet person.
   Óн споко́йно живёт.
   Óн споко́йный челове́к.
   Óн про́сто живёт.
   Óн просто́й челове́к.
   (странно, скучно, интересно, свободно)

2. *It was a warm day today.*
   Today was warm.
   Сего́дня бы́л тёплый де́нь.
   Сего́дня бы́ло тепло́.
   Сего́дня бы́л хоро́ший де́нь.
   Сего́дня бы́ло хорошо́.
   (холодный, жаркий, отличный, прекрасный, трудный, скучный, плохой)

3. *Tomorrow will be warm.*
   It'll be a warm day tomorrow.
   За́втра бу́дет тепло́.
   За́втра бу́дет тёплый де́нь.
   За́втра бу́дет жа́рко.
   За́втра бу́дет жа́ркий де́нь.
   (холодно, неплохо, хорошо, тепло, жарко)

4. *I have a quiet room.*
   I feel peaceful there.
   У меня́ споко́йная ко́мната.
   Мне́ та́м споко́йно.
   У меня́ плоха́я ко́мната.
   Мне́ та́м пло́хо.
   (хорошая, тёплая, холодная, неудобная, неплохая)

5. *He's an excellent secretary.*
   He does excellent work. (Lit. *He works excellently.*)
   Óн отли́чный секрета́рь.
   Óн отли́чно рабо́тает.
   Óн хоро́ший секрета́рь.
   Óн хорошо́ рабо́тает.
   (плохо́й, прекра́сный, неплохо́й, хоро́ший, отли́чный)

6. *This is so boring!*
   This is such a boring essay!
   Э́то та́к ску́чно!
   Э́то тако́й ску́чный о́черк!
   Э́то та́к интере́сно!
   Э́то тако́й интере́сный о́черк!
   (так хорошо́, так стра́нно, так пло́хо, так ску́чно, так интере́сно)

7. *That's an interesting business* (or *affair*).
   That's interesting.
   Э́то интере́сное де́ло.
   Э́то интере́сно.
   Э́то плохо́е де́ло.
   Э́то пло́хо.
   (ску́чное, просто́е, лёгкое, тру́дное, стра́нное)

ЧТЕ́НИЕ И ПИСЬМО́

В клу́бе бы́ло о́чень жа́рко. Зи́на и Оле́г до́лго танцева́ли, и она́ уста́ла. Оле́г предложи́л ей сту́л, но Зи́на не хоте́ла сиде́ть, она́ хоте́ла вы́йти на све́жий во́здух.

Ко́ля и Воло́дя хорошо́ игра́ют в ша́хматы. Они́ ча́сто хо́дят в клу́б игра́ть, но сего́дня там кино́. Идёт ста́рый фи́льм „Челове́к из рестора́на." Они́ хотя́т его́ посмотре́ть.

Сего́дня они́ не игра́ли в ша́хматы. Ка́тя о́чень уста́ла, ей жа́рко. Она́ хо́чет вы́пить воды́. Влади́мир говори́т, что принесёт ей лимонада. В буфете очередь; ему надо немного подождать. Катя берёт „Огонёк" и читает.

Зина опять забыла, что она и Олег на „ты" и сказала ему: „Дайте мне вашу книгу." Олег просит её не забывать, что они на „ты". Ему, конечно, тоже трудно помнить это, но всё-таки он молодец и не забывает, как Зина.

Вечером Нина и Семён идут в кино, а сейчас им надо отдохнуть. Вот они взяли в библиотеке книги и журналы, сидят и читают. А за столом у окна студент и студентка играют в шахматы. Ей, кажется, скучно, и она часто смотрит в окно. Наверно, студент скоро даст ей мат.

Николай голоден, ему давно пора идти обедать, но надо кончить работу. Ему трудно кончить её. Вчера Галя была здесь, и они вместе работали, а сегодня её нет. Он сделал ошибку, а где — не знает. Теперь он сидит и ищет эту ошибку. Вот досада!

Олег спросил меня о Хитрове, и когда я сказал, что Хитров болен, он позвонил ему. К телефону подошла жена Хитрова и сказала, что он уже вполне здоров и работает. Олег хочет вечером зайти к нему и поговорить о работе.

Нина не ожидала встретить Козлова в клубе. Она не знала, что он часто ходит туда. Ей интересно, что он там делает. Может быть пьёт? Нет, конечно. В клубе не пьют. Там играют в шахматы, слушают музыку, иногда танцуют. Козлов говорит ей, что часто играет в шахматы вон там, за этим столом. Он спрашивает, не хочет ли Зина посмотреть, как он и товарищ будут играть. Но она говорит, что ей будет скучно, она не играет и не понимает этой игры.

— Не хочется сегодня обедать дома.
— А я как раз хотел предложить тебе пойти в ресторан.
— С удовольствием. В какой?
— Здесь на углу есть хороший.
— Я знаю. Я там раз была.
— Так пойдём туда, хорошо?
— Хорошо.

— Хо́чешь, пойдём вме́сте в библиоте́ку?

— А что́ тебе́ та́м ну́жно взя́ть?

— Рома́н «На́ши знако́мые».

— У меня́ есть э́тот рома́н. Хо́чешь, я тебе́ да́м?

— А тебе́ он не ну́жен?

— Не́т, я его́ уже́ чита́л.

— Вы́ уже́ сказа́ли ре́ктору обо мне́?

— Не́т, ещё не говори́л. Я хоте́л предложи́ть ва́м пойти́ к нему́ вме́сте.

— Ва́м ка́жется, что та́к бу́дет лу́чше? Я́ немно́го бою́сь его́.

— Ну что́ вы́! Он о́чень просто́й и ми́лый челове́к. Пойдёмте!

— Ва́м не ску́чно сиде́ть всё вре́мя до́ма?

— Не́т, я слу́шаю му́зыку.

— Стра́нно, что вы́ лю́бите сиде́ть во́т та́к, слу́шать му́зыку и ничего́ не де́лать. Я та́к не могу́.

— Зна́чит, вы́ не лю́бите му́зыку. Заче́м ва́м тогда́ ва́ш прои́грыватель?

— Пра́вда, он мне́ не ну́жен. Хоти́те, я ва́м его́ да́м?

— Спаси́бо.

— То́лько он о́чень ста́рый.

— Э́то ничего́.

— Га́ля, что́ ты́ ду́маешь о Петро́ве?

— Никола́е и́ли Оле́ге?

— Я его́ и́мени не зна́ю. Ви́дела то́лько два́ ра́за. У него́ си́ние глаза́.

— Зна́чит, э́то Оле́г. Я его́ ви́жу ка́ждый де́нь на ле́кциях.

— Я хоте́ла с ни́м познако́миться.

— Я могу́ тебя́ познако́мить. То́лько бою́сь, что тебе́ бу́дет с ни́м ску́чно. Он всё вре́мя что́-то чита́ет и да́же, ка́жется, пи́шет стихи́.

— Э́то интере́сно. Познако́мь на́с, пожалуйста.

— Хорошо́.

— Интере́сно смотре́ть, ка́к они́ игра́ют, пра́вда?

— Вы́ зна́ете э́ту игру́, во́т ва́м и интере́сно, а я ничего́ не понима́ю, и мне́ ску́чно.

— Тогда́ почему́ бы ва́м не взя́ть журна́л? Во́т после́дний но́мер «Огонька́», хоти́те?

— Спаси́бо, я с удово́льствием посмотрю́.

— Та́м, кста́ти, есть о́черк об Аме́рике.

— Смотри́те, во́т проводни́к. Скажи́те ему́.

— Сейча́с. Проводни́к! Я проси́ла в ка́ссе да́ть мне́ ни́жнее ме́сто. Наверху́ мне́ неудо́бно спа́ть.

— Но ва́м да́ли ве́рхнее, и я ничего́ не могу́ сде́лать. Мо́жет бы́ть, э́тот граждани́н мо́жет спа́ть наверху́.

— Коне́чно, могу́. Мину́тку, я сейча́с возьму́ свои́ ве́щи. Во́т, пожа́луйста.

— Спаси́бо.

NOTES

Поéдем к нáм на канѝкулы

канѝкулы, канѝкул (pl only)
на канѝкулы

Поéдем к нáм на канѝкулы.
плáн
Какѝе у вáс плáны на канѝкулы?

покá
никакóй
Покá никакѝх.

А у вáс какѝе плáны?

родѝтели, –ей
Мы éздим к родѝтелям.
колхóз
Мы éздим к родѝтелям в колхóз.
мы с брáтом
Мы с брáтом éздим к родѝтелям в
колхóз.
обы́чный (adv обы́чно)
Мы с брáтом обы́чно éздим к родѝтелям в
колхóз.

отсю́да
киломéтр
пятьдеся́т [piḍḍiṣát]
Э́то пятьдеся́т киломéтров отсю́да.

пригласѝть (pfv II), приглашу́,
приглáсишь, –я́т
Мы ду́мали вáс пригласѝть.

далёкий (adv далекó)
Пятьдеся́т киломéтров — э́то далекó.
Спасѝбо. Но пятьдеся́т киломéтров — э́то
далекó.

vacation
on (*or* for) a vacation, to spend a
vacation
Let's go to our place on our vacation.
plan; map (of city)
What plans do you have for vacation?

for the time being, meanwhile, while
not . . . any, none at all
None at all for the time being.

And what plans do you have?

parents
We go to see our parents.
kolkhoz, collective farm, village
We go to the kolkhoz to see our parents.
my brother and I
My brother and I go to the kolkhoz to see
our parents.
usual, usually
My brother and I usually go to the kolkhoz
to see our parents.

from here, hence
kilometer, three-fifths of a mile
fifty
It's fifty kilometers from here.

to invite

We thought of inviting you.

far, far away, distant
Fifty kilometers is a long way off.
Thanks, but fifty kilometers is a long way
off.

разрешéние	permissiom, authorization, permit
Мнé не дадýт разрешéния.	They won't give me a permit.
нельзя́	[it's] impossible, one can't, one must not
иностра́нец, –нца	foreigner
Иностра́нцам нельзя́ свобóдно éздить.	[It's] impossible for foreigners to travel freely.
по (*plus* dat)	about, to (different places), in, via, along, around, through, up and down
страна́, –ы́; стра́ны, стра́н	country
Иностра́нцам нельзя́ свобóдно éздить по странé.	Foreigners can't travel about the country freely.
Я́ и забы́ла, что иностра́нцам нельзя́ свобóдно éздить по странé.	I forgot that foreigners can't travel about the country freely.
жа́ль	too bad, pity, sorry
Да́, óчень жа́ль.	Yes, it's really too bad *or* I'm very sorry.
Я́ ва́ших колхóзов ещё не ви́дел.	I haven't seen your kolkhozes yet.
Я́ ведь ва́ших колхóзов ещё не ви́дел.	After all, I haven't seen your kolkhozes yet.
сни́мок, –мка	snapshot, picture
У меня́ éсть мнóго сни́мков.	I have a lot of snapshots.
У меня́ éсть мнóго сни́мков на́шего колхóза.	I have a lot of snapshots of our kolkhoz.
Послýшайте, у меня́ éсть мнóго сни́мков на́шего колхóза.	Listen, I have a lot of snapshots of our kolkhoz.
показа́ть (pfv I) (*like* сказа́ть)	to show
Хоти́те, покажý?	I'll show [them to you if] you like (*lit.* You want, I'll show).
Да́, пожа́луйста.	Yes, please do.
цветнóй	colored, in color
нéкоторый	some, certain
Ó, нéкоторые да́же цветны́е!	Oh, some are even in color!
снима́ть (I), снима́ю, –ешь, –ют	to take off, take (a picture)
са́м, –а́, –ó, са́ми	oneself
Вы́ са́ми снима́ли?	Did you take them yourself?
аппара́т	apparatus, camera
Да́, у меня́ нóвый аппара́т.	Yes, I have a new camera.
Зóркий	Zorky (name of camera)
Да́, у меня́ нóвый аппара́т «Зóркий».	Yes, I have a new Zorky camera.
вы́шел, вы́шла, –о, –и (past tense of вы́йти)	
Сни́мки óчень неплóхо вы́шли.	The pictures came out very well.
поря́док, –дка	order, arrangement, sequence
по поря́дку	in succession, in sequence, one by one
Дава́йте смотрéть по поря́дку.	Let's take them one by one.

в поря́дке	in order, all right, O.K.
Всё в поря́дке?	Is everything all right?
бли́зкий (adv бли́зко)	near, close
бли́зко от	close to, near
Вы живёте совсе́м бли́зко	You live quite close to us.
от на́с.	
недалеко́	close, near, not far
Мы живём недалеко́ от го́рода.	We live close to (or not far from) town.
приглаша́ть (I)	to invite
Они́ обы́чно приглаша́ют меня́	They usually invite me to their place
к себе́ на кани́кулы.	for vacation.
ми́ля, –и; –и, миль	mile
Ско́лько ми́ль отсю́да до	How many miles is it from here to the
вокза́ла?	station?
отту́да	from there
Ско́лько киломе́тров отту́да	How many kilometers is it from there to
до Москвы́?	Moscow?

Пое́дем к на́м на кани́кулы

Г. — Га́ля   Ф. — Фили́пп

Г. 1 Фили́пп, каки́е у ва́с пла́ны на кани́кулы?

Ф. 2 Пока́ никаки́х. А у ва́с?

Г. 3 Мы с бра́том обы́чно е́здим к роди́телям в колхо́з. Это пятьдеся́т киломе́тров отсю́да.[1] Ду́мали ва́с пригласи́ть.

Ф. 4 Спаси́бо, но пятьдеся́т киломе́тров — э́то далеко́. Мне́ не даду́т разреше́ния.[2]

Г. 5 Я и забы́ла, что иностра́нцам нельзя́ свобо́дно е́здить по стране́.

Ф. 6 Да́, о́чень жа́ль. Я ведь ва́ших колхо́зов ещё не ви́дел.

Г. 7 Послу́шайте, у меня́ е́сть мно́го сни́мков на́шего колхо́за. Хоти́те, покажу́?

Ф. 8 Да́, пожа́луйста. О́, не́которые да́же цветны́е! Вы́ са́ми снима́ли?

Г. 9 Да́, у меня́ но́вый аппара́т «Зо́ркий».[3]

Ф. 10 Сни́мки о́чень непло́хо вы́шли. Дава́йте смотре́ть по поря́дку.

NOTES

[1] **Колхо́з** is derived from **коллекти́вное хозя́йство** *collective farm*. The word **колхо́з** has almost entirely replaced the old word **дере́вня**, in the sense of *village*. Russian villages usually consist of one long street lined with wooden huts on both sides. Behind each hut is a small garden patch and, as a rule, a small, log bathhouse.

² Exchange students in the U.S.S.R. can travel within a thirty-kilometer radius from the city where they live; to travel farther, they must apply for a special permit. It is unlikely that such a permit would be granted to visit a collective farm.

³ The Zorky is a German-made camera and is very popular in the U.S.S.R. In Russian **зо́ркий** means *sharp-sighted* or *vigilant*.

PREPARATION FOR CONVERSATION	Га́ля пока́зывает Фили́ппу сни́мки
пока́зывать (I)	to show
Га́ля пока́зывает Фили́ппу сни́мки.	Galya shows Philip snapshots.
о́бщий, –ая, –ее, –ие	general, over-all, common
вид	view, aspect
Вот о́бщий вид.	Here's an over-all view.
по́ле, –я; поля́, –е́й	field
Вот о́бщий вид: тут поля́.	Here's an over-all view: over here are the fields.
колхо́зный	kolkhoz, collective farm (adj)
Вот о́бщий вид: тут колхо́зные поля́.	Here's an over-all view: over here are the kolkhoz fields.
о́зеро, –а; озёра, озёр	lake
лес, –а; леса́, –о́в	forest, wood(s)
вдали́	in the distance
Тут поля́, а вдали́ лес и о́зеро.	Over here are the fields, and in the distance the woods and the lake.
ви́ден, видна́, ви́дно, видны́	visible, can be seen
Вдали́ видны́ лес и о́зеро.	In the distance the woods and the lake can be seen.
Вот о́бщий вид: тут поля́, а вдали́ видны́ лес и о́зеро.	Here's an over-all view: over here are fields and in the distance you can see the woods and the lake.
изба́, –ы́; и́збы, изб	village house, hut, cottage, farmhouse
А вот на́ша изба́.	And here is our house.
деревя́нный	wooden, made of wood
О, деревя́нная?!	Oh, made of wood?
А э́то что́ на у́лице?	And what's that in the street?
коло́дец, –дца	well
Э́то коло́дец.	That's the well.
водопрово́д	running water, plumbing
У на́с не́т водопрово́да.	We don't have running water.

338   LESSON 15

ведро́, –а́; вёдра, вёдер
вёдрами
носи́ть (II), ношу́, но́сишь, –ят
На́до во́ду носи́ть вёдрами.

представля́ть себе́ (I)
ина́че (*or* и́наче)
Я́ ина́че представля́л себе́
колхо́з.
А я́, зна́ете, ина́че представля́л
себе́ колхо́з.

ка́менный
Вы́ ду́мали, наве́рно, дома́
ка́менные, да́?
электри́чество
Вы́ ду́мали, наве́рно: дома́
ка́менные, электри́чество, да́?

стро́ить (II), стро́ю, –ишь, –ят
Тепе́рь стро́ят дома́.
Тепе́рь стро́ят дома́ для
колхо́зников.
Я́ чита́л в «Огоньке́», каки́е
тепе́рь стро́ят дома́ для
колхо́зников.
Да́. Я́ по́мню чита́л в «Огоньке́»,
каки́е тепе́рь стро́ят дома́
для колхо́зников.

А́, зна́ю.
тури́ст
Таки́е пока́зывают тури́стам.
А́, зна́ю. Таки́е пока́зывают тури́стам.

семья́, –и́; се́мьи, семе́й
Во́т ту́т вся́ на́ша семья́.
Во́т ту́т вся́ на́ша семья́ за столо́м.
фо́то (*indecl n*)
А на э́том фо́то вся́ на́ша семья́ за
столо́м.

висе́ть (II), виси́т, вися́т
ико́на
У ва́с, я́ ви́жу, ико́ны вися́т.

Бо́г, –а
ве́рить (II) (*plus* dat)
ве́рить в (*plus* acc)
Ра́зве вы́ ве́рите в Бо́га?

Мы́ с бра́том не ве́рим.

pail, bucket
by (*or* in) pails, in (*or* by) buckets
to carry
We have to carry water in buckets *or* Water
  has to be carried in buckets.

to imagine, envisage, picture
otherwise, differently
I imagined the kolkhoz would be
  different.
You know, I imagined the kolkhoz
  would be different.

stone, brick
You probably thought the houses would be
  brick, didn't you?
electricity, lights
You probably thought the houses would
  be brick and [that] there'd be electricity,
  didn't you?

to build, construct
They're building houses now.
They're building houses now for farmers.

I read in *Ogonyok* the kind of houses
  they're building now for farmers.

Yes, I remember reading in *Ogonyok* [about]
  the kind of houses they're building now
  for farmers.

Oh yes, I know.
tourist
That's the kind they show to tourists.
Oh yes, I know. That's the kind they show
  to tourists.

family
Here is our whole family.
Here is our whole family at the table.
photograph, picture
And in this picture our whole family is at
  the table.

to be hanging, to hang
icon, holy picture
I see you have icons hanging.

God
to believe, trust
to believe in, have faith in
Do you really believe in God?

My brother and I don't believe.

отéц, отцá	father
мáть, мáтери; мáтери, –éй	mother
вéрующий	one who believes, believer
Отéц и мáть у нáс вéрующие.	Father and mother are the believers in our family.
цéрковь, цéркви; –и, –éй	church
Отéц и мáть хóдят в цéрковь.	Father and mother go to church.
У вáс и цéрковь тáм éсть?	Do you have a church there?
Тáк у вáс и цéрковь тáм éсть?	Then you do have a church there?
селó, –á; сёла, сёл	village
сосéдний, –яя, –ее, –ие	neighboring, next
Éсть в сосéднем селé.	There is one in the next village.
Éсть, тóлько не у нáс, а в сосéднем селé.	There is one, only [it is] not in ours, but in the neighboring village.
Пóсле войны́ откры́ли.	It was opened after the war.

SUPPLEMENT

дорóга	road, way, route
Дорóга не óчень хорóшая.	The road isn't very good.
Нáш дóм óчень блúзко от дорóги.	Our house is very close to the road.
Вы́ знáете дорóгу к óзеру?	Do you know the way to the lake?
по дорóге	along the road, on the way
По дорóге шёл какóй-то человéк.	A man was walking along the road.
По дорóге домóй я́ купúл газéту.	On my way home I bought a paper.
нáм по дорóге	we're going the same way
Кáжется, нáм по дорóге.	Looks like we're going the same way.
пострóить (pfv II) (*like* стрóить)	to build
Здéсь скóро пострóят нóвые домá.	They'll soon build new houses here.
повéрить (pfv II) (*plus* dat)	to believe
Повéрьте мнé, óн хорóший человéк.	Believe me, he's a good man.
сосéд, –а; сосéди, –ей[1]	neighbor
Онú нáши сосéди.	They're our neighbors.
сосéдка	neighbor (f)
Нáша сосéдка принеслá нáм э́то.	Our neighbor brought us this.
вéра	faith, confidence
вéра в (*plus* acc)	faith in, confidence in
У негó нéт вéры в себя́.	He has no faith (*or* confidence) in himself.
колхóзница	collective-farm worker (f)
Моя́ мáть колхóзница.	My mother is a collective-farm worker.

---

[1] Note that the final stem consonant of сосéд *neighbor*, which is hard throughout the singular, becomes soft in the plural. Compare the singular: сосéд, сесéда [saşét, saşédə] with the plural: сосéди, сосéдей, о сосéдях, сосéдям [saşéḓi, saşéḓij, asaşéḓəx, saşéḓəm].

Гáля покáзывает Фили́ппу сни́мки

Г. — Гáля
Ф. — Фили́пп

Г. 1 Вóт óбщий ви́д: тýт колхóзные поля́, а вдали́ видны́ лéс и óзеро. А вóт нáша избá.

Ф. 2 Ó, деревя́нная?! А э́то чтó такóе на ýлице?

Г. 3 Э́то колóдец. У нáс нет водопровóда, нáдо вóду носи́ть вёдрами.[1]

Ф. 4 А я́, знáете, инáче представля́л себé колхóз.

Г. 5 Вы́ дýмали, навéрно: домá кáменные, электри́чество, дá?[2]

Ф. 6 Дá. Я́ пóмню читáл в «Огонькé», каки́е тепéрь стрóят домá для колхóзников.[3]

Г. 7 Á, знáю. Таки́е покáзывают тури́стам. А на э́том фóто вся́ нáша семья́ за столóм.[4]

Ф. 8 У вáс, я́ ви́жу, икóны вися́т. Рáзве вы́ вéрите в Бóга?

Г. 9 Нéт, мы́ с брáтом не вéрим, но отéц и мáть у нáс вéрующие, хóдят в цéрковь.[5]

Ф. 10 Тáк у вáс и цéрковь тáм éсть?

Г. 11 Éсть, тóлько не у нáс, а в сосéднем селé. Пóсле войны́ откры́ли.[6]

NOTES

[1] In Russian cities there was running water (at least cold) even before the Revolution; however, it is still nonexistent in rural areas.

[2] Electric lights are usually not found in rural Russia. Note that the term **кáменный**, literally *stone*, refers to all nonwooden buildings, i.e., brick, stone, stucco, and so forth.

[3] In some villages, two-family and multi-family houses have been erected under Khrushchev's program to modernize the villages.

[4] Russians usually use the word **фóто** (short for **фотогрáфия**), rather than **сни́мок**, in reference to snapshots of people.

[5] The noun **цéрковь** (f) *church* has a soft final stem consonant except in certain plural cases where a hard [v] occurs. Compare the nominative plural **цéркви** [cérkγi] with the prepositional **о церквáх** [acirkváx] and with the dative **церквáм** [cirkvám].

[6] **Селó** is a large village. Characteristically it had a church in pre-Revolution times, but this is not necessarily true today.

Basic sentence patterns

1. Привет жене!   Say hello to your wife.
_____ сестре!   _____ sister.
_____ мужу!   _____ husband.
_____ отцу!   _____ father.
_____ брату!   _____ brother.
_____ матери!   _____ mother.
_____ родителям!   _____ parents.
_____ друзьям   _____ friends.
_____ братьям!   _____ brothers.
_____ сёстрам!   _____ sisters.

2. Покажите Филиппу снимки.   Show Philip the snapshots.
_____ Николаю _____.   ____ Nikolay _____.
_____ отцу _____.   ____ Father _____.
_____ сестре _____.   ____ Sister _____.
_____ матери _____.   ____ Mother _____.
_____ родителям _____.   ____ your parents _____.
_____ друзьям _____.   ____ your friends _____.
_____ туристам _____.   ____ the tourists _____.

3. На каникулы я обычно езжу к родителям.   On my vacation I usually go to see my parents.
_____ к друзьям.   _____ friends.
_____ к брату.   _____ brother.
_____ к сестре.   _____ sister.

А я езжу в колхоз.   And I go to the kolkhoz.
_____ в село.   _____ to the village.
_____ в Киев.   _____ to Kiev.
_____ в Одессу.   _____ to Odessa.

4. Дайте эти фото Гранту.   Give these pictures to Grant.
_____ профессору.   _____ to the professor.
_____ учителю.   _____ to the teacher.
_____ туристам.   _____ to the tourists.
_____ Зине.   _____ to Zina.
_____ учительнице.   _____ to the teacher.

5. Мне не дадут разрешения.   They won't give me a pass.
Коле _____.   _____ Kolya _____.
Гале _____.   _____ Galya _____.
Николаю _____.   _____ Nikolay _____.
Брату _____.   _____ Brother _____.
Отцу _____.   _____ Father _____.
Нам _____.   _____ us _____.
Филиппу _____.   _____ Philip _____.

6. Мне надо больше спать.   I need more sleep.
Зине _____.   Zina needs _____.
Олегу _____.   Oleg needs _____.
Студентам _____.   The students need _____.
Мужу _____.   My husband needs _____.

Сестре́ на́до бо́льше спа́ть.	My sister needs more sleep.
Отцу́ _____.	My father needs _____.
Бра́тьям _____.	My brothers need _____.

7. Иностра́нцам нельзя́ свобо́дно е́здить
по СССР.
_____ по стране́.
_____ по Кита́ю.

Foreigners can't travel about freely
in the U.S.S.R.
_____ in the country.
_____ in China.

8. Мы́ ходи́ли по па́рку.
_____ по́ полю.[1]
_____ по́ лесу.
_____ по колхо́зу.
_____ по го́роду.
_____ по селу́.
_____ по вокза́лу.

We walked all around the park.
_____ the field.
_____ the woods.
_____ the kolkhoz.
_____ the city.
_____ the village.
_____ the station.

9. Мне́ его́ жа́ль.
____ её _____.
____ ва́с _____.
____ и́х _____.
____ тебя́ _____.
Мне́ жа́ль Зи́ну.
_____ Ко́лю.
_____ Фили́ппа.
_____ колхо́зников.

I feel sorry for him.
_____ her.
_____ you.
_____ them.
_____ you.
_____ Zina.
_____ Kolya.
_____ Philip.
_____ the collective farmers.

10. У ни́х не́т ве́ры в себя́.
_____ в э́то де́ло.
_____ в люде́й.
_____ в челове́ка.

They have no faith in themselves.
_____ in this thing.
_____ in people.
_____ in man.

11. Каки́е у ва́с пла́ны на кани́кулы?
_____ на за́втра?
_____ на воскресе́нье?
_____ на э́ту суббо́ту?
_____ на э́ту неде́лю?
_____ на э́тот ве́чер?

What are your plans for the vacation?
_____ for tomorrow?
_____ for Sunday?
_____ for this Saturday?
_____ for this week?
_____ for this evening?

12. Роди́тели живу́т далеко́ от Москвы́.
_____ недалеко́ от Москвы́.
_____ бли́зко от Москвы́.
_____ пятьдеся́т киломе́тров
отсю́да.
_____ далеко́ отсю́да.
_____ недалеко́ отсю́да.

My parents live a long way from Moscow.
_____ not far from Moscow.
_____ close to Moscow.
_____ fifty kilometers from here.
_____ a long way from here.
_____ not far away from here.

13. Мы́ прошли́ ми́лю.
_____ о́коло ми́ли.
_____ две́ ми́ли.
_____ три́ ми́ли.
_____ пя́ть ми́ль.

We've covered (or walked) a mile.
_____ about a mile.
_____ two miles.
_____ three miles.
_____ five miles.

---

[1] Note that **по** occasionally takes the stress from the noun: **по́ полю** [pópəļu], **по́ лесу** [póļisu].

Мы́ прошли́ киломе́тр.	We've covered (or walked) about a kilometer.
_____ о́коло киломе́тра.	_____ about a kilometer.
_____ два́ киломе́тра.	_____ two kilometers.
_____ четы́ре киломе́тра.	_____ four kilometers.
_____ пя́ть киломе́тров.	_____ five kilometers.

14. Они́ уже́ прошли́ пя́ть уро́ков. They've already covered five lessons.
    _____ во́семь _____. _____ eight _____.
    _____ де́сять _____. _____ ten _____.

15. Доро́га идёт к о́зеру. The road goes to the lake.
    _____ шла_____. _____ went _____.
    Авто́бус идёт в колхо́з. The bus is going to the kolkhoz.
    _____ шёл _____. _____ was going _____.
    _____ пришёл _____. _____ arrived at _____.

16. Дава́йте игра́ть в ка́рты. Let's play cards.
    _____ в ша́хматы. _____ chess.
    _____ в футбо́л. _____ soccer.
    _____ в бейсбо́л. _____ baseball.
    _____ в те́ннис. _____ tennis.
    _____ в хокке́й. _____ hockey.

17. Лу́чше не бу́дем игра́ть в ка́рты. We'd better not play cards.
    _____ в ша́хматы. _____ chess.
    _____ в футбо́л. _____ soccer.
    _____ в бейсбо́л. _____ baseball.
    _____ в те́ннис. _____ tennis.
    _____ в хокке́й. _____ hockey.

18. Та́к не сидя́т. People don't sit like that or That's no way to sit.
    _____ говоря́т. _____ talk _____ or _____ to talk.
    _____ танцу́ют. _____ dance _____ or _____ to dance.
    _____ хо́дят. _____ walk _____ or _____ to walk.
    _____ игра́ют. _____ play _____ or _____ to play.

19. Две́ри уже́ открыва́ют. They're opening the doors already.
    _____ закрыва́ют. They're closing _____.
    Уже́ выхо́дят из це́ркви. People are coming out of church already.
    Про́пусков бо́льше не даю́т. Passes are no longer being given.
    Таки́х рома́нов бо́льше не пи́шут. They don't write such novels anymore.
    Его́ стихо́в бо́льше не чита́ют. People don't read his poetry anymore.

20. Тури́сты обы́чно снима́ют Tourists usually take pictures
    на́ши колхо́зы. of our farms.
    _____ на́ши озёра. _____ of our lakes.
    _____ на́ши ка́менные дома́. _____ of our stone houses.
    _____ на́ши и́збы. _____ of our huts.
    _____ на́ши деревя́нные це́ркви. _____ of our wooden churches.
    _____ на́шу деревя́нную це́рковь. _____ of our wooden church.
    _____ на́ши ру́сские сёла. _____ of our Russian villages.
    _____ на́ших колхо́зников. _____ of our collective farmers.
    _____ на́ших колхо́зниц. _____ of our collective-farm women.

21. На э́том фо́то моя́ семья́. My family is in this picture.
_____ мо́й оте́ц. My father is _____.
_____ мои́ роди́тели. My parents are _____.
_____ моя́ ма́ть. My mother is _____.
_____ моя́ сосе́дка. My neighbor (f) is_____.
_____ мо́й сосе́д. My neighbor is _____.
_____ мои́ сосе́ди. My neighbors are _____.
_____ на́ши колхо́зники. Our collective farmers are _____.

Pronunciation practice: consonant clusters with [l] or [ļ]

A. Clusters with [l] or [ļ] in second position.

[blánk] бла́нк [vļáşţ] вла́сть [mļéčnij] мле́чный
blank power milky
[bļískə] бли́зко [vļéşţ] вле́зть [plán] пла́н
close to crawl into plan
[bļúdə] блю́до [kļáşţ] кля́сть [plóxə] пло́хо
platter, dish to curse it's bad
[vlážnij] вла́жный [mláčšij] мла́дший [plíţ] плы́ть
humid younger to be swimming

B. Clusters with [l] or [ļ] in initial position.

[lbá] лба́ [lžót] лжёт [ļdínə] льди́на
of the forehead he's lying ice floe
[lbí] лбы́ [lží] лжи́ [ļná] льна́
foreheads of the lie of flax
[lgáţ] лга́ть [ļvá] Льва́ [ļşţíţ] льсти́ть
to lie of Lev to flatter
[lgún] лгу́н [ļdá] льда́ [ļščú] льщу́
liar of ice I flatter

C. Clusters witц [l] or [ļ] in final position.

[ρérl] пе́рл [ansámbļ] анса́мбль [ótrəsļ] о́трасль
pearl ensemble branch
[smísl] смы́сл [žurávļ] жура́вль [zárəsļ] за́росль
sense crane brushwood
[rúbļ] ру́бль [sρiktákļ] спекта́кль [mísļ] мы́сль
ruble show thought
[karávļ] кора́бль [ϸinókļ] бино́кль [vópļ] во́пль
ship binoculars outcry

D. Clusters with [l] or [ļ] immediately before the final consonant.

[stólp] сто́лб [šólk] шёлк [púļs] пу́льс
post silk pulse
[dólk] до́лг [pólk] по́лк [áļt] а́льт
duty regiment alto
[póls] по́лз [žólč] жёлчь [kúļt] ку́льт
he crawled bile cult
[vólk] во́лк [váļs] ва́льс [fáļš] фа́льшь
wolf waltz falsehood

The dative of nouns: singular and plural

MODELS

Фили́ппу ну́жен про́пуск. — Philip needs a pass.
Влади́миру _____. — Vladimir _____.
Евге́нию _____. — Evgeny _____.
Никола́ю _____. — Nikolay _____.
Ко́ле _____. — Kolya _____.
Ма́ше _____. — Masha _____.
Ири́не _____. — Irina _____.
Мари́и _____. — Maria _____.

Принеси́ отцу́ стака́н воды́. — Bring Father a glass of water.
_____ бра́ту _____. — _____ Brother _____.
_____ америка́нцу _____. — _____ the American (m) _____.
_____ учи́телю _____. — _____ the teacher _____.
_____ секретарю́ _____. — _____ the secretary _____.
_____ учи́тельнице _____. — _____ the teacher _____.
_____ америка́нке _____. — _____ the American (f) _____.
_____ Ни́не _____. — _____ Nina _____.
_____ Мари́и _____. — _____ Maria _____.

Подойди́те к телефо́ну. — Come (or go) to the telephone.
_____ к столу́. — _____ to the table.
_____ к шка́фу. — Come (or go) over to the cupboard.
_____ к окну́. — _____ to the window.
_____ к доске́. — _____ to the blackboard.
_____ к две́ри. — _____ to the door.
_____ к ка́рте. — _____ to the map.

О́н чита́ет ле́кции по му́зыке. — He lectures on music.
_____ по матема́тике. — _____ on mathematics.
_____ по литерату́ре. — _____ on literature.
_____ по фи́зике. — _____ on physics.
_____ по хи́мии. — _____ on chemistry.
_____ по исто́рии. — _____ on history.
_____ по геогра́фии. — _____ on geography.

Позвони́те студе́нтам в понеде́льник. — Call the students on Monday.
_____ студе́нткам _____. — _____ coeds _____.
_____ певца́м _____. — _____ singers _____.
_____ певи́цам _____. — _____ singers (f) _____.
_____ учи́тельницам _____. — _____ teachers _____.
_____ отца́м _____. — _____ fathers _____.
_____ матеря́м _____. — _____ mothers _____.
_____ роди́телям _____. — _____ parents _____.
_____ учителя́м _____. — _____ teachers _____.
_____ секретаря́м _____. — _____ secretaries _____.

По понеде́льникам я всегда́ до́ма.	On Mondays I'm always home.
По вто́рникам _____ .	On Tuesdays _____ .
По среда́м _____ .	On Wednesdays _____ .
По четверга́м _____ .	On Thursdays _____ .
По пя́тницам _____ .	On Fridays _____ .
По суббо́там _____ .	On Saturdays _____ .
По воскресе́ньям _____ .	On Sundays _____ .

NOUN ENDINGS IN THE DATIVE			
SINGULAR –у, –ю		–е	–и
сто́л- and окно́-nouns		жена́-nouns (except –ия nouns)	две́рь-nouns, жена́-nouns ending in –ия, и́мя-nouns
Hard stems and stems ending in ч and щ	*Soft stems*		
–у	–ю	–е	–и
столу́	дню	жене́	две́ри
бра́ту	Никола́ю	сестре́	ма́тери
Козло́ву	учи́телю	Ната́ше	о́череди
телефо́ну	па́рню	Ко́ле	исто́рии
отцу́	Кита́ю	Га́ле	ле́кции
това́рищу	пла́тью	де́вушке	Мари́и
ключу́	собра́нию	продавщи́це	и́мени
ме́сту			вре́мени
окну́			

PLURAL –ам	–ям
Hard stems and stems ending in ч and щ	*Soft stems*
–ам	–ям
утра́м	бра́тьям
города́м	дверя́м
гости́ницам	парня́м
де́вушкам	ле́кциям
ребя́там	собра́ниям
жёнам	учителя́м
сёстрам	очередя́м
о́кнам	пе́сням
стола́м	друзья́м
ка́ртам	сту́льям
това́рищам	лаборато́риям

Repeat the given models, noting the pattern of endings for nouns in the dative case.

■ CUED QUESTION-ANSWER DRILLS

1. (*Vladimir*)   *Who needs tickets?*
                 Vladimir.
   (Влади́мир)   Кому́ нужны́ биле́ты?
                 Влади́миру.
   (де́вушки)   Кому́ нужны́ биле́ты?
                 Де́вушкам.
   (америка́нка, студе́нты, секрета́рь,
   Алексе́ев, Ната́ша, её подру́ги,
   това́рищ Волко́в)

2. (*Zina*)   *Who are you selling your camera to?*
             To Zina.
   (Зи́на)   Кому́ вы продаёте ваш аппара́т?
             Зи́не.
   (Евге́ний)   Кому́ вы продаёте ваш аппара́т?
             Евге́нию.
   (профе́ссор Орло́в, Га́ля, америка́нец,
   учи́тель, друзья́, това́рищ, Никола́й,
   Мари́я)

3. (*friends*)   *Who did you call on?*
              Friends.
   (друзья́)   К кому́ вы заходи́ли?
             К друзья́м.
   (роди́тели)   К кому́ вы заходи́ли?
             К роди́телям.
   (профе́ссор Орло́в, америка́нка,
   учи́тель, Зи́на, студе́нты, Оля,
   америка́нцы, Грант)

4. (*conveniences*)   *What's he accustomed to?*
                 Conveniences.
   (удо́бства)   К чему́ он привы́к?
             К удо́бствам.
   (джаз)   К чему́ он привы́к?
             К джа́зу.
   (Аме́рика, уда́чи, Евро́па, про́сьбы,
   рабо́та, Кита́й)

■ RESPONSE DRILLS

1. *Masha's thirsty* or *Masha wants a drink.*
   Bring Masha a glass of water.
   Ма́ша хо́чет пи́ть.
   Принеси́ Ма́ше стака́н воды́.
   Оте́ц хо́чет пи́ть.
   Принеси́ отцу́ стака́н воды́.
     (сестра́, Оле́г, секрета́рь, певи́ца,
     това́рищ Семёнов, певе́ц, господи́н
     Грант)

2. *Oleg is asking where the lake is.*
   Tell Oleg where the lake is.
   Оле́г спра́шивает, где́ о́зеро.
   Скажи́те Оле́гу, где́ о́зеро.
   Учи́тель спра́шивает, где́ о́зеро.
   Скажи́те учи́телю, где́ о́зеро.
     (её подру́га, студе́нты, его́ друг, его́
     жена́, его́ това́рищ, Га́ля, сёстры)

3. *Doesn't Philip have a permit?*
   Give Philip a permit.
   У Фили́ппа не́т разреше́ния?
   Да́йте Фили́ппу разреше́ние!

   У Ко́ли не́т разреше́ния?
   Да́йте Ко́ле разреше́ние!
     (америка́нцев, господи́на Гра́нта,
     америка́нки, учителе́й, Козло́ва, Зи́ны)

■ QUESTION-ANSWER DRILLS

1. *Isn't Oleg going to come?*
   No, Oleg would be bored there.
   Оле́г не придёт?
   Не́т, Оле́гу бу́дет та́м ску́чно.
   Зи́на не придёт?
   Не́т, Зи́не бу́дет та́м ску́чно.
     (студе́нты, её подру́га, их друзья́,
     его́ брат, Ко́ля, профе́ссор,
     америка́нец, певи́ца)

2. *Does your friend have your camera?*
Yes, I gave it to my friend.
Твóй аппарáт у товáрища?
Дá, я егó дáл товáрищу.
Твóй аппарáт у сестры́?
Дá, я егó дáл сестрé.
    (друзéй, профéссора, её подрýги,
    товáрища по кóмнате, америкáнца,
    Зи́ны, брáта)

3. *Did Nikolay buy an atlas?*
No, Nikolay no longer needs an atlas.
Николáй купи́л áтлас?
Нéт, Николáю áтлас ужé не нýжен.
Зи́на купи́ла áтлас?
Нéт, Зи́не áтлас ужé не нýжен.
    (ребя́та, профéссор Курóчкин, отéц,
    сестрá, Фили́пп, учи́тельница)

4. *Is he a professor of music?*
Yes, he lectures on music.
Óн профéссор мýзыки?
Да, óн читáет лéкции по мýзыке.
Óн профéссор матемáтики?
Да, óн читáет лéкции по матемáтике.

(профéссор фи́зики, профéссор хи́мии,
профéссор геогрáфии, профéссор литерату́ры, профéссор истóрии)

■ STRUCTURE REPLACEMENT DRILL

He'll come on Saturday.
He usually comes Saturdays.
Óн придёт в суббóту.
Óн обы́чно прихóдит по суббóтам.
Óн придёт в срéду.
Óн обы́чно прихóдит по средáм.

(в четвéрг, в воскресéнье, в пя́тницу, во
втóрник, в понедéльник, в суббóту, в
срéду)

DISCUSSION: NOUN ENDINGS IN THE DATIVE

Singular

1. Those **стóл-** and **окнó-**nouns taking –a in the genitive singular take –y in the dative singular; those taking –я in the genitive singular take –ю in the dative singular.

2. **Женá-** and **двéрь-**nouns have identical forms in the dative singular and the prepositional singular; so, too, do the nouns **и́мя** and **врéмя.**

Plural

Nouns taking –ах in the prepositional plural take –ам in the dative plural; those taking –ях in the prepositional plural take –ям in the dative plural.

Stress

1. Stress in the dative singular is the same as that in the genitive and prepositional singular.

NOM SG	GEN SG	PREP SG	DAT SG
стóл	столá	столé	столý
отéц	отцá	отцé	отцý
окнó	окнá	окнé	окнý
женá	жены́	женé	женé
Гáля	Гáли	Гáле	Гáле
двéрь	двéри	двéри	двéри
óчередь	óчереди	óчереди	óчереди
врéмя	врéмени	врéмени	врéмени
мáть	мáтери	мáтери	мáтери

2. Stress in the dative plural is the same as that in the prepositional plural.

NOM PL	GEN PL	PREP PL	DAT PL
слова́	слов	слова́х	слова́м
столы́	столо́в	стола́х	стола́м
отцы́	отцо́в	отца́х	отца́м
о́кна	о́кон *or* око́н	о́кнах	о́кнам
до́ски	досо́к	доска́х	доска́м
жёны	жён	жёнах	жёнам
сёстры	сестёр	сёстрах	сёстрам
па́рни	парне́й	парня́х	парня́м
две́ри	двере́й	двера́х	двера́м
о́череди	очереде́й	очередя́х	очередя́м
времена́	времён	времена́х	времена́м
ма́тери	матере́й	матеря́х	матеря́м
ру́ки	рук	рука́х	рука́м
го́ловы	голо́в	голова́х	голова́м

Dative constructions with на́до

MODELS

Мне́ на́до пойти́ на по́чту.	I need to go to the post office.
Ему́ _____.	He needs _____.
Ей _____.	She needs _____.
Им _____.	They need _____.
Ва́м _____.	You need _____.
На́м _____.	We need _____.
Тебе́ _____.	You need _____.

Мне́ на́до бы́ло пойти́ в библиоте́ку.	I had to go to the library.
Ему́ _____.	He _____.
Ей _____.	She _____.
Им _____.	They _____.
Ва́м _____.	You _____.
На́м _____.	We _____.
Тебе́ _____.	You _____.

Мне́ на́до бу́дет е́хать к роди́телям.	I'll have to go to my parents.
Ему́ _____.	He'll have _____ his _____.
Ей _____.	She'll have _____ her _____.
Им _____.	They'll have _____ their _____.
Ва́м _____.	You'll have _____ your _____.
На́м _____.	We'll have _____ our _____.
Тебе́ _____.	You'll have _____ your _____.

■ REPETITION DRILL

Repeat the given models, noting that **на́до** is typically used in infinitive constructions together with the dative.

1. *Is Zina going to the collective farm?*
   Yes, she has to go there.
   Зи́на е́дет в колхо́з?
   Да́, ей на́до туда́ е́хать.
   Оле́г е́дет в колхо́з?
   Да́, ему́ на́до туда́ е́хать.
   (ребя́та, учи́тель, её подру́га, оте́ц, его́ роди́тели, Га́ля, бра́т)

2. *Did the secretary often go to the village?*
   Yes, he had to go there often.
   Секрета́рь ча́сто е́здил в село́?
   Да́, ему́ ча́сто на́до бы́ло туда́ е́здить.
   Пётр ча́сто е́здил в село́?
   Да́, ему́ ча́сто на́до бы́ло туда́ е́здить.
   (студе́нты, учи́тельница, това́рищ Цара́пкин, Ма́ша, оте́ц, её друзья́, сестра́)

■ RESPONSE DRILLS

1. *Is it possible Orlov doesn't know Galya yet?*
   Orlov has got to meet her.
   Ра́зве Орло́в ещё не зна́ет Га́лю?
   Орло́ву на́до с ней познако́миться.
   Ра́зве Воло́дя ещё не зна́ет Га́лю?
   Воло́де на́до с ней познако́миться.
   (Са́ша, его́ бра́т, его́ сестра́, де́вушки, Зи́на, ребя́та, ты, оте́ц)

2. *Galya heard there was an interesting movie playing.*
   She'll have to see it.
   Га́ля слы́шала, что идёт интере́сный фи́льм.
   Ей на́до бу́дет его́ посмотре́ть.
   Бра́т слы́шал, что идёт интере́сный фи́льм.
   Ему́ на́до бу́дет его́ посмотре́ть.
   (ты, сёстры, мы, жена́, профе́ссор, я, продавщи́ца, шофёр, студе́нты)

3. *Masha didn't manage (or have time) to order tickets.*
   She has to go and order tickets.
   Ма́ша не успе́ла заказа́ть биле́ты.
   Ей на́до пойти́ заказа́ть биле́ты.
   Профе́ссор не успе́л заказа́ть биле́ты.
   Ему́ на́до пойти́ заказа́ть биле́ты.
   (оте́ц, вы, бра́тья, ма́ть, мы, подру́ги, я, Семён, ты)

4. *Oleg wanted to speak English.*
   He had to study English.
   Оле́г хоте́л говори́ть по-англи́йски.
   Ему́ на́до бы́ло учи́ть англи́йский язы́к.
   Певе́ц хоте́л говори́ть по-англи́йски.
   Ему́ на́до бы́ло учи́ть англи́йский язы́к.
   (де́вушки, её подру́га, его́ това́рищ, их друзья́, сестра́, оте́ц, бра́т, студе́нтка)

5. *Kolya's parents are ill.*
   He must go to see his parents.
   Роди́тели Ко́ли больны́.
   Ему́ на́до е́хать к роди́телям.
   Роди́тели Ма́ши больны́.
   Ей на́до е́хать к роди́телям.
   (Козло́ва, О́ли, вахтёра, Никола́я, Мари́и, Воло́ди, шофёра)

6. *I was at the station.*
   I had to buy tickets.
   Я́ бы́л на ста́нции.
   Мне́ на́до бы́ло купи́ть биле́ты.
   Она́ была́ на ста́нции.
   Ей на́до бы́ло купи́ть биле́ты.
   (он, они́, ты, она́, вы, мы, я)

■ QUESTION-ANSWER DRILL

Why is Kolya in such a hurry?
He has to make it to the post office in time.
Почему́ Ко́ля та́к спеши́т?
Ему́ на́до успе́ть на по́чту.
Почему́ они́ та́к спеша́т?
Им на́до успе́ть на по́чту.

(вы, твои́ това́рищи, её сестра́, э́ти де́вушки, э́тот па́рень, твои́ друзья́, продавщи́ца, ты, Воло́дя)

На́до is an unchanging form used chiefly with infinitives to express an urgent need to perform some activity. The dative which usually accompanies **на́до** focuses on the person for whom the action is necessary. In the past tense **на́до** is followed by **бы́ло**; in the future by **бу́дет.**

Ему́ **на́до бы́ло** пойти́ в го́род.	He had to go downtown.
Ему́ **на́до бу́дет** пойти́ в го́род.	He'll have to go downtown.

In colloquial Russian the infinitive is sometimes omitted. This is especially common with verbs of motion where the destination is mentioned.

Мне́ **на́до** на по́чту.	I need to go to the post office.
Мне́ **на́до бы́ло** на уро́к.	I had to go to class.

The combination **не на́до** is often used as a plea that the addressee *not* do something. Infinitives used with **не на́до** are always imperfective.

Не на́до об э́том говори́ть.	*Don't* talk about that.
Мо́жно откры́ть о́кна?	Is it all right to open the windows?
— Не́т, **не на́до** (открыва́ть о́кон).	No, *don't* (open the windows).

Note that **на́до** and the short-form neuter adjective **ну́жно** are often interchangeable in infinitive constructions.

Ему́ **ну́жно бы́ло** спеши́ть.	He had to hurry.
Ему́ **на́до бы́ло** _____.	He had _____.
Мне́ **ну́жно** пойти́ на по́чту.	I've got to go to the post office.
Мне́ **на́до**_____.	I've got_____.

The past tense of the imperfective verb идти́ and its prefixed perfective derivatives

MODELS

Что́ шло́ в кино́?	What was playing at the movies?
— Шёл америка́нский фи́льм.	An American film was playing.
— Шла́ америка́нская карти́на.	An American picture was playing.
— Шли́ америка́нские фи́льмы.	American films were playing.

По́сле ле́кции о́н пошёл домо́й.	After the lecture he went home.
_____ она́ пошла́ _____.	_____ she went ____.
_____ они́ пошли́ _____.	_____ they went ____.

Ка́к прошёл уро́к?	How did the lesson go?
____ прошло́ собра́ние?	____ did the meeting go?
____ прошла́ ле́кция?	____ did the lecture go?
____ прошли́ экза́мены?	____ did the exams go?

О́н вошёл в ко́мнату.	He entered the room.
Она́ вошла́ _____.	She entered _____.
Они́ вошли́ _____.	They entered _____.

Он на минýтку зашёл в библиотéку.	He dropped by the library for a minute.
Онá _____ зашлá _____.	She dropped by _____.
Мы _____ зашлú _____.	We dropped by _____.
Он пришёл пóсле обéда.	He came after lunch (*or* in the afternoon).
Онá пришлá _____.	She came _____.
Онú пришлú _____.	They came _____.
Олéг тóлько что вышел.	Oleg just stepped out.
Зúна _____ вышла.	Zina ___ stepped out.
Дéвушки _____ вышли.	The girls ____stepped out.

■ REPETITION PRACTICE

Repeat the above models, noting particularly that all perfective verbs derived from **идти** are patterned alike in the past tense.

■ SUBSTITUTION DRILLS

1. *How did your lesson go?*
   Кáк у вáс прошёл **урóк**?
   Кáк у вáс прошлó **собрáние**?
   (экзáмены, обéд, лéкция, ýтро, врéмя, недéля, суббóта, тáнцы)

2. *Volodya entered the dining hall.*
   Волóдя вошёл в столóвую.
   Онú вошлú в столóвую.
   (онá, студéнты, Зúна и Олéг, учúтель Семёнов, Натáша, Кáтя и Нúна)

■ STRUCTURE REPLACEMENT DRILLS

1. *I'm on my way to the station.*
   I was on my way to the station.
   Я идý на стáнцию.
   Я шёл на стáнцию.
   Он идёт на стáнцию.
   Он шёл на стáнцию.
   (онú, вы, онá, егó товáрищ, мы, пáрень, брáтья)

2. *The lesson will go well.*
   The lesson went well.
   Урóк пройдёт хорошó.
   Урóк прошёл хорошó.
   Собрáние пройдёт хорошó.
   Собрáние прошлó хорошó.
   (эта зимá, эта недéля, экзáмены, врéмя, лéкция, вéчер, суббóта, обéд)

3. *He'll stop by the library.*
   He stopped by the library.
   Он зайдёт в библиотéку.
   Он зашёл в библиотéку.
   Онú зайдýт в библиотéку.
   Онú зашлú в библиотéку.
   (ты, онá, вы, студéнты, профéссор, учителя́, учúтельница, твоú товáрищи)

4. *They'll enter the coach.*
   They entered the coach.
   Онú войдýт в вагóн.
   Онú вошлú в вагóн.
   Мáша войдёт в вагóн.
   Мáша вошлá в вагóн.
   (учúтельница, её сёстры, её брат, твоú товáрищи, мы, он, вы, ты, Олéг)

■ STRUCTURE REPLACEMENT DRILLS

1. *I had to stop by the house.*
   I stopped by the house.
   Мнé нáдо было зайтú домóй.
   Я зашёл домóй.
   Нáм нáдо было зайтú домóй.
   Мы зашлú домóй.
   (профéссору, подрýгам, тебé, женé, вам, шофёру, америкáнке)

2. *Katya had to go out of the house.*
   Katya went out of the house.
   Кáте нáдо было выйти úз дому.
   Кáтя вышла úз дому.
   Отцý нáдо было выйти úз дому.
   Отéц вышел úз дому.
   (Олéгу, сёстрам, мáтери, вам, учúтелю, нам, дéвушкам, ей)

3. *I didn't want to go over to him.*
I didn't go over to him.
Я не хоте́л к нему́ подойти́.
Я к нему́ не подошёл.

Мы́ не хоте́ли к нему́ подойти́.
Мы́ к нему́ не подошли́.

(мать, оте́ц, сестра́, бра́тья, друг,
роди́тели, Ко́ля, друзья́)

■ QUESTION-ANSWER DRILLS

1. *Where were you hurrying to last night?*
I was on my way to the movies.
Куда́ ты́ спеши́л вчера́ ве́чером?
Я шёл в кино́.
Куда́ ва́ша сестра́ спеши́ла вчера́
ве́чером?
Она́ шла́ в кино́.

(вы, он, они, твоя учительница, твой
товарищ Петров, студенты, этот
парень)

2. *Will Kolya go to the post office?*
He has already gone.
Ко́ля пойдёт на по́чту?
Он уже́ пошёл.
Его́ жена́ пойдёт на по́чту?
Она́ уже́ пошла́.

(он, их уборщица, твои братья,
Любовь Петровна, твой товарищ)

■ STRUCTURE REPLACEMENT DRILL

She's walking along the street.
She was walking along the street.
Она́ идёт по у́лице.
Она́ шла́ по у́лице.

Подру́ги иду́т по у́лице.
Подру́ги шли́ по у́лице.

(мы, продавщица, вы, Володя, сёстры,
отец, мать, Олег)

DISCUSSION

The past tense of **идти́** *to be going* is based on an alternate root and has the following forms:

(m)	шёл	(f)	шла́	(n)	шло́	(pl)	шли́

All the prefixed perfective derivatives of **идти́** have pasts built on these same forms. With the exception of **вы́шел, вы́шла, вы́шло,** and **вы́шли** (from **вы́йти** *to go out*), where the stress is consistently drawn to the prefix **вы́–**, the stress is always on the last syllable of the past tense form.

PAST				INFINITIVE	
пошёл	пошла́	пошло́	пошли́	**пойти́**	to go
вошёл	вошла́	вошло́	вошли́	**войти́**	to enter
зашёл	зашла́	зашло́	зашли́	**зайти́**	to drop in
пришёл	пришла́	пришло́	пришли́	**прийти́**	to come
прошёл	прошла́	прошло́	прошли́	**пройти́**	to pass, go, go by, go through
подошёл	подошла́	подошло́	подошли́	**подойти́**	to go up to, approach
перешёл	перешла́	перешло́	перешли́	**перейти́**	to go across, cross

Suggestions that include the speaker:
part II—imperfective verbs

Давáйте смотрéть снúмки.	Let's look at snapshots!
_____ игрáть в кáрты.	____ play cards!
_____ слýшать пластúнки.	____ listen to records!
_____ обéдать в столóвой.	____ eat dinner in the dining hall!
_____ пúть чáй.	____ drink tea!
_____ рабóтать вмéсте.	____ work together!
_____ петь пéсни.	____ sing some songs!

Давáйте бýдем смотрéть снúмки.	Let's look at snapshots!
_____ игрáть в кáрты.	____ play cards!
_____ слýшать пластúнки.	____ listen to records!
_____ обéдать в столóвой.	____ eat dinner in the dining hall!
_____ пúть чáй.	____ drink tea!
_____ рабóтать вмéсте.	____ work together!
_____ пéть пéсни.	____ sing some songs!

Давáйте не бýдем об э́том говорúть.	Let's not talk about it!
_____ ходúть на егó лéкции.	_____ go to his lecture!
_____ обéдать в столóвой.	_____ eat dinner in the dining hall!
_____ рабóтать по суббóтам.	_____ work on Saturdays!
_____ открывáть óкон.	_____ open the windows!
_____ тудá éздить.	_____ go there!

Лýчше не бýдем сегóдня рабóтать.	We'd better not work today.
_____ сегóдня танцевáть.	_____ dance today.
_____ сегóдня спáть на дворé.	_____ sleep outdoors today.
_____ бóльше тудá éздить.	_____ go there anymore.
_____ бóльше с нúми игрáть.	_____ play with them anymore.
_____ бóльше об э́том дýмать.	_____ think about it anymore.

■ REPETITION PRACTICE

Repeat the given models, noting the alternate ways in which suggestions that include the speaker
and employ imperfective verbs may be expressed.

■ QUESTION-ANSWER DRILLS

1. *Want to look at snapshots?*
   Fine, let's look at snapshots.
   Хотúте смотрéть снúмки?
   Хорошó, давáйте смотрéть снúмки.
   Хотúте пúть чáй?
   Хорошó, давáйте пúть чáй.
   (слушать пластинки, читать стихи,
   учить русский язык, работать вечером,
   играть в карты, обедать в столовой,
   петь песни)

2. *Shall we talk about it?*
   No, let's not talk about it
   Мы́ бýдем говорúть об э́том?
   Нéт, давáйте не бýдем говорúть об э́том.
   Мы́ бýдем писáть об э́том?
   Нéт, давáйте не бýдем писáть об э́том.
   (спрашивать об этом, его ждать,
   слушать радио, играть в шахматы,
   ему звонить, стоять в очереди, ему
   отвечать)

3. *Do you want to work today?*
   No, let's not work today.
   Вы́ хоти́те сего́дня рабо́тать?
   Не́т, лу́чше не бу́дем сего́дня рабо́тать.
   Вы́ хоти́те сего́дня игра́ть в ка́рты?
   Не́т, лу́чше не бу́дем сего́дня игра́ть в ка́рты?
   (писа́ть заявле́ние, чита́ть стихи́,
   обе́дать в столо́вой, танцева́ть, спа́ть
   на дворе́, пе́ть рома́нсы)

4. *Shall we read today?*
   No, let's read tomorrow instead.
   Мы́ бу́дем сего́дня чита́ть?
   Не́т, лу́чше бу́дем чита́ть за́втра.
   Мы́ бу́дем сего́дня слу́шать джа́з?
   Не́т, лу́чше бу́дем слу́шать за́втра.
   (учи́ть слова́, писа́ть письмо́, игра́ть в
   ша́хматы, смотре́ть сни́мки, танцева́ть,
   иска́ть рабо́ту)

■ RESPONSE DRILL

They're playing tennis.
Let's play too!
Они́ игра́ют в те́ннис.
Дава́й то́же игра́ть!

Они́ чита́ют журна́л.
Дава́й то́же чита́ть!
(смо́трят сни́мки, танцу́ют, обе́дают,
спя́т, и́щут кни́гу)

DISCUSSION

In affirmative suggestions that include the speaker and use imperfective verbs, **дава́й** (*or* **дава́йте**) may be followed either by the infinitive alone or by **бу́дем** plus the infinitive: Дава́й чита́ть (*or* Дава́й бу́дем чита́ть) *Let's read!*

In negative suggestions employing imperfective verbs, **бу́дем** cannot be omitted. **Лу́чше** is often used instead of **дава́й** (**дава́йте**): Дава́й не бу́дем чита́ть (*or* Лу́чше не бу́дем чита́ть) *Let's not read!*

Impersonal constructions using the subjectless third person plural verb

MODELS

Говоря́т, вчера́ бы́ло собра́ние.
Мне́ говори́ли, что вчера́ бы́ло собра́ние.
Уже́ **открыва́ют** две́ри.
Зде́сь **продаю́т** ры́бу.
Ско́ро **откро́ют** две́ри.
Мне́ **не даду́т** разреше́ния.
Таки́е дома́ **пока́зывают** тури́стам.
Тепе́рь **стро́ят** дома́ для колхо́зников.

They say there was a meeting yesterday.
I was told there was a meeting yesterday.
They're already *opening* the doors.
Fish *is sold* here *or They sell* fish here.
They'll soon *open* the doors.
They won't give me a pass.
That's the kind of houses *they show* tourists.
Houses *are* now *being built* for the farmers.

■ STRUCTURE REPLACEMENT DRILLS

1. *They sell fish.*
   They sell fish here or Fish is sold here.
   Они́ продаю́т ры́бу.
   Зде́сь продаю́т ры́бу.
   Они́ пока́зывают фи́льмы.
   Зде́сь пока́зывают фи́льмы.

   Они́ говоря́т по-англи́йски.
   Они́ понима́ют по-ру́сски.
   Они́ даю́т пропуска́.
   Они́ отдыха́ют ле́том.
   Они́ продаю́т поде́ржанные ве́щи.

2. *Who told him?*
   Why was he told?
   Ктó емý сказáл?
   Почемý емý сказáли?
   Ктó емý разрешѝл?
   Почемý емý разрешѝли?
   (послал, дал, показал, продал, звонил,
   написал, открыл, заплатил,
   предложил)

3. *We'll close the doors.*
   They'll soon close the doors or *The doors*
   will soon close.
   Мы́ закрóем двéри.
   Скóро закрóют двéри.
   Мы́ открóем двéри.
   Скóро открóют двéри.
   Мы́ напѝшем об э́том в газéте.
   Мы́ разрешѝм éздить во Владивостóк.
   Мы́ покáжем э́ту картѝну.
   Мы́ открóем собрáние.
   Мы́ принесём обéд.

4. *The administrator will give us a room.*
   They'll give us a room or *We'll be given a*
   room.
   Администрáтор нáм дáст нóмер.
   Нáм дадýт нóмер.
   Администрáтор нáм открóет двéрь.
   Нáм открóют двéрь.
   Администрáтор нáм позвонѝт в чáс.

Администрáтор нáм покáжет теáтр.
Администрáтор нáм об э́том напѝшет.
Администрáтор нáм разрешѝт тудá
   поéхать.
Администрáтор нáм посовéтует кудá
   пойтѝ.
Администрáтор нáм об э́том скáжет.

■ RESPONSE DRILL

Who sits like that?
That's no way to sit! or *People don't sit*
   like that!
Ктó тáк сидѝт?
Тáк не сидя́т!
Ктó тáк рабóтает?
Тáк не рабóтают!
   (пишет, читает, играет, стоит,
   танцует, говорит)

■ QUESTION-ANSWER DRILL

Will they give you a pass?
They already did.
Тебé дадýт прóпуск?
Мнé ужé дáли.
Тебé напѝшут об э́том?
Мнé ужé написáли.
Тебé разрешáт изменѝть ѝмя?
Тебé отвéтят из посóльства?
Тебé позвоня́т с рабóты?
Тебé покáжут снѝмки?
Тебé кýпят портфéль?

■ STRUCTURE REPLACEMENT DRILLS

1. *I can't sleep.*
   They don't let me sleep.
   Я́ не могý спáть.
   Мнé не даю́т спáть.
   Я́ не могý рабóтать.
   Мнé не даю́т рабóтать.
   (писать, читать, слушать, думать,
   играть)

2. *He couldn't speak.*
   They wouldn't let him speak.
   Óн не мóг говорѝть.
   Емý не давáли говорѝть.
   Óн не мóг спросѝть.
   Емý не давáли спросѝть.
   Óн не мóг отвечáть.
   Óн не мóг открѝть собрáние.
   Óн не мóг слýшать рáдио.
   Óн не мóг отдохнýть.
   Óн не мóг ходѝть в кинó.

The third person plural verb without a subject is used when the action is attributed to an indefinite group. The speaker either does not know the source of the action or finds it convenient not to mention the source, for example, if it is attributed to officials in power. Such constructions may be rendered variously in English, for example, **говорят** *they say, people say, it's said.*

Such constructions are often used where English would use the passive voice.

Мне говорили, что завтра будет экзамен.	I was told there'd be an exam tomorrow.
Уже открывают двери.	The doors are being opened already.
Здесь говорят по-русски.	Russian is spoken here.

ЧТЕНИЕ И ПИСЬМО

— Вы уже довольно хорошо говорите по-русски. Теперь вам нужно только больше читать. — Я каждый день читаю „Вечернюю Москву". — Это хорошо. Но вам надо ещё и говорить по-русски каждый день. Вот на вашем курсе есть милая девушка Зина. Вы её знаете? — Да, но мне с ней очень трудно говорить. Когда я с ней говорю, я всё забываю и только смотрю на неё.

Олег должен посмотреть этот фильм. В нём играет его сестра. Она много писала ему об этом фильме, и ему очень интересно его посмотреть. Но сегодня он всё утро был на лекциях, после лекций пошёл к товарищу, и они долго вместе читали. Нет, сегодня ему будет трудно пойти в кино, он устал. Лучше он пойдёт завтра.

— Борис Михайлович, у вас нет деревянного ящика?

— Есть, а зачем он вам?

— Мне нужно послать родителям проигрыватель.

— А разве у них в колхозе есть электричество?

— Да, есть. Я давно хотел купить им проигрыватель и вот купил. Думаю, что это будет хороший подарок для них.

— Скажите, Николай, у вас в колхозе хорошие избы?

— Да, очень хорошие.

— И водопровод есть?

— Нет, водопровода нет. Но у нас много колодцев и хорошее озеро. Да и люди наши привыкли носить воду, им не трудно.

— Мне странно это слышать. У нас в Америке всё совсём иначе.

— Что это там строят?

— Кажется дома для колхозников.

— О, каменные!

— Да. В «Огоньке» недавно был об этом очерк.

— Ах да, я читал, но не знал, что это об этом колхозе.

— Да, в этих новых домах, говорят, будет электричество и даже водопровод.

— Да ну? И всё удобства? Ванные, уборные?

— Этого я не знаю.

— А телефон?

— Не думаю.

— Знаешь, Олег, я уже привык здесь, в городе, к электричеству и радио, а вот приехал недавно в наш колхоз и — ничего там нет. Странно даже, как люди могут жить без этих удобств!

— А ведь ты сам так жил, когда дома был.

— Да я уже и не помню об этом — так давно это было.

— А вот кончишь университет, может быть будешь в своём колхозе работать. Опять привыкнешь.

— Нет! Я в колхозе работать не буду, не хочу. Впрочем, когда я кончу, может быть там уже будет электричество.

— Галя, помните, я вам показывал снимки фабрики, где работает мой отец?

— Да. Я себе иначе представляла американские фабрики.

— Вы даже, кажется, не поверили мне, правда?

— Нет, Филипп, я вам поверила, только я уже привыкла иначе думать об Америке.

— А знаете, когда я сюда ехал, я тоже всё себе иначе представлял.

— Ваши студенты учат английский язык?

— Да, и некоторые уже неплохо говорят. Вы с ними разве не говорили?

— Говорил, но по-русски. Так жаль! Я не знал, что они говорят по-английски.

— Да, а я как раз думал спросить вас, господин Грант, как они говорят.

— Я завтра зайду к вам и поговорю с ними.

NOTES

PREPARATION FOR CONVERSATION

Несчáстный слýчай

слýчай [slúčij]	case, occasion, incident, event, chance
несчáстный [ɲiščásnij]	unhappy, unfortunate
несчáстный слýчай	accident, unfortunate incident
Юрий Николáевич, давнó вáс не вѝдел!	Yury Nikolaevich, I haven't seen you for a long time!
чтó это [štóetə]	why, why is it, how come
А чтó это вы́ тáк идёте?	But why are you walking like that?
Вы́ рáзве не слы́шали?	You mean you haven't heard?
ногá (acc sg нóгу)	leg, foot
сломáть (pfv I), сломáю, –ешь, –ют	to break
Я сломáл себé нóгу.	I broke my leg.
упáсть (pfv I) (fut упадý, –ёшь, –ýт; past упáл, –а, –о, –и)	to fall, fall down
Я упáл и сломáл себé нóгу.	I fell and broke my leg.
чýть не	almost, all but, nearly
Я чýть не сломáл себé нóгу.	I almost broke my leg.
Я упáл и чýть не сломáл себé нóгу.	I fell and almost broke my leg.
Бóже мóй!	good heavens! my goodness! my God!
Áх ты́, Бóже мóй!	Oh for heaven's sake!
случѝться (pfv II)	to happen
Кáк же э́то случѝлось?	How in the world did it happen?
представить (pfv II), представлю, –вишь, –вят	to present, introduce
представить себé	to imagine
Представьте себé!	Imagine! or Just imagine!
лéстница [ḷésɲicə]	stairway, stairs, ladder
Представьте себé! Э́то случѝлось на лéстнице.	Imagine! It happened on the stairway.

внизы
вни́з по ле́стнице
Я шёл вни́з по ле́стнице.
вдру́г
и вдру́г упа́л
Я шёл вни́з по ле́стнице и вдру́г упа́л.
Предста́вьте себе́, шёл вни́з по на́шей ле́стнице и вдру́г упа́л.

несча́стье [ɲiščástjə]
Во́т несча́стье!
действи́тельно
Во́т, действи́тельно, несча́стье!

глу́пость (f)
Про́сто глу́пость!
шестна́дцать [šisnátcət]
ле́т (gen pl of год *year*)
шестна́дцать ле́т
Шестна́дцать ле́т хожу́ по э́той ле́стнице.
осторо́жный, осторо́жно
(*short form* осторо́жен, –жна, –о, –ы)

Шестна́дцать ле́т хожу́ по э́той ле́стнице, всегда́ та́к осторо́жен, а ту́т вдру́г упа́л!

вся́кий
со вся́ким
Э́то со вся́ким мо́жет случи́ться.

обрати́ться (pfv II) [abraṭítcə]
обращу́сь, обрати́шься, –ятся
Вы́ к кому́ обрати́лись?

К О́сипову.

вра́ч, –а́; –и́, –е́й
О́н хоро́ший вра́ч.
несимпати́чный
О́н хоро́ший вра́ч, но челове́к несимпати́чный.

безду́шный

како́й-то
О́н безду́шный како́й-то.

душа́
Да зачём ва́м душа́?

специали́ст
Ва́м специали́ст ну́жен.

down, downstairs
down the stairs
I was going down the stairs.
suddenly, all of a sudden
and suddenly fell
I was going down the stairs and suddenly fell.
Imagine! I was going down our stairs and suddenly fell.

bad luck, misfortune, unhappiness
What an unlucky break!
really, indeed
That was really an unlucky break!

foolishness, stupidity, nonsense
It was plain stupidity!
sixteen
years
sixteen years
I've been walking up and down those stairs for sixteen years.
careful, carefully

I've been walking up and down those stairs for sixteen years, always [being] so careful, and all of a sudden I fall!

anyone, anybody, any
to anybody (*lit.* with anybody)
It can happen to anybody.

to consult, turn to, address

Whom did you consult? *or* What doctor did you see?

Osipov.

physician, doctor
He's a good physician.
not likable, not nice, not personable
He's a good physician, but not a likable person.

unfeeling, cold, impersonal (*lit.* without soul, heartless)
a, an; kind of, some kind of
He's kind of cold and unfeeling.

soul, heart, feeling
What's feeling got to do with it?

specialist
You need a specialist.

прáв, –á, –о, –ы	right
Вы́ прáвы, конéчно.	You're right, of course.

дóктор, –а; докторá, –óв	doctor
Я не люблю́ ходи́ть к докторáм.	I don't like going to doctors *or* I hate going to doctors.
Кáк я́ не люблю́ ходи́ть к докторáм!	How I hate going to doctors!

SUPPLEMENT

во вся́ком слу́чае	in any case, anyway, in any event
Во вся́ком слу́чае, я́ в Москву́ не поéду.	In any case, I won't go to Moscow.
навéрх	up, upstairs
Пойдём ко мнé навéрх.	Let's go upstairs to my room.
глу́пый	foolish, silly, dumb, stupid
Какáя онá глу́пая!	How foolish she is!
у́мный	wise, intelligent, smart, clever
Онá такáя у́мная!	She's so clever (*or* wise)!
симпати́чный	nice, likable
Óн óчень симпати́чный человéк.	He's a very nice person.
гóд, –а	year
в э́том году́	this year
Рáз в гóд я́ éзжу в Я́лту.	Once a year I go to Yalta.
В э́том году́ я́ тудá не поéду.	This year I won't go there.
мéсяц	month; moon
в э́том мéсяце	this month
Двá рáза в мéсяц мы́ éздили в гóрод.	Twice a month we went to the city.
В э́том мéсяце мы́ тудá не поéдем.	This month we won't go there.

Несчáстный слу́чай

С.П. — Сергéй Пáвлович   Ю.Н. — Ю́рий Николáевич

С.П. 1 Ю́рий Николáевич, давнó вáс не ви́дел! А чтó э́то вы́ тáк идёте?[1]

Ю.Н. 2 Вы́ рáзве не слы́шали? Я́ упáл и чу́ть не сломáл себé нóгу.

С.П. 3 Áх ты́, Бóже мóй![2] Кáк же э́то случи́лось?

Ю.Н. 4 Предстáвьте себé, шёл вни́з по нáшей лéстнице и вдру́г упáл.

С.П. 5 Вóт, действи́тельно, несчáстье!

Ю.Н. 6 Прóсто глу́пость! Шестнáдцать лéт хожу́ по э́той лéстнице, всегдá тáк остарóжен, а ту́т вдру́г упáл![3]

С.П. 7 Э́то со вся́ким мóжет случи́ться. Вы́ к кому́ обрати́лись?

Ю.Н.   8 К Óсипову. Óн хорóший врáч, но человéк несимпатúчный. Бездýшный какóй-то.

С.П.   9 Да зачéм вáм душá?⁴ Вáм специалúст нýжен.

Ю.Н. 10 Вы́ прáвы, конéчно. Кáк я не люблю́ ходúть к докторáм!

NOTES
¹ **Чтó это, чтó** and even **чегó** in a more colloquial style are often substituted for **почемý** *why* in spoken Russian. Stylistically this is something akin to the colloquial English *how come:* **Чтó это вы́ к нáм не захóдите?** *How come you don't drop in to see us?*

² **Бóг** *God* is one of the few Russian nouns with a vocative form: **Бóже!** The expression **Бóже мóй!** is a stock phrase with its own special word order. It is not as strong as the English *My God!* but is rather like *Good heavens!* or *My goodness!* In Soviet publications, the word for God is written with a small initial letter.

³ The form **лéт**, which functions as the genitive plural of **гóд** *year* with numbers and adverbs of quantity, is actually the genitive plural of **лéто** *summer.* Compare **одúн гóд** with **мнóго лéт, шестнáдцать лéт.** (Consider the poetic use of English *summers* as, for example, in "She was sixteen *summers* old.") The regular genitive plural form **годóв** is very rarely used. **Гóд** also has alternate forms in the nominative plural: **гóды** and **годá.**

⁴ Although **душá** literally means *soul,* it is often best translated as *heart,* in the sense of empathy or sympathetic character. Note that the adjective **бездýшный** is formed from **без** *without* and **душá.**

PREPARATION FOR CONVERSATION   **У дóктора**

чýвствовать себя́ (i)¹	to feel
чýвствую, чýвствуешь, –ют	
Как вы́ себя́ чýвствуете?	How do you feel?
горáздо	by far, much, considerably
Горáздо лýчше, дóктор.	Much better, doctor.
Я почтú свобóдно хожý.	I have almost no trouble walking. (*Lit.* I walk almost freely.)
Дáже смóг пешкóм к вáм прийтú.	I was even able to come to your office on foot.
сойтú (pfv i) (*like* пойтú)	to go off, get off, come (*or* go) down
ýм, –á	mind, sense
сойтú с умá	to go (*or* be) out of one's mind, to go (*or* be) crazy
Вы́ с умá сошлú?	Are you out of your mind?

¹ Forms of **чýвствовать** are simplified in speech. The first **в** should never be pronounced. The second **в** may also be dropped so that in rapid speech **чýвствуете** is usually pronounced [čústujţi]. (Compare this with **здрáвствуйте**, which is usually pronounced [zdrástujţi] or, in very rapid speech, [zdráşşţi].)

Я вáм сказáл ходúть тóлько
по кóмнате.
    полчасá
    в дéнь

I told you to walk only about the room.
    half an hour
    per day, a day

Вáм мóжно ходúть тóлько
полчасá в дéнь.
    тó

You can walk only half an hour a day.
    then

**Я же вáм сказáл ходúть тóлько
по кóмнате и тó не бóльше,
чéм полчасá в дéнь.**

But I told you to walk only about the room
and then not more than half an hour
a day.

    становúться (II) [stənaɣítcə]
      становлю́сь, станóвишься, –ятся

    to become, get, grow, step

Мнé станóвится лýчше.
    чéм . . . тéм . . .
    чéм бóльше, тéм лýчше

I'm getting better *or* I'm improving.
    the . . . the . . .
    the more the better

Чéм бóльше я́ хожý, тéм лýчше
мнé станóвится.
    казáться (I) (past казáлось, pres кáжется)

The more I walk, the better I get.
    to seem

Мнé казáлось, что мнé станóвится
лýчше.

It seemed to me I was improving.

**Извинúте, дóктор, но мнé казáлось, что
чéм бóльше я́ хожý, тéм лýчше
мнé станóвится.**

Excuse me, doctor, but it seemed to
me the more I walked, the more
I improved.

    обращáться (I) [abraščátcə]
      обращáюсь, обращáешься, –ются

    to consult, turn to, address, go (*or* come) to

Зачéм вы́ ко мнé обращáлись?
    вообщé

Why did you consult me?
    in general, at all

Зачéм вы́ вообщé ко мнé обращáлись?

Why did you [bother to] consult me
at all?

    нрáвиться (II) [nráɣitcə]
      нрáвлюсь, нрáвишься, –ятся
    тáк, кáк вáм нрáвится
    éсли

    to like, please, appeal to

    just as you please, exactly as you like
    if

**Éсли вы́ дéлаете тáк, кáк вáм
нрáвится, тó зачéм вы́ тогдá
вообщé ко мнé обращáлись?**

If you do just as you please, then
why do you bother to consult me
at all?

    сердúться (II) [şirḍítcə]
      сержýсь, сéрдишься, –ятся

    to be angry, to be mad

Не сердúтесь, дóктор.
    тóчный; тóчно

Don't be angry, doctor.
    exact, precise; exactly, precisely

Я бýду дéлать всё тóчно тáк,
кáк вы́ скáжете.

I'll do everything exactly as you say.

**Не сердúтесь, дóктор, я́ бýду
дéлать всё тóчно тáк, кáк вы́
скáжете.**

Don't be angry, doctor; I'll do
everything exactly as you say.

Ну́, хорошо́. Покажи́те мне́ но́гу. Да́, непло́хо.	Well, all right. Show me your leg. Yes, not bad.
боле́ть (II)	to ache, hurt, pain
У меня́ боли́т нога́.	My leg (or foot) hurts.
Она́ у меня́ почти́ совсе́м не боли́т.	It's almost stopped hurting altogether.
масса́ж	massage
де́лать масса́ж	to massage
по утра́м	in the mornings, mornings
На́до де́лать по утра́м масса́ж.	You have to massage it in the mornings.
продолжа́ть (I)	to continue, keep on
Продолжа́йте де́лать по утра́м масса́ж.	Continue massaging it in the mornings.
ма́зь (f)	ointment, salve
реце́пт	prescription, recipe
Я́ ва́м да́м но́вый реце́пт на ма́зь.	I'll give you a new prescription for ointment.
помога́ть (I) (*plus* dat)	to help
Спаси́бо. Э́та ма́зь мне́ о́чень помога́ет.	Thanks. The ointment really helps me.
Когда́ мне́ прийти́?	When am I to come? *or* When should I come?
Когда́ мне́ прийти́ опя́ть, в сре́ду?	When should I come again, on Wednesday?
коне́ц, конца́; –ы́, –о́в	end
уезжа́ть (I)	to go away, leave (by vehicle)
Не́т, я уезжа́ю в конце́ э́той неде́ли.	No, I'm going away the end of this week.
че́рез пя́ть дне́й	in five days
дне́й че́рез пя́ть	in about five days
Я уезжа́ю дне́й че́рез пя́ть.	I'm going away in about five days.
верну́ться (pfv I) [γirnútcə] верну́сь, верне́шься, –у́тся	to come back, return
Я верну́сь дне́й че́рез пя́ть.	I'll return in about five days.
ра́ньше	earlier, before
Я верну́сь дне́й че́рез пя́ть, не ра́ньше.	I'll return in about five days, not before.
Я уезжа́ю в конце́ э́той неде́ли и верну́сь дне́й че́рез пя́ть, не ра́ньше.	I'm going away the end of this week and will return in about five days, not before.
назна́чить (pfv II)	to set, designate, appoint, assign
назна́чить де́нь	to give an appointment, set a date
Я́ ва́м назна́чу де́нь.	I'll give you an appointment.
Позвони́те мне́ че́рез неде́лю, и я́ ва́м назна́чу де́нь.	Phone me in a week and I'll give you an appointment.

ху́же | worse

Я чу́вствую себя́ гора́здо ху́же, до́ктор. | I feel much worse, doctor.

рассерди́ться (pfv II) (*like* серди́ться) | to become angry, get mad

Почему́ о́н та́к на меня́ рассерди́лся? | Why did he become so angry with me?

помо́чь (pfv I) (*like* мо́чь) (*plus* dat) | to help

О́н, наве́рно, ва́м помо́жет. | He'll probably help you.

уе́хать (pfv I) (*like* е́хать) | to go away, leave (by vehicle)

Когда́ о́н уе́хал из Москвы́? | When did he leave Moscow?

Я ско́ро уе́ду в Ленингра́д. | I'll soon leave for Leningrad.

нача́ло | beginning, start

О́н уе́хал в нача́ле э́той неде́ли. | He went away at the beginning of the week.

возвраща́ться (I) | to return, come (*or* go) back

Оте́ц возвраща́ется домо́й в ше́сть. | Father returns home at six.

по́зже | later, later on

Они́ приду́т по́зже. | They'll come later.

в конце́ концо́в [fkancé kancóf] | finally, in the end, in the long run, after all

В конце́ концо́в, о́н получи́л разреше́ние. | He finally got a permit.

У до́ктора

О. — О́сипов

Ю.Н. — Ю́рий Никола́евич

О. 1 Здра́вствуйте! Ка́к вы́ себя́ чу́вствуете?

Ю.Н. 2 Гора́здо лу́чше, до́ктор. Я почти́ свобо́дно хожу́. Да́же смо́г пешко́м к ва́м прийти́.

О. 3 Вы́ с ума́ сошли́? Я же ва́м сказа́л ходи́ть то́лько по ко́мнате и то́ не бо́льше, чéм полчаса́ в де́нь.

Ю.Н. 4 Извини́те, до́ктор, но мне́ каза́лось, чéм бо́льше я хожу́, тéм лу́чше мне́ стано́вится.

О. 5 Éсли вы́ де́лаете та́к, ка́к ва́м нра́вится, то заче́м вы́ тогда́ вообще́ ко мне́ обраща́лись?!

Ю.Н. 6 Не серди́тесь, до́ктор, я бу́ду де́лать всё то́чно та́к, ка́к вы́ ска́жете.[1]

О. 7 Ну́, хорошо́. Покажи́те мне́ но́гу. Да́, непло́хо.

Ю.Н. 8 Она́ у меня́ почти́ совсе́м не боли́т.

О. 9 Хорошо́, но продолжа́йте де́лать по утра́м масса́ж. Я́ ва́м да́м но́вый рецéпт на ма́зь.

Ю.Н. 10 Спаси́бо. Э́та ма́зь мне́ о́чень помога́ет. Когда́ мне́ прийти́ опя́ть, в сре́ду?

О. 11 Не́т, я уезжа́ю в конце́ э́той неде́ли и верну́сь дне́й че́рез пя́ть, не ра́ньше.[2] Позвони́те мне́ че́рез неде́лю, и я́ ва́м назна́чу де́нь.

NOTES

[1] Although **вра́ч** and **до́ктор** can sometimes be used interchangeably, only **до́ктор** is used as a form of address or with names: **У до́ктора О́сипова**, "Скажи́те, до́ктор . . ." **Вра́ч** and **до́ктор** apply to both men and women.

> О́н (она́) хоро́ший вра́ч.   He's (she's) a good doctor.
> Э́то до́ктор Петро́ва.   This is Dr. Petrov (f).

General practitioners are mostly women, as are the majority of dentists and oculists in the Soviet Union.

[2] Note the word order in the expression **дне́й че́рез пя́ть**. The placement of a numeral after the noun which it modifies serves to express approximation. Compare **два́ часа́** *two hours* with **часа́ два́** *about two hours*; **сейча́с во́семь часо́в** *it's eight o'clock now* with **сейча́с часо́в во́семь** *it's about eight o'clock now*; and **в де́вять часо́в** *at nine* with **часо́в в де́вять** *around nine*.

Basic sentence patterns

1. Ка́к ва́м понра́вился э́тот вра́ч? How did you like that doctor?
_____ понра́вилась э́та ма́зь? _____ like that ointment?
_____ понра́вилось его́ пе́ние? _____ like his singing?
_____ понра́вились его́ роди́тели? _____ like his parents?

2. Ка́жется, я́ ей нра́влюсь. I guess she likes me.
_____ мы́ __ нра́вимся. _____ likes us.
_____ о́н __ нра́вится. _____ likes him.
_____ ты́ __ нра́вишься. _____ likes you.
_____ они́ __ нра́вятся. _____ likes them.
_____ вы́ __ нра́витесь. _____ likes you.

3. Она́ ча́сто заходи́ла к свое́й сосе́дке. She often called on her neighbor.
_____ к свои́м сосе́дям. _____ on her neighbors.
_____ к своему́ учи́телю. _____ on her teacher.
_____ к свое́й сестре́. _____ on her sister.
_____ к свои́м знако́мым. _____ on her acquaintances.
_____ к своему́ бра́ту. _____ on her brother.
_____ к свои́м подру́гам. _____ on her girl friends.

4. Он обрати́лся к хоро́шему врачу́.

_____ к ру́сскому специали́сту.

_____ к но́вому до́ктору.

_____ к америка́нскому профе́ссору.

_____ к ча́стному врачу́.

He consulted a good physician.

_____ the Russian specialist.

_____ the new doctor.

_____ the American professor.

_____ a private physician.

5. Мы́ шли́ по краси́вой доро́ге.

_____ ста́рой _____.

_____ но́вой _____.

_____ хоро́шей _____.

_____ прямо́й _____.

_____ како́й-то _____.

We were walking along a lovely road.

_____ an old _____.

_____ a new _____.

_____ a good _____.

_____ a straight _____.

_____ some kind of __.

6. Покажи́те э́тот фи́льм ва́шим студе́нтам.

_____ свои́м _____.

_____ мои́м _____.

_____ но́вым _____.

_____ ста́рым _____.

_____ америка́нским __.

_____ хоро́шим _____.

Show the film to your students.

_____ your _____.

_____ my _____.

_____ the new _____.

_____ the old _____.

_____ the American _____.

_____ the good _____.

7. Позвони́те э́той же́нщине.

_____ э́тому челове́ку.

_____ э́тим лю́дям.

_____ э́тому врачу́.

_____ э́той де́вушке.

_____ э́тим молоды́м лю́дям.

Give this woman a call.

____ this man _____.

____ these people _____.

____ this doctor _____.

____ this girl _____.

____ these young people _____.

8. Не станови́тесь туда́!

Не сади́тесь туда́!

Не бо́йтесь!

Не серди́тесь!

Не обраща́йтесь к ни́м!

Не возвраща́йтесь к ни́м!

Don't stand (or step) there!

Don't sit (down) there!

Don't be afraid!

Don't be angry!

Don't consult them!

Don't go back to them!

9. Я́ удивля́юсь, что вы́ к нему́ обрати́лись.

Она́ удивля́ется_____.

Мы́ удивля́емся_____.

Оле́г удивля́ется_____.

Они́ удивля́ются_____.

Ты́ не удивля́ешься, что я́ к нему́ обрати́лся?

Вы́ не удивля́етесь_____?

I'm surprised that you consulted him.

She's surprised_____.

We're surprised_____.

Oleg is surprised_____.

They're surprised_____.

You're not surprised that I consulted him?

You're not surprised_____?

10. Когда́ она́ вернётся?

_____ты́ вернёшься?

_____вы́ вернётесь?

Я́ верну́сь че́рез неде́лю.

Он вернётся_____.

Они́ верну́тся_____.

When will she be back?

____ will you be back?

____ will you be back?

I'll be back in a week.

He'll be back_____.

They'll be back_____.

11. Они́ всегда́ возвраща́ются в ча́с.
    Вы_____ возвраща́етесь_____.
    Я_____ возвраща́юсь_____.
    Ты_____ возвраща́ешься_____.
    Мы_____ возвраща́емся____.
    До́ктор____ возвраща́ется_____.

They always return at one.
    You_____ return_____.
    I_____ return_____.
    You_____ return_____.
    We _____ return _____.
    The doctor _____ returns _____.

12. Вы́ мне́ помо́жете?
    — Да́, я́ ва́м помогу́.
    О́н ва́м помо́жет?
    — Да́, о́н мне́ помо́жет.
    Они́ на́м помо́гут?
    — Да́, они́ на́м помо́гут.
    О́н ва́м помо́г?
    — Да́, помо́г.
    Она́ ва́м помогла́?
    — Да́, помогла́.
    Они́ ва́м помогли́?
    — Да́, помогли́.

Will you help me?
Yes, I'll help you.
Will he help you?
Yes, he'll help me.
Will they help us?
Yes, they'll help us.
Did he help you?
Yes, he did.
Did she help you?
Yes, she did.
Did they help you?
Yes, they did.

13. Когда́ мне́ лу́чше прийти́?
  _____ прие́хать?
  _____ уе́хать?
  _____ зайти́?
  _____ пойти́?
  _____ войти́?
  _____ верну́ться?

When's the best time for me to come?
  _____ to arrive?
  _____ to leave?
  _____ to stop by?
  _____ to go?
  _____ to go in?
  _____ to return?

14. Куда́ мне́ пойти́?
  _____ звони́ть?
  _____ э́то положи́ть?
  _____ пое́хать?
  _____ смотре́ть?
  _____ писа́ть?
  _____ поступа́ть?
  _____ е́хать?

Where am I to (or should I) go?
  _____ call?
  _____ put this?
  _____ drive to?
  _____ look?
  _____ write?
  _____ enroll?
  _____ go?

15. Мне́ стано́вится лу́чше.
  _____ ху́же.
  Мне́ станови́лось лу́чше.
  _____ ху́же.
  Стано́вится хо́лодно.
  _____ жа́рко.
  _____ тепло́.
  _____ свежо́
  _____ ску́чно.
  _____ интере́сно.

I'm getting better.
  _____ worse.
I was getting better.
  _____ worse.
It's getting cold.
  _____ hot.
  _____ warm.
  _____ chilly.
  _____ boring.
  _____ interesting.

16. Ка́к вы́ себя́ чу́вствуете?
    — Я́ себя́ чу́вствую пло́хо.
  _____ хорошо́.
  _____ лу́чше.
  _____ гора́здо лу́чше.
  _____ ху́же.
  _____ гора́здо ху́же.

How do you feel?
I don't feel well.
I feel fine.
  ____ better.
  ____ much better.
  ____ worse.
  ____ much worse.

17. Ка́к по-тво́ему, результа́ты хоро́шие?	What do you think, are the results good?
— Да́, по-мо́ему, результа́ты о́чень хоро́шие.	Yes, in my opinion, the results are very good.
Ка́к по-ва́шему, результа́ты хоро́шие?	What do you think, are the results good?
— Да́, по-мо́ему, результа́ты о́чень хоро́шие.	Yes, in my opinion, the results are very good.

18. Позвони́те мне́ через неде́лю.	Call me up in a week.
_____ две́ неде́ли.	_____ two weeks.
_____ три́ _____.	_____ three _____.
_____ четы́ре _____.	_____ four _____.
_____ пя́ть неде́ль.	_____ five _____.
_____ ше́сть неде́ль.	_____ six _____.
_____ ме́сяц.	_____ a month.
_____ два́ ме́сяца.	_____ two months.
_____ ше́сть ме́сяцев.	_____ six months.

Pronunciation practice: the voicing of ordinarily unvoiced consonants

Contrast the following sets in which к, с, and т are first pronounced voiceless and then are voiced.

A. The letter к pronounced [k]	The letter к pronounced [g]
[kpáru] к па́ру	[gbáru] к ба́ру
to the steam	to the bar
[któmu] к то́му	[gdómu] к до́му
to the volume	to the house
B. The letter с pronounced [s]	The letter с pronounced [z]
[spít] спи́т	[zb̦ít] сби́т
sleeps	knocked down
[spór] спо́р	[zbór] сбо́р
argument	harvesting
C. The letter т pronounced [t]	The letter т pronounced [d]
[atšárə] от ша́ра	[adžárə] от жа́ра
from the sphere	from the heat
[atkatáț] откати́ть	[adgadáț] отгада́ть
to roll off	to guess

STRUCTURE AND DRILLS

Prepositions requiring the dative: к and по

MODELS

Я́ иду́ к до́ктору.	I'm on my way to the doctor's.
_____ к бра́ту.	_____ to my brother's place.
_____ к сестре́.	_____ to my sister's place.
_____ к отцу́.	_____ to my father's place.
_____ к ма́тери.	_____ to my mother's place.
_____ к роди́телям.	_____ to my parents' place.

Подойди́ к телефо́ну.

_____ к столу́.

_____ к окну́.

_____ к доске́.

_____ к ка́рте.

Подойди́ ко мне́.

_____ к на́м.

Э́то на́до сде́лать к обе́ду.

_____ к ве́черу.

_____ ко вто́рнику.

_____ к среде́.

_____ к пя́тнице.

_____ к концу́ ме́сяца.

_____ к нача́лу неде́ли.

Вы́ гото́вы к экза́мену?

_____ к уро́ку?

_____ к ле́кции?

_____ к рабо́те?

_____ к экза́менам?

_____ к заня́тиям?

_____ к ле́кциям?

_____ к обе́ду.

По вечера́м мы́ гуля́ем в па́рке.

По утра́м _____.

По воскресе́ньям _____.

По суббо́там _____.

По среда́м _____.

Не ходи́ по па́рку!

_____ по́ лесу!

_____ по у́лицам!

_____ по́ полю!

_____ по поля́м!

_____ по селу́!

_____ по го́роду!

_____ по доро́ге!

_____ по у́лице!

О́н чита́ет ле́кции по ру́сской му́зыке.

_____ по матема́тике.

_____ по исто́рии СССР.

_____ по геогра́фии.

_____ по ру́сской литерату́ре.

_____ по ру́сскому языку́.

Go (or come) to the phone.

_____ to the table.

_____ to the window.

_____ to the blackboard.

_____ up to the map.

Come over here to me.

_____ to us.

This has to be done by noon.

_____ by evening.

_____ by Tuesday.

_____ by Wednesday.

_____ by Friday.

_____ by the end of the month.

_____ by the beginning of the
week.

Are you prepared (or ready) for the exam?

_____ for the lesson?

_____ for the lecture?

_____ for the work?

_____ for the exams?

_____ for the classes?

_____ for the lectures?

_____ for the dinner?

In the evenings we stroll in the park.

In the mornings _____.

On Sundays _____.

On Saturdays _____.

On Wednesdays _____.

Don't walk (or wander) around in the park!

_____ in the woods!

_____ in the streets!

_____ in the field!

_____ in the fields!

_____ in the village!

_____ in the city!

_____ in the road!

_____ in the street!

He gives lectures on Russian music.

_____ on mathematics.

_____ on the history of the U.S.S.R.

_____ on geography.

_____ on Russian literature.

_____ on the Russian language.

У нáс бы́л экзáмен по рýсскому языкý.	We had an exam on the Russian language.
_____ по фи́зике.	_____ in physics.
_____ по хи́мии.	_____ in chemistry.
_____ по истóрии.	_____ in history.
_____ по геогрáфии.	_____ in geography.
_____ по литератýре.	_____ in literature.
Они́ товáрищи по кýрсу.	They're classmates.
_____ по кóмнате.	_____ roommates.
_____ по шкóле.	_____ schoolmates.
_____ по университéту.	_____ fellow university students.
_____ по рабóте.	_____ co-workers.
_____ по слýжбе.	_____ co-workers.
Онá лю́бит ходи́ть по толкýчкам.	She loves to make the rounds of the flea markets.
_____ по магази́нам.	_____ of the stores.
_____ по ресторáнам.	_____ of the restaurants.
_____ по библиотéкам.	_____ of the libraries.
_____ по докторáм.[1]	_____ of the doctors.

■ REPETITION DRILL

Repeat the given models, noting the various usages of **к** and **по**, both of which require the dative case.

■ STRUCTURE REPLACEMENT DRILLS

1. *On the right was the door.*
   He went over (or *up*) *to the door.*
   Напрáво былá двéрь.
   Óн подошёл к двéри.
   Напрáво бы́л телефóн.
   Óн подошёл к телефóну.
   (окно, стол, лестница, полка, касса, буфет)

2. *On Wednesday we went to the movies.*
   On Wednesdays we used to go to the movies.
   В срéду мы́ ходи́ли в кинó.
   По средáм мы́ ходи́ли в кинó.
   В четвéрг мы́ ходи́ли в кинó.
   По четвергáм мы́ ходи́ли в кинó.
   (в пятницу, в воскресенье, в понедельник, в субботу, во вторник)

3. *I was at my brother's* (*place*).
   I'm going to see my brother.
   Я́ бы́л у брáта.
   Я́ идý к брáту.
   Я́ бы́л у дóктора.
   Я́ идý к дóктору.
   (у врача, у учителя, у Зины, у друга, у американца, у сестры, у Гали, у товарища, у продавщицы, у Наташи)

4. *It'll be ready before noon.*
   It'll be ready by noon.
   Э́то бýдет готóво до обéда.
   Э́то бýдет готóво к обéду.
   Э́то бýдет готóво до четвергá.
   Э́то бýдет готóво к четвергý.
   (до пятницы, до субботы, до понедельника, до среды, до воскресенья, до начала следующей недели, до дня его рождения)

---

[1] Note that there is a slight difference between **ходи́ть к докторáм** and **ходи́ть по докторáм**. The first is neutral, *to go to doctors;* the second means *to go from one doctor to another, to run to different doctors.*

5. *We have a Russian language lesson.*
   We have a lesson on the Russian language.
   У на́с уро́к ру́сского языка́.
   У на́с уро́к по ру́сскому языку́.
   У на́с уро́к исто́рии.
   У на́с уро́к по исто́рии.
   (геогра́фии, хи́мии, фи́зики,
   матема́тики, исто́рии СССР, му́зыки,
   ру́сской литерату́ры)

6. *They entered the hall.*
   They walked (or wandered) about the hall.
   Они́ вошли́ в за́л.
   Они́ ходи́ли по за́лу.
   Они́ вошли́ в теа́тр.
   Они́ ходи́ли по теа́тру.
   (лаборато́рию, па́рк, ко́мнату, до́м,
   библиоте́ку, вокза́л, магази́н, клу́б,
   горсове́т)

7. *She loves flea markets.*
   She loves to make the rounds of the flea markets.
   Она́ лю́бит толку́чки.
   Она́ лю́бит ходи́ть по толку́чкам.

   Она́ лю́бит магази́ны.
   Она́ лю́бит ходи́ть по магази́нам.
   (библиоте́ки, клу́бы, рестора́ны,
   теа́тры, конце́рты)

■ CUED QUESTION-ANSWER DRILL

(*room*)   *Are they acquainted?*
          Yes, they're roommates.
(ко́мната) Они́ знако́мы?
     Да́, они́ това́рищи по ко́мнате.

(ку́рс)   Они́ знако́мы?
     Да́, они́ това́рищи по ку́рсу.
(университе́т, шко́ла, рабо́та, ко́мната,
ку́рс)

DISCUSSION

1. К (Ко)

The preposition **к** always requires the dative. With motion verbs **к** must be used if the destination is a person. In this use it is the destinational opposite of the locational preposition **у**.

| Где́ вы́ бы́ли? — У бра́та. | Where were you? At my brother's. |
| Куда́ вы́ идёте? — К бра́ту. | Where are you going? To my brother's. |

When the destination is a place or object, **в** or **на** plus the accusative is used if complete attainment of the goal is implied. However, **к** plus the dative may be used to describe movement toward the goal, i.e., limited attainment of the goal.

Я́ иду́ в па́рк.	I'm going to the park.
Я́ иду́ к па́рку.	I'm walking toward the park.
Иди́те в до́м.	Go into the house.
Иди́те к до́му.	Go up toward the house.

К is also used with time nouns in the sense of *by* or *toward*.

Я́ прие́ду к концу́ ме́сяца.	I'll come toward (*or* by) the end of the month.
К утру́ стано́вится хо́лодно.	Toward morning it gets cold.
Я́ э́то сде́лаю к суббо́те.	I'll get it done by Saturday.
Я́ э́то сде́лаю ко вто́рнику.	I'll get it done by Tuesday.

In conjunction with nouns describing activities, **к** is used in the sense of *for*.

| Мы́ ещё не гото́вы к экза́мену. | We're not prepared for the exam yet. |
| Что́ ты́ купи́л к обе́ду? | What did you buy for dinner? |

2. По

По is a preposition used mostly with the dative; it has many meanings, for example, *over*, *along* (the surface of), *to* (various goals), *on, in, via, by, according to, apiece, per person.* Some of these are illustrated below.

по вечера́м, по утра́м	[in the] evenings, [in the] mornings
по среда́м	on Wednesdays
по ра́дио, по телефо́ну	by (*or* over) the radio, by phone
звони́ть по телефо́ну	to call on the phone
по исто́рии, по литерату́ре	on (the subject of) history, literature
по привы́чке, по пла́ну, по оши́бке	by habit, by plan, by mistake
по́ лесу, по́ полю, по го́роду	about the woods, field, city
по доктора́м	to one doctor after another
по магази́нам	to one store after another
по стака́ну, по ча́шке	a glass apiece, a cup apiece

A number of adverbial expressions are formed by prefixing **по**.

по-мо́ему	in my opinion
по-ва́шему	in your opinion
по-ру́сски	in Russian
по-англи́йски	in English

The dative endings of э́тот, чей, and the possessive pronoun modifiers

THE ENDINGS		
SINGULAR		PLURAL
Masculine and Neuter	Feminine	
–ому, –ему	–ой, –ей	–им

MODELS

Кто́ помо́жет э́тому студе́нту?	Who will help this student?
_____ па́рню?	_____ lad?
_____ э́той студе́нтке?	_____ this girl student?
_____ же́нщине?	_____ woman?
_____ э́тим студе́нтам?	_____ these students?
_____ лю́дям?	_____ people?

Позвони́те э́тому врачу́.	Give this (*or* that) physician a call.
_____ до́ктору.	_____ doctor _____.
_____ челове́ку.	_____ man _____.
_____ учи́телю.	_____ teacher _____.
_____ э́той же́нщине.	_____ this (*or* that) woman _____.
_____ де́вушке.	_____ girl _____.
_____ э́тим студе́нткам.	_____ these (*or* those) girl students _____.
_____ де́вушкам.	_____ girls _____.
_____ парня́м.	_____ lads _____.

Пойдём к моему́ дру́гу. | Let's go to my friend's place.
_____ това́рищу. | _____ friend's _____.
_____ бра́ту. | _____ brother's _____.
_____ к мое́й сестре́. | _____ to my sister's _____.
_____ ма́тери. | _____ mother's _____.
_____ подру́ге. | _____ girl friend's _____.
_____ к мои́м роди́телям. | _____ to my parents' _____.
_____ друзья́м. | _____ friends' _____.
_____ това́рищам. | _____ friends' _____.

Приве́т ва́шему му́жу. | Give my regards to your husband.
_____ твоему́ _____. | _____ your _____.
_____ ва́шей жене́. | _____ your wife.
_____ твое́й _____. | _____ your _____.
_____ ва́шим роди́телям. | _____ your parents.
_____ твои́м _____. | _____ your _____.

Мы́ привы́кли к на́шему профе́ссору. | We're used to our professor.
_____ учи́телю. | _____ teacher.
_____ сосе́ду. | _____ neighbor.
_____ к на́шей учи́тельнице. | _____ to our teacher (f).
_____ сосе́дке. | _____ neighbor (f).
_____ к на́шим студе́нтам. | _____ to our students.
_____ профессора́м. | _____ professors.
_____ сосе́дям. | _____ neighbors.
_____ учителя́м. | _____ teachers.

EXPANSION DRILLS

1. *Come over to the window!*
   Come over to this window!
   Подойди́ к окну́!
   Подойди́ к э́тому окну́!
   Подойди́ к по́лке!
   Подойди́ к э́той по́лке!
   (ли́фту, коло́дцу, две́ри, ка́ссе, избе́, ка́рте, ваго́ну, буфе́ту)

2. *Give the tourists a pass!*
   Give these tourists a pass!
   Да́йте тури́стам про́пуск!
   Да́йте э́тим тури́стам про́пуск!
   Да́йте певи́це про́пуск!
   Да́йте э́той певи́це про́пуск!
   (иностра́нцу, тури́сту, америка́нке, студе́нту, учителя́м, продавщи́це)

3. *Don't walk* (or *wander*) *around in the park!*
   Don't walk (or *wander*) *around in this park!*
   Не ходи́ по па́рку!
   Не ходи́ по э́тому па́рку!
   Не ходи́ по у́лице!
   Не ходи́ по э́той у́лице!
   (по поля́м, по доро́ге, по го́роду, по у́лицам, по́ полю, по́ лесу)

4. *I'm used to the teacher.*
   I'm used to our teacher.
   Я́ привы́к к учи́телю.
   Я́ привы́к к на́шему учи́телю.
   Я́ привы́к к учи́тельнице.
   Я́ привы́к к на́шей учи́тельнице.
   (к сосе́дкам, к сосе́ду, к сосе́дям, к профе́ссору, к студе́нтам, к америка́нцу)

■ RESPONSE DRILLS

1. *We came up* (or *went over*) *to her window.*
   To whose window?
   Мы́ подошли́ к её окну́.
   К чьему́ окну́?

   Мы́ подошли́ к её дверя́м.
   К чьи́м дверя́м?
   (две́ри, сту́лу, столу́, по́лке, шкафу́, ко́мнате)

2. *She's gone to visit their brother.*
Whose brother?
Она́ пое́хала к и́х бра́ту.
К чьему́ бра́ту?
Она́ пое́хала к и́х сестре́.
К чье́й сестре́?

(родителям, другу, подруге, товарищам, отцу, друзьям, учительнице)

■ EXPANSION DRILLS

1. *He bought his father a present.*
He bought a present for his (own) father.
Óн купи́л пода́рок отцу́.
Óн купи́л пода́рок своему́ отцу́.
Óн купи́л пода́рок сестре́.
Óн купи́л пода́рок свое́й сестре́.

(родителям, другу, подруге, брату, товарищу, жене, учителю, учительнице)

2. *I went over to the desk.*
I went over to my desk.
Я́ подошёл к столу́.
Я́ подошёл к моему́ столу́.
Я́ подошёл к окну́.
Я́ подошёл к моему́ окну́.

(дверям, шкафу, полкам, лаборатории, вагону, школе, общежитию, дому)

■ STRUCTURE REPLACEMENT DRILLS

1. *I returned to my work.*
We returned to our work.
Я́ верну́лся к мое́й рабо́те.
Мы́ верну́лись к на́шей рабо́те.
Я́ верну́лся к моему́ о́черку.
Мы́ верну́лись к на́шему о́черку.

(моим занятиям, моему роману, моей книге, моему сочинению, моей просьбе, моему плану)

2. *Are you going to see your neighbor?*
Ты́ пойдёшь к твое́й сосе́дке?
Вы́ пойдёте к ва́шей сосе́дке?
Ты́ пойдёшь к твоему́ сосе́ду?
Вы́ пойдёте к ва́шему сосе́ду?

(твоему учителю, твоей подруге, твоей учительнице, твоим друзьям, твоему отцу, твоей сестре, твоим товарищам)

■ STRUCTURE REPLACEMENT DRILL

This student wants to go away.
This student has to go away.
Э́тот студе́нт хо́чет уе́хать.
Э́тому студе́нту на́до уе́хать.
Э́та америка́нка хо́чет уе́хать.
Э́той америка́нке на́до уе́хать.

(этот профессор, эти туристы, этот доктор, эта девушка, этот иностранец, эта певица, эти соседи, этот певец)

NOM (m)	этот	чей	мой	твой	свой	наш	ваш
(n)	это	чьё	моё	твоё	своё	наше	ваше
DAT	этому	чьему	моему	твоему	своему	нашему	вашему
NOM (f)	эта	чья	моя	твоя	своя	наша	ваша
DAT	этой	чьей	моей	твоей	своей	нашей	вашей
NOM (pl)	эти	чьи	мои	твои	свои	наши	ваши
DAT	этим	чьим	моим	твоим	своим	нашим	вашим

The dative endings for **чей**, **э́тот**, and the possessive pronoun modifiers are distributed as follows:

1. The masculine and neuter dative singular ending is –ему for all except э́тот and э́то, which take –ому. Compare моему́, ва́шему, чьему́ with э́тому.
2. The feminine dative singular ending is –ей for all except э́та, which takes –ой. Compare мое́й, ва́шей, чье́й with э́той.
3. The dative plural ending for *all* these modifiers is –им: мои́м, ва́шим, чьи́м, э́тим.[1]

The dative endings of adjectives: singular and plural

THE ENDINGS		
SINGULAR		PLURAL
Masculine and Neuter	*Feminine*	
–ому, –ему	–ой, –ей	–ым, –им

MODELS

О́н не привы́к к чёрному хле́бу.	He's not used to black bread.
_____ бе́лому хле́бу.	_____ white bread.
_____ америка́нскому джа́зу.	_____ American jazz.
_____ холо́дному ча́ю.	_____ cold tea.
_____ большо́му го́роду.	_____ the big city.
_____ горя́чему молоку́.	_____ hot milk.
_____ вече́рнему ча́ю.	_____ evening tea.
_____ све́жему во́здуху.	_____ fresh air.
Она́ привы́кла к тако́й рабо́те.	She's used to such work.
_____ ру́сской пи́ще.	_____ Russian food.
_____ но́вой ко́мнате.	_____ the new room.
_____ большо́й кварти́ре.	_____ a big apartment.
_____ горя́чей пи́ще.	_____ hot food.
_____ вече́рней рабо́те.	_____ evening work.
Мы́ привы́кли к краси́вым веща́м.	We're used to beautiful things.
_____ тёплым зи́мам.	_____ warm winters.
_____ таки́м заявле́ниям.	_____ such applications.
_____ таки́м оши́бкам.	_____ such mistakes.
_____ больши́м удо́бствам.	_____ great conveniences.
_____ ма́леньким ко́мнатам.	_____ small rooms.
_____ све́жим огурца́м.	_____ fresh cucumbers.
_____ вече́рним заня́тиям.	_____ evening classes.
_____ тру́дным экза́менам.	_____ difficult exams.

---

[1] Note that in all cases э́тот shows a regular alternation of hard-stem [t] in the singular (э́тот, э́того, э́тому, э́та, э́той) with soft-stem [ţ] in the plural (э́ти, э́тих, э́тим).

Но́вому студе́нту нужна́ ко́мната.	The new student needs a room.
Молодо́му челове́ку _____.	The young man _____.
Америка́нскому тури́сту _____.	The American tourist _____.
Молодо́й де́вушке _____.	The young lady _____.
Но́вой студе́нтке _____.	The new student _____.
Ста́рой же́нщине _____.	The old woman _____.
Но́вым студе́нтам нужны́ ко́мнаты.	The new students need rooms.
Молоды́м лю́дям _____.	The young people _____.
Америка́нским тури́стам _____.	The American tourists _____.

■ REPETITION DRILL

Repeat the given models, noting the pattern of adjective endings in the dative case.

■ STRUCTURE REPLACEMENT DRILLS

1. *This is a new student.*
   Let's help this new student.
   Э́то но́вый студе́нт.
   Помо́жем э́тому но́вому студе́нту.
   Э́то плохо́й студе́нт.
   Помо́жем э́тому плохо́му студе́нту.
   (симпатичный, хороший, глупый, американский, неплохой, молодой, умный, русский)

2. *A new professor has arrived.*
   The new professor needs a room.
   Прие́хал но́вый профе́ссор.
   Но́вому профе́ссору нужна́ ко́мната.
   Прие́хала но́вая учи́тельница.
   Но́вой учи́тельнице нужна́ ко́мната.
   (новые студенты, наши старые друзья, молодой человек, наш общий друг, американский турист, русские специалисты, английский профессор)

■ STRUCTURE REPLACEMENT DRILLS

He wrote to these beautiful girls.
He wrote to this beautiful girl.
О́н написа́л э́тим краси́вым де́вушкам.
О́н написа́л э́той краси́вой де́вушке.
О́н написа́л э́тим ми́лым де́вушкам.
О́н написа́л э́той ми́лой де́вушке.
   (симпатичным, русским, интересным, молодым, хорошим, красивым)

■ CUED QUESTION-ANSWER DRILL

(*cold water*)   *What's she gotten used to?*
                     To cold water.
(холо́дная вода́) К чему́ она́ привы́кла?
                     К холо́дной воде́.
(све́жие огурцы́) К чему́ она́ привы́кла?
                     К све́жим огурца́м.
(горячее молоко, бесплатные обеды, вкусные вещи, лёгкая удача, такая работа, трудные экзамены, красивые вещи, свежая рыба, свежие огурцы, свежий воздух)

SINGULAR				PLURAL	
Masculine and Neuter		*Feminine*			
–ому	–ему	–ой	–ей	–ым	–им
молодо́му	си́нему	молодо́й	си́ней	молоды́м	больши́м
большо́му	вече́рнему	большо́й	вече́рней	но́вым	си́ним
но́вому	све́жему	но́вой	све́жей	ста́рым	вече́рним
ста́рому	хоро́шему	ста́рой	хоро́шей	краси́вым	све́жим
краси́вому		краси́вой			хоро́шим
ру́сскому		ру́сской			ру́сским
друго́му		друго́й			други́м

DISTRIBUTION OF ENDINGS

In the dative singular masculine-neuter, the ending is spelled –ому after hard stems and –ему after soft stems. Compare краси́вому, молодо́му with вече́рнему. Mixed stems take –ому, except where the ending is unstressed and preceded by ш, ж, ч, or щ, in which case it is spelled –ему. Compare друго́му, ру́сскому, большо́му with хоро́шему, све́жему.

In the dative singular feminine, the ending is spelled –ой after hard stems and –ей after soft stems. Compare молодо́й, но́вой with вече́рней. Mixed stems take –ой except where the ending is unstressed and preceded by ш, ж, ч, or щ, in which case it is spelled –ей. Compare друго́й, ру́сской, большо́й with хоро́шей, све́жей. Note that these are the same endings as in the genitive and prepositional singular.

In the dative plural, the endings are spelled –ым for hard stems and –им for soft stems and *all* mixed stems. Compare краси́вым, молоды́м with ру́сским, больши́м, хоро́шим, вече́рним.

Reflexive verbs: part I

MODELS

Я́ верну́сь че́рез неде́лю.	I'll return in a week.
Ты́ вернёшься_____.	You'll return _____.
О́н вернётся _____.	He'll return _____.
Мы́ вернёмся _____.	We'll return _____.
Вы́ вернётесь _____.	You'll return _____.
Они́ верну́тся _____.	They'll return _____.

Оте́ц верну́лся из Москвы́.	Father has returned from Moscow.
Ма́ть верну́лась из го́рода.	Mother has returned from the city.
Роди́тели верну́лись в колхо́з.	Our parents have returned to the kolkhoz.

Я́ сержу́сь на Зи́ну.	I'm mad at Zina.
Ты́ се́рдишься____.	You're _____.
О́н се́рдится _____.	He's _____.
Мы́ се́рдимся ____.	We're _____.
Вы́ се́рдитесь ____.	You're _____.
Они́ се́рдятся ____.	They're _____.

Он на меня рассердил**ся**.   He became angry with me.
Она _____ рассерди́ла**сь**.   She became angry with_____.
Они́ _____ рассерди́ли**сь**.   They became angry with ___.

Note that the verbs **серди́ться, рассерди́ться** are accompanied by **на** plus the accusative to indicate the object of one's anger.

■ REPETITION DRILL

Repeat the given models, observing that reflexive verbs are exactly like nonreflexives structurally except for the addition of the particle **–ся** (after consonants including **й**) or **–сь** (after vowels).

■ SUBSTITUTION DRILL

I usually return at one.
Я обы́чно возвраща́юсь в ча́с.
До́ктор обы́чно возвраща́ется в ча́с.
    (она, мы, они, вы, я, ты, он)

■ STRUCTURE REPLACEMENT DRILLS

1. *It was getting warm.*
   It's getting warm.
   Станови́лось тепло́.
   Стано́вится тепло́.
   Станови́лось свежо́.
   Стано́вится свежо́.
       (жарко, интересно, скучно, трудно, легко)

2. *I'm getting cold.*
   I was getting cold.
   Мне́ стано́вится хо́лодно.
   Мне́ станови́лось хо́лодно.
   Мне́ стано́вится ску́чно.
   Мне́ станови́лось ску́чно.
       (тепло, жарко, холодно, лучше, хуже, интересно, неудобно)

3. *She was angry with him.*
   She's angry with him.
   Она́ на него́ серди́лась.
   Она́ на него́ се́рдится.
   Оте́ц на него́ серди́лся.
   Оте́ц на него́ се́рдится.
       (вы, Олег, мать, ты, я, твои родители, сестра, брат)

4. *He became angry with her.*
   He'll become angry with her.
   О́н на неё рассерди́лся.
   О́н на неё рассе́рдится.
   Ма́ть на неё рассерди́лась.
   Ма́ть на неё рассе́рдится.
       (мои подруги, соседка, отец, мать, вы, мы, я, сосед, профессор)

5. *Sergey returned on Wednesday.*
   Sergey will return on Wednesday.
   Серге́й верну́лся в сре́ду.
   Серге́й вернётся в сре́ду.

   Бра́тья верну́лись в сре́ду.
   Бра́тья верну́тся в сре́ду.
       (я, все, уборщица, секретарь, мы, туристы, Юра и Олег, вы)

■ RESPONSE DRILL

I'm always well.
I never go to the doctor.
Я́ всегда́ здоро́в.
Я никогда́ не обраща́юсь к врачу́.

Ты́ всегда́ здоро́ва.
Ты́ никогда́ не обраща́ешься к врачу́.
    (учителя́, вы, сестра, Николай, Наташа, мы, девушки)

DISTRIBUTION OF THE REFLEXIVE PARTICLE –ся OR –сь		
	SINGULAR	PLURAL
PRES-FUT	first person –сь second person –ся third person –ся	first person –ся second person –сь third person –ся
PAST	(m) –ся (n) –сь (f) –сь	(pl) –сь
IMPER	–ся (after consonants [including й]) –сь (after vowels)	

DISCUSSION

Reflexive verbs are those ending in the particle –ся or –сь, with –ся occurring after consonants (including й) and –сь occurring after vowels. Many Russian verbs have both reflexive and non-reflexive forms. Some, like **нра́виться**, are never used without the reflexive particle.

Reflexive verbs cannot have an accusative direct object; from the historical standpoint, the direct object is the attached particle –ся or –сь, which is derived from the reflexive pronoun **себя**. However, the accusative may be used if preceded by a preposition: **О́н рассерди́лся на Ни́ну** *He got mad at Nina.*

Most of the other cases may accompany reflexive verbs, both with and without prepositions, for example:

GEN	О́н бои́тся **Ни́ны**.	He's afraid of Nina.
DAT	О́н удивля́ется **Ни́не**.	He's amazed at Nina.
DAT	Обрати́сь к **О́сипову**!	Consult Osipov!
INSTR	Хоти́те познако́миться с **не́й**?	Want to meet her?

Note on pronunciation: Many Russian speakers do not pronounce the **с** of –ся or –сь soft, despite its spelling. It should *never* be pronounced soft in the infinitive and third person forms where –ть and –т precede it. In this position it combines in a long, hard, unreleased [c], which we indicate in the transcription by [tc]. Thus, for example, both the infinitive **верну́ться** and the third person plural **верну́тся** are pronounced exactly alike: [ɣirnútcə].

Reflexive verbs encountered and drilled in this lesson are given below in all their forms.

1. First conjugation

обраща́ться (ipfv) (к + dat) *to turn to, consult, go to*
    PAST   обраща́лся, обраща́лась, обраща́лось, обраща́лись
    PRES   обраща́юсь, обраща́ешься, –ется, –емся, –етесь, –ются
    IMPER обраща́йся! обраща́йтесь!

возвраща́ться (ipfv) (к + dat) *to return, come back*
    PAST   возвраща́лся, возвраща́лась, –ось, –ись
    PRES   возвраща́юсь, возвраща́ешься, –ется, –емся, –етесь, –ются
    IMPER возвраща́йся! возвраща́йтесь!

верну́ться (pfv) (imperfective **возвраща́ться**) *to return, come back*
- PAST   верну́лся, верну́лась, –ось, –ись
- FUT   верну́сь, вернёшься, –ётся, –ёмся, –ётесь, –у́тся
- IMPER верни́сь! верни́тесь!

каза́ться (ipfv) (mostly used impersonally with the dative) *to seem, appear*
- PAST   каза́лся, каза́лась, –ось, –ись
- PRES   кажу́сь, ка́жешься, –ется, –емся, –етесь, –утся
- IMPER (not used)

2. Second conjugation

обрати́ться (pfv) (imperfective **обраща́ться**) *to turn to, consult, go to*
- PAST   обрати́лся, обрати́лась, –ось, –ись
- FUT   обращу́сь, обрати́шься, –и́тся, –и́мся, –и́тесь, –я́тся
- IMPER обрати́сь! обрати́тесь!

серди́ться (ipfv) (**на** + acc) *to become angry, to get mad*
- PAST   серди́лся, серди́лась, –ось, –ись
- FUT   сержу́сь, се́рдишься, –ится, –имся, –итесь, –ятся
- IMPER [не] серди́сь! [не] серди́тесь!

рассерди́ться (pfv) (conjugated like the imperfective **серди́ться**) *to become angry, to get mad*

станови́ться (ipfv) *to stand, get, become*
- PAST   станови́лся, станови́лась, –ось, –ись
- PRES   становлю́сь, стано́вишься, –ится, –имся, –итесь, –ятся
- IMPER станови́сь! станови́тесь!

случи́ться (pfv) (used only in the third person) *to happen*
- PAST   случи́лся, случи́лась, –ось, –ись
- PRES   случи́тся, случа́тся

Нра́виться, понра́виться

MODELS

Что́ вам понра́вилось?	What did you like?
— Мне́ понра́вился «Евге́ний Оне́гин».	I liked *Eugene Onegin.*
— Мне́ понра́вилась «Война́ и мир».	I liked *War and Peace.*
— Мне́ понра́вилось нача́ло э́того фи́льма.	I liked the beginning of the movie.
— Мне́ понра́вились ру́сские пе́сни.	I liked the Russian songs.
Кто́ тебе́ понра́вился?	Whom did you like?
— Мне́ понра́вился Влади́мир.	I liked Vladimir.
— Мне́ понра́вилась Ната́ша.	I liked Natasha.
— Мне́ понра́вились твои́ сёстры.	I liked your sisters.
Как вам понра́вился фи́льм?	How did you like the movie?
— На́м фи́льм о́чень понра́вился.	We really enjoyed the movie.
Как вам понра́вилась карти́на?	How did you like the picture?
— На́м карти́на о́чень понра́вилась.	We really enjoyed the picture.

Как вáм понрáвилось её пéние?	How did you like her singing?
— Нáм её пéние óчень понрáвилось.	We really enjoyed her singing.
Как вáм понрáвились пластíнки?	How did you like the records?
— Нáм пластíнки óчень понрáвились.	We really enjoyed the records.

Тебé нрáвится истóрия?	Do you like history?
— Нéт, мнé не нрáвится истóрия.	No, I don't care for history.
Тебé нрáвится фíзика?	Do you like physics?
— Нéт, мнé не нрáвится фíзика.	No, I don't care for physics.
Тебé нрáвятся егó стихí?	Do you like his poetry?
— Нéт, мнé не нрáвятся егó стихí.	No, I don't like his poetry.
Тебé нрáвятся э́ти картíны?	Do you like these pictures?
— Нéт, мнé не нрáвятся э́ти картíны.	No, I don't like these pictures.

Ей понрáвится э́тот костю́м.	She'll like this suit.
_____ э́тот подáрок.	_____ this present.
_____ э́та пластíнка.	_____ this record.
_____ э́та кóмната.	_____ this room.
_____ э́та у́лица.	_____ this street.
_____ э́то плáтье.	_____ this dress.

Ей понрáвятся э́ти пéсни.	She'll like these songs.
_____ э́ти кнíги.	_____ these books.
_____ э́ти чáшки.	_____ these cups.

Вы́ мнé нрáвитесь.	I like you.
Óн мнé нрáвится.	I like him.
Ты́ мнé нрáвишься.	I like you.
Онá мнé нрáвится.	I like her.
Онí мнé нрáвятся.	I like them.
Я́ вáм нрáвлюсь?	Do you like me?
Мы́ вáм нрáвимся?	Do you like us?

■ REPETITION DRILL

Repeat the given models illustrating **нрáвиться, понрáвиться**. Note that the one who performs the liking is in the dative case and that the object of the liking is in the nominative case in Russian.

■ QUESTION-ANSWER DRILL

What don't you like?
I don't like this camera.
Чтó вáм не нрáвится?
Мнé не нрáвится э́тот аппарáт.
Чтó емý не нрáвится?
Емý не нрáвится э́тот аппарáт.
   (ей, тебе, им, ему, вам)

■ STRUCTURE REPLACEMENT DRILL

He loves to sing loudly.
He likes to sing loudly.
Óн лю́бит грóмко пéть.
Емý нрáвится грóмко пéть.
Я́ люблю́ грóмко пéть.
Мнé нрáвится грóмко пéть.
   (мы, она, ты, они, я, он, мы)

■ STRUCTURE REPLACEMENT DRILLS

1. *We really like that girl.*
   We really liked that girl.
   Нáм óчень нрáвится э́та дéвушка.
   Нáм óчень нрáвилась э́та дéвушка.
   Нáм óчень нрáвится твóй брáт.
   Нáм óчень нрáвился твóй брáт.

(ваша сестра, ваш аппарат, эта пластинка, этот очерк, ваш сосед, ваша соседка)

2. *He'll like this novel.*
   He liked this novel.
   Ему́ понра́вится э́тот рома́н.
   Ему́ понра́вился э́тот рома́н.
   Ему́ понра́вится на́ше о́зеро.
   Ему́ понра́вилось на́ше о́зеро.

(их кварти́ра, её пе́ние, э́ти певцы́, её исполне́ние, её карти́ны, Оде́сса, Владиво́сток, Я́лта)

■ RESPONSE DRILLS

1. *She's reading* Doctor Zhivago.
   She likes Doctor Zhivago.
   Она́ чита́ет «До́ктора Жива́го».
   Ей нра́вится «До́ктор Жива́го».
   Она́ чита́ет стихи́ Пу́шкина.
   Ей нра́вятся стихи́ Пу́шкина.
   (рома́н Толсто́го, э́то сочине́ние, о́черк о США, рабо́ты студе́нтов, э́ту кни́гу, рома́ны, «Войну́ и мир», «Евге́ния Оне́гина»)

2. *They brought him kasha.*
   He didn't like (or *care for*) *kasha.*
   Ему́ принесли́ ка́шу.
   Ка́ша ему́ не понра́вилась.
   Ему́ принесли́ бо́рщ.
   Бо́рщ ему́ не понра́вился.
   (чай, атла́сы, ка́рту, портфе́ль, мазь, сту́лья, кни́гу, слова́рь)

■ SUBJECT REVERSAL DRILL

I don't like that doctor.
That doctor doesn't like me.
Э́тот до́ктор мне́ не нра́вится.
Я э́тому до́ктору не нра́влюсь.

Э́та убо́рщица мне́ не нра́вится.
Я э́той убо́рщице не нра́влюсь.
(она́, его́ сестра́, э́та учи́тельница, э́тот профе́ссор, Влади́мир, э́тот учи́тель)

DISCUSSION

The verb **нра́виться** (perfective **понра́виться**) is best translated into English as *to like, enjoy, care for*, but is structurally closer to the English *to appeal to*. Like **ну́жен**, it is used in nominative-dative constructions which appear backward to the English-speaking student: **Вы́ мне́ нра́витесь** *I like you.* (Lit. *You appeal to me*).

As compared with **люби́ть** *to like, love, be fond of*, **нра́виться** expresses a milder attitude on the part of the speaker. **Нра́виться** is more typical of situations describing one's immediate emotional reaction, whereas **люби́ть** describes a more permanent emotional attitude on one's part.

Ва́м нра́вится э́тот рома́н?
— Да́. Я его́ о́чень люблю́. Мно́го ра́з его́ чита́л.

Do you like this novel?
Yes, I'm very fond of it. I've read it many times.

ЧТЕ́НИЕ И ПИСЬМО́

Бы́ло воскресе́нье, и Влади́мир предложи́л Ка́те пое́хать к его́ роди́телям в колхо́з. Ей давно́ хоте́лось с ни́ми познако́миться, посмотре́ть как они живут. Но в это воскресенье Кате надо было много работать. Тогда Владимир спросил насчёт следующего воскресенья. Катя была согласна, и они так и договорились.

Орлов только что пришёл с работы. Он очень устал, но его жена этого не понимает. Она хочет пойти в магазин и купить себе платье. Орлов говорит ей, что он не хочет идти в магазин, что ему это совсем не интересно. Он просит жену не сердиться, но она говорит, что он бездушный человек.

Осипов был болен, но теперь он чувствует себя гораздо лучше. Вчера доктор сказал, что ему уже можно читать, но не больше, чем полчаса в день. Он забыл об этом, и читал сегодня всё утро. Такая глупость! Ведь он всегда осторожен и точно делает всё, что говорит доктор.

— Интере́сно, кто́ стро́ил э́ту це́рковь?
— Не зна́ю, она́ о́чень ста́рая.
— Тепе́рь таки́х не стро́ят.
— Тепе́рь, по-мо́ему, церкве́й вообще́ не стро́ят.
— Не́т, стро́ят, но ма́ло и не таки́е, коне́чно, как э́та.
— А каки́е же?
— Не зна́ю. Ту́т в сосе́днем селе́, ка́жется, стро́ят. Поезжа́й и посмотри́.

— Зна́ете, в наш го́род прие́хал америка́нский врач. Я вчера́ с ним познако́мился.

— Вот интере́сно! Он прие́хал сюда́ жить?

— Нет, он прие́хал посмотре́ть, как рабо́тают на́ши врачи́.

— И что ж, ему́ понра́вилось?

— Не зна́ю, мы бо́льше говори́ли об Аме́рике, чем о врача́х.

— Фили́пп, покажи́те мне ваш аппара́т, пожа́луйста.

— Вы ещё не ви́дели америка́нских аппара́тов?

— Нет. Он хорошо́ снима́ет?

— Да, я дово́лен. По́мните, я вам пока́зывал цветны́е сни́мки?

— А, по́мню: ви́ды ле́са, о́зера, поле́й.

— Неплохи́е, пра́вда?

— Да, о́чень хоро́шие. У меня́ таки́е не выхо́дят.

— А како́й у вас аппара́т?

— «Зо́ркий».

— Вы ча́сто хо́дите пешко́м?

— Нет, о́чень ре́дко.

— Вот сра́зу ви́дно, что вы америка́нец.

— А почему́ вы ду́маете, что америка́нцы ма́ло хо́дят?

— Мне так говори́ли. И тури́сты из Аме́рики всегда́ то́лько е́здят, никогда́ не хо́дят.

— Ну, тури́сты — э́то друго́е де́ло. Хотя́ вы пра́вы: мы лю́бим е́здить.

Оле́г о́чень хоро́ший студе́нт, и това́рищи обраща́ются к нему́, когда́ не понима́ют ле́кций. Он им всегда́ помога́ет. Но сего́дня он не по́мнит, о чём говори́л профе́ссор. Он всё вре́мя смотре́л на Зи́ну и ничего́ не слы́шал. Э́то о́чень стра́нно. Впро́чем, э́то со вся́ким мо́жет случи́ться.

Воло́дя ду́мает, что пора́ идти́ домо́й. Сейча́с уже́ по́здно, он уста́л, а за́втра ему́ на́до мно́го рабо́тать. Но Га́ля не хо́чет идти́ домо́й, ей хо́чется ещё погуля́ть. Ей нра́вится э́тот лес и о́зеро, во́здух тако́й све́жий. Но что де́лать? Е́сли на́до идти́, то, коне́чно, она́ пойдёт.

— Ну вот, аппара́т гото́в. Сади́сь, Ка́тя, здесь. Я хочу́ ви́деть тебя́, э́то о́зеро и наш дом.

— Всё сра́зу?

— Коне́чно.

— А сни́мки бу́дут цветны́е?

— Да. То́лько сиди́, пожа́луйста, свобо́дно и не ду́май о том, что я тебя́ снима́ю.

— Хорошо́, я бу́ду ду́мать об экза́менах, и у меня́ бу́дет ску́чный вид.

— Не говори́ глу́пости. Ду́май, наприме́р о та́нцах вчера́ в клу́бе.

— И как я там упа́ла? Ну, не серди́сь. Я бу́ду ду́мать о тебе́. Хо́чешь?

— Вот э́то друго́е де́ло. Э́то мне нра́вится.

NOTES

PREPARATION FOR CONVERSATION   **За гриба́ми**

гри́б, –а́	mushroom
за (*plus* instr)	for, after (to get); behind, beyond, across
Пое́дем в ле́с за гриба́ми.	Let's go to the woods after mushrooms.
найти́ (pfv I) (*like* пойти́)	to find
Смотри́, каки́е я нашёл грибы́!	Look what mushrooms I found!
то́чка	dot, point, period
с (*plus* instr)	with, together with, and
Смотри́, каки́е я нашёл грибы́: **кра́сные с бе́лыми то́чками.**	Look what mushrooms I found: red ones with white dots!
вы́бросить (pfv II) вы́брошу, вы́бросишь, –ят	to throw out (*or* away), discard
Э́то плохи́е, вы́брось!	Those are bad; throw them away!
Во́т доса́да!	Darn it!
расти́ (I) (pres расту́, растёшь, –у́т; past ро́с, росла́, –о́, –и́)	to grow
Й́х ту́т мно́го растёт!	There are lots of them growing here!
ёлка	fir tree, spruce tree; Christmas tree
А и́х ту́т под ёлками мно́го **растёт.**	There are lots of them growing here under the fir trees.
рука́, –и́ (acc sg ру́ку); ру́ки, ру́к	hand, arm
вы́тереть (pfv I) (fut вы́тру, вы́трешь, –ут; past вы́тер, вы́терла, –о, –и)	to wipe, wipe off, wipe dry
Вы́три ру́ки.	Wipe your hands off.
плато́к, –тка́	handkerchief, kerchief
Во́т плато́к, вы́три ру́ки.	Here's a handkerchief; wipe your hands off.
поде́лать (pfv I) (*like* де́лать)	to do
что́ ж поде́лаешь!	it can't be helped! what can you do!
Что́ ж поде́лаешь! Во́т плато́к, **вы́три ру́ки.**	It can't be helped! Here's a handkerchief; wipe your hands off.
что́-нибудь (gen чего́-нибудь)	anything
А ты́, Та́ня, нашла́ что́-нибудь?	And how about you, Tanya, have you found anything?

Да́, бе́лые.
Оди́н большо́й и четы́ре ма́леньких.

А во́н то́т гри́б, хоро́ший?

    де́рево, –а; дере́вья, –ьев
А во́н то́т гри́б, за де́ревом,
    хоро́ший?

    не́сколько (*plus* gen)
    ещё не́сколько
Да́. А во́н та́м ещё не́сколько.
    ли́ст, –а́; ли́стья, ли́стьев
    под (*plus* instr)

А во́н та́м под ли́стьями
    ещё не́сколько.

Я́ пойду́ посмотрю́.

    трава́
Ай, что́ э́то ту́т в траве́?
    ползти́ (I) (pres ползу́, –ёшь, –у́т;
    past по́лз, ползла́, –о́, –и́)
Ай, что́ э́то ту́т в траве́ ползёт?

    змея́, –и́; зме́и, змей
Где́? Э́то змея́!

    дли́нный
У́х, кака́я дли́нная!

    па́лка
    би́ть (I), бью́, бьёшь, бью́т
Бе́й её па́лкой!
    скоре́е (*or* скоре́й)

Скоре́е! Бе́й её па́лкой!
    ка́мень, ка́мня; –и, –е́й (m)
А я́ ка́мнем.
Скоре́е бе́й её па́лкой,
    а я́ — ка́мнем.

    убива́ть (I), убива́ю, –ешь, –ют
Оста́вьте её, заче́м убива́ть?
    де́ти, дете́й
Оста́вьте её, де́ти, заче́м убива́ть?
    пу́сть
Пу́сть она́ живёт.
Оста́вьте её, де́ти, заче́м убива́ть?
    Пу́сть живёт.

    уползти́ (pfv I) (*like* ползти́)
Ну́ во́т, змея́ уползла́.

Yes, white ones.
One big one and four little ones.

How about that mushroom over there;
    is it a good one?

    tree
How about that mushroom over there
    behind the tree; is it a good one?

    several, some, a few
    a few more, several more, some more
Yes, and over yonder are a few more.
    leaf
    under, underneath, beneath;
      near (a city)
And over yonder under the leaves are
    a few more.

I'll go take a look.

    grass
Hey, what's this in the grass here?
    to be crawling (*or* creeping)

Hey, what's this crawling in the grass here?

    snake?
Where? It's a snake!

    long
Ooh, how long it is!

    stick
    to beat, hit, strike
Hit it with a stick!
    quick, hurry up (*lit.* sooner,
      faster, more quickly)
Quick! Hit it with a stick!
    stone, rock
And I'll use a rock. (*Lit.* And I with a rock.)
Quick, hit it with a stick and I'll use
    a rock.

    to kill
Leave it alone; why kill it?
    children
Leave it alone, children; why kill it?
    let
Let it live!
Leave it alone, children; why kill it?
    Let it live!

    to crawl away, creep off
See now, the snake got away.

мешáть (I) — to disturb, hinder, interfere, butt in; mix, stir

Ты́, мáма, всегдá мешáешь. — You're always butting in, mamma.

невозмóжно — impossible
с тобóй — with you
С тобóй невозмóжно ходи́ть в лéс. — It's impossible going to the woods with you.
С тобóй прóсто невозмóжно ходи́ть в лéс. — It's just impossible going to the woods with you.

SUPPLEMENT

сы́н, –а; сыновья́, сыновéй — son
Скóлько у вáс сыновéй? — How many sons do you have?
дóчь, дóчери; –и, –éй — daughter
Скóлько у вáс дочерéй? — How many daughters do you have?
дя́дя, –и; –и, –ей — uncle
Скóлько у вáс дя́дей? — How many uncles do you have?
тётя, –и; –и, –ей — aunt
Скóлько у вáс тётей? — How many aunts do you have?
дéдушка (gen pl дéдушек) — grandfather
Гдé живёт вáш дéдушка? — Where does your grandfather live?
бáбушка (gen pl бáбушек) — grandmother
Гдé живёт вáша бáбушка? — Where does your grandmother live?
находи́ть (II) (like ходи́ть) — to find
Я всегдá нахожý здéсь грибы́. — I always find mushrooms here.
находи́ться (II), нахóдится, нахóдятся — to be located, to be situated
Гдé нахóдится вáш колхóз? — Where is your collective farm located?
зá город [zágərət] — to the country, out of town, to the suburbs
Поéдем зá город. — Let's drive to the country!
зá городом [zágərədəm] — out of town, in the country, in the suburbs
Мы́ живём зá городом. — We live out of town or We live in the country.
корóткий — short
Я напишý емý корóткое письмó. — I'll write him a short letter.
возмóжный (adv возмóжно) — possible
Возмóжно, что óн ужé вернýлся. — It's possible he's already returned.

За грибáми

Сы́н 1 Смотри́, каки́е я нашёл грибы́: крáсные с бéлыми тóчками.

Мáть 2 Это плохи́е, вы́брось![1]

Сы́н 3 Вóт досáда! А и́х тýт под ёлками мнóго растёт!

Мáть 4 Чтó ж подéлаешь! Возьми́ платóк, вы́три рýки.[2,3] А ты́, Тáня, нашлá чтó-нибудь?

Дóчь 5 Дá, бéлые.[4] Оди́н большóй и четы́ре мáленьких.

Сын	6	Ма́ма, а во́н то́т гри́б, за де́ревом, хоро́ший?
Ма́ть	7	Да́. А во́н та́м под ли́стьями ещё не́сколько.
До́чь	8	Я пойду́ посмотрю́. Ай, что́ э́то ту́т в траве́ ползёт?
Сын	9	Где́? Э́то змея́! У́х, кака́я дли́нная! Скоре́е бе́й её па́лкой, а я́ — ка́мнем!
Ма́ть	10	Оста́вьте её, де́ти, заче́м убива́ть?[5] Пу́сть живёт!
Сын	11	Ну́ во́т, уползла́. Ты́, ма́ма, всегда́ меша́ешь. С тобо́й про́сто невозмо́жно ходи́ть в ле́с.

NOTES

[1] Russians are great mushroom lovers and usually know how to tell a good mushroom from a bad one. The red ones with the white spots picked by the son are the poisonous **мухомо́ры** *toadstools* (lit. *flykillers*).

[2] After touching poisonous mushrooms one must wash, or at least wipe, one's hands clean.

[3] **Ру́ки** means both *hands* and *arms*; likewise **но́ги** means both *feet* and *legs*.

[4] **Бе́лый гри́б** *edible Boletus* is considered a delicacy by Russians. It has a brown cap which is spongy underneath. The mushroom is called *white* because of the color it acquires when dried; most other species turn dark.

[5] The noun **де́ти** *children* has an archaic singular form **дитя́** *baby*, *child*. In modern Russian the word used for *baby* or *child* is **ребёнок**; its grammatical plural **ребя́та** is used in the special sense of *kids*, *guys*, or *fellows*.

PREPARATION FOR CONVERSATION **Пиро́г с гриба́ми**

пиро́г, –а́	pirog (kind of pie)
пиро́г с гриба́ми	pirog filled with mushrooms
Вы́ лю́бите пиро́г с гриба́ми?	Do you like pirog with mushrooms?
стуча́ть (II), стучу́, –и́шь, –а́т	to knock, bang, rap, pound
Та́м, ка́жется, стуча́т.	Someone seems to be knocking.
Алёша! Та́м, ка́жется, стуча́т.	Alyosha, someone seems to be knocking.
Пойди́, пожа́луйста, откро́й.	Please go open the door.
оде́т, –а, –о, –ы	dressed
Я́ не оде́та.	I'm not dressed.
А́, э́то ты́, Лю́ба! Заходи́.	Ah, it's you Lyuba. Come in!
стира́ть (I)	to wash, launder
Ва́ля стира́ет.	Valya's doing the laundry.
Она́ сейча́с придёт.	She'll be right in.
мину́тка (var. of мину́та)	a minute
на мину́тку	for a minute (*or* moment)
Я́ на мину́тку.	I can only stay a moment.
с на́ми	with us, together with us

Я зашла́ пригласи́ть ва́с с на́ми пообе́дать.	I dropped in to invite you to have dinner with us.
Здра́вствуй, ми́лая.	Hello, dear.
Когда́ ты верну́лась?	When did you get back?
с детьми́	with the children, and the children
Когда́ ты с детьми́ верну́лась?	When did you and the children get back?
наза́д	ago, back
Ча́с наза́д.	An hour ago.
двухчасово́й	two-o'clock (adj), two-hour (adj)
Ча́с наза́д, двухчасовы́м по́ездом.	An hour ago, on the two-o'clock train.
ша́пка	cap
потеря́ть (pfv I), потеря́ю, –ешь, –ют	to lose
Пе́тя потеря́л ша́пку.	Petya lost his cap.
бы (unstressed particle)	would, would have
Мы́ бы ра́ньше верну́лись, но Пе́тя потеря́л ша́пку.	We'd have returned earlier, but Petya lost his cap.
прийти́сь (pfv I) (used with dat)	to have to, to be forced to
На́м придётся иска́ть ша́пку.	We'll have to look for the cap.
На́м пришло́сь иска́ть ша́пку.	We had to look for the cap.
Мы́ бы ра́ньше верну́лись, но Пе́тя потеря́л ша́пку, и на́м пришло́сь её иска́ть.	We'd have returned earlier, but Petya lost his cap and we had to hunt for it.
Ну́ ка́к? Мно́го грибо́в нашли́?	Well, how about it; did you find many mushrooms?
ма́сса	mass, lots, plenty, a great many
Ма́ссу.	Loads.
испе́чь (pfv I) (fut испеку́, испечёшь, испеку́т; past испёк, испекла́, –о́, –и́)	to bake
Я́ уже́ испекла́ пиро́г.	I've already baked a pirog.
свари́ть (pfv II), сварю́, сва́ришь, –ят	to cook (by boiling)
су́п	soup
Я́ уже́ испекла́ пиро́г и свари́ла су́п.	I've already baked a pirog and made soup.
Приходи́те к на́м на обе́д.	Come to our place for dinner.
Большо́е спаси́бо.	Thanks very much.
как то́лько	as soon as
Придём, как то́лько я́ ко́нчу стира́ть.	We'll come just as soon as I finish washing.
оста́ться (pfv I), оста́нусь, –ешься, –утся	to be left, to remain
А тебе́ ещё мно́го оста́лось?	And do you have much left to do?
руба́шка	shirt, slip
ю́бка	skirt
Не́т, одна́ ю́бка и две́ руба́шки.	No, one skirt and two shirts.
Ну́, конча́й скоре́й, и приходи́те.	Well, hurry and finish and come on over!
Бу́дем ва́с жда́ть.	We'll be expecting you.

сáхар	sugar
Вы́ пьёте чáй с сáхаром?	Do you drink your tea with sugar?
лимóн	lemon
Я пью́ чáй с лимóном.	I drink my tea with lemon.
ухá	fish soup, fish chowder
Мы́ óчень лю́бим уху́.	We like fish chowder very much.
лапшá (sg only)	noodles
су́п с лапшóй	noodle soup
Кáк вáм нрáвится су́п с лапшóй?	How do you like the noodle soup?
бульóн	consommé, bouillon soup, broth
Принеси́те мнé, пожáлуйста, бульóн.	Bring me consommé, please.
бу́лка	large roll, small loaf of French bread
Купи́те двé бу́лки.	Buy two loaves of French bread.
бу́лочка	roll
Купи́те, пожáлуйста, бу́лочек.	Please buy some rolls.
Женá испеклá э́ти бу́лочки.	My wife baked these rolls.
печéнье	cookies
Я вáм куплю́ печéнья.	I'll buy you some cookies.
тóрт	cake
Какóй вку́сный тóрт!	What a delicious cake!
пéчь (I) (*like* испéчь)	to bake
Вáша женá чáсто печёт?	Does your wife bake often?
вари́ть (II) (*like* свари́ть)	to cook (by boiling)
Вы́ ужé вáрите обéд?	Are you already cooking dinner?
теря́ть (I) (*like* потеря́ть)	to lose, waste
Не теря́йте на э́то врéмени.	Don't waste time on that.
тому́ назáд	ago
Э́то случи́лось гóд тому́ назáд.	It happened a year ago.
автору́чка	fountain pen
Пиши́те автору́чкой.	Write with a fountain pen.
мéл	chalk
Пиши́те мéлом.	Write with chalk.
недовóлен, –льна, –о, –ы	dissatisfied, displeased
Óн недовóлен результáтами.	He's dissatisfied with the results.

Пирóг с грибáми

Вáля (Валенти́на)
Алёша (Алексéй, её му́ж)
Лю́ба (Любóвь, и́х сосéдка)

Вáля   1 Алёша! Тáм, кáжется, стучáт. Пойди́, пожáлуйста, открóй. Я не одéта.

Алёша   2 А́, э́то ты́, Лю́ба. Заходи́, Вáля стирáет, онá сейчáс придёт.

Люба	3	Я на минутку. Зашла пригласить вас с нами пообедать.
Валя	4	Здравствуй, милая. Когда ты с детьми вернулась?
Люба	5	Час назад, двухчасовым поездом.[1] Мы бы раньше вернулись, но Петя потерял шапку, и нам пришлось её искать.
Алёша	6	Ну как? Много грибов нашли?
Люба	7	Массу. Я уже испекла пирог и сварила суп.[2] Приходите к нам на обед.
Валя	8	С большим удовольствием. Придём, как только я кончу стирать.
Алёша	9	А тебе ещё много осталось?
Валя	10	Нет, одна юбка и две рубашки.
Люба	11	Ну, кончай скорей, и приходите. Будем вас ждать.

NOTES

[1] It is not uncommon for Russians to take a train to the country, and then go to the forest to pick berries or mushrooms, or just to hike.

[2] Пирог is a kind of pie, usually rectangular in shape, which contains any of various fillings, for example, meat, cabbage, mushrooms, rice, eggs, carrots, or any combination of these ingredients. The sweet variety with a fruit filling is called **сладкий пирог** *sweet pie* and usually does not have a crust on top. Small individual ones encased in dough are called **пирожки** (singular **пирожок**) or, if slightly larger, **пироги**.

Basic sentence patterns

1. Кем он доволен?
   — Тобой.
   — Мной.
   — Вами.
   — Владимиром.
   — Им.
   — Таней.
   — Ей (ею).
   — Студентами.
   — Ими.

   With whom is he pleased?
   With you
   With me.
   With you.
   With Vladimir.
   With him.
   With Tanya.
   With her.
   With the students.
   With them.

2. Чем мне писать?
   — Этим карандашом.
   — Этой авторучкой.

   What should I write with?
   Use this pencil.
   Use this fountain pen.

Чём мне наре́зать хлеб?	What should I cut the bread with?
—Э́тим ножо́м.	Use this knife.
Чём мне вы́тереть ру́ки?	What should I wipe my hands with?
—Э́тим платко́м.	Use this handkerchief.
Чём мне меша́ть су́п?	What am I to stir the soup with?
—Э́той ло́жкой.	Use this spoon.

3. С кем оста́нутся де́ти?   With whom are the children going to stay?

— Со мно́й.	With me.
— С ма́терью.	With their mother.
— С роди́телями.	With their parents.
— С отцо́м.	With their father.
— С ба́бушкой.	With their grandmother.
— С дя́дей.	With their uncle.
— С де́душкой.	With their grandfather.
— С тётей.	With their aunt.

4. Я́ пое́ду вме́сте с Оле́гом.   I'll go along (or together) with Oleg.

＿＿＿＿＿ с роди́телями.	＿＿＿＿＿ with my parents.
＿＿＿＿＿ с детьми́.	＿＿＿＿＿ with the children.
＿＿＿＿＿ с э́тими людьми́.	＿＿＿＿＿ with these people.
＿＿＿＿＿ с сы́ном.	＿＿＿＿＿ with my son.
＿＿＿＿＿ с до́черью.	＿＿＿＿＿ with my daughter.
＿＿＿＿＿ с ба́бушкой.	＿＿＿＿＿ with grandmother.

5.
Пиши́те карандашо́м.	Write with (or in) pencil.
＿＿＿ ме́лом.	＿＿＿ chalk.
＿＿＿ ру́чкой.	＿＿＿ pen.
＿＿＿ авторру́чкой.	＿＿＿ fountain pen.
＿＿＿ перо́м.	＿＿＿ pen.
Не стучи́ ножо́м!	Don't rap with your knife!
＿＿＿ ло́жкой!	＿＿＿ spoon!
＿＿＿ ви́лкой!	＿＿＿ fork!
Не стучи́те нога́ми!	Don't tap with your feet!
Наре́жь хлеб э́тим ножо́м!	Slice the bread with this knife!
＿＿＿ огурцы́＿＿＿!	＿＿ the cucumbers＿＿＿!
Меша́йте су́п э́той деревя́нной ло́жкой!	Stir the soup with this wooden spoon!

6.
Вы́ пьёте ча́й с лимо́ном?	Do you drink your tea with lemon?
— Не́т, без лимо́на.	No, without lemon.
Вы́ пьёте ча́й с са́харом?	Do you drink your tea with sugar?
— Не́т, без са́хара.	No, without sugar.
Вы́ пьёте ча́й с молоко́м?	Do you drink your tea with milk?
— Не́т, без молока́.	No, without milk.
Вы́ пьёте ча́й с лимо́ном и са́харом?	Do you drink your tea with lemon and sugar?
— Не́т, без ничего́.	No, without anything.

7. Ба́бушка испекла́ пиро́г с гриба́ми.   Grandmother baked a mushroom pirog.

＿＿＿＿＿ пиро́г с ры́бой.	＿＿＿＿＿ a fish pirog.
＿＿＿＿＿ два́ пирога́.	＿＿＿＿＿ two pirogs.
＿＿＿＿＿ не́сколько пирого́в.	＿＿＿＿＿ several pirogs.

Бабушка испекла́ бу́лочки.   Grandmother baked rolls.

_____ бу́лку.   _____ a loaf of white bread.

_____ бу́лки.   _____ large rolls.

8. Жена́ свари́ла су́п.   My wife cooked soup.

_____ вку́сный су́п.   _____ a delicious soup.

_____ су́п с лапшо́й.   _____ noodle soup.

_____ су́п с гриба́ми.   _____ soup with mushrooms.

_____ бульо́н.   _____ consommé.

_____ бо́рщ.   _____ borsch.

_____ лапшу́.   _____ noodles.

9. Зи́на хо́чет с тобо́й познако́миться.   Zina wants to meet you.

— Со мно́й?!   Me?

Познако́мьтесь, э́то Фили́пп Гра́нт,   I'd like you to meet each other; Philip Grant,
    э́то Ле́в Никола́евич.   Lev Nikolaevich.

Фили́пп, познако́мься со Льво́м   Philip, meet Lev Nikolaevich.
    Никола́евичем.

— Мы́ уже́ знако́мы.   We're already acquainted.

Ле́в Никола́евич, познако́мьтесь   Lev Nikolaevich, meet Philip Grant.
    с Фили́ппом Гра́нтом.

— Мы́ уже́ вчера́ познако́мились.   We already met yesterday.

10. Познако́мь меня́ с Мари́ей.   Introduce me to Maria.

_____ с Серге́ем.   _____ Sergey.

_____ с твои́ми сыновья́ми.   _____ your sons.

_____ дочерьми́.   _____ daughters.

_____ детьми́.   _____ children.

О́чень прия́тно с ва́ми познако́миться.   I'm very glad to meet you.

Вы́ знако́мы с мое́й кни́гой?   Are you familiar with my book?

_____ с мои́м рома́ном?   _____ with my novel?

_____ с мои́ми рабо́тами?   _____ with my works?

11. О́н мне́ меша́ет.   He bothers me.

Они́ мне́ меша́ют.   They bother me.

Я́ ва́м не меша́ю?   I'm not disturbing you, am I?

Вы́ мне́ не меша́ете.   You're not disturbing (or bothering) me.

Ты́ мне́ не меша́ешь.   You're not disturbing (or bothering) me.

12. Вы́ потеря́ете мно́го вре́мени.   You'll lose (or waste) a lot of time.

О́н потеря́ет _____.   He'll lose (or waste)_____.

Я́ потеря́ю _____.   I'll lose (or waste)_____.

Они́ потеря́ют _____.   They'll lose (or waste)_____.

О́н потеря́л ша́пку.   He lost his cap.

Она́ потеря́ла плато́к.   She lost her [hand]kerchief.

Они́ потеря́ли пя́ть рубле́й.   They lost five rubles.

13. На́м придётся пойти́ в магази́н.   We'll have to go to the store.

_____ рабо́тать в суббо́ту.   _____ to work on Saturday.

_____ иска́ть рабо́ту.   _____ to look for work.

_____ вы́бросить э́ти лимо́ны.   _____ to throw these lemons out.

На́м придётся стира́ть э́ти руба́шки.	We'll have to wash these shirts.
_____ оста́ться ту́т ещё неде́лю.	_____ to stay here another week.
_____ до́лго жда́ть.	_____ to wait a long time.
_____ и́х пригласи́ть.	_____ to invite them.

14. Óн стоя́л за де́ревом. — He stood behind the tree.

_____ до́мом.	_____ the house.
_____ избо́й.	_____ the hut.
_____ кио́ском.	_____ the newsstand.
_____ столо́м.	_____ the table.
_____ две́рью.	_____ the door.
_____ дверьми́.	_____ the doors.

15. Ключи́ под две́рью. — The keys are under the door.

_____ портфе́лем.	_____ the briefcase.
_____ коро́бкой.	_____ the box.
_____ журна́лом.	_____ the magazine.
_____ сни́мками.	_____ the snapshots.
_____ кни́гами.	_____ the books.

16. Где́ нахо́дится ва́ш до́м? — Where's your house located?

— За́ городом.	Out of town.
— За ле́сом.	Beyond the forest.
— За па́рком.	Across the park.
— За о́зером.	Across the lake.

17. До́чь верну́лась неде́лю тому́ наза́д. — The daughter returned a week ago.

_____ пя́ть неде́ль тому́ наза́д.	_____ five weeks ago.
_____ ме́сяц тому́ наза́д.	_____ a month ago.
_____ го́д тому́ наза́д.	_____ a year ago.
_____ два́ го́да тому́ наза́д.	_____ two years ago.

18. Мы́ договори́лись на сре́ду. — We made a date for Wednesday.

_____ за́втра.	_____ tomorrow.
_____ сле́дующий понеде́льник.	_____ next Monday.
_____ сле́дующую пя́тницу.	_____ next Friday.
_____ ча́с.	_____ one.
_____ де́вять часо́в.	_____ nine o'clock.

Pronunciation practice: the unvoicing of ordinarily voiced consonants

The unvoicing of ordinarily voiced consonants in word final position.

A. The letter **б** pronounced [b] or [b̦]

[xl̦ébə] хле́ба
of the bread
[rabí] рабы́
slaves
[gólub̦i] го́луби
pigeons

The letter **б** pronounced [p]
The letters **бь** pronounced [p̦]

[xl̦ép] хле́б
bread
[ráp] ра́б
slave
[gólup̦] го́лубь
pigeon

B. The letter **в** pronounced [v] or [ɣ]

    [slévə] слéва
    on the left
    [sḷívə] слúва
    plum
    [ɣétɣi] вéтви
    branches

The letter **в** pronounced [f]
The letters **вь** pronounced [f̡]

    [léf] лéв
    lion
    [sḷíf] слúв
    of plums
    [ɣétf̡] вéтвь
    branch

C. The letter **г** pronounced [g] or [g̡]

    [səpag̡í] сапогú
    high boots
    [vrag̡í] врагú
    enemies
    [kṇígə] кнúга
    book

The letter **г** pronounced [k]

    [sapók] сапóг
    high boot
    [vrák] врáг
    enemy
    [kṇík] кнúг
    of books

D. The letter **д** pronounced [d] or [d̡]

    [górədə] гóрода
    of the city
    [gódi] гóды
    years
    [m̡éd̡i] мéди
    of copper

The letter **д** pronounced [t]
The letters **дь** pronounced [t̡]

    [gorət] гóрод
    city
    [gót] гóд
    year
    [m̡ét̡] мéдь
    copper

E. The letter **ж** pronounced [ž]

    [naží] ножú
    knives
    [kóži] кóжи
    hides

The letter **ж** pronounced [š]

    [nóš] нóж
    knife
    [kóš] кóж
    of hides

The unvoicing of ordinarily voiced consonants in a non-final position.

A. The letter **б** pronounced [b]

    [abd̡irát̡] обдирáть
    to peel off
    [abžít̡] обжúть
    to make livable

The letter **б** pronounced [p]

    [apt̡irát̡] обтирáть
    to wipe off
    [apšít̡] обшúть
    to saw

B. The letter **в** pronounced [v]

    [vbár̡i] в бáре
    in a bar
    [vzór] взóр
    glance

The letter **в** pronounced [f]

    [fpár̡i] в пáре
    in a pair
    [fsór] в сóр
    into rubbish

C. The letter **д** pronounced [d]

    [pədgarój] под горóй
    at the foot of a mountain
    [padžít̡] поджúть
    to heal up

The letter **д** pronounced [t]

    [pətkarój] под корóй
    under bark
    [patšít̡] подшúть
    to line

Nouns in the instrumental case

The instrumental case without a preposition designates the means by which some action is accomplished. It may specify the tool, instrument, conveyance, agency, or means used to effect the act; or it may indicate the manner in which the act was accomplished.

Наре́жь хлеб э́тим ножо́м.	Cut the bread *with this knife.*
Чём вы́ пи́шете, карандашо́м?	What are you writing with, *a pencil?*
Ка́к вы́ прие́хали, по́ездом?	How did you come? *By train?*

Several prepositions require the instrumental case, the most common of which is **c** (**co**) in the meaning *with, in accompaniment with.*

Я́ говори́л с отцо́м.	I was talking with father.
О́н пойдёт с Ко́лей.	He'll go along with Kolya.

Note: The preposition **c** must not be used to translate the English *with* in the sense of *by means of;* the instrumental case form alone expresses the English *with* in such situations: **Пиши́те ру́чкой!** *Write with a pen!*

NOUN ENDINGS IN THE INSTRUMENTAL CASE		
SINGULAR		PLURAL
Masculine and Neuter	*Feminine*	
–ом, –ём, –ем	–ой, –ёй, –ей, –ью	–ами, –ями, –ьми́

MODELS

Поговори́те с сосе́дом.	Have a talk with your neighbor.
_____ с бра́том.	_____ your brother.
_____ с отцо́м.	_____ your father.
_____ с секретарём.	_____ your secretary.
_____ с учи́телем.	_____ your teacher.
_____ с иностра́нцем.	_____ the stranger.
_____ с америка́нцем.	_____ the American.

Я́ нашёл биле́ты под столо́м.	I found the tickets under the table.
_____ под письмо́м.	_____ under the letter.
_____ под словарём.	_____ under the dictionary.
_____ под шка́фом.	_____ under the cupboard.
_____ под портфе́лем.	_____ under the briefcase.
_____ под заявле́нием.	_____ under the application.
_____ под сочине́нием.	_____ under the composition.

Она́ верну́лась с газе́той.	She came back with the paper.
_____ с ры́бой.	_____ with the fish.
_____ с кни́гой.	_____ with the book.
_____ с водо́й.	_____ with the water.
_____ с семьёй.	_____ with her family.
_____ с квита́нцией.	_____ with the receipt.

Она́ уже́ говори́ла с подру́гой.	She has already talked with her friend.
_____ с сосе́дкой.	_____ with her neighbor.
_____ с ба́бушкой.	_____ with her grandmother.
_____ с учи́тельницей.	_____ with her teacher.
_____ с продавщи́цей.	_____ with the saleslady.
_____ с певи́цей.	_____ with the singer.
Она́ до́лго говори́ла с ма́терью.	She talked for a long time with her mother.
_____ с до́черью.	_____ with her daughter.
Плато́к бы́л под две́рью.	The handkerchief was under the door.
_____ под тетра́дью.	_____ under the notebook.
_____ под коро́бкой с ма́зью.	_____ under the box with ointment.
Не стучи́ карандашо́м!	Don't rap with your pencil!
_____ ножо́м!	_____ knife!
_____ ме́лом!	_____ chalk!
_____ ло́жкой!	_____ spoon!
_____ ви́лкой!	_____ fork!
_____ ного́й!	_____ foot!
_____ па́лкой!	_____ stick (or cane)!
Я пойду́ за газе́тами.	I'll go get the papers.
_____ за огурца́ми.	_____ the cucumbers.
_____ за бу́лочками.	_____ the rolls.
_____ за лимо́нами.	_____ the lemons.
_____ за кни́гами.	_____ the books.
_____ за журна́лами.	_____ the magazines.
_____ за ша́хматами.	_____ the chess set.
_____ за словаря́ми.	_____ the dictionaries.
_____ за сту́льями.	_____ the chairs.
Я игра́л в ка́рты с това́рищами.	I was playing cards with friends.
_____ со студе́нтами.	_____ with the students.
_____ с де́вушками.	_____ with the girls.
_____ со студе́нтками.	_____ with the students.
_____ с сёстрами.	_____ with my sisters.
_____ с друзья́ми.	_____ with my friends.
_____ с роди́телями.	_____ with my parents.
_____ с бра́тьями.	_____ with my brothers.
_____ с сыновья́ми.	_____ with my sons.
_____ с учителя́ми.	_____ with the teachers.
_____ с дочерьми́.	_____ with my daughters.
_____ с детьми́.	_____ with the children.
Вы дово́льны студе́нтами?	Are you pleased with the (or your) students?
_____ студе́нтками?	_____ the (or your) students?
_____ профессора́ми?	_____ the (or your) professors?
_____ учителя́ми?	_____ the (or your) teachers?
_____ сосе́дями?	_____ the (or your) neighbors?
_____ секретаря́ми?	_____ the (or your) secretaries?

Here's chalk.
Write with chalk.
Во́т ме́л.
Пиши́те ме́лом.

Во́т авторучка.
Пиши́те авторучкой.
(каранда́ш, перо́, ру́чка, ме́л, авторучка)

■ CUED SUBSTITUTION DRILLS

1. (*bookshelf*) *He found his cap behind the bookshelf.*
   (по́лка) Óн нашёл ша́пку за по́лкой.
   (шка́ф) Óн нашёл ша́пку за **шка́фом.**
   (две́рь, изба́, до́м, буфе́т, це́рковь, де́рево, коро́бка, я́щик)

2. (*sideboard*) *Did you look under the sideboard?*
   (буфе́т) Вы́ иска́ли под **буфе́том?**
   (ли́стья) Вы́ иска́ли под **ли́стьями?**
   (окно́, шка́ф, де́рево, тетра́ди, коро́бка, сту́лья, сто́л)

■ STRUCTURE REPLACEMENT DRILLS

1. *Go with your brother.*
   Go with your brothers.
   Поезжа́й с бра́том!
   Поезжа́й с бра́тьями!
   Поезжа́й с подру́гой!
   Поезжа́й с подру́гами!
   (с америка́нцем, с това́рищем, с певи́цей, с америка́нкой, с певцо́м, с тури́стом, с секретарём, с учи́телем, с проводнико́м)

2. *I'm acquainted with her uncles.*
   I'm acquainted with her uncle.
   Я́ знако́м с её дя́дями.
   Я́ знако́м с её дя́дей.
   Я́ знако́м с её бра́тьями.
   Я́ знако́м с её бра́том.
   (тётями, подру́гами, друзья́ми, сёстрами, сосе́дями, учи́тельницами, сосе́дками, дя́дями)

3. *He returned with the newspapers.*
   He returned with the newspaper.
   Óн верну́лся с газе́тами.
   Óн верну́лся с газе́той.
   Óн верну́лся со словаря́ми.
   Óн верну́лся со словарём.
   (ка́ртами, журна́лами, заявле́ниями, сни́мками, па́лками, биле́тами, бу́лками, квита́нциями)

4. *I'll stop by for my neighbors.*
   I'll stop by for my neighbor.
   Я́ зайду́ за сосе́дками.
   Я́ зайду́ за сосе́дкой.
   Я́ зайду́ за това́рищами.
   Я́ зайду́ за това́рищем.
   (студе́нтами, америка́нцами, сосе́дями, подру́гами, учи́тельницами, друзья́ми, певи́цами, доктора́ми)

■ RESPONSE DRILLS

1. *We have no milk.*
   I'll go get the milk.
   У на́с не́т молока́.
   Я́ пойду́ за молоко́м.
   У на́с не́т бу́лочек.
   Я́ пойду́ за бу́лочками.
   (хле́ба, огурцо́в, са́хара, воды́, ча́я, бу́лки, пече́нья, ры́бы, лимо́нов)

2. *Grandfather knows the way.*
   Follow Grandfather.
   Де́душка зна́ет доро́гу.
   Иди́ за де́душкой.
   Ю́рий зна́ет доро́гу.
   Иди́ за Ю́рием.
   (его́ оте́ц, его́ де́ти, его́ ба́бушка, Евге́ний, его́ дя́дя, его́ роди́тели, его́ тётя, сосе́д, америка́нец)

1. *Is herring sold here?*
   Yes, this is the line for herring.
   Тут продаю́т селёдку?
   Да́, э́то о́чередь за селёдкой.
   Тут продаю́т лимо́ны?
   Да́, э́то о́чередь за лимо́нами.
   (хлеб, сахар, билеты, рубашки, молоко, лимона́д, платки, пластинки, печенье)

2. *Don't you have a fountain pen?*
   I don't like to write with a fountain pen.
   У тебя́ не́т авторучки?
   Я́ не люблю́ писа́ть авторучкой.
   У тебя́ не́т карандаша́?
   Я́ не люблю́ писа́ть карандашо́м.
   (нет ручки, нет пера, нет мела, нет авторучки, нет карандаша)

3. *Is Alyosha going too?*
   Yes, Alyosha and I are going together.
   Алёша то́же е́дет?
   Да́, мы́ с Алёшей е́дем вме́сте.
   Тво́й бра́т то́же е́дет?

   Да́, мы́ с бра́том е́дем вме́сте.
   (дети, Люба, твой дядя, Таня, твой отец, твои родители, врач, Сергей, твоя мама)

1. *He has met Zina.*
   Óн познако́мился с Зи́ной.
   Óн познако́мился с Зи́ной.
   ___ (пригласи́л) _____.
   Óн пригласи́л Зи́ну.
   _____ (её де́душку).
   ___ (знако́м с) _____.
   ___ (жда́л) _____.
   _____ (дете́й).
   ___ (игра́л с) _____.
   ___ (иска́л) _____.
   _____ (грибы́).
   ___ (свари́л су́п с) _____.

2. *I saw my uncle.*
   Я увидел дя́дю.
   Я́ увидел дя́дю.
   ___ (гуля́л с) _____.
   Я́ гуля́л с дя́дей.
   ___ (встре́тил) _____.
   _____ (друзе́й).
   ___ (пое́хал с) _____.
   ___ (пригласи́л) _____.
   _____ (её отца́).
   ___ (познако́мился с) ___.
   ___ (узна́л) _____.
   _____ (Серге́я).
   ___ (рабо́тал с) _____.

DISCUSSION

INSTRUMENTAL SINGULAR OF NOUNS		
сто́л- and окно́-nouns stressed –о́м, –ём unstressed –ом, –ем	жена́-nouns –о́й, –е́й –ой, –ей	две́рь-nouns only –ью (never stressed)
столо́м словарём	жено́й семьёй	две́рью
угло́м учи́телем	зимо́й змеёй	Любо́вью
автобусом Никола́ем	сестро́й ле́кцией	о́чередью
ме́лом му́жем	душо́й исто́рией	тетра́дью
ножо́м америка́нцем	пого́дой Ната́шей	ве́щью
карандашо́м па́рнем	по́чтой Воло́дей	ма́терью
ключо́м собра́нием	кни́гой неде́лей	до́черью
перо́м пла́тьем	ша́пкой Мари́ей	
де́лом вре́менем	Зи́ной уда́чей	

1. Hard-stem **стол-** and **окно́-**nouns have the instrumental singular ending –**ом**; soft-stem **стол-** and **окно́-**nouns have the ending –**ём** if stressed, –**ем** if unstressed. Stems ending in **ч, щ, ш, ж,** and **ц** spell their ending –**óм** if stressed and –**ем** if unstressed. Compare **борщо́м** with **това́рищем**.

2. Hard-stem **жена́-**nouns have the instrumental singular ending –**ой**; soft-stem **жена́-**nouns have the ending –**ей** if stressed, –**ей** if unstressed. Stems ending in **ч, щ, ш, ж,** and **ц** spell their ending –**о́й** if stressed and –**ей** if unstressed. Compare **душо́й** with **ка́шей**. There are also alternate endings –**ою**, –**ёю**, and –**ею** which are mostly encountered in literary works: **жено́ю, семьёю,** and **Ната́шею**.

3. All **две́рь-**nouns have the instrumental singular ending –**ью**, always unstressed.

4. **Вре́мя-** and **и́мя-**nouns take the unstressed instrumental singular ending –**ем**: **вре́менем** and **и́менем**.

INSTRUMENTAL PLURAL OF NOUNS	
Hard stems and stems ending in **ч** *and* **щ** –**ами**	*Soft stems* –**ями**
стола́ми	учителя́ми
жёнами	неде́лями
о́кнами	роди́телями
города́ми	сочине́ниями
доктора́ми	бра́тьями
сёстрами	сту́льями
ножа́ми	зда́ниями
ключа́ми	
това́рищами	

1. Nouns which take –**ах** in the prepositional plural and –**ам** in the dative plural take –**ами** in the instrumental plural. Their stress is identical in all three cases: **стола́х, стола́м, стола́ми**; **жёнах, жёнам, жёнами**.

2. Nouns which take –**ях** in the prepositional plural and –**ям** in the dative plural take –**ями** in the instrumental plural. Their stress is also identical in all three cases: **учителя́х, учителя́м, учителя́ми**; **бра́тьях, бра́тьям, бра́тьями**.

3. The nouns **две́рь** and **до́чь** have an alternate instrumental plural ending –**ьми́**: **дверьми́** (ог **дверя́ми**), **дочерьми́** (ог **дочеря́ми**).

4. The nouns **лю́ди** *people* and **де́ти** *children* have *only* the instrumental plural ending –**ьми́**: **людьми́** and **детьми́**.

The instrumental of кто́, что́, the personal pronouns, and the reflexive personal pronoun себя́

NOM	кто́	что́	я	ты́	(no nom)	о́н, оно́	она́	мы́	вы́	они́
INSTR	ке́м	че́м	мно́й	тобо́й	собо́й	и́м,(ни́м)	ею,(не́й)	на́ми	ва́ми	и́ми, (ни́мн)

Notes

1. Third person alternate forms **ни́м, не́й,** and **ни́ми** occur only with prepositions, for example, **с ни́м, за ни́м, с не́й, за не́й, с ни́ми, за ни́ми**.

2. In addition to **мной, тобой, собой,** and **ней,** there are also the alternate instrumental forms **мно́ю, тобо́ю, собо́ю,** and **не́ю.** These are encountered primarily in literature, especially poetry.

MODELS

Я хочу́ с **ни́м** поговори́ть.	I want to have a talk with him.
_____ с **ней** _____.	_____ with her.
_____ с **ва́ми** _____.	_____ with you.
_____ с **ни́ми** _____.	_____ with them.
_____ с **тобо́й** _____.	_____ with you.

Ре́ктор хо́чет с **на́ми** поговори́ть.	The chancellor wants to have a talk with us.
_____ со **мно́й** _____.	_____ with me.

Возьми́те с **собо́й** каранда́ш и тетра́дь.

Take a pencil and a notebook along (*lit.* with yourself).

С **чём** вы́ пьёте ча́й?

What do you take in your tea? *or* With what do you drink tea?

— С молоко́м.

Milk.

С **кём** вы́ хоти́те говори́ть?

With whom do you want to speak?

— С ва́ми.

With you.

Чём вы́ пи́шете, карандашо́м?

What are you writing with, a pencil?

Ке́м вы́ дово́льны? — **Ва́ми.**

With whom are you pleased? You.

Я **собо́й** недово́лен.

I'm dissatisfied with myself.

Ке́м вы́ недово́льны, **мно́й**?

With whom are you dissatisfied, me?

— Не́т, **и́м.**

No, him.

— Не́т, **е́ю.**

No, her.

— Не́т, **собо́й.**

No, myself.

■ CUED QUESTION-ANSWER DRILL

With whom will she go?
With him.

(о́н) С ке́м она́ пойдёт?
       С ни́м.
(я) С ке́м она́ пойдёт?
       Со мно́й.
(они́, она́, мы́, я́, о́н, вы́, она́, ты́, я́)

■ QUESTION-ANSWER DRILLS

1. *Do you know Oleg?*
   No, I don't know him.
   Ты́ знако́м с Оле́гом?
   Не́т, я́ с ни́м не знако́м.
   Ты́ знако́м с Ва́лей?
   Не́т, я́ с ней не знако́м.
     (с Ю́рием, с её сосе́дями, с америка́н-
     цем Гра́нтом, с его́ сёстрами, с его́
     ба́бушкой, с его́ де́душкой, с его́ дя́дей,
     с его́ тётей)

2. *Is he pleased with the exams?*
   Yes, he is.
   О́н дово́лен экза́менами?
   Да́, о́н и́ми дово́лен.
   О́н дово́лен тобо́й?
   Да́, о́н мно́й дово́лен.
     (учи́тельницей, шофёром, детьми́,
     мно́й, рабо́той, ва́ми, учи́телем, собо́й,
     на́ми, студе́нтами)

She's displeased with her son.
She's displeased with him.
Она́ сы́ном недово́льна.
Она́ им недово́льна.
Она́ сестро́й недово́льна.
Она́ е́ю недово́льна.
 (детьми́, уборщицей, вахтёром,
 студе́нтами, учи́телем, до́черью)

I was sitting behind you.
You were sitting behind me.
Я сиде́л за ва́ми.
Вы сиде́ли за мно́й.
Мы сиде́ли за не́й.
Она́ сиде́ла за на́ми.
Вы сиде́ли за не́й.
Он сиде́л за не́й.
Ты сиде́л за не́й.
Они́ сиде́ли за не́й.
Я сиде́л за не́й.
Мы сиде́ли за не́й.

The instrumental of э́тот, чей, and the possessive modifiers

SINGULAR		PLURAL
Masculine and Neuter	*Feminine*	
–им	–ой, –ей	–ими

MODELS

Не говори́те с э́тим америка́нцем.   Don't talk to that American.
_____ студе́нтом.   _____ student.
_____ тури́стом.   _____ tourist.
_____ с э́той америка́нкой.   _____ American woman.
_____ студе́нткой.   _____ student.
_____ с э́тими студе́нтами.   _____ those students.
_____ америка́нцами.   _____ Americans.
_____ тури́стами.   _____ tourists.

С чьи́м дру́гом вы танцева́ли?   Whose friend did you dance with?
_____ бра́том _____?   _____ brother _____?
С чье́й до́черью _____?   _____ daughter _____?
_____ сестро́й _____?   _____ sister _____?
С чьи́ми друзья́ми _____?   _____ friends _____?
_____ дочерьми́ _____?   _____ daughters _____?

Де́ти оста́нутся со свои́м отцо́м.   The children will stay with their father.
_____ со свое́й ма́терью.   _____ with their mother.
_____ со свои́ми роди́телями.   _____ with their parents.

Они́ до́лго говори́ли с мои́м бра́том.   They talked with my brother for a long time.
_____ с мои́м отцо́м.   _____ with my father _____.
_____ с мои́м дя́дей.[1]   _____ with my uncle _____.
_____ с мои́м де́душкой.[1]   _____ with my grandfather _____.

---

[1] Note that although дя́дя and де́душка are жена́-class nouns and decline as such, they are still treated as masculine in terms of agreement.

 Мо́й де́душка жи́л в Москве́.   My grandfather lived in Moscow.
 Вы говори́ли с мои́м дя́дей?   Did you talk with my uncle?

This is true of all such жена́-class nouns referring to males, for example, мужчи́на, Ко́ля, and Воло́дя.

Они́ до́лго говори́ли с мое́й сестро́й.

_____ с мое́й ма́терью.

_____ с мои́ми роди́телями.

Учи́тель не о́чень дово́лен твои́м о́черком.

_____ твои́м

сочине́нием.

_____ твое́й рабо́той.

_____ твои́ми отве́тами.

За на́шим до́мом растёт мно́го дере́вьев.

За на́шим общежи́тием _____.

За на́шей избо́й _____.

За на́шими дома́ми _____.

They talked with my sister for a long time.

_____ with my mother _____.

_____ with my parents _____.

The teacher isn't very happy with your essay.

_____ with your

composition.

_____ with your work.

_____ with your answers.

There are lots of trees growing behind our house.

_____ behind our

dormitory.

_____ behind our hut.

_____ behind our houses.

■ REPETITION DRILL

Repeat the given models, noting the pattern of endings in the instrumental case.

■ STRUCTURE REPLACEMENT DRILLS

1. *I'm acquainted with your uncle.*
   Я знако́м с ва́шим дя́дей.
   Я знако́м с твои́м дя́дей.
   Я знако́м с ва́шей тётей.
   Я знако́м с твое́й тётей.
   (роди́телями, сосе́дкой, де́душкой,
   подру́гой, друзья́ми, ма́мой, семьёй)

2. *Alyosha is satisfied with my work.*
   Alyosha is satisfied with your work.
   Алёша дово́лен мое́й рабо́той.
   Алёша дово́лен ва́шей рабо́той.
   Алёша дово́лен мои́м сочине́нием.
   Алёша дово́лен ва́шим сочине́нием.
   (игро́й, о́черком, кни́гой, стиха́ми,
   рома́ном, ку́рсом, ле́кцией)

3. *Did you talk with your father?*
   Вы говори́ли с ва́шим отцо́м?
   Вы говори́ли со свои́м отцо́м?
   Вы говори́ли с ва́шими друзья́ми?
   Вы говори́ли со свои́ми друзья́ми?
   (проводнико́м, сосе́дом, сосе́дями,
   ре́ктором, секретарём, студе́нтами)

4. *We'll go with her uncle.*
   We'll go with our uncle.
   Мы пое́дем с её дя́дей.
   Мы пое́дем с на́шим дя́дей.
   Мы пое́дем с её това́рищами.
   Мы пое́дем с на́шими това́рищами.
   (учи́телем, детьми́, друзья́ми,
   ребя́тами, сы́ном, тётей)

■ EXPANSION DRILLS

1. *The newsstand stood behind the school.*
   The newsstand stood behind this school.
   Кио́ск стоя́л за шко́лой.
   Кио́ск стоя́л за э́той шко́лой.
   Кио́ск стоя́л за рестора́ном.
   Кио́ск стоя́л за э́тим рестора́ном.
   (дере́вьями, до́мом, зда́нием,
   гости́ницей, теа́тром, клу́бом)

2. *The letter is under the newspaper.*
   The letter is under this newspaper.
   Письмо́ под газе́той.
   Письмо́ под э́той газе́той.
   Письмо́ под журна́лом.
   Письмо́ под э́тим журна́лом.
   (ка́ртой, ка́ртами, коро́бкой, кни́гой,
   словарём, заявле́нием, квита́нциями,
   бума́гой)

1. *That fellow bothers me.*
What am I to do with that fellow?
Э́тот па́рень мне́ меша́ет.
Что́ мне́ де́лать с э́тим па́рнем?
Э́та студе́нтка мне́ меша́ет.
Что́ мне́ де́лать с э́той студе́нткой?
(дети, сосед, девушка, люди,
господин, граждане, певица, человек)

2. *This soup doesn't taste good.*
What should be done with this soup?
Э́тот су́п невку́сный.
Что́ де́лать с э́тим су́пом?
Э́та ры́ба невку́сная.
Что́ де́лать с э́той ры́бой?
(огурцы, каша, бульон, печенье, грибы,
уха, борщ, лапша)

3. *An accident happened to her son.*
Whose son?
С её сы́ном случи́лось несча́стье.
С чьи́м сы́ном?
С её тётей случи́лось несча́стье.
С чье́й тётей?
(родителями, сестрой, дедушкой, дядей,
бабушкой, братьями, отцом)

DISCUSSION

			э́тот, че́й, AND THE POSSESSIVE MODIFIERS					
NOM	(m)	э́тот	че́й	мо́й	тво́й	сво́й	на́ш	ва́ш
	(n)	э́то	чьё	моё	твоё	своё	на́ше	ва́ше
INSTR		э́тим	чьи́м	мои́м	твои́м	свои́м	на́шим	ва́шим
NOM	(f)	э́та	чья́	моя́	твоя́	своя́	на́ша	ва́ша
INSTR		э́той	чье́й	мое́й	твое́й	свое́й	на́шей	ва́шей
NOM	(pl)	э́ти	чьи́	мои́	твои́	свои́	на́ши	ва́ши
INSTR		э́тими	чьи́ми	мои́ми	твои́ми	свои́ми	на́шими	ва́шими

DISTRIBUTION OF ENDINGS

1. The masculine and neuter instrumental singular ending is exactly like that of the dative plural of these forms: –им.

2. The feminine instrumental singular ending is like that of the genitive, dative, and prepositional cases: –ой in э́той and –ей in all the rest.

Alternate endings –ою and –ею may also be encountered in older works of literature and in poetry.

3. The instrumental plural ending is –ими.

Reflexive verbs—part II

MODELS

Я́ ему́ удивля́юсь.
Она́ ____ удивля́ется.
Мы́ ____ удивля́емся.

I'm surprised at him.
She's surprised _____.
We're surprised _____.

Чему́ ты́ удивля́ешься?	What are you surprised at?
Чему́ они́ удивля́ются?	What are they surprised at?
Чему́ вы́ удивля́етесь?	What are you surprised at?
О́н не удивля́лся на́шим успе́хам.	He wasn't surprised at our success.
Она́ не удивля́лась _____.	She wasn't surprised _____.
Они́ не удивля́лись _____.	They weren't surprised _____.

Note that **удивля́ться** is accompanied by the dative case without a preposition, to express the source of surprise or astonishment.

Я́ бою́сь экза́менов.	I'm afraid of the exams.
Ты́ бои́шься _____.	You're afraid _____.
Она́ бои́тся _____.	She's afraid _____.
Мы́ бои́мся _____.	We're afraid _____.
Вы́ бои́тесь _____.	You're afraid _____.
Они́ боя́тся _____.	They're afraid _____.
О́н боя́лся ма́тери.	He was afraid of his mother.
Она́ боя́лась отца́.	She was afraid of her father.
Они́ боя́лись роди́телей.	They were afraid of their parents.

Note that **боя́ться** is accompanied by the genitive case without a preposition, to express the source of fear.

Мы́ сади́мся обе́дать.	We're sitting down to eat dinner.
Я́ сажу́сь _____.	I'm sitting down _____.
Вы́ сади́тесь _____.	You're sitting down _____.
Она́ сади́тся _____.	She's sitting down _____.
Ты́ сади́шься _____.	You're sitting down _____.
Они́ садя́тся _____.	They're sitting down _____.
О́н уже́ познако́мился с не́й.	He's already been introduced to her.
Ты́ ___ познако́милась _____.	You've ___ been introduced _____.
Мы́ ___ познако́мились _____.	We've ___ been introduced _____.
Я́ познако́млюсь с ни́ми.	I'll make their acquaintance.
Мы́ познако́мимся _____.	We'll make _____ acquaintance.
О́н познако́мится _____.	He'll make _____ acquaintance.
Они́ познако́мятся _____.	They'll make _____ acquaintance.
Когда́ ты́ познако́мишься с ни́ми?	When are you going to meet them?
Когда́ вы́ познако́митесь с ни́ми?	When are you going to meet them?
Познако́мься с мое́й сестро́й.	Meet my sister.
Познако́мьтесь с мои́м бра́том.	Meet my brother.
Не бо́йся!	Don't be afraid!
Не бо́йтесь!	Don't be afraid!
Не удивля́йся!	Don't be surprised!
Не удивля́йтесь!	Don't be surprised!
Не серди́сь!	Don't get mad! *or* Don't be angry!
Не серди́тесь!	Don't get mad! *or* Don't be angry!

What are you afraid of?
We're afraid of the exams.
Чего́ вы́ бои́тесь?
Мы́ бои́мся экза́менов.

Чего́ Зи́на бои́тся?
Зи́на бои́тся экза́менов.
    (ты, студенты, эти девушки, вы, этот
    парень, твоя сестра, твои братья)

■ STRUCTURE REPLACEMENT DRILLS

1. *We reached an agreement on this.*
   We'll reach an agreement on this.
   Мы́ договори́лись об э́том.
   Мы́ договори́мся об э́том.
   Они́ договори́лись об э́том.
   Они́ договоря́тся об э́том.
      (ты, они, вы, я, мы, он, они)

2. *We don't feel like going to the lake.*
   We didn't feel like going to the lake.
   На́м не хо́чется е́хать на о́зеро.
   На́м не хоте́лось е́хать на о́зеро.
   На́м не хо́чется е́хать в ле́с.
   На́м не хоте́лось е́хать в ле́с.
      (в колхоз, в село, в Москву, на вокзал)

3. *I stayed home.*
   I'll stay home.
   Я́ оста́лся до́ма.
   Я́ оста́нусь до́ма.
   О́н оста́лся до́ма.
   О́н оста́нется до́ма.
      (мы, дети, ты, сын, вы, дочь, соседи,
      мать)

4. *There'll still be a piece of pirog left.*
   There's still a piece of pirog left.
   Ещё оста́нется кусо́к пирога́.
   Ещё оста́лся кусо́к пирога́.
   Ещё оста́нутся пироги́.
   Ещё оста́лись пироги́.
      (немного каши, суп, грибы, уха, молоко,
      бульон, немного борща, много грибов)

5. *I was getting acquainted with the town.*
   I'm getting acquainted with the town.
   Я́ знако́мился с го́родом.
   Я́ знако́млюсь с го́родом.

О́н знако́мился с го́родом.
О́н знако́мится с го́родом.
    (мы, сын, её дочери, ты, её родители,
    брат, вы)

■ RESPONSE DRILLS

1. *You've got to meet him.*
   I will.
   Тебе́ на́до с ни́м познако́миться.
   Я́ познако́млюсь.
   Зи́не на́до с ни́м познако́миться.
   Она́ познако́мится.
      (твоим родителям, вам, её сыну, нам,
      её дочерям, ребятам, мне)

2. *Don't be afraid!*
   I'm not afraid.
   Не бо́йся!
   Я́ не бою́сь.
   Не серди́сь!
   Я́ не сержу́сь.
   Не удивля́йся!
   Не сади́сь!
   Не обраща́йся к нему́!
   Не станови́сь в о́чередь!

3. *Don't be mad!*
   We're not.
   Не серди́тесь!
   Мы́ не се́рдимся.
   Не сади́тесь!

   Мы́ не сади́мся.
   Не обраща́йтесь к нему́!
   Не бо́йтесь!
   Не станови́тесь туда́!
   Не удивля́йтесь э́тому!

1. *We'll be eating dinner.*
   We're sitting down to eat dinner.
   Мы́ бу́дем обе́дать.
   Мы́ сади́мся обе́дать.
   Сестра́ бу́дет обе́дать.
   Она́ сади́тся обе́дать.
   (отец и мать, брат, туристы, я,
   уборщица, вы, американцы, ты)

2. *It's time for you to sit down and eat dinner.*
   Sit down and eat dinner.
   Тебе́ пора́ сади́ться обе́дать.
   Сади́сь обе́дать.
   Тебе́ пора́ с ни́ми познако́миться.
   Познако́мься с ни́ми.
   Тебе́ пора́ верну́ться домо́й.
   Тебе́ пора́ договори́ться об э́том.
   Тебе́ пора́ обрати́ться к врачу́.
   Тебе́ пора́ сади́ться за сто́л.
   Тебе́ пора́ познако́миться с мои́ми
   роди́телями.

3. *You mustn't be afraid of it.*
   Don't be afraid of it!
   Вы́ не должны́ э́того боя́ться.
   Не бо́йтесь э́того!
   Вы́ не должны́ к нему́ обраща́ться.
   Не обраща́йтесь к нему́!
   Вы́ не должны́ э́тому удивля́ться.
   Вы́ не должны́ на него́ серди́ться.

   Вы́ не должны́ с ни́ми знако́миться.
   Вы́ не должны́ туда́ возвраща́ться.
   Вы́ не должны́ его́ боя́ться.

Reflexive verbs reviewed and drilled in this lesson are given below in all their forms:

1. First conjugation

   оста́ться (pvf) *to remain, stay, be left*
PAST	оста́лся, оста́лась, –ось, –ись
FUT	оста́нусь, оста́нешься, –ется, –емся, –етесь, –утся
IMPER	оста́нься! оста́ньтесь!

   удивля́ться (ipfv) (+ dat) *to be surprised* (or *amazed*)
PAST	удивля́лся, удивля́лась, –ось, –ись
PRES	удивля́юсь, удивля́ешься, –ется, –емся, –етесь, –ются
IMPER	[не] удивля́йся! [не] удивля́йтесь!

   хоте́ться (ipfv) (used impersonally with the dative and the infinitive) *to feel like*
PAST	хоте́лось
PRES	хо́чется
IMPER	(not used)

2. Second conjugation

   боя́ться (ipfv) (+ gen) *to fear, to be afraid*
PAST	боя́лся, боя́лась, –ось, –ись
PRES	бою́сь, бои́шься, –и́тся, –и́мся, –и́тесь, –я́тся
IMPER	[не] бо́йся! [не] бо́йтесь!

   знако́миться (ipfv) (с + instr) *to meet, become acquainted with*
PAST	знако́мился, знако́милась, –ось, –ись
PRES	знако́млюсь, знако́мишься, –ится, –имся, –итесь, –ятся
IMPER	знако́мься! знако́мьтесь!

   познако́миться (pfv) (conjugated like imperfective **знако́миться**) *to meet, become acquainted with*

   сади́ться (ipfv) *to sit down, take a seat*
PAST	сади́лся, сади́лась, –ось, –ись
PRES	сажу́сь, сади́шься, –и́тся, –и́мся, –и́тесь, –я́тся
IMPER	сади́сь! сади́тесь!

договори́ться (pfv) (c + instr) *to come to an agreement, make a date* (or *appointment*)

PAST	договори́лся, договори́лась, –ось, –ись
FUT	договорю́сь, договори́шься, –и́тся, –и́мся, –и́тесь, –я́тся
IMPER	договори́сь! договори́тесь!

Nouns with declension irregularities:
ма́ть, до́чь, сы́н, де́рево, ли́ст

MODELS

У неё краси́вая до́чь.	She has a beautiful daughter.
_____ краси́вый сы́н.	_____ a handsome son.
У неё краси́вые до́чери.	She has beautiful daughters.
_____ краси́вые сыновья́.	_____ handsome sons.

Како́е краси́вое де́рево!	What a beautiful tree!
Како́й краси́вый ли́ст!	What a beautiful leaf!
Каки́е краси́вые дере́вья!	What beautiful trees!
Каки́е краси́вые ли́стья!	What beautiful leaves!

Та́м бы́ло мно́го ли́стьев.	There were lots of leaves there.
_____ дере́вьев.	_____ trees _____.

Я́ ви́дел в го́роде ва́шу до́чь.	I saw your daughter in town.
_____ ма́ть.	_____ mother _____.
_____ ва́шего сы́на.	._____ your son _____.
_____ дру́га.	_____ friend _____.
_____ и́х дочере́й.	_____ their daughters _____.
_____ матере́й.	_____ mothers _____.
_____ сынове́й.	_____ sons _____.
_____ друзе́й.	_____ friends _____.

Я́ говори́л с ва́шей до́черью.	I was talking to your daughter.
_____ ма́терью.	_____ mother.
_____ с ва́шим сы́ном.	_____ to your son.
_____ дру́гом.	_____ friend.
_____ с и́х дочерьми́.	_____ to their daughters.
_____ матеря́ми.	_____ mothers.
_____ сыновья́ми.	_____ sons.
_____ друзья́ми.	_____ friends.

Они́ живу́т у до́чери.	They live with their daughter.
_____ у ма́тери.	_____ mother.
_____ у сы́на.	_____ son.
_____ у дру́га.	_____ friend.
_____ у дочере́й.	_____ daughters.
_____ у матере́й.	_____ mothers.
_____ у сынове́й.	_____ sons.
_____ у друзе́й.	_____ friends.

1. *Is this your pen?*
   Are these your pens?
   Это ва́ше перо́?
   Это ва́ши пе́рья?
   Это ваш стул?
   Это ва́ши сту́лья?
   (ваша дочь, ваш брат, ваша мать, ваш муж, ваш сын, ваш друг)

2. *Don't forget about their mother.*
   Don't forget about their mothers.
   Не забу́дьте об и́х ма́тери.
   Не забу́дьте об и́х матеря́х.
   Не забу́дьте о ва́шем дру́ге.
   Не забу́дьте о ва́ших друзья́х.
   (о её сыне, об их дочери, о вашем брате, об этом дереве)

3. *She's going to visit her son.*
   They're going to visit their sons.
   Она́ е́дет к сы́ну.
   Они́ е́дут к сыновья́м.
   Она́ е́дет к бра́ту.
   Они́ е́дут к бра́тьям.
   (к матери, к другу, к дочери, к мужу, к сыну, к брату)

Where are their brothers?
I didn't see their brothers.
Где́ и́х бра́тья?
Я не ви́дел и́х бра́тьев.
Где́ и́х сыновья́?
Я не ви́дел и́х сынове́й.
(дочери, мужья, братья, матери, друзья)

There's only one leaf here.
There are lots of leaves there.
Ту́т то́лько оди́н лист.
А та́м мно́го ли́стьев.
Ту́т то́лько одно́ де́рево.
А та́м мно́го дере́вьев.
(один стул, одно перо, один лист, одно дерево)

1. *Their friends invited us to dinner.*
   We invited their friends to dinner.
   Их друзья́ пригласи́ли на́с на обе́д.
   Мы́ пригласи́ли их друзе́й на обе́д.
   Их сыновья́ пригласи́ли на́с на обе́д.
   Мы́ пригласи́ли их сынове́й на обе́д.
   (их матери, их друзья, их дочь, их братья, их мать, их дочери, их мужья)

2. *Her sons aren't acquainted with him.*
   He's not acquainted with her sons.
   Её сыновья́ с ни́м не знако́мы.
   Он не знако́м с её сыновья́ми.
   Её ма́ть с ни́м не знако́ма.
   О́н не знако́м с её ма́терью.
   (её дочь, её друзья, её муж, её дочери, её сын, её братья)

DISCUSSION

1. The nouns **мать** *mother* and **дочь** *daughter* are **дверь**-nouns with an alternate stem for the nominative and accusative singular, as opposed to that of all the other cases singular and plural.

	SINGULAR			PLURAL	
NOM-ACC	ма́ть	до́чь	**NOM**	ма́тери	до́чери
GEN-PREP-DAT	ма́тери	до́чери	**ACC-GEN**	матере́й	дочере́й
INSTR	ма́терью	до́черью	**PREP**	о матеря́х	о дочеря́х
			DAT	матеря́м	дочеря́м
			INSTR	матеря́ми	дочерьми́

Note that the instrumental plural of **до́чь** is **дочерьми́** (like **детьми́** and **людьми́**). An alternate form **дочеря́ми** also exists in conversational Russian.

2. The noun **сы́н** *son* has an expanded stem in the plural. It declines as a hard stem in the singular and as a soft stem in the plural.

SINGULAR		PLURAL	
NOM	сы́н	NOM	сыновья́
ACC-GEN	сы́на	ACC-GEN	сынове́й
PREP	о сы́не	PREP	о сыновья́х
DAT	сы́ну	DAT	сыновья́м
INSTR	сы́ном	INSTR	сыновья́ми

Note especially the genitive and accusative plural **сынове́й** with inserted vowel **e** and with the [j] of the plural stem written **й**.

3. The nouns **ли́ст** *leaf* and **де́рево** *tree* have expanded stems in the plural, following the declension pattern of **бра́т**, **сту́л**, and **перо́**; all such nouns decline as hard stems in the singular and as soft stems in the plural.

SINGULAR			PLURAL		
NOM-ACC	ли́ст	де́рево	NOM-ACC	ли́стья	дере́вья
GEN	листа́	де́рева	GEN	ли́стьев	дере́вьев
PREP	о листе́	о де́реве	PREP	о ли́стьях	о дере́вьях
DAT	листу́	де́реву	DAT	ли́стьям	дере́вьям
INSTR	листо́м	де́ревом	INSTR	ли́стьями	дере́вьями

Ли́ст also means *sheet*. In this meaning it has a regular plural, for example, **листы́**, **листо́в**, **о листа́х**: Да́йте мне́ не́сколько **листо́в** бума́ги. (Give me a few *sheets* of paper.)

ЧТЕ́НИЕ И ПИСЬМО́

Никола́й с Га́лей е́здил домо́й в колхо́з, где живу́т и рабо́тают их роди́тели. Это пятьдеся́т киломе́тров от го́рода. Колхо́з небольшо́й, то́лько не́сколько изб. За изба́ми поля́, ле́с и небольшо́е о́зеро. В э́том о́зере ма́сса ры́бы. Бра́т и сестра́ лю́бят ходи́ть в ле́с и на о́зеро. Они́ всегда́ прино́сят мно́го грибо́в и ры́бы, и ма́ть ва́рит для ни́х уху́ и печёт пироги́ с гриба́ми.

В лесу много грибов, только не всякий их найдёт. Иногда их под листьями сразу не увидишь. И надо знать, какие грибы хорошие, а какие плохие. Петя как раз этого не знает. Он увидел какие-то красные грибы с белыми точками и они ему понравились. Он взял их в руки и показал матери. Мать сказала, что они плохие и их надо выбросить. Вдруг Таня увидела в траве длинную чёрную змею. Петя хотел убить змею камнем или палкой. Но мать посоветовала детям не убивать её. Змея уползла. Петя рассердился на маму и долго не мог забыть об этом.

Николай и Гáля приéхали домóй к родúтелям. Родúтели бы́ли рáды вúдеть свойх детéй: ведь онú éздят домóй рéдко, тóлько на канúкулы. За обéдом отéц говорúл о колхóзных делáх, спрáшивал сы́на и дóчь, кáк онú живýт в Москвé. После обéда Гáля с Николáем пошлú к бáбушке и дéдушке в сосéднее селó.

— Я слы́шала, что вы́ с сосéдкой вчерá éздили в лéс за грибáми.
— Дá, с нéй и с её дóчерью.
— Вы́ на тó же мéсто éздили, гдé мы́ с вáми бы́ли?
— Дá.
— Нý кáк, мнóго нашлú грибóв?
— Ó, дá! Я сварúла сýп и дáже испеклá большóй пирóг.
— Вóт кáк! Тогдá мы́ тóже поéдем в лéс в слéдующее воскресéнье.
— Тóлько не ищúте óколо óзера: тáм грибóв нéт.
— Дá, я знáю. Я тáм нéсколько рáз искáла и ничегó не находúла.

— Дéти, покажúте вáши грибы́.
— Этот грúб я нашёл вон тáм, под дéревом.
— Это как рáз плохóй. Вы́брось егó и вы́три рýки. А кáк твой делá, Тáня?
— Я, кáжется, нашлá бéлые грибы́ — трú большúх и двá мáленьких. Вóт, смотрú.
— Нéт, это не бéлые, но онú тóже хорóшие, возьмём úх.
— Вóт досáда, что я такúх не нашёл!
— Ничегó, Пéтя, Мы́ ведь тóлько что пришлú в лéс. Ты́ ещё найдёшь.

— Это бе́лый гриб, ма́ма?

— Да́, Та́ня, э́то бе́лый. Посмотри́, Пе́тя. По́мнишь, мы́ ви́дели таки́е грибы́ в магази́не?

— Да́, по́мню. Они́ бы́ли о́чень дороги́е.

— И́х ведь тру́дно находи́ть.

— А где́ они́ расту́т?

— Под дере́вьями, но на́до зна́ть места́. Во́т бу́дем ходи́ть, и ты́ уви́дишь.

— Ма́ма, смотри́, уже́ о́зеро ви́дно.

— Где́? Я́ не ви́жу.

— Во́н та́м напра́во, за дере́вьями.

— Пойдём туда́, хорошо́?

— Я́ согла́сна, я́ уже́ уста́ла ходи́ть по́ лесу. А ка́к ты́, Та́ня?

— Я́ то́же. Пойдём отдохнём на траве́.

— То́лько возьмём с собо́й па́лку, та́м во́зле о́зера мно́го зме́й.

— Каки́х зме́й? Что́ ты́, Пе́тя, говори́шь глу́пости?

— Э́то не глу́пости, пра́вда, ма́ма?

— Я́ не зна́ю. Ты́ и́х ви́дел?

— Не́т, но мне́ дя́дя Алёша сказа́л.

— А́, е́сли дя́дя Алёша сказа́л, то э́то пра́вда.

— Ва́ля, что́ у на́с сего́дня на обе́д?

— Су́п с лапшо́й и ка́ша.

— Опя́ть? Неуже́ли ты́ не могла́ свари́ть что́-нибудь друго́е, наприме́р уху́?

— А отку́да я́ возьму́ ры́бу? Я́ два́ часа́ стоя́ла в магази́не, а когда́ пришла́ моя́ о́чередь, ры́бы уже́ не́ было.

— Во́т доса́да! Та́к хо́чется ры́бы! Я́ на э́ту ка́шу уже́ смотре́ть не могу́ — вчера́ ка́ша, сего́дня ка́ша. Я́ лу́чше совсе́м не бу́ду обе́дать.

— Ну́ не серди́сь, Алёша. Подожди́, я́ пойду́ к сосе́дке, мо́жет бы́ть она́ мне́ да́ст ры́бы. Я́ зна́ю, она́ доста́ла.

— Мне́ ну́жно зайти́ к Алёше Во́лкову. Пе́тя, пойдёшь со мно́й? Я́ тебя́ с ни́м познако́млю.

— А где́ о́н живёт?

— На у́лице Толсто́го.

— Э́то далеко́ отсю́да?

— Не́т, мину́т де́сять ну́жно идти́.

— Ну́, ла́дно, пойдём. Э́тот Во́лков, ка́жется, но́вый па́рень, из села́?

— Да́, о́н ме́сяц тому́ наза́д прие́хал в го́род. О́н мне́ нра́вится: просто́й тако́й и ви́дно, что с хоро́шей душо́й. Тако́му мо́жно ве́рить.

— Ну́, ты́ лу́чше бу́дь осторо́жен, ты́ ведь его́ ещё ма́ло зна́ешь.

— Да́, но я́ чу́вствую, что о́н хоро́ший челове́к. И, зна́ешь, всё вре́мя говори́ть себе́ «осторо́жно» — э́то ску́чно. Та́к жи́ть нельзя́. Э́то ра́ньше на́ши отцы́ боя́лись говори́ть откры́то, боя́лись люде́й, да́же бли́зких знако́мых. А тепе́рь ина́че, тепе́рь всё свобо́дно говоря́т то́, что ду́мают.

— Ну́, э́то ещё не совсе́м та́к, но, пожа́луй, ты́ пра́в. На́ши отцы́ боя́лись бо́льше, чем мы́.

— Скажи́те пожа́луйста, где́ кварти́ра Бори́са Миха́йловича Ку́рочкина?

— На пя́том этаже́. Я́ то́же та́м живу́. На́м на́до идти́ по ле́стнице, ли́фт не рабо́тает.

— А́, знако́мая исто́рия. У нас в до́ме уже́ четы́ре ме́сяца ли́фт не рабо́тает: де́ти слома́ли две́рь. Я́ ка́ждый де́нь по́сле рабо́ты до́лжен ползти́ наве́рх на пя́тый эта́ж. Уже́ привы́к.

— А вы́ с Бори́сом Миха́йловичем вме́сте рабо́таете?

— Не́т, я то́лько что прие́хал из Москвы́. Мы́ с Бори́сом ста́рые друзья́. Я́ прие́хал сюда́ на неде́лю и во́т хочу́ его́ уви́деть.

— Ка́жется Бори́са Миха́йловича не́т до́ма. Стучу́ уже́ пя́ть мину́т и не́т отве́та.

— А́х, да́, о́н говори́л, что у ни́х сего́дня како́е-то собра́ние.

— Ничего́ не поде́лаешь. Придётся подожда́ть.

— Заходи́те ко мне́, е́сли хоти́те. Поговори́м, познако́мимся.

— Большо́е спаси́бо. А я́ ва́м не бу́ду меша́ть?

— Не́т, что́ вы́! Я́ бу́ду о́чень ра́д.

— Вы́ не зна́ете, почему́ Петро́в вчера́ и сего́дня не́ был на рабо́те?

— О́н о́чень бо́лен. Его́ жена́ звони́ла ча́с наза́д. Сказа́ла, что о́н и за́втра не придёт.

— Что́ с ни́м? Вы́ у него́ бы́ли?

— Не́т. Хочу́ зайти́ по́сле рабо́ты.

— А что́ его́ жена́ сказа́ла?

— Что у него́ всё боли́т.

— Ка́к всё? Не мо́жет бы́ть! Наве́рно, о́н про́сто хо́чет отдохну́ть.

— Что́ с ва́ми? У ва́с что́-нибудь боли́т?

— Я́ то́лько что упа́л и, ка́жется, слома́л себе́ ру́ку.

— Что́ вы́ говори́те! Иди́те скоре́е к врачу́. Хоти́те я́ ва́м помогу́?

— Да́, пожа́луйста. Позвони́те до́ктору О́сипову на кварти́ру. Его́ но́мер телефо́на два́-четы́ре-пя́ть-ше́сть.

— А вы́ ду́маете, о́н сейча́с до́ма?

— Да́. У него́ сего́дня свобо́дный де́нь.

— Я́ сейча́с позвоню́.

— Вчера́ мы́ бы́ли у сосе́дей на обе́де. У и́х до́чери Та́ни бы́л де́нь рожде́ния, и они́ на́с к себе́ пригласи́ли.

— Хоро́шии бы́л обе́д?

— Прекра́сный! Была́ уха́, пиро́г с гриба́ми, вку́сные бу́лочки, то́рт...

— Э́то действи́тельно обе́д!

— А каки́е пода́рки э́та Та́ня от свои́х роди́телей получи́ла! Вы́ да́же не пове́рите!

— Каки́е?

— Но́вый прои́грыватель, аппара́т «Зо́ркий» и авторучку!

— Всё сра́зу? Ну́, зна́ете, э́то да́же глу́по.

— Я́ с ва́ми согла́сен. Я́ свое́й до́чери никогда́ не покупа́ю та́к мно́го пода́рков.

NOTES

PREPARATION FOR CONVERSATION   Прощай, школа!

прощай! прощайте!
Прощай, школа!
     окончен, –а, –о, –ы
Вот и окончена школа.

     свобода
     чувство   [čústvə]
Какое чувство свободы!

     поступить (pfv II)
          поступлю, поступишь, –ят
     вуз
Ты сможешь сразу в вуз поступить.
     отличник
Ты отличник, сможешь сразу
     в вуз поступить.
     захотеть (pfv like хотеть)
Это для тебя свобода: ты
     отличник, если захочешь —
     сможешь сразу в вуз поступить.

     производство
     работать на производстве
А я должен работать на
     производстве.
     целый
А я целые два года должен
     работать на производстве.

     техника

farewell! good-bye!
Farewell, school!
     finished, over, done with
Well, so school is finished.

     freedom, liberty
     feeling
What a feeling of freedom!

     to enter, enroll, join (an institution);
          to behave, act
     college
You can enter college immediately.
     "A" student
You're an "A" student; you can go
     straight on to college.
     to want, feel like
It's freedom for you: You're an "A"
     student; if you want, you can go straight
     on to college.

     production, manufacture
     to work in a factory
But I have to work in a factory.

     entire, whole
But I have to work two whole years in
     a factory.

     engineering, technology, technical things,
          equipment

интересова́ться (I) (*plus* instr)   to be interested in
    интересу́юсь, интересу́ешься, –ются
Ты́ всегда́ интересова́лся   You've always been interested in technical
    те́хникой.   things.
Но ведь, ты́ всегда́ интересова́лся   But you've always been interested in
    те́хникой.   technical things.

    мя́со   meat
    мясокомбина́т   meat-packing plant
А мясокомбина́т?   What about the meat-packing plant?
Подожди́, То́ля, а мясокомбина́т?   Wait a minute, Tolya; what about the meat-
      packing plant?

    дире́ктор   director
    помо́щник   assistant, aide
    помо́щник дире́ктора   assistant director
У тебя́ та́м е́сть знако́мый,   You do have a friend there, the assistant
    помо́щник дире́ктора.   director.
    са́м помо́щник дире́ктора   the assistant director himself
У тебя́ та́м е́сть знако́мый,   You do have a friend there, the assistant
    са́м помо́щник дире́ктора.   director himself.

    уже́ не́т (уже́ не)   no longer, not any longer (*or* more)
Его́ уже́ та́м не́т.   He's not there anymore.
    где́-то   somewhere
Его́ уже́ та́м не́т, где́-то   He's not there anymore; he works somewhere
    в друго́м ме́сте рабо́тает.   else.

    научи́ться (pfv II) (*plus* dat)   to learn
    научу́сь, нау́чишься, –атся
Чему́ я́ та́м научу́сь?   What will I learn there?
    всё равно́   anyway, it doesn't matter
И, всё равно́, чему́ я́ та́м   And anyway, what will I learn there?
    научу́сь?

    рабо́чий, –его   worker
    просто́й рабо́чий   unskilled worker, ordinary worker
Ведь меня́ просты́м рабо́чим   After all, they'll send me as an ordinary
    пошлю́т.   worker.

    весёлый (adv ве́село)   merry, lively, gay, jolly
    э́то ве́село   it's fun
Да́, э́то не ве́село.   Yes, that's no fun.
    осо́бенный   special, particular
Да́, э́то не осо́бенно ве́село.   Yes, that's no particular fun.

    бы́стрый   quick, fast, rapid
Ну, ничего́. Два́ го́да   Well, never mind. Two years will go by
    пройду́т бы́стро.   quickly.

    жи́знь (f)   life
    устро́ить (pfv II)   to arrange, establish, organize, fix up
    пото́м   afterward, later on, then
Пото́м ты́ устро́ишь свою́ жи́знь,   Later on you'll arrange your life the
    ка́к захо́чешь.   way you want to.

Что́ мне́ «пото́м»?	What good is "later on" to me?
учи́ться (II)	to learn, study
учи́ться в ву́зе	to go to college
Мне́ уже́ тепе́рь хо́чется учи́ться в ву́зе.	I want to go to college now.
профе́ссия	profession, calling, skill, trade
получи́ть профе́ссию	to enter a profession, learn a trade, acquire a skill
А каку́ю ты́ хо́чешь получи́ть профе́ссию?	What profession do you want to enter?
инжене́р	engineer
ста́ть (pfv I), ста́ну, ста́нешь, –ут	to become, get, grow; stop
Ты́ хо́чешь ста́ть инжене́ром?	Do you want to become an engineer?
Всё ещё хо́чешь ста́ть инжене́ром?	Do you still want to become an engineer?
мечта́ть (I)	to dream
Не́т, я́ об э́том бо́льше не мечта́ю.	No, I don't dream of that anymore.
что́бы [štóbi] or [štəbi]	in order to, to
Что́бы ста́ть инжене́ром, ну́жно пя́ть ле́т учи́ться.	In order to be an engineer you've got to study for five years.
сли́шком	too
Э́то сли́шком до́лго.	That's too long.
пра́ктика	practical experience, practice
Всё-таки полу́чишь пра́ктику.	Anyway, you'll gain practical experience.
да́ром	for nothing, gratis, with no return, in vain, to no avail
пропа́сть (pfv I) (like упа́сть)	to be lost, missing, wasted; to perish
Вре́мя не пропадёт да́ром	The time won't be totally wasted.
И заче́м тебе́ профе́ссия?	And what do you need a profession for?
месте́чко (var of ме́сто)	spot, place, job; small town
тёплое месте́чко	a soft spot, a nice cushy job
устро́иться (pfv II), устро́юсь, устро́ишься, –ятся	to get a job, to get settled, to get fixed up (or established)
Я́ хочу́ устро́иться на тёплое месте́чко.	I want to get myself a nice cushy job.
гла́вный	main, chief
гла́вное	the main thing
Гла́вное — устро́иться на тёплое месте́чко.	The main thing is to get yourself set up in a nice cushy job.
знако́мство	acquaintance, familiarity
по знако́мству	by knowing the right people, through friends
Гла́вное — устро́иться по знако́мству на тёплое месте́чко.	The main thing is to get yourself set up in a nice cushy job by knowing the right people.
нача́ть (pfv I) (past на́чал, –о, –и, [f] начала́; fut начну́, начнёшь, –у́т)	to start, begin
зараба́тывать (I)	to earn (or make) [money]

Мне хо́чется нача́ть зараба́тывать.	I want to start earning [money].
Гла́вное — устро́иться по знако́мству на тёплое месте́чко, нача́ть хорошо́ зараба́тывать.	The main thing is to get yourself set up in a nice cushy job by knowing the right people and start earning good [money].
серьёзный	serius
наде́яться (I) (на *plus* acc)	to hope, count on, rely on
Наде́юсь, ты́ э́то не серьёзно говори́шь.	I hope you're not serious in saying that.
Не́т, серьёзно.	Yes, I am.
Я́ са́м хочу́ та́к сде́лать.	I myself want to do just that.
Не́т, серьёзно. Я́ са́м хочу́ та́к сде́лать.	Yes, I am serious. That's what I want to do.
де́ньги, де́нег (pl only)	money
больши́е де́ньги	good money, lots of money
Я́ бу́ду зараба́тывать больши́е де́ньги.	I'll be gaking good money.
маши́на	car, machine
е́здить на маши́не	to drive a car, go by car
Я́ хочу́ е́здить на свое́й маши́не.	I want to drive my own car.
Бу́ду зараба́тывать больши́е де́ньги, е́здить на свое́й маши́не.	I'll be earning good money [and] driving my own car.
успе́х	success, luck
жела́ть (I)	to wish
жела́ть кому́-нибудь успе́ха	to wish someone luck
Ну, жела́ю тебе́ успе́ха.	Well, I wish you luck.

SUPPLEMENT

де́лать больши́е успе́хи	to do very well, to make excellent progress
Он де́лает больши́е успе́хи в ру́сском языке́.	He's doing very well in Russian.
мне́ всё равно́	I don't care, it's all the same to me, it makes no difference to me
Ты́ опозда́ешь на ле́кцию.	You'll be late to the lecture.
— Мне́ всё равно́.	I don't care.
ме́дленный	slow
Вре́мя шло́ та́к ме́дленно.	The time went very slowly.
занима́ться (I) (*plus* instr), занима́юсь, –ешься, –ются	to busy oneself, to occupy oneself, to study
Он занима́ется ру́сским языко́м.	He's studying Russian.

Проща́й, шко́ла

В. — Ви́ктор   А. — Анато́лий (То́ля)   И. — И́горь

В. 1 Во́т и око́нчена шко́ла. Како́е чу́вство свобо́ды!

А. 2 Э́то для тебя́ свобо́да: ты́ отли́чник, е́сли захо́чешь — смо́жешь сра́зу в ву́з поступи́ть.[1] А я́ це́лые два́ го́да до́лжен ра́ньше рабо́тать на произво́дстве.[2]

В. 3 Но ведь ты' всегда́ интересова́лся те́хникой.

И. 4 Подожди́, То́ля, а мясокомбина́т? У тебя́ та́м есть знако́мый, са́м помо́щник дире́ктора.

А. 5 Его́ уже́ та́м не́т, где́-то в друго́м ме́сте рабо́тает. И, всё равно́, чему́ я та́м научу́сь? Ведь меня́ просты́м рабо́чим пошлю́т.

В. 6 Да́, э́то не осо́бенно ве́село. Ну́, ничего́, два́ го́да пройду́т бы́стро, а пото́м устро́ишь свою́ жи́знь, ка́к захо́чешь.

А. 7 Что́ мне́ «пото́м»? Мне́ уже́ тепе́рь хо́чется учи́ться в ву́зе![3]

И. 8 А каку́ю ты́ хо́чешь получи́ть профе́ссию? Всё ещё хо́чешь ста́ть инжене́ром?

А. 9 Не́т, я об э́том бо́льше не мечта́ю. Что́бы ста́ть инжене́ром, ну́жно пя́ть ле́т учи́ться. Э́то сли́шком до́лго.

В. 10 Всё-таки полу́чишь пра́ктику — вре́мя не пропадёт да́ром.

И. 11 И заче́м тебе́ профе́ссия? Гла́вное — устро́иться по знако́мству на тёплое месте́чко, нача́ть хорошо́ зараба́тывать.[4]

А. 12 Наде́юсь, ты́ э́то не серьёзно говори́шь.

И. 13 Не́т, серьёзно. Я са́м хочу́ та́к сде́лать. Бу́ду зараба́тывать больши́е де́ньги, е́здить на свое́й маши́не.

В. 14 Ну́, жела́ю тебе́ успе́ха![5]

NOTES

[1] Ву́з is comparable to an American college or university; the word itself is another example of one formed from initial letters, in this case, вы́сшее уче́бное заведе́ние *higher educational institution*.

[2] All high school graduates with the exception of отли́чники "*A*" *students* are required to do two years of manual work, usually at a factory or kolkhoz, to which they are assigned by the government.

[3] Compare the three Russian verbs meaning *to study*: учи́ть, учи́ться, and занима́ться.

Я учу́ ру́сский язы́к.	I'm studying Russian.
Я учу́сь ру́сскому языку́.	I'm studying Russian.
Я занима́юсь ру́сским языко́м.	I'm studying Russian.

The verb учи́ть usually implies assiduous study and memorization, i.e., real effort: Я учу́ э́ти ру́сские слова́ *I'm studying these Russian words*. The verb учи́ться is broader in its meaning: Я учу́сь игра́ть в ша́хматы *I'm learning how to play chess*; Сы́н у́чится чита́ть *My son is learning to read*. The verb занима́ться indicates study on a higher level, usually in connection with a specific field or discipline: Он занима́ется фи́зикой *He's studying physics*; Он занима́ется исто́рией Кита́я (or Он специали́ст по исто́рии Кита́я) *He's doing research on the history of China* (or *He's a specialist in the history of China*).

Note that while ходи́ть в шко́лу may be used in the sense *to attend school*, one cannot use the verb ходи́ть in reference to a college or university. Compare Он ýчится (or занимáется) в вýзе *He goes to college*; Óн ýчится (or занимáется) в университéте *He attends the university*; with Óн хóдит в шкóлу *He goes to school.*

⁴ The notion of **тёплое местéчко** means not only a *sinecure* or *easy job*, but often one in which the person can make a little extra money on the side through bribery or illegal dealings.

⁵ The verb **желáть** is used with the dative for the person (to whom it is wished) and with the genitive for the thing wished. Such expressions as **спокóйной нóчи**, **всегó хорóшего**, and **счастлúвого путú** are all in the genitive case and have been shortened from the longer phrase containing the verb **желáть**: **Желáю вáм (тебé) спокóйной нóчи** *I wish you a restful night.*

PREPARATION FOR CONVERSATION **Прощáльная вечерúнка**

вечерúнка	party (informal evening gathering)
прощáльный	farewell (adj)
прощáльная вечерúнка	farewell party
У нáс бýдет прощáльная вечерúнка.	We're going to have a farewell party.
сбóр	gathering, assembly
в сбóре	together, present, here
Кáжется, всё ужé в сбóре.	I guess everybody's here now.
Нéт, Óля ещё не пришлá.	No, Olya hasn't come yet.
Онá звонúла. Придёт немнóго пóзже.	She phoned. She'll come a little later.
женúх, –á; –ú, –óв	fiancé, bridegroom-to-be
И знáете с кéм? Со своúм женихóм.	And you know with whom? With her fiancé.
выходúть зáмуж	to get married (said of women only)
Рáзве онá выхóдит зáмуж?	You mean she's getting married?
С женихóм? Рáзве онá выхóдит зáмуж?	With her fiancé? You mean she's getting married?
Это и для меня нóвость.	That's news even to me.
счáстье [ščášţji]	happiness, luck
Давáйте вы́пьем за её счáстье.	Let's drink a toast to her happiness!
Вы́пьем.	Let's do that!
бýдущее, –его	future
А тепéрь — за нáше бýдущее.	And now, to our future.
винó, –á; вúна, вúн	wine
налúть (pfv I), налью́, нальёшь, –ю́т	to pour, fill (by pouring)
Налéй мнé ещё винá, Вáня.	Pour me some more wine, Vanya!
фúзик	physicist
собирáться (I), собирáюсь, –ешься, –ются	to plan, intend, prepare, get ready; to gather, assemble
Мы́ собирáемся бы́ть фúзиками.	We're planning to be physicists.
Мы́ с Нáдей собирáемся бы́ть фúзиками.	Nadya and I are planning to be physicists.
А ты́, Бóря, кéм хóчешь бы́ть?	How about you, Borya, what do you want to be?
учёный, –ого	scientist, scholar, learned man

А ты, Бо́ря, ке́м хо́чешь бы́ть, учёным?

How about you, Borya, what do you want to be, a scientist?

космона́вт
Я хочу́ бы́ть космона́втом.
   хоте́л бы   [xaţélbi]
Я хоте́л бы бы́ть космона́втом.

astronaut, cosmonaut
I want to be a cosmonaut.
   would like
I'd like to be a cosmonaut.

ма́сло
переда́ть (pfv *like* да́ть)   (past пе́редал,
   –о, –и; [f] –а́)
Переда́й мне́ ма́сло.
   колбаса́, –ы́; колба́сы, колба́с
Переда́й мне́ колбасу́.
Переда́й мне́ ма́сло и колбасу́.

butter
to pass, hand, give, pass on

Pass me the butter.
   sausage
Pass me the sausage.
Pass me the butter and sausage.

полете́ть (pfv II), полечу́, полети́шь, –я́т
   Ма́рс
Хо́чешь полете́ть на Ма́рс?
   земля́, –и́; зе́мли, земе́ль (acc sg зе́млю)
   вокру́г (*plus* gen)
Хо́чешь полете́ть вокру́г Земли́?
**Хо́чешь полете́ть вокру́г Земли́ и́ли пря́мо
  на Ма́рс?**

to fly
Mars
You want to fly to Mars?
   earth, land
   around
You want to fly around the Earth?
You want to fly around the Earth, or straight to Mars?

не сто́ит
На Ма́рс не сто́ит, там то́же жи́зни не́т.

it's not worthwhile, why bother, it's no use
No use going to Mars; there's no life there either.

шу́тка
Э́то уже́ ста́рая шу́тка.

joke
That joke's already an old one.

салфе́тка
Ви́тя, переда́й мне́ салфе́тки.

napkin
Vitya, hand me the napkins.

лежа́ть (II), лежу́, лежи́шь, –а́т
   перед (*or* передо) (*plus* instr)
Они́ перед тобо́й лежа́т.

to be lying
in front of, before
They're lying in front of you.

просну́ться (pfv I), просну́сь,
   проснёшься, –у́тся
Ви́тя!!! Просни́сь!
   заду́маться (pfv I)

to wake up

Vitya, wake up!
   to become lost in thought, fall into
     reverie, daydream

Ви́тя!!! Просни́сь! Ты́ о чём заду́мался?

Vitya, wake up! What were you daydreaming about?

реши́ть (pfv II), решу́, реши́шь, –а́т
Да́ не могу́ реши́ть, куда́ мне́ идти́.
   ника́к (не)
Да́ ника́к не могу́ реши́ть, куда́ мне́ идти́.

to decide, make a decision
Why, I can't decide where I ought to go.
   by no means, in no way (*lit.* nohow)
I can't for the life of me decide where I ought to go.

интересова́ть (I), интересу́ю,
   интересу́ешь, –ют
Меня́ всё интересу́ет.

to interest

Everything interests me.

институ́т	institute
пединститу́т [pedinsţitút]	teachers college
Поступа́й в пединститу́т.	Enroll in a teachers college.
литфа́к	department of literature
на литфа́к	to study literature
что́-ли	maybe, perhaps, possibly
Куда́ мне́ поступи́ть?	Where should I enroll?
В пединститу́т что́ ли, на литфа́к?	Perhaps in a teachers college, to study literature?
мысль (f)	idea, thought
Хоро́шая мы́сль.	That's a good idea.
Я то́же туда́ ду́маю.	I'm thinking of going there, too.
преподава́тель (m)	teacher, instructor
По-мо́ему, бы́ть преподава́телем о́чень интере́сно.	In my opinion, being a teacher is very interesting.

SUPPLEMENT

хи́мик	chemist
Я хочу́ ста́ть хи́миком.	I want to become a chemist.
исто́рик	historian
Я хочу́ ста́ть исто́риком.	I want to become a historian.
те́хник	technician
Он ста́нет те́хником.	He'll be a technician.
нау́ка	science, knowledge, study, lesson
Меня́ интересу́ют то́чные нау́ки.	The exact sciences interest me.
Во́т тебе́ нау́ка!	Let that be a lesson to you!
нау́чный	scientific, scholarly
Он пи́шет нау́чную рабо́ту.	He's writing a scientific (or scholarly) work.
преподава́ть (I) (like дава́ть)	to teach, instruct
Он преподаёт ру́сский язы́к.	He teaches Russian.
око́нчить (pfv II)	to finish, graduate from
Он око́нчил ву́з два́ го́да тому́ наза́д.	He graduated from college two years ago.
просыпа́ться (I)	to wake up
Я обы́чно просыпа́юсь в ше́сть.	I usually wake up at six.
про́шлый	past, last
Они́ прие́хали на про́шлой неде́ле.	They arrived last week.
про́шлое, –ого	the past
Забу́дь о про́шлом!	Forget about the past!
литерату́рный	literary
Вы́ чита́ете «Литерату́рную газе́ту»?	Do you read the *Literary Gazette?*

Проща́льная вечери́нка[1]

Наде́жда (На́дя)   Ве́ра   Ива́н (Ва́ня)   Ви́ктор (Ви́тя)   Бори́с (Бо́ря)

На́дя   1 Ка́жется, всё уже́ в сбо́ре. Не́т, О́ля ещё не пришла́.

Ве́ра   2 Она́ звони́ла. Придёт немно́го по́зже. И зна́ете с ке́м? Со свои́м женихо́м.[2]

Ваня	3	С женихóм? Рáзве онá выхóдит зáмуж?
Витя	4	Это и для меня нóвость. Давáйте вы́пьем за её счáстье.
Бóря	5	Вы́пьем. А тепéрь — за нáше бýдущее. Налéй мне ещё винá, Вáня.³
Ваня	6	Вóт мы с Нáдей собирáемся бы́ть физиками.⁴ А ты, Бóря, кéм хóчешь бы́ть? Учёным?⁵
Бóря	7	Нéт, я хотéл бы бы́ть космонáвтом. Передáй мне мáсло и колбасý. Спасúбо.
Нáдя	8	Космонáвтом? Вокрýг Землú хóчешь полетéть úли прямо на Мáрс?
Вáня	9	На Мáрс не стóит, тáм тóже жúзни нéт . . .
Нáдя	10	Это ужé стáрая шýтка.⁶ Витя, передáй мне салфéтки, онú перед тобóй лежáт. Витя!!! Проснúсь! Ты́ о чём задýмался?
Витя	11	Да никáк не могý решúть, кудá мне идтú: меня всё интересýет. В пединститýт чтó ли, на литфáк?⁷
Вéра	12	Хорóшая мы́сль! Я тóже тудá дýмаю. По-мóему, бы́ть преподавáтелем óчень интерéсно.⁸

NOTES

[1] Russians use the word **вéчер** to mean both *evening* and *party*. In the latter sense, **вéчер** refers to a formal or institutional evening gathering. For a private party, however, **вечерúнка** is more commonly used. The preposition **на** (*plus* prepositional *or* accusative) is used with both **вéчер** and **вечерúнка** in this sense:

Я познакóмился с ни́м в клýбе **на вéчере.**	I met him *at a party* at the club.
Приходúте к нáм **на вечерúнку.**	Come *to a party* at our place.

[2] The word **женúх** *fiancé, bridegroom-to-be* and **невéста** *fiancée, bride-to-be* have come back into official usage, following the return of the tradition of engagements in the U.S.S.R. In an effort to discourage church weddings, the Soviet government has been trying to make civil wedding ceremonies more attractive and has even established special **дворцы́ счáстья** *palaces of happiness*, one in Moscow and one in Leningrad. The whole ceremony—champagne included—takes about five minutes. There is always a waiting line of young couples, many of whom have traveled great distances in order to be married there.

[3] The Russian language is rich in variants of names which reflect the attitude or relationship of the speaker to the person named. Thus **Вúктор** may be called **Вúтя** informally, **Вúтька** to show superiority or contempt, or **Вúтенька** to show affectionate regard. Similarly, **Ивáн** is called **Вáня, Вáнька,** or **Вáнечка; Николáй** becomes **Кóля, Кóлька,** and **Кóлечка** (*or* **Кóленька**). **Óльга** is informally called **Óля** and affectionately **Óлечка; Вéра** is affectionately **Вéрочка,** but pejoratively **Вéрка; Борúс** is informally **Бóря,** pejoratively **Бóрька,** and affectionately **Бóречка.**

[4] Many **стóл**-nouns designating professions may apply to women as well as to men:

Онá фúзик.	She's a physicist.
Онá хорóший врáч.	She's a good physician.

Товáрищ Орлóва — профéссор матемáтики.	Comrade Orlov (f) is a professor of mathematics.
Онá хи́мик.	She's a chemist.
Онá большóй специали́ст.	She's a great specialist.

[5] Note that Russian uses the pronoun **ктó** while English uses *what* in referring to work or professions:

Ктó óн, хи́мик?	*What* is he, a chemist?
Кéм ты́ хóчешь бы́ть?	*What* do you want to be?
Кéм ты́ стáнешь, инженéром?	*What* are you going to be, an engineer?

[6] "На Мáрсе **тóже жи́зни нéт**" is the punch line from a recent space-age anti-Soviet joke. A cosmonaut, on returning from Mars, is asked if there is any life there and replies, "No, there's no life on Mars *either*."

[7] **Пединститýт** (short for **педагоги́ческий институ́т**) serves the same function as an American teachers college. Students in the **пединститýт** specialize in one field only. For example, Vera hopes to major in literature, i.e., enroll in the department of literature **поступи́ть на литфáк** (*full form* **литерату́рный факульте́т**).

[8] The term **преподавáтель** is applied to instructors at the secondary or university level. The rank of **преподавáтель** is used at the university level for an instructor without an advanced degree who teaches basic or introductory courses.

The term **учи́тель**, on the other hand, is limited to the elementary and secondary-school levels, or refers to a teacher who gives private lessons, for example, in music or dancing.

Basic sentence patterns

1. Мóй дя́дя бы́л инженéром.
   _____ хи́миком.
   _____ фи́зиком.
   _____ истóриком.
   _____ дирéктором пединститýта.
   _____ преподавáтелем истóрии.

   My uncle was an engineer.
   _____ a chemist.
   _____ a physicist.
   _____ a historian
   _____ the director of a teacher's college.
   _____ a history teacher.

2. Óн бы́л помóшником дирéктора.
   _____ профéссора.
   _____ врачá.

   He was the director's assistant.
   _____ the professor's assistant.
   _____ the doctor's assistant.

3. Ты́ интересу́ешься жи́знью в колхóзе?
   _____ истóрией?
   _____ хи́мией?
   _____ геогрáфией?
   _____ фи́зикой?
   _____ литерату́рой?
   _____ э́той рабóтой?
   _____ рабóтой на мясокомбинáте?

   Are you interested in life on the kolkhoz?
   _____ history?
   _____ chemistry?
   _____ geography?
   _____ physics?
   _____ literature?
   _____ this work?
   _____ a job in the meat-packing plant?

4. Я собира́юсь ста́ть врачо́м.	I plan to become a doctor.
_____ инжене́ром.	_____ an engineer.
_____ те́хником.	_____ a technician.
_____ космона́втом.	_____ a cosmonaut.
_____ преподава́телем.	_____ a teacher.
_____ учёным.	_____ a scientist.
5. Ке́м о́н рабо́тает?	What kind of work does he do?
— О́н рабо́тает вахтёром.	He works as a custodian.
_____ носи́льщиком.	_____ porter.
_____ шофёром.	_____ chauffeur.
_____ администра́тором.	_____ administrator.
_____ секретарём.	_____ secretary.
6. Я нахожу́ э́то интере́сным.	I find this interesting.
_____ тру́дным.	_____ difficult.
_____ лёгким.	_____ easy.
_____ возмо́жным.	_____ possible.
_____ невозмо́жным.	_____ impossible.
7. О́н каза́лся ста́рым.	He seemed old.
_____ молоды́м.	_____ young.
_____ симпати́чным.	_____ nice.
_____ стра́нным.	_____ strange.
_____ споко́йным.	_____ quiet.
8. Э́тот челове́к мне́ ка́жется глу́пым.	That man seems stupid to me.
_____ у́мным.	_____ intelligent __.
_____ безду́шным.	_____ heartless ___.
_____ симпати́чным.	_____ likable _____.
_____ несча́стным.	_____ unhappy ____.
_____ знако́мым.	_____ familiar ____.
9. Вода́ ста́ла холо́дной.	The water became (*or* turned) cold.
_____ горя́чей.	_____ hot.
_____ тёплой.	_____ warm.
_____ кра́сной.	_____ red.
_____ си́ней.	_____ blue.
_____ чёрной.	_____ black.
10. Они́ бы́ли молоды́ми врача́ми.	They were young doctors.
_____ хоро́шими специали́стами.	_____ good specialists.
_____ ста́рыми знако́мыми.	_____ old acquaintances.
_____ прекра́сными певца́ми.	_____ excellent singers.
_____ ста́рыми людьми́.	_____ old people.
11. О́н бы́л знако́м с Толсты́м.	He was acquainted with Tolstoy.
_____ с Чайко́вским.	_____ with Tschaikovsky.
_____ с Маяко́вским.	_____ with Mayakovsky.
_____ с Достое́вским.	_____ with Dostoevsky.
_____ с Го́рьким.	_____ with Gorky.
_____ с Толсты́ми.	_____ with the Tolstoys.
_____ с Достое́вскими.	_____ with the Dostoevskys.

12. Какого цвета ваша машина?
    — Чёрная с белым.
    _____ с зелёным.
    _____ с синим.
    _____ с жёлтым.

What color is your car?
Black and white.
_____ green.
_____ blue.
_____ yellow.

13. Какого цвета ваш костюм?
    — Белый с красным.
    _____ с голубым.
    _____ с синим.

What color is your costume?
White and (*or* with) red.
_____ blue.
_____ dark blue.

14. Зайдите ко мне перед обедом.
    _____ перед экзаменом.
    _____ перед уроком.
    _____ перед лекцией.
    _____ перед концертом.
    _____ перед работой.
    _____ перед собранием.
    _____ перед началом каникул.

Drop in to see me before dinner.
_____ before the exam.
_____ before the lesson.
_____ before the lecture.
_____ before the concert.
_____ before work.
_____ before the meeting.
_____ before the beginning of vacation.

15. Перед магазином масса людей.
    _____ зданием_____.
    _____ дверьми_____.
    _____ домом _____.
    _____ кассой _____.
    _____ горсоветом _____.
    _____ гостиницей _____.

There are lots of people in front of the store.
_____ the building.
_____ the doors.
_____ the house.
_____ the box office.
_____ the city hall.
_____ the hotel.

16. Как ты это устроил?
    _____ заработал?
    _____ решил?
    _____ нашёл?
    _____ потерял?

How did you arrange it?
_____ earn it?
_____ decide (*or* solve) it?
_____ find it?
_____ lose it?

17. Так ты никогда не научишься.
    _____ устроишься.
    _____ проснёшься.
    _____ с ней не познакомишься.

You'll never learn anything that way.
_____ get a job _____.
_____ wake up _____.
_____ meet her _____.

18. Мне не хочется просыпаться.
    _____ собираться.
    _____ этим заниматься.
    _____ учиться.
    _____ возвращаться.
    _____ садиться.
    _____ с ней знакомиться.

I don't feel like waking up.
_____ getting ready.
_____ doing (*or* studying) that.
_____ studying.
_____ going back.
_____ sitting down.
_____ meeting her.

19. Я немного посплю.
    Он _____ поспит.
    Они _____ поспят.
    Она немного поспала.
    Он _____ поспал.

I'll take a little nap.
He'll take _____.
They'll take_____.
She took a little nap.
He took_____.

20.	Когда́ вы́ обы́чно просыпа́етесь?	When do you usually wake up?
	_____ ты́ _____ просыпа́ешься?	_____ do you _____ wake up?
	Я́ обы́чно просыпа́юсь в се́мь.	I usually wake up at seven.
	Мы́ _____ просыпа́емся _____.	We_____ wake up _____.
	Они́ _____ просыпа́ются_____.	They __ wake up _____.

21.	О́н ско́ро проснётся.	He'll wake up soon.
	Они́ _____ просну́тся.	They'll wake up _____.
	Я́ то́лько что просну́лся.	I just woke up.
	Она́ _____ просну́лась.	She _____ woke up.
	Они́ _____ просну́лись.	They _____ woke up.

22.	Порабо́тай немно́го!	Do a little bit of work!
	Поспи́ немно́го!	Take a little nap!
	Потанцу́й немно́го!	Dance a bit!
	Поживи́ та́м немно́го!	Live there for a while!
	Побу́дь со мно́й!	Stay with me!
	Посиди́ немно́го!	Sit awhile! _or_ Stay awhile!
	Полежи́ немно́го!	Stay in bed awhile! _or_ Lie down for awhile!
	Погуля́й немно́го!	Go for a little stroll!
	Походи́ немно́го!	Walk a bit!

23.	Вы́ у́читесь ру́сскому языку́?	Are you studying (_or_ learning) Russian?
	Ты́ у́чишься_____?	Are you studying (_or_ learning) _____?
	Я́ учу́сь англи́йскому языку́.	I'm studying (_or_ learning) English.
	О́н у́чится_____.	He's studying (_or_ learning) _____.
	Они́ у́чатся_____.	They're studying (_or_ learning)____.

24.	Я́ мно́гое узна́л.	I found out a lot _or_ I learned a lot.
	Ты́ мно́гому нау́чишься.	You'll learn a lot.
	Мы́ о мно́гом говори́ли.	We talked about a lot of things.
	Я́ ко мно́гому привы́к.	I'm used to a lot of things.
	Она́ мно́гого бои́тся.	She's afraid of a lot of things.
	Она́ со мно́гим не согла́сна.	There's a lot she doesn't agree with.

25.	Я́ э́то переда́м ва́шему знако́мому.	I'll pass this on to your friend.
	_____ ва́шим знако́мым.	_____ your friends.
	_____ ва́шей знако́мой.	_____ your friend.
	_____ на́шим рабо́чим.	_____ our workers.

Pronunciation practice: clusters beginning with the letters с and з

Clusters beginning with the letter с.

A. с + с = long с

[ssóɲij] с Со́ней
with Sonya

[ʂʂévəm] с се́вом
with the sowing

[ssáləm] с са́лом
with fat

[ʂʂíɲij] с си́ней
with blue

[ssúpəm] с су́пом
with soup

B. с + з = long з

[ẓẓimój] с зимо́й
with winter
[zzáḑi] сза́ди
from behind

[zzáɣiṣṭju] с за́вистью
with envy
[zzólətəm] с зо́лотом
with gold

[zzóni] с зо́ны
from the zone
[zziváṭ] сзыва́ть
to call together

C. с + ш = long ш

[raššiḅítcə] расшиби́ться
to break to pieces
[ššíṭ] сши́ть
to sew
[ššárəm] с ша́ром
with a ball
[ššútkəj] с шу́ткой
with a joke

[ššíləm] с ши́лом
with an awl
[pəššibáṭ] посшиба́ть
to knock down
[ššápkəj] с ша́пкой
with a cap
[ššérṣṭju] с ше́рстью
with wool

[ššiṛinój] с ширино́й
with the width
[raššítij] расши́тый
embroidered

D. с + ж = long ж

[žžíṭ] сжи́ть
worry to death
[žžárəm] с жа́ром
animatedly
[žžútkəj] с жу́ткой
with horrible
[žžírəm] с жи́ром
with fat

[pəžžímáṭ] посжима́ть
to squeeze together
[žžápkəj] с жа́бкой
with a small toad
[žžéṣṭju] с же́стью
with a tin plate
[žžinój] с жено́й
with wife

E. с + ч = шч (щ)

[ščáṣṭji] сча́стье
happiness
[ščitáṭ] счита́ть
to count
[naščót] насчёт
concerning
[iščiṣláṭ] исчисля́ть
to calculate

[rəščisáṭ] расчеса́ть
to comb apart
[ščáškəj] с ча́шкой
with a cup
[ščužím] с чужи́м
with a foreign
[ščístim] с чи́стым
with clean

[ščimadánəm] с чемода́ном
with a suitcase
[ščilavékəm] с челове́ком
with a man
[ṇiščém] ни с чём
with nothing

Clusters beginning with the letter з.

A. з + з = long з

[izzáɣiṣṭi] из за́висти
from envy
[izzóbə] из зо́ба
from the craw

[izzáṛivə] из за́рева
from the glow
[izzóni] из зо́ны
from the zone

[iẓẓirná] из зерна́
from grain
[raẓẓivátcə] раззева́ться
to yawn

B. з + с = long с

[issádə] из са́да
from the orchard
[iṣṣéṃiṇi] из се́мени
from the seed

[issúpə] из су́па
from soup
[issarátəvə] из Сара́това
from Saratov

[issipúčij] из сыпу́чей
from the quicksand
[iṣṣól] из сёл
from villages

C. з + ж = long ж

[ižžáləʂʈi]   из жа́лости
  from pity
[ižžógə]   изжо́га
  heartburn

[ižžáɹiʈ]   изжа́рить
  to fry
[ižžilútkə]   из желу́дка
  from the stomach

[ižžirlá]   из жерла́
  from the muzzle
[ražživát]   разжева́ть
  to chew apart

D. з + ш = long ш

[iššerʂʈi]   из ше́рсти
  from wool
[iššírmi]   из ши́рмы
  from a screen

[iššárə]   из ша́ра
  from a sphere
[iššútḳi]   из шу́тки
  from a joke

[iššólkə]   из шёлка
  from silk
[iššiʈjá]   из шитья́
  from sewing

E. з + ч = шч (щ)

[iščásʈi]   из ча́сти
  from the part
[iščužóvə]   из чужо́го
  from foreign
[iščislá]   из числа́
  from the number

[iščimadánə]   из чемода́на
  from the suitcase
[iščášḳi]   из ча́шки
  from a cup
[iščivó]   из чего́
  from what

STRUCTURE AND DRILLS

Use of the instrumental in the predicate with verbs of *being* and *becoming*

MODELS

О́н бы́л дире́ктором заво́да.	He was plant director.
_____ до́ктором.	_____ a doctor.
_____ преподава́телем.	_____ an instructor.
_____ певцо́м.	_____ a singer.
_____ учи́телем.	_____ a teacher.
_____ профе́ссором исто́рии.	_____ a history professor.
_____ мои́м сосе́дом.	_____ my neighbor.
Она́ была́ фи́зиком.	She was a physicist.
_____ хи́миком.	_____ a chemist.
_____ мое́й сосе́дкой.	_____ my neighbor.
_____ учи́тельницей му́зыки.	_____ a music teacher.
_____ убо́рщицей.	_____ a cleaning woman.
_____ продавщи́цей.	_____ a saleslady.
_____ специали́стом в э́том де́ле.	_____ a specialist in this field.
Я́ бу́ду врачо́м.	I'm going to be a doctor.
_____ инжене́ром.	_____ an engineer.
_____ те́хником.	_____ a technician.
_____ исто́риком.	_____ a historian.
_____ космона́втом.	_____ an astronaut.

Она́ ста́нет инжене́ром.	She'll become an engineer.
_____ до́ктором.	_____ a doctor.
_____ певи́цей.	_____ a singer.
_____ учи́тельницей.	_____ a teacher.

Мы́ с сестро́й бу́дем фи́зиками.	My sister and I are going to be physicists.
_____ хи́миками.	_____ chemists.
_____ преподава́телями.	_____ instructors.
_____ учителя́ми.	_____ teachers.
_____ инжене́рами.	_____ engineers.
_____ доктора́ми.	_____ doctors.

■ REPETITION DRILL

Repeat the given models, noting that the instrumental case is used in the predicate after verbs such as **бы́ть** and **ста́ть** to describe what one was in the past or expects to be in the future.

■ STRUCTURE REPLACEMENT DRILLS

1. *She's a high-school teacher.*
   She was a high-school teacher.
   Она́ учи́тельница.
   Она́ была́ учи́тельницей.
   Он помо́щник дире́ктора.
   Он был помо́щником дире́ктора.
   (он химик, она врач, он учитель, он директор завода, она певица, она моя соседка, они певцы, он отличник, она студентка)

2. *I'm a chemist.*
   I'm going to be a chemist.
   Я́ хи́мик.
   Я́ бу́ду хи́миком.
   Я́ до́ктор.
   Я́ бу́ду до́ктором.
   (певец, историк, директор фабрики, профессор химии, преподаватель музыки, учитель, студент вуза)

■ RESPONSE DRILLS

1. *My friend is a physicist.*
   His father also was a physicist.
   Мо́й дру́г фи́зик.
   Его́ оте́ц то́же бы́л фи́зиком.
   Мо́й дру́г учи́тель.
   Его́ оте́ц то́же бы́л учи́телем.
   (историк, техник, проводник, шофёр, носильщик, колхозник)

2. *I'm not a professor.*
   But I hope to become one.
   Я́ не профе́ссор.
   Но́ я́ наде́юсь ста́ть профе́ссором.
   Я́ не инжене́р.
   Но́ я́ наде́юсь ста́ть инжене́ром.
   (доктор, физик, космонавт, отличник, директор)

3. *I'm interested in the work of a doctor.*
   It's interesting to be a doctor.
   Я́ интересу́юсь рабо́той до́ктора.
   Интере́сно бы́ть до́ктором.
   Я́ интересу́юсь рабо́той инжене́ра.
   Интере́сно бы́ть инжене́ром.
   (техника, историка, химика, преподавателя, врача, учителя)

4. *A doctor's profession is very interesting.*
   I want to become a doctor.
   Профе́ссия врача́ о́чень интере́сна.
   Я́ хочу́ ста́ть врачо́м.
   Профе́ссия учи́теля о́чень интере́сна.
   Я́ хочу́ ста́ть учи́телем.
   (профессия инженера, профессия доктора, профессия химика, профессия физика, профессия историка)

(*cosmonauts*)　*What do they plan to become?*
　　　　　　Cosmonauts.
(космона́вты)　Ке́м они́ собира́ются бы́ть?
　　　　　　Космона́втами.
(инжене́р)　　Ке́м о́н собира́ется бы́ть?
　　　　　　Инжене́ром.
(преподаватели, учительница,
инженеры, продавщица, певец,
учитель, врачи, певица)

■ QUESTION-ANSWER DRILLS

1. *Is she a physician?*
   Yes, and her sons will also be physicians.
   Она́ вра́ч?
   Да́, и её сыновья́ то́же бу́дут врача́ми.
   Она́ хи́мик?
   Да́, и её сыновья́ то́же бу́дут хи́миками.
   　(инженер, физик, доктор, техник,
   　директор фабрики)

2. *Was your son interested in technology?*
   Yes, and he became a technician.
   Ва́ш сы́н интересова́лся те́хникой?
   Да́, и о́н ста́л те́хником.
   Ва́ш сы́н интересова́лся пе́нием?
   Да́, и о́н ста́л певцо́м.
   　(физикой, химией, историей, местом
   　секретаря, местом помощника ди-
   　ректора)

3. *Is her daughter a college student?*
   Yes, she recently became one.
   Её до́чь — студе́нтка ву́за?
   Да́, она́ неда́вно ста́ла студе́нткой.
   Её до́чь — инжене́р?
   Да́, она́ неда́вно ста́ла инжене́ром.
   　(уборщица, врач, заочница, про-
   　давщица, профессор химии, учи-
   　тельница)

■ DISCUSSION

Whereas the nominative case is used in simple, definition statements in the present tense, the instrumental case is generally required in past or future definitions.

Compare	О́н инжене́р.	He's an engineer.
with	О́н бы́л инжене́ром.	He was an engineer.
	О́н ста́нет инжене́ром.	He'll become an engineer.
	О́н хо́чет бы́ть инжене́ром.	He wants to be an engineer.

In such instances, the instrumental usually describes a situation which is impermanent—one that was or is to become.

Note that one uses the nominative, however, if he views the situation described as permanent.

О́н бы́л америка́нец.	He was an American.
Э́та же́нщина была́ моя́ ма́ть.	That woman was my mother.

The instrumental of adjectives

THE ENDINGS		
SINGULAR		PLURAL
Masculine and Neuter	*Feminine*	
–ым, –им	–ой, –ей	–ыми, –ими

MODELS

Ка́к ты́ мо́жешь бы́ть таки́м споко́йным?	How can you be so calm?
_____ мя́гким?	_____ soft?
_____ ску́чным?	_____ dull?
_____ холо́дным?	_____ cold?
_____ безду́шным?	_____ heartless?
_____ глу́пым?	_____ silly?

О́зеро каза́лось споко́йным.	The lake seemed calm.
_____ больши́м.	_____ large.
_____ си́ним.	_____ dark blue.
_____ зелёным.	_____ green.

Вода́ ста́ла холо́дной.	The water's gotten cold.
_____ тёплой.	_____ warm.
_____ горя́чей.	_____ hot.

Она́ на́м ка́жется глу́пой.	She seems silly to us.
_____ у́мной.	_____ intelligent _____.
_____ несча́стной.	_____ unhappy_____.
_____ симпати́чной.	_____ likeable _____.

Како́го цве́та ва́ш костю́м?	What color is your costume?
—Чёрный с бе́лым.	Black and white.
_____ с кра́сным.	_____ red.
_____ с голубы́м.	_____ light blue.
_____ с жёлтым.	_____ yellow.
_____ с си́ним.	_____ blue.

—Бе́лый с чёрными то́чками.	White with black polka dots.
_____ с кра́сными _____.	_____ red _____.
_____ с голубы́ми _____.	_____ light blue _____.
_____ с си́ними _____.	_____ blue _____.
_____ с зелёными _____.	_____ green _____.

■ REPETITION DRILL

Repeat the given models, noting that the instrumental form of the adjective is often used to focus on a temporary condition.

1. *He's nice.*
   He seems nice to me.
   Óн симпати́чный.
   Óн мне́ ка́жется симпати́чным.
   Она́ ми́лая.
   Она́ мне́ ка́жется ми́лой.
   (они умные, он глупый, он умный,
   они симпатичные, она холодная, она
   скучная, они бездушные, он
   спокойный)

2. *The lake is calm.*
   The lake seems calm.
   Óзеро спокóйное.
   Óзеро ка́жется спокóйным.
   Дорóга дли́нная.
   Дорóга ка́жется дли́нной.
   Лéс большóй.
   Ýлица спокóйная.
   Селó большóе.
   Дорóга корóткая.
   Земля́ чёрная.
   Хлéб вку́сный.

3. *The meeting was an interesting one.*
   The meeting seemed interesting to me.
   Собра́ние бы́ло интерéсное.
   Собра́ние мне́ каза́лось интерéсным.
   Экза́мен бы́л трýдный.
   Экза́мен мне́ каза́лся трýдным.

   Лéкция была́ дли́нная.
   Экза́мены бы́ли трýдные.
   Урóк бы́л корóткий.
   Результа́ты бы́ли интерéсные.

How do you find the soup?
I find it very delicious.
Ка́к вы́ нахóдите сýп?
Я́ егó нахожý óчень вку́сным.
Ка́к вы́ нахóдите пироги́?
Я́ и́х нахожý óчень вку́сными.
(борщ, уху, торт, рыбу, печенье,
грибы, бульон, лапшу, булочки, пирог)

Are you acquainted with her girl friend?
Are you acquainted with her nice girl friend?
Ты́ знакóм с её подрýгой?
Ты́ знакóм с её симпати́чной подрýгой?
Ты́ знакóм с э́тим па́рнем?
Ты́ знакóм с э́тим симпати́чным па́рнем?
(этими студентами, нашим
инженером, этой учительницей, этими
ребятами, этой продавщицей, её
женихом, этой женщиной)

1. *The chairs are old.*
   They have to be replaced with new ones.
   Сту́лья ста́рые.
   И́х на́до замени́ть нóвыми.
   Ли́фт ста́рый.
   Егó на́до замени́ть нóвым.
   (лестница, вилки, словарь, полка,
   карты, атлас, пластинка, телефоны,
   дверь)

2. *But these things are secondhand.*
   They seem too expensive to me.
   Ведь э́ти вéщи подéржанные.
   Они́ мне́ ка́жутся сли́шком дороги́ми.
   Ведь э́тот костю́м подéржанный.
   Óн мне́ ка́жется сли́шком дороги́м.
   (эта вещь, этот стол, эта рубашка,
   эти платья, эта шапка, эти стулья)

3. *He answered me in a direct way.*
   I'm pleased with his direct answer.
   Óн мне пря́мо отвéтил.
   Я́ довóлен егó пря́мым отвéтом.

   Óн мне прекра́сно отвéтил.
   Я́ довóлен егó прекра́сным отвéтом.
   (правильно, спокойно, быстро, хорошо,
   просто, тепло, осторожно, коротко)

They were young men then.

He was a young man then.

Они́ тогда́ бы́ли молоды́ми людьми́.

Óн тогда́ бы́л молоды́м челове́ком.

Йх дя́ди бы́ли стра́нными.

Йх дя́дя бы́л стра́нным.

Йх ба́бушки бы́ли о́чень ста́рыми.

Йх бра́тья бы́ли споко́йными людьми́.

Йх до́чери бы́ли ещё ма́ленькими.

Йх сыновья́ бы́ли ещё ма́ленькими.

Йх де́душки бы́ли симпати́чными людьми́.

Йх ма́тери бы́ли просты́ми же́нщинами.

SINGULAR				PLURAL	
Masculine and Neuter		*Feminine*			
–ым	–им	–ой	–ей	–ыми	–ими
молоды́м	си́ним	молодо́й	си́ней	молоды́ми	си́ними
но́вым	вече́рним	но́вой	вече́рней	ста́рыми	вече́рними
ста́рым	ру́сским	ста́рой	све́жей	но́выми	ру́сскими
	други́м	ру́сской	хоро́шей		други́ми
	све́жим	друго́й			больши́ми
	хоро́шим	большо́й			све́жими
	больши́м				хоро́шими

DISTRIBUTION OF ENDINGS

1. In the masculine-neuter instrumental singular, the ending is spelled –ым for hard stems and –им for soft and mixed stems. Compare молоды́м, ста́рым with си́ним, други́м, ру́сским, хоро́шим, больши́м.

2. In the feminine instrumental singular, the ending is spelled –ой for hard stems and –ей for soft stems. Compare молодо́й, но́вой with си́ней, вече́рней. Mixed stems take the ending –ой, except where the ending is unstressed and preceded by ш, ж, ч, or щ, in which case it is spelled –ей. Compare ру́сской, друго́й, большо́й with хоро́шей, све́жей.[1]

3. In the instrumental plural, the ending is spelled –ыми for hard stems and –ими for soft and mixed stems. Compare молоды́ми, но́выми with си́ними, больши́ми, хоро́шими, ру́сскими, други́ми.

Adjectives and pronouns (in adjectival form) which function as nouns

MODELS

Гдé столо́вая?

___ ва́нная?

___ убо́рная?

___ комиссио́нный?

Столо́вая ужé откры́та.

В **столо́вой** опя́ть щи и ка́ша.

Пойдём в **столо́вую.**

Where's the *dining room* (or *dining hall*)?

_____ the *bathroom?*

_____ the *toilet?*

_____ the *commission store?*

The *dining hall* is already open.

Again, it's shchi and kasha at the *dining hall.*

Let's go to the *dining hall.*

---

[1] In addition to the regular feminine endings –ой and –ей, there are also longer endings –ою and –ею, found mostly in older literary works and in poetry.

Я ви́дел э́ти ве́щи в комиссио́нном.	I saw these things in the *commission store.*
Я доста́л э́ти ве́щи че́рез знако́мых.	I got these things through *friends.*
Он мой хоро́ший знако́мый.	He's a close *acquaintance* of mine.
Она́ моя́ хоро́шая знако́мая.	She's a close *acquaintance* of mine.
Вы́пьем за на́ше бу́дущее.	Let's drink to our *future.*
Забу́дь про́шлое, ду́май то́лько о бу́дущем!	Forget the *past*; think only of the *future!*
Кем ты хо́чешь бы́ть, учёным?	What do you want to be, a *scientist?*
Гла́вное — у него́ хоро́шее ме́сто.	The *main thing* is he has a good job.
Не́которые лю́бят ча́й с молоко́м.	*Some (people)* like tea with milk.
Вы ви́дите в лю́дях то́лько хоро́шее.	You see only the *good* in people.
_____ плохо́е.	_____ *bad* _____.
О чём же ты хо́чешь говори́ть?	What then do you want to talk about?
— О мно́гом.	About a *lot* of things.
— О про́шлом.	About *the past.*
— О бу́дущем.	About *the future.*
— О друго́м.	About *something else.*
Э́то со вся́ким мо́жет случи́ться.	That can happen to *anyone.*
Не ка́ждый мо́жет э́то сде́лать.	Not *everyone* can do that.
Я о́чень люблю́ Толсто́го.	I'm extremely fond of *Tolstoy.*
_____ Достое́вского.	_____ *Dostoevsky.*
_____ Чайко́вского.	_____ *Tschaikovsky.*
_____ Страви́нского.	_____ *Stravinsky.*
_____ Го́рького.	_____ *Gorky.*
_____ Маяко́вского.	_____ *Mayakovsky.*
Моя́ ба́бушка зна́ла Толсту́ю.	My grandmother knew *Mrs. Tolstoy.*
_____ Достое́вскую.	_____ *Dostoevsky.*
_____ Страви́нскую.	_____ *Stravinsky.*
_____ Толсты́х.	_____ *the Tolstoys.*
_____ Достое́вских.	_____ *Dostoevskys.*
_____ Страви́нских.	_____ *Stravinskys.*

■ CUED SUBSTITUTION DRILLS

1. (*our friends*)   *We had dinner at our friends' place.*
   (на́ши знако́мые) Мы́ обе́дали у на́ших знако́мых.
   (э́ти ру́сские) **Мы́ обе́дали у э́тих ру́сских.**
   (наш знако́мый, э́тот учёный, э́тот рабо́чий, э́ти ру́сские, на́ша знако́мая)

2. (*dining hall*)   *He came out of the dining hall* (or *room*).
   (столо́вая) Он вы́шел из столо́вой.
   (ва́нная) **Он вы́шел из ва́нной.**
   (убо́рная, комиссио́нный, столо́вая, ва́нная)

3. (*the past*)   *It's not worth talking about the past.*
   (про́шлое) Не сто́ит говори́ть о про́шлом.
   (бу́дущее) **Не сто́ит говори́ть о бу́дущем.**
   (друго́е, мно́гое, её знако́мый, э́ти рабо́чие, его́ знако́мые, э́тот учёный)

4. (*Mayakovsky*)   *Do you know this work of Mayakovsky's?*
   (Маяко́вский) Вы́ зна́ете э́ту ве́щь Маяко́вского?
   (Достое́вский) **Вы́ зна́ете э́ту ве́щь Достое́вского?**
   (Чайко́вский, Го́рький, Толсто́й, Страви́нский)

1. *They became scientists.*
   He became a scientist.
   Они стáли учёными.
   Óн стáл учёным.
   Брáтья стáли рабóчими.
   Брáт стáл рабóчим.
   Эти америкáнки стáли нáшими
     знакóмыми.
   Эти студéнты стáли нáшими знакóмыми.
   Её брáтья стáли учёными.

2. *She met Mrs. Tolstoy.*
   She met the Tolstoys.
   Онá познакóмилась с Толстóй.
   Онá познакóмилась с Толстыми.
   Онá познакóмилась со Стравúнским.
   Онá познакóмилась со Стравúнскими.
   (Маякóвским, Достоéвской, Чай-
   кóвским, Стравúнской, Толстым)

DISCUSSION

Many Russian adjectives function as nouns. This includes such names as **Толстóй, Достоéвский, Чайкóвский, Маякóвский, Стравúнский.** All such names have a feminine form ending in –ая and a plural form ending in –ые (or –ие): **Толстáя** *Miss or Mrs. Tolstoy,* **Толстые** *the Tolstoys;* **Достоéвская** *Miss or Mrs. Dostoevsky,* **Достоéвские** *the Dostoevskys.*

Those referring to persons may, but do not always, have feminine counterparts: **рýсский** *Russian (man),* **рýсская** *Russian (woman),* **больнóй** *sick man, patient,* **больнáя** *sick woman, patient* (f). The word **рабóчий** *working man, laborer* is used only in the masculine form and refers only to a man. Compare it with **учёный,** which in its masculine form may also refer to a woman: **Онá большóй учёный.**

Besides the adjectives which function as nouns, there are a number of pronouns, adjectival in form, which also function as nouns, for example, **кáждый** *everyone,* **всякий** *anyone,* **нéкоторые** *some (people),* **мнóгое** *much,* **мнóгие** *many (people).*

The gender of such words is usually determined by the noun omitted or understood, for example, **столóвая (столóвая кóмната), комиссиóнный (комисиóнный магазúн), прóшлое (прóшлое врéмя), кáждый (кáждый человéк).**

Some words referring to abstract concepts, however, are neuter and are not associated with any specific noun, for example, **нóвое** *that which is new,* **глáвное** *the main thing,* **интерéсное** *that which is interesting.* Compare the neuter singular **мнóгое** *many things, a lot of things* with the plural **мнóгие** *many people.*

Reflexive verbs—part III

MODELS

Я интересýюсь мýзыкой.
Óн интересýется _____.
Мы интересýемся _____.
Вы интересýетесь _____.
Они интересýются _____.
Ты интересýешься _____.

I'm interested in music.
He's interested in ____.
We're interested in ____.
You're interested in __.
They're interested in __.
You're interested in __.

Óн интересовáлся хúмией.
Онá интересовáлась _____.
Они интересовáлись _____.

He was interested in chemistry.
She was interested in _____.
They were interested in _____.

Ты у́чишься англи́йскому языку́?	Are you studying (*or* learning) English?
Вы у́читесь _____?	Are you studying (*or* learning) _____?
Я учу́сь ру́сскому языку́.	I'm studying (*or* learning) Russian.
Она́ у́чится _____.	She's studying (*or* learning) _____.
Мы у́чимся _____.	We're studying (*or* leaning) _____.
Они́ у́чатся _____.	They're studying (*or* learning) ____.
Он научи́лся е́здить на маши́не.	He learned to drive a car.
Она́ научи́лась _____.	She learned _____.
Они́ научи́лись _____.	They learned _____.
Ты собира́ешься уезжа́ть?	Are you getting ready (*or* planning) to go away?
Вы собира́етесь _____?	Are you getting ready (*or* planning)_____?
Я собира́юсь уезжа́ть.	I'm getting ready (*or* planning) to go away.
Он собира́ется _____.	He's getting ready (*or* planning) _____.
Мы собира́емся ____.	We're getting ready (*or* planning) _____.
Студе́нты собира́ются.	The students are getting ready (*or* planning) ____.
Сего́дня он просну́лся ра́но.	He woke up early today.
_____ она́ просну́лась _____.	She woke up _____.
_____ мы просну́лись _____.	We woke up _____.
Когда́ вы за́втра проснётесь?	When will you wake up tomorrow?
_____ ты _____ проснёшься?	_____ will you wake up_____?
За́втра я просну́сь ра́но.	Tomorrow I'll wake up early.
_____ она́ проснётся _____.	_____ she'll wake up _____.
_____ мы проснёмся _____.	_____ we'll wake up _____.
_____ они́ просну́тся _____.	_____ they'll wake up _____.
Я обы́чно просыпа́юсь в се́мь.	I usually wake up at seven.
Ты _____ просыпа́ешься _____.	You ___ wake up _____.
Он _____ просыпа́ется _____.	He _____ wakes up _____.
Мы _____ просыпа́емся _____.	We ___ wake up_____.
Вы _____ просыпа́етесь _____.	You ___ wake up _____.
Они́ _____ просыпа́ются _____.	They ___ wake up_____.
Ты занима́ешься ру́сским языко́м?	Are you studying the Russian language?
Вы занима́етесь _____?	Are you studying _____?
Я занима́юсь ру́сским языко́м.	I'm studying the Russian language.
Он занима́ется _____.	He's studying _____.
Мы занима́емся _____.	We're studying _____.
Они́ занима́ются _____.	They're studying _____.

■ STRUCTURE REPLACEMENT DRILLS

1. *I'm interested in geography.*
   I was interested in geography.
   Я интересу́юсь геогра́фией.
   Я интересова́лся геогра́фией.
   Я интересу́юсь геогра́фией.
   Я интересова́лась геогра́фией.
   (он, вы, они, она, мы, ты, он)

2. *I'm planning to enter college.*
   I was planning to enter college.
   Я собира́юсь поступи́ть в ву́з.
   Я собира́лся поступи́ть в ву́з.
   Я собира́юсь поступи́ть в ву́з.
   Я собира́лась поступи́ть в ву́з.
   (они, мы, Га́ля, Ви́тя, вы, он, она, ты)

3. *I'm studying physics.*
   I was studying physics.
   Я занима́юсь фи́зикой.
   Я занима́лся фи́зикой.
   Я занима́юсь фи́зикой.
   Я занима́лась фи́зикой.
   (вы, На́дя, мы, они́, Ва́ня, она́, я, ты)

4. *I was learning how to play chess.*
   I learned how to play chess.
   Я учи́лся игра́ть в ша́хматы.
   Я научи́лся игра́ть в ша́хматы.
   Я учи́лась игра́ть в ша́хматы.
   Я научи́лась игра́ть в ша́хматы.
   (сын, до́чери, Ната́ша, мы, вы, он, ты, они́)

5. *I wake up at seven.*
   I'll wake up at seven.
   Я просыпа́юсь в се́мь.
   Я просну́сь в се́мь.
   Она́ просыпа́ется в се́мь.
   Она́ проснётся в се́мь.
   (мы, ты, вы, они́, я, она́)

6. *He got himself a nice soft job.*
   He'll get himself a nice soft job.
   Он устро́ился на тёплое месте́чко.
   Он устро́ится на тёплое месте́чко.
   Вы устро́ились на тёплое месте́чко.
   Вы устро́итесь на тёплое месте́чко.
   (мы, ты, она́, я, они́, он, вы)

■ QUESTION-ANSWER DRILLS

1. *Would that seem interesting to you?*
   Yes, I'm interested in that.
   Тебе́ э́то бу́дет интере́сно?
   Да́, я э́тим интересу́юсь.
   Ему́ э́то бу́дет интере́сно?
   Да́, он э́тим интересу́ется.
   (вам, им, ей, тебе́, ему́)

2. *Are you students?*
   Yes, we go to college.
   Вы студе́нты?
   Да́, мы у́чимся в ву́зе.
   Она́ студе́нтка?
   Да́, она́ у́чится в ву́зе.
   (Они́ студе́нты? Она́ студе́нтка? Вы студе́нты? Он студе́нт? Ты студе́нт? Они́ студе́нты?)

3. *Are you leaving already?*
   Yes, I'm getting ready to leave.
   Ты уже́ уезжа́ешь?
   Да́, я собира́юсь уезжа́ть.
   Вы уже́ уезжа́ете?
   Да́, мы собира́емся уезжа́ть.
   (она́, ты, они́, он, вы, она́, они́)

4. *Do you drive a car already?*
   Not yet, but I'll learn.
   Ты уже́ е́здишь на маши́не?
   Не́т ещё, но я научу́сь.
   Он уже́ е́здит на маши́не?
   Не́т ещё, но он научится.
   (вы, она́, ты, они́, он, вы, она́)

■ MIXED STRUCTURE REPLACEMENT DRILLS

Plural to singular and vice versa.

1. *We'll wake up early.*
   I'll wake up early.
   Мы проснёмся ра́но.
   Я просну́сь ра́но.
   Он проснётся ра́но.
   Они́ просну́тся ра́но.
   (ты, мы, она́, вы, я, он, мы, ты)

2. *What were you thinking about?*
   О чём ты заду́мался?
   О чём вы заду́мались?
   О чём де́вушки заду́мались?
   О чём де́вушка заду́малась?
   (па́рни, она́, он, вы, он, ты)

3. *I'm studying Russian.*
   We're studying Russian.
   Я занима́юсь ру́сским языко́м.
   Мы занима́емся ру́сским языко́м.

   Э́та америка́нка занима́ется ру́сским языко́м.
   Э́ти америка́нки занима́ются ру́сским языко́м.
   (вы, мы, ты, я, она́, студе́нты)

4. *Wake up!*
Просыпа́йся!
Просыпа́йтесь!
Просни́сь!
Просни́тесь!

Учи́тесь ру́сскому языку́!
Занима́йся ру́сским языко́м!
Научи́тесь е́здить на маши́не!
Интересу́йся бо́льше заня́тиями!

■ RESPONSE DRILL

You're not awake yet?
Wake up!
Ты́ ещё не просну́лся?
Просни́сь!
Ты́ ещё не научи́лся?
Научи́сь!

Ты́ ещё не собира́ешься?
Ты́ с ни́м не познако́мился?
Ты́ не у́чишься?
Ты́ не занима́ешься?

DISCUSSION

The verb **интересова́ться** is accompanied by the instrumental case without a preposition to indicate the thing one becomes interested in: **Óн интересу́ется ру́сской литерату́рой** *He's interested in Russian literature.*

The verb **занима́ться** is accompanied by the instrumental without a preposition to indicate the thing with which one is occupied or the thing one is studying: **Óн занима́ется ру́сским языко́м** *He's studying Russian*; **Я́ занима́юсь чте́нием пи́сем** *I'm busy reading letters.*

Учи́ться and **научи́ться** are accompanied by the infinitive or the dative without a preposition to indicate the thing studied or learned: **Óн у́чится ру́сскому языку́** *He's studying Russian*; **Она́ научи́лась говори́ть по-англи́йски** *She learned to speak English.*

The verb **устро́иться** is followed by **на** plus the accusative in the sense of getting established in a position or job: **Óн устро́ился на хоро́шую рабо́ту** *He got himself a good job.* In describing the place where one works or settles, however, **в** or **на** plus the prepositional is used.

Óн устро́ился в Москве́.	He settled in Moscow *or* He got himself a job in Moscow.
Я́ устро́юсь на заво́де.	I'll get a job at a factory.
Она́ удо́бно устро́илась в но́вой кварти́ре.	She's comfortably settled in her new apartment.

Perfectivization by prefix по–
to indicate a limited amount of the activity

MODELS

Óн рабо́тал це́лый де́нь.	He worked the whole day.
Óн порабо́тал полчаса́.	He did half an hour's work.
Мы́ мно́го танцева́ли.	We danced a lot.
Мы́ потанцева́ли немно́го.	We danced for awhile.
Она́ до́лго спала́.	She slept for a long time.
Она́ поспала́ о́коло ча́са.	She got about an hour's sleep.

Вы́ до́лго сиде́ли в па́рке?	Did you sit in the park long?
—Не́т, мы́ посиде́ли о́коло ча́са, а пото́м уе́хали.	No, we sat about an hour and then drove away.
Ты́ до́лго стоя́ла в о́череди?	Did you stand in line long?
— Да́, мне́ пришло́сь постоя́ть мину́т два́дцать.	Yes, I had to stand for about twenty minutes.
Вы́ до́лго иска́ли ша́пку?	Did you spend a long time looking for the cap?
— Не́т, мы́ поиска́ли мину́т де́сять и нашли́.	No, we hunted about ten minutes and found it.
О́н бы́л у на́с про́шлой зимо́й.	He was at our place last winter.
О́н побы́л у на́с два́ дня́ и уе́хал.	He spent two days with us and left.
Мы́ та́м жи́ли два́ го́да.	We lived there for two years.
Мы́ та́м недо́лго пожи́ли, а пото́м нашли́ но́вую ко́мнату.	We lived there for awhile, then found a new room.
Вы́ бу́дете игра́ть всё у́тро?	Will you be playing all morning?
— Не́т, мы́ то́лько немно́го поигра́ем.	No, we'll just play a little.

■ QUESTION-ANSWER DRILLS

1. *How much longer will I have to stand?*
   Stand a little longer.
   Ка́к до́лго мне́ ещё ну́жно стоя́ть?
   Посто́й ещё немно́го.
   Ка́к до́лго мне́ ещё ну́жно ходи́ть?
   Походи́ ещё немно́го.
      (рабо́тать, сиде́ть, стуча́ть, меша́ть
      суп, занима́ться, гуля́ть, лежа́ть)

2. *Were you able to get a good nap?*
   No, I only slept for half an hour.
   Вы́ смогли́ хорошо́ поспа́ть?
   Не́т, я́ поспа́л то́лько полчаса́.
   Вы́ смогли́ хорошо́ пое́здить?
   Не́т, я́ пое́здил то́лько полчаса́.
      (погуля́ть, потанцева́ть, порабо́тать,
      поспа́ть, пое́здить)

3. *Are you off to look for work?*
   Yes, I'll go do a bit of looking.
   Ты́ идёшь иска́ть рабо́ту?
   Да́, пойду́ поищу́.
   Ты́ идёшь стира́ть?
   Да́, пойду́ постира́ю.

      (рабо́тать, игра́ть в футбо́л, гуля́ть,
      спа́ть, смотре́ть на и́х игру́, слу́шать
      но́вости)

■ STRUCTURE REPLACEMENT DRILLS

1. *We were strolling.*
   We strolled a bit.
   Мы́ гуля́ли.
   Мы́ немно́го погуля́ли.
   Мы́ рабо́тали.
   Мы́ немно́го порабо́тали.
      (стуча́ли, спа́ли, сиде́ли, лежа́ли,
      е́здили на но́вой маши́не, стоя́ли в
      о́череди, слу́шали ра́дио)

2. *I'll dance with her.*
   I'll dance with her awhile.
   Я́ бу́ду с не́й танцева́ть.
   Я́ с не́й потанцу́ю.
   Я́ бу́ду с не́й говори́ть.
   Я́ с не́й поговорю́.
   Я́ бу́ду зде́сь сиде́ть.
   Я́ бу́ду зде́сь стоя́ть.
   Я́ бу́ду с ва́ми рабо́тать.
   Я́ бу́ду с ва́ми гуля́ть.
   Я́ бу́ду с ва́ми слу́шать пласти́нки.
   Я́ бу́ду иска́ть ва́м ме́сто.

DISCUSSION

Although **по-** sometimes provides what may be considered the basic perfective for an imperfective verb (**смотре́ть, посмотре́ть**), very often it is not the primary perfective, but rather a secondary perfective focusing on the limited duration of the activity.

Compare **чита́ть** (ipfv) *to read, to be reading*
прочита́ть (pfv) *to finish reading, read* (*through to the end*)

with **почита́ть** (pfv) *to do a bit of reading, read for a while*

Вы ко́нчили чита́ть э́ту газе́ту?	Have you finished reading this paper?
— Да, я сё уже́ прочита́л.	Yes, I've already read it.
— Нет, я ещё не всю́ прочита́л.	No, I haven't read it all yet.
— Нет, я ещё чита́ю.	No, I'm still reading it.
— Да, я **почита́л** немно́го и уста́л.	Yes, I read awhile and got tired.

Among the verbs already encountered which may take perfectives with the prefix **по-** are the following: стоя́ть, сиде́ть, лежа́ть, говори́ть, ду́мать, слу́шать, рабо́тать, бы́ть, жи́ть, танцева́ть, иска́ть, стуча́ть, е́здить, ходи́ть, гуля́ть, спа́ть, пи́ть, игра́ть, стира́ть, занима́ться.

ЧТЕ́НИЕ И ПИСЬМО́

Шко́ла око́нчена. Де́сять лет прошли́ так бы́стро! Ви́ктор и Анато́лий учи́лись вме́сте и бы́ли больши́ми друзья́ми, но Ви́ктор был отли́чник, а Анато́лий — нет. Хорошо́ Ви́ктору: он мо́жет сра́зу поступи́ть в вуз. Анато́лий же до́лжен рабо́тать два го́да на произво́дстве просты́м рабо́чим. Это не осо́бенно ве́село. Но Ви́ктор говори́т Анато́лию, что ещё не всё пропа́ло: Анато́лий лю́бит те́хнику, вот э́ти два го́да и не пропаду́т, бу́дут хоро́шей пра́ктикой. А пото́м он смо́жет устро́ить свою́ жизнь, как ему́ нра́вится.

Ива́н хо́чет устро́иться на тёплое месте́чко, что́бы сра́зу нача́ть хорошо́ зараба́тывать, как говоря́т, ста́ть на но́ги. Ра́ньше он хоте́л стать инжене́ром, но тепе́рь уже́ не мечта́ет об э́том: э́то сли́шком до́лго и тру́дно.

У него теперь другие планы: устроиться на хорошую работу. Тогда и профессия не будет нужна. Как устроиться? Очень просто: по знакомству. Виктор слушает и не верит, что Иван действительно мечтает об этом. Он его хорошо знает и понимает, что Иван не думает серьёзно о „тёплом местечке", а хотел бы тоже учиться дальше. Но Виктор всё-таки желает ему успеха.

На прощáльной вечери́нке всё бы́ли в сбóре: Нáдя, Вéра, Вáня, Бóря, Ви́тя. Тóлько Óля опоздáла: онá звони́ла Вéре и сказáла, что óчень занятá и придёт немнóго пóзже вмéсте со свои́м женихóм. Всё вы́пили за её счáстье, а потóм за своё бýдущее. Говори́ли о профéссиях, ктó кéм хóчет бы́ть. Вáня с Нáдей сказáли, что собирáются бы́ть фи́зиками, а Бóря сказáл, что хотéл бы стáть космонáвтом.

Ви́тя никáк не мóжет реши́ть, кудá емý идти́: емý кáжется всё интерéсным. Он не знáет, кéм стáть. Вéра хóчет поступи́ть в пединститýт на литфáк и совéтует Ви́те тóже тудá идти́. Онá дýмает, что преподавáть óчень интерéсно. Это онá тепéрь тáк дýмает, когдá шкóла ужé окóнчена. Тепéрь всё учителя́ кáжутся таки́ми хорóшими, а и́х рабóта — такóй интерéсной.

— Когдá я бы́л мáленьким, я óчень люби́л читáть об Амéрике. Я прочитáл всé ромáны Джéка Лóндона и Фенимóра Кýпера.
— И, навéрно, мечтáли уéхать в Амéрику?
— Конéчно. Я реши́л поéхать пря́мо в Нью-Йóрк. Нóчью вы́шел и́з дому, пошёл на вокзáл, купи́л билéт до Ки́ева и поéхал.
— Почемý же до Ки́ева? Нáдо бы́ло до Владивостóка, ведь вы́ жи́ли в Ташкéнте?
— Дá. Как ви́дите, я плóхо знáл геогрáфию. Пóзже нáш учи́тель геогрáфии óчень серди́лся и удивля́лся, что я тáк мáло научи́лся на егó урóках.
— Нý, и далекó вы́ уéхали?
— Нéт, тóлько пятьдеся́т киломéтров от Ташкéнта. Меня́ замéтил проводни́к и спроси́л, кудá я éду. Я скáзал: «В Нью-Йóрк, в Амéрику». Óн, конéчно, позвони́л моéй мáтери, онá приéхала и взялá меня́ домóй.

— Знáешь, Алёша, у нáс тепéрь нóвые сосéди Орлóвы: отéц, мáть и мáленькая дóчь.
— Дá, я с ни́м ужé познакóмился. Óн рабóтает на мясокомбинáте помóщником дирéктора.
— Вóт кáк! А мнé егó женá сказáла, что óн дирéктор.
— Навéрно онá мечтáет, что óн стáнет дирéктором. Вóт éй и кáжется, что óн ужé дирéктор.

— Да, наве́рно. А зна́ешь, ке́м она́ рабо́тает? Продавщи́цей в кио́ске. Продаёт лимона́д.

— Что́? Жена́ помо́щника дире́ктора и рабо́тает продавщи́цей? Тру́дно пове́рить.

— Да, пра́вда, э́то немно́го стра́нно. Му́ж её хорошо́ зараба́тывает, у ни́х своя́ маши́на, шофёр.

— Подожди́, а кто́ тебе́ насчёт э́того лимона́да сказа́л?

— Их ма́ленькая до́чь Та́ня.

— Ну́, я ду́маю, что на́шей ма́ленькой сосе́дке не сли́шком мо́жно ве́рить.

— Да, пожа́луй. Познако́мимся с ни́ми как сле́дует, лу́чше их узна́ем. Мо́жет бы́ть они́ и неплохи́е лю́ди.

— Да, наде́юсь, что мы́ бу́дем хоро́шими сосе́дями.

— Ка́к прошёл ве́чер у твои́х знако́мых?

— Ничего́, то́лько вы́пить как сле́дует нельзя́ бы́ло: да́ли не вино́, а каку́ю-то кра́сную во́ду. А о во́дке и не спра́шивай — не́ было совсе́м.

— А кто́ был, интере́сно?

— Все́ на́ши ребя́та и ещё оди́н америка́нец.

— Како́й америка́нец?

— Фили́пп Гра́нт. Он со мно́й на одно́м ку́рсе.

— А, Гра́нт! Я о нём слы́шал. Ка́к у него́ с ру́сским языко́м?

— Тепе́рь вполне́ хорошо́. Всё понима́ет и говори́т совсе́м свобо́дно.

— Скажи́те, до́ктор, что́ я до́лжен де́лать?

— Лежа́ть, немно́го ходи́ть, и по утра́м де́лать масса́ж.

— Ох, ка́к не люблю́ масса́жа!

— Без масса́жа вы́ никогда́ не смо́жете хорошо́ ходи́ть.

— А ско́лько вре́мени мне́ ещё ну́жно сиде́ть до́ма?

— Ещё неде́лю, е́сли то́чно бу́дете де́лать всё, что я сказа́л. А е́сли не бу́дете, тогда́, пожа́луй, ещё две́ неде́ли не смо́жете ходи́ть на рабо́ту.

— Я не ду́мал, что э́то серьёзно.

— Ничего́, э́то ва́м бу́дет нау́ка.

— Да, в сле́дующий ра́з бу́ду осторо́жен.

— Стра́нно, я то́лько что до́ма пообе́дал и уже́ го́лоден.

— Неуже́ли? Хоти́те, я ва́м принесу́ немно́го борща́?

— Пожа́луйста. Я борща́ давно́ не ви́дел!

— Так сади́тесь. А ка́к насчёт ры́бы?

— Не́т, спаси́бо, не хо́чется.

— Хорошо́. Во́т бо́рщ, а во́т пироги́.

— Пироги́ я о́чень люблю́. О, о́чень вку́сные!

— Я ра́да, что они́ ва́м нра́вятся. Бери́те ещё.

— Не́т, спаси́бо, уже́ дово́льно.

APPENDIX

Reference guide to the pronunciation of Cyrillic letters

The alphabet is given below in its conventional order, together with examples illustrating the various possible pronunciations of each letter and explanatory notes.

А

а	[a]	and, but	
та́к	[ták]	so	
ва́с	[vás]	you	
ка́к	[kák]	how	
да́	[dá]	yes	
давно́	[davnó]	for long	
куда́	[kudá]	where (to)	
та́м	[tám]	there	
авто́бус	[aftóbus]	bus	
па́па	[pápə]	papa	
ма́ма	[mámə]	mamma	
по́чта	[póčtə]	post office	

Russian **a** is pronounced with its full value [a] not only when it is stressed, but also in the syllable immediately before the stressed syllable and in the initial position. Otherwise it is reduced to [ə], the final sound in English sof*a*.

Б

ба́ба	[bábə]	old woman	
ба́к	[bák]	tank	
бы́ло	[bílə]	was	
бы́л	[bíl]	was	
рабо́та	[rabótə]	work	
собра́ние	[sabráņijə]	meeting	
авто́бус	[aftóbus]	bus	
бума́га	[bumágə]	paper	
би́л	[ḅíl]	hit	
бе́лая	[ḅéləjə]	white	
обе́д	[aḅét]	dinner	
в клу́бе	[fklúḅi]	at the club	
на слу́жбе	[naslúžḅi]	on the job	
бюро́	[ḅuró]	bureau	
у тебя́	[uṭiḅá]	you have	
клу́б	[klúp]	club	
гри́б	[gṛíp]	mushroom	
общежи́тие	[apščižíṭijə]	dormitory	
коро́бка	[karópkə]	box	

Before hard-series vowel letters (**a, э, o, ы, у**) the letter **б** is pronounced hard, somewhat like the *b* in English *b*ook. Before soft-series vowel letters (**я, е, и, ё, ю**) it is pronounced soft, somewhat like the *b* in *b*eauty.

In the final position and before certain consonants **б** is pronounced like the *p* in sto*p*, but without the puff of breath that accompanies the English sound.

В

ва́с	[vás]	you	
вы́	[ví]	you	

Before hard-series vowel letters the Russian **в** is pronounced hard, somewhat

завόд	[zavót]	plant, factory	
здорόва	[zdaróvə]	healthy, well	
вόт	[vót]	here, there	
Ивάн	[iván]	Ivan	
привέт	[pɾiɣét]	greetings, regards	
извинήте	[izɣiɳíṭi]	excuse [me]	
до свидάния	[dəsɣidáɳijə]	good-bye	
вчерά	[fčirá]	yesterday	
автόбус	[aftóbus]	bus	
в клýбе	[fklúþi]	at the club	
всё	[fṣó]	all	
всю зήму	[fṣú źímu]	all winter	
Лέв	[ḷéf]	Lev	
здорόв	[zdaróf]	healthy, well	

like the *v* in *v*ote. Before soft-series vowels it is pronounced soft, somewhat like the *v* in *v*iew.

Before certain consonants and at the end of a word **в** is pronounced like the *f* in *f*olk.

Г

гόрод	[górət]	city, town	
Гάля	[gáḷə]	Galya	
бумάга	[bumágə]	paper	
газέта	[gaẓétə]	newspaper	
ГУМ	[gúm]	GUM (dept. store)	
дόлго	[dólgə]	long	
никогдά	[ɳikagdá]	never	
гимнάзия	[gimnáẓijə]	secondary school	
Евгέний	[jivɣéɳij]	Evgeny	
Олέг	[aḷék]	Oleg	
дрýг	[drúk]	friend	
всегό	[fṣivó]	[of] all	
хорόшего	[xaróšivə]	[of] good	
Толстόго	[talstóvə]	[of] Tolstoy	

Russian **г** is pronounced like the *g* in *g*oal before **о, а,** and **у** and like the *g* in ar*g*ue before **е** and **и**. (It is not written before **ё, я, ю, ы,** or **э**.)

Before certain consonants and at the end of a word **г** is pronounced like the *k* in *sk*ill.

Note: In the genitive case endings **–ого** and **–его, г** is pronounced like the *v* in *v*ote.

Д

дά	[dá]	yes	
кудά	[kudá]	where (to)	
идý	[idú]	I'm going	
до свидάния	[dəsɣidáɳijə]	good-bye	
рάды	[rádi]	glad	
дόлго	[dólgə]	long	
идёт	[iḍót]	is going	
на завόде	[nəzavóḍi]	at the plant	
дέло	[ḍélə]	thing, matter	
завόд	[zavót]	plant, factory	
гόрод	[górət]	city	
вόдка	[vótkə]	vodka	

Before hard-series vowel letters the letter **д** is pronounced hard, somewhat like the *d* in English woo*d* but with the tongue touching the teeth. Before soft-series vowel letters it is pronounced soft, somewhat like the *d* in *d*uty (pronounced in the British way with a y-like glide).

At the end of a word and before certain consonants the letter **д** is pronounced like the *t* in *st*ool.

Е

привέт	[pɾiɣét]	greetings, regards	
нέт	[ɳét]	no	
пέния	[ṗéɳijə]	[of] singing	
вчерά	[fčirá]	yesterday	
в клýбе	[fklúþi]	at the club	
на завόде	[nəzavóḍi]	at the plant	
всегό	[fṣivó]	[of] all	
έсли	[jéṣḷi]	if	
έсть	[jéṣṭ]	to eat	
знάет	[znájit]	knows	
рабόтает	[rabótəjit]	works	

After a consonant Russian **е** is pronounced like the *e* in m*e*t or th*ey* only when it is stressed. Unstressed, it is pronounced more like the *e* in *e*mote or the *i* in *i*ndustrious. The consonant preceding **е** is typically pronounced soft. When **е** occurs in the initial position or immediately after a vowel it has the same vocalic value as elsewhere, but is preceded by the consonant [j] (as in *y*es).

Ё

всё	[fṣó]	all	
Семён	[ṣiṃón]	Semyon	
идёт	[iḍót]	is going	
ещё	[jiščó]	yet, still	
её	[jijó]	her	
моё	[majó]	my	
ёлка	[jólkə]	fir	
ёж	[jóš]	hedgehog	

After a consonant the letter **ё** is pronounced like *o* in sp*o*rt. The consonant preceding **ё** is typically pronounced soft. In the initial position or after another vowel **ё** is pronounced like the *yo* in *Yo*rk.[1]

---

[1] The letter **ё** always indicates a stressed syllable. When the stress shifts to another syllable **ё** is replaced by **е**. Compare всё [fṣó] with всегό [fṣivó].

Ж	скажи́те	[skažíṭi]	say! tell [me]!	The letter ж is pronounced somewhat like the s in leisure or pleasure, but is articulated farther back in the mouth than the English sound.
	уже́	[užé]	already, by now	
	жена́	[žiná]	wife	
	жёлтый	[žóltij]	yellow	
	на слу́жбе	[naslúžḅi]	on the job	
	мо́жно	[móžnə]	it's possible	In the final position and before certain consonants it is pronounced somewhat like the sh in shore. It is always pronounced hard, even when followed by e, ё, и, or ь, which normally indicate that a soft consonant precedes.
	у́ж	[uš]	already	
	му́ж	[múš]	husband	
	мужчи́на	[muščínə]	man	
	наре́жь	[naṛéš]	cut!	

З	заво́д	[zavót]	plant, factory	The Russian з is pronounced hard (as in zoo) before hard-series vowel letters and soft (somewhat like the s in the British pronunciation of resume) before soft-series vowel letters.
	здоро́ва	[zdaróvə]	healthy, well	
	за́втра	[záftrə]	tomorrow	
	зна́ете	[znájiṭi]	you know	
	зима́	[ẓimá]	winter	
	всю зи́му	[fṣú ẓimu]	all winter	In the final position and before certain consonants з is pronounced like the s in swim.
	взя́л	[vẓál]	took	
	зе́ркало	[ẓérkələ]	mirror	
	ра́з	[rás]	time, once	
	ска́зка	[skáskə]	tale	

И	и	[i]	and	Initially and after a consonant the letter и is pronounced like the i in machine or the e in emote.
	приве́т	[pṛiɣét]	greetings, regards	
	Ни́на	[ṇínə]	Nina	
	иду́	[idú]	I'm going	
	мой	[mají]	my	After a vowel it has the same vocalic value, but is preceded by the consonant [j] (as in yeast). In rapid speech, however, the [j] sound tends to disappear, especially in the combination ии.
	сто́ило	[stójilə]	cost	
	в Росси́и	[vraṣí(j)i]	in Russia	

Й	домо́й	[damój]	home	The letter й sounds like the y in yes and boy. It occurs almost exclusively after a vowel letter when no vowel follows. It occurs between vowel letters only in words of foreign origin.
	мо́й	[mój]	my	
	поступа́йте	[pəstupájṭi]	enter, join	
	войти́	[vajṭí]	to come in	
	майо́р	[majór]	major	
	фойе́	[fojé]	foyer	

К	куда́	[kudá]	where (to)	The Russian к is pronounced like the k in skill before the letters о, а, and у, and like the k in askew before е and и. (It does not usually occur before ё, я, ю, ы, or э).
	уро́к	[urók]	lesson	
	ка́к	[kák]	how	
	Ко́ля	[kólə]	Kolya	
	Кири́лл	[ḳiṛíl]	Kirill	
	на по́лке	[napólḳi]	on the shelf	
	ви́лки	[ɣílḳi]	forks	

Л	дела́	[d̦ilá]	things	The letter л is pronounced somewhat like the l in belt or middle before hard-series vowel letters and like l in milieu (or ll in million) before both soft-series vowel letters and ь.
	слы́шал	[slíšəl]	heard	
	бы́ло	[bílə]	was	
	бы́ли	[bíḷi]	were	
	на столе́	[nəstaḷé]	on the table	
	О́ля	[óḷə]	Olya	
	О́лю	[óḷu]	Olya	
	О́ле	[óḷi]	to Olya	
	бо́льше	[bólʃi]	more	
	портфе́ль	[partʃéḷ]	briefcase	
	больны́	[baḷní]	sick	

М	письмо́	[ṗiṣmó]	letter	The Russian м is pronounced like the m in moose before hard-series vowel letters and like the m in amuse before both soft-series vowel letters and ь.
	мо́й	[mój]	my	
	та́м	[tám]	there	
	зи́му	[ẓímu]	winter	
	мы́	[mí]	we	
	Семён	[ṣiṃón]	Semyon	
	в ГУ́Ме	[vgúṃi]	in GUM	

	Ми́ла	[m̦ílə]	Mila
	меня́	[m̦iná]	me
	вре́мя	[vr̦ém̦ə]	time
	се́мь	[șém̦]	seven

Н

на уро́к	[nəurók]	to class
но	[no]	but
ну́	[nú]	well
студе́нт	[stud̦ént]	student
жёны	[žóni]	wives
Ни́на	[n̦ínə]	Nina
не́т	[n̦ét]	no
собра́ние	[sabrán̦ijə]	meeting
до свида́ния	[dəșyidán̦ijə]	good-bye
Ни́не	[n̦ín̦i]	for Nina
не́ было	[n̦ébilə]	there wasn't
извини́те	[izyin̦íti]	excuse [me]
о́чень	[óčin̦]	very
де́нь	[d̦én̦]	day

Before hard-series vowel letters the Russian **н** is pronounced somewhat like the *n* in *noon* but with the tongue touching the teeth. Before soft-series vowel letters it is pronounced somewhat like the *ny* in ca*ny*on or the *n* in me*n*u.

О

О́ля	[ólə]	Olya
уро́к	[urók]	lesson
на по́чту	[napóčtu]	to the post office
мо́й	[mój]	my
домо́й	[damój]	home
общежи́тие	[apščižíțijə]	dormitory
собра́ние	[sabrán̦ijə]	meeting
до свида́ния	[dəșyidán̦ijə]	good-bye
бы́ло	[bílə]	was
спаси́бо	[spaṣíbə]	thanks

The Russian **о** is pronounced with its full value (like the *o* in p*o*rt) only when it is stressed. In the initial position and just before the stressed syllable it is pronounced [a]; otherwise it is reduced to [ə], the final sound in sof*a*.

П

по́чта	[póčtə]	post office
Па́вел	[páyil]	Pavel
су́пу	[súpu]	some soup
спаси́бо	[spaṣíbə]	thanks
вполне́	[fpaln̦é]	completely
беспла́тно	[b̦isplátnə]	free
пра́вда	[právdə]	truth
ти́пы	[țípi]	types
пе́ние	[p̦én̦ijə]	singing
тепе́рь	[țip̦ér̦]	now
спешу́	[sp̦išú]	I'm hurrying
опя́ть	[ap̦áț]	again
пёк	[p̦ók]	he baked
пи́ли	[p̦íl̦i]	drank
сте́пь	[șțép̦]	steppe

Before hard-series vowel letters **п** is pronounced somewhat like the *p* in *poor*; before both soft-series vowel letters and **ь** it is pronounced more like the *p* in *pure*.

Р

ра́д	[rát]	glad
уро́к	[urók]	lesson
вчера́	[fčirá]	yesterday
собра́ние	[sabrán̦ijə]	meeting
хорошо́	[xərašó]	good, well
конце́рт	[kancért]	concert
университе́т	[un̦iyír̦ṣițét]	university
орёл	[aról]	eagle
ря́д	[r̦át]	row
приве́т	[pr̦iyét]	greetings, regards
Кири́лл	[k̦ir̦íl]	Kirill
говоря́т	[gəvar̦át]	they say
тепе́рь	[țip̦ér̦]	now
две́рь	[dyér̦]	door

Before hard-series vowel letters the Russian **р** is pronounced with a tongue trill somewhat like the Scotch *r*. Before both soft-series vowel letters and **ь** it is pronounced trilled but soft, and it has somewhat the effect of a y-like glide following.

С

студе́нт	[stud̦ént]	student
студе́нтка	[stud̦éntkə]	coed
собра́ние	[sabrán̦ijə]	meeting
ва́с	[vás]	you

Before hard-series vowel letters the Russian **с** is pronounced like the *s* in *soon*. Before both soft-series vowels and **ь** it is pronounced somewhat like the *ss* in

	интере́сно	[inṭiṛésnə]	interesting	assume (pronounced in the British way with a y-like glide).
	су́п	[súp]	soup	
	автобусы	[aftóbusi]	buses	
	спаси́бо	[spaşíbə]	thanks	
	Семён	[şimón]	Semyon	
	всю́ зи́му	[fşú zímu]	all winter	
	всё у́тро	[fşó útrə]	all morning	
	ве́сь ве́чер	[γéş γéčir]	all evening	
	письмо́	[ṛişmó]	letter	

Т

привет	[pṛiγét]	greetings, regards	Before hard-series vowel letters the Russian т is pronounced somewhat like the *t* in s*t*ool but with the tongue touching the teeth. Before both soft-series vowel letters and ь, it sounds somewhat like *t* with a y-like glide (as in the British cos*t*ume and *t*une).
та́м	[tám]	there	
на по́чту	[napóčtu]	to the post office	
ты́	[tí]	you	
автобус	[aftóbus]	bus	
идёте	[iḓóṭi]	you're going	
тепе́рь	[ṭiṛéṛ]	now	
хоти́те	[xaṭíṭi]	you want	
тётя	[ṭóṭə]	aunt	
слы́шать	[slíšəṭ]	to hear	
посла́ть	[pasláṭ]	to send	
опя́ть	[aṛáṭ]	again	

У

куда́	[kudá]	where (to)	The Russian у is pronounced everywhere somewhat like the *u* in Sch*u*bert. (It is never pronounced like the *u* in *u*niversity, i.e. with a [j] preceding it.)
уже́	[užé]	already, by now	
уро́к	[urók]	lesson	
иду́	[idú]	I'm going	
на по́чту	[napóčtu]	to the post office	
автобус	[aftóbus]	bus	

Ф

фа́кт	[fákt]	fact	The Russian ф is found mostly in words of foreign origin. It is pronounced hard (like the *f* in *f*arm) before hard-series vowel letters and soft (somewhat like the *f* in *f*ew) before both soft-series vowel letters and ь.
фо́рма	[fórmə]	form, uniform	
фами́лия	[famíḽijə]	last name	
жира́ф	[žiráf]	giraffe	
портфе́ль	[partṭéḽ]	briefcase	
Фили́пп	[fiḽíp]	Filipp	

Х

хорошо́	[xərašó]	good, well	The Russian х has no counterpart in English. Before а, о, and у it is pronounced hard, somewhat like the *ch* in German a*ch* and Ba*ch*; before е or и it is pronounced soft, somewhat like the *ch* in German i*ch*.
заходи́те	[zəxaḓíṭi]	drop in! come in!	
а́х	[áx]	oh!	
ху́же	[xúži]	worse	
хоти́те	[xaṭíṭi]	you want	
Хитро́в	[xitróf]	Khitrov	
бронхи́т	[branxít]	bronchitis	
схе́ма	[sxémə]	scheme, plan	

Ц

конце́рт	[kancért]	concert	The Russian ц is always pronounced hard (somewhat like the *ts* in ca*ts*), even when it is followed by е or и, which normally indicate that a soft consonant precedes.
Цара́пкин	[carápķin]	Tsarapkin	
огурцы́	[agurcí]	cucumbers	
в канцеля́рии	[fkənciḽáṛiji]	in an office	
ца́рь	[cáṛ]	tsar	
оте́ц	[aṭéc]	father	

Ч

на по́чту	[napóčtu]	to the post office	The Russian ч is always pronounced soft (somewhat like the *ch* in *ch*eese), even when it is followed by а, о, or у, which normally indicate that a hard consonant precedes.
вчера́	[fčirá]	yesterday	
ча́й	[čáj]	tea	
«О́чи чёрные»	[óči čórnijə]	"Dark Eyes"	
о́чень	[óčiṇ]	very	
в о́череди	[vóčiṛiḓi]	in line	
плечо́	[pḽičó]	shoulder	
чу́дно	[čúdnə]	wonderful	

Ш

слы́шал	[slíšəl]	heard	The Russian ш is always pronounced hard (somewhat like the *sh* in *sh*ip but articulated farther back in the mouth), even when it is followed by ь, е, or и,
хорошо́	[xərašó]	good, well	
хоро́шего	[xaróšivə]	[of] good	
спешу́	[sṛišú]	I'm hurrying	

	спеши́те	[sp̧išíṭi]	you're hurrying
	ка́ша	[kášə]	kasha
	ша́пка	[šápkə]	cap
	ше́сть	[šéṣṭ]	six
Щ	бо́рщ	[bóršč]	borsch
	ещё	[jiščó]	yet, still
	щи́	[ščí]	schi
	в я́щике	[vjáščiķi]	in the drawer
	борща́	[barščá]	some borsch
	щу́ка	[ščúka]	pike
Ъ	съе́л	[sjél]	ate
	отъе́зд	[atjést]	departure
Ы	ты́	[ti]	you
	вы́	[ví]	you
	бы́ло	[bílə]	was
	бы́л	[bíl]	was
	бы́ть	[bíṭ]	to be
	слы́шал	[slíšəl]	heard
	мы́	[mí]	we
Ь	посла́ть	[paslát]	to send
	портфе́ль	[partfél]	briefcase
	письмо́	[p̧iṣmó]	letter
	бо́льше	[bólši]	more, bigger
	о́чень	[óčiņ]	very
	семья́	[ṣimjá]	family
Э	э́то	[étə]	this
	э́тот	[étət]	this
	э́ти	[éṭi]	these
	экза́мен	[igzámin]	exam
	элеме́нт	[iļimént]	element
Ю	всю́ неде́лю	[fṣú ņiḍéļu]	all week
	говорю́	[gəvaŗú]	I speak
	стою́	[stajú]	I stand
	рабо́таю	[rabótəju]	I work
	пью́	[p̧jú]	I drink
	о́сенью	[óṣiņju]	in the fall
Я	говоря́т	[gəvaŗát]	they say
	опя́ть	[ap̧áṭ]	again
	в канцеля́рии	[fkənciļáŗiji]	in an office
	портфе́ля	[partféļə]	[of the] briefcase
	стоя́ли	[stajáļi]	stood
	до свида́ния	[dəsẏidáņjə]	good-bye
	пе́ния	[p̧éņijə]	[of] singing
	язы́к	[jizík]	language
	тяжело́	[ṭižiló]	hard

which normally indicate that a soft consonant precedes.

The Russian **щ** is a long, soft consonant pronounced somewhat like the *shch* in fre*sh ch*eese, spoken without a break. It is always pronounced soft, even when it is followed by **a** or **y**, which normally indicate that a hard consonant precedes.

The symbol **ъ** (hard sign) has no sound value of its own. It is used between prefixes that end in a consonant and word roots beginning with **е, я, ю,** or **ё** to indicate that these vowel letters are pronounced with a preceding [j] (as in *y*es).

The letter **ы** varies in pronunciation ranging from something like the vowel in b*i*t to the *i* of mach*i*ne. After lip consonants **б, в, п, ф,** and **м,** many speakers pronounce a w-like glide before **ы** so that it sounds somewhat like the English *we,* except shorter.

The letter **ы** never appears in the initial position in a word.

The symbol **ь** (soft sign) has no sound value of its own. It serves to indicate the softness of a preceding consonant at the end of a word or immediately before another consonant letter.

It also serves (like **ъ**) to indicate that the soft-series vowel letter which follows is pronounced with a preceding [j] (as in *y*es).

The letter **э** occurs mostly in words of foreign origin, usually in the initial position. When stressed it is pronounced like the *e* in *E*ric; when not stressed it is apt to be pronounced like the *e* in *e*mote or the *i* in *i*llegal, although many speakers pronounce it as [e] wherever it occurs.

The letter **ю,** both when stressed and unstressed, is pronounced like the *u* in t*u*ne after a consonant letter (which is pronounced soft); it is pronounced like the *u* in *u*nion after a vowel letter, **ъ,** or **ь,** or when it is in the initial position.

After a consonant the stressed letter **я** is pronounced somewhat like the *a* in f*a*r. In unstressed syllables **я** is usually pronounced like **и,** except in certain grammatical endings where it sounds like the *a* in English sof*a*. The consonant preceding **я** is always pronounced soft. When **я** occurs in the initial position or following a vowel, **ъ,** or **ь,** it has the same vocalic value as elsewhere, but is preceded by the consonant sound [j] (as in *y*es).

Noun declension

1. стол-nouns

		table	city	knife	tea	student	teacher	day
					SINGULAR			
N		стол	город	нож	чай	студент	учитель	день
A		стол	город	нож	чай	студента	учителя	день
G		стола́	го́рода	ножа́	ча́я	студе́нта	учи́теля	дня́
P		столе́	го́роде	ноже́	ча́е	студе́нте	учи́теле	дне́
D		столу́	го́роду	ножу́	ча́ю	студе́нту	учи́телю	дню́
I		столо́м	го́родом	ножо́м	ча́ем	студе́нтом	учи́телем	днём
					PLURAL			
N		столы́	города́	ножи́	чаи́	студе́нты	учителя́	дни́
A		столы́	города́	ножи́	чаи́	студе́нтов	учителе́й	дни́
G		столо́в	городо́в	ноже́й	чаёв	студе́нтов	учителе́й	дней
P		стола́х	города́х	ножа́х	чая́х	студе́нтах	учителя́х	дня́х
D		стола́м	города́м	ножа́м	чая́м	студе́нтам	учителя́м	дня́м
I		стола́ми	города́ми	ножа́ми	чая́ми	студе́нтами	учителя́ми	дня́ми

2. окно́-nouns

		window	word	letter	meeting	dress	field
					SINGULAR		
N		окно́	сло́во	письмо́	собра́ние	пла́тье	по́ле
A		окно́	сло́во	письмо́	собра́ние	пла́тье	по́ле
G		окна́	сло́ва	письма́	собра́ния	пла́тья	по́ля
P		окне́	сло́ве	письме́	собра́нии	пла́тье	по́ле
D		окну́	сло́ву	письму́	собра́нию	пла́тью	по́лю
I		окно́м	сло́вом	письмо́м	собра́нием	пла́тьем	по́лем
					PLURAL		
N		о́кна	слова́	пи́сьма	собра́ния	пла́тья	поля́
A		о́кна	слова́	пи́сьма	собра́ния	пла́тья	поля́
G		о́кон	слов	пи́сем	собра́ний	пла́тьев	поле́й
P		о́кнах	слова́х	пи́сьмах	собра́ниях	пла́тьях	поля́х
D		о́кнам	слова́м	пи́сьмам	собра́ниям	пла́тьям	поля́м
I		о́кнами	слова́ми	пи́сьмами	собра́ниями	пла́тьями	поля́ми

3. жена́-nouns

		wife	girl	sister	street	earth, land	lecture	uncle
					SINGULAR			
N		жена́	де́вушка	сестра́	у́лица	земля́	ле́кция	дя́дя
A		жену́	де́вушку	сестру́	у́лицу	зе́млю	ле́кцию	дя́дю
G		жены́	де́вушки	сестры́	у́лицы	земли́	ле́кции	дя́ди
P		жене́	де́вушке	сестре́	у́лице	земле́	ле́кции	дя́де
D		жене́	де́вушке	сестре́	у́лице	земле́	ле́кции	дя́де
I		жено́й	де́вушкой	сестро́й	у́лицей	землёй	ле́кцией	дя́дей
					PLURAL			
N		жёны	де́вушки	сёстры	у́лицы	зе́мли	ле́кции	дя́ди
A		жён	де́вушек	сестёр	у́лицы	зе́мли	ле́кции	дя́дей
G		жён	де́вушек	сестёр	у́лиц	земе́ль	ле́кций	дя́дей
P		жёнах	де́вушках	сёстрах	у́лицах	зе́млях	ле́кциях	дя́дях
D		жёнам	де́вушкам	сёстрам	у́лицам	зе́млям	ле́кциям	дя́дям
I		жёнами	де́вушками	сёстрами	у́лицами	зе́млями	ле́кциями	дя́дями

4. дверь-nouns

			SINGULAR			
	door	*notebook*	*line, turn*	*thing*	*mother*	*daughter*
N	две́рь	тетра́дь	о́чередь	ве́щь	ма́ть	до́чь
A	две́рь	тетра́дь	о́чередь	ве́щь	ма́ть	до́чь
G	две́ри	тетра́ди	о́череди	ве́щи	ма́тери	до́чери
P	две́ри	тетра́ди	о́череди	ве́щи	ма́тери	до́чери
D	две́ри	тетра́ди	о́череди	ве́щи	ма́тери	до́чери
I	две́рью	тетра́дью	о́чередью	ве́щью	ма́терью	до́черью

			PLURAL			
N	две́ри	тетра́ди	о́череди	ве́щи	ма́тери	до́чери
A	две́ри	тетра́ди	о́череди	ве́щи	матере́й	дочере́й
G	двере́й	тетра́дей	очереде́й	веще́й	матере́й	дочере́й
P	дверя́х	тетра́дях	очередя́х	веща́х	матеря́х	дочеря́х
D	дверя́м	тетра́дям	очередя́м	веща́м	матеря́м	дочеря́м
I	дверя́ми / дверьми́	тетра́дями	очередя́ми	веща́ми	матеря́ми	дочерьми́ / дочеря́ми

5. и́мя-nouns (neuter)

	SINGULAR			PLURAL	
	name	*time*		*names*	*times*
N	и́мя	вре́мя	N	имена́	времена́
A	и́мя	вре́мя	A	имена́	времена́
G	и́мени	вре́мени	G	имён	времён
P	и́мени	вре́мени	P	имена́х	времена́х
D	и́мени	вре́мени	D	имена́м	времена́м
I	и́менем	вре́менем	I	имена́ми	времена́ми

6. Nouns with declension irregularities

			SINGULAR			
	church	*neighbor*	*brother*	*chair*	*leaf*	*pen*
N	це́рковь	сосе́д	бра́т	сту́л	ли́ст	перо́
A	це́рковь	сосе́да	бра́та	сту́л	ли́ст	перо́
G	це́ркви	сосе́да	бра́та	сту́ла	листа́	пера́
P	це́ркви	сосе́де	бра́те	сту́ле	листе́	пере́
D	це́ркви	сосе́ду	бра́ту	сту́лу	листу́	перу́
I	це́рковью	сосе́дом	бра́том	сту́лом	листо́м	перо́м

			PLURAL			
N	це́ркви	сосе́ди	бра́тья	сту́лья	ли́стья	пе́рья
A	це́ркви	сосе́дей	бра́тьев	сту́лья	ли́стья	пе́рья
G	церкве́й	сосе́дей	бра́тьев	сту́льев	ли́стьев	пе́рьев
P	церква́х	сосе́дях	бра́тьях	сту́льях	ли́стьях	пе́рьях
D	церква́м	сосе́дям	бра́тьям	сту́льям	ли́стьям	пе́рьям
I	церква́ми	сосе́дями	бра́тьями	сту́льями	ли́стьями	пе́рьями

(cont.)

		SINGULAR			
		tree	*husband*	*son*	*friend*	*citizen*
N		де́рево	му́ж	сы́н	дру́г	граждани́н
A		де́рево	му́жа	сы́на	дру́га	граждани́на
G		де́рева	му́жа	сы́на	дру́га	граждани́на
P		де́реве	му́же	сы́не	дру́ге	граждани́не
D		де́реву	му́жу	сы́ну	дру́гу	граждани́ну
I		де́ревом	му́жем	сы́ном	дру́гом	граждани́ном

		PLURAL			
N		дере́вья	мужья́	сыновья́	друзья́	гра́ждане
A		дере́вья	муже́й	сынове́й	друзе́й	гра́ждан
G		дере́вьев	муже́й	сынове́й	друзе́й	гра́ждан
P		дере́вьях	мужья́х	сыновья́х	друзья́х	гра́жданах
D		дере́вьям	мужья́м	сыновья́м	друзья́м	гра́жданам
I		дере́вьями	мужья́ми	сыновья́ми	друзья́ми	гра́жданами

		SINGULAR			
		Mr.	*Georgian*	*man*	*baby, child*
N		господи́н	грузи́н	челове́к	ребёнок
A		господи́на	грузи́на	челове́ка	ребёнка
G		господи́на	грузи́на	челове́ка	ребёнка
P		господи́не	грузи́не	челове́ке	ребёнке
D		господи́ну	грузи́ну	челове́ку	ребёнку
I		господи́ном	грузи́ном	челове́ком	ребёнком

		PLURAL			
N		господа́	грузи́ны	лю́ди	де́ти
A		госпо́д	грузи́н	люде́й	дете́й
G		госпо́д	грузи́н	люде́й	дете́й
P		господа́х	грузи́нах	лю́дях	де́тях
D		господа́м	грузи́нам	лю́дям	де́тям
I		господа́ми	грузи́нами	людьми́	детьми́

7. Nouns used in the plural

		chess	*kids, guys*	*money*	*schi*
N		ша́хматы	ребя́та	де́ньги	щи́
A		ша́хматы	ребя́т	де́ньги	щи́
G		ша́хмат	ребя́т	де́нег	ще́й
P		ша́хматах	ребя́тах	деньга́х	ща́х
D		ша́хматам	ребя́там	деньга́м	ща́м
I		ша́хматами	ребя́тами	деньга́ми	ща́ми

Adjective declension

MASCULINE AND NEUTER				*Singular*			
N (m) нóвый	молодóй	сѝний	другóй	рýсский	большóй	хорóший
N (n) нóвое	молодóе	сѝнее	другóе	рýсское	большóе	хорóшее
A (animate = genitive; inanimate = nominative)							
G нóвого	молодóго	сѝнего	другóго	рýсского	большóго	хорóшего
P нóвом	молодóм	сѝнем	другóм	рýсском	большóм	хорóшем
D нóвому	молодóму	сѝнему	другóму	рýсскому	большóму	хорóшему
I нóвым	молодьм	сѝним	другѝм	рýсским	большѝм	хорóшим

FEMININE							
N нóвая	молодáя	сѝняя	другáя	рýсская	большáя	хорóшая
A нóвую	молодýю	сѝнюю	другýю	рýсскую	большýю	хорóшую
G P D I } нóвой	молодóй	сѝней	другóй	рýсской	большóй	хорóшей

				Plural			
N нóвые	молодьіе	сѝние	другѝе	рýсские	большѝе	хорóшие
A (animate = genitive; inanimate = nominative)							
G P } нóвых	молодьіх	сѝних	другѝх	рýсских	большѝх	хорóших
D нóвым	молодьім	сѝним	другѝм	рýсским	большѝм	хорóшим
I нóвыми	молодьіми	сѝними	другѝми	рýсскими	большѝми	хорóшими

Pronoun declension

1. Personal pronouns and interrogatives ктó and чтó

N	я	ты	óн, онó	онá	мы	вы	онѝ	ктó	чтó
A	меня	тебя	егó, негó	её, неё	нáс	вáс	ѝх, нѝх	когó	чтó
G	меня	тебя	егó, негó	её, неё	нáс	вáс	ѝх, нѝх	когó	чегó
P	мнé	тебé	нём	нéй	нáс	вáс	нѝх	кóм	чём
D	мнé	тебé	емý, немý	éй, нéй	нáм	вáм	ѝм, нѝм	комý	чемý
I	мнóй / мнóю	тобóй / тобóю	ѝм, нѝм	éй, нéй / éю, нéю	нáми	вáми	ѝми, нѝми	кéм	чём

Note: The reflexive personal pronoun **себя** has no nominative form; it declines like **ты**: **себя, себé, собóй.**

2. Possessive pronoun modifiers and interrogative чей *whose*

MASCULINE AND NEUTER				*Singular*		
N (m) чéй	мóй	твóй	свóй	нáш	вáш
N (n) чьё	моё	твоё	своё	нáше	вáше
A (animate = genitive; inanimate = nominative)						
G чьегó	моегó	твоегó	своегó	нáшего	вáшего
P чьём	моём	твоём	своём	нáшем	вáшем
D чьемý	моемý	твоемý	своемý	нáшему	вáшему
I чьѝм	мойм	твойм	свойм	нашѝм	вашѝм

FEMININE						
N чья	моя	твоя	своя	нáша	вáша
A чью	мою	твою	свою	нáшу	вáшу
G P D I } чьéй	моéй	твоéй	своéй	нáшей	вáшей

		Plural				
N	чья́	мой	твой	свой	на́ши	ва́ши
A	(animate = genitive; inanimate = nominative)					
G P	чья́х	мой́х	твой́х	свой́х	на́ших	ва́ших
D	чья́м	мой́м	твой́м	свой́м	на́шим	ва́шим
I	чья́ми	мой́ми	твой́ми	свой́ми	на́шими	ва́шими

Note: The third person possessives **его́**, **её**, and **их** do not decline.

3. Declension of оди́н *one*, э́тот *this*, то́т *that*, and ве́сь *all*

	MASCULINE AND NEUTER		*Singular*		
N	(*m*)	оди́н	э́тот	то́т	ве́сь
	(*n*)	одно́	э́то	то́	все́
A	(animate = genitive; inanimate = nominative)				
G		одного́	э́того	того́	всего́
P		одно́м	э́том	то́м	всём
D		одному́	э́тому	тому́	всему́
I		одни́м	э́тим	те́м	всём

	FEMININE				
N	одна́	э́та	та́	вся́
A	одну́	э́ту	ту́	всю́
G P D I	одно́й	э́той	то́й	все́й

		Plural			
N	одни́	э́ти	те́	все́
A	(animate = genitive; inanimate = nominative)			
G P	одни́х	э́тих	те́х	все́х
D	одни́м	э́тим	те́м	все́м
I	одни́ми	э́тими	те́ми	все́ми

Verb conjugation

1. First conjugation verbs

	IMPERFECTIVE ASPECT					
INFINITIVE	чита́ть *read*	писа́ть *write*	ползти́ *crawl*	пе́чь *bake*	сове́товать *advise*	просыпа́ться *wake up*
PAST	чита́л	писа́л	по́лз	пёк	сове́товал	просыпа́лся
	чита́ла	писа́ла	ползла́	пекла́	сове́товала	просыпа́лась
	чита́ло	писа́ло	ползло́	пекло́	сове́товало	просыпа́лось
	чита́ли	писа́ли	ползли́	пекли́	сове́товали	просыпа́лись
PRESENT	чита́ю	пишу́	ползу́	пеку́	сове́тую	просыпа́юсь
	чита́ешь	пи́шешь	ползёшь	печёшь	сове́туешь	просыпа́ешься
	чита́ет	пи́шет	ползёт	печёт	сове́тует	просыпа́ется
	чита́ем	пи́шем	ползём	печём	сове́туем	просыпа́емся
	чита́ете	пи́шете	ползёте	печёте	сове́туете	просыпа́етесь
	чита́ют	пи́шут	ползу́т	пеку́т	сове́туют	просыпа́ются
IMPERATIVE	чита́й	пиши́	ползи́	пеки́	сове́туй	просыпа́йся
	чита́йте	пиши́те	ползи́те	пеки́те	сове́туйте	просыпа́йтесь

Note: The imperfective future is formed by combining the future forms of **бы́ть** with the imperfective infinitive: **бу́ду чита́ть**, **бу́дешь чита́ть**, and so forth.

PERFECTIVE ASPECT						
INFINITIVE	прочита́ть *read*	написа́ть *write*	уползти́ *crawl away*	испе́чь *bake*	посове́товать *advise*	просну́ться *wake up*
PAST	прочита́л прочита́ла прочита́ло прочита́ли	написа́л написа́ла написа́ло написа́ли	упо́лз уползла́ уползло́ уползли́	испёк испекла́ испекло́ испекли́	посове́товал посове́товала посове́товало посове́товали	просну́лся просну́лась просну́лось просну́лись
FUTURE	прочита́ю прочита́ешь прочита́ет прочита́ем прочита́ете прочита́ют	напишу́ напи́шешь напи́шет напи́шем напи́шете напи́шут	уползу́ уползёшь уползёт уползём уползёте уползу́т	испеку́ испечёшь испечёт испечём испечёте испеку́т	посове́тую посове́туешь посове́тует посове́туем посове́туете посове́туют	просну́сь проснёшься проснётся проснёмся проснётесь просну́тся
IMPERATIVE	прочита́й прочита́йте	напиши́ напиши́те	уползи́ уползи́те	испеки́ испеки́те	посове́туй посове́туйте	просни́сь просни́тесь

Note: Perfective verbs are not used in the present tense.

2. Second conjugation verbs

IMPERFECTIVE ASPECT							
INFINITIVE	ве́рить *believe*	учи́ться *study*	смотре́ть *look*	стоя́ть *stand*	люби́ть *love*	проси́ть *ask*	серди́ться *be angry*
PAST	ве́рил ве́рила ве́рило ве́рили	учи́лся учи́лась учи́лось учи́лись	смотре́л смотре́ла смотре́ло смотре́ли	стоя́л стоя́ла стоя́ло стоя́ли	люби́л люби́ла люби́ло люби́ли	проси́л проси́ла проси́ло проси́ли	серди́лся серди́лась серди́лось серди́лись
PRESENT	ве́рю ве́ришь ве́рит ве́рим ве́рите ве́рят	учу́сь у́чишься у́чится у́чимся у́читесь у́чатся	смотрю́ смо́тришь смо́трит смо́трим смо́трите смо́трят	стою́ стои́шь стои́т стои́м стои́те стоя́т	люблю́ лю́бишь лю́бит лю́бим лю́бите лю́бят	прошу́ про́сишь про́сит про́сим про́сите про́сят	сержу́сь се́рдишься се́рдится се́рдимся се́рдитесь се́рдятся
IMPERATIVE	верь ве́рьте	учи́сь учи́тесь	смотри́ смотри́те	стой сто́йте	люби́ люби́те	проси́ проси́те	серди́сь серди́тесь

Note: The imperfective future is formed by combining the future forms of **быть** with the infinitive: **бу́ду ве́рить, бу́дешь ве́рить,** and so forth.

PERFECTIVE ASPECT							
INFINITIVE	пове́рить *believe*	научи́ться *learn*	посмотре́ть *look*	постоя́ть *stand*	оста́вить *leave*	попроси́ть *ask*	рассерди́ться *become angry*
PAST	пове́рил пове́рила пове́рило пове́рили	научи́лся научи́лась научи́лось научи́лись	посмотре́л посмотре́ла посмотре́ло посмотре́ли	постоя́л постоя́ла постоя́ло постоя́ли	оста́вил оста́вила оста́вило оста́вили	попроси́л попроси́ла попроси́ло попроси́ли	рассерди́лся рассерди́лась рассерди́лось рассерди́лись
FUTURE	пове́рю пове́ришь пове́рит пове́рим пове́рите пове́рят	научу́сь научи́шься научи́тся научи́мся научи́тесь нау́чатся	посмотрю́ посмо́тришь посмо́трит посмо́трим посмо́трите посмо́трят	постою́ постои́шь постои́т постои́м постои́те постоя́т	оста́влю оста́вишь оста́вит оста́вим оста́вите оста́вят	попрошу́ попро́сишь попро́сит попро́сим попро́сите попро́сят	рассержу́сь рассе́рдишься рассе́рдится рассе́рдимся рассе́рдитесь рассе́рдятся
IMPERATIVE	пове́рь пове́рьте	научи́сь научи́тесь	посмотри́ посмотри́те	постой постойте	оста́вь оста́вьте	попроси́ попроси́те	рассерди́сь рассерди́тесь

Note: Perfective verbs are not used in the present tense.

3. Irregular verbs

	INFINITIVE	хоте́ть (ipfv) *want*		да́ть (pfv) *give*
	PAST	хоте́л хоте́ла хоте́ло хоте́ли		да́л дала́ да́ло да́ли
	PRESENT	хочу́ хо́чешь хо́чет хоти́м хоти́те хотя́т	FUTURE	да́м да́шь да́ст дади́м дади́те даду́т
	IMPERATIVE	(none)		да́й да́йте

Other verbs conjugated similarly are: **захоте́ть** (pfv), **прода́ть** (pfv), **пода́ть** (pfv), **переда́ть** (pfv), and all other perfective verbs formed by adding prefixes to the above basic verbs.

Reference list of verbs[1]

Б
би́ть I (pfv по-)   17 — hit
боле́ть II (pfv по-)   16 — ache
боя́ться II (pfv по-)   14 — fear
бра́ть I (pfv взя́ть)   13 — take
бы́ть (pfv по-)   4 — be

В
вари́ть II (pfv с-)   17 — cook
ве́рить II (pfv по-)   15 — believe
верну́ться I (ipfv возвраща́ться)   16 — return
взя́ть I (ipfv бра́ть)   6 — take
ви́деть II (pfv у-)   2, 6 — see
висе́ть II (pfv по-)   15 — be hanging
возвраща́ться I (pfv верну́ться)   16 — return
войти́ I (ipfv входи́ть)   4 — enter
встре́тить II (ipfv встреча́ть)   11 — meet
вы́бросить II (ipfv выбра́сывать)   17 — discard, throw out
вы́говорить II (ipfv выгова́ривать)   11 — pronounce, utter
вы́йти I (ipfv выходи́ть)   14 — go (*or* come) out
вы́пить I (ipfv пи́ть)   13 — drink
вы́тереть I (ipfv вытира́ть)   17 — wipe
выходи́ть II (pfv вы́йти)   14 — go (*or* come) out
выходи́ть (вы́йти) за́муж   18 — get married

Г
говори́ть II (pfv по- *or* сказа́ть)   1 — speak, say
гуля́ть I (pfv по-)   14 — stroll

Д
дава́ть I (pfv да́ть)   14 — give
да́ть (ipfv дава́ть)   13 — give
де́лать I (pfv с- *or* по-)   3 — do, make
договори́ться II (ipfv догова́риваться)   11 — agree, come to terms
достава́ть I (pfv доста́ть)   13 — get hold of
доста́ть I (ipfv достава́ть)   4 — get hold of
ду́мать I (pfv по-)   6 — think

Е
е́здить II (pfv по-)   12 — go (by vehicle)
е́хать I (pfv по-)   12 — be going (by vehicle)

Ж
жда́ть I (подо-)   9 — wait
жела́ть I (по-)   18 — wish
жи́ть I (по-)   9 — live

З
забыва́ть I (pfv забы́ть)   14 — forget
забы́ть I (ipfv забыва́ть)   7 — forget
заду́маться I (ipfv заду́мываться)   18 — sink into reverie
зайти́ I (ipfv заходи́ть)   13 — drop in, go behind
заказа́ть I (ipfv зака́зывать)   12 — order
закры́ть I (ipfv закрыва́ть)   3 — close
замени́ть II (ipfv заменя́ть)   4 — replace
заме́тить II (ipfv замеча́ть)   13 — notice
замо́лвить сло́во (*or* слове́чко) II (pfv)   9 — put in a good word
занима́ться I (pfv по- *or* заня́ться)   18 — study, busy oneself
заплати́ть II (ipfv плати́ть)   12 — pay
зараба́тывать I (pfv зарабо́тать)   18 — earn
заходи́ть II (pfv зайти́)   4 — drop in, go behind
захоте́ть II (ipfv хоте́ть)   18 — want
зва́ть I (pfv по-)   11 — call
звони́ть II (pfv по-)   7 — phone
зна́ть I (ipfv)   3 — know

---

[1] Roman numerals I and II refer to the first and second conjugations. Arabic numerals refer to the lesson in which the verb was initially presented (usually in the Preparation for Conversation).

The other member of the aspect pair is indicated parenthetically; for the sake of completeness some verbs not formally presented or drilled in the text are included here. The translations given are the most basic ones.

И

игра́ть I (сыгра́ть *or* по-) 11	play
идти́ I (pfv пойти́) 1	be going
извини́ть II (ipfv извиня́ть) 1	excuse
измени́ть II (ipfv изменя́ть) 4	change
интересова́ть I (pfv за-) 18	interest
интересова́ться I (pfv за-) 18	be interested
иска́ть I (pfv по-) 12	seek
испе́чь I (ipfv пе́чь) 17	bake
итти́ I (*see* идти́) 1	be going

К

каза́ться I (pfv по-) 6	seem
конча́ть I (pfv ко́нчить) 14	finish
ко́нчить II (ipfv конча́ть) 14	finish
куши́ть II (ipfv покупа́ть) 4	buy

Л

лежа́ть II (pfv по-) 18	lie
люби́ть II (pfv по-) 10	love

М

мечта́ть I (pfv по-) 18	dream
меша́ть I (pfv по-) 17	disturb, stir
мо́чь I (pfv с-) 7	be able, can

Н

наде́яться I (pfv по-) 18	hope
назва́ть I (ipfv называ́ть) 10	name
назна́чить II (ipfv назнача́ть) 16	set, designate
найти́ I (ipfv находи́ть) 17	find
нали́ть I (ipfv налива́ть) 18	pour
написа́ть I (ipfv писа́ть) 4, 7	write
наре́зать I (ipfv нареза́ть) 5	slice
научи́ться II (ipfv учи́ться) 18	learn
находи́ть II (pfv найти́) 17	find
находи́ться II (pfv найти́сь) 17	be situated
нача́ть I (ipfv начина́ть) 18	begin
носи́ть II (pfv по-) 15	carry
нра́виться II (pfv по-) 11, 16	like

О

обе́дать I (pfv по-) 5	eat dinner
обрати́ться II (ipfv обраща́ться) 16	consult
обраща́ться I (pfv обрати́ться) 16	consult
ожида́ть I (ipfv) 8	expect
око́нчить II (ipfv ока́нчивать) 18	finish
опа́здывать I (pfv опозда́ть) 11	be late
опозда́ть I (ipfv опа́здывать) 11	be late
оста́вить II (ipfv оставля́ть) 7	leave
оста́ться I (ipfv остава́ться) 17	remain, be left
отве́тить II (ipfv отвеча́ть) 3	answer
отвеча́ть I (pfv отве́тить) 3	answer
отдохну́ть I (ipfv отдыха́ть) 14	rest
отдыха́ть I (pfv отдохну́ть) 14	rest
открыва́ть I (pfv откры́ть) 11	open
откры́ть I (pfv открыва́ть) 3, 7	open

П

переда́ть (ipfv передава́ть) 18	hand over, pass
перейти́ I (ipfv переходи́ть) 14	cross, switch, go over
переходи́ть II (pfv перейти́) 14	cross, switch, go over
пе́ть (pfv с-) 13	sing
пе́чь I (pfv ис- *or* с-) 17	bake
писа́ть I (pfv на-) 4, 7	write
ши́ть I (pfv вы́-) 5	drink
плати́ть II (pfv за-) 12	pay
побы́ть I (ipfv быть) 18	be (for a while)
пове́рить II (ipfv ве́рить) 15	believe
повтори́ть II (ipfv повторя́ть) 1	repeat
поговори́ть II (ipfv говори́ть) 11	talk
погуля́ть I (ipfv гуля́ть) 14	stroll
пода́ть (ipfv подава́ть) 9	give, submit

поде́лать I (ipfv де́лать) 17	do
подожда́ть I (ipfv жда́ть) 8	wait
подойти́ I (ipfv подходи́ть) 7	approach
поду́мать I (ipfv ду́мать) 7	think
пое́здить II (ipfv е́здить) 18	drive (a bit)
пое́хать I (ipfv е́хать) 12	go (by vehicle)
пожи́ть I (ipfv жи́ть) 18	live (for a while)
позанима́ться I (ipfv занима́ться) 18	study, be busy (for a while)
позвони́ть II (ipfv звони́ть) 7	phone
познако́мить II (ipfv знако́мить) 10	introduce
познако́миться II (ipfv знако́миться) 6	meet
поигра́ть I (ipfv игра́ть) 18	play (for a while)
поиска́ть I (ipfv иска́ть) 18	look for
пойти́ I (ipfv идти́, итти́) 3	go
показа́ть I (ipfv пока́зывать) 15	show
пока́зывать I (pfv показа́ть) 15	show
покупа́ть I (pfv купи́ть) 4	buy
полежа́ть II (ipfv лежа́ть) 18	lie (for a while)
полете́ть II (ipfv лете́ть) 18	fly
ползти́ I (pfv по-) 17	be crawling
положи́ть II (ipfv кла́сть) 12	put, lay
получи́ть II (ipfv получа́ть) 9	get
по́мнить II (pfv вс-) 11	remember
помога́ть I (pfv помо́чь) 16	help
помо́чь I (ipfv помога́ть) 16	help
понима́ть I (pfv поня́ть) 6	understand
понра́виться II (ipfv нра́виться) 11	like
пообе́дать I (ipfv обе́дать) 5	eat dinner
попроси́ть II (ipfv проси́ть) 7	ask, request
порабо́тать I (ipfv рабо́тать) 18	work (for a while)
посиде́ть II (ipfv сиде́ть) 18	sit (for a while)
посла́ть I (ipfv посыла́ть) 1	send
послу́шать I (ipfv слу́шать) 13	listen
посмотре́ть II (ipfv смотре́ть) 4	take a look
посове́товать I (ipfv сове́товать) 13	advise
поспа́ть II (ipfv спа́ть) 18	sleep (for a while), take a nap
постира́ть I (ipfv стира́ть) 18	do the wash
постоя́ть II (ipfv стоя́ть) 18	stand (for a while)
постро́ить II (ipfv стро́ить) 15	build
поступа́ть I (pfv поступи́ть) 3	join, enroll; act, behave
поступи́ть II (ipfv поступа́ть) 18	join, enroll; act, behave
постуча́ть II (ipfv стуча́ть) 18	knock, rap
потанцева́ть I (ipfv танцева́ть) 18	dance (for a while)
потеря́ть I (ipfv теря́ть) 17	lose
походи́ть II (ipfv ходи́ть) 18	walk a bit
предлага́ть I (pfv предложи́ть) 14	suggest
предложи́ть II (ipfv предлага́ть) 9	suggest
предста́вить II (ipfv представля́ть) 16	present
представля́ть I (pfv предста́вить) 15	present
представля́ть (or предста́вить) себе́ 15	imagine
преподава́ть I (ipfv) 18	instruct
привы́кнуть I (ipfv привыка́ть) 14	get used to
пригласи́ть II (ipfv приглаша́ть) 15	invite
приглаша́ть I (pfv пригласи́ть) 15	invite
прие́хать I (ipfv приезжа́ть) 12	arrive (by vehicle)
прийти́ I (ipfv приходи́ть) 14	come, arrive
прийти́сь I (ipfv приходи́ться) 17	have to
принести́ I (ipfv приноси́ть) 8	bring
приноси́ть II (pfv принести́) 13	bring
приходи́ть II (pfv прийти́) 14	come, arrive
продава́ть I (pfv прода́ть) 13	sell
продолжа́ть I (pfv продо́лжить) 16	continue
пройти́ I (ipfv проходи́ть) 6	pass, go through
пропа́сть (ipfv пропада́ть) 18	vanish, be lost
проси́ть II (pfv по-) 12	request, ask
просну́ться I (ipfv просыпа́ться) 18	wake up

	просыпа́ться I (pfv просну́ться) 18	wake up
	проходи́ть II (pfv пройти́) 9	pass
	прочита́ть I (ipfv чита́ть) 13	read
Р	рабо́тать I (pfv по-) 2	work
	разреши́ть II (ipfv разреша́ть) 12	permit
	рассерди́ться II (ipfv серди́ться) 16	become angry
	расти́ I (pfv вы́-) 17	grow
	реши́ть II (ipfv реша́ть) 18	decide, solve
С	сади́ться II (pfv се́сть) 14	sit down
	свари́ть II (ipfv вари́ть) 17	cook
	сде́лать I (ipfv де́лать) 9	do
	серди́ться II (pfv рас-) 16	be angry
	сиде́ть II (pfv по-) 10	sit
	сказа́ть I (ipfv говори́ть) 1	say, tell
	слома́ть I (ipfv лома́ть) 16	break
	случи́ться II (ipfv случа́ться) 16	happen
	слу́шать I (pfv по-) 7	listen
	слы́шать II (pfv у-) 2	hear
	смотре́ть II (pfv по-) 5	look
	смо́чь I (ipfv мочь) 7	be able
	снима́ть I (pfv сня́ть) 15	take off, take a picture
	собира́ться I (pfv собра́ться) 18	gather, get ready, plan
	сове́товать I (pfv по-) 13	advise
	сойти́ I (ipfv сходи́ть) 16	go off, get off (or down)
	спа́ть II (pfv по-) 12	sleep
	спеши́ть II (pfv по-) 2	hurry
	спра́шивать I (pfv спроси́ть) 8	ask, inquire
	спроси́ть II (ipfv спра́шивать) 8	ask, inquire
	станови́ться II (pfv ста́ть) 16	become, get, step, stand
	ста́ть I (ipfv станови́ться) 18	become, get, step, stand
	стира́ть I (pfv по- or вы́-) 17	wash, launder
	сто́ить II (ipfv) 12	cost
	стоя́ть II (pfv по-) 4	stand
	стро́ить II (pfv по-) 15	build
	стуча́ть II (pfv по-) 17	knock
	счита́ть I (pfv со-) 10	count, consider
	сыгра́ть I (ipfv игра́ть) 14	play
Т	танцева́ть I (pfv по-) 10	dance
	теря́ть I (pfv по-) 17	lose
У	убива́ть I (pfv уби́ть) 17	kill
	уви́деть II (ipfv ви́деть) 10	see
	удивля́ться I (pfv удиви́ться) 12	be surprised
	уезжа́ть I (pfv уе́хать) 16	go away (by vehicle)
	уе́хать I (ipfv уезжа́ть) 16	go away (by vehicle)
	узна́ть I (ipfv узнава́ть) 7	find out, recognize
	упа́сть I (ipfv па́дать) 16	fall
	уползти́ I (ipfv уполза́ть) 17	crawl away
	услы́шать II (ipfv слы́шать) 13	hear
	успе́ть I (ipfv успева́ть) 11	succeed, manage, have time
	уста́ть I (ipfv устава́ть) 11	get (or be) tired
	устро́ить II (ipfv устра́ивать) 18	arrange, set up
	устро́иться II (ipfv устра́иваться) 18	be arranged, get settled
	учи́ть II (pfv на-) 6	learn, teach
	учи́ться II (pfv на-) 18	learn, study
Х	ходи́ть II (pfv по-) 11	go, walk, attend
	хоте́ть (pfv за-) 3	want
	хоте́ться (pfv за-) 5	feel like
Ч	чита́ть I (pfv про- or по-) 1	read
	чу́вствовать I (pfv по-) 16	feel

Russian-English Vocabulary

Arabic numerals refer to the lesson in which the word was introduced or discussed.

Nouns are given in their nominative singular form, or, if used only in the plural, in their nominative plural form. Where an inserted vowel occurs in the nominative singular, the genitive singular is also indicated.

Verbs are given in their infinitive form, with the third person plural present-future sometimes also provided. Perfective verbs are marked pfv; imperfective verbs are not marked. Roman numerals I and II refer to the first and second conjugations.

Long-form adjectives are given only in the nominative singular masculine form except for soft stems, where feminine and neuter forms are also provided.

Prepositions are accompanied by a parenthetical indication of the case they require.

А а

а and, but, by the way, how about 1
а́ ah, oh 2
авто́бус bus 1
авторучка fountain pen 17
ага́ [ahá] aha! ahhh! 7
администра́тор clerk, administrator 12
Алёша (var. of Алексе́й) Alyosha (Alex) 17
алло́ hello (telephone only) 7
Аме́рика America 6
америка́нец, –нца American (m) 6
америка́нка American (f) 6
америка́нский American (adj) 6
Анато́лий Anatoly (Anatole) 18
аппара́т apparatus, camera 15
а́тлас atlas 8
аудито́рия lecture room, auditorium, classroom 6
а́х oh! 4

Б б

ба́бушка grandmother 17
бага́ж luggage, baggage 12
бага́жник baggage compartment, trunk 12
без, безо (*plus* gen) without 9
безду́шный unfeeling, heartless 16
бейсбо́л baseball 11
бе́лый white 13
беру́, берёшь (pres of бра́ть) 13
беспла́тно free 3

библиоте́ка library 6
биле́т ticket 12
би́ть, бью́т (I) to beat, hit, strike 17
бли́зкий close, near 15
Бо́г God 15
  Бо́же мо́й! good heavens! my God! 16
бо́лен, больна́, больны́ sick, ill 2, 3
боле́ть, боля́т (II) to ache, hurt 16
больны́ (*see* бо́лен) 2, 3
бо́льше more, bigger 5
  бо́льше не́т there isn't any more 5
большо́й large, big 6
  большо́е спаси́бо thanks very much 9
Бори́с Boris 7
бо́рщ borsch (beet soup) 5
Бо́ря (var. of Бори́с) Borya 18
боя́ться, боя́тся (II) to be afraid 14
бра́т brother 6
бра́ть, беру́т (I) to take, get 13
бра́тья (pl of бра́т) 7
бу́ду, бу́дешь (fut of бы́ть) 10
бу́дущее the future 18
бу́лка large roll, small loaf of French bread 17
бу́лочка roll, bun 17
бульо́н consommé, bouillon soup 17
буфе́т snack bar, sideboard 14
бы, б (conditional particle) would 17
бы́л, была́, бы́ло, бы́ли (past tense of бы́ть) 1
бы́стрый fast, quick, rapid 18
бы́ть to be 4

В в

в, во (*plus* prep *or* acc)   in, into, at, to 1
вагóн   railroad car 12
Вáля (var. of Валентина)   Valya 17
вáм, вáми (dat, instr of вы) 9, 12
вáнная   bathroom 12
Вáня (var. of Ивáн)   Vanya (Johnny) 18
варить (II)   to cook (by boiling) 17
вáс (acc, gen of вы) 2
вахтёр   custodian (m) 7
вахтёрша   custodian (f) 7
вáш, вáша, вáше, вáши   your, yours 6
вдали   in the distance 15
вдвоём   two together 14
вдруг   suddenly 16
ведрó   pail, bucket 15
ведь   after all, but, you know 9
вездé   everywhere 13
вéра   faith, confidence 15
Вéра   Vera 18
вéрить (II)   to believe, trust 15
вернýться (pfv I)   to come back, return 16
вéрующий   believer 15
вéрхний, –яя, –ее,   upper 12
весёлый   merry, gay, jolly 18
   вéсело   it's fun 18
веснá   spring 11
   веснóй   in spring 11
вéсь, вся, всё, всё   all, whole 2, 7
вéчер   evening, party (formal) 10
   по вечерáм   in the evenings 16
вечеринка   party (informal) 18
вечéрний, –яя, –ее,   evening (adj) 13
   «Вечéрняя Москвá»   *Evening Moscow* (newspaper) 13
вéчером   in the evening 10
   сегóдня вéчером   this evening 10
вéщь (f)   thing 12
взять, возьмýт (pfv I)   to take, get 6
вид   view, aspect 15
видел, видела, –о, –и (past of видеть) 2
виден, виднá, –о, –ы   visible, can be seen 15
видеть (II)   to see 6
вижу (first person sg of видеть) 5
Виктор   Victor 18
вилка   fork 5
винó   wine 18
висéть (II)   to be hanging 15
Витя (var. of Виктор)   Vitya 18
вкýсный   tasty, good, delicious 13
Владивостóк   Vladivostok 12
Владимир   Vladimir 8
вмéсте   together 10
   всé вмéсте   all together 1
вмéсто (*plus* gen)   instead of, in place of 14
вниз   down, downstairs 16
   внизý   downstairs, below 12
водá   water 12
водопровóд   running water, plumbing 15
возвращáться (I)   to return, come (*or* go) back 16
вóздух   air 14
возмóжный   possible 17
возьмý, возьмёшь (fut of взять) 6
войнá   war 10
войти, войдýт (pfv I)   to enter, come (*or* go) in 4
вокзáл   station, terminal 12

вокрýг (*plus* gen)   around 18
Вóлков   Volkov (last name) 9
Волóдя (var. of Владимир)   Volodya 10
вóн   there, yonder 6
   вóн тáм   over there, over yonder 6
   вóн тóт   that person over there 6
вообщé   in general, at all 16
вóсемь   eight 10
воскресéнье   Sunday 10
вóт   here('s), there('s) 1
   вóт кáк!   is that so! 7
   вóт чтó!   so that's it! 9
вошёл, вошлá, –ó, –и (past tense of войти) 15
вполнé   completely, fully 2
впрóчем   however, but then again 14
врáч   physician, doctor 16
врéмени, врéменем, etc. (*see* врéмя) 10
врéмя   time 10
все, всё, вся, всю, etc. (*see* вéсь) 2, 7
всё ещё   still, yet 2
   всё равнó   anyway, it doesn't matter 18
всегдá   always 5
всегó хорóшего   good-bye 2
всё-таки   nevertheless, still, just the same 8
встрéтить (pfv II)   to encounter, meet 11
всю, вся, etc. (*see* вéсь) 2
всякий   any, anyone, anybody 16
   во всяком слýчае   in any case 16
втóрник   Tuesday 10
вуз   college 18
вчерá   yesterday 1
вы   you 1
выбросить (pfv II)   to throw out, discard 17
выговорить (pfv II)   to pronounce, say 11
выйти, выйдут (pfv I)   to go out, get off 14
выпить, выпьют (pfv I)   to drink, have a drink 13
вытереть, вытрут (pfv I)   to wipe, wipe off 17
выходить (II)   to go out, get off 14
   выходить (выйти) зáмуж   to get married 18
вышел, вышла, etc. (past of выйти) 15

Г г

газéта   newspaper 13
Гáля (var. of Галина)   Galya 6
гдé   where (at what place) 2
гдé-нибудь   anywhere 18
гдé-то   somewhere 18
геогрáфия   geography 8
глáвный   main, chief 18
   глáвное   the main thing 18
глаз   eye 13
глýпость (f)   foolishness, stupidity 16
глýпый   foolish, stupid 16
говорить (II)   to speak, talk 1, 6
гóд   year 16
   в этом годý   this year 16
гóлоден, голоднá, гóлодны   hungry 5
голубóй   light blue 13
гораздо   by far, much, considerably 16
гóрод   city, town 4
   в гóрод (*or* в гóроде)   downtown 4
горсовéт   gorsovet (city soviet *or* council) 2
горячий   hot 12
господá   ladies and gentlemen, everybody 3
господин   Mr. 3

госпожа́   Miss, Mrs. 3
гости́ница   hotel 12
гото́в   ready 6
гра́ждане (pl of граждани́н)   citizens 12
гри́б   mushroom 17
гро́мче   louder 1
грузи́н   Georgian 7
гру́ппа   group, section 7
гуля́ть (I)   to stroll 14
ГУМ   GUM (dept. store in Moscow) 4

Д д

да   and 5
да́   yes 2
да ну́!   no kidding! 13
дава́ть, даю́т (I)   to give, let 14
давно́   for a long time, a long time ago 2
дади́м, дади́те, даду́т (see да́ть) 13
да́же   even 5
да́й, да́йте (imper of да́ть) 13
далёкий   far, far away, distant 15
да́льше   further; continue! go on! 4
да́м, да́шь, да́ст (see да́ть) 13
да́ром   gratis, for nothing 18
да́ть (pfv with irreg fut: да́м, да́шь, да́ст, дади́м,
   дади́те, даду́т)   to give 13
два́, две́   two 6, 10
две́рь (f)   door 4
дво́р   courtyard, yard 14
   на дворе́   outdoors, outside, in the yard 14
двухчасово́й   two-o'clock (adj) 17
де́вушка   young lady, girl 9
де́вять   nine 6
де́душка   grandfather 17
действи́тельно   really, indeed 16
де́лать (I)   to do, make 3
де́ло   thing, matter, business 2
   в чём де́ло?   what's the matter? 7
де́нь, дня́ (m)   day 4
де́нь рожде́ния   birthday 4
де́ньги   money 18
де́рево   tree 17
дере́вья (pl of де́рево) 17
деревя́нный   wooden 15
де́сять   ten 10
де́ти   children 17
джа́з   jazz, American-style popular music 13
дире́ктор   director 18
дли́нный   long 17
для (plus gen)   for 9
дни́ (pl of де́нь) 7
до (plus gen)   before, until, up to 9
до свида́ния   good-bye, I'll be seeing you 1
до́брый   kind, good 11
   до́брый ве́чер   good evening 11
дово́лен, –льна, etc.   pleased 7
дово́льно   rather, quite, enough 14
договори́ться (pfv II)   to come to terms 11
до́ктор   doctor 16
до́лго   long, a long time 4
до́лжен, должна́, etc.   must, have to 8
до́м   house, building 9
дома́ (pl of до́м) 9
до́ма   at home 10
домо́й   home, homeward 1
доро́га   road, way, route 15

дорого́й   expensive, dear 8
доса́да   annoyance 5
   во́т доса́да!   how annoying! what a nuisance! 5
доска́   board, blackboard 4
достава́ть, достаю́т (I)   to get (hold of) 13
доста́ть, доста́нут (pfv I)   to get (hold of) 4
до́чери, до́черью, etc. (see до́чь) 17
до́чь   daughter 17
дру́г   friend 9
друго́й   other, different 5
друзья́ (pl of дру́г) 9
ду́мать (I)   to think 6
душа́   soul, heart 16
дя́дя   uncle 17

Е е

Евге́ний   Evgeny (Eugene) 1
его́   him, it, his 6, 10
её   her, it, hers 6, 10
е́здить (II)   to go (by vehicle) 12
е́й (dat of она́) 14
ему́ (dat of о́н) 17
е́сли   if 16
е́сть   there is, there are 5
е́хать, е́дут (I)   to be going (by vehicle) 12
ещё   still, yet, more 5
   всё ещё   still, yet 2
   ещё ка́к!   and how! 14
   ещё раз   once again, once more 1
е́ю (instr of она́) 17

Ё ё

ёлка   fir tree, Christmas tree 17

Ж ж

жа́ль   too bad, pity, sorry 15
жа́ркий   hot 14
   жа́рко   [it's] hot 14
жда́ть, жду́т (I)   to wait 9
же (unstressed emphatic particle)   but 5
жела́ть (I)   to wish 18
жёлтый   yellow 13
жена́   wife 2
жени́х   fiancé, bridegroom 18
же́нщина   woman 12
жёсткий   hard 12
   жёсткий ваго́н   second-class coach 12
жи́знь (f)   life 18
жи́ть, живу́т (I)   to live 9
журна́л   magazine, journal 13

З з

за (acc, instr)   for, at, behind, after 9
   за́ город (or за́ городом)   out of town 17
   за меня́   for me, in my behalf 9
   за столо́м   at the table 14
забыва́ть (I)   to forget 14
забы́ть, забу́дут (pfv I)   to forget 7
заво́д   plant, factory 1
за́втра   tomorrow 4
заду́маться (pfv I)   to daydream 18
зайти́, зайду́т (pfv I)   to drop in, stop by 13
заказа́ть, зака́жут (pfv I)   to order 12

закрыть, закроют (pfv I)   to close, shut 3
зал   hall, room 6
заменить (pfv II)   to substitute 4
заметить (pfv II)   to notice 13
замолвить словечко   to put in a good word 9
заниматься (I)   to occupy oneself, to study 18
занят, занята, заняты   busy, occupied 3
занятия   studies, classes 8
заочница (*full form* студентка-заочница)   corres-
    pondence-school student (f) 9
заперт, -а, etc.   locked 4
заплатить (pfv II)   to pay 12
зарабатывать (I)   to earn, make [money] 18
заходить (II)   to drop in, stop by 4
захотеть, захотят (irreg)   to want, feel like 18
захочу, захочешь, захочет, захотим, захотите, etc.
    (irreg fut of захотеть) 18
зачем   why, what for 6
   зачем тебе   why do you need 6
заявление   application 9
звать, зовут (I)   to call 11
   как тебя (*or* вас) зовут?   what's your name? 11
звонить (II)   to ring, phone 7
звонок, -нка   bell 7
здание   building 7
здесь   here 7
здоров, -а, -ы   healthy, well 2
здравствуй, здравствуйте   hello 3
зелёный   green 13
земля   earth, land 18
зима   winter 2
   зимой   in winter 11
Зина (var. of Зинаида)   Zina 10
змея   snake 17
знаком, -а, -ы   acquainted, familiar 10
знакомство   acquaintance, familiarity 18
   по знакомству   by knowing the right person,
     through friends 18
знакомый (m), знакомая (f)   [an] acquaintance,
    [a] friend 13
знать (I)   to know 3
значить (II)   to mean 10
   значит   it means, so, then 10

И и

и   and, also, too 1
Иван   Ivan (John) 7
   Иванович (patronymic, son of Иван) 9
   Ивановна (patronymic, daughter of Иван) 7
игра   game, play 14
играть (I)   to play 11
   играть в карты   to play cards 11
идём   let's go 5
идти, идут (I)   to be going 1
из, изо (gen)   from, out of 9
изба   hut, village house 15
известия   news, news report 13
   «Известия»   *Izvestia* (*News*) (newspaper) 13
извините   excuse [me] 1
изменить (pfv II)   to change 4
икона   holy picture, icon 15
или   or 10
   или ... или ...   either ... or 10
им (dat of они, instr of он) 7, 14, 17
имени, именем, имена, etc. (*see* имя) 11

имя   name, first name 11
иначе (*or* иначе)   otherwise, differently 15
инженер   engineer 18
иногда   sometimes 3
иностранец, -нца   foreigner 15
институт   institute 18
интересно   [that's] interesting, [I] wonder 3
интересовать, -суют (I)   to interest 18
интересоваться (I)   to be interested in 18
Ирина   Irina (Irene) 9
искать, ищут (I)   to look for, seek 12
испечь, испекут (pfv I)   to bake 17
исполнение   performance 13
   в исполнении   performed by 13
историк   historian 18
история   history 8
итти (var. of идти) 1
их   their, them 6, 10

К к

к, ко (dat)   toward, to, to see 4, 7
каждый   each, every 11
кажется   [it] seems 6
казаться, кажутся (I)   to seem 16
как   how, as, like 2
   как дела?   how is everything? 2
   как раз   just, it just happens, the very thing 5, 9
как только   as soon as 17
какой   what, which 9
какой-то   some sort of, a, an, kind of 8, 16
каменный   [made of] stone, [made of] brick 15
камень, камня   stone, rock 17
каникулы (pl only)   vacation 15
карандаш   pencil 6
карта   map, card 8
картина   picture 11
касса   ticket window, box office, cash register 12
Катя (var. of Екатерина)   Katya (Kathy) 10
каша   kasha (mush, cooked cereal) 5
квартира   apartment 9
квитанция   receipt, claim check 12
Киев   Kiev 12
километр   kilometer (three-fifths of a mile) 15
кино   movies, cinema 10
киоск   stand, newsstand 8
Кирилл   Kirill (Cyril) 2
Китай   China 8
клуб   club 1
ключ   key 7
книга   book 3
когда   when, while 10
кого (gen, acc of кто) 8
кое-что   a thing or two 8
Козлов   Kozlov (last name) 7
колбаса   sausage 18
колодец, -дца   well 15
колхоз   kolkhoz, collective farm 15
   колхозник   collective-farm worker (m) 15
   колхозница   collective-farm worker (f) 15
   колхозный   collective farm (adj) 15
Коля (var. of Николай)   Kolya (Nick) 6
комиссионный (магазин)   secondhand store 13
комната   room 9
конец, -нца   end 16
   в конце концов   finally, in the end 16

коне́чно of course, sure, certainly 4
конце́рт concert 3
конча́ть (I) to finish, end 14
ко́нчить (pfv II) to finish, end 14
копе́йка kopeck 12
коро́бка box (cardboard) 4
коро́ткий short 17
космона́вт cosmonaut, astronaut 18
костю́м suit, costume 4
кото́рый which, what, that 13
ко́фе (indecl) coffee 5
краси́вый lovely, pretty, handsome 4
кра́сный red 13
   кра́сный уголо́к recreation room (*lit.* red corner) 13
кста́ти incidentally, apropos, by the way 3
кто́ who 4
куда́ where (to) 1
купе́ (indecl) compartment 12
купи́л, –а, etc. (past of купи́ть) 4
купи́ть (pfv II) to buy 4
Ку́рочкин Kurochkin (last name) 7
ку́рс class (year), course 10
кусо́к, куска́ piece, slice 8

Л л

лаборато́рия laboratory 3
ла́дно O.K., fine, all right 14
лапша́ noodles 17
Лёв, Льва́ Lev (Leo) 3
лёгкий easy, light 13
   легко́ [it's] easy, easily 13
лежа́ть (II) to be lying, to lie in bed 18
ле́кция lecture, class 6
Ленингра́д Leningrad 12
ле́с forest, woods 15
ле́стница stairway, stairs, ladder 16
ле́т (gen pl of го́д) 16
ле́то summer 11
   ле́том in summer 11
ли whether, if (question particle) 7
лимо́н lemon 17
лимона́д lemonade, soft drink 14
ли́ст leaf; sheet 17
листы́ sheets 17
ли́стья leaves 17
литерату́ра literature 8
   литерату́рный literary, literature (adj) 18
литфа́к department of literature 18
ли́фт elevator 12
ло́жка spoon 5
лу́чше better, rather 1
лу́чший best, better 7
Лю́ба (var. of Любо́вь) Lyuba 17
люби́ть (II) to love, like, to be fond of 10
любо́вь, любви́ (f) love 17
Любо́вь Lyubov (Amy) 17
лю́ди people 13
лю́кс deluxe class 12

М м

магази́н store 8
ма́зь (f) ointment, salve 16
ма́ленький small, little 9

ма́ло little, few, too little 10
ма́ма mamma, mom 17
Мари́я Maria (Mary) 7
Ма́рс Mars 18
ма́сло butter, oil 18
ма́сса lots, mass, plenty 17
масса́ж massage 16
ма́т checkmate 14
матема́тика mathematics 8
ма́тери, матере́й, etc. (*see* ма́ть) 15
материа́л material 4
   материа́л на костю́м suit material 4
   материа́л на пла́тье dress material 4
ма́ть, ма́тери, etc. mother 15
Ма́ша (var. of Мари́я) Masha 7
маши́на car, machine 18
ме́дленный slow 18
ме́жду (*plus* instr) between, among
   ме́жду про́чим by the way 13
ме́л chalk 17
мело́дия melody, tune 13
меня́ (gen, acc of я́) 8
месте́чко spot, place, job, small town 18
   тёплое месте́чко a soft spot, a nice cushy job 18
ме́сто place, seat, berth, job 12
ме́сяц month; moon 16
мечта́ть (I) to dream 18
меша́ть (I) to disturb, hinder, mix 17
Ми́ла (var. of Людми́ла) Mila 3
ми́лый nice, kind, dear, darling 9
ми́ля mile 15
мину́тка minute, moment 7
   [одну́] мину́тку just a minute 7
ми́р peace, world 10
   «Война́ и ми́р» *War and Peace* 10
Миха́йлович (patronymic, son of Миха́ил) 7
мне́ (prep, dat of я́) 3
мно́го a lot, lots, much 7
   мно́гое many things, lots of things 11
могу́, мо́жешь, мо́жет, etc. (pres of мо́чь) 7
мо́жет бы́ть maybe, perhaps 6
мо́жно it's possible, one may 4
мой, моя́, моё, мои́ my, mine 1, 6
молоде́ц, –дца́ one who does an outstanding job 7
молодо́й young 13
молоко́ milk 5
Москва́ Moscow 9
мо́чь, мо́гут (I) to be able, can 7
му́ж husband 2
мужчи́на man 12
мужья́ (pl of му́ж) 7
му́зыка music 13
мы́ we 1
мы́сль (f) idea, thought 18
мя́гкий soft 12
   мя́гкий ваго́н first-class coach 12
мя́со meat 18
мясокомбина́т meat-packing plant 18

Н н

на (*plus* acc *or* prep) on, onto, to, at, in, for 1
наве́рно probably, likely 8
наве́рх up, upstairs 16
   наверху́ upstairs, on top, in the upper 12

наде́жда   hope 18
Наде́жда   Nadezhda (Hope) 18
наде́яться, наде́ются (I)   to hope, count on 18
на́до   [it's] necessary, one has to 9
   не на́до!   don't! 15
На́дя (var. of Наде́жда)   Nadya 18
наза́д   back, ago 17
   тому́ наза́д   ago 17
назва́ть, назову́т (pfv I)   to name 10
назна́чить (pfv II)   to set, designate, appoint 16
найти́, найду́т (pfv I)   to find 17
нале́во   on the left, to the left 12
нали́ть, налью́т (pfv I)   to pour, fill 18
на́м (dat of мы) 14
на́ми (instr of мы) 17
написа́ть, напи́шут (pfv I)   to write 4, 7, 12
напиши́те (imper of написа́ть) 4
напра́во   on (or to) the right 12
наприме́р   for example 11
наре́жь, наре́жьте (imper of наре́зать) 5
наре́зать, наре́жут (pfv I)   to cut, slice 12
наро́д   people 7
   наро́дный   folk, popular, people's 13
на́с (gen, acc, prep of мы) 5
   у на́с [есть]   we have 5
насчёт (plus gen)   about 5
Ната́ша (var. of Ната́лья)   Natasha 11
нау́ка   science, knowledge 18
   во́т тебе́ нау́ка!   let that be a lesson to you! 18
научи́ться (pfv II)   to learn 18
нау́чный   scientific, scholarly 18
находи́ть (II)   to find 17
находи́ться (II)   to be located 17
нача́ло   beginning, start 16
нача́ть, начну́т (pfv I)   to start, begin 18
на́ш, на́ша, на́ше, на́ши   our, ours 5, 7
не   not (negative particle) 1
небольшо́й   small, not large 12
невозмо́жно   impossible 17
него́ (gen, acc of о́н and оно́)
   у него́   he has, at his place 8
неда́вно   recently, not long ago 5
недалеко́   not far, close, near 15
неде́ля   week 8
недово́лен, -льна, etc.   dissatisfied, displeased 17
неё (gen, acc of она́) 4, 8, 10
   у неё [есть]   she has 4, 7
не́й (prep, dat, instr of она́) 7, 14, 17
не́который   some, certain 15
нельзя́   [it's] impossible, one can't 15
нём (prep of о́н and оно́) 7
немно́го   a little, somewhat 10
нему́ (dat of о́н and оно́) 14, 16
непло́хо   not badly 6
   неплохо́й   not half bad, pretty good 7
непра́вильно   [it's] wrong, [it's] incorrect 3
несимпати́чный   not nice, not likable 16
не́сколько   several, some, a few 17
несча́стный   unhappy, unfortunate 16
   несча́стье   bad luck, misfortune, unhappiness 16
не́т   no; there's no, there isn't any 1, 7
неудо́бный   uncomfortable, inconvenient 12
неуже́ли!   really! you don't say! 13
ни   not (negative particle) 13
   ни . . . ни . . .   neither . . . nor 13
нигде́   nowhere, not . . . anywhere 7

ни́жний, -яя, -ее, lower 12
ника́к   in no way, by no means 9
никако́й   not . . . any, none at all 15
Ники́тич (patronymic, son of Ники́та) 9
никогда́   never 3
Никола́евич (patronymic, son of Никола́й) 7
Никола́й   Nikolay (Nicholas) 6
ни́м (dat of они́, instr of о́н and оно́) 10, 14
   с ни́м   with him (or it) 10
   к ни́м   to them 14
ни́ми (instr of они́) 10
   с ни́ми   with them 10
Ни́на   Nina 1
ни́х (gen, acc, prep of они́) 7, 8, 10
   у ни́х [есть]   they have 8
ничего́   nothing; all right 4, 6
но   but 1
но́вость (f)   news, novelty 13
но́вый   new 13
   что́ но́вого?   what's new? 13
нога́   leg, foot 16
но́ж   knife 5
но́мер   hotel room, issue, number 12
носи́льщик   porter 12
носи́ть   to carry, wear 15
но́чь (f)   night 11
   по нача́м   nights 16
   споко́йной но́чи   good night 11
   но́чью   at night, during the night 11
нра́виться (II)   to like, please, appeal to 11, 16
ну́   well, why 1
   ну́, ка́к?   well, how about it? 11
   ну́, что́ вы́!   why, what do you mean! 6
   ну́, что́ та́м!   whatever for! not at all! 9
ну́жен, нужна́, -о, -ы́   necessary 8
   мне́ нужна́ ка́рта Евро́пы   I need a map of Europe 8

О о

о, об, обо (plus prep)   about, concerning 7
о́!   oh! 12
обе́д   dinner, noon 5
   до обе́да   before noon 9
   по́сле обе́да   after noon, in the afternoon 9
обе́дать (I)   to dine, eat dinner 5
обрати́ться (pfv II)   to consult, turn to 16
обраща́ться (I)   to consult, turn to 16
общежи́тие   dormitory 4
о́бщий   general, over-all, common 15
объявле́ние   notice, announcement 13
обы́чно   usually 15
обы́чный   usual 15
огонёк, -нька́   small light 13
   «Огонёк»   Ogonyok (magazine) 13
огурцы́ (pl of огуре́ц)   cucumbers 5
Оде́сса   Odessa 12
оде́т, -а, -ы   dressed 17
оди́н, одна́, одно́   one, a, one and the same, alone 6
ожида́ние   waiting, wait, expectation 12
   за́л ожида́ния   waiting room 12
ожида́ть (I)   to expect, wait 8
о́зеро   lake 15
окно́   window 5
о́коло (plus gen)   near, by, about 9
око́нчен, -а, -о, -ы   finished, over, done with 18

окóнчить (pfv II)   to finish, graduate from 18
Олéг   Oleg 5
Óля (var. of Óльга)   Olya 4
óн   he, it 1
онá   she, it 1
онú   they 1
онó   it 1
опáздывать (I)   to come (or be) late 11
опоздáть (pfv I)   to be late 11
опя́ть   again 5
Орлóв   Orlov (last name) 7
Орлóва   Miss Orlov, Mrs. Orlov 7
óсень (f)   fall, autumn 2
   óсенью   in fall, in autumn 11
Óсипов   Osipov (last name) 16
осóбенно   especially, particularly 18
осóбенный   special, particular 18
остáвить (pfv II)   to leave 7
остáться, остáнутся (pfv I)   to remain, to be left 17
осторóжен, –жна, etc.   careful 16
осторóжный   careful 16
от, ото (plus gen)   from, away from 9
отвéт   answer 13
отвéтить (pfv II)   to answer, reply 3
отвечáть (I)   to answer, reply 3
отдохнýть (pfv I)   to rest 14
отдыхáть (I)   to rest 14
отéц, отцá   father 15
открывáть (I)   to open 11
откры́т, –а, –о, –ы   open, opened 5
откры́ть, открóют (pfv I)   to open 3, 7
откýда   from where 9
отлúчник   "A" student 18
отлúчно   excellent, excellently 7
отсю́да   from here, hence 15
оттýда   from there 15
óтчество   patronymic 11
   кáк вáше úмя [и] óтчество?   what are your first name and patronymic? 11
óчень   very, very much, really 4
óчередь (f)   line, turn 4
óчерк   sketch, essay, feature story 13
óчи (poetic for глазá)   eyes 13
   «Óчи чёрные»   "Dark Eyes" (song) 13
ошúбка   mistake, error 12

П п

Пáвлович (patronymic, son of Пáвел) 2
пáлка   stick 17
пáрень, пáрня   fellow, lad, boy 10
пáрк   park 9
певéц, певцá   singer (m) 13
певúца   singer (f) 13
пединситýт   teachers college 18
пéй, пéйте (imper of пúть) 13
пéние   singing 1
   урóк пéния   singing lesson 1
пéрвый   first 6
перед, передо (plus instr)   in front of, before 18
передáть, передадýт (pfv irreg like дáть)   to pass, hand 18
перейтú, перейдýт (pfv I)   to go across, go over, to switch 14
переходúть (II)   to go across, go over 14
перó   pen point, pen 6

пéсня   song 13
Пётр   Pyotr (Peter) 9
Петрóв   Petrov (last name) 11
Петрóва   Miss Petrov, Mrs. Petrov 7
Петрóвич (patronymic, son of Пётр) 11
Петрóвна (patronymic, daughter of Пётр) 9
пéть, поют́ (I)   to sing 13
Пéтя (var. of Пётр)   Petya (Pete) 17
печéнье   cookies 17
пéчь, пекýт (I)   to bake 17
пешкóм   on foot 12
пирóг   pirog 17
писáть, пúшут (I)   to write 4, 7, 12
письмó   letter, writing 1
пúть, пьют́ (I)   to drink 5, 12
пишúте (imper of писáть) 4
пúща   fare, food, diet 5
плáн   plan, map (of city) 15
пластúнка   record (phonograph) 13
платúть (II)   to pay 12
платóк, –ткá   handkerchief, kerchief 17
плáтье   dress 4
   материáл на плáтье   dress material 4
плóхо   poorly 1
плохóй   poor, bad 14
по (plus dat)   by, on, about, in, via, along, around, through 15
по–англúйски   [in] English 6
побы́ть, побýдут (pfv I)   to be, spend some time 18
повéрить (pfv II)   to believe 15
повторúть (pfv II)   to repeat 1
поговорúть (pfv II)   to have a talk, talk 11
погóда   weather 14
погуля́ть (pfv I)   to go for a walk, stroll 14
под, подо (plus instr or acc)   under, underneath, beneath 17
подáрок, –рка   present, gift 4
подáть, подадýт (pfv irreg like дáть)   to give, serve, submit 9
подéлать (pfv I)   to do 17
   чтó ж подéлаешь!   it can't be helped! what can you do! 17
подéржанный   secondhand 13
подождáть, подождýт (pfv I)   to wait (for a while) 8
подойтú, подойдýт (pfv I)   to go up to, come over to, approach 7
   подойдúте к телефóну!   answer the phone! 7
подрýга   girl friend 13
подýмать (pfv I)   to think 7
пóезд   train 12
поéздить, поéздят (pfv II)   to do some riding 18
поезжáй! позжáйте!   drive! go (by vehicle)! 12
поéхать, поéдут (pfv I)   to go (by vehicle) 12
пожáлуй   perhaps, that's an idea 14
пожáлуйста   please, don't mention it, you first 1
пожúть, поживýт (pfv I)   to live (for a while) 18
позанимáться (pfv I)   to study 18
позвонúть (pfv II)   to call, to telephone 7
пóздно   late 3
пóзже   later, later on 16
познакóмить (pfv II)   to introduce 10
познакóмиться (pfv II)   to meet, to be introduced 6
поигрáть (pfv I)   to play (for a while) 18
поискáть, поúщут (pfv I)   to look for 18
пóй, пóйте (imper of пéть) 15
пойдём   let's go 10

пойти́, пойду́т (pfv I) to go (on foot) 3, 6
пока́ so long; while, meanwhile 6
показа́ть, пока́жут (pfv I) to show 15
пока́зывать (I) to show 15
покупа́ть (I) to buy 4
по́ле field 15
полежа́ть (pfv II) to lie down (for a while) 18
полете́ть (pfv II) to fly 18
ползти́, ползу́т (I) to be crawling, to be creeping 17
по́лка shelf, bookcase 6
положи́ть (pfv II) to put, lay 12
получи́ть (pfv II) to receive, get 9
полчаса́ half an hour 16
по́мнить (II) to remember 11
помога́ть (I) to help 16
по-мо́ему in my opinion, I think 7
помо́чь, помо́гут (pfv I) to help 16
помо́щник assistant, aide 18
понеде́льник Monday 10
понима́ние understanding, grasp 11
понима́ть (I) to understand 3
понра́виться (pfv II) to like 11, 16
пообе́дать (pfv I) to eat dinner 5
попроси́ть (pfv II) to ask, request 7
попу́тчик traveling companion, fellow traveler 12
пора́ time, it's time 6
порабо́тать (pfv I) to work (a bit) 18
портфе́ль (m) briefcase 4
по-ру́сски [in] Russian 6
поря́док, –дка order, arrangement 6, 15
  всё в поря́дке everything's O.K. 6
посиде́ть (pfv II) to sit (for a while) 18
посла́ть, пошлю́т (pfv I) to send 1, 12
по́сле (plus gen) after 8
после́дний, –яя, –ее last, latest 13
послеза́втра day after tomorrow 10
послу́шать (pfv I) to listen (to) 13
посмотре́ть (pfv II) to take a look 4
посове́товать, –уют (pfv I) to advise 13
посо́льство embassy 13
поспа́ть, поспя́т (pfv II) to sleep (for a while) 18
постира́ть (pfv I) to do the wash 18
постоя́ть (pfv II) to stand (for a while) 18
постро́ить (pfv II) to build 15
поступа́ть (I) to enroll, enter; behave 3
поступи́ть (pfv II) to enroll, enter; behave 18
постуча́ть (pfv II) to knock 18
потанцева́ть, –у́ют (pfv I) to dance (for a while) 18
потеря́ть (pfv I) to lose 17
пото́м afterward, later on, then 18
походи́ть (pfv II) to walk (a bit) 18
почему́? why? 10
по́чта post office, mail 1
почти́ almost 6
пошёл, пошла́, etc. (past of пойти́) 8, 15
пошли́! let's go! 6
пою́, поёшь, etc. (pres of пе́ть) 15
пра́в, –а́, –о, –ы right 16
пра́вда truth; that's true, isn't it, isn't that so 4, 6
  «Пра́вда» Pravda (Truth) (newspaper) 13
пра́вильно right, that's right 3
пра́ктика practice, practical experience 18
предлага́ть (I) to suggest, propose, offer 14
предложи́ть (pfv II) to suggest, propose, offer 9
предста́вить (pfv II) to present, introduce 16
  предста́вить себе́ to imagine 16

представля́ть (I) to present, introduce 15
  представля́ть себе́ to imagine 15
прекра́сно fine, excellent, splendid 12
преподава́тель (m) instructor, teacher 18
преподава́ть, преподаю́т (I) to instruct, teach 18
приве́т greetings! regards! hi! 1
привы́к, –ла (past of привы́кнуть) 14
привы́кнуть (pfv I) to get used to 14
привы́чка habit 14
пригласи́ть (pfv II) to invite 15
приглаша́ть (I) to invite 15
прие́хать, прие́дут (pfv I) to arrive (by vehicle) 12
прийти́, приду́т (pfv I) to come, arrive (on foot) 14
прийти́сь (pfv I) to have to, to be forced to 17
принести́, принесу́т (pfv I) to bring (on foot) 8
приноси́ть (II) to bring (on foot) 13
приходи́ть (II) to come, arrive (on foot) 14
пришёл, пришла́, etc. (past of прийти́) 15
пришло́сь (past of прийти́сь) 17
прия́тно pleased, [it's] nice 6
проводни́к conductor, guide 12
продава́ть, продаю́т (I) to sell 13
продавщи́ца saleslady 8
продолжа́ть (I) to continue, keep on 16
прои́грыватель (m) record player 13
произво́дство production, manufacture 18
  рабо́тать на произво́дстве to work in a factory 18
происше́ствие happening, occurrence, accident, event, incident 13
пройти́, пройду́т (pfv I) to pass, go by 6
пропа́сть, пропаду́т (pfv I) to be lost, to perish 18
про́пуск pass, entry permit 13
проси́ть (II) to request, ask for 12
просну́ться (pfv I) to wake up 18
про́сто just, simply 13
просто́й simple 13
  просто́й рабо́чий unskilled worker, ordinary worker 18
просыпа́ться (I) to wake up 18
про́сьба request, favor 9
про́тив (plus gen) opposite, across from, against 6
профе́ссия profession, calling 18
профе́ссор professor 7
проходи́ть (II) to pass, go by 9
прочита́ть (pfv I) to read (through), finish reading 13
прошёл, прошла́, etc. (past of пройти́) 6
про́шлое the past 18
про́шлый past, last 18
  на про́шлой неде́ле last week 18
проща́льный farewell (adj) 18
проща́й, проща́йте good-bye, farewell 18
пря́мо straight, straight ahead, directly, just 12
пусть let 17
пя́тница Friday 10
пя́тый fifth 12
пять five 10
пятьдеся́т fifty 15

Р р

рабо́та work, written paper 7
рабо́тать to work 2
рабо́чий worker 18
  просто́й рабо́чий unskilled worker 18

рад, –а, –ы   glad 2, 3
радио (indecl)   radio 13
раз   occasion, time; once 5
   как раз   just, it just happens 5
   на этот раз   this time 10
разве   really; is it possible! 8
разве что   unless maybe 11
разговор   conversation 4
разрешение   permission, permit 15
разрешить (pfv II)   to permit, allow 12
рано   early 3
раньше   earlier, before 16
распродан, –а, –о, –ы   sold out 13
рассердиться (pfv II)   to become angry, 16
расти, растут (I)   to grow 17
ребёнок, –нка   baby, child 17
ребята   kids, fellows, guys 5
редко   rarely, seldom 3
результат   result 7
реклама   advertisement, publicity 13
ректор   chancellor, president 6
ресторан   restaurant 9
рецепт   prescription, recipe 16
решить (pfv II)   to decide, solve 18
родители   parents 15
рождение   birth 4
   день рождения   birthday 4
роман   novel 10
романс   love song 13
рос, росла, etc. (irreg past of расти) 17
рубашка   shirt, slip 17
рубль (m)   ruble 12
рука   hand, arm 17
русский   Russian 6
ручка   penholder, pen 6
рыба   fish 5

С с

с, со (gen)   since, from 2, 9
с, со (instr)   with, together with 10, 17
садиться (II)   to sit down 14
салфетка   napkin 18
сам, –а, –о, сами   oneself (myself, yourself, etc.) 15
сахар   sugar 17
Саша (var. of Александр, –дра)   Sasha (Sandy) 4
сбор   gathering, assembly 18
   в сборе   together, present 18
сварить (pfv II)   to cook (by boiling) 17
свежий   fresh 14
свежо   cool, chilly, fresh 14
свобода   freedom, liberty 18
свободно   freely, fluently 16
свободный   free, unoccupied 14
свой   one's own (my own, your own, etc.) 7
сделать (pfv I)   to do, get done 9, 11
себя   oneself (reflexive personal pronoun) 9
   у себя   in one's room (or office) 9
сегодня   today 5
сейчас   now, right away 6
секретарь (m)   secretary 9
селёдка   herring 5
село   village 15
Семён   Semyon (Simon) 2
Семёнов   Semyonov (last name) 8
семь   seven 10
семья   family 15

Сергей   Sergey 16
сердиться (II)   to be angry, to be mad 16
серьёзный   serious 18
сестра   sister 6
сидеть (II)   to sit, to be sitting 10
симпатичный   nice, likable 16
синий, –яя, –ее   dark blue 13
скажите (imper of сказать) 1
сказать, скажут (pfv I)   to say, tell 12
сколько   how much, how many 10
   во сколько   at what time 10
скорее, скорей   quick, hurry up; sooner, faster 17
скоро   soon 11
скучно   dull, boring 3
следующий   next 8
   на следующей неделе   next week 8
слишком   too, too much 18
словарь (m)   dictionary, vocabulary 8
словечко (var. of слово) 9
   замолвите за меня словечко!   put in a good word for me! 9
слово   word 9
сломать (pfv I)   to break 16
служба   job, service, work 4
случай   case, occasion, incident, event, chance 16
   во всяком случае   in any case, in any event 16
случиться (pfv II)   to happen 16
слушать (I)   to listen 7
слушаю   hello (on telephone) 7
слышать (II)   to hear 2
смогу, сможешь, etc. (fut of смочь) 7
смотреть (II)   to look, see 5
смочь, смогут (pfv I)   to be able, can 7
снимать (I)   to take off, take a picture 15
снимок, –мка   snapshot, picture 15
собираться (I)   to gather; to plan 18
собрание   meeting, gathering, collection 1
советовать, советуют (I)   to advise 13
совсем   completely, quite, altogether 7
согласен, –сна, etc.   agreed, agreeable 14
сойти, сойдут (pfv I)   to go off, get off, come down, go down 16
   сойти с ума   to be out of one's mind, to go crazy 16
   вы с ума сошли!   you're out of your mind! 16
сосед   neighbor (m) 15
соседка   neighbor (f) 15
соседний, –яя, –ее   neighboring, next 15
сочинение   composition 7
спасибо   thanks, thank you 2
   большое спасибо   thanks very much 9
спать, спят (II)   to sleep, to be asleep 12, 13
специалист   specialist 16
спешить (II)   to hurry 2
сплю, спишь, спит, etc. (pres of спать) 12, 13
спокойный   calm, quiet 11
   спокойной ночи   good night 11
спрашивать (I)   to ask (a question), inquire 8
сразу   immediately, right 8
среда   Wednesday 10
СССР (Союз Советских Социалистических Республик)   U.S.S.R. 7
стакан   glass 8
становиться (II)   to stand, become, grow, get, step 16

ста́нция   station 12

ста́рый   old 9

стать, ста́нут (pfv I)   to stand, become, grow, get, step 18

стира́ть (I)   to launder, wash 17

стихи́   verses, poetry 10

сто́ить (II)   to cost 12

   ско́лько э́то сто́ит?   how much is this? 12

   не сто́ит   it's no use, it isn't worthwhile 18

сто́л   table, desk 5

столо́вая   dining hall, dining room, cafe 5

стоя́ть (II)   to be standing, to stand 4

страна́   country 15

стра́нный   strange 13

стро́ить (II)   to build 15

студе́нт   student (m) 1

студе́нтка   student (f), coed 1

сту́л   chair 7

сту́лья (pl of сту́л) 7

стуча́ть (II)   to knock, rap, pound 17

суббо́та   Saturday 10

су́п   soup 17

сча́стье   happiness, luck 18

счита́ть (I)   to count, consider 10

США (Соединённые Шта́ты Аме́рики)   U.S.A. 13

сыгра́ть (pfv I)   to play a game 14

сы́н   son 17

сыновья́ (pl of сы́н) 17

сюда́   here, over here 10

Т т

та́к (unstressed)   then, in that case 3

та́к   so, as, that way, thus 3

та́к, ка́к   just as 16

тако́й   such, so 11

такси́ (indecl)   taxi 12

та́м   there 1

та́нец (sg of та́нцы) 10

танцева́ть, танцу́ют (I)   to dance 10

та́нцы   dance, dances, dancing 10

Та́ня (var. of Татья́на)   Tanya 17

Ташке́нт   Tashkent 12

тво́й, твоя́, твоё, твои́   your(s) 6

те́ (pl of то́т) 13

те́ же   the same 13

теа́тр   theater 9

   театра́льный   theatrical, theater (adj) 13

тебе́ (prep, dat of ты́) 6, 14

тебя́ (gen, acc of ты́) 6, 9, 10

телефо́н   telephone, phone 7

   звони́т телефо́н   the phone's ringing 7

   звони́ть по телефо́ну   to phone 16

   подойди́(те) к телефо́ну!   answer the phone! 7

те́ннис   tennis 11

тепе́рь   now 2

тёплый   warm 14

   тепло́   [it's] warm 14

   тёплое месте́чко   a nice cushy job 18

теря́ть (I)   to lose 17

тетра́дь (f)   notebook 6

тётя   aunt 17

те́хник   technician 18

те́хника   technology, engineering 18

тобо́й (instr of ты́) 17

това́рищ   comrade, friend, colleague 9

   това́рищ по ко́мнате   roommate 10

тогда́   then, in that case 6

то́же   too, also, either 2, 8

толку́чка   flea market, secondhand market 13

Толсто́й, Лёв   Tolstoy, Leo (writer) 11

то́лько   only, just 5

   то́лько что   just, just now 8

То́ля (var. of Анато́лий)   Tolya 18

тому́ наза́д   ago 17

то́рт   cake 17

то́т, та́, то́   that, that one, the one 6

то́т же, та́ же, то́ же   the same 13

то́чка   dot, point, period 17

то́чный   exact, precise 16

трава́   grass 17

три́   three 10

три́дцать   thirty 12

тру́дный   hard, difficult 13

туда́   there, to that place 5

тури́ст   tourist 15

ту́т   here 4

ты́   you 1

У у

у (plus gen)   at, by, on, from, at the place of 4

   у на́с [е́сть]   we have 5

   у него́ [е́сть]   he has 8

   у неё [е́сть]   she has 4

   у ни́х [е́сть]   they have 8

убива́ть (I)   to kill 17

убо́рная   toilet, lavatory 12

убо́рщица   cleaning woman 7

уви́деть (pfv II)   to see, catch sight of 10

у́гол, угла́   corner, angle 8

уголо́к, –лка́   little corner 13

   кра́сный уголо́к   recreation room (lit. red corner) 13

уда́ча   luck, good luck 11

удивля́ться (I)   to be surprised 12

удо́бный   convenient, comfortable 12

удо́бство   convenience, comfort 12

удово́льствие   pleasure 3

   с удово́льствием   with pleasure, gladly 3

уезжа́ть (I)   to go away (by vehicle) 16

уе́хать, уе́дут (pfv I)   to go away (by vehicle) 16

уже́   already, by now 2

   уже́ не   no longer, not ... anymore 18

узна́ть (pfv I)   to find out, learn, recognize 7

«Украи́на»   The Ukraine (hotel) 12

укра́инец, –нца   Ukrainian 7

у́лица   street 13

у́м   mind, sense 16

   вы́ с ума́ сошли́!   you're out of your mind! 16

у́мный   wise, smart, intelligent 16

университе́т   university 3

упа́сть, упаду́т (pfv I)   to fall, fall down 16

уползти́, уползу́т (pfv I)   to crawl away, creep off 17

уро́к   lesson, class 1

услы́шать (pfv II)   to hear 13

успе́ть (pfv I)   to manage in time, succeed 11

успе́х   success, luck 18

   де́лать больши́е успе́хи   to do very well, make excellent progress 18

уста́ть, уста́нут (pfv I)   to be tired, to get tired 14

устро́ить (pfv II)   to arrange, fix up, organize 18

устро́иться (pfv II)   to get fixed up, get established, get settled 18

у́тро morning 4
  по утра́м in the mornings 16
уф! ugh! ooh! 14
уха́ fish soup, fish chowder 17
учёный scholar, learned man, scientist 18
учи́тель (m) teacher 7
учи́тельница teacher (f) 7
учи́ть (II) to teach; to study 6
учи́ться (II) to learn, study 18

Ф ф

фа́брика factory 9
факульте́т department 7
фами́лия last name, family name 11
фи́зик physicist 18
фи́зика physics 8
Фили́ппович (patronymic, son of Фили́пп) 2
фи́льм film, movie 10
фо́то photograph, picture 15
футбо́л soccer 11
  игра́ть в футбо́л to play soccer 11

X x

Ха́рьков Kharkov 12
хи́мик chemist 18
хи́мия chemistry 8
Хитро́в Khitrov (last name) 2
хле́б bread 5
ходи́ть (II) to go, attend, walk 11
хокке́й hockey 11
холо́дный cold 14
  хо́лодно [it's] cold 14
хоро́ший good 9
хорошо́ good, fine, well, nice 1
хоте́ть (irreg pres: хочу́, хо́чешь, хо́чет, хоти́м,
  хоти́те, хотя́т) to want 3-5
хотя́ although 14
  хотя́ бы even if only 14
хо́чется [one] feels like 5
хочу́, хо́чешь, хо́чет, etc. (see хоте́ть) 3-5
ху́же worse 16

Ц ц

Цара́пкин Tsarapkin (last name) 2
цве́т color 13
  цветно́й in color, colored 15
це́лый entire, whole 18
це́рковь, це́ркви (f) church 15

Ч ч

ча́й tea 5
ча́с hour 10
ча́стный private, personal 13
ча́сто often, frequently 3
ча́шка cup 8
чей, чья, чьё, чьи whose 6
челове́к person, human being, man 13
чём than 3
  лу́чше по́здно, чём никогда́ better late than
    never 3

чём (instr of что́) 17
че́рез (plus acc) through, across, in 13
че́рез ча́з in an hour 13
чёрный black 13
четве́рг Thursday 10
четы́ре four 10
чита́ть (I) to read 1, 10
что that, who, which 6
что́ what 3
  что́ вы́! you're not serious! 3
что́ ли perhaps, possibly, maybe 18
что́ но́вого? what's new? 13
что́ это why is it, how come 16
что́бы in order to, to 18
что́-нибудь anything, something or other 9
что́-то something 14
чу́вство feeling 18
чу́вствовать, чу́вствуют (I) to feel 16
  чу́вствовать себя́ to be feeling 16
чу́ть не all but, darned near, almost 16
чьё (n of чей) 6
чьи (pl of чей) 6
чья (f of чей) 6

Ш ш

ша́пка cap 17
ша́хматы chess, chess board 14
  игра́ть в ша́хматы to play chess 14
шёл, шла́, шло́, шли́ (past of идти́) 12, 15
шестна́дцать sixteen 16
ше́сть six 10
шка́ф cupboard, dresser 5
шко́ла school 6
шофёр driver (of car) 12
шу́тка joke 18

Щ щ

щи schi (cabbage or sauerkraut soup) 5

Э э

экза́мен examination, exam 7
электри́чество lights, electricity 15
эта́ж floor, story 12
э́ти these, those 6
э́то it, this, that 2
э́тот, э́та, э́то this, that 7

Ю ю

ю́бка skirt 17
Ю́рий Yury (George) 16

Я я

я́ I 1
язы́к language, tongue 6
яку́т Yakut 7
Я́лта Yalta 12
я́щик drawer, box (wooden) 5

INDEX

Russian words are in boldface and English translations in italics. The numbers refer to pages on which the items are discussed and drilled. The following abbreviations are used:

acc	accusative		m-d	multidirectional
adj	adjective, adjectival		N	note
adv	adverb, adverbial		n	neuter
aff	affirmative		neg	negative, negation, negated
asp	aspect		nom	nominative
con	consonant		obj	object
conj	conjugation		pers	person, personal
constr	construction		pfv	perfective
dat	dative		pl	plural
decl	declension, declensional		poss	possessive
demonstr	demonstrative		pred	predicate
dir obj	direct object		prep	preposition, prepositional
f	feminine		pres	present
fn	footnote		pres-fut	present-future
fut	future		pron	pronoun
gen	genitive		refl	reflexive
imper	imperative		reg	regular
impers	impersonal		sg	singular
indecl	indeclinable		subj	subject
inf	infinitive		u-d	unidirectional
instr	instrumental		var	variant
interrog	interrogative		vb	verb
ipfv	imperfective		vs	versus
irreg	irregular		vwl	vowel
m	masculine			

305, **купи́ть** *to buy* 215, **оста́вить** *to leave* 215, **позвони́ть** *to phone* 302, **познако́мить** *to introduce* 215, **спроси́ть** *to ask* 215; of two-stem 1st conj vbs: **доста́ть** *to get*, **забы́ть** *to forget*, **заказа́ть** *to order*, **закры́ть** *to close*, **написа́ть** *to write*, **наре́зать** *to slice*, **откры́ть** *to open*, **посла́ть** *to send*, **прие́хать** *to arrive* 263–66; vs ipfv fut 218

personal pronouns: dat of refl pers pron 318–20; declension: in acc 208–10, in dat 318–20, in gen 156–58, in instr 404–06, in nom 11, 72–73, in prep 133–35; instr of refl pers pron 404–06; refl pers pron **себе́** 228 N

plural-polite *or* formal-plural (*see also* familiar): **вы** vs familiar sg **ты** 11 fn, 55 fn; imper with unstressed suffix **–те** 105, 291

possessive modifiers: declension: in dat sg and pl 375–78, in instr sg and pl 406–08; in nom, acc, gen, prep, sg and pl 299–302, in nom pl 125–27, in nom sg 98–101; use of **у** plus gen as substitute for 182

predicate: use of instr case with vbs of *being* and *becoming* 433–35

prefix *or* prefixation: past tense of prefixed pfv derivatives of **идти́** *to be going* 352–54; perfectivization by prefix **по–** 443–45; use of to distinguish between vb aspects 38 N

prepositional case: of adjs, sg and pl 295–99; of nouns, sg and pl 127–30; of pers and interrog prons 133–35; of **чей** and poss modifiers 299–302; special prep sg ending in **–у** 144 N; primary function of 54; with preps **в** and **на** 131–33

prepositions: **на** vs **в** in meaning *at* 13 N, 131–33; **на** vs **в** in meaning *to* 58; with acc case: **в** and **на** 57–58, 213, 220–21; with dat case: **к** and **по** 371–75; with gen case: **из**, **с**, and **от** 182–85, **у** 151, 179–82, others requiring gen case 185–87; with instr case: **с** 400; with prep case: **в**, **на**, and **о** (**об**) 128–33

present tense (*see also* aspects, conjugation, verbs): of 1st conj verbs: **де́лать** *to do* 240, **ду́мать** *to think* 240, **жда́ть** *to wait* 240, **жи́ть** *to live* 240, **зна́ть** *to know* 240, **идти́** *to be going* 14–17, 237, **мо́чь** *to be able* 188–90, **обе́дать** *to dine* 240, **ожида́ть** *to expect* 240, **покупа́ть** *to buy* 240, **понима́ть** *to understand* 240, **рабо́тать** *to work* 25–27, 237, **слу́шать** *to listen* 240, **спра́шивать** *to ask* 240, **чита́ть** *to read* 240; of irreg vbs: **дава́ть** *to speak* 325–27, **хоте́ть** *to want* 75; of 2nd conj vbs: **ви́деть** *to see* 104–05, **говори́ть** *to speak* 45, 97–98, **люби́ть** *to love* 215, **проси́ть** *to request* 302, 305, **слы́шать** *to hear* 45, 302, **смотре́ть** *to look* 305, **спеши́ть** *to hurry* 43–45, 105, **стоя́ть** *to stand* 45, 302; of two-stem 1st conj vbs: **иска́ть** *to look for* 263, **е́хать** *to be going (by vehicle)*, **писа́ть** *to write*, **пи́ть** *to drink*, **танцева́ть** *to dance* 264; use of gen case in pres fut constrs 158–60; use of in Russian where English uses past tense or pres perfect 227 N

present-future (*see also* conjugation, perfective future, present tense, verbs): comparison between endings of 1st and 2nd conj vbs 45, 304–305; definition of 103; of 2nd conj vbs with stem con change in 1st pers sg 213–15; of 1st conj vbs patterned like **рабо́тать** *to work* and **идти́** *to be going* 237–40; stress patterns in the pres-fut 215, 305

professions: use of nouns for both men and women in professions 427–28 N; use of pronoun **кто́** when English uses *what* in referring to one's work 428 N

pronouns: demonstr pron **э́тот**: in dat 375–78, in instr 406–08, in nom, acc, gen, and prep 248–50; function of refl poss pron modifier **свой** 112 N, 302; interrog prons **кто́** and **что́**: in acc 208–10, in dat 318–20, in gen 156–58, in instr 404–06, in nom 73–74, in prep 133–35; pers prons: in acc 208–10, in dat 318–20, in gen 156–58, in instr 404–06, in nom 11, 72–73, in prep 133–35; placement of obj pron before vb 38 N; refl pers pron **себя́** 228 N, 318–20, 404–06; **чей** and poss modifiers: in dat sg and pl 375–78, in instr sg and pl

406–08, in nom, acc, gen, and prep, sg and pl 299–302, in nom pl 125–27, in nom sg 98–101

pronunciation (*see also* Russian sound system, consonants, vowels): of clusters beginning with letters **с** and **з** 431–33; of clusters with [l] or [ḷ] 345; of double cons 234; of final clusters with [r] or [ṛ] 317–18; of hard [k], [g], [x] and soft counterparts [ķ], [g], [x̧] 176–77; of hard [l] in sg and soft [ḷ] in pl of past tense 76; of initial clusters with [r] or [ṛ] 289–90; of letter **г** as [v] 22 N, 61 fn; of paired hard and soft cons 3–4; of reflexive particle **–ся** (**–сь**) 382; of special clusters [čš], [čč], [dž], [tc] 262–63; of **США** 283 N; of unpaired hard cons [š], [ž], [c] and unpaired soft cons [č], [šč], [j] 204–06; of voiced and voiceless cons 39–43, 371, 398–99; of [b] vs [ḅ] 118; of [d] vs [ḍ] 68–69; of [f] vs [f̧] 148; of [l] vs [ḷ] 148; of [m] vs [m̧] 119; of [n] vs [ṇ] 69; of [p] vs [p̧] 118; of [r] vs [ṛ] 92; of [s] vs [ş] 91; of [t] vs [ţ] 68; of [v] vs [γ] 147; of [z] vs [z̧] 91; simplification of certain con clusters in pronunciation 35 fn, 364 fn

рабо́тать *to work*: as typical "j-stem" vb 27; pres-fut of 1st conj vbs patterned like 237–40; pres tense of 25–27

reflexive pronouns: refl poss pron modifier **свой** 112 N, 299–302; refl pers pron **себя́** 228 N, 318–20, 404–06

reflexive verbs: **нра́виться**, **понра́виться** *to like* 228 fn, 230 N, 383–85; other refl vbs 380–83, 408–12, 440–43

Russian handwriting system: 28–33

Russian *or* Cyrillic alphabet: and the writing system 5–7

Russian sound system: cons 3–5; correspondance between vowel letters and vowel sounds 23–25; discrepancies between sound system and writing system 8–10; vowels 3

second conjugation (*see also* conjugation, present-future, verbs): pfv fut of **встре́тить** *to meet* 305, **купи́ть** *to buy* 215, **оста́вить** *to leave* 215, **позвони́ть** *to phone* 302, **познако́мить** *to introduce* 215, **спроси́ть** *to ask* 215; pres tense of: **ви́деть** *to see* 104–05, 215, **говори́ть** *to speak* 45, 97–98, 105, **люби́ть** *to love* 215, **проси́ть** *to request* 302, 305, **слы́шать** *to hear* 45, 302, **смотре́ть** *to look* 305, **спеши́ть** *to hurry* 43–45, **стоя́ть** *to stand* 45, 302; review of 302–05; vbs with stem con change in 1st pers sg pres-fut 213–15

segment (*see also* intonation): major segment 7–8, 92

short-form adjectives (*see also* adjectives, long-form adjectives): m, f, and pl forms of **за́нят**, **ра́д**, **здоро́в**, and **бо́лен** 45–47

soft consonants (*see also* pronunciation): cons always pronounced soft 5; use of "soft-series" vowel letters to indicate softness of preceding con 8 9; use of soft sign to indicate softness of preceding con 9–10; vs hard cons 3–5

soft sign **мя́гкий знак**: 4 fn; convention of using after hard con **ш** in 2nd pers sg vb 17 fn; functions of 9–10

"soft-series" vowel letters: functions of 8–9; use of in conjugation with hard sign 10

спеши́ть *to hurry*: as 2nd conj verb model 43–45

stems (*see also* endings, "j-stem" verbs): alternation of stems in pres-fut of 2nd conj vbs 305; inserted vwls and alternation of stems 124–25; noun stems ending in [j] in pl 125, 241–42; nouns with expanded stems in pl 125; nouns with pl stem differing from sg stem 121, 124–25, 256 N, 266–68, 340 fn, 341 N; pres-fut stem contrasted with inf-past stem in 1st conj vbs **жи́ть** *to live* and **взя́ть** *to take* 240; pres-fut stem vs inf-past stem 305; pres tense of vb **дава́ть** *to give*, based on stem [daj-] 327; remarks on endings and 54–55; stem cons change in 1st pers sg of 2nd conj vbs 213–15; two-stem 1st conj vbs 263–66

stress (*see also* intonation): in past tense 78; in past tense of 2nd conj vbs 215; in short-form n adjs and advs ending in **–о** compared with that of long-form adjs

LaVergne, TN USA
26 August 2009

156058LV00005B/68/A